GRAMMAR FOR LANGUAGE LEARNING

ELEMENTS *of* SUCCESS

ANNE M. EDIGER

LINDA LEE

JENNI CURRIE SANTAMARIA

2

OXFORD
UNIVERSITY PRESS

SHAPING learning TOGETHER

We would like to thank the following classes for piloting *Elements of Success*:

University of Delaware English Language Institute
Teacher: Kathleen Vodvarka
Students: Ahmad Alenzi, Bandar Manei Algahmdi, Fadi Mohammed Alhazmi, Abdel Rahman Atallah, Anna Kuzmina, Muhanna Sayer Aljuaid, Coulibaly Sita

ABC Adult School, Cuerritos, CA
Teacher: Jenni Santamaria
Students: Gabriela A. Marquez Aguilar, Yijung Chen, Laura Gomez, Terry Hahn, EunKyung Lee, Subin Lee, Sunmin Lee, Jane Leelachat, Lilia Nunezuribe, Gina Olivar, Young Park, Seol Hee Seok, Kwang Mi Song

---

During the development of *Elements of Success*, we spoke with teachers and professionals who are passionate about teaching grammar. Their feedback led us to create *Elements of Success: Grammar for Language Learning*, a course that solves teaching challenges by presenting grammar clearly, simply, and completely. We would like to acknowledge the advice of teachers from

USA • BRAZIL • CANADA • COSTA RICA • GUATEMALA • IRAN • JAPAN • MEXICO • OMAN • RUSSIA
SAUDI ARABIA • SOUTH KOREA • TUNISIA • TURKEY • UKRAINE • THE UNITED ARAB EMIRATES

Mehmet Abi, Mentese Anatolian High School, Turkey; **Anna-Marie Aldaz**, Doña Ana Community College, NM; **Diana Allen**, Oakton Community College, IL; **Marjorie Allen**, Harper College, IL; **Mark Alves**, Montgomery College, Rockville, MD; **Kelly Arce**, College of Lake County, IL; **Irma Arencibia**, Union City Adult Learning Center, NJ; **Arlys Arnold**, University of Minnesota, MN; **Marcia Arthur**, Renton Technical College, WA; **Alexander Astor**, Hostos Community College, NY; **Chris Atkins**, CHICLE Language Institute, NC; **Karin Avila-John**, University of Dayton, OH; **Ümmet Aydan**, Karabuk University, Iran; **Fabiana Azurmendi**; **John Baker**, Wayne State University, MI; **Sepehr Bamdadnia**; **Terry Barakat**, Missouri State University, MO; **Marie Bareille**, Borough of Manhattan Community College, NY; **Eileen Barlow**, SUNY Albany, NY; **Denise Barnes**, Madison English as a Second Language School, WI; **Kitty Barrera**, University of Houston, TX; **Denise Barsotti**, EID Training Solutions, FL; **Maria Bauer**, El Camino College; **Christine Bauer-Ramazani**, Saint Michael's College, VT; **Jamie Beaton**, Boston University, MA; **Gena Bennett**, Cornerstone University, NE; **Linda Berendsen**, Oakton Community College, IL; **Carol Berteotti**; **Grace Bishop**, Houston Community College, TX; **Perrin Blackman**, University of Kansas, KS; **Mara Blake-Ward**, Drexel University English Language Center, PA; **Melissa Bloom**, ELS; **Alexander Bochkov**, ELS, WA; **Marcel Bolintiam**, University of Colorado, CO; **Nancy Boyer**, Golden West College, CA; **T. Bredl**, The New School, NY; **Rosemarie Brefeld**, University of Missouri, MO; **Leticia Brereton**, Kingsborough Community College, NY; **Deborah Brooks**, Laney College, CA; **Kevin Brown**, Irvine Community College, CA; **Rachel Brown**, Center for Literacy, NY; **Tracey Brown**, Parkland College, IL; **Crystal Brunelli**, Tokyo Jogakkan Middle and High School, Japan; **Tom Burger**, Harris County Department of Education, TX; **Thom Burns**, Tokyo English Specialists College, Japan; **Caralyn Bushey**, Maryland English Institute, MD; **Gül Büyü**, Ankara University, Turkey; **Scott Callaway**, Community Family Centers, TX; **Adele Camus**, George Mason University, VA; **Nigel Caplan**, University of Delaware, DE; **Nathan Carr**, California State University, CA; **Christina Cavage**, Savannah College of Art and Design,

GA; **Neslihan Çelik**, Özdemir Sabancı Emirgan Anatolian High School, Turkey; **Shelley Cetin**, Kansas City Kansas Community College, KS; **Hoi Yuen Chan**, University of Wyoming, WY; **Esther Chase**, Berwyn Public Library, IL; **Suzidilara Çınar**, Yıldırım Beyazıt University, Turkey; **Diane Cirino**, SUNY Suffolk, NY; **Cara Codney**, Emporia State University, KS; **Catherine Coleman**, Irvine Valley College, CA; **Jenelle Collins**, Washington High School, AZ; **Greg Conner**, Orange Coast Community College, CA; **Ewelina Cope**, The Language Company, PA; **Jorge Cordon**, Colegio Montessori, Guatemala; **Kathy Cornman**, University of Michigan, MI; **Barry Costa**, Castro Valley Adult and Career Education, CA; **Cathy Costa**, Edmonds Community College, WA; **Julia Cote**, Houston Community College NE, TX; **Eileen Cotter**, Montgomery College, MD; **Winnie Cragg**, Mukogawa Fort Wright Institute, WA; **Douglas Craig**, Diplomatic Language Services, VA; **Elizabeth Craig**, Savannah College of Art and Design, GA; **Ann Telfair Cramer**, Florida State College at Jacksonville, FL; **R. M. Crocker**, Plano Independent School District, TX; **Virginia Cu**, Queens Adult Learning Center, CT; **Marc L. Cummings**, Jefferson Community and Technical College, KY; **Roberta Cummings**, Trinidad Correctional Facility, CO; **David Dahnke**, Lone Star College-North Harris, TX; **Debra Daise**, University of Denver, CO; **L. Dalgish**, Concordia College, NY; **Kristen Danek**, North Carolina State University, NC; **April Darnell**, University of Dayton, OH; **Heather Davis**, OISE Boston, MA; **Megan Davis**, Embassy English, NY; **Jeanne de Simon**, University of West Florida, FL; **Renee Delatizky**, Boston University, MA; **Sonia Delgadillo**, Sierra Community College, CA; **Gözde Burcu Demirkul**, Orkunoglu College, Turkey; **Stella L. Dennis**, Longfellow Middle School, NY; **Mary Diamond**, Auburn University, AL; **Emily Dibala**, Bucks County Community College, PA; **Cynthia Dieckmann**, West Chester East High School, PA; **Michelle DiGiorno**, Richland College, TX; **Luciana Diniz**, Portland Community College, OR; **Özgür Dirik**, Yıldız Technical University, Turkey; **Marta O. Dmytrenko-Arab**, Wayne State University, MI; **Margie Domingo**, Intergenerational Learning Community, CO; **Kellie Draheim**, Hongik University, South Korea; **Ilke Buyuk Duman**, Sehir University, Turkey; **Jennifer Eick-Magan**, Prairie State College, IL;

Juliet Emanuel, Borough of Manhattan Community College, NY; **David Emery**, Kaplan International Center, CA; **Patricia Emery**, Jefferson County Literacy Council, WI; **Eva Engelhard**, Kaplan International Center, WA; **Nancey Epperson**, Harry S. Truman College, IL; **Ken Estep**, Mentor Language Institute, CA; **Cindy Etter**, University of Washington, WA; **Rhoda Fagerland**, St. Cloud State University, MN; **Anrisa Fannin**, Diablo Valley College, CA; **Marie Farnsworth**, Union Public Schools, OK; **Jim Fenton**, Bluegrass Community Technical College, KY; **Lynn Filazzola**, Nassau BOCES Adult Learning Center, NY; **Christine Finck**, Stennis Language Lab; **Mary Fischer**, Texas Intensive English Program, TX; **Mark Fisher**, Lone Star College, TX; **Celeste Flowers**, University of Central Arkansas, AR; **Elizabeth Foss**, Washtenaw Community College, MI; **Jacqueline Fredericks**, West Contra Costa Adult Education, CA; **Patricia Gairaud**, San Jose City College, CA; **Patricia Gallo**, Delaware Technical Community College, DE; **Beverly Gandall**, Coastline Community College, CA; **Alberto Garrido**, The Community College of Baltimore County, MD; **Debbie Garza**, Park University, MO; **Karen Gelender**, Castro Valley Adult and Career Education, CA; **Ronald Gentry**, Suenos Compartidos, Mexico; **Kathie Madden Gerecke**, North Shore Community College, MA; **Jeanne Gibson**, Colorado State University, CO; **A. Elizabeth Gilfillan**, Houston Community College, TX; **Melanie Gobert**, The Higher Colleges of Technology, UAE; **Ellen Goldman**, West Valley College, CA; **Jo Golub**, Houston Community College, TX; **Maria Renata Gonzalez**, Colegio Montessori, Guatemala; **Elisabeth Goodwin**, Pima Community College, AZ; **John Graney**, Santa Fe College, FL; **Karina Greene**, CUNY in the Heights, NY; **Katherine Gregorio**, CASA de Maryland, MD; **Claudia Gronsbell**, La Escuelita, NY; **Yvonne Groseil**, Hunter College, NY; **Alejandra Gutierrez**, Hartnell College, CA; **Eugene Guza**, North Orange County Community College District, CA; **Mary Beth Haan**, El Paso Community College, TX; **Elizabeth Haga**, State College of Florida, FL; **Saeede Haghi**, Ozyegin University, Turkey; **Laura Halvorson**, Lorain County Community College, OH; **Nancy Hamadou**, Pima Community College, AZ; **Kerri Hamberg**, Brookline Community and Adult Education, MA;

Katia Hameg, L'Envol Des Langues, Québec, Canada; **Sunsook Han**, King Abdulaziz University, Saudi Arabia; **Aniko Harrier**, Valencia College, FL; **James M. Harris**, University of Texas-Pan American, TX; **Susan Haskins-Doloff**, Pratt Institute, NY; **Olcay Havalan**, Bursa Anadolu Erkek Lisesi, Turkey; **Marla Heath**, Sacred Heart University, CT; **Jean Hendrickson**, SUNY Stony Brook, NY; **Tracy Henninger-Willey**, Lane Community College, OR; **Emily Herrick**, University of Nebraska, NE; **Jan Hinson**, Carson Newman University, TN; **Lisa Hockstein**, SUNY Westchester, NY; **Sarah Hodge**, Defense Language Institute, TX; **Kristie Hofelich**, Brown Mackie College, KY; **Harry Holden**, North Lake Community College, TX; **Elke Holtz**, Escuela Sierra Nevada, Mexico; **Hirofumi Hosokawa**, Fukuoka Jo Gakuin University, Japan; **Elisa Hunt**, North Dakota State University, ND; **Lutfi Hussein**, Mesa Community College, AZ; **Curt Hutchison**, Leeward Community College, HI; **Elizabeth Iannotti**, LaGuardia Community College, NY; **Barbara Inerfeld**, Rutgers University, NJ; **Julie Ingber**, Columbia University, NY; **Debbie Janysek**, Victoria College, TX; **Joan Jarrett**, Feather River College, CA; **Shawn Jarvis**, St. Cloud State University, MN; **Justin Jernigan**, Georgia Gwinnett College, GA; **Melanie Jipping**, Tokyo International University of America, OR; **Catherine Jones**, Excellent Interpreting, CO; **Jackie Jones**, Wayne State University, MI; **Irene Juzkiw**, University of Missouri, MO; **Aysegul Liman Kaban**, Gedik University, Turkey; **Vivian Kahn**, Long Island University, NY; **Eleanor Kamataris**, Harris Middle School, TX; **Gursharan Kandola**, University of Houston, TX; **Emily Kaney**, Northern Michigan University, MI; **Krystal Kaplan**, Pace University, NY; **Linda Karlen**, Oakton Community College, IL; **Katherine Katsenis**, Lyceum Tutorial Services, LLC, CA; **Martha Kehl**, Ohlone College, CA; **Scott Keller**, Literacy Volunteers of Leon County, FL; **Robert Kelso**, Miami Dade College, FL; **Alicia N. Kenter**, City College of San Francisco, CA; **Paul Kern**, Green River Community College, WA; **Mignon Kery**, H-B Woodlawn Secondary Program, VA; **Candace Khanna**, Laney College, CA; **Joy Kidstry**, University of Phoenix, AZ; **Cynthia Kilpatrick**, The University of Texas at Arlington, TX; **Doe-Hyung Kim**, Georgia Gwinnett College, GA; **Kindra Kinyon**, Los Angeles Trade-Technical College, CA; **James Kirchner**, Macomb Community College, MI; **Renee La Rue**, Lone Star College-Montgomery, TX; **Marjorie Labe**, Montgomery County Community College, PA; **Peter LaFontaine**, Alexandria Adult Learning Center, VA; **Katie Land**, St. Giles International, Canada; **Renee Lane**, Oxnard Adult School, CA; **Alan Lanes**, The Higher Colleges of Technology, UAE; **Stephanie Lange**, Cuyamaca College, CA; **T. Jonathan Lathers**, Macomb Community College, MI; **Margaret Vera Layton**, University of Nevada, NV; **Susan Leckart**, Middlesex County College, NJ; **Suzanne Leduc**, The New America College, CO; **Judy Lee**, Central Connecticut State University, CT; **Joy Leventhal**, Cuyahoga Community College, OH; **Helen Lin**, University of Florida, FL; **Amy Lindstrom**, University of New Mexico, NM; **Gytis Liulevicius**, Wellstone International High School, MN; **Robyn Lockwood**, Stanford University, CA; **Victoria Loeb**, Houston Community College, TX; **Janet Long**, University of Missouri, MO; **Roland Lopez**, Santa Monica College, CA; **Alexandra Lowe**, Westchester Community College (SUNY), NY; **Mary Lozano**, Pierce College, CA; **Gail Lugo**, Trine University, IN; **Joanna Luper**, Liberty University, VA; **Jaime Lyon**, University of Northern Iowa, IA; **Doris Macdonald**, Northern Illinois University, IL; **Bridgette MacFarlane**, Brewster Technical Center, FL; **Kevin Mackie**, Austin Community College, TX; **Mercedes Martinez**, Global Language Institute, MN; **Tetiana Maslova**, Kyiv Polytechnic Institute, Ukraine; **Terry Masters**, American School for Women and Children, OH; **Maryann Matheny**, Campbellsville University, KY; **Jennifer Maxwell**, Daytona State College, FL; **Halina Mazurak**, Cleveland State University, OH; **Susan McAlister**, University of Houston, TX; **Luke McCarthy**, Norwalk Community College, CT; **Marlo McClurg**, Cosumnes River College, CA; **Deb McCormick**, Doña Ana Community College, NM; **Chris McDaniel**, Yale University, CT; **Bridget McDonald**, Independent Learning Services, MA; **Deborah McGraw**, Syracuse University, NY; **Lisa McHenry**, GEOS Languages Plus, CA; **Deirdre McMurtry**, University of Nebraska at Omaha, NE; **Aziah McNamara**, Kansas State University, KS; **Ellen Measday**, Middlesex County College, NJ; **Nancy Megarity**, Collin College, TX; **Diane Mehegan**, Harvard University, MA; **Michelle Merritt**, Harmony School of Innovation, TX; **Nila Middleton**, Lone Star College-Cypress, TX; **Brandon Mills**, ELS Language Center, ND; **Malgorzata Moll**, St. Louis Community College, MO; **Kathleen Molzan**, Cuyahoga Community College, OH; **Adrienne Monaco**, Erie 1 BOCES, NY; **Beth Montag**, University of Nebraska at Kearney, NE; **Elisabete Montero**, Val Hala escola de idiomas, Brazil; **Do Sik Moon**, Hanyang Cyber University, South Korea; **Diane Mora**, Johnson County Community College, KS; **Micheline Morena**, College of the Desert, CA; **Gloria Munson**, University of Texas, TX; **Gino Muzzatti**, Santa Rosa Junior College, CA; **Myo Myint**, Mission College, CA; **Kathy Najafi**, Houston Community College, TX; **Patricia Nation**, Miami Dade College, FL; **Elizabeth Neblett**, Union County College, NJ; **Karen Nelson**, Pittsburgh State University, PA; **Marley Nelson**, English Center USA, IL; **Anastasia Nizamova**, New York University, NY; **Sharon Nunn**, Englishdom; **Karla Odenwald**, Boston University, MA; **Tina O'Donnell**, Language Center International, MI; **Ann O'Driscoll**, Southern Oregon University, OR; **Donna Ogle**, Arkansas Tech University, AR; **Nastaran Ohadi**, Ganjineh Danesh, Iran; **Iris Oriaro**, Arkansas State University, AR; **Fernanda Ortiz**, University of Arizona, AZ; **Susan Osuch**, Englishworks, Inc., TX; **Kris Oswald**, Kansas State University, KS; **Stephanie Owens**, ELS, CT; **Gorkem Oztur**, Özel Manavgat Bahcesehir Anadolu Lisesi, Turkey; **Ümit Öztürk**, İzmir-Torbalı Anatolian Teacher Training High School, Turkey; **Murat Ozudogru**, Maltepe University, Turkey; **Marilyn Padgett**, Calhoun Middle School, NY; **Bilsev Pastakkaya**, Yalova University, Turkey; **Angela Pastore-Nikitenko**, Embassy English, CA; **Wendy Patriquin**, Parkland College, IL; **Irina Patten**, Lone Star College, TX; **Jennifer Paz**, Auburn University, AL; **Mary Peacock**, Richland College, TX; **Randi Lynn Peerlman**, Texas A&M University, TX; **Jeanne Peine**, University of Houston, TX; **Nuran Peker**, Nazilli High School, Turkey; **Susan Pelley**, Doña Ana Community College, NM; **Jorge Perez**, Southwestern College, CA; **Kim Perkins**, Boston University, MA; **William Phelps**, Southern Illinois University, IL; **Tom Pierce**, Central New Mexico Community College, NM; **Jennifer Piotrowski**, Language Center International, MI; **Carole Poppleton-Schrading**, Johns Hopkins University, MD; **Valentina Portnov**, Kingsborough Community College, NY; **Nancy Price**, University of Missouri, MO; **Catherine Ramberg**, Albany Adult School, CA; **Brian Ramey**, Sehir University, Turkey; **Steven Rashba**, University of Bridgeport, CT; **Victoria Reis**, Language Studies International, NY; **Amy Renehan**, University of Washington, WA; **Elizabeth Reyes**, Elgin Community College, IL; **Kathleen Reynolds**, Harper College, IL; **Tom Riedmiller**, University of Northern Iowa, IA; **Dzidra Rodins**, DePaul University, IL; **Ana Rodriguez**, Elliston School of Languages, FL; **Ann Roemer**, Utah State University, UT; **Margot Rose**, Pierce College, WA; **David Ross**, Houston Community College, TX; **Robert Ruddy**, Northeastern University, MA; **Peter Ruggiero**, Boston University, MA; **Phil Ruggiero**, The University of Missouri, MO; **Anne Sadberry**, The Language Company, OK; **Jessica Saigh**, University of Missouri-St. Louis, MO; **Irene Sakk**, Northwestern University, IL; **Kamila Salimova**, TGT, Russia; **Chari Sanchinelli**, Colegio Valle Verde, Guatemala; **Christen Savage**, University of Houston, TX; **Boutheina Sayadi**, Virtual University of Tunis, Tunisia; **Rosemary Schmid**, University of North Carolina, NC; **Diana Schoolman**, St. John's University, NY; **Myrna Schwarz**, La Roche College, PA; **Karen Schwenke**, Biola University, CA; **Dilek Batur Secer**, Toros University, Turkey; **Diana Sefchik**, Raritan Valley Community College, NJ; **Ertan Selimoglu**, Yildiz Technical University, Turkey; **Rene Serrano**, Universidad Nacional Autónoma de México, Mexico; **Gul Shamim**, Amir Sharifi, California State University, CA; **Caroline Sharp**, University of Maryland, MD; **Shixian Sheng**, Boston Chinatown Neighborhood Center, MA; **Oksana Shevchenko**, Horlivka Language School, Ukraine; **A. Shipley**, Academy of Art University, CA; **D. H. Shreve**, University of North Texas, TX; **Meire Silva**, Celebration Language Institute, FL; **Fiore Sireci**, Hunter College, NY; **Anita Teresa Smith**, Majan College, Oman; **Jacqueline Smith**, The New School, NY; **Jeff Smith**, Ohio Northern University, OH; **Lorraine Smith**, Queens College, NY; **Barbara Smith-Palinkas**, Hillsborough Community College, FL; **Kimberly Spallinger**, Bowling Green State University, OH; **James Stakenburg**, Rennert International, NY; **Katrina Tamura**, Palomar College, CA; **Dan Tannacito**, Indiana University of Pennsylvania, PA; **Jamie Tanzman**, Northern Kentucky University, KY; **Tara Tarpey**, New York University, NY; **Amy Tate**, Houston Community College, TX; **Rose Tauscher**, Skyline High School, TX; **Tamara Taylor**, University of North Texas-IELI, TX; **Cihan Tekin**, İMKB 24 Kasım Anadolu Lisesi, Turkey; **Kelly Tennison**, Roseville Area High School, MN; **Abby Thomas**, Northern Essex Community College, MA; **Brett Thomas**, Sacramento City College, CA; **Linda Thomas**, Lone Star College-Montgomery, TX; **Edith Thompson**, Purdy R-II School District, MO; **Sylwia Thorne**, Kent State University, OH; **Donna Tooker**, Miramar College, CA; **Beth Topping**, Auburn University, AL; **Carolyn Trachtova**, Webster University, MO; **William Trudeau**, Ohio Northern University, OH; **Kathy Truman**, Haverford High School, PA; **Karen Tucker**, Georgia Institute of Technology, GA; **Gretchen Twohig**, ASC English, MA; **Blanca Ugraskan**, Del Mar Community College, TX; **Serkan Ülgü**, Air Force Academy, Turkey; **Mecit Uzun**, Gaziosmanpaşa, Turkey; **Cynthia Valdez**, Palisade High, CO; **Kanako Valencia Suda**, De Anza College, CA; **Michelle Van de Sande**, Arapahoe Community College, CO; **Sharon Van Houte**, Lorain County Community College, OH; **Sara Vandenberg**, University of Colorado, CO; **Lillian Vargas**, University of Florida, FL; **Tara Vassallo**, Pace University, NY; **Stephanie Viol**, Palm House; **Kathleen Vodvarka**, University of Delaware, DE; **Kerry Vrabel**, GateWay Community College, AZ; **Carol Wachana**, ELS Language School; **Christine Waddail**, Johns Hopkins University, MD; **Christina Wade**, Liberty University, VA; **Wendy Walsh**, College of Marin, CA; **Colin Ward**, Lone Star College-North Harris, TX; **Mary Kay Wedum**, Colorado State University, CO; **Linda Wesley**, Pennsylvania State University, PA; **Lynne Wilkins**, The English Center, CA; **Betty Williams**; **Jeff Wilson**, Irvine Community College, CA; **Lori Wilson-Patterson**, Ivy Tech Community College, IN; **Kirsten Windahl**, Cuyahoga Community College, OH; **Aleasha Winters**, Lingo TEFL Language Institute, Costa Rica; **Jing Zhou**, Defense Language Institute, CA; **Yelena Zimon**, Fremont Adult School, CA; **Koraljka Zunic**, Grossmont College, CA

Contents

3 | Nouns and Articles

4 | Pronouns and Determiners

5 | Future Forms

6 | Modals

7 | Gerunds and To- Infinitives

8|Present Perfect and Past Perfect

9|Modals II

10|Adjectives and Other Forms That Describe Nouns

11 | Adverbs and Prepositional Phrases

12 | Adverb Clauses

13 | Comparisons

14 | Sentence Patterns

1 Simple Present and Present Progressive

If we don't change, we don't grow. If we don't grow, we aren't really living.

—GAIL SHEEHY, JOURNALIST, LECTURER, AND AUTHOR (1937–)

Talk about It Do you agree or disagree with the quotation above? Why?

WARM-UP

A Read these sentences and check (✓) *True* or *False*. Then compare answers with your classmates. What was the most common answer for each question?

Speaking English

	TRUE	FALSE
1. I **am taking** an English course this year.	☐	☐
2. My teacher only **uses** English in the classroom.	☐	☐
3. I **study** hard.	☐	☐
4. I **like** to talk in class.	☐	☐
5. My English **is getting** better.	☐	☐
6. Many jobs **require** knowledge of another language.	☐	☐
7. One out of six people in the world **speaks** English.	☐	☐
8. Other languages **are** now **borrowing** many words from English.	☐	☐

B Answer these questions about the verbs in the sentences above.

1. The verbs in **blue** are simple present verbs. Some end in *-s* and some do not. Why is that?
2. The verbs in green are present progressive verbs. How are they different from the simple present verbs?

C Look back at the quotation on page 2. Identify any present verb forms.

1.1 Using the Simple Present

A

TIMELESS TRUTHS AND GENERAL STATEMENTS **1** Most Canadians **speak** English. **2** The earth **moves** around the sun. **3** New York City **is** truly a unique place. **4** There **are** about 7 billion people in the world.	We use the **simple present** for timeless truths and general statements, as in **1 – 4**.

B

HABITS AND ROUTINES **5** My brother **works** five days a week. **6** My sister never **gets** home before 7:00. **7** The bank **opens** at 8:00 on Saturday.	We also use the simple present to describe habits and routines—things that take place regularly, as in **5 – 7**.

C

HOW SOMEONE OR SOMETHING IS (STATES)
8 A: How's your back?
   B: It **feels** worse today.
9 A: Is Jenn OK?
   B: Yeah, she **seems** fine now.
10 A: I **like** this movie a lot.
    B: Really? I **think** it's kind of strange.
	We can also use the simple present with non-action verbs to describe how someone or something is now, as in **8 – 10**. Some common non-action verbs are:

be	have	look	remember
believe	hear	love	seem
contain	know	need	think
feel	like	own	want

GRAMMAR TERM: Non–action verbs are also called **stative verbs** because they describe states instead of actions. For a list of non-action verbs, see the Resources, page R-2.

1 | Noticing the Simple Present in General Statements Underline the simple present verbs. Then complete each sentence with an idea from the box. `1.1 A`

PROVERBS

1. Age and time <u>do not wait</u> _for people_ _____ .	a thousand words
2. An apple a day keeps _____ .	always right
3. Two heads are _____ .	better than one
4. Bad news travels _____ .	fast
5. A picture paints _____ .	for people
6. A good companion shortens _____ .	his tools
7. The customer is _____ .	louder than words
8. Actions speak _____ .	perfect
9. The bad worker always blames[1] _____ .	the doctor away
10. Practice makes _____ .	the longest road

Think about It We call the sentences above "proverbs." Why do you think we use the simple present form of verbs with proverbs?

Talk about It Take turns reading the proverbs above aloud with a partner. What do you think each proverb means? Do you agree or disagree?

[1] **blame:** to say that something else is the cause of a problem

4

2 | Noticing the Simple Present Underline the simple present verbs in these statements. Which country do the sentences describe? Choose from the list. (You will not use all the countries.) `1.1 A`

Descriptions of Countries

COUNTRY 1 _____

    a. It <u>is</u> the second largest country in the world.

    b. It borders the United States.

    c. The three biggest cities are Toronto, Montreal, and Vancouver.

COUNTRY 2 _____

    d. People in this country speak Arabic.

    e. The capital city of this country is Muscat.

    f. This country produces oil.

COUNTRY 3 _____

    g. This country shares borders with Belgium, Germany, Luxembourg, Switzerland, Spain, and Italy.

    h. The island of Corsica belongs to this country.

    i. A flight from this country to New York takes about six hours.

COUNTRY 4 _____

    j. This country has the longest river in South America.

    k. It produces 80 percent of the world's orange juice.

    l. The largest cities are São Paulo, Rio de Janeiro, and Salvador.

Brazil

Japan

Oman

Canada

France

Kenya

Write about It Write three facts about another country. Read your facts to your classmates, and ask them to guess the country.

3 | Describing Habits and Routines Underline the simple present verbs in these statements. Then check (✓) the statements that describe you. `1.1 B`

EATING HABITS

☐ 1. I <u>eat</u> a lot of fruit.

☐ 2. I drink a lot of coffee.

☐ 3. I eat breakfast every morning.

☐ 4. I eat slowly.

☐ 5. I avoid junk food.

☐ 6. I often skip meals[2].

☐ 7. I often eat late at night.

☐ 8. I drink a lot of water during the day.

SLEEPING HABITS

☐ 9. I sleep fewer than seven hours a night.

☐ 10. I get up at the same time every day.

☐ 11. I almost always go to bed late.

☐ 12. I sometimes fall asleep in front of the television.

PHYSICAL HABITS

☐ 13. I sit for many hours during the day.

☐ 14. I take a long walk almost every day.

☐ 15. I play a sport regularly.

[2] **skip meals:** to not eat meals

Think about It Circle the time expressions in the sentences in Activity 3. Which time expressions come before the verb? Which come after? Write each time expression in the chart below.

Time expressions before the verb	Time expressions after the verb
often	*every morning*

Talk about It Look at the sentences you checked in Activity 3. Which are healthy habits, and which are unhealthy habits? Tell a partner. Then think of three more healthy and unhealthy habits.

"My healthy habits are: I eat a lot of fruit...."   *"My unhealthy habits are: I drink a lot of coffee...."*

4 | Identifying Non-Action Verbs
Underline the seven non-action verbs in these comments. Then match the sentences with non-action verbs to the pictures below. **1.1 C**

COMMENTS

1. "She <u>feels</u> cold."
2. "He needs a haircut."
3. "He's tired."
4. "She has a headache."
5. "They dance very well."

6. "They look alike."
7. "She knows the answer."
8. "He drives a big car."
9. "They like ice cream."
10. "She usually wears black."

a. _6_

b. ____

c. ____

d. ____

e. ____

f. ____

g. ____

Write about It Think of another comment for each picture above. Ask your classmates to identify the action and non-action verbs in your comments. (Look at Chart 1.1 for a list of non-action verbs you can use.)

They have red shirts. They seem friendly.

1.2 Simple Present Statements

A

The simplest form of a verb is the **base form**. We use the base form for the simple present of most verbs, as in **1 – 3** and **5**. We add **-s** or **-es** when the subject is *he, she, it,* or a singular noun, as in **4**.

FIRST PERSON

	base form	
1 I	**live**	there.

	base form	
2 Dan and I / We	**live**	there.

SECOND PERSON

	base form	
3 You	**live**	there.

THIRD PERSON

	base form + -s / -es	
4 He/She/It / My friend	**lives**	there.

	base form	
5 They / My parents	**live**	there.

For spelling rules of third-person singular verbs, see Activity 6, page 8.
For the simple present of the verb *be*, see Chart 1.4, page 16.

B

For negative statements, we use *do not / does not* + the **base form of a main verb**, as in **6 – 10**.
When we use the verb **do** in this way, we call it a **helping verb**.

	do + not	base form	
6 I	**do not** / **don't**	**like**	it.

	do + not	base form	
7 We	**do not** / **don't**	**like**	it.

	do + not	base form	
8 You	**do not** / **don't**	**like**	it.

	does + not	base form	
9 He/She/It	**does not** / **doesn't**	**like**	it.

	do + not	base form	
10 They	**do not** / **don't**	**like**	it.

We often use the contractions *don't* or *doesn't* instead of *do not* or *does not*, especially in conversation.

C

11 My sister **doesn't work** here.
12 I **do** the dishes, and my kids **do** the laundry.
13 I **don't do** anything on Saturdays.

The verb *do* is special. We can use the verb *do* as:
- a **helping verb**, as in **11**
- a **main verb**, as in **12**

It's even possible to use the helping verb *do* with the main verb *do*, as in **13**.

D

CORRECT THE COMMON ERRORS (See page R-13.)

14 ✗ She don't have time for this.
15 ✗ He email his family a lot.
16 ✗ She is a housewife and have three children.
17 ✗ It make me happy.

GO ONLINE

---

5 | Using the Correct Form Complete these sentences with the correct form of the verb in parentheses. Then check (✓) *True* or *False*. **1.2 A**

DESCRIBING PEOPLE IN YOUR CLASS	TRUE	FALSE
1. My classmates and I _____*talk*_____ a lot in class. (talk/talks)	☐	☐
2. My teacher _____ glasses. (wear/wears)	☐	☐
3. My classmates _____ the same music I _____ . (like/likes)	☐	☐
4. Nobody _____ a musical instrument. (play/plays)	☐	☐
5. One person _____ in a hospital. (work/works)	☐	☐
6. I _____ pretty good today. (feel/feels)	☐	☐
7. Two people _____ to class every day. (drive/drives)	☐	☐
8. I _____ to class on Tuesdays and Thursdays. (come/comes)	☐	☐

	TRUE	FALSE
9. In class, we _____ in chairs in a circle. (sit/sits)	☐	☐
10. A few of my classmates _____ Chinese. (speak/speaks)	☐	☐
11. Everybody _____ a lot of words in English. (know/knows)	☐	☐
12. Everyone _____ more than one language. (speak/speaks)	☐	☐

Think about It Which statements in Activity 5 describe a habit or routine?

Sentence 1 describes a habit or routine.

> **F Y I**
>
> Indefinite pronouns such as *everybody*, *somebody*, and *nobody* are always singular.
>
> **Everybody** in my class speaks English.

6 | Spelling Note: Third-Person Singular Verbs Read the note. Then do Activity 7.

To form the third-person singular *(he/she/it)* for the simple present:

1 Add -*es* to verbs that end in -*sh*, -*ch*, -*ss*, -*s*, -*x*, or -*z*.

finish	finishes	touch	touches	pass	passes	relax	relaxes

2 For verbs ending in a consonant + -*y*, change the -*y* to -*i* and add -*es*.

study	studies	worry	worries	deny	denies	fly	flies

3 Three verbs have a special spelling:

go	goes	do	does	have	has

4 For all other verbs, add -*s*.

like	likes	buy	buys	see	sees	speak	speaks

7 | Forming Third-Person Singular Verbs Complete these statements with the correct form of the bold verb. `1.2 A`

HOW ARE YOU AND YOUR SPOUSE DIFFERENT?

1. I **watch** a lot of movies on TV, and my husband _____*watches*_____ a lot of news programs.

2. I **belong** to a basketball team, and he _____ to a soccer team.

3. I **wash** the dishes, and he _____ the clothes.

4. I **do** karate for exercise, and he _____ weight-lifting.

5. I **worry** about money, and he _____ about the future.

6. I **go** to work by subway, and he _____ by bus.

7. I **get up** early on weekends, but my wife _____ late.

8. I **have** a lot of books, and she _____ a lot of videos.

9. I **fly** to Los Angeles once a month, and she _____ to New York every other week.

10. I **finish** work at 6:00, and she _____ at 5:00.

11. I **buy** a lot of clothes, and my wife _____ a lot of jewelry.

12. I always **carry** a briefcase with me, and she always _____ a purse.

Write about It Think of a friend or family member. How are you different? Write three sentences like the ones in Activity 7.

I have short hair, and my sister has long hair.

8 | Pronunciation Note: Third-Person Singular Verbs Listen to the note. Then do Activity 9.

We usually pronounce the -s or -es ending on a verb as a /s/ or /z/ sound. Notice that in a sentence, it's often difficult to hear the difference between the two sounds.

1 He eats here every day.   **3** He always leaves before me.
2 She makes a lot of money.   **4** She worries too much.

We pronounce the -es ending as /əz/ with an extra syllable when the base form of the verb ends in a hissing or buzzing sound. (These words are often spelled with a final -ce, -ge, -se, -ze, -ch, -sh, and -ss).

5 She really misses him.   **7** The company publishes good books.   **9** He teaches math.
6 He chooses his own clothes.   **8** She arranges all of our meetings.

9 | Pronouncing Third-Person Singular Verbs How do you pronounce the -s or -es ending on these **bold** verbs? Check (✓) your ideas. Then listen and confirm your answers. **1.2 A**

	/s/ OR /z/	AN EXTRA SYLLABLE /əz/
1. She **watches** a lot of TV.	☐	☑
2. He always **relaxes** on the weekend.	☐	☐
3. She usually **takes** a nap around 3:00.	☐	☐
4. He **hopes** to finish soon.	☐	☐
5. She **expresses** herself well.	☐	☐
6. He always **shares** his lunch with me.	☐	☐
7. He never **raises** his hand in class.	☐	☐
8. She **notices** everything.	☐	☐
9. He **shakes** hands with everyone.	☐	☐
10. She **washes** her clothes by hand.	☐	☐
11. He never **finishes** on time.	☐	☐
12. Our boss **makes** us come in early on Fridays.	☐	☐
13. He **manages** his money well.	☐	☐
14. My job **involves** a lot of travel.	☐	☐
15. Your dinner **includes** soup and a salad.	☐	☐
16. Canada **produces** a lot of oil.	☐	☐

10 | Using *Don't or Doesn't* Complete these descriptions with the negative form of the verb in parentheses. `1.2 B`

TYPES OF PEOPLE

1. Vegetarians _____ *don't eat* _____ meat. (eat)
2. A couch potato _____ anything all day. (do)
3. A technophobe _____ to use computers or technology. (like)
4. A conformist _____ to be different from other people. (want)
5. A night owl _____ at night. (sleep)
6. A pacifist _____ in war. (believe)
7. Pessimists _____ the positive in things. They only see the negative. (see)
8. Homebodies _____ to go out or travel. They prefer to stay home. (like)
9. Early birds _____ in bed in the morning. They get up early. (stay)
10. Optimists _____ when things go wrong. They believe that everything will be OK. (worry)

Talk about It Do any of the words above describe you? Why? Tell a partner.

"I'm a night owl because I like to stay up late."

11 | Making Negative Statements Rewrite these sentences to describe a bad job. Use the negative form of the verb. `1.2 B`

Characteristics of a good job	Characteristics of a bad job
1. You get a lot of vacation time.	1. *You don't get a lot of vacation time.*
2. You have a long time for lunch.	2. _____
3. The company provides good health insurance.	3. _____
4. The office has good lighting.	4. _____
5. The company pays overtime[3].	5. _____
6. The company lets people work flexible hours.	6. _____
7. You get a big bonus at the end of the year.	7. _____
8. The office has its own gym.	8. _____
9. You get out early on Friday.	9. _____
10. You enjoy the work.	10. _____
11. Your co-workers do their work on time.	11. _____

Write about It Write two other characteristics of a good job and a bad job.

[3] **overtime:** extra hours worked

12 | Helping Verb or Main Verb? Is the **bold** verb a helping verb or a main verb? Check (✓) your answers. `1.2 C`

PERSONAL HABITS	HELPING VERB	MAIN VERB
1. I don't usually **do** my homework.	☐	☑
2. I don't **do** anything on the weekend.	☐	☐
3. I **do**n't have a lot of close friends.	☐	☐
4. I **do** most of the cooking at home.	☐	☐
5. I **do** a lot for other people.	☐	☐
6. I **do**n't cause trouble at school.	☐	☐
7. I don't always **do** the right thing.	☐	☐
8. I **do**n't talk a lot in class.	☐	☐
9. I rarely **do** the dishes at home.	☐	☐
10. I always **do** my best on tests.	☐	☐
11. I **do**n't drink a lot of coffee.	☐	☐
12. I **do** the laundry at home.	☐	☐
13. I **do** my shopping online.	☐	☐
14. I **do**n't exercise every day.	☐	☐

Think about It Why does *do* appear twice in three of the sentences above?

Talk about It Which sentences above describe you? Tell a partner.

13 | Error Correction Correct any errors in these sentences. (Some sentences may not have any errors.)

FAMILY MEMBERS

1. My mother is get up early every day and cook breakfast for everyone.

   My mother gets up early every day and cooks breakfast for everyone.

2. My father works hard and help all of his neighbors. I am very much respect him.
3. My mother help me in many ways, but I don't rely on her for everything.
4. My brother is not eat meat. He's a vegetarian.
5. My older brother work every day. At home, he take care of his baby daughter.
6. My parents are my security. They accepts my ideas or at least they doesn't show their disagreement.
7. My father is also my good friend. He and I do a lot of things together and we talk a lot.
8. My father is a helpful person, and he give me lots of advice. For example, he often talk to me about my future. He ask me lots of questions and listen carefully.
9. My grandmother tell great stories, and she always make me laugh. She also make great cookies and cakes. I am sad every time I leave her.
10. My brother is a nurse. He works very hard, but he still find time to visit our parents almost every week. He is a good son, unlike his younger brother (me). I live far away, so I only visits my parents once a year.
11. One of my favorite people is my aunt. We talk on the phone almost every day. My aunt don't like to fly, so I don't get to see her often. In fact, I only see her on holidays when I fly home. Unfortunately, that don't happen very often.

1.3 Questions with the Simple Present

We use the helping verb *do* to ask questions with the simple present.

For *yes/no* questions, we use *do / does* and the **base form of a main verb**, as in **1 – 3**. We can give short answers to *yes/no* questions with *do / does*, as in **4 – 9**. In negative short answers, we often use contractions, as in **7 – 9**.

A

YES/NO QUESTIONS

	do / does	subject	base form
1	Do	I you	work?
2	Does	he she it	work?
3	Do	we you they	work?

SHORT ANSWERS

			do / does
4	Yes,	you I	do.
5	Yes,	he she it	does.
6	Yes,	you we they	do.

			do / does + not
7	No,	you I	don't.
8	No,	he she it	doesn't.
9	No,	you we they	don't.

For *wh-* questions, we use a **wh- word** + *do / does* and the **base form of a main verb**, as in **10 – 21**.

B

WH- QUESTIONS

	wh- word	do	subject	base form
10	What		you	want?
11	Where		they	live?
12	When	do	the stores	open?
13	Why		we	exercise?
14	Who		you	know?
15	How		I	begin?

	wh- word	does	subject	base form
16	What		he	want?
17	Where		Sarah	live?
18	When	does	it	open?
19	Why		Tom	exercise?
20	Who		she	know?
21	How		the movie	begin?

When the **wh- word** is the subject, don't use *do* or *does*. Use the base form + **-s** or **-es**, as in **22 – 23**.

WH- QUESTIONS ABOUT THE SUBJECT

	subject	base form + -s / -es	
22	Who	lives	there?
23	What	happens	in the morning?

For information about forming questions with the verb *be*, see Chart 1.4, page 16.

14 | Choosing *Do* or *Does* Complete the questions with *Do* or *Does*. Then say where you might hear each question. Check (✓) one or more places. **1.3 A**

PERSONAL HABITS	RESTAURANT	CLOTHING STORE	AIRPORT
1. _____Do_____ you have this in size 12?	☐	☐	☐
2. _____ the chicken come with a salad?	☐	☐	☐
3. _____ you take credit cards?	☐	☐	☐
4. _____ we need a reservation?	☐	☐	☐
5. _____ this shirt come in other colors?	☐	☐	☐
6. _____ you have your ticket?	☐	☐	☐

	RESTAURANT	CLOTHING STORE	AIRPORT
7. _____ you want a table near the window?	☐	☐	☐
8. _____ you sell shoes?	☐	☐	☐
9. _____ soup come with this?	☐	☐	☐
10. _____ you have any luggage?	☐	☐	☐

Think about It What is the main verb in each question in Activity 14? Circle it.

Talk about It Work with a partner. Choose one of the questions in Activity 14 and use it to create a short conversation. Present your conversation to the class.

A: Do you have this in size 12?
B: No, I'm sorry, we don't. Do you want to try size 10 or size 14?
A: Sure.

15 | Forming *Yes/No* Questions with *Do* or *Does* Choose verbs from the boxes to complete these conversations. Use the correct form. Then practice with a partner. `1.3 A`

1. A: _____*Do*_____ you _____*know*_____ Philip Winski?

   B: No, I don't. _____ he _____ here?

   A: Yes, he _____ the mail room.

   | know |
   | manage |
   | work |

2. A: What's the matter with the printer?

   B: I _____ _____ .

   A: _____ it _____ paper?

   B: Yes, I _____ so.

   | have |
   | not/know |
   | think |

3. A: _____ you _____ Anne's number?

   B: No, I don't, but I _____ it on my phone.

   _____ you _____ me to get it?

   A: Please.

   | have |
   | remember |
   | want |

4. A: _____ Jen _____ Mexican food?

   B: I think so. Why?

   A: Because tomorrow's her birthday, and Ben and I _____ to take her out.

   B: _____ you _____ a good Mexican restaurant?

   A: Yeah. People say Café Central _____ good Mexican food.

   | know |
   | like |
   | serve |
   | want |

5. A: How's the new baby girl?

   B: Great, but Dan and I are both pretty tired.

   A: _____ she _____ through the night yet?

   B: No, but she's healthy, and she _____ happy.

   A: That's good.

   | seem |
   | sleep |

Think about It Which verbs above describe a state (how someone or something is) rather than an action?

16 | Asking *Wh-*Questions Complete these quiz questions with a *wh-* word (*when, who, where, what, how long,* or *how often*). Then circle your answers. `1.3 B`

The Olympic Games Quiz

1. _____How often_____ do the Olympic Games take place?

   a. every year
   b. every two years
   c. every ten years

2. _____ do the Games last?

   a. about one week
   b. about two weeks
   c. about four weeks

3. _____ does the host country[4] do?

   a. It organizes the Games.
   b. It chooses the winners of the events.
   c. It selects the athletes.

4. _____ marches in the opening parade?

   a. one athlete from each country
   b. only the athletes from the host country
   c. athletes from all countries

5. _____ does the winner of an event get?

   a. a medal
   b. some money
   c. a new uniform

6. _____ leads the opening parade?

   a. athletes from Afghanistan
   b. athletes from Greece
   c. athletes from the host country

7. _____ do the athletes live during the Games?

   a. in the Olympic Village
   b. in nearby cities
   c. in private hotels

8. _____ chooses the athletes?

   a. the Olympic Committee
   b. each country
   c. the host country

9. _____ do the Olympic Games take place?

   a. in Greece
   b. in Asia
   c. in a different country each time

10. _____ do the skiing events take place?

   a. in the Winter Games
   b. in the Summer Games
   c. in the Winter Games and Summer Games

Answers: 1. b; 2. b; 3. a; 4. c; 5. a; 6. b; 7. a; 8. b; 9. c; 10. a

Think about It What is the main verb in each question above? Underline it.

17 | Pronunciation Note: Question Intonation Listen to the note. Then do Activities 18 and 19.

Yes/No questions usually end with rising intonation.

1 Do you work?   **2** Do you play soccer?   **3** Does she need some money?

Wh- questions usually end with falling intonation.

4 What do you do?   **5** Where do you live?   **6** Where does he go to school?

[4]**host country:** the country where the Games take place

18 | Listening for Question Intonation Listen to each question. Circle ⤴ (rising intonation) or ⤵ (falling intonation). Then listen again and repeat the questions. `1.3 A–B`

1. (⤴) ⤵	4. ⤴ ⤵	7. ⤴ ⤵	10. ⤴ ⤵	13. ⤴ ⤵
2. ⤴ ⤵	5. ⤴ ⤵	8. ⤴ ⤵	11. ⤴ ⤵	14. ⤴ ⤵
3. ⤴ ⤵	6. ⤴ ⤵	9. ⤴ ⤵	12. ⤴ ⤵	15. ⤴ ⤵

19 | Using Question Intonation Read these questions and mark them ⤴ (for rising intonation) or ⤵ (for falling intonation). Then listen and repeat the questions. `1.3 A–B`

TWELVE COMMON QUESTIONS IN CONVERSATION

1. Do I make myself clear? ⤴
2. Do you mind? ____
3. How do you like this weather? ____
4. Does anyone know? ____
5. How do you do? ____
6. What does that prove? ____
7. Who do you want to talk to? ____
8. What does it matter? ____
9. Does it work for you? ____
10. Who do you think you are? ____
11. Do you understand? ____
12. What do you mean? ____

RESEARCH SAYS...

We often use these verbs in the simple present form:

doubt	mind
know	suppose
matter	think
mean	

CORPUS

Think about It In what situations do people use the questions above? Share ideas with your classmates.

20 | Pronunciation Note: Reduced Words Listen to the note. Then do Activity 21.

We usually pronounce *Do you* as "Duh yuh" or "D'yuh" except in very formal speech.

1 Do you like this?	*sounds like*	"D'yuh like this?"
2 Do you have a minute?	*sounds like*	"Duh yuh have a minute?"

We also pronounce *wh-* questions with "Duh yuh" or "D'yuh" except in very formal speech.

3 What **do you** need?	*sounds like*	"What-d'yuh need?"
4 Where **do you** live?	*sounds like*	"Where duh yuh live?"
5 Why **do you** ask?	*sounds like*	"Why duh yuh ask?"

21 | Listening for Reduced Words Listen and repeat. Then ask a partner the questions. `1.3 A–B`

QUESTIONS FROM PERSONALITY TESTS

1. Do you talk a lot?
2. Do you get angry easily?
3. Do you make friends easily?
4. Do you like animals?
5. Do you work hard?
6. Do you usually show your feelings?
7. How much time do you spend on the Internet?
8. What do you do for fun?
9. How do you handle a disagreement?
10. How do you handle stress?
11. Where do you like to go on vacation?
12. Where do you go for advice?

A: *Do you talk a lot?*
B: *I do! I love to sit in a café and talk for hours.*

The simple present of *be* has three forms: *am*, *is*, and *are*, as in **1 – 5**.

A

FIRST PERSON

		be	
1	I	am 'm	fine.
2	We	are 're	ready.

SECOND PERSON

		be	
3	You	are 're	alone.

THIRD PERSON

		be	
4	He/She/It	is 's	right.
5	They	are 're	good.

B

We add **not** after *am* / *is* / *are* for negative statements, as in **6 – 10**.

		be + not	
6	I	am not 'm not	sure.
7	We	are not 're not aren't	certain.

		be + not	
8	You	are not 're not aren't	careful.

		be + not	
9	He/She/It	is not 's not isn't	ready.
10	They	are not 're not aren't	alone.

C

We put *am* / *is* / *are* before the subject to ask *yes/no* questions, as in **11 – 12**.
We can give short answers to *yes/no* questions, as in **13 – 16**.
In negative short answers, we often use contractions, as in **15 – 16**.

YES/NO QUESTIONS

	be	subject	
11	**Am**	I	late?
	Are	you	
	Is	he she it	
12	**Are**	we you they	OK?

SHORT ANSWERS

			be
13	Yes,	you	are.
		I	am.
		he she it	is.
14	Yes,	you we they	are.

			be + not
15	No,	you	're not. aren't.
		I	'm not.
		he she it	's not. isn't.
16	No,	you we they	're not. aren't.

WARNING! We don't use contractions with short yes answers.
(NOT: ~~Yes, you're.~~)

D

For *wh-* questions, we use a **wh- word** + *am* / *is* / *are*, as in **17 – 22**.
In conversation, we often use a contraction, as in **23 – 28**.

WH- QUESTIONS

	wh- word	*be*	
17	What		his name?
18	Where	is	my computer?
19	When		your birthday?
20	Who		that?
21	Why	are	we here?
22	How		you?

CONTRACTIONS WITH WH- WORDS

	wh- word + *be*	
23	What's	his name?
24	Where's	my computer?
25	When's	your birthday?
26	Who's	that?
27	Why're	we here?
28	How're	you?

GO ONLINE

22 | Choosing *Is* or *Are* Describe some of your favorite things. Use *is* or *are* in your sentences. `1.4 A`

FAVORITE THINGS

1. My favorite colors ____are____ _____ .

2. My favorite day of the week _____ _____ .

3. My favorite sports to watch on TV _____ _____ .

4. Two of my favorite movies _____ _____ .

5. My favorite website _____ _____ .

6. My favorite sport _____ _____ .

7. My favorite hot drinks _____ _____ .

8. My favorite school subject _____ _____ .

9. My favorite cities _____ _____ .

10. My favorite kind of music _____ _____ .

> **WARNING!**
>
> In English, every complete sentence needs a subject and a verb. We can't leave out the verb *be* as we can in some other languages.
>
> She is happy.
> (NOT: ~~She happy.~~)

Talk about It Compare the statements you wrote above with a partner. How many of your favorite things are the same?

23 | Using *Is/Isn't* and *Are/Aren't* Complete these facts with the correct form of the verb *be*. Use the negative form of the verb in the first sentence of each pair. (Use a contraction where possible.) `1.4 B`

○ ○ ○

Ten Facts about Geography

1. The earth ____isn't____ flat. It ___'s____ round.

2. The national language of Brazil _____ Spanish. It _____ Portuguese.

3. The Mississippi River _____ the longest river in the world. The Nile _____ .

4. The world's two highest mountains _____ in Europe. They _____ in Asia.

5. The Atlantic Ocean _____ the largest ocean in the world. The Pacific _____ .

6. Canada's official languages _____ English and Spanish. They _____ English and French.

7. Canada _____ the biggest country in the world. Russia _____ .

8. The world's two largest cities _____ in South America. They _____ in Asia.

9. The world's largest desert _____ the Sahara Desert. It _____ Antarctica.

10. Mars _____ the hottest planet in our solar system. Venus _____ .

Think about It Read each sentence above aloud two times. Use different negative contractions in each reading.

"The earth isn't flat. It's round."   *"The earth's not flat. It's round."*

Talk about It What other geography facts do you know? Share information with your classmates.

24 | Using _Be_ in _Yes/No_ Questions and Answers Complete these conversations with the positive or negative form of the verb _be_. (Use a contraction where possible.) Then practice with a partner. `1.4 C`

ON AN AIRPLANE

1. A: Excuse me, but I think you __'re__

   in my seat.

   B: _____ you sure?

   A: Yes, I _____ pretty sure.

2. A: _____ the restroom in the back of

   the plane?

   B: No, it _____ in the front.

IN A STORE

3. A: _____ you open on Sundays?

   B: No, we _____. We _____ only

   open from Monday to Saturday.

4. A: _____ this shirt on sale?

   B: Yes, it _____. It _____

   50 percent off.

   A: Ooh! That _____ a good price.

5. A: Excuse me. _____ women's shoes

   on the first floor?

   B: No, they _____ on the second floor.

   A: Thanks.

AT AN AIRPORT

6. A: _____ Flight 245 on time?

   B: Yes, it _____.

7. A: _____ this your suitcase?

   B: Yes, it _____.

   A: I _____ sorry, but it _____

   too big to carry on the plane.

ON THE TELEPHONE

8. A: _____ Amanda there?

   B: No, she _____ here right now.

9. A: _____ this David?

   B: Yes, it _____. _____ that you,

   Carlos?

   A: Yeah. Hi, David.

IN A RESTAURANT

10. A: _____ you ready to order?

    B: Yes, I think so.

11. A: _____ everything OK?

    B: Yes, the food _____ delicious.

25 | Understanding _Wh-_ Questions Complete these questions with _is_ or _are_. `1.4 D`

TWELVE COMMON WH- QUESTIONS WITH IS AND ARE

1. What _____ new?
2. How _____ you?
3. What _____ the matter?
4. Who _____ that guy?
5. What _____ the problem?
6. Where _____ you?
7. Where _____ my keys?
8. What _____ on your mind?
9. How _____ your food?
10. Who _____ your friend?
11. How _____ things with you?
12. How _____ the weather?

Talk about It Work with a partner. Choose one of the questions above and use it to create a short conversation. (Use a contraction where possible.) Present your conversation to the class.

A: What's new?
B: I have a new job. I really like it.
A: Great!
B: What about you?

26 | Usage Note: *How* Questions Read the note. Then do Activity 27.

We use the question word *how* in special ways. We can use:

1	***How*** + an adjective	**How old** are you? **How serious** is it? **How important** is this test?
2	***How*** + an adverb	**How often** does your class meet? **How well** does she speak English?
3	***How*** + ***many*** + a plural count noun	**How many students** are here today? **How many times** a day do you eat?
4	***How*** + ***much*** + a noncount noun	**How much money** is in the desk? **How much water** do you usually drink?

27 | Asking *Wh-* Questions with *Be* Complete the questions about each place. Use a *wh-* word from the box and *is* or *are*. (You will use some *wh-* words more than once.) 1.4 D

how big	how far	how many	how old	what	where

BRASILIA

1. Question: ___*Where is*___ Brasilia?

   Answer: It's in Brazil.

2. Question: _____ the population of Brasilia?

   Answer: About 1,750,000 people.

3. Question: _____ Brasilia from São Paulo?

   Answer: 544 miles or 875 kilometers.

4. Question: _____ the city?

   Answer: About 70 years old.

5. Question: _____ special about Brasilia?

   Answer: It's an example of modern architecture and urban planning.

Brazilian National Congress
building in Brasilia

CAVE PAINTINGS OF LASCAUX

6. Question: _____ the cave paintings?

   Answer: In southwestern France.

7. Question: _____ they?

   Answer: Up to 20,000 years old.

8. Question: _____ the animals in the paintings?

   Answer: Some are huge—10 to 15 feet long.

9. Question: _____ animals _____ in the pictures?

   Answer: Horses, deer, and bulls.

10. Question: _____ pictures _____ in the cave?

    Answer: About 2,000.

cave paintings of Lascaux

Write about It Write a *wh-* question about a place. Find the answer online and report to the class.

28 | Error Correction Correct any errors in these sentences. (Some sentences may not have any errors.)

1. She always late.
2. Is you OK?
3. I very proud of my parents.
4. Why we are here?
5. Sometimes she very strong, and sometimes she very weak.

6. My parents they are always very busy, but they always ready to help me.
7. It hard to raise a family.
8. My parents happy with their life? Yes, I think so.
9. The weather in Moscow colder than in Berlin.

1.5 Using Time Expressions with the Simple Present

A

ADVERBS OF FREQUENCY

always 100%	almost always	usually often frequently	sometimes occasionally	hardly ever rarely seldom	almost never	never 0%
				negative adverbs of frequency		

1 We **almost always** eat at home.
2 We **hardly ever** eat out.
3 It **almost never** rains here.
(NOT: ~~It doesn't never rain here.~~)

Adverbs of frequency are one kind of time expression.
- We use adverbs of frequency with the simple present to say how often something happens, as in **1 – 3**.
- We don't use *not* with a negative adverb, as in **3**.

B

4	This room	is	usually	open.
5	Vacations	aren't	always	fun.

6	We	don't	usually	meet	on Friday.
7	She	doesn't	always	know	the answer.

8	The game	almost never	starts	on time.
9	She		always	does	her work.

10 **Do** you **ever feel** sleepy in class?
11 She **doesn't ever call** me.

Adverbs of frequency usually come:
- after the **main verb *be***, as in **4 – 5**
- after a **helping verb** like *do*, as in **6 – 7**
- before other **main verbs**, as in **8 – 9**

We use *ever* most often in questions and negative statements, as in **10 – 11**.

ever = at any time	not ever = never

C

MULTI-WORD TIME EXPRESSIONS
12 Do you go there **every day**?
13 I get my hair cut **once a month**.
14 A: How often does the class meet?
   B: **Two times a week**.
15 A: Are you open **on Saturdays**?
   B: Yes, we're open **all day**.

We often use **multi-word time expressions** when we talk about current habits, as in **12 – 15**. Some common examples are:

every	+	morning/day/week/year/Sunday/time
once/twice a	+	day/week/month/year
two times a	+	day/week/month/year
on	+	weekdays/weekends/Mondays
all	+	day/week/the time

D

CORRECT THE COMMON ERRORS (See page R-13.)
16 ✗ He walks to school usually every morning.
17 ✗ They always are busy.

18 ✗ They always don't leave a tip.
19 ✗ John don't never visit us.

29 | Choosing Adverbs of Frequency Complete these statements with an adverb of frequency. (Make the statements true for you.) 1.5 A

YOUR HABITS

1. I _____ get up before 7:00 in the morning.
2. In the evening, I _____ play games on the computer.
3. I am _____ sleepy during the day.
4. I _____ eat a big breakfast.
5. I am _____ ready for a test.
6. I _____ do all of my homework for class.
7. I am _____ late to class.
8. I _____ listen carefully in class.
9. I _____ keep my promises.
10. I _____ make bad decisions.
11. I _____ argue with other people.
12. I _____ pay my bills.
13. I am _____ calm in difficult situations.
14. I _____ feel angry.
15. I _____ forget to do things.

> **FYI**
>
> For emphasis, we sometimes use the adverbs *usually, often, sometimes,* and *occasionally* at the beginning of a sentence.
>
> **Sometimes** he gets home really late.
>
> We can also use *often* and *sometimes* at the end of a sentence.
>
> We watch that program **sometimes**.

Talk about It Compare your statements above with a partner. How many of your statements are the same?

30 | Placement of Adverbs of Frequency Add the adverbs in parentheses to these statements. Then check (✓) *True* or *False* for your class. 1.5 B

DESCRIBING YOUR CLASS	TRUE	FALSE
1. Our teacher ^never^ gives tests. (never)	☐	☐
2. Our classroom is too hot. (frequently)	☐	☐
3. We watch movies in class. (rarely)	☐	☐
4. We listen to music in class. (often)	☐	☐
5. We don't have homework. (ever)	☐	☐
6. We study grammar in class. (sometimes)	☐	☐
7. It's quiet in my classroom. (almost never)	☐	☐
8. Some students are late to class. (almost always)	☐	☐
9. We don't speak in our first language. (usually)	☐	☐
10. Our teacher isn't tired. (ever)	☐	☐
11. A few students fall asleep in class. (occasionally)	☐	☐
12. Our teacher asks questions. (hardly ever)	☐	☐

Think about It Think of a way to restate the information in sentences 1, 5, 10, and 12 in Activity 30.

1. Our teacher doesn't ever give us tests.

Write about It Rewrite the false statements in Activity 30. Make them true for your class.

Our teacher often gives us tests.

31 | Using Adverbs of Frequency Underline the adverbs of frequency in these sentences. Then rewrite them. Replace the **bold** words with the words in parentheses, and use a different adverb of frequency.
`1.5 A–B`

COMPLAINTS AND CRITICISMS

1. It's <u>almost always</u> **rainy** here. (sunny)

   It's almost never sunny here.

2. It's usually **noisy** here at night. (quiet)
3. The weather is always **bad** on the weekend. (nice)
4. My friends are usually **late**. (early)
5. You always **criticize** me. (praise)
6. You hardly ever **remember** to do your homework. (forget)
7. The bus is almost never **on time**. (late)
8. It's lonely in this town. I never **go out**. (stay at home)
9. You rarely **understand** me. (misunderstand)
10. He seldom **tells the truth**. (lie)

32 | Using Multi-Word Time Expressions Use this calendar to write six sentences about Isabel's schedule. Use a multi-word time expression in each sentence. `1.5 C`

Isabel goes to class twice a week.

SUNDAY	MONDAY	TUESDAY	WEDNESDAY	THURSDAY	FRIDAY	SATURDAY
11:00 PM–6:00 AM	11:00 PM–6:00 AM	11:00 PM–6:00 AM	11:00 PM–6:00 AM	11:00 PM–6:00 AM	11:00 PM–6:00 AM	11:00 PM–6:00 AM
Sleep	Sleep	Sleep	Sleep	Sleep	Sleep	Sleep
12:30 PM	8:30 AM–12:30 PM	9:00–11:00AM	8:30 AM–12:30 PM	8:30 AM–12:30 PM	8:30 AM–12:30 PM	9:00–11:00 AM
Meet Mom	Work	Volunteer	Work	Work	Work	Volunteer
2:00–6:00 PM	2:00–4:00 PM		2:00–4:00 PM	2:00–6:00 PM	2:00–6:00 PM	
Volunteer	Volunteer		Volunteer	Volunteer	Volunteer	
	4:30–6:00 PM		4:30–6:00 PM	7:00–9:00 PM		
	Class		Class	Study		

Write about It Write three to four sentences about your weekly schedule.

33 | Error Correction Correct any errors in these sentences. (Some sentences may not have any errors.)

1. When I get presents, I always am happy.
2. I enjoy usually board games.
3. She don't have often time to read.
4. He all the time is tired.
5. We don't do ever anything.
6. My sister doesn't never have time to visit me.
7. I only have class once week.
8. She studies here all the day.

1.6 Present Progressive Statements

A

1 A: Hey, John. Your phone's **ringing.** B: Thanks. **2** A: How **are** you **feeling** today? B: A little better, thanks. **3** Engineers **are looking** for ways to build better cars.	We use the **present progressive** form of a verb to show that something is: • in progress now and • temporary, or lasting for a limited time Now can be exactly at this moment or more general (*today, this week, this year,* etc.) as in **1 – 3**.

CHANGING STATES OR SITUATIONS **4** We **are** all **getting** older. **5** The price of food **is increasing.** **6** I'm **getting** tired.	We also use the present progressive to describe changing states or situations, as in **4 – 6**. Common verbs we use this way are: | become	decrease	get	grow	increase | **GRAMMAR TERM:** The present progressive is also called the **present continuous**.

B

For the present progressive, we use *am* / *is* / *are* + (**not**) + the **-ing form of a main verb**, as in **7 – 11**. With the present progressive, *be* is a helping verb.

FIRST PERSON

		be (+ not)	verb + -ing
7	I	am 'm am not 'm not	working.
8	We	are 're are not 're not aren't	working.

SECOND PERSON

		be (+ not)	verb + -ing
9	You	are 're are not 're not aren't	working.

THIRD PERSON

		be (+ not)	verb + -ing
10	He She It	is 's is not 's not isn't	working.
11	We	are 're are not 're not aren't	working.

For a list of spelling rules for the *-ing* form of verbs, see Activity 35, page 24.

GRAMMAR TERM: The *-ing* form of a verb is sometimes called the **present participle**.

34 | Noticing Present Progressive Verbs Underline the present progressive verbs in these sentences. Then check (✓) *True* or *False*.   1.6 A

	TRUE	FALSE
1. I'm feeling pretty good today.	☐	☐
2. I'm just sitting at home right now.	☐	☐
3. We're still studying verbs in class this week.	☐	☐
4. My English is getting better and better.	☐	☐
5. I'm making a lot of new friends these days.	☐	☐
6. The weather is getting colder now.	☐	☐
7. The price of gasoline is increasing again.	☐	☐
8. The days⁵ are getting shorter now.	☐	☐
9. My understanding of English is improving.	☐	☐
10. I'm finding a lot of interesting things to do these days.	☐	☐
11. I'm spending a lot of money this year.	☐	☐
12. I'm taking an interesting course this semester.	☐	☐

> **F Y I**
>
> We sometimes use the adverbs *just* and *still* with present progressive verbs.
>
> He is **just** finishing his homework now.
> (just = at this moment)
>
> She is **still** eating dinner.
> (still = something continuing until now, often longer than expected)

Think about It Which verbs above describe a changing state or situation?

Think about It Circle the time expressions above that we use with the present progressive.

Write about It Rewrite the false statements above to make them true. Then compare ideas with your classmates.

I'm feeling pretty tired today.

35 | Spelling Note: *-ing* Verbs Read the note. Then do Activity 36.

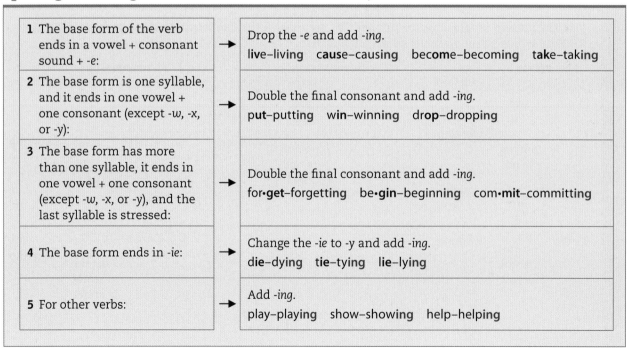

1 The base form of the verb ends in a vowel + consonant sound + -*e*:	Drop the -*e* and add -*ing*. live–living cause–causing become–becoming take–taking
2 The base form is one syllable, and it ends in one vowel + one consonant (except -*w*, -*x*, or -*y*):	Double the final consonant and add -*ing*. put–putting win–winning drop–dropping
3 The base form has more than one syllable, it ends in one vowel + one consonant (except -*w*, -*x*, or -*y*), and the last syllable is stressed:	Double the final consonant and add -*ing*. for·**get**–forgetting be·**gin**–beginning com·**mit**–committing
4 The base form ends in -*ie*:	Change the -*ie* to -*y* and add -*ing*. die–dying tie–tying lie–lying
5 For other verbs:	Add -*ing*. play–playing show–showing help–helping

⁵ **days:** the amount of daylight during the day

36 | Spelling -ing Verbs Write the -ing form of these verbs. `1.6 B`

Base form	-ing form	Base form	-ing form	Base form	-ing form
1. run	_____	11. leave	_____	21. increase	_____
2. shop	_____	12. wait	_____	22. decrease	_____
3. make	_____	13. sit	_____	23. get	_____
4. rain	_____	14. stand	_____	24. improve	_____
5. bring	_____	15. wear	_____	25. change	_____
6. buy	_____	16. hold	_____	26. look	_____
7. carry	_____	17. live	_____	27. watch	_____
8. come	_____	18. stay	_____	28. feel	_____
9. cry	_____	19. joke	_____	29. stare	_____
10. laugh	_____	20. talk	_____	30. refer	_____

37 | Using Present Progressive Verbs Write the present progressive form of the verb in parentheses. Use contractions. Then practice with a partner. `1.6 B`

1. A: Where's Matt Jacobs? I never see him anymore.

   B: He _'s living_ in Thailand this year. (live)

2. A: Are you OK?

   B: Yeah, I ____ just _____ a little tired. (feel)

3. A: Let's go. It _____ late. (get)

   B: But I _____ fun. (have)

4. A: What's the matter?

   B: Dad _____ dinner. (cook)

   A: Why?

   B: Because Mom _____ late. (work)

5. A: Why is it so quiet in here?

   B: Shhh. James and Toshi _____ chess. (play)

   A: Why does James look so unhappy?

   B: Because Toshi _____ . (win)

6. A: What's that noise?

   B: It's Anna. She _____ the piano. (play)

7. A: This is a great picnic.

   B: I'm glad you _____ yourself. (enjoy)

8. A: What's the problem?

   B: My phone _____ again. (not/work)

   A: Do you want to use mine?

   B: Thanks.

9. A: Where's your brother?

   B: He ____ still _____ dressed. (get)

   A: But it's already 8:00. We need to leave now.

10. A: Do you like your new boss?

    B: Yes, but he's about 200 years old.

    A: I think you _____ . (exaggerate)

    B: OK, so maybe he's 70.

38 | Describing Changing Things Write a sentence telling how each item in the box is changing. 1.6 A–B

airplanes	computers	the Internet		the price of gasoline
cell phones	newspapers	the number of cars on the road		TV sets

TV sets are getting thinner and bigger. OR *The picture on a TV set is getting better.*

Talk about It Compare ideas from your sentences with your classmates.

1.7 Questions with the Present Progressive

To form present progressive *yes/no* questions, we put **am / is / are** before the subject and use the **-ing form of a main verb**, as in **1 – 2**. We can give short answers to *yes/no* questions with *am / is / are*, as in **3 – 6**.

A

YES/NO QUESTIONS

	be	subject	verb + -ing
1	Am	I	working?
	Are	you	
	Is	he she it	

	be	subject	verb + -ing
2	Are	we you they	losing?

SHORT ANSWERS

			be
3	Yes,	you	are.
		I	am.
		he she it	is.

			be
4	Yes,	you we they	are.

			be + not
5	No,	you	're not. aren't.
		I	'm not.
		he she it	's not. isn't.

6	No,	you we they	're not. aren't.

WARNING! We don't use contractions with short *yes* answers.

B

For *wh-* questions, we use a **wh- word + am / is / are** and the **-ing form of a main verb**, as in **7 – 18**. In **17 – 18**, the *wh-* word is the subject.

WH- QUESTIONS

	wh- word	be	subject	verb + -ing
7	Where	am	I	going?
8	How		I	doing?
9	Why		you	laughing?
10	Who	are	they	calling?
11	What		your kids	doing?

	wh- word	be	subject	verb + -ing
12	Where		Tom	going?
13	How		she	doing?
14	Why	is	he	laughing?
15	Who		Sarah	calling?
16	What		it	doing?

WH- QUESTIONS ABOUT THE SUBJECT

	subject	be	verb + -ing
17	What	is	happening?
18	Who		calling?

39 | Asking *Yes/No* Questions Use the words in parentheses to write short conversations. Use the present progressive form of the **bold** verb. Then practice with a partner. `1.7 A`

1. A: _Is it getting late?_ (it/**get**/late?)
   B: _Yes, it is._ (yes)

2. A: _____ (you/**listen**/to me?)
   B: _____ (yes)

3. A: _____ (I/**talk**/too loudly?)
   B: _____ (no)

4. A: _____
   _____ (anyone else in your family/**take**/an English class?)
   B: _____ (no)

5. A: _____ (I/**bother**/you?)
   B: _____ (no)

6. A: _____ (it/**rain**?)
   B: _____ (yes)

7. A: _____ (they/**pay**/attention/now?)
   B: _____ (yes)

8. A: _____ (you/**speak**/to me?)
   B: _____ (yes)

9. A: _____ (he/**wait**/for the bus?)
   B: _____ (yes)

10. A: _____ (you/**worry**/about the test?)
    B: _____ (no)

Think about It Underline the main verbs in the conversations above. Circle the helping verbs.

Talk about It Ask a partner the questions you wrote above. Use your own ideas to give answers.

40 | Pronunciation Note: Contractions with *Wh-* Words Listen to the note. Then do Activity 41.

> In conversation, we usually contract (or shorten) the verb *be* in *wh-* questions.
>
> | Contracted, spoken form | Full, written form |
> |---|---|
> | **1** What's she reading? | What is she reading? |
> | **2** Where're you living? | Where are you living? |
> | **3** Who's talking? | Who is talking? |

41 | Listening for Contractions Listen and repeat the questions. Then write the full, written form of each question. `1.7 B`

CONTRACTED, SPOKEN FORM	FULL, WRITTEN FORM
1. Why's she crying?	_Why is she crying?_
2. How're they doing?	_____

CONTRACTED, SPOKEN FORM	FULL, WRITTEN FORM

3. Who's calling me? _____

4. What're they making? _____

5. How's she feeling? _____

6. Why're we leaving now? _____

7. Why're you being so rude? _____

8. What's he talking about? _____

9. Who's singing? _____

10. Why's she doing that? _____

11. Who're you talking to? _____

12. Where's his computer? _____

13. What's making that noise? _____

14. Who's cooking dinner? _____

Talk about It Work with a partner. Choose three of the questions in Activity 41 and create short conversations.

A: Why's she crying?
B: She failed the test!

42 | Forming *Wh-* Questions Complete these conversations with a *wh-* word and the present progressive form of the verb in parentheses. Then practice with a partner. **1.7 B**

1. A: _What are you doing_____? (do)

   B: I'm watching a movie. What about you?

2. A: _____? (cry)

   B: Because his stomach hurts.

3. A: _____ that noise? (make)

   B: It's Dad. He's building something outside.

4. A: _____ for a job? (look)

   B: Because she needs the money.

5. A: _____? (live)

   B: In an apartment with her mother.

6. A: _____ in school? (do)

   B: Great. I'm learning a lot.

7. A: _____ in school? (study)

   B: She's majoring in engineering.

8. A: _____ that away? (throw)

   B: Because I don't need it anymore.

9. A: _____ now? (work)

   B: At a bank. I really like it.

10. A: _____ my phone? (use)

    B: Not me. Maybe Rob has it.

RESEARCH SAYS...

The present progressive form of verbs is much more common in conversation than in writing.

CORPUS

43 | Error Correction Correct any errors in these sentences. (Some sentences may not have any errors.)

1. Where she going?

2. Who you talking to?

3. They leaving?

4. What he is doing?

5. What are you do with my computer?

6. Why is she leaving?

7. Are you talk to me?

8. What happening?

1.8 Comparing the Simple Present and Present Progressive

A

SIMPLE PRESENT

We use the **simple present** to describe things that are habitual or generally true, as in **1a** – **4a**.

1a You **make** me nervous.
   (= It's always true. You always make me nervous.)

2a He **cooks** dinner, not me.
   (= It's habitual. He always cooks dinner.)

3a She's rude.
   (= It's always true. She's always rude.)

4a The cost of living **increases** every year.
   (= It's generally true. It increases.)

PRESENT PROGRESSIVE

We use the **present progressive** to describe temporary things in progress now, as in **1b** – **3b**, or changing states or situations, as in **4b**.

1b You **are making** me nervous.
   (= It's temporary. You are making me nervous now.)

2b He's **cooking** dinner.
   (= It's in progress. He's cooking now.)

3b She's **being** rude.
   (= It's temporary. She's being rude right now.)

4b The cost of living **is increasing**.
   (= The cost of living is changing now.)

B

We use different **time expressions** with the simple present and present progressive, as in **5 – 6**.

Common time expressions used with the simple present include:

always	every day	once a day
never	every month	twice a day
usually	on Saturday	

Common time expressions used with the present progressive include:

now	this week	today
right now	this month	these days
at the moment	this year	nowadays

5a My sister **usually** **drives** me to school.

6a I **work** **every day**.

5b I'm **taking** the bus to school **today**.

6b I'm **working** every day **this week**.

C

CORRECT THE COMMON ERRORS (See page R-14.)

7 ✗ I'm usually going to school on Monday.

8 ✗ He cooks dinner right now.

9 ✗ You're always make fun of me.

10 ✗ They watching TV every evening.

GO ONLINE

44 | Distinguishing the Simple Present and Present Progressive Circle the simple present verbs in these paragraphs. Underline the present progressive verbs. `1.8 A`

THE TRADITIONAL ROLES OF FATHERS AND MOTHERS

1. I (think) that the traditional role of fathers <u>is changing</u>. It's not common yet, but more and more fathers are leaving their careers. They are staying home and taking care of the children while their wives go to work.

2. The traditional role of fathers is slowly changing. In many homes today, both parents work outside the home. This means that fathers need to do some of the work at home. For example, my father does the food shopping, and he usually washes the dishes; my mother cooks all the food.

3. In many countries, the traditional role of mothers is changing very little or not at all. In my country, many women prefer to stay at home. They don't want to work outside the home.

4. Many people think that mothers belong at home when they have young children. I don't agree with this. I have two young children, but I still work five days a week. My children go to a good daycare center every day.

RESEARCH SAYS...

With some verbs, we rarely use the present progressive form. For example:

Action verbs rarely used with the progressive

convince	reply
find	shut
promise	thank

Non-action verbs rarely used with the progressive

agree	mean
believe	own
belong	prefer
hear	want
know	

CORPUS

Think about It Why does the writer use the simple present or present progressive above? Choose a reason from the chart below. Write the number of the reason over the verb. (More than one answer may be possible for each verb.)

Reasons for using the simple present	Reasons for using the present progressive
1. for habits and routines 2. for timeless truths and general statements 3. for states—how someone or something is (These are also a kind of general statement.)	4. for temporary actions in progress now 5. for changing states or situations

45 | Usage Note: Verbs with Active and Non-Active Meanings Read the note. Then do Activity 46.

Some verbs have both active and non-active meanings. We use the present progressive with the active meaning of these verbs to show that something is temporary.

Active meaning

He **is being** friendly.
(= He is behaving in a friendly way right now.)

I'm **thinking** about it. (= I am using my mind.)

We're **having** a lot of fun. (= We are experiencing fun.)

Non-active meaning

He **is** friendly.
(= He is always friendly.)

I **think** you are right. (= In my opinion, you are right.)

He **has** my book. (= He possesses my book.)

46 | Choosing the Correct Meaning Match the **bold** verbs with the dictionary definitions. Write the letter of the definition. (Some definitions can be used more than once.) `1.8 A`

_a_ 1. A: Do you know how to use this computer?

B: What do you mean?

A: Well, it's turned on, but I**'m** not **seeing** anything on the screen.

____ 2. A: I don't want to go to that movie tonight.

B: I **see**. Is there something else you want to do?

____ 3. A: I **see** you as a famous scientist someday.

B: Me? Really?

A: Yeah. You're really smart, and you work really hard.

____ 4. A: Do you **see** that big bird over there?

B: Yeah. What is it?

____ 5. A: Please **see** that the children do their homework.

B: No problem.

____ 6. A: What time is it?

B: I **think** it's about 3:00.

____ 7. A: What **are** you **thinking** about?

B: Nothing special. Just my work.

____ 8. A: What are you **thinking** of cooking for dinner?

B: What about chicken?

A: Sounds good.

____ 9. A: Do you **think** Jon is OK?

B: Yeah, I **think** he's just tired.

____10. A: Do you **have** a cell phone?

B: Yeah. Do you need it?

____11. A: Are you **having** fun?

B: Yes. This is a great football game.

____12. A: What's the matter?

B: Nothing, really. I just **have** a headache.

____13. A: Why is everybody here?

B: Because we**'re having** a picnic.

> **see** /si/ _verb_ (**saw**, **seen**, **see·ing**)
>
> **a.** to notice something using your eyes
> **b.** to understand
> **c.** to imagine
> **d.** to make sure

> **think** /θɪŋk/ _verb_ (**thought**, **thought**, **think·ing**)
>
> **a.** to use your mind
> **b.** to believe; to have as an opinion
> **c.** to plan

> **have** /hæv/ _verb_ (**had**, **had**, **hav·ing**)
>
> **a.** to own; to possess
> **b.** to be sick with
> **c.** to experience something
> **d.** to hold or organize an event

47 | Present Progressive or Simple Present? Complete these conversations. Use the present progressive or simple present form of the verb in parentheses. Then practice with a partner. `1.8 A–B`

1. A: (_telephone rings_) Hello.

B: Hi, Sam. It's me. Are you busy?

A: Yeah, I ___'m making___ dinner. (make)

2. A: Why don't you like Mr. Jones?

B: I don't know. He _____ me nervous. (make)

3. A: How do you get to work?

B: I usually _____. (drive)

4. A: Who _____ me to school today? (drive)

B: Ask your father.

5. A: How is the baby?

B: Fine, but she still _____ through the night. (not/sleep)

6. A: Can I talk to Emma?

B: She _____ right now. (sleep)

7. A: _____ you usually _____ a
   suit to work? (wear)

   B: No, thank goodness.

8. A: Why _____ you _____ a suit
   today? (wear)

   B: I have an important meeting.

9. A: What _____ you _____ ? (drink)

   B: It's just water.

10. A: Do you want some coffee?

    B: Thanks, but I _____ coffee.
    (not/drink)

11. A: _____ you _____ a lot?
    (travel)

    B: No, only a few times a year.

12. A: Where's Hassan?

    B: He _____ this week. (travel)

Think about It Circle the time expressions in the conversations in Activity 47.

48 | Choosing the Simple Present or Present Progressive Choose verbs from the boxes to
complete these paragraphs. Use the simple present or present progressive form. `1.8 A-B`

FAMOUS PEOPLE WHO HELP

1. The actor Leonardo DiCaprio _____*believes*_____ that
   the environment[6] is a very important issue. Right now he
   _____ a television series about a town in the U.S.
   The people in this community _____ their town
   to be environmentally healthy. DiCaprio _____
   this town is a good model for the rest of the world.

   | believe |
   | produce |
   | rebuild |
   | think |

2. The actors Gwyneth Paltrow and Cameron Diaz
   _____ to a group called the Union of Concerned
   Scientists. This group _____ environmental
   scientists, famous people, and regular people. These days, they
   _____ together on issues such as global warming
   and nuclear power.

   | belong |
   | include |
   | work |

3. Russell Simmons _____ to help children.
   He _____ art and education programs for
   children in New York City. Simmons is a famous rap music
   producer, and he _____ a lot about music and
   how it affects the lives of children. This year his organization
   _____ money to build a large arts education
   center.

   | know |
   | raise |
   | run |
   | want |

Think about It Underline each time expression above. Think of a different time expression you
could use.

---

[6] **the environment:** the air, water, land, animals, and plants around us

32

49 | Error Correction Correct any errors in these sentences. (Some sentences may not have any errors.)

1. We are going there every day.
2. You work too hard.
3. My mother is usually cooking dinner.
4. He is a vegetarian, so he is not eating any meat.
5. When I have a problem, I'm thinking of him.
6. The earth is dying because it's more and more trash building up.
7. When I feeling sad, she tell me a funny story and I laugh.
8. He is running his business well.
9. Every month she receive money and is sending it to her family at home.
10. I feel good every time I am answering an email.
11. The universities in my country are getting better.

1.9 Imperatives

<table>
<tr><td rowspan="2">A</td><td>
1 **Stop** it!
2 **Turn** right at the corner.
3 **Remember** to call your father.
4 **Watch** out! There's glass on the floor.
5 **Get** home safely.
</td><td>
We can use the **base form of a verb** to:
• give commands, as in **1**
• give instructions, as in **2**
• give advice, as in **3**
• give a warning, as in **4**
• wish something, as in **5**

We call these sentences **imperatives**. The subject of an imperative statement is always *you*, but we don't say or write *you*.
</td></tr>
<tr><td>
6 Please **help** me.
7 Please **stop** talking.
</td><td>
We often use the word *please* to soften an imperative, as in **6 – 7**.
</td></tr>
<tr><td>B</td><td>
8 **Don't open** that.
9 **Don't forget** your sister's birthday.
10 **Don't worry** about it.
11 **Don't be** late.
</td><td>
We use *don't* + the **base form of a verb** for a negative imperative, as in **8 – 11**.
</td></tr>
</table>

 ONLINE

50 | Using Imperatives Write each imperative under the correct group in the chart below. (Some may fit in both groups.) **1.9 A**

Be a good girl.	Leave your sister alone.	Repeat after me.	Stop talking.
Eat your vegetables.	Please be quiet.	Say "please."	Take out your books.
Go to your room.	Please pass in your papers.	Sit up straight.	Turn to page 43.

Things teachers say to students	Things parents say to their children
Please be quiet.	*Please be quiet.*

Write about It Add three more imperative sentences to each group in Activity 50.

Think about It Which of the statements in Activity 50 are commands? Which are instructions?

51 | Understanding Informal Expressions Match each imperative to an informal expression with a similar meaning. `1.9 A–B`

IMPERATIVES

1. Please start eating. _e_
2. Have a good night's sleep. ____
3. Be careful. ____
4. Don't say anything. ____
5. Wait. Slow down. Be patient. ____
6. Go away. ____
7. Don't stop. ____
8. Stop doing that. ____
9. Stop complaining. ____
10. Relax. ____

INFORMAL EXPRESSIONS

a. Cut it out.
b. Get lost.
c. Sleep tight.
d. Chill out.
e. Dig in.
f. Watch your step.
g. Quit your moaning.
h. Hang in there.
i. Hold your horses.
j. Hold your tongue.

> **WARNING!**
>
> Be careful how you use informal expressions like the ones in Activity 51. Some of them may sound impolite if you use them in the wrong situation.

52 | Giving Advice Choose verbs from the boxes to complete the advice. (You will need to use *don't* in some of your answers.) `1.9 A–B`

USEFUL ADVICE

I don't sleep well at night. How can I get more sleep?

1. _____Don't drink_____ a lot of coffee.
2. _____ regularly.
3. _____ a nap during the day.
4. _____ to bed at the same time every night.
5. _____ a big meal just before you go to bed.

| drink |
| eat |
| exercise |
| go |
| take |

What's the best way to learn a foreign language?

1. _____ interesting books and magazines.
2. _____ afraid to make mistakes.
3. _____ some people to practice with.
4. _____ in a country where people speak the language.
5. _____ about having an accent.

| be |
| find |
| live |
| read |
| worry |

Write about It Write two other pieces of advice to answer each question above. Use imperatives.

53 | Giving Written Advice Complete the advice on page 35 with the verbs from the box. `1.9 A–B`

be	be	circle	imitate	talk	talk
be	buy	collect	read	talk	talk

ADVICE ON WRITING FROM THE POET GWENDOLYN BROOKS

Gwendolyn Brooks, winner of the Pulitzer Prize for Poetry, 1950

In your poems, _____*talk*_____ about what you know. _____
                         1   2
about what you think. _____ about what you feel.
                              3
_____ about what you wonder. _____ words!
         4   5
_____ your own dictionary. _____ your dictionary
         6   7
every day. _____ exciting words. The more words you know, the
                    8
better you will be able to express yourself, your thoughts.

_____ yourself. Do not _____ other poets. You are
         9   10
as important as they are. Do not _____ afraid to say something
                                         11
new. In some of your poems, _____ a little mysterious. Surprise
                                    12
yourself and your reader.

1.10 Using the Present in Speaking

A	**1** Nice shirt. (= That's a nice shirt.) **2** Ready to go? (= Are you ready to go?) **3** You see that guy? (= Do you see that guy?) **4** You doing anything? (= Are you doing anything?) **5** See that man? (= Do you see that man?) **6** Looking for something? (= Are you looking for something?)	In everyday conversation, we often shorten statements and questions. We can sometimes leave out: • the subject and main verb *be*, as in **1 – 2** • a helping verb, like *do* or *be*, as in **3 – 4** • a helping verb and the subject, as in **5 – 6**
B	**7** A: Are you ready? B: **Uh-huh.** **8** A: Are you sleeping? B: **Nope.** **9** A: Do you have your cell phone? B: **I think so.**	In everyday conversation, we sometimes use these words to answer *yes/no* questions, as in **7 – 9**. **POSITIVE ANSWERS**: Yep. Sure. Yeah. I think so. Uh-huh. Of course. **NEGATIVE ANSWERS**: Nah. I don't think so. Nope. I doubt it. Uh-uh. Of course not.
C	**10** A: Are you watching this program? B: Yes, **it's really interesting.** **11** A: Are you calling Tina? B: No, **I'm calling Paul.** **12** A: Does your rent include heat and electricity? B: No, **I pay extra for them.**	In conversation, we often answer a *yes/no* question with *yes* or *no* and more information, as in **10 – 12**.

🔊 **54 | Understanding Shortened Sentences** Listen and complete the shortened sentences. Then listen again and repeat the sentences. `1.10 A`

1. _____New_____ sweater?
2. _____ now?
3. _____ that?
4. _____ tired?
5. _____ OK?
6. _____ anything?
7. _____ for that job interview tomorrow?
8. _____ to know something?
9. _____ this?
10. _____ to see you.
11. _____ answer.
12. _____ car.

Think about It What words did the speaker leave out in each sentence above? Share ideas with your classmates. (More than one answer may be possible.)

1. _Is that a new sweater?_
2. _____
3. _____
4. _____
5. _____
6. _____
7. _____
8. _____
9. _____
10. _____
11. _____
12. _____

55 | Shortening Statements and Questions Complete the conversations by shortening the statements in parentheses. (More than one answer may be possible.) Then practice with a partner. `1.10 A`

1. A: This is my friend John.
   B: _Pleased to meet you._____ (I'm pleased to meet you.)
2. A: How's everything?
   B: _____ (Everything is fine.)
3. A: What smells so good?
   B: Spaghetti. _____ (Do you want some?)
4. A: Let's have sushi for dinner.
   B: _____ (That's an interesting choice.)
5. A: _____ (Do you want my dessert?)
   B: Sure. Thanks.
6. A: _____ (Are you listening to this?)
   B: No, turn it off.
7. A: _____ (Are you talking to me?)
   B: No, I'm talking to myself.
8. A: _____ (Is everybody here?)
   B: Yes, I think so.
9. A: _____ (Do you need some more paper?)
   B: No, I have plenty.
10. A: _____ (Is this your coat?)
    B: No, I think it's David's.

36

56 | Understanding Positive and Negative Answers Listen to these questions and answers. Does the speaker give a positive answer or a negative answer? Check (✓) your answers. `1.10 B`

	Positive	Negative
1.	☐	✓
2.	☐	☐
3.	☐	☐
4.	☐	☐
5.	☐	☐
6.	☐	☐
7.	☐	☐
8.	☐	☐
9.	☐	☐
10.	☐	☐
11.	☐	☐
12.	☐	☐
13.	☐	☐
14.	☐	☐
15.	☐	☐

PRONUNCIATION

Uh-huh means "yes." It is pronounced with stress on the second syllable. *Uh-uh* means "no." It is pronounced with stress on the first syllable.

A: Are you ready?
B: **Uh-HUH.** (= yes)

A: Are you ready?
B: **UH-uh.** (= no)

57 | Answering *Yes/No* Questions Match the questions with the answers. Then practice with a partner. `1.10 C`

QUESTIONS

1. Does your class meet every day? _e_
2. Are you listening to me? ____
3. Are you hungry? ____
4. Do you feel OK? ____
5. Are you studying? ____
6. Do you drink coffee? ____
7. Is your sister here? ____
8. Does it ever snow here in the winter? ____
9. Are stores here closed on Sunday? ____
10. Is anyone using this computer? ____

ANSWERS

a. Yes, but I think you're wrong.
b. Yes, I'm starving.
c. No, she's at home.
d. No, they're usually open.
e. No, only on Tuesday and Thursday.
f. No, it's all yours.
g. No, it's too warm here.
h. No, I prefer tea.
i. Yeah, I'm doing my math homework.
j. Yes, I'm fine.

Talk about It Think of two more ways to answer each question above.

Question: Does your class meet every day?
Answers: Yes, but I don't go on Saturday or Sunday./No, it doesn't meet on Friday.

1.11 Using the Present in Writing

A	**WRITING DESCRIPTIONS** **1** A pyramid **is** a shape with a flat bottom and three sides. The sides **come** to a point at the top. **2** A dictionary **explains** the meaning of words from A to Z. Nowadays, many people **use** online dictionaries. **3** An internist **is** a doctor of internal medicine. Internists **specialize** in treating adults. Many internists **get** more training in another specialty. For example, a cardiologist **is** an internist with extra training in diseases of the heart.	We often use the **simple present** when we write descriptions of people and things, as in **1 – 3**.
B	**WRITING SUMMARIES** **4** The book *Mama's Bank Account* by Kathryn Forbes **tells** the story of an immigrant Norwegian family in San Francisco in the early 1900s. In one episode, Mama's daughter and son **need** to bring food to school for their classmates. . . .	Writers often use the simple present to review or summarize the plot of a book or movie, as in **4**.
C	**WRITING LISTS AND INSTRUCTIONS** **5** • **buy** some milk • **call** Ben • **pay** bills **6** **Jog** with your shoulders back and your arms and hands relaxed. **Bend** your elbows at your waist, and **let** your arms swing naturally.	We use **imperatives** to make written lists of things to do, as in **5**. We also use imperatives to give written instructions, as in **6**.

58 | Using the Simple Present in Descriptions Read these descriptions and add the simple present form of the verb in parentheses. **1.11 A**

Descriptive Paragraphs

1. Accidents often _____*happen*_____ at home. The Consumer Product Safety Commission
   (happen)

   _____ that the five most dangerous things in the house _____: stairs, glass
   (report)   (be)

   doors, cutlery[7], glass bottles and jars, and home power tools.

2. A bistro _____ a type of restaurant. These small restaurants _____ good food
   (be)   (serve)

   in a friendly atmosphere. However, don't expect to get your meal quickly. Bistros _____ not
   (be)

   fast-food restaurants. Bistros _____ French in origin, but they _____ now more
   (be)   (be)

   popular in other countries as well.

[7] **cutlery:** tableware (knives, forks, etc.)

3. Every airplane _____ a black box or flight data recorder. The black box _____
                       (carry)   (be / not)

   actually black—it _____ orange. Inside the box, a stainless-steel tape _____
                                    (be)   (contain)

   information on the airplane's airspeed and altitude[8]. A second orange box _____ a tape of
                                                                               (have)

   the last half-hour of conversation between the pilots in the cockpit.

Write about It Write a short description of something that interests you.

59 | Using the Present in Summaries Read these movie summaries and underline the verbs. `1.11 B`

Movie Plots

The movie *Girl with a Pearl Earring* <u>takes place</u> in the seventeenth century in Holland. It tells the story of the famous painter Johannes Vermeer and a young woman, his servant. In the movie, Vermeer decides to paint the young woman's picture, and he asks her to wear a pair of pearl earrings for the painting. Unfortunately, the earrings belong to Vermeer's wife. She becomes very jealous, and she begins to make the young woman's life difficult. In the end . . .

The movie *The English Patient* takes place in Italy during World War II. At the beginning of the movie, Hana, a nurse from Canada, is taking care of a badly injured pilot. The pilot says he doesn't remember his name or anything else about himself. Because he has an English accent, the doctors and nurses call him "the English patient." Over time, Hana learns more about the patient, and in the end . . .

FYI

Sometimes a verb is more than one word. The two or more words work like a single verb. Some examples are:

go on
take care of
take place
watch out

Write about It Complete each summary above in your own words. (If you haven't seen the movies, make up your own endings.)

Write about It Choose a movie or book. Write a short summary of it. Answer these questions.

1. Where does the story take place?
2. When does the story take place?
3. What important things happen in the story?

[8]**altitude:** elevation; height in the sky

SIMPLE PRESENT AND PRESENT PROGRESSIVE   **39**

60 | Writing Lists List ten things you need to do this week. `1.11 C`

Things to Do This Week	
1.	6.
2.	7.
3.	8.
4.	9.
5.	10.

Talk about It Talk to different classmates. Look for people who have the same things on their list.

A: *Do you have "Study for the test" on your list?*
B: *Yes, I do. Do you have "Get some exercise" on your list?*

WRAP-UP Demonstrate Your Knowledge

A | SURVEY Ask your classmates questions to find the information below. When someone answers "Yes," write the person's name in the box.

A: *Do you speak Spanish?*   A: *Do you speak Spanish?*
B: *No, I speak Arabic and English.*   C: *Yes, I do.*

FIND SOMEONE WHO . . .

1. speaks Spanish Name: _____	4. lives near here Name: _____	7. feels good today Name: _____
2. usually drives to school Name: _____	5. likes sports Name: _____	8. has a sister Name: _____
3. never studies on the weekend Name: _____	6. is looking for a job Name: _____	9. is having a good time in class Name: _____

B | PRESENTATION Think of a famous person who is alive today. Write sentences describing this person but don't name the person. Read your description aloud and let your classmates ask you more questions about the person. Then ask your classmates to identify the person.

This person is a famous athlete. He lives in . . .

C | WRITING Think of something that you like to do. Then answer these questions in a short piece of writing.

QUESTIONS

1. What is one of your favorite fun activities?
2. How often do you do this activity?
3. Why do you like to do this activity? How does it make you feel?

I like to watch movies—especially comedies. I usually watch three or four movies every week. I do this because movies relax me and make me feel happy. I also like to watch movies because they help me improve my English.

1.12 Summary of the Simple Present and Present Progressive

SIMPLE PRESENT

STATEMENTS		
I	work.	
You We They	do not work. don't work.	
He She It	works. does not work. doesn't work.	

YES/NO QUESTIONS			
Do	I / you / we / they	work?
Does	he / she / it	

WH- QUESTIONS			
Where	do	I / you / we / they	work?
	does	he / she / it	
Who	works	here?	

USES

We use the **simple present**:
- for timeless truths and general statements
- to describe current habits and routines

SIMPLE PRESENT OF THE VERB *BE*

STATEMENTS		
I	am am not 'm not	
You We They	are are not aren't 're not	here.
He She It	is is not isn't 's not	

YES/NO QUESTIONS		
Am	I	
Are	you / we / they	here?
Is	he / she / it	

WH- QUESTIONS		
Where	am	I?
	are	you / we / they?
	is	he / she / it?
Who	is	here?

USES

We use the simple present of the **verb *be*** to describe current states and conditions.

PRESENT PROGRESSIVE

STATEMENTS		
I	am am not 'm not	
You We They	are are not aren't 're not	working.
He She It	is is not isn't 's not	

YES/NO QUESTIONS		
Am	I	
Are	you / we / they	working?
Is	he / she / it	

WH- QUESTIONS		
Where	am	I
	are	you / we / they	working?
	is	he / she / it
Who	is working?	

USES

We use the **present progressive** to show that something is:
- in progress now
- temporary, or lasting for a limited time

Simple Past and Past Progressive

I was working on . . .
one of my poems all
morning and took out a
comma. In the afternoon,
I put it back again.

—OSCAR WILDE,
WRITER AND POET
(1854–1900)

Talk about It What do you think the quotation above means?

WARM-UP

A | Match the beginnings of these descriptions with their endings. Which of these habits do you think is the most unusual?

Work Habits of Famous People

1. The movie director Ingmar Bergman (1918–2007) **hated** lateness. ____

2. The playwright Arthur Miller (1915–2005) **had** a destructive[1] routine. He usually **wrote** for several hours in the morning. ____

3. The architect Le Corbusier (1887–1965) **stayed** late in the office when his work **was going** well. ____

4. The mathematician Paul Erdos (1913–1996) **got up** early and **worked** for 19 hours straight[2]. ____

5. The philosopher Immanuel Kant (1724–1804) **didn't like** to get up early in the morning. ____

a. Then he **tore up** everything.

b. While he **was working**, he **drank** cup after cup of coffee.

c. Rehearsals[3] **began** promptly at 10:30, lunch **was** at 12:45, and work **finished** at 3:30.

d. Despite this, he **got up** at 5:00 a.m. every day.

e. When his work **wasn't going** very well, he **left** the office early.

B | Answer these questions about the sentences above.

1. Do the sentences describe people in the present or past? How do you know?
2. The words in **blue** are simple past verbs. Which of these verbs end in -ed? Which do not?
3. Which simple past verb above has a negative form?
4. The words in **green** are past progressive verbs. What is similar about the form of these three verbs?
5. Which past progressive verb has a negative form?

C | Look back at the quotation on page 42. Identify any past verb forms.

[1] **destructive:** causing damage
[2] **straight:** without stopping

[3] **rehearsals:** times when you practice something before a public performance

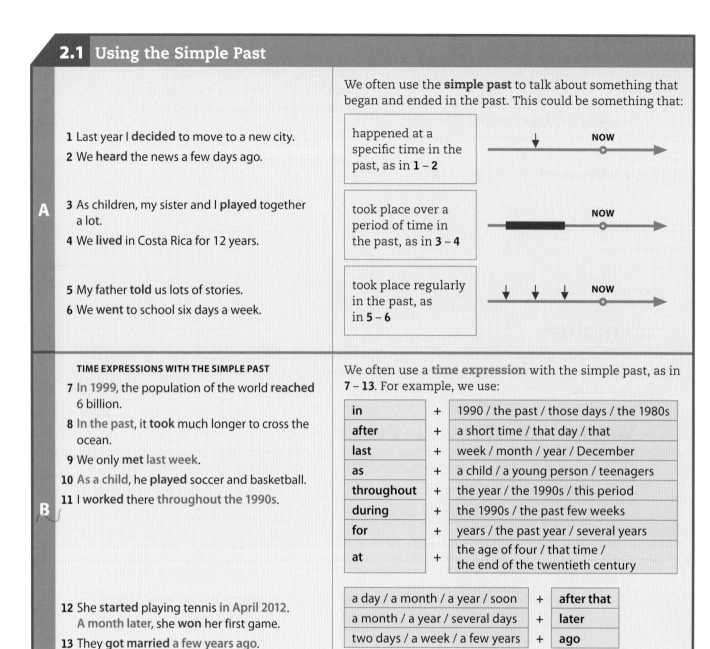

2.1 Using the Simple Past

A

1 Last year I **decided** to move to a new city.
2 We **heard** the news a few days ago.

3 As children, my sister and I **played** together a lot.
4 We **lived** in Costa Rica for 12 years.

5 My father **told** us lots of stories.
6 We **went** to school six days a week.

We often use the **simple past** to talk about something that began and ended in the past. This could be something that:

| happened at a specific time in the past, as in **1 – 2** |
| took place over a period of time in the past, as in **3 – 4** |
| took place regularly in the past, as in **5 – 6** |

B

TIME EXPRESSIONS WITH THE SIMPLE PAST

7 **In 1999**, the population of the world **reached** 6 billion.
8 **In the past**, it **took** much longer to cross the ocean.
9 We only **met** **last week**.
10 **As a child**, he **played** soccer and basketball.
11 I **worked** there **throughout the 1990s**.

12 She **started** playing tennis **in April 2012**. **A month later**, she **won** her first game.
13 They **got married** **a few years ago**.

We often use a **time expression** with the simple past, as in **7 – 13**. For example, we use:

in	+	1990 / the past / those days / the 1980s
after	+	a short time / that day / that
last	+	week / month / year / December
as	+	a child / a young person / teenagers
throughout	+	the year / the 1990s / this period
during	+	the 1990s / the past few weeks
for	+	years / the past year / several years
at	+	the age of four / that time / the end of the twentieth century

a day / a month / a year / soon	+	**after that**
a month / a year / several days	+	**later**
two days / a week / a few years	+	**ago**

---

1 | Noticing Simple Past Verbs Underline the simple past verbs in these sentences. The number in parentheses shows the number of simple past verbs. **2.1 A**

INTERESTING FACTS ABOUT FAMOUS PEOPLE

1. For many years, the French writer Voltaire <u>drank</u> 30 cups of coffee a day. (1)

2. When Ludwig van Beethoven wrote his nine symphonies, he sometimes poured water over his head. That kept him awake. (3)

3. The French painter Paul Cézanne had a parrot[4]. He taught it to say, "Cézanne is a great painter!" (2)

4. When the Russian painter Marc Chagall bought things, he usually paid by check. Because he was very famous, people rarely cashed his checks[5], so he got a lot of things free. (5)

a painting by Marc Chagall

[4] **parrot:** a bird, often brightly colored, that can copy people's words   [5] **cash a check:** to get money for a check

44

5. The American writer Jack London did many adventurous[6] things while he was young. Later in life, however, he stayed in bed all day and wrote his books. (4)

6. When the British writer Anthony Burgess was 39, his doctors told him that he had only 1 more year to live. Burgess decided to write 10 novels in that year. During the year, Burgess wrote 5½ novels, and his illness disappeared. Burgess lived for 37 more years and wrote many more books. (8)

Think about It Look at the sentences in Activity 1. When did each action or event take place? Write each one under the correct group in the chart below. (More than one answer may be possible.)

Specific time in the past	Over a period of time in the past	Regularly in the past
		drank 30 cups of coffee a day

2 | Choosing Time Expressions Underline the simple past verbs and choose a time expression to complete each sentence. Check (✓) your answer. Then compare with a partner. `2.1 B`

FAMOUS MOMENTS IN HISTORY

1. The first modern Olympic Games <u>took</u> place ____.
   - ☐ a. last year
   - ☐ b. during the 1950s
   - ☑ c. in 1896

2. Russians sent the first man into space ____.
   - ☐ a. during the 1950s
   - ☐ b. in the early 1960s
   - ☐ c. in 1971

3. The population of Earth reached 1 billion ____.
   - ☐ a. more than 200 years ago
   - ☐ b. during the 1980s
   - ☐ c. in 1900

4. Dinosaurs disappeared ____.
   - ☐ a. a few days ago
   - ☐ b. a very long time ago
   - ☐ c. in the 1200s

5. Teaching at Oxford University began ____.
   - ☐ a. in 1096
   - ☐ b. a short time ago
   - ☐ c. during the 1800s

6. Uruguay hosted the first World Cup games ____.
   - ☐ a. a few years ago
   - ☐ b. at the end of the nineteenth century
   - ☐ c. in 1930

7. The bicycle first became popular ____.
   - ☐ a. during the 1800s
   - ☐ b. 65 million years ago
   - ☐ c. in the twentieth century

8. Elizabeth I was queen of England ____.
   - ☐ a. throughout the late 1500s
   - ☐ b. in the 1800s
   - ☐ c. a few years ago

"I think the first modern Olympic Games took place in 1896. What do you think?"

[6]**adventurous:** enjoying exciting and dangerous things

3 | Identifying Time Expressions Read this text. Underline the time expressions with the simple past.

2.1 B

Working Together in Space

In 1986, the Russian space station *Mir* began to orbit Earth. During its lifetime, the space station was a temporary home to travelers from many different countries. In 1987, astronauts from Syria, Bulgaria, and Afghanistan spent time on *Mir*. Then, in 1990, a journalist from Japan, Toyohiro Akiyama, visited the space station and filed news reports from there.

In 1991, Helen Sharman, a British chemist, traveled to the space station *Mir*. She was the winner of a contest with a prize of eight days on the *Mir* space station, and she became the first British astronaut. During her visit to *Mir*, Sharman did medical tests and other types of research. Throughout the 1990s, researchers and astronauts from different countries continued to visit and work on the Russian space station.

> **RESEARCH SAYS...**
>
> The most common time word used with the simple past is *then*. The most common time phrases use the prepositions *in*, *during*, *for*, and *throughout*.
>
> CORPUS

Write about It Complete this timeline with information from the text above. Try to use your own words. Then compare with a partner. Were your timelines the same or different?

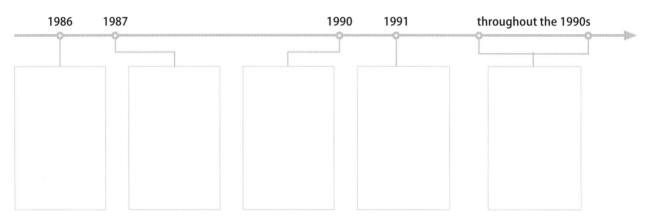

1986   1987   1990   1991   throughout the 1990s

Think about It Which time expressions from the text above can you also use with the simple present? Which ones cannot be used with the simple present?

2.2 Simple Past Statements with Regular and Irregular Verbs

There are two types of **simple past** verb forms: regular and irregular.

A

SIMPLE PAST WITH REGULAR VERBS

1 They **asked** me a lot of questions.
2 Somebody **called** late last night.
3 My sister **helped** me a lot.

For the simple past of regular verbs, we add *-d* or *-ed* to the base form, as in **1 – 3**.

REGULAR VERBS			
base form	simple past	base form	simple past
ask	ask**ed**	finish	finish**ed**
call	call**ed**	help	help**ed**
decide	decide**d**	move	move**d**

4 We **studied** a number of surveys.
5 They **planned** everything carefully.
6 He **regretted** buying a used car.

A few regular verbs have a special spelling, as in **4 – 6**.

For a list of spelling rules, see Activity 9, page 50. For information on the pronunciation of *-ed* endings, see Activity 5, page 48.

B

SIMPLE PAST WITH IRREGULAR VERBS

7 She **sat** alone in the room.
8 I **forgot** my wallet.
9 Somebody **took** my lunch.
10 I needed to study, but I **went** out instead.
11 I **had** a great time.

About 200 verbs have an irregular past form, as in **7 – 11**. Some common irregular verbs are:

IRREGULAR VERBS			
base form	simple past	base form	simple past
get	**got**	say	**said**
go	**went**	see	**saw**
have	**had**	sit	**sat**
know	**knew**	take	**took**
make	**made**	think	**thought**

For a list of irregular verbs, see the Resources, page R-3.

C

CORRECT THE COMMON ERRORS (See page R-14.)

12 ✗ He attend, but he fail.
13 ✗ He teached me everything.
14 ✗ I sat and think for a while.
15 ✗ My grandfather dead five years ago.

GO ONLINE

4 | Using the Simple Past of Regular Verbs Complete these sentences with the simple past form of the **bold** verb. 2.2 A

1. As a child, I _____*played*_____ a lot of football, but now I don't **play** anymore.

2. As children, my friends and I _____ the same things, and we still **enjoy** the same things.

3. My mother doesn't **help** me with my homework now, but she _____ me a lot in the past.

4. Ten years ago, I _____ a horse, but now I **want** a motorcycle.

5. As children, my brothers and I _____ a lot, and we still **laugh** a lot.

6. As a child, I _____ a lot of TV, but now I never **watch** TV.

7. I _____ hard in school when I was a child, but I don't **work** hard now.

8. As a child, I usually _____ to school, but now I never **walk** to school.

9. I don't often **stay up** late, but last night I _____ until two in the morning.

10. Our class **starts** at ten, but yesterday it _____ at eleven.

11. I usually **listen** to music in the morning, but yesterday I _____ to the news.

12. I don't usually **ask** questions in class, but yesterday I _____ several.

13. I don't typically **call** my husband at work, but yesterday I _____ him twice.

14. I usually **finish** my homework before class, but last week I _____ it in class.

Talk about It Are any of the statements in Activity 4 true for you? Tell a partner.

5 | Pronunciation Note: -ed Verb Endings Listen to the note. Then do Activities 6–8.

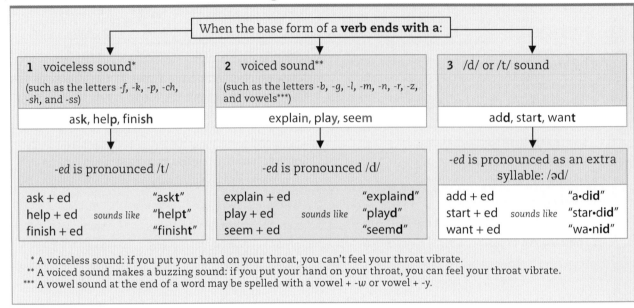

When the base form of a **verb ends with a**:		
1 voiceless sound* (such as the letters -f, -k, -p, -ch, -sh, and -ss)	**2** voiced sound** (such as the letters -b, -g, -l, -m, -n, -r, -z, and vowels***)	**3** /d/ or /t/ sound
ask, help, finish	explain, play, seem	add, start, want
-ed is pronounced /t/	*-ed* is pronounced /d/	*-ed* is pronounced as an extra syllable: /əd/
ask + ed "askt" help + ed sounds like "helpt" finish + ed "finisht"	explain + ed "explaind" play + ed sounds like "playd" seem + ed "seemd"	add + ed "a•did" start + ed sounds like "star•did" want + ed "wa•nid"

* A voiceless sound: if you put your hand on your throat, you can't feel your throat vibrate.
** A voiced sound makes a buzzing sound: if you put your hand on your throat, you can feel your throat vibrate.
*** A vowel sound at the end of a word may be spelled with a vowel + -w or vowel + -y.

6 | Pronouncing -ed Verb Endings Write each past verb under the correct group in the chart below. Then listen and confirm your answers. **2.2 A**

agreed	decided	listened	needed	showed	walked
believed	liked	looked	promised	suggested	watched

-ed ending sounds like /t/	*-ed* ending sounds like /d/	*-ed* ending sounds like /əd/
	agreed	

Think about It Listen and complete these sentences with the verbs above. Why are these verb endings difficult to hear in normal speech?

1. He ____*agreed*____ to go.
2. I _____ some help.
3. We _____ to the store.
4. They _____ to go.
5. He _____ it a lot.
6. I _____ a great movie.

7. She _____ me.
8. We _____ for a long time.
9. She _____ out the window.
10. He _____ to call.
11. She _____ her passport.
12. They _____ several good restaurants.

7 | Listening for the -ed Ending on Regular Verbs Listen for the simple past verb in each sentence. Check (✓) the ending you hear. `2.2 A`

	/t/ **or** /d/	/əd/		/t/ **or** /d/	/əd/
1. acted	☐	✓	10. encouraged	☐	☐
2. agreed	☐	☐	11. enjoyed	☐	☐
3. allowed	☐	☐	12. introduced	☐	☐
4. arranged	☐	☐	13. lasted	☐	☐
5. avoided	☐	☐	14. passed	☐	☐
6. burned	☐	☐	15. pointed	☐	☐
7. completed	☐	☐	16. separated	☐	☐
8. counted	☐	☐	17. talked	☐	☐
9. decided	☐	☐	18. waited	☐	☐

Talk about It Work with a partner. One person says the base form of a verb in the chart above. The other person says the simple past form.

A: Complete.
B: Completed.

8 | Present or Past? In normal speech, it is sometimes difficult to hear the difference between the simple present and simple past of regular verbs. Listen to the sentences and circle the verb you hear. `2.2 A`

1. She **works** / (**worked**) here.
2. They **like** / **liked** me.
3. She **agrees** / **agreed** with me.
4. He usually **arrives** / **arrived** at ten.
5. They **ask** / **asked** a lot of questions.
6. We **allow** / **allowed** everyone to go.
7. I always **enjoy** / **enjoyed** his company.
8. They always **finish** / **finished** before me.
9. We **discuss** / **discussed** lots of things.
10. She **calls** / **called** me every day.
11. We **move** / **moved** every year.
12. We never **talk** / **talked** about it.
13. I always **watch** / **watched** her games.
14. She **smiles** / **smiled** a lot.

> **F Y I**
>
> We can use some time expressions with more than one verb form. For example:
>
> **Simple Present**
> I **work** at home **every day**.
> I **usually study** at night.
>
> **Simple Past**
> I **worked** at home **every day**.
> I **usually studied** at night.

Talk about It Take turns reading the sentences above to a partner. Use either verb. Ask your partner to point to the verb you used.

A: She works here.
B: [Points to "works."]

9 | Spelling Note: Simple Past of Regular Verbs Read the note. Then do Activity 10.

	SPELLING RULES	base form	simple past
1	When the base form of a regular verb ends in -e, **add -d**.	close refuse	closed refused
2	When the base form ends in a consonant + **-y**, **change the -y to -i and add -ed**.	study worry identify	studied worried identified
3	When the base form has one syllable and ends in a **c**onsonant + **v**owel + **c**onsonant (CVC), **double the final consonant and add -ed**. (Warning! Do not double a final w, x, or y: play / played, wax / waxed, row / rowed.)	plan jog drop	planned jogged dropped
4	When the base form of a two-syllable verb ends in a **c**onsonant + **v**owel + **c**onsonant (CVC) and the last syllable is stressed, **double the final consonant and add -ed**.	re·**fer** re·**gret**	referred regretted
5	For all other regular verbs, **add -ed**.	open destroy	opened destroyed

10 | Spelling Simple Past Regular Verbs Write the simple past form of each verb. 2.2 A

Rule 1	Rule 2	Rule 3	Rule 4	Rule 5
agree	carry	drip	admit	avoid
agreed	_____	_____	_____	_____
continue	copy	grin	commit	cook
_____	_____	_____	_____	_____
damage	reply	hug	control	end
_____	_____	_____	_____	_____
describe	try	rub	prefer	order
_____	_____	_____	_____	_____

Think about It Add the simple past form of these verbs to the chart above.

| dry | empty | enjoy | happen | increase | occur | permit | start | stop | wrap |

11 | Using Irregular Verbs Write the simple past form of each verb. (For a list of irregular verbs, see the Resources, page R-3.) 2.2 B

1. begin _____began_____
2. buy _____bought_____
3. come _____came_____
4. cut _____cut_____
5. eat _____ate_____
6. fall _____fell_____

7. fly _____flew_____
8. get _____got_____
9. give _____gave_____
10. go _____went_____
11. have _____had_____
12. know _____knew_____

13. leave _____left_____
14. run _____ran_____
15. see _____saw_____
16. sleep _____slept_____
17. win _____won_____
18. write _____wrote_____

Write about It Use ten of the verbs in Activity 11 to write sentences about your childhood. (Look back at Chart 2.1B for help with time expressions.)

I began school at the age of 5.

12 | Using Regular and Irregular Past Forms   Complete this story with the simple past form of the verbs in parentheses.   2.2 A–B

○ ○ ○

Sailing Around the World

Zac Sunderland ____*learned*____
(1. learn)
to sail a boat at the age of 4! Thirteen

years later, Zac __*became*__
(2. become)
one of the youngest people to

sail around the world by himself.

Zac __*grew up*__ by the
(3. grow up)
water in California. As a child, he

__*spent*__ many hours sailing, surfing, and rock climbing.
(4. spend)

His father, Laurence, __*passed on*__ a love of exploration to
(5. pass on)

his son. Laurence __*took*__ Zac and his seven brothers
(6. take)

and sisters around Mexico, Australia, and New Zealand by sailboat.

After that, Zac __*worked*__ hard to buy his own sailboat and
(7. work)

__*began*__ planning his trip around the world. At the age
(8. begin)

of 16, Zac __*left*__ on his journey. The trip was hard, and
(9. leave)

Zac __*sailed*__ through a lot of bad weather. He sometimes
(10. sail)

__*felt*__ lonely, but he __*finished*__ his journey in 13
(11. feel)   (12. finish)

months and two days.

STUDY STRATEGY

When you are learning irregular verbs, group them into categories that make sense to you. For example:

Verbs with different spelling but the same vowel sound

make	**made**
send	**sent**

Verbs with different spelling and different vowel sounds

feel	**felt**
say	**said**

Verbs that have the same spelling and pronunciation

cut	**cut**
put	**put**

Talk about It Close your book. Write three things you learned about Zac Sunderland. Then compare ideas with your classmates.

Think about It What time expressions did the writer use in the story above? Circle them. What other time expressions can you use in the sentences?

In sentence 2, you can use "At the age of 17" instead of "Thirteen years later."

13 | Error Correction Correct any errors in these sentences. (Some sentences may not have any errors.)

1. For several years, she worked during the day and attend college at night.

2. I sat and think for a long time. Then I remembered the answer.

3. He try hard to finish college.

4. I told my parents and they agree with me.

5. At that time, not many people like her paintings. Later they admire her pictures a lot.

6. My uncle teached me everything about his work.

7. I meet him last year when I start my first class.

8. As a child, I usually finish all my homework and do well in school.

2.3 Simple Past Negative Statements and Questions

A

NEGATIVE STATEMENTS

	did + not	base form
I You He She It We You They	**did not** **didn't**	**go.**

(1)

We use the **helping verb** *did* + **not** + the **base form of a main verb** for simple past negative statements, as in **1**. In conversation, we usually use the contraction *didn't*.

B

YES/NO QUESTIONS

	did	subject	base form
2	**Did**	I you he she it we you they	**go?**

SHORT ANSWERS

			did (+ not)
3	Yes,	you I he she it	**did.**
	No,	you we they	**didn't.**

We use *did* and the **base form of a main verb** to form simple past *yes/no* questions, as in **2**.

We use *did* to give a short answer to a *yes/no* question, as in **3**. In negative short answers, we often use contractions.

C

WH- QUESTIONS

	wh- word	did	subject	base form
4	What		I	do?
5	Where		you	live?
6	When	did	he	leave?
7	Why		she	quit?
8	Who		it	hurt?
9	How long		they	stay?

For *wh-* questions, we use a **wh- word** + *did* and the **base form of a main verb**, as in **4 – 9**.

WH- QUESTIONS ABOUT THE SUBJECT

	subject	past verb form
10	What	happened?
11	Who	called?

When the *wh-* word is the subject, we use a **wh- word** + the **past form of a main verb**, as in **10 – 11**. We don't use *did*.

D

CORRECT THE COMMON ERRORS (See page R-14.)

12 ✗ They don't go shopping last weekend.

13 ✗ I no hear the news last night.

14 ✗ Who go with you?

15 ✗ When you get there?

52

14 | Using Positive and Negative Statements Complete these conversations with the positive or negative simple past form of the verb in parentheses. Then practice with a partner. `2.3 A`

1. A: What's the matter? You look upset.

   B: It's Amanda. She passed me on the street, but she _____*didn't*_____

   even _____*say*_____ hello. (say)

   A: Maybe she ___*didn't see*___ you. (see)

2. A: Are you OK?

   B: I'm just a little worried. I left a message for David, but he
   ___*didn't call*___ me back. (call)

   A: Maybe he just _____*got*_____ too busy. (get)

3. A: Why are you angry with Anna?

   B: Because she took my car, but she ___*didn't ask*___ first. (ask)

   A: Maybe she asked, but you ___*didn't hear*___ her. (hear)

4. A: Why are you firing Toshi?

   B: Because he _____*made*_____ a lot of mistakes last week. (make)

   A: Maybe he ___*didn't understand*___ the task. (understand)

   B: That's possible, but he ___*didn't come*___ to me with any questions either. (come)

5. A: Don't you think it's strange?

   B: What?

   A: John and Emma came all the way down here, and they ___*didn't stop*___ to visit us. (stop)

   B: Maybe they ___*didn't have*___ time. (have)

6. A: Why is the front door unlocked?

   B: Maybe you ___*forgot*___ to lock it this morning. (forget)

   A: But I'm sure I did.

FYI

We sometimes use the word *even* to show that something is surprising.

He saw me, but he didn't **even** say hello.

She can't **even** remember my name.

15 | Asking *Yes/No* Questions about the Past Complete these conversations with the words in parentheses. Then practice with a partner. `2.3 B`

1. A: _____*Did anyone call*_____? (anyone/call)

   B: Yes, your wife called about an hour ago.

2. A: These cookies are delicious. ___*did you make*___ them? (you/make)

   B: No, I bought them.

3. A: ___*did your friend*___ this photo? (your friend/take)

   B: Uh-huh. Do you like it?

   A: Yes. It's really nice.

4. A: ___*did you have*___ a good trip? (you/have)

   B: Yeah. We really enjoyed Sydney.

   A: ___*did you go*___ anywhere else in Australia? (you/go)

   B: Yes, we spent a week in Perth.

5. A: _did every one do_ the homework for today? (everyone/do)

    B: What homework?

6. A: _did I tell_ you about my award? (I/tell)

    B: Yes, three times.

7. A: _did you see_ that? (you/see)

    B: See what?

    A: That car. It just went through a red light.

    B: _did you get_ the license plate number? (you/get)

    A: No, it's too dark.

8. A: _did you get_ my email? (you/get)

    B: What email? _did you send_ me something? (you/send)

    A: Yeah, I sent an email this morning. It was important.

    B: Well, I didn't get it.

9. A: The food tasted good, but the waiter was kind of rude.

    B: Yeah. _did you leave_ him a tip? (you/leave)

    A: Yes, but not a very big one.

10. A: _did you bring_ anything to eat? (you/bring)

    B: No, I forgot.

Think about It Write each past verb in Activity 15 under the correct group in the chart below.

Regular simple past verbs	Irregular simple past verbs
called	bought

16 | Asking *Wh-* Questions about the Past Complete these questions with *you* and the simple past form of the verb in parentheses. `2.3 C`

ASKING QUESTIONS ABOUT A TRIP

1. Where _did you go_? (go)
2. When _did you take_ this trip? (take)
3. How _dne get there_ there? (get)
4. Who _did you travel_ with? (travel)
5. What _did you do_ there? (do)
6. What _did you like_ best about the trip? (like)
7. What problems _did you have_ on the trip? (have)

Write about It Choose a trip you took in the past. Write your own answers to the questions in Activity 16. Then ask and answer them with a partner.

A: *Where did you go?*
B: *I went to Thailand.*

17 | Asking *Yes/No* and *Wh-* Questions about the Past Read one person's personal timeline and complete the questions. Then match the questions with the answers below. `2.3 B–C`

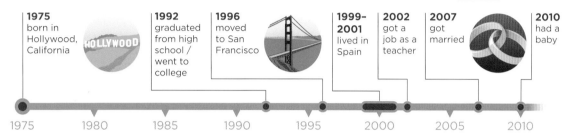

1975	1992	1996	1999–2001	2002	2007	2010
born in Hollywood, California	graduated from high school / went to college	moved to San Francisco	lived in Spain	got a job as a teacher	got married	had a baby

1975   1980   1985   1990   1995   2000   2005   2010

QUESTIONS   ANSWERS

1. ___*Did*___ you ___*get*___ good grades in high school? (get)   _g_

2. _____ _____ you _____ to college? (where/go)   ____

3. _____ _____ you _____ in college? (what/study)   ____

4. _____ _____ you _____ to San Francisco? (why/move)   ____

5. _____ you _____ your time in San Francisco? (enjoy)   ____

6. _____ _____ you _____ best about Spain? (what/like)   ____

7. _____ _____ you _____ in 2002? (what/teach)   ____

8. _____ you _____ at a high school or college? (work)   ____

9. _____ you _____ a big wedding? (have)   ____

10. _____ you _____ a girl or a boy? (have)   ____

11. _____ _____ in 2008? (what/happen)   ____

> **ANSWERS**
>
> a. I taught Spanish.
> b. Yes, I did, but it's an expensive city.
> c. No, we had a very small wedding.
> d. The people and the food.
> e. I studied history and languages.
> f. To look for a job.
> g. Yes, I did. I was a pretty good student.
> h. Nothing special.
> i. In New York.
> j. A girl.
> k. At a high school.

Talk about It Add dates and ten facts about your life to the timeline below. Exchange timelines with a partner and ask your partner questions to get more information. Tell your classmates what you learned about your partner.

TIMELINE

18 | Error Correction Correct any errors in these sentences. (Some sentences may not have any errors.)

1. On that day, we didn't had anything to eat.
2. What kind of car do you buy?
3. Who did came?
4. They not do anything about the problem last week.
5. What go wrong yesterday?
6. Did he had much fun on the trip?
7. What happen to you yesterday?
8. Who took my books?

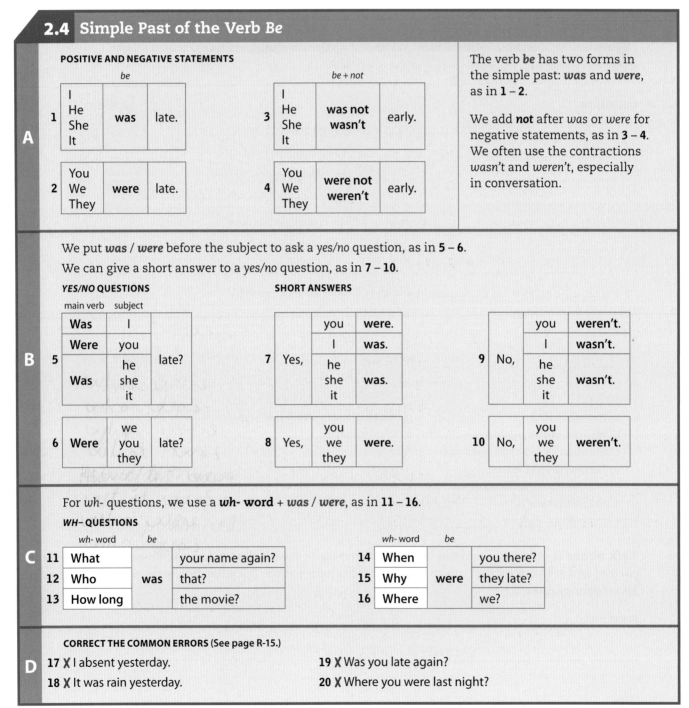

2.4 Simple Past of the Verb *Be*

A

POSITIVE AND NEGATIVE STATEMENTS

be

1 | I / He / She / It | **was** | late. |

2 | You / We / They | **were** | late. |

be + not

3 | I / He / She / It | **was not** / **wasn't** | early. |

4 | You / We / They | **were not** / **weren't** | early. |

The verb *be* has two forms in the simple past: **was** and **were**, as in **1 – 2**.

We add **not** after *was* or *were* for negative statements, as in **3 – 4**. We often use the contractions *wasn't* and *weren't*, especially in conversation.

B

We put **was / were** before the subject to ask a *yes/no* question, as in **5 – 6**.

We can give a short answer to a *yes/no* question, as in **7 – 10**.

YES/NO QUESTIONS

main verb | subject

5 | Was | I | late? |
| Were | you | |
| Was | he / she / it | |

6 | Were | we / you / they | late? |

SHORT ANSWERS

7 Yes, | you | **were.** |
| I | **was.** |
| he / she / it | **was.** |

9 No, | you | **weren't.** |
| I | **wasn't.** |
| he / she / it | **wasn't.** |

8 Yes, | you / we / they | **were.** |

10 No, | you / we / they | **weren't.** |

C

For *wh-* questions, we use a **wh- word** + **was / were**, as in **11 – 16**.

WH- QUESTIONS

wh- word | be

11 | What | was | your name again? |
12 | Who | | that? |
13 | How long | | the movie? |

wh- word | be

14 | When | were | you there? |
15 | Why | | they late? |
16 | Where | | we? |

D

CORRECT THE COMMON ERRORS (See page R-15.)

17 ✗ I absent yesterday.

18 ✗ It was rain yesterday.

19 ✗ Was you late again?

20 ✗ Where you were last night?

GO ONLINE

56

19 | Was or Were? Circle *was* or *were* in the first part of each sentence. Then match the beginnings of the sentences with the endings. (More than one answer may be possible, but only one is correct.) `2.4 A`

London in 1850

1. In 1850, London (**was**) / were ___e___
2. Charles Dickens **was / were** ____
3. Music, drama, and opera **was / were** ____
4. Many people in London **was / were** ____
5. Coal[7] **was / were** ____
6. The air in London **was / were** ____
7. Clean water **was / were** ____
8. Wages[8] **was / were** ____
9. In 1850, the population of London **was / were** ____
10. Horse-drawn buses **was / were** ____

a. popular forms of entertainment.
b. not available for most people.
c. a common form of transportation.
d. more than 2 million people. By 1875, it was more than 4 million.
e. the largest city in Europe.
f. very dirty.
g. the main source of energy.
h. unemployed[9].
i. a famous author in London at that time.
j. very low for most people.

20 | Positive or Negative? Complete these sentences with *was, wasn't, were,* or *weren't.* `2.4 A`

WHAT WAS YOUR FIRST SCHOOL LIKE?

1. My first school _____ very big.
2. The school building _____ very new.
3. The desks _____ very comfortable.
4. The teachers _____ very strict.
5. Sports _____ very important at my school.
6. Music _____ important at my school.
7. My first teacher _____ a man.
8. Girls and boys _____ in separate classes.
9. We _____ in school all day.
10. Summer vacation _____ very long.
11. My favorite school subject back then _____ math.
12. My grades in school _____ very good.

Talk about It Compare your sentences above with a partner. How were your schools similar?

"Our schools were very big."
"The desks at our schools weren't very comfortable."

---

[7]**coal:** a black mineral used as fuel
[8]**wages:** payment for work; salary

[9]**unemployed:** without a job

21 | Asking *Yes/No* Questions with *Was* and *Were* For each statement, think of a follow-up *yes/no* question with *was* or *were*. Use a word from the list on the right. (Many different questions may be possible.) `2.4 B`

1. Kate didn't go to work yesterday. *Was she sick?* _____

2. I lost Matt's phone. _____

3. Mary spoke in front of 200 people last night. _____

4. We missed the bus this morning. _____

5. My brother didn't get on the football team. _____

6. My boss yelled at me. _____

7. I slept all day yesterday. _____

8. We went on a school picnic last week. _____

9. We watched a movie last night. _____

10. It was very hot during the last Olympic Games. _____

11. Nobody called or texted Rob yesterday. _____

12. Mr. Lee didn't come to class last week. _____

angry
disappointed
early
excited
fun
good
late
nervous
sick
there
tired
upset

Talk about It Work with a partner. Use the statements and questions above to make your own conversations. Add answers to the questions you wrote.

A: Kate didn't go to work yesterday.
B: Really? Was she sick?
A: No, one of her kids was sick.

22 | Asking *Wh-* Questions with *Was* and *Were* Complete these questions with a *wh-* word (*what, where, who,* or *how often*) and *was* or *were*. `2.4 C`

QUESTIONS ABOUT YOUR CHILDHOOD

1. _____*What was*_____ your favorite sport as a child?
2. __What were__ your favorite TV programs?
3. __Who was__ your best childhood friend?
4. __Where were__ you on your first birthday?
5. __What was__ your favorite toy as a child?
6. __How often were__ you in trouble?
7. __What was__ your favorite food?
8. __Who were__ your childhood heroes?
9. __Who was__ your oldest relative?
10. __What was__ one of your childhood accomplishments?
11. __Where was__ your first school?
12. __How often were__ your parents angry at you?

Talk about It Ask a partner the questions above. Then tell your classmates something interesting you learned about your partner.

A: What was your favorite sport as a child?
B: I didn't really play sports, but I watched a lot of basketball.

58

2.5 Using *And / But / So* with the Simple Past

A

1 I **called** and **made** an appointment.

2 She **read** books and **watched** movies about mountain climbing.

3 The car **skidded**, **hit** a wall, **and turned** over.

We use *and* to connect two verb phrases, as in **1 – 2**. We use the same form for both verbs—in this case, the **simple past**.

When we connect three or more verb phrases, we use **commas (,)** + *and*, as in **3**.

B

4

subject	verb		subject	verb
We	**drove**	and	John	**walked**.
main clause			main clause	

5

The computer	**was** old	but	it **worked**.

6

No one **came**	so	we **canceled** the meeting.

7 Life **wasn't** easy in 1900, **and** the average person **didn't live** very long.

8 A few people **had** cars, **but** most people **traveled** by electric streetcar.

We use *and*, *but*, or *so* to connect two main clauses, as in **4 – 6**. Each main clause has a subject and a verb. We use

- *and* to connect two similar and equally important ideas, as in **4**
- *but* to connect two contrasting ideas, as in **5**
- *so* to say the result of something, as in **6**

We put a **comma (,)** before *and*, *but*, or *so* when it connects two longer clauses, as in **7 – 8**.

GRAMMAR TERM: A **main clause** is a group of words with a subject and a verb. A sentence with two main clauses connected by *and*, *but*, or *so* is called a **compound sentence**.

 GO ONLINE

23 | Using More Than One Verb Complete each sentence with a verb phrase from the box. Remember to use the simple past form of the verb. [2.5 A]

1. He went home and ____took a nap____.
2. He opened the refrigerator and _____.
3. They sat down at the table and _____.
4. She opened the car door and _____.
5. I turned around and _____.
6. He put on his coat and _____.
7. I pulled up a chair and _____.
8. He picked up a rock and _____.
9. He put his clothes in the washing machine and _____.
10. She turned on her computer and _____.
11. We opened our books and _____.
12. I went outside without a coat and _____.
13. The ball went through the window, hit the mirror, and _____.
14. The thief grabbed the money, put it in his pocket, and _____.

begin studying	see him behind me
break it	sit down
catch a cold	start eating
get in	take a nap
leave immediately	take out some food
read her emails	throw it
run out of the store	turn it on

Talk about It Think of a different way to complete each sentence above.

"He went home and went to bed."
"He went home and watched a movie."
"He went home and had something to eat."

24 | Combining Sentences In each pair of sentences, the subject is the same. Use *and* to combine the information in each pair of sentences. Make one sentence with one subject and two verbs. `2.5 A`

LIFE EVENTS

1. I grew up in Thailand. I moved to China in 2007 after college.

    I grew up in Thailand and moved to China in 2007 after college.

2. My grandfather left his parents in Poland. He started a new family here.
3. As children, we played together. We had a lot of fun.
4. He met many people on his trip. He made friends everywhere.
5. He graduated from college. He went to work for CARE International.
6. My brother studied engineering at school. He had many different jobs there.
7. I graduated from high school in 2010. I started college the next year.
8. At my first job, I checked business contracts. I also studied business disputes[10].
9. Two months later, I left Iran. I went to Turkey.
10. My father worked for a shipping company. He traveled a lot.

Think about It When you combine the sentences above, why can you leave out the second subject?

25 | Distinguishing *And, But,* and *So* Complete these sentences with the simple past. Then explain why the speaker used *and, but,* or *so*. Choose a reason from the box below. `2.5 B`

BEST EXCUSES FOR NOT DOING YOUR HOMEWORK   REASON

1. I ___opened___ the car window, and my essay ___fell out___.   _a_
   (open)   (fall out)
2. I _tried_ to finish my homework, but I _fell_ asleep.   ____
   (try)   (fall)
3. My mother _thought_ it was trash, so she _threw_ it out.   ____
   (think)   (throw)
4. My computer _crashed_, and I _lost_ all my work.   ____
   (crash)   (lose)
5. I _wanted_ to do my homework, but I _forgot_ my book.   ____
   (want)   (forget)
6. I _wrote_ my essay, but my printer _ran out of_ ink.   ____
   (write)   (run out of)
7. My friend _broke_ my glasses, so I _didn't see_ the homework assignment.   ____
   (break)   (not see)
8. I _hit_ my head and _lost_ my memory, so I _forgot_ to do it.   ____
   (hit)   (lose)   (forget)
9. I _put_ it in my shirt pocket, and then my mother _washed_ my shirt.   ____
   (put)   (wash)
10. My brother _made_ it into a paper airplane, and it _landed_ on the roof.   ____
    (make)   (land)
11. My friend _promised_ to do it for me, but she _got_ busy.   ____
    (promise)   (get)
12. I _wanted_ to do it but I _was_ too tired.   ____
    (want)   (be)

REASON

The second part of the sentence is:
  a. a similar and equally important idea
  b. a contrasting idea
  c. a result of something

F Y I

We sometimes use *and + then* to show that one action comes after another action.

I did all my homework, **and then** my brother spilled a glass of water on it.

---

[10] **disputes:** disagreements; debates

Write about It Write three other excuses like the ones in Activity 25. Try to use *and, but,* or *so.*

happy birthday

26 | Connecting Ideas with *And, But,* or *So* Which clause best completes each sentence? Match each main clause on the left with a main clause on the right. `2.5 B`

1. I had a headache, but ___c___
2. I had a headache, so ___c___
3. I had a headache, and ___b___

   a. I didn't go to the meeting.
   b. my back hurt.
   c. I went to the meeting anyway.

4. We found a wallet on the street, but ___a___
5. We found a wallet on the street, so ___b___
6. We found a wallet on the street, and ___c___

   a. it didn't have anyone's name inside.
   b. we called the police.
   c. it had a lot of money inside.

7. I called my mother, but ___c___
8. I called my mother, so ___a___
9. I called my mother, and ___b___

   a. now she's happy.
   b. she answered right away.
   c. she didn't answer.

10. The kids were naughty, but ___b___
11. The kids were naughty, so ___a___
12. The kids were naughty, and ___c___

   a. their mother sent them to bed early.
   b. their parents didn't do anything.
   c. they thought it was funny.

13. My brother didn't like school, but ___a___
14. My brother didn't like school, so ___c___
15. My brother didn't like school, and ___b___

   a. he was a good student.
   b. his teachers knew it.
   c. he didn't go to college.

Write about It Choose one group of sentences above. Think of a different way to complete each sentence in the group.

I had a headache, but it wasn't very bad.
I had a headache, so I took some aspirin.
I had a headache, and my sister had a stomachache.

27 | Choosing *And, But,* or *So* Complete these sentences with *and, but,* or *so.* `2.5 B`

FOOD IN HISTORY

1. Plates weren't available for most people in fourteenth-century England, _____so_____ they ate their food on thick slices of bread instead.

2. In the 1800s in the U.S., many people bought tomato sauce, _____ they didn't put it on their food. They thought tomato sauce was a medicine, _____ they drank it when they were sick.

a fourteenth-century baker

3. Today, potatoes are popular in many parts of the world, _____ in the 1500s, they weren't. People thought potatoes were poisonous[11], _____ they refused to eat them.

4. When the first Europeans saw an avocado, they thought it was a pear, _____ they ate it for dessert. They told everyone that the avocado was delicious, _____ for a long time, people in Europe didn't want to eat this fruit.

SPORTS IN HISTORY

5. A football (soccer ball) in the 1870s was very heavy, _____ it was impossible to kick it very far, _____ hitting the ball with your head was very dangerous.

6. Golf was an Olympic sport in 1900 and 1904, _____ in 1908, the organizers of the Olympics decided to remove this sport from the Games.

7. The first modern Olympic Games took place in 1896. There were 311 male athletes, _____ there weren't any female competitors.

a football game in nineteenth-century England

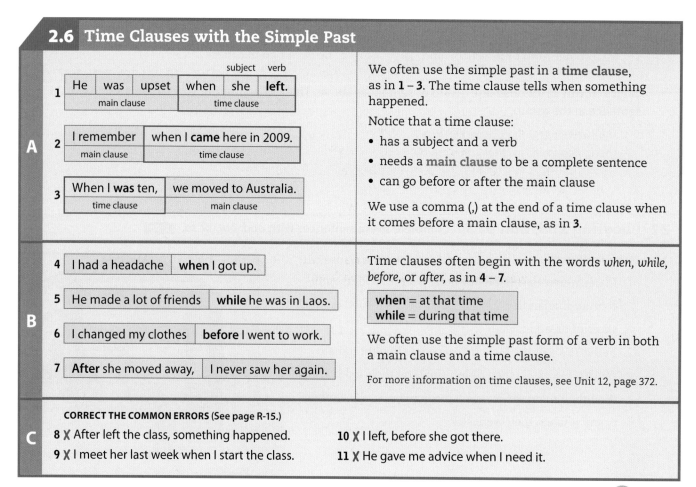

2.6 Time Clauses with the Simple Past

A

			subject	verb	
1	He	was	upset	when	she	left.

main clause / time clause

2 | I remember | when I **came** here in 2009. |

main clause / time clause

3 | When I **was** ten, | we moved to Australia. |

time clause / main clause

We often use the simple past in a **time clause**, as in **1 – 3**. The time clause tells when something happened.

Notice that a time clause:
- has a subject and a verb
- needs a **main clause** to be a complete sentence
- can go before or after the main clause

We use a comma (,) at the end of a time clause when it comes before a main clause, as in **3**.

B

4 | I had a headache | **when** I got up. |

5 | He made a lot of friends | **while** he was in Laos. |

6 | I changed my clothes | **before** I went to work. |

7 | **After** she moved away, | I never saw her again. |

Time clauses often begin with the words *when, while, before,* or *after,* as in **4 – 7.**

when = at that time
while = during that time

We often use the simple past form of a verb in both a main clause and a time clause.

For more information on time clauses, see Unit 12, page 372.

C

CORRECT THE COMMON ERRORS (See page R-15.)

8 ✗ After left the class, something happened.

9 ✗ I meet her last week when I start the class.

10 ✗ I left, before she got there.

11 ✗ He gave me advice when I need it.

GO ONLINE

[11] **poisonous:** harmful; dangerous to eat or drink

28 | Noticing Time Clauses Underline the time clauses in these sentences. Then answer the questions below. `2.6 A`

Great Achievements

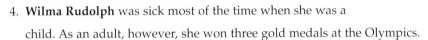

1. **Tamae Watanabe** was 63 years old <u>when she climbed Mount Everest for the first time</u>. Then, when she was 73 years old, she climbed Mount Everest again.

2. When **Zac Sunderland** was just 16 years old, he sailed alone around the world.

3. **Isaac Asimov** wrote more than 400 books during his life, but he started late. He was 30 years old when he wrote his first one.

4. **Wilma Rudolph** was sick most of the time when she was a child. As an adult, however, she won three gold medals at the Olympics.

5. **Ching-He Huang** had her first TV cooking program when she was 27 years old. The next year she wrote her first cookbook.

6. **Dikembe Mutombo** came to the U.S. to study, and then he became a professional basketball player. When he had enough money, he built a hospital in his native country.

7. **Bill Gates** was just 19 years old when he co-founded Microsoft.

8. **Farrah Gray** started his first business when he was 6 years old. What was his business? He painted rocks by hand and sold them. He later started his own radio program and wrote several books. Today Gray is a wealthy man.

QUESTIONS

1. What are the subject and verb in each time clause?
2. What are the subject and verb in each main clause?
3. In some of the sentences, the writer put the time clause before the main clause. Can you think of any reasons for doing this?
4. Which person is the most interesting to you? Why?

29 | Adding Time Clauses Complete each time clause with information about your childhood. (Many different answers are possible.) Then compare with a partner. `2.6 A`

WHEN I WAS A CHILD . . .

1. I started school when _____.
2. I had a lot of friends when _____.
3. I had fun when _____.
4. I began studying English when _____.
5. I sometimes got angry when _____.
6. I was ten years old when _____.
7. I hated it when _____.
8. As a child, I was always happy when _____.

30 | Using the Simple Past in Time Clauses Read this text. Complete the story with the simple past. Then complete the sentences below with *when, while, before,* or *after.* [2.6 B]

THE BURNING AIRPLANE

During World War II, Nicholas Alkemade was in the

British Royal Air Force. On March 25, 1944, he was on

a mission¹² when his airplane _____*caught*_____ fire.
(1. catch)

When the fire _____ to spread, the pilot
(2. start)

and the other crew members quickly _____
(3. put on)

their parachutes and _____ out of the
(4. jump)

burning plane. Nicholas turned to get his parachute and _____ that it was on fire. He
(5. see)

had to make a quick decision—burn in the airplane or jump without a parachute?

Nicholas _____ to jump. When he jumped, his plane _____ 6,000 meters
(6. decide) (7. be)

above the ground. He _____ quickly, moving at about 185 kilometers per hour, but he
(8. fall)

didn't die. Nicholas was very lucky. The thick branches of some trees _____ his fall
(9. slow)

before he _____ on the deep snow below. Amazingly, Nicholas was not seriously injured.
(10. land)

He _____ burns on his legs, hands, and feet from the fire. He _____ his back
(11. have) (12. hurt)

and knee when he landed, but he didn't break any bones. Nicholas Alkemade survived the war and

_____ to be an old man.
(13. live)

SENTENCES

1. _____ he was in the Air Force, Nicholas flew on many missions.

2. The pilot jumped from the airplane _____ Nicholas turned to get his parachute.

3. His parachute caught on fire _____ he could put it on.

4. _____ Nicholas jumped from the airplane, the fire burned his legs.

5. Nicholas was not seriously injured _____ he landed on the ground.

6. He lived for many years _____ the war ended.

Think about It What other time expressions did the writer use in the story above? Circle them.

31 | Error Correction Correct any errors in these sentences. (Some sentences may not have any errors.)

1. I met her last month when I start this class.

2. When I came here, I study very hard.

3. When I got here, my friends always help me.

4. When I saw the picture.

5. After I get to know him, we became very good friends.

6. I didn't speak any English before I came here.

7. When I was 15, my father take a job far away from my home.

8. When I was in a bad mood, my friends always make me laugh.

¹²**mission:** a trip to do a special job

2.7 Using the Past Progressive

1 I **was** still **doing** my homework at ten last night.

10 O'CLOCK

NOW

I WAS DOING MY HOMEWORK.

2 We **were** just **talking** about you.

3 The trains **weren't running** all day yesterday.

We use the **past progressive** to describe something in progress at a particular time in the past, as in **1 – 3**.

A

POSITIVE AND NEGATIVE STATEMENTS

		be (+ not)	verb + -ing	
4	I He She It	was was not wasn't	working	yesterday.
5	We You They	were were not weren't	working	yesterday.

We form the past progressive with *was / were* + (**not**) + the **-ing form of a main verb**, as in **4 – 5**.

With the past progressive, *was / were* (the past of *be*) are helping verbs.

For a list of spelling rules for the *-ing* form of verbs, see the Resources, page R-4.

B

PAST PROGRESSIVE IN TIME CLAUSES

6 I **was thinking** about her **while** she **was driving** across the country. (= I was thinking about her during the time she was driving.)

7 She **called while** I **was thinking** about her.
(= She called during the time I was thinking about her.)

8 I **was thinking** about her **when** she **called**.
(= I was thinking about her and then she called.)

We often use the **past progressive** in a sentence with a time clause. We sometimes use:

- **while** to connect two activities in progress at the same time, as in **6**
- **while** + the past progressive to show that an activity was in progress when another action (usually in the **simple past**) took place, as in **7**
- **when** + the simple past to show that an action interrupted an activity in progress, as in **8**

C

YES/NO QUESTIONS

	be	subject	verb + -ing
9	Was	I / he / she / it	sleeping?
10	Were	you / we / they	sleeping?

To form *yes/no* questions, we put *was / were* before the subject and use the **-ing form of a main verb**, as in **9 – 10**.

D

To form *wh-* questions, we use a **wh- word** + *was / were* and the **-ing form of a main verb**, as in **11 – 14**. In **15 – 16**, the *wh-* word is the subject.

WH- QUESTIONS

	wh- word	be	subject	verb + -ing
11	How	was	she	doing?
12	Why	was	he	laughing?
13	Where	were	you	going?
14	Why	were	they	laughing?

WH- QUESTIONS ABOUT THE SUBJECT

	subject	be	verb + -ing
15	What	was	happening?
16	Who	was	laughing?

32 | Using the Past Progressive in Statements Complete the sentences below with the past progressive form of the verb in parentheses. Then read Sam's schedule and check (✓) *True* or *False*. 2.7 A

Wi-Fi 🛜		7:30 AM			65% 🔋
YESTERDAY	8 a.m.	take children to school	2 p.m.	interview new staff member	
	10 a.m.	doctor's appointment	4 p.m.	project meeting	
	12 p.m.	lunch with client	6 p.m.	football game at high school	

WHAT WAS SAM DOING AT THESE TIMES YESTERDAY?   TRUE   FALSE

1. At 8 in the morning, Sam _____*was taking*_____ his children to school. (take)   ☐   ☐

2. At 10:30, he _____ in the doctor's office. (sit)   ☐   ☐

3. At 12:30 yesterday, he _____ lunch at his desk. (have)   ☐   ☐

4. At 2:15 in the afternoon, he _____ a new staff member. (interview)   ☐   ☐

5. At 4:30 in the afternoon, he _____ his son's football game. (watch)   ☐   ☐

6. At 6:30 in the evening, he _____ a project meeting. (attend)   ☐   ☐

Talk about It Work with a partner. Talk about what you were doing at the same times yesterday.

"At 8 in the morning, I was riding the train to school."

33 | Noticing Past Progressive Verbs Read this text. Underline the past progressive verbs. 2.7 A–B

Lightning Strikes Twice!

Does lightning ever hit the same thing twice? Absolutely. Just ask Roy Sullivan. In fact, lightning struck him four times! When lightning hit Sullivan the first time, he was climbing down from a lookout tower in a U.S. national park. Then, 27 years later, lightning hit Sullivan again. This time Sullivan was driving a truck. The next time lightning struck Sullivan, he was standing in his yard. Several years later, Sullivan was working at a campsite when lightning hit him again. Amazingly, lightning never seriously injured Roy Sullivan.

Think about It What are the four actions in progress in the story above? List them in the chart below. Then identify the specific action that interrupts each one.

Action in progress	Specific event that interrupts the action in progress
1.	
2.	
3.	
4.	

34 | Simple Past or Past Progressive? Complete these sentences with the verbs in parentheses. Use the simple past or the past progressive. `2.7 A–B`

ACCIDENTS

1. One time I _____*cut*_____ my finger while I ____*was making*____ a sandwich.
   (cut)   (make)
2. My father once ____*hurt*____ his back when he ____*fell*____ off the roof of our house.
   (hurt)   (fall)
3. I ____*was walking*____ to my car when I ____*slipped*____ on the ice and ____*fell*____ down.
   (walk)   (slip)   (fall)
4. Back in 2009, a horse ____*stepped*____ on my foot and ____*broke*____ my toe.
   (step)   (break)
5. My best friend ____*was cooking*____ something at the stove when her shirt ____*caught*____ on fire.
   (cook)   (catch)
6. One time I ____*was riding*____ my bike when a dog ____*ran*____ into the street and ____*bit*____
   (ride)   (run)   (bite)
   my leg.
7. I ____*touched*____ the stove and ____*burned*____ my arm while I ____*was making*____ dinner.
   (touch)   (burn)   (make)
8. My brother ____*broke*____ his arm when a boy ____*ran*____ into him while they
   (break)   (run)
   ____*were playing*____ baseball.
   (play)
9. My best friend ____*twisted*____ his ankle while he ____*was walking*____ in his sleep.
   (twist)   (walk)
10. One time at the gym, I ____*was running*____ on a treadmill when I ____*lost*____ my footing and
    (run)   (lose)
    ____*fell*____ down.
    (fall)

Talk about It Work with a partner. Take turns telling about an accident you had in the past. Ask questions to get more information.

A: *One time I cut my leg while I was swimming.*
B: *Where were you swimming?*
A: *In a pool.*
B: *How did you cut your leg?*

35 | Using Time Clauses Use each group of words to write a sentence. More than one sentence may be possible. `2.7 B`

1. I/hear a loud noise outside/talk on the phone/when

   I was talking on the phone when I heard a loud noise outside.

2. My friends/drive home from school/see something terrible/while
3. My friend/hurt his leg/walk to school/while
4. I/a customer/start yelling/work at the restaurant one night/while
5. I/the lights go out/work on my laptop/when
6. My brother/jump into the swimming pool/wear his new suit/when
7. I/stand on a street corner/hear someone call my name/when
8. I/listen to the radio/drive my car/while

Write about It Choose one or more of the sentences above. What do you think happened? Write your ideas.

I was talking on the phone when I heard a loud noise outside. I looked outside and saw two men next to a car. The car had a big dent in it, and the men were yelling at each other.

36 | Simple Past or Past Progressive? Complete these conversations with the simple past or the past progressive. (More than one answer may be possible.) Then practice with a partner. `2.7 C-D`

1. A: ___Did___ you ___talk___ to James yesterday? (talk)

   B: Yeah, we had lunch together.

2. A: ___Were___ you ___talking___ to someone when I called you yesterday? (talk)

   B: Yeah. Isabel was here, and we were planning our vacation.

3. A: ___Was___ your brother ___watching___ TV when you got home last night? (watch)

   B: No, he was already in bed.

4. A: ___did___ you ___watch___ the football game last night? (watch)

   B: Yeah, it was a great game.

5. A: What ___were___ you ___doing___ when you fell down? (do)

   B: I was running down the stairs to answer the door.

6. A: What ___did___ you ___do___ when you cut your hand? (do)

   B: I put pressure on the cut.

7. A: Why ___were___ you and Mika ___sleeping___ while I was giving my speech? (sleep)

   B: Sorry about that. We were up all night last night studying.

8. A: ___Did___ you ___sleep___ OK last night? (sleep)

   B: Yes. I didn't wake up once.

9. A: ___Did___ you ___go___ to Jen's house yesterday? (go)

   B: Yes, but I didn't stay very long.

10. A: Did I see your car downtown yesterday?

    B: Maybe. I was there in the afternoon.

    A: Where ___were___ you ___going___? (go)

    B: To the movies.

37 | Error Correction Correct any errors in these sentences. (Some sentences may not have any errors.)

1. While I going to that school, I also had a job.
2. When I was deciding to leave, I made $10 an hour.
3. One week later, I was getting a new job.
4. She tried to wake me while I slept.
5. I felt sick when I got up this morning.
6. I was plan to go there, but then my mother called and asked me to help her.
7. Why you were laughing when I came in?
8. He looked at me while I fell down, but he didn't help me up.
9. She turned around while I was looking at her.
10. Where you going when I saw you yesterday?

2.8 Using Past Forms in Speaking

A

ASKING FOR REPETITION

1 A: Her number is 666-4549.
   B: **Did you say** 4549?

2 A: I put your keys on the table.
   B: Sorry. What **was** that?

3 A: Your dinner's on the stove.
   B: Sorry. What **did you say**?

We often use the **simple past** when we ask for repetition, as in **1 – 3**.

B

USING *DID* IN POSITIVE STATEMENTS

4 A: I thought you had a key to the office.
   B: I **did have** one, but I lost it.

5 A: Why didn't you buy coffee at the store?
   B: I **did buy** coffee.

In a positive statement, we sometimes add the helping verb **did** before the main verb to give extra emphasis or show a contrast, as in **4 – 5**.

Remember: We use the base form of the main verb after *did*.

USING *DID NOT* AND *WAS NOT*

6 A: You ate all the ice cream.
   B: I **did not**.

7 A: You were late.
   B: I **was not**.

In conversation, we often use the contractions *didn't* and *wasn't*. However, we sometimes use **did not** and **was not** for extra emphasis, as in **6 – 7**.

C

CONNECTING SEVERAL CLAUSES

8 Sorry I'm late, **but** I had a bunch of stuff to deal with at home, **and** the traffic was bumper to bumper, **and** it was a real nightmare.

When people talk about past experiences in everyday conversation, they connect several clauses using *and*, **but**, or *so*, as in **8**. We don't do this in writing.

38 | Asking for Repetition Listen and write the missing question in each conversation. Then practice with a partner. **2.8 A**

1. A: Tom just called.
   B: _What was that?_
   A: Tom just called. He needs Sue's phone number.
   B: Oh, OK.

2. A: Hurry up. The train leaves at ten.
   B: _____
   A: Yes, ten.

3. A: Where's Sun-Hee?
   B: She's at the library.
   A: _____
   B: That's right.

4. A: Did you talk to Hassan this morning?
   B: _____
   A: Did you talk to Hassan?
   B: Yep.

5. A: John wants you to call him at 555-1212.
   B: _____
   A: No, I said 555-1212.

6. A: Could you get some milk at the store?
   B: _____
   A: Milk. Could you pick up some milk?
   B: Sure. No problem.

7. A: Did you go anywhere fun on vacation?
   B: Yeah. We went to China.
   A: _____
   B: Yeah. We spent three weeks there.

8. A: Please turn down the TV.
   B: _____
   A: I said, turn the TV down.
   B: Oh, OK.

🔊 39 | Adding Emphasis Listen and write the missing words. Then practice with a partner. `2.8 B`

1. A: Why didn't you call last night?

    B: _I did call_____, but you didn't answer.

2. A: I thought you had a headache.

    B: _____, but now I feel better.

3. A: I heard you didn't go to school today.

    B: But _____.

4. A: Matt said you fell asleep in class again.

    B: Yeah, _____ for a few minutes, but that's all.

5. A: Why were you downtown this morning?

    B: I wasn't downtown.

    A: Yes, you were.

    B: _____

6. A: I can't believe it. You ate my sandwich.

    B: No, I didn't.

    A: But you did.

    B: _____

7. A: Where's the remote?

    B: I put it on the table.

    A: Well, it's not there now.

    B: But _____.

8. A: That's my pen. You took it.

    B: I _____. This is my pen. Yours is on the floor over there.

🔊 40 | Noticing Long Sentences Listen and write the missing words: *and*, *but*, or *so*. `2.8 C`

SPOKEN DESCRIPTIONS

1. I left on time, ____*but*____ the traffic was terrible, _____ then I was late to that meeting, _____ it was important, _____ my boss was so angry.

2. Kate and I got together last night, _____ we were trying to do the homework, _____ it was really hard, _____ the instructions weren't clear, _____ we finally gave up.

3. This weather is weird, like it's hot out, _____ then the wind blows _____ it's cold, _____ I don't even know what to wear.

4. I was watching this movie, _____ then I had to go somewhere or something, _____ it was just when you called.

5. I didn't see Khalid today, _____ he called, _____ we decided to meet tomorrow, _____ I didn't go anywhere all day.

6. I saw Tom downtown, _____ I waved to him, _____ he didn't wave back, _____ maybe he didn't even see me. I don't know.

2.9 Using Past Forms in Writing

	COMPARE	Good writers combine information in different ways and use different sentence lengths to make their writing more interesting. This is true for stories and historical accounts about the past, as in **1a**.
A	**1a** When J. Paul Getty died in 1976, he was one of the richest people in the world. He was also one of the stingiest. For example, Getty refused to turn on the heat in his home when he had visitors. He also installed a pay phone at home for his guests.	
	1b J. Paul Getty died in 1976. He was one of the richest people in the world. He was also one of the stingiest. He refused to turn on the heat in his home. He also installed a pay phone at home for his guests.	Using a lot of short sentences can be repetitive and boring, as in **1b**.
B	**2** Vanessa-Mae had her first piano lesson **when she was only three years old. Two years later**, she started playing the violin. **Then, at the age of eight**, she had to choose between the piano and the violin.	We often use **time expressions** and **time clauses** when we write about a sequence of events, as in **2**. They help us connect ideas from one sentence to the next. This helps the reader follow our ideas.
C	**3** One evening my brothers and I were sitting around the dinner table. Suddenly we heard a loud noise outside, and smoke began to fill the house. . . .	We sometimes use the **past progressive** to set the scene for a story, as in **3**. We then use the **simple past** to describe the events in the story.

41 | Noticing Sentence Variety Read two versions of the same story. Answer these questions. `2.9 A`

1. Which version of the story has fewer sentences? Why?
2. How many time clauses do you see in each version? Underline them.
3. Which version do you prefer? Why?
4. Choose one of the paragraphs in Version 1. Rewrite it in a different way.

Version 1

My father took a new job in Saudi Arabia. I was eight years old. I didn't want to leave my school to go there. I didn't want to leave my friends.

We arrived in Saudi Arabia. I was very nervous. I didn't know anybody there. The food tasted very different. I didn't speak the language. Then I started school. I quickly made a lot of new friends. It was fun to visit my classmates' homes. I discovered that the food was really delicious! I also began to study Arabic. I learned the language quickly.

This experience gave me the opportunity to meet new people. I also got to do new things. As a result, I now love to travel. I am also more adventurous. I meet new people, but I don't feel so shy. Sometimes I don't want to do something. Then I think about my time in Saudi Arabia. I remember that it is important to try new things.

Version 2

When I was eight years old, my father took a new job in Saudi Arabia. I didn't want to leave my school and my friends to go there.

When we first arrived in Saudi Arabia, I was very nervous. I didn't know anybody there. The food tasted very different, and I didn't speak the language. However, when I started school, I quickly made a lot of new friends. It was fun to visit my classmates' homes, and I discovered that the food was really delicious! I also began to study Arabic, and I learned the language quickly.

This experience gave me the opportunity to meet new people and do new things. As a result, I now love to travel, and I am more adventurous. I am also not so shy when I meet new people. Now, when I don't want to do something, I think about my time in Saudi Arabia, and I remember that it is important to try new things.

42 | Adding Sentence Variety Rewrite these paragraphs. Add more variety and use different sentence lengths. You can leave out words or add new words. (Many different answers are possible.) 2.9 A

A TRIP TO COSTA RICA

In 2010, I spent six months in Costa Rica. I was 26 years old. I wanted to learn Spanish. I also wanted to make friends with people from a different culture.

I didn't know anyone at first. I was very lonely. None of the other students at my school spoke my language (German). I didn't have anyone to talk to. Many of the students were native speakers of English. They spent a lot of time together after class. Unfortunately, my English isn't very good. I didn't want to hang out with them.

After a few weeks, I made friends with a Costa Rican family. I went to their house every weekend for dinner. They taught me how to make some Costa Rican dishes. They helped me speak Spanish. They took me to a beautiful beach. They introduced me to some Costa Rican students. Before long I was speaking Spanish pretty well.

43 | Connecting Ideas in a Piece of Writing Read this story. Circle the time expressions. Underline the time clauses. 2.9 B

From Bookworm to World Adventurer

When Lei Wang was young, no one thought she would become a world adventurer. She was a "bookworm[13]," her mother said. Wang did well in school, and after she earned an undergraduate degree at Tsinghua University in Beijing, she moved to the U.S. to study computer science at the University of North Carolina.

After Wang got her master's degree in computer science, she took a job in New York. Then, in 2001, she decided to go back to school to get a graduate degree. While she was in school, she went on a mountain-climbing trip in Ecuador. That trip excited her about mountain climbing. Soon after the trip, Wang began working out at the gym to build her strength. She also read books and watched movies about mountaineering. She was determined to excel[14] at her new sport.

Of course, most serious mountain climbers want to climb Mount Everest, and Wang was no exception. To prepare for Everest, she climbed the highest mountain on the six other continents. Then, in May of 2010, Wang climbed to the top of the highest mountain in the world.

Write about It Rewrite the story about Lei Wang above. For example, you might want to combine the information in different ways and use different time expressions and time clauses.

No one thought Lei Wang would become a world adventurer when she was a child. . . .

[13] **bookworm:** a person who loves to read books
[14] **excel:** to succeed; to do very well

44 | Setting the Scene Number the sentences in this story in order from 1 (first) to 7 (last). **2.9 C**

THE LITTLE MICE

____ The cat heard the barking of a dog and ran away.

____ The mother mouse turned to her children and said, "You see, it's very important to know a second language."

____ Then she yelled, "Woof, woof, woof[15]!"

____ They were looking for something to eat when they heard a loud noise. "Meow[16]! Hiss! Meow!" It was a cat!

____ The cat ran toward the mother mouse, but she didn't move.

_1_ One day a mother mouse and her young children were walking in the garden.

____ Instead, she looked him in the eye and raised her paw.

Think about It Which words helped you to know the order of the sentences in the story above?

WRAP-UP Demonstrate Your Knowledge

A | INTERVIEW Think of ten things you did yesterday. List them below. Use the simple past form of the verb.

Things I Did Yesterday
1.
2.
3.
4.
5.
6.
7.
8.
9.
10.

Exchange your list above with a partner. Ask your partner questions to get more details about each activity.

A: I walked for an hour yesterday.
B: Where did you walk?

[15] **woof:** the sound a dog makes
[16] **meow:** the sound a cat makes

B | SURVEY Ask a partner about the times in the chart below and complete it with the information. (You can also ask follow-up questions.)

Yesterday								
	8 a.m.	10 a.m.	Noon	2 p.m.	4 p.m.	6 p.m.	8 p.m.	10 p.m.
Where?								
What?								
How?								

A: *Where* were you at 8 a.m. yesterday?
B: *At home.*
A: *What were you doing?*
B: *I was reading.*
A: *What were you reading?*
B: *A magazine.*
A: *How were you feeling at the time?*
B: *Very good.*

A: *Where* were you at ____ yesterday?
B: ____
A: *What* were you doing?
B: ____
A: *How* were you feeling at the time?
B: ____

How good was your partner's day yesterday? Use your partner's answers to make a line graph. Then show the graph to the class. For example:

	8 a.m.	10 a.m.	Noon	2 p.m.	4 p.m.	6 p.m.	8 p.m.	10 p.m.
HOW?	Very good	Good	Good	Very good	Very good	Terrible	Very good	Good
Very good								
Good								
OK								
So-so								
Terrible								

C | WEB SEARCH Choose one of the people mentioned in this unit. Think of three more things you want to know about this person. Write questions. Then look for the information online and write the answers.

PERSON:

Questions	Answers

EXAMPLE: *Ingmar Bergman*

What movies did he direct?   *What was his most famous movie?*   *Where was he from?*

D | WRITING Choose a topic from the box or think of your own. Write four to five sentences on your topic. Then read a classmate's writing. Think of three more things you would like to know about your classmate's story. Write your ideas as questions and give them to your classmate.

a childhood memory

a favorite game

a favorite teacher

a gift you received

2.10 Summary of the Simple Past and Past Progressive

SIMPLE PAST

STATEMENTS	I You He She It We They	worked. did not work. didn't work.

	USES	We use the **simple past** for something that: • began and ended at a specific time in the past • took place over a period of time in the past • took place regularly in the past

YES / NO QUESTIONS	Did	I / you / he / she / it / we / they	work?

WH- QUESTIONS	Where	did	I / you / he / she / it / we / they	work?

Who	worked	here?

SIMPLE PAST OF THE VERB *BE*

STATEMENTS	I He She It	was was not wasn't	there.
	You We They	were were not weren't	

	USES	The simple past uses of the verb *be* are similar to the simple past uses of other verbs—see above.

YES / NO QUESTIONS	Was	I / he / she / it	there?
	Were	you / we / they	

WH- QUESTIONS	Where	was	I / he / she / it?
		were	you / we / they?
	Who	was	that?

PAST PROGRESSIVE

STATEMENTS	I He She It	was was not wasn't	working.
	You We They	were were not weren't	

	USES	We use the **past progressive** to show that something was in progress: • at a particular time in the past • when another event (usually in the simple past) took place

YES / NO QUESTIONS	Was	I / he / she / it	working?
	Were	you / we / they	

WH- QUESTIONS	Where	was	I / he / she / it	working?
		were	you / we / they	

Who	was working?

3 Nouns and Articles

I find television very educational. The minute somebody turns it on, I go to the library and read a good book.

—GROUCHO MARX,
COMEDIAN
(1890–1977)

Talk about It What does the quotation above mean? Do you think television is educational? Why or why not?

WARM-UP

A | Circle one answer for each question. Then compare answers with your classmates. Which answer to each question was the most popular?

Personal Preferences

1. What do you usually eat for **breakfast**?
   a. **some cereal**
   b. **an egg** and **some toast**
   c. nothing
   d. other: _____

2. What is your favorite **school subject**?
   a. **math**
   b. **history**
   c. **English**
   d. other: _____

3. What do you like to do in your free time?
   a. watch **television**
   b. read **a book**
   c. get together with **friends**
   d. other: _____

4. Which **place** would you most like to visit?
   a. **the moon**
   b. **Antarctica**
   c. **Paris**
   d. **Australia**

5. What is most important to you?
   a. **money**
   b. **love**
   c. **friendship**
   d. other: _____

6. What do you worry about most?
   a. **the economy**
   b. **the environment**
   c. **crime**
   d. other: _____

B | Answer these questions about the words in the survey above.

1. The words in **blue** are **nouns**. Are any nouns capitalized? Which ones?

2. The words in **green** are **articles**. What are the words?

3. Do we always use an article before a noun?

C | Look back at the quotation on page 76. Identify any nouns or articles.

3.1 Overview of Nouns

A

Nouns are labels or names for people, places, things, and ideas.

PEOPLE		PLACES		THINGS		IDEAS	
child	friend	city	Japan	book	money	advice	power
Dr. Sanchez	Mary	country	library	computer	movie	fun	problem
father	sister	hospital	Sydney	game	television	peace	work

B

We use nouns in different places in a sentence, as in **1 – 4**.

1. [subject] **Friendship** | is | important.

2. I | have | [object of verb] **friends** | here.

3. I | went out | with | [object of preposition] **friends**.

4. We | are | [complement] **friends**.

C

NOUN PHRASE			
articles	adjectives	nouns	prepositional phrase
5		information	
6 a		computer	
7 some		money	
8 an	excellent	dinner	
9 the		members	of a team
10	serious	problems	

Sometimes we use nouns alone, as in **5**. We can also use nouns together with other "describing" words. For example:

- We can use nouns with *a/an, the,* and *some,* as in **6 – 9**. (These words are called articles.)
- We can use nouns with adjectives, as in **8** and **10**. Adjectives explain "what kind of" noun.
- We can add a prepositional phrase after a noun, as in **9**.

1 | Grouping Nouns Read this information about symbols. Write each **bold** noun under the correct group in the chart on page 79. (Some nouns may fit into more than one group.) `3.1 A`

1. **People** wear green **ribbons** to show their **concern** for the **environment**.

2. The **rings** on the Olympic **flag** represent the five main **regions**[1] of the **world**.

3. The two olive **branches** on the United Nations flag represent **peace**.

4. The **eagle**, a kind of **bird**, represents **courage**[2], **power**, and **strength**.

5. A wedding ring is a **symbol** of **love** and **commitment**[3].

6. The **Taj Mahal** in **India** is the **tomb**[4] of the wife of **Emperor Shah Jahan**. The **building** is a symbol of the emperor's love.

[1] **regions:** areas
[2] **courage:** the ability to do something difficult or dangerous
[3] **commitment:** a promise to do something
[4] **tomb:** burial place

People	Places	Things you can see, hear, or touch	Ideas
people			

Write about It Add five more nouns to each group in the chart above. Then share ideas with your classmates.

2 | Using Nouns in Sentences Choose nouns from the box to complete each fact. `3.1 B`

ball	event	sport	television	women
countries	players	teams	Uruguay	the United States

TEN FACTS ABOUT FOOTBALL

Noun as subject

1. Only 8 _____*countries*_____ have won the World Cup.
2. _____ run for 3.5 or 4.5 kilometers during a game.
3. Today, more than 20 million _____ play football.

Noun as complement

4. Football is the most popular team _____ in the world.
5. Football became an Olympic _____ in 1908.

Noun as object of preposition

6. In _____, football is called soccer.
7. The World Cup was not on _____ until 1954.
8. The first World Cup took place in 1930 in _____.
9. Football players cannot run with the _____ in their hands.

Noun as object of verb

10. Only 13 countries sent _____ to the first World Cup.

Think about It We use a **complement** (not an object) after a linking verb to rename or describe the subject of the sentence. What are the linking verbs in sentences 4 and 5 above?

Write about It Work with a partner. Choose a different sport and write two facts like the ones above. Read your facts to your classmates. Ask them to identify the nouns in each one.

Ice hockey is the most popular sport in Canada.

3 | Usage Note: Prepositional Phrases Read the note. Then do Activities 4–5.

on the table	
in my house	= **preposition** + **noun phrase** = a prepositional phrase
in the world	

We often use a prepositional phrase to tell *where* or *when* something happens.

    I usually study **at the library.** (where)   My class is **on Monday nights.** (when)

We can also use a noun phrase + a prepositional phrase. The prepositional phrase gives more information about the noun phrase.

The library at my school	is always quiet.
noun phrase	

The capital of Canada	is Ottawa.
noun phrase	

Notice: a noun phrase + a prepositional phrase = one long noun phrase

4 | Using Nouns with Describing Words Listen and write the missing word(s) in each question. `3.1 C`

	Article	Adjective	Noun	Prepositional phrase
1. Do you have	*a*		car?	
2. How expensive is	a		computer?	
3. How much is	a		cell phone?	
4. What is	the	largest	city	?
5. Do you like		scary	?	
6. What's the name of	an		movie?	
7. Do you like to wear		expensive	?	
8. Are you		hard	worker?	
9. Do you know			people	?
10. Do you want to be			engineer?	
11. What is	the			of a famous university?
12. What is	the	best	restaurant	?
13. Did you eat			breakfast?	
14. Would you like	some		?	

Talk about It Ask a partner the questions above.

A: Do you have a car?
B: No, I don't. I don't like to drive.

Think about It Look at the questions above. When do English speakers use *an* instead of *a*?

5 | Prepositions + Nouns Circle the nouns in each **bold** noun phrase. Then listen and add the missing prepositions. `3.1 C`

TORONTO, CANADA

1. Toronto is **the largest (city)** _in_ **(Canada)**.

2. **The population** ___ **Toronto** is 2.48 million people.

3. Toronto is **one of the most multicultural cities** _in_ the world.

4. **Twenty percent** _of_ **all immigrants** _in_ Canada live in Toronto.

5. There are **more than 1,400 parks** _in_ Toronto.

6. Yonge Street in Toronto is **the longest street** _in_ the world.

7. **More than 30 percent of the people** _in_ Toronto speak a foreign language at home.

8. According to *Fortune Magazine,* Toronto was **the safest city** _in_ North America in 1996.

9. **Over half** _in_ the workforce has a university degree or college diploma.

10. The Toronto International Film Festival takes place **every year** _in_ September.

RESEARCH SAYS...

The most common prepositions are *of, in,* and *to.*

CORPUS

Write about It Choose a city and write two sentences about it. Try to use a prepositional phrase in each sentence.

Beibei is a small city in China.

3.2 Proper Nouns and Common Nouns

A

PROPER NOUNS	Names of unique people, places, things, and ideas are called **proper nouns** (or proper names). We always capitalize proper nouns, as in **1** – **2**.
1 Montreal is in Canada.	
2 Canadians celebrate Thanksgiving in October.	
COMMON NOUNS	All other nouns are called **common nouns**, as in **3** – **5**. We capitalize a common noun at the beginning of a sentence, as in **5**.
3 My university is in a big city.	
4 Our next holiday is in a month.	
5 Holidays are a good time to relax.	

B

content words

6 | I study at | the | University | of | London.
function words

Many proper names have two or more words. We capitalize content words in proper names, as in **6** – **7**. We do not usually capitalize function words.

content words

7 | The | Office | for | Student | Affairs | is closed.
function words

WARNING! We capitalize any word at the beginning of a sentence, as in **7**.

8 | My favorite book is | *Sense* | *and* | *Sensibility*.

9 | Did you see the film | *And* | *the* | *Ship* | *Sails* | *On*?

We capitalize the content words in titles of books, movies, etc., as in **8** – **9**. We capitalize the first and last word, even if they are function words, as in **9**.

C

COMPARE	**WARNING!** The same noun can be a proper noun or a common noun, as in **10a** – **10b**.
10a My favorite teacher is **Professor Jones**. She's teaching **Economics 101** this semester.	
10b Sarah Jones is a **professor** at Brown College. She teaches **economics**.	

ONLINE

6 | Noticing Proper and Common Nouns Underline the nouns in these sentences. Then write each noun under the correct group in the chart below. `3.2 A`

BIOGRAPHICAL INFORMATION

1. My first <u>name</u> is Linda.
2. I was born in Mexico in the month of August.
3. I have one brother. His name is Manuel.
4. I speak two languages: Spanish and English.
5. My first teacher was Mrs. Vargas.
6. I have classes on Wednesdays and Fridays.
7. I'd like to travel to Hawaii with a good friend.
8. I'm interested in science and art.

Proper nouns	Common nouns
	name

Write about It Change any of the nouns in the sentences above to make the sentences true for you.

My first name is _____ .

7 | Exploring Categories of Proper Nouns Add one more proper noun to each category. Then share ideas with your classmates. `3.2 A–B`

1. **Names of countries:** Turkey, Brazil, _____
2. **Names of towns and cities:** Tokyo, San Salvador, _____
   _____
3. **Names of specific streets:** Abbey Road, Yonge Street, _____
   _____
4. **Names of rivers, lakes, etc.:** the Nile, the Indian Ocean, _____
   _____
5. **Months of the year:** February, October, _____
6. **Days of the week:** Wednesday, Saturday, _____
7. **Names of holidays:** Ramadan, New Year's Day, _____
   _____
8. **Nationalities:** Italian, Costa Rican, _____
9. **Names of languages:** Russian, Arabic, Farsi, _____
10. **Names of schools:** Oxford University, _____
11. **Names of school courses:** Intro to Astronomy, _____
    _____
12. **People's names:** Albert Einstein, _____
13. **Titles before people's names:** Dr. Smith, Mr. Jones, _____
    _____
14. **Titles of books, movies, etc.:** *Never Let Me Go,* _____
    _____

> **F Y I**
>
> We use *the* before some proper nouns. These include:
>
> - rivers, lakes, etc.
>   the Amazon
>   the Pacific Ocean
>
> - plural geographical names
>   the United Arab Emirates
>   the Solomon Islands
>
> - most newspapers and some magazines
>   *The Manchester Guardian*
>   *The New Republic*

15. **Names of organizations:** the United Nations (UN), _____

    _____

16. **Abbreviations of academic degrees:** MA (master of arts), _____

    _____

17. **Brand names:** Apple, Coke, _____

8 | Identifying Proper Nouns Underline the proper nouns in each paragraph. Then match each proper noun with a category from Activity 7. Write the number of the category above the proper noun. **3.2 A–B**

Excerpts from a University Catalog

<u>The School of Liberal Arts and Sciences</u> offers courses in biology, chemistry, English, history, mathematics, music, psychology, and Spanish. This school is near Central Lake—only two hours away from the city of Portland. The university bus system provides[5] free transportation between the downtown area and the campus. Buses run from Thursday to Sunday (Friday to Sunday in July and August) except during holidays.

Professor Nancy Lim is the director of the English Language Institute. Professor Lim is from Korea. After receiving her MA and PhD in the United States, she taught English in Costa Rica. In addition to her responsibilities as the director of the program, Professor Lim teaches English Composition. She is the author of _Developing Your Writing Skills._

Think about It In the information above, the following nouns are NOT capitalized: _history, city, university, downtown,_ and _director._ Why is that?

9 | Capitalizing Words Rewrite these sentences and capitalize the correct words. **3.2 B**

1. my friend likes the magazine _reader's digest_.

   My friend likes the magazine Reader's Digest.

2. one of my favorite books is _the sea_ by john banville.
3. my sister and I just watched the movie _beauty and the beast_.
4. my brother is a student at the university of california.
5. the london school of economics is a famous school.
6. aravind adiga wrote _the white tiger_.
7. we saw a great exhibit at the museum of modern art.
8. the president of brazil lives in the palace of the dawn.

> **F Y I**
>
> When we write on a computer, we usually _italicize_ the titles of books, magazines, newspapers, films, etc. When we write by hand, we usually <u>underline</u> a title.

---

[5] **provide:** to offer; to give

10 | Capitalizing Words Read these paragraphs. Capitalize the correct words. `3.2 A–B`

AUSTRALIA

1. australia is the sixth largest country in the world. in fact, it's 50 percent larger than europe. australia also has more beaches than any other country in the world. bondi beach, one of the most famous beaches in the world, is on the east coast of australia.

2. australia is a multicultural country. the most common languages after english are mandarin, italian, arabic, and cantonese.

3. one of the most famous australian writers is colleen McCullough. she studied medicine before she became a writer, and for ten years she taught at yale medical school in the united states. she wrote her first two books while she was there. her second book, *the thorn birds*, was made into a miniseries in 1983.

4. one of the most famous buildings in the world is the sydney opera house. this beautiful building was designed by a danish architect, jorn utzon. queen elizabeth II came to australia in 1973 to open the building. the first performance at the opera house was *war and peace* by sergei prokofiev.

Write about It Choose a country and write several sentences about it. Share your writing with your classmates and ask if you capitalized all the necessary words.

Hungary is a small country in Europe. The capital of Hungary is Budapest.

11 | Writing Common and Proper Nouns Ask a classmate these questions and write your classmate's answers. Be sure to capitalize the correct words. `3.2 A–B`

1. Where were you born?
2. What's your favorite kind of car?
3. What's the name of a good movie?
4. What's your favorite school subject?
5. Where did you live last year?
6. What is your favorite month of the year?
7. What languages did you study in school?
8. What city do you want to visit someday?
9. What is the name of a website you often visit?
10. What is your favorite holiday?

Write about It Write three sentences with information about a classmate. Collect the papers and mix them up. Then take turns reading the sentences aloud. The rest of the class can guess the person.

This person's favorite school subject is math. Last year, this person lived in Canada.
This person often uses Facebook.

12 | Proper Noun or Common Noun? Rewrite these sentences and correct any errors in capitalization. (Some sentences may not have any errors.) `3.2 C`

1. a. One of my Professors always looks at my papers and gives me advice.
   b. I have a meeting with professor Henley on Friday.
2. a. What do you know about president Dilma Rousseff of brazil?
   b. Dilma Rousseff was the first female president of brazil.

Dilma Rousseff

3. a. My house is the first house on Castro street, next to the library.

   b. We live on a beautiful street with lots of trees.

4. a. I want to study Business in college.

   b. Between my final math 101 and spanish 201 exams, I drove home.

5. a. When the problems began in my country, I was still a student. I wanted to leave the University, but my parents told me to stay there.

   b. My parents visited North Carolina last year because my brother is studying engineering at Duke university.

6. a. My favorite movies are *the King's speech* and *Raiders Of The Lost Ark*.

   b. I always take my rings off when I go swimming.

> **FYI**
>
> We capitalize the names of specific school courses. We don't capitalize the names of school subjects.
>
> My favorite course last semester was **History 302**.
>
> My favorite school subject is **history**.

3.3 Singular Nouns and Plural Nouns

A

singular	plural
one computer	two computers
one place	two places
one class	two classes

1

To form most **plural** nouns, add *-s* or *-es* to the **singular** form, as in **1**.

singular	plural
one life	two lives
one family	two families
one city	two cities

2

In some nouns, a letter changes when we add *-s* or *-es*, as in **2**.

For a complete list of spelling rules for plural nouns, see Activity 16, page 87.

B

singular	irregular plural
one child	two children
one foot	two feet
one man	two men
one person	two people
one tooth	two teeth
one woman	two women

3

A few nouns have irregular plural forms, as in **3**.

one fish	two fish
one species	two species

4

Some nouns have the same form for the singular and plural, as in **4**. These are often words for animals.

C

COMPARE NOUNS AND VERBS

5a Do you want a **copy** of this? (singular noun)

5b Please don't **copy** my paper. (verb)

5c Why do people **copy** me? (verb)

6a How many **watches** do you own? (plural noun)

6b My sister **watches** a lot of TV. (verb)

WARNING! Nouns and verbs can look the same.

• A singular noun can look like a verb, as in **5a** – **5c**.

• A plural noun can look like a verb, as in **6a** – **6b**.

D

7 The French are proud of their history.

(the French = all French people)

8 Are **the rich** different from you and me?

(the rich = all rich people)

We can use *the* + an adjective to describe a group of people that share one quality, as in **7** – **8**. *The* + adjective functions as a plural noun.

13 | Singular or Plural Noun? It is sometimes difficult to hear the *-s* or *-es* ending on plural nouns. Listen and circle the letter of the sentence that you hear. `3.3 A`

1. a. Please write the **name** on the envelope.
   b. Please write the **names** on the envelope.
2. a. Don't forget to put your **paper** on my desk.
   b. Don't forget to put your **papers** on my desk.
3. a. Bring your **friend** to the meeting tonight.
   b. Bring your **friends** to the meeting tonight.
4. a. Please call the **number** below.
   b. Please call the **numbers** below.
5. a. Forward the **email** to my new address.
   b. Forward the **emails** to my new address.
6. a. Please pick up the **package** on my desk.
   b. Please pick up the **packages** on my desk.

7. a. Please finish the **report** by next week.
   b. Please finish the **reports** by next week.
8. a. Don't forget to leave the **box** on the table.
   b. Don't forget to leave the **boxes** on the table.
9. a. Please close the **window** when you leave.
   b. Please close the **windows** when you leave.
10. a. Make a copy of the **document** you found.
    b. Make a copy of the **documents** you found.
11. a. Leave the completed **form** on my desk.
    b. Leave the completed **forms** on my desk.
12. a. Did you find the **message** I left on your desk?
    b. Did you find the **messages** I left on your desk?

14 | Pronunciation Note: *-s* and *-es* Endings Listen to the note. Then do Activity 15.

Usually the plural ending *-s* or *-es* is just a consonant sound: /s/ or /z/.

	SINGULAR	PLURAL	
1	one night	two nights	/ s /
2	one note·book	two note·books	
3	one her·o	two her·oes	/ z /
4	one cit·y	two cit·ies	

When a singular noun ends in a hissing or buzzing sound, the plural *-s* or *-es* ending adds another syllable: / əz /. (These words are often spelled with a final *-s*, *-x*, *-z*, *-ce*, *-ge*, *-se*, *-ze*, *-sh*, and *-ss*.)

	SINGULAR	PLURAL	
5	one wish	two wish·es	+ 1 syllable
6	one size	two siz·es	/ əz /
7	one page	two pag·es	
8	one sen·tence	two sen·ten·ces	

15 | Pronouncing Plural Nouns Listen to each pair of words. Check (✓) the ending you hear. `3.3 A`

			/ s / OR / z /	/ əz /				/ s / OR / z /	/ əz /
1.	sport	sports	☐	☐	9.	language	languages	☐	☐
2.	college	colleges	☐	☐	10.	similarity	similarities	☐	☐
3.	symbol	symbols	☐	☐	11.	glass	glasses	☐	☐
4.	discovery	discoveries	☐	☐	12.	beach	beaches	☐	☐
5.	campus	campuses	☐	☐	13.	game	games	☐	☐
6.	movie	movies	☐	☐	14.	name	names	☐	☐
7.	course	courses	☐	☐	15.	business	businesses	☐	☐
8.	place	places	☐	☐	16.	suitcase	suitcases	☐	☐

Talk about It Work with a partner. One person reads aloud the singular nouns above. The other person listens and says the plural form. Then change roles.

Write about It Write three questions using plural nouns from the list above. Then ask your partner the questions.

How many movies did you watch last week?   *What are the similarities between Mexico and Spain?*

16 | Spelling Note: -s and -es Endings Read the note. Then do Activities 17–19.

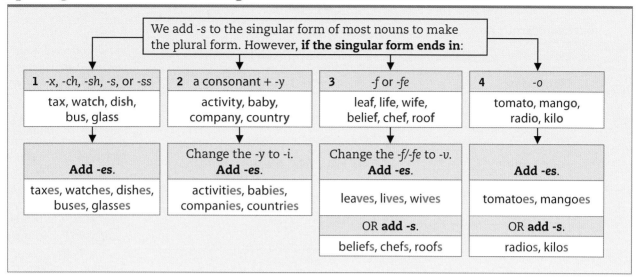

We add -s to the singular form of most nouns to make the plural form. However, **if the singular form ends in**:

1 -x, -ch, -sh, -s, or -ss	**2** a consonant + -y	**3** -f or -fe	**4** -o
tax, watch, dish, bus, glass	activity, baby, company, country	leaf, life, wife, belief, chef, roof	tomato, mango, radio, kilo
Add -es.	Change the -y to -i. **Add -es.**	Change the -f/-fe to -v. **Add -es.**	**Add -es.**
taxes, watches, dishes, buses, glasses	activities, babies, companies, countries	leaves, lives, wives	tomatoes, mangoes
		OR **add -s.**	OR **add -s.**
		beliefs, chefs, roofs	radios, kilos

17 | Spelling Plural Nouns Write the plural form of each noun. `3.3 A`

SINGULAR	PLURAL		SINGULAR	PLURAL
1. family	_____		10. lady	_____
2. dress	_____		11. match	_____
3. video	_____		12. hero	_____
4. story	_____		13. bush	_____
5. essay	_____		14. copy	_____
6. potato	_____		15. party	_____
7. box	_____		16. knife	_____
8. city	_____		17. chief	_____
9. day	_____		18. photo	_____

Think about It Work in a group of three. Each person checks the plural spelling of six words above.

18 | Exploring Plural Nouns Write two more plural nouns for each category. `3.3 A`

1. Three things that people read: _magazines_ _____
2. Three things that people watch: _videos_ _____
3. Three things that people wear in cold weather: _coats_ _____
4. Three things that grow outdoors: _flowers_ _____
5. Three types of electronic devices: _cell phones_ _____
6. Three things you might see in a school: _students_ _____
7. Three kinds of fruit: _bananas_ _____
8. Three things you can use for cutting: _scissors_ _____

Write about It Compare your lists above with a partner and add any additional words.

Think about It Which of the words in your lists above changed spelling when you added -s or -es?

19 | Using Plural Nouns Complete each question with the plural form of the noun in parentheses. Then choose an answer from the box below. `3.3 A–B`

QUESTIONS ABOUT NUMBERS

a. How many _____sides_____ does a square have? (side)   4

b. How many _____ are in the number 1 million? (zero)

c. How many _____ are in one U.S. dollar? (penny)

d. How many _____ are there on a piano? (key)

e. How many _____ are there in a circle? (degree)

f. On average, how many years do _____ live? (elephant)

g. How many _____ are in a yard[6]? (foot)

h. How many _____ does a normal adult have? (tooth)

i. How many _____ does it take to make a whole? (half)

j. How many _____ do most humans have? (vertebra[7])

k. Approximately how many _____ are in 100 pounds? (kilo)

l. Approximately how many _____ are born in the world every second? (baby)

m. Approximately how many _____ in the world have more than 1 million people? (city)

> **F Y I**
>
> Words borrowed from other languages sometimes have an **irregular plural form**. For example:
>
> | Singular | Plural |
> |---|---|
> | crisis | crises |
> | hypothesis | hypotheses |
>
> In some cases, both the irregular plural form and the regular -s form are acceptable. For example:
>
> | Singular | Plural |
> |---|---|
> | appendix | appendixes |
> | | appendices |
> | vertebra | vertebrae |
> | | vertebras |

ANSWERS TO QUESTIONS ABOUT NUMBERS

2   3   4   4.5   6   32   33   45   60   88   100   360   480

Talk about It Work in a group of four. Ask and answer the questions above.

Write about It In your group, write three more questions with numbers for answers. Then ask another group the questions.

How many days are there in the longest month?

20 | Distinguishing Nouns and Verbs Decide if the **bold** word is a noun or a verb. Write *N* (noun) or *V* (verb) above each word. `3.3 C`

1. Do you have a middle **name**? *(N)*

2. How did your parents choose your **name**?

3. Can you **name** the continents?

4. Do you have a **watch**?

5. Do you **watch** a lot of TV?

6. Who **watches** the most TV in your family?

7. Why are fewer people wearing **watches** these days?

8. Does your teacher **grade** all of your homework?

9. Are **grades** important to you?

[6] **yard:** a measure of length
[7] **vertebra:** a small bone in your back

10. Do you have a **plan** for your future?

11. What do you **plan** to do tomorrow?

12. Do you like to make **plans**?

13. Who **plans** the meals in your family?

14. What do family members sometimes **fight** about?

15. What is a good way to end a **fight**?

16. What are the basic **needs** of a baby?

17. How much water do you **need** to drink every day?

18. Do you ever feel the **need** to sleep during the day?

19. How many hours do you **need** to sleep at night?

Talk about It Ask a partner the questions in Activity 20.

A: Do you have a middle name?
B: No, I don't. But I have two last names.

21 | Using Adjectives as Nouns Use *the* + an adjective from the box to complete each question below. (You will use some adjectives more than once. Many different questions are possible.) `3.3 D`

educated	elderly[8]	poor	rich	uneducated	unemployed	young

QUESTIONS ABOUT GROUPS OF PEOPLE

1. Are _____ happier than other people?

2. Should _____ be allowed to make their own decisions?

3. Are _____ getting poorer?

4. Do _____ have more health problems than other people?

5. Are _____ likely to earn high salaries[9]?

6. Are _____ lazy?

7. Should _____ pay more taxes than other people?

8. Should young people take care of _____?

9. Is it difficult for _____ to find work these days?

Talk about It Choose one of your questions above and interview six classmates. Then report their answers to the class.

"I asked six classmates, 'Do the poor have more health problems than other people?'
Five people answered 'Yes' and one person answered 'No.'"

[8] **elderly:** old
[9] **salaries:** money that people receive for their work

3.4 Count Nouns and Noncount Nouns

When you use a noun, ask yourself, "Can I count this?" The things you can count are called **count nouns**. The things you can't count are called **noncount nouns**.

A

COUNT NOUNS

2 glasses

4 men

4 trees

NONCOUNT NOUNS

water

PEACE

flour

For a list of common noncount nouns, see the Resources, page R-10.

B

COUNT NOUNS

1 I have one **class** on Monday and two **classes** on Tuesday.

2 We spent a **day** in Boston and three **days** in New York.

NONCOUNT NOUNS

3 The **information** was correct. (NOT: ~~informations~~)

4 Your **advice** was very helpful. (NOT: ~~advices~~)

5 Did you buy some **furniture**? (NOT: ~~furnitures~~)

A count noun has a singular form and a plural form, as in **1 – 2**.

A noncount noun does not have a plural form because we think of it as a whole thing, as in **3 – 5**.

Sometimes "a whole thing" can have many parts, as in **5**. When we use a noncount noun, we are talking about all of the parts together.

C

COMPARE

6a Can I have three **coffees**, please? (coffees = cups of coffee)

6b Do you drink **coffee**? (coffee = the liquid drink)

7a I had a bad **experience** yesterday.
(experience = one separate event)

7b How much **experience** do you have with computers?
(experience = the skill or knowledge you learn)

Many nouns have a count meaning and a noncount meaning.

- Nouns have a count meaning when they are single, separate things, as in **6a** and **7a**.

- A noun has a noncount meaning when it is a thing or idea in general, as in **6b** and **7b**.

 ONLINE

22 | Can You Count It? Think about each noun in this list. Is it something you can count? Check (✓) *Count* or *Noncount*. **3.4 A–B**

	COUNT	NONCOUNT		COUNT	NONCOUNT
1. tomato	✓		10. information		✓
2. chemistry		✓	11. knowledge		✓
3. child	✓		12. region	✓	
4. problem		✓	13. university	✓	
5. advice		✓	14. jewelry		✓
6. excitement		✓	15. library	✓	
7. job	✓		16. furniture	✓	✓
8. fun			17. money		✓
9. computer	✓		18. holiday	✓	

Think about It Write the plural form of each count noun above.

tomatoes

23 | Distinguishing Count and Noncount Nouns Is the **bold** word in each question a singular count noun, a plural count noun, or a noncount noun? Check (✓) your answers. `3.4 A–B`

COMMON QUESTIONS FOR TEACHERS	SINGULAR COUNT	PLURAL COUNT	NONCOUNT
1. Did we have any **homework** for today?	☐	☐	✓
2. Do I need to bring my book to **school** every day?	☐	☐	☐
3. What **advice** do you have for someone studying English?	☐	☐	☐
4. Do I need a learner's **dictionary**?	☐	☐	☐
5. What is your **opinion** of electronic dictionaries?	☐	☐	☐
6. How often do you give **tests**?	☐	☐	☐
7. When is the next **holiday**?	☐	☐	☐
8. Why do we need to study **grammar**?	☐	☐	☐
9. How many **books** do we need for this class?	☐	☐	☐
10. Can we drink **coffee** in class?	☐	☐	☐
11. Does reading **literature** help you learn a new language?	☐	☐	☐
12. Can we work in **groups** today?	☐	☐	☐
13. Can we listen to some **music** today?	☐	☐	☐
14. Do we need to take **notes** in class?	☐	☐	☐

Talk about It Ask your teacher the questions above.

Student: Did we have any homework for today?
Teacher: No, but we're having a quiz!

24 | Identifying Count Nouns There is one count noun in each group of **bold** nouns. Circle the count noun. `3.4 A–B`

1. Do you like to talk about (**grammar** / the **weather** / **shopping** / (**books**))?
2. Do you like (**fruit** / **meat** / **sugar** / **beans**)?
3. Do you need special (**tools** / **equipment** / **clothing** / **knowledge**) to fix a car?
4. Do you hope to have (**money** / a good **job** / good **health** / **happiness**) in the future?
5. Do you like to watch (**baseball** / **movies** / **football** / **tennis**)?
6. Do you eat a lot of (**carrots** / **cheese** / **meat** / **bread**)?
7. Is it important to have (**courage** / good **health** / **friends** / **confidence**)?
8. Do you spend a lot of money on (**entertainment** / **books** / **clothing** / **food**)?
9. Did you buy any (**furniture** / **equipment** / **gasoline** / **shoes**) yesterday?
10. Where can you get (good **information** / good **advice** / a good **meal** / good **coffee**)?

Think about It What helped you to identify the count nouns above?

Talk about It Ask a partner the questions above. Use any of the **bold** nouns.

A: Do you like to talk about movies?
B: Sure. Do you like to talk about the weather?
A: Not really.

🔊 **25 | Listening for Count and Noncount Nouns** Listen and write the missing words. Then decide where each conversation takes place. Write your ideas in the boxes. (More than one answer is possible.)

3.4 A–B

1. Employee: Next, please.

   Customer: ___*Tickets*___ for one adult and two _____, please.

   Employee: There you go. That will be seventeen _____.

1. Where?

2. Employee: Do you need some _____?

   Customer: Yes, do you sell _____?

   Employee: Yes, we do. Luggage is on the third _____.

2. Where?

3. Customer: Excuse me.

   Employee: Yes?

   Customer: I'm looking for some _____ about popular music in the 1960s.

   Employee: Did you look it up on the _____?

   Customer: Yes, I did, but I didn't have any _____.

3. Where?

4. Customer: Excuse me. How much are these _____?

   Employee: Let me look on the box. Um, it says five hundred dollars.

   Customer: Five hundred dollars! That's a lot of _____.

4. Where?

5. Employee: Are you ready to order?

   Customer: Yes, I'd like the broiled _____, please.

   Employee: Do you want that with _____ or _____?

5. Where?

6. Employee: Can I help you?

   Customer: I need to withdraw some _____, but I don't have my ATM card.

   Employee: Can I see some identification, please?

   Customer: Sure. Here's my _____.

6. Where?

7. Customer: Excuse me, where's the _____?

   Employee: It's in that aisle, next to the _____.

   Customer: Thanks.

7. Where?

8. Employee: How many _____ are you checking?

   Customer: Just one.

   Employee: Is that your _____? Do you want to check it, too?

   Customer: No, my _____ is in it.

8. Where?

Think about It Circle all of the nouns in the conversations in Activity 25. Then write each noun under the correct group in the chart below.

Count nouns	Noncount nouns
tickets	

> **WARNING!**
> We can't count *money* (NOT: ~~one money, two moneys~~), but we can count *dollars, pounds, yen,* etc.
>
> A: I only have **five dollars**.
> B: That's not a lot of **money**.

Write about It Work with a partner. Write another conversation for one of the places in Activity 25.

26 | Using Noncount Nouns
Use the nouns in the box to complete the quotations below. (More than one noun may be possible, but only one is correct.) `3.4 A–B`

advice	education	information	music	money
	education	information	music	money
	education	information	music	money

FAMOUS QUOTATIONS

1. All _____*music*_____ is beautiful. (*Billy Strayhorn, composer*)

2. _____ is only a tool. (*Ayn Rand, writer*)

3. _____ is not knowledge. (*Albert Einstein, physicist*)

4. _____ is a fantastic[10] peacekeeper of the world. (*Xun Zi, philosopher*)

5. _____ is the most powerful weapon which you can use to change the world.
   (*Nelson Mandela, president of South Africa*)

6. _____ is the universal language of mankind. (*Henry Wadsworth Longfellow, writer*)

7. _____ is only useful when you get rid of[11] it. (*Evelyn Waugh, writer*)

8. _____ is seldom[12] welcome, and those who need it the most, like it the least.
   (*Lord Chesterfield, statesman*)

9. _____ is the oxygen of the modern age. (*Ronald Reagan, U.S. president*)

10. _____ is the root of[13] all evil. (*Louisa May Alcott, writer*)

11. _____ is a source of[14] learning. (*William Pollard, physicist*)

12. _____ is not preparation for life; _____ is life itself. (*John Dewey, philosopher*)

Talk about It Take turns reading the quotations above aloud with a partner. What does each quotation mean? Do you agree or disagree?

Think about It Do an online search for other quotations about money, music, information, education, or advice and share them with your classmates.

---

[10]**fantastic:** excellent; very good
[11]**get rid of:** to throw away or use up
[12]**seldom:** not often

[13]**the root of:** the cause of
[14]**a source of:** a person or thing that something comes from

27 | Choosing the Correct Meaning Match the **bold** words with the dictionary definitions. Write the number of the definition. `3.4 C`

> **or·gan·i·za·tion** 🔑 /ˌɔrgənəˈzeɪʃn/ *noun*
> **1** [*count*] a group of people who work together for a special purpose: *He works for an organization that helps old people.*
> **2** [*noncount*] the activity of planning or arranging something; the way that something is planned or arranged: *She's busy with the organization of her daughter's wedding.*

> **room** 🔑 /rum/ *noun*
> **1** [*count*] one of the spaces in a building that has walls around it: *How many rooms do you have in your house?* • *a classroom*
> **2** [*noncount*] space; enough space: *There's no room for you in the car.*

1. The United Nations is an international **organization**. __1__
2. I belong to a student **organization** at my school. ____
3. Your desk needs a bit of **organization**. ____
4. She volunteers at an **organization** for the homeless. ____
5. Success in school depends on good **organization**. ____
6. We aren't all good at **organization**. ____
7. My apartment only has two **rooms**. ____
8. Is there **room** for 50 chairs in your classroom? ____
9. A hotel **room** in New York can be expensive. ____
10. My car only has **room** for four people. ____
11. There isn't **room** on my shelf for another book. ____
12. I'm renting a **room** in a private house. ____

Dictionary entries are from the *Oxford Basic American Dictionary for learners of English* © Oxford University Press 2011.

28 | Count or Noncount Meaning? Decide if the **bold** word in each sentence has a count meaning or a noncount meaning. Check (✓) your answers. `3.4 C`

	COUNT	NONCOUNT
1. a. Do you like **football**?	☐	✓
b. Do you own a **football**?	✓	☐
2. a. Are you interested in studying **law**?	☐	✓
b. Is there a **law** against talking on your cell phone while driving?	✓	☐
3. a. We had many **adventures** on our trip to the Arctic.	☐	✓
b. She had lots of excitement and **adventure** in her life.	☐	✓
4. a. Please don't make so much **noise**!	☐	✓
b. I heard a loud **noise**.	✓	☐
5. a. She felt a sharp **pain** in her stomach.	✓	☐
b. We could see the **pain** in her eyes.	☐	☐
6. a. We took a tour bus to see the **sights** of Paris.	✓	☐
b. Don't let the children get out of **sight**.	☐	✓
7. a. I hope you have **success** in your new job.	☐	✓
b. The dinner was a great **success**.	✓	☐

Think about It What helped you identify the count nouns above?

Write about It Look up one of the words below in a learner's dictionary. Write sentences using the count and noncount meanings. Read your sentences to your classmates and ask them to identify the count and noncount meanings.

action	alarm	authority	chocolate	danger	production

3.5 Subject-Verb Agreement

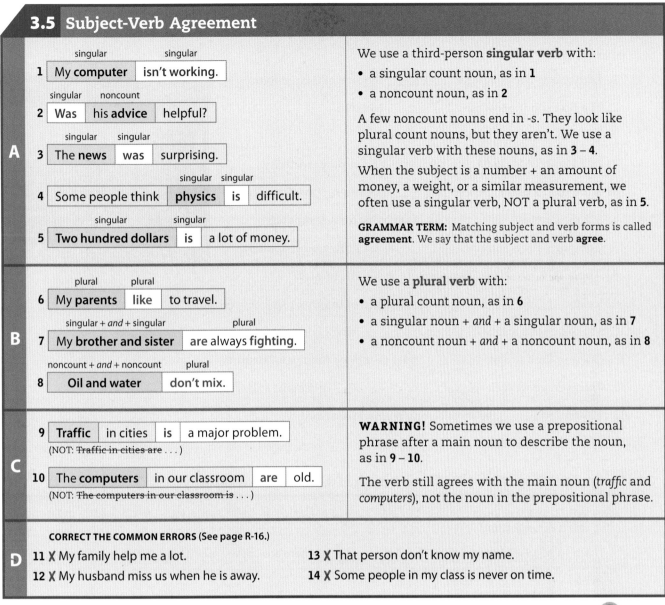

A

singular   singular
1 My **computer** | isn't working.

singular   noncount
2 Was | his **advice** | helpful?

singular   singular
3 The **news** | was | surprising.

singular   singular
4 Some people think | **physics** | is | difficult.

singular   singular
5 **Two hundred dollars** | is | a lot of money.

We use a third-person **singular verb** with:
- a singular count noun, as in **1**
- a noncount noun, as in **2**

A few noncount nouns end in -s. They look like plural count nouns, but they aren't. We use a singular verb with these nouns, as in **3 – 4**.

When the subject is a number + an amount of money, a weight, or a similar measurement, we often use a singular verb, NOT a plural verb, as in **5**.

GRAMMAR TERM: Matching subject and verb forms is called **agreement**. We say that the subject and verb **agree**.

B

plural   plural
6 My **parents** | like | to travel.

singular + *and* + singular   plural
7 My **brother and sister** | are always **fighting**.

noncount + *and* + noncount   plural
8 **Oil and water** | don't mix.

We use a **plural verb** with:
- a plural count noun, as in **6**
- a singular noun + *and* + a singular noun, as in **7**
- a noncount noun + *and* + a noncount noun, as in **8**

C

9 **Traffic** | in cities | is | a major problem.
(NOT: ~~Traffic in cities are . . .~~)

10 The **computers** | in our classroom | are | old.
(NOT: ~~The computers in our classroom is . . .~~)

WARNING! Sometimes we use a prepositional phrase after a main noun to describe the noun, as in **9 – 10**.

The verb still agrees with the main noun (*traffic* and *computers*), not the noun in the prepositional phrase.

D

CORRECT THE COMMON ERRORS (See page R-16.)

11 ✗ My family help me a lot.
12 ✗ My husband miss us when he is away.
13 ✗ That person don't know my name.
14 ✗ Some people in my class is never on time.

29 | Noticing Singular Subjects and Verbs Circle the subject and underline the verb(s) in these questions. `3.5 A`

1. <u>Is</u> (fruit) good for you?
2. What is a popular sport in your country?
3. How important is money to you?
4. When is the news on TV?
5. Is physics an interesting subject?
6. Is anger ever useful?
7. What is your favorite movie?
8. Does your mother speak English?
9. What makes a good home?
10. Is exercise an important part of your life?

Talk about It Ask a partner the questions above. Then ask each question again with a different subject.

A: *Is fruit good for you?*
B: *Yes, it is.*

A: *Is ice cream good for you?*
B: *No, it isn't, but it's delicious.*

Think about It Look back at the subjects you circled in the questions above. Write *SC* over the singular count nouns. Write *NC* over the noncount nouns.

30 | Distinguishing Singular and Plural Subjects Complete these sentences with the correct form of the verb. `3.5 A–B`

COMPUTERS

1. Early electronic computers ___were___ the size of a large room.
   (was / were)
2. The first computer mouse ___was___ wooden.
   (was / were)
3. A laptop ___is___ a portable computer.
   (is / are)
4. ROM and RAM ___are___ two types of computer memory.
   (is / are)
5. More than 2 billion people ___use___ the Internet worldwide.
   (uses / use)
6. 512 megabytes ___isn't___ a lot of memory for a computer.
   (isn't / aren't)
7. Computer programming ___is___ a fast-growing occupation.
   (is / are)
8. Apple ___wasn't___ the first company to sell the mouse.
   (wasn't / weren't)
9. Iceland ___has___ the highest percentage of Internet users: 95 percent.
   (has / have)
10. My cell phone and MP3 player ___have___ small computers inside.
    (has / have)
11. One hundred dollars ___isn't___ a lot of money for a new computer.
    (isn't / aren't)
12. The average worker ___sends___ or ___receives___ 110 emails a day.
    (sends / send)   (receives / receive)
13. 123456 ___is___ the most common email password.
    (is / are)

31 | Language Note: *There is/There are* Read the note. Then do Activity 32.

We sometimes use *there + be* at the beginning of a sentence. In these sentences, *there* has little meaning. We call it "empty *there*."

| There's | no place like home. |

| There are | many opportunities for work here. |

Notice that the verb *be* agrees with the main noun after it.

| There is | too much **information** on the Internet. |

| There are | over 20 billion **Web pages** on the Internet. |

There + be signals that new information is coming next. It often introduces a new topic.

There are many ways to greet people. For example, you can . . .

32 | Using *There + Be* Write *There is* or *There are* to complete these sentences. Is each sentence true or false? Check (✓) your answer and then compare with a partner. `3.5 A–B`

TOPIC SENTENCES		TRUE	FALSE
1. _There is_ a possibility of rain tomorrow.		☐	☐
2. _There are_ 30 days in February.		☐	☐
3. _there are_ many different ways to lose weight.		☐	☐
4. _there is_ very little sugar in candy.		☐	☐
5. _there are_ many interesting things to do in a big city.		☐	☐
6. _There are_ beautiful places in every country.		☐	☐
7. _There is_ always a danger of war.		☐	☐

8. I think _____ a connection between cell phones and cancer. ☐   ☐

9. I think _____ a lot of ads on TV. ☐   ☐

10. _____ few living things in the oceans. ☐   ☐

11. _____ life on Mars. ☐   ☐

12. _____ a difference between happiness and joy. ☐   ☐

Think about It Which of the sentences in Activity 32 could you use as a topic sentence for a paragraph or longer pieces of writing? Why?

33 | Using Prepositional Phrases Complete each sentence with a phrase from the box. `3.5 C`

in Africa	in South America	in your body	of India	of the earth
in North America	in 2 billion	of art	of Mount Everest	of the horse

1. The ancestors[15] _____*of the horse*_____ were only a foot tall.

2. The longest river _____ is the Amazon.

3. The longest rivers _____ are the Nile and the Congo.

4. The diameter _____ is 12,756 kilometers (7,926 miles).

5. The height _____ is 8,848 meters (29,029 feet).

6. The earliest works _____ are animal paintings in a cave in France.

7. The capital _____ is New Delhi.

8. One person _____ will live to be 116 or older.

9. The highest mountain _____ is in Alaska.

10. The longest bone _____ is in the leg.

34 | Singular or Plural Verb? Choose verbs from the boxes to complete the article. `3.5 A–C`

Common Surnames[16] in the United States

There _____ now six million different surnames in the U.S. The most common
            1

surname _____ Smith. More than two million people _____ that
            2   3

name. Johnson, Williams, Brown, Jones, Miller, and Davis _____ the next
                                                          4

most common surnames. More than a million people _____ each of those
                                                 5

names. Garcia and Rodriguez, two Hispanic surnames, _____ now on the list
                                                    6

of the top 10 surnames in the U.S. The surname Lee _____ on the list of the
                                                   7

top 25 most common names. Many people with the surname Lee _____ of
                                                           8

Asian descent.

1. is/are
2. is/are
3. has/have
4. is/are
5. has/have
6. is/are
7. is/are
8. is/are

[15] **ancestors:** the animals in the past that developed into modern animals   [16] **surnames:** family names

Talk about It Activity 34 lists some common surnames in the U.S. What are some common surnames in other countries? Share ideas with your classmates.

"The most common surnames in Argentina are Fernandez, Rodriguez, and Gonzalez."

35 | Error Correction Correct any errors in these sentences. (Some sentences may not have any errors.)

1. My friends likes me a lot, but they are also a little jealous of me.

   My friends like me a lot, but they are also a little jealous of me.

2. The blue stripes on the Nicaraguan flag represents the Pacific Ocean and Caribbean Sea.
3. Many people wants a good job, but they don't have the necessary skills.
4. The news are always very bad.
5. The programs on television isn't very good.
6. Fresh food keep you healthy.
7. Computers make it easier to learn about other countries without traveling.
8. A college education provide you with the tools to get a good job.
9. My brother have a serious problem.
10. When children is young, they don't understand money.
11. Four dollars is a lot of money for a cup of coffee.
12. Food and water is all we need.
13. The food in most restaurants here is expensive.
14. There are some moneys for you on the table.

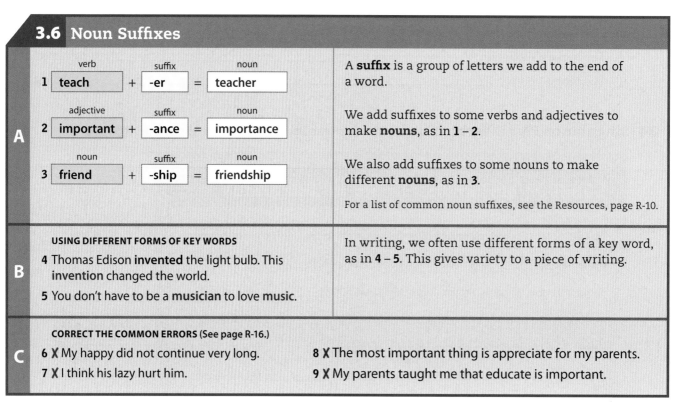

3.6 Noun Suffixes

A

verb		suffix		noun
1 teach	+	-er	=	teacher

adjective		suffix		noun
2 important	+	-ance	=	importance

noun		suffix		noun
3 friend	+	-ship	=	friendship

A **suffix** is a group of letters we add to the end of a word.

We add suffixes to some verbs and adjectives to make **nouns**, as in **1 – 2**.

We also add suffixes to some nouns to make different **nouns**, as in **3**.

For a list of common noun suffixes, see the Resources, page R-10.

B

USING DIFFERENT FORMS OF KEY WORDS

4 Thomas Edison **invented** the light bulb. This **invention** changed the world.

5 You don't have to be a **musician** to love **music**.

In writing, we often use different forms of a key word, as in **4 – 5**. This gives variety to a piece of writing.

C

CORRECT THE COMMON ERRORS (See page R-16.)

6 ✗ My happy did not continue very long.

7 ✗ I think his lazy hurt him.

8 ✗ The most important thing is appreciate for my parents.

9 ✗ My parents taught me that educate is important.

36 | Identifying Suffixes Complete this chart. Write the missing noun or suffix. 3.6 A

Verb + suffix	= Noun
1. achieve + -ment	= *achievement*
2. act + ____ion____	= action
3. appear + _____	= appearance
4. arrange + -ment	=
5. connect + _____	= connection
6. contain + -er	=
7. develop + _____	= development
8. differ + -ence	=
9. direct + -ion	=
10. disagree + _____	= disagreement
11. discuss + _____	= discussion
12. employ + _____	= employer
13. excite + _____	= excitement
14. fail + _____	= failure
15. lead + _____	= leader
16. press + -ure	=

Adjective + suffix	= Noun
17. difficult + -y	=
18. free + -dom	=
19. kind + _____	= kindness
20. real + -ity	=
21. sad + -ness	=
22. similar + _____	= similarity
23. weak + _____	= weakness

Noun + suffix	= New noun
24. art + -ist	=
25. child + _____	= childhood
26. music + -ian	=
27. office + _____	= officer
28. poet + _____	= poetry
29. prison + -er	=
30. relation + -ship	=

Think about It Use a dictionary to check the meaning of any words above that you don't know.

37 | Spelling Note: Noun Suffixes Read the note. Then do Activities 38–39.

Some words need a spelling change when we add a suffix. For example:

VERB		NOUN	VERB		NOUN
decide	(-de + -sion)	= **decision**	describe	(-be + -ption)	= **description**
combine	(-e + -ation)	= **combination**	argue	(-e + -ment)	= **argument**
compare	(-e + -ison)	= **comparison**	behave	(-e + -ior)	= **behavior**

There is no easy way to know which suffix to add to a word. You learn suffixes by seeing the words (by reading a lot) and practicing them. You can also look in a dictionary. Notice that the noun is often listed separately from the verb.

re·duce 🔑 /rɪ'dus/ *verb* (re·duc·es, re·duc·ing, re·duced)
to make something smaller or less: *This shirt was reduced from $50 to $30.* ◆ *Reduce speed now* (= words on a road sign). ⊃ ANTONYM **increase**

re·duc·tion
/rɪ'dʌkʃn/ *noun*
[count]
making something smaller or less: *price reductions* ◆ *a reduction in the number of students*

Dictionary entries are from the *Oxford Basic American Dictionary for learners of English* © Oxford University Press 2011.

38 | Using Noun Suffixes Complete these test prompts with the noun form of the words in parentheses. Use a dictionary if necessary. **3.6 A**

COMMON TEST PROMPTS

1. What are some qualities of a good _____supervisor_____? (supervise)
2. If you were an employer, for what reasons would you fire an _____? (employ)
3. _____ is the most important factor in the _____ of a country. Do you agree? (educate/develop)
4. Do the benefits of study abroad justify the _____? (difficult)
5. Money can't buy _____. Do you agree? (happy)
6. Should the _____ spend money on space _____? (govern/explore)
7. How do movies and television influence people's _____? (behave)
8. There will always be _____ in the world. Agree or disagree? (violent)
9. Should foreign language _____ begin in kindergarten? Why or why not? (instruct)
10. Parents should make important _____ for their older (15- to 18-year-old) children. Agree or disagree? (decide)

Talk about It Talk about one of the questions above with a partner.

A: What are some qualities of a good supervisor?
B: Well, I think a supervisor should be patient. . . .

39 | Using Different Forms of a Word Complete these sentences with the noun form of the **bold** word. (You can use a dictionary if necessary.) **3.6 B**

ESSAY BEGINNINGS

1. The Internet has changed the way people **interact**. For example, today there is less need for face-to-face _____interaction_____.
2. My friends are **similar** in a number of ways. Perhaps the most important _____ is their love of sports.
3. It's not easy to **decide** what to do with your life, but it's a _____ we all have to make.
4. If you want your children to **behave** well, you should pay attention to your own _____.
5. Football and soccer **differ** in several ways. One important _____ is how the players use the ball.
6. My parents **collect** old jazz records. Their _____ fills an entire room.
7. Awards and prizes **motivate** people to work hard. Simple praise can also be a good _____.
8. It may take years to **recover** from a brain injury, but a complete _____ is possible.
9. For homework, we had to **describe** a beautiful place. I decided to write a _____ of my hometown.
10. We all **fail** sometimes. We just can't allow _____ to discourage us.

Write about It Choose one of the essay beginnings above. What do you think the writer says next? Write your idea in a sentence. (You don't need to use the bold word in your sentence.)

The Internet has changed the way people interact. For example, today there is less need for face-to-face interaction. People don't need to meet in person to make friends.

40 | Error Correction Correct any errors in these sentences. (Some sentences may not have any errors.)

1. The organize of my paragraph wasn't very good.

   The organization of my paragraph wasn't very good.

2. Last year I took a course in art appreciate.

3. There are many different between my language and English.

4. When I was young, my brother always tried to protect me from dangerous.

5. I think confident makes us perform better.

6. It is not easy to accept the true sometimes.

7. The behave of many people on airplanes is very surprising.

8. When does adult begin? Is it when a person can drive a car?

9. The organization and develop of my essay need improvement.

10. I failed the exam because of its difficultness.

11. Teachers and their teenaged students discuss lots of different things in class. That's why teenagers and their teachers have a special relation.

12. Everyone fails sometimes. When you know the cause of your fail, you can change your actions.

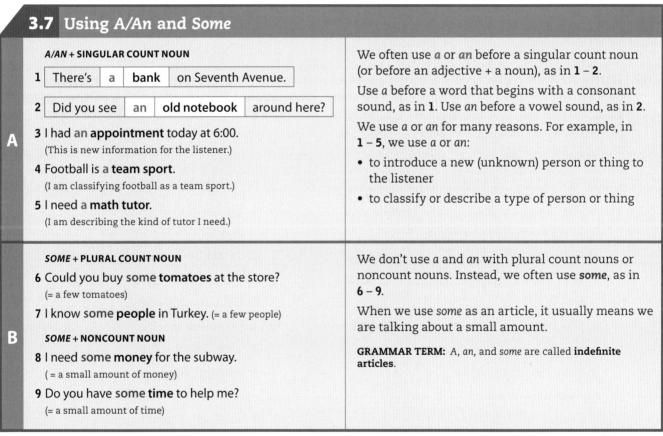

3.7 Using A/An and Some

A

A/AN + SINGULAR COUNT NOUN

1. | There's | a | bank | on Seventh Avenue. |

2. | Did you see | an | old notebook | around here? |

3. I had **an appointment** today at 6:00.
   (This is new information for the listener.)

4. Football is **a team sport**.
   (I am classifying football as a team sport.)

5. I need **a math tutor**.
   (I am describing the kind of tutor I need.)

We often use *a* or *an* before a singular count noun (or before an adjective + a noun), as in **1 – 2**.

Use *a* before a word that begins with a consonant sound, as in **1**. Use *an* before a vowel sound, as in **2**.

We use *a* or *an* for many reasons. For example, in **1 – 5**, we use *a* or *an*:

- to introduce a new (unknown) person or thing to the listener
- to classify or describe a type of person or thing

B

SOME + PLURAL COUNT NOUN

6. Could you buy **some tomatoes** at the store?
   (= a few tomatoes)

7. I know **some people** in Turkey. (= a few people)

SOME + NONCOUNT NOUN

8. I need **some money** for the subway.
   (= a small amount of money)

9. Do you have **some time** to help me?
   (= a small amount of time)

We don't use *a* and *an* with plural count nouns or noncount nouns. Instead, we often use *some*, as in **6 – 9**.

When we use *some* as an article, it usually means we are talking about a small amount.

GRAMMAR TERM: *A*, *an*, and *some* are called **indefinite articles**.

41 | Using *A* and *An* Complete these sentences with *a* or *an*. 3.7 A

SPORTS

1. Gymnastics is _an_ ancient[17] sport.
2. Football is ____ team sport.
3. Golf is ____ individual sport, not a team sport.
4. Car racing is ____ dangerous sport.
5. Volleyball is ____ awesome[18] sport.
6. Kite flying is ____ professional sport in Thailand.
7. Golf was ____ Olympic sport in 1900 and 1904.
8. You can't play polo without ____ horse.
9. A football game lasts for about ____ hour and a half.
10. The World Cup takes place in ____ different country every four years.
11. There are six players on ____ ice hockey team.

> **PRONUNCIATION**
>
> For words that begin with the letter *u*:
>
> - use *an* when the *u* has a vowel sound:
>   **an u**nusual sport, **an u**mbrella
>
> - use *a* when the *u* has a consonant sound:
>   **a u**nique sport, **a u**niversity
>
> For words that begin with the letter *h*:
>
> - use *an* when the *h* is silent:
>   **an h**our, **an h**onest man
>
> - use *a* when the *h* is pronounced:
>   **a h**ospital, **a h**ard test

Write about It Write your own sentences about six different sports. Then share ideas with your classmates.

_____ is (a/an) _____ sport.
(name of sport)   (adjective)

42 | Using *A/An* + Adjective + Noun Choose an adjective to complete each conversation below. (More than one adjective may be possible for some conversations.) Then practice with a partner. 3.7 A

| academic | delicious | good | interesting | nice | only | unusual |
| attractive | extra | hard | new | old | strange | used |

1. A: That's a _____nice_____ sweater.
   B: Thanks. I'm glad you like it.
2. A: Did you have a _____ evening?
   B: Yeah, I watched an _____ movie on TV.
3. A: This is a _____ sandwich. Did you make it?
   B: Yeah. I'm glad you like it.
4. A: I admire you a lot.
   B: Really? Why's that?
   A: Because you're a _____ worker.
5. A: Is there anything good on TV tonight?
   B: Yeah, there's an _____ program about Antarctica at 8:00.

6. A: Do you plan to get an _____ degree?
   B: Of course. I want to be an engineer.
7. A: That's an _____ suit.
   B: Thank you. It's new.
8. A: Do you have an _____ pen?
   B: Sure. Take this one.
9. A: Why did you buy a _____ car?
   B: Because I couldn't afford a _____ car.
10. A: Are you an _____ child?
    B: No, I have two brothers.

[17] **ancient:** very old

[18] **awesome:** very good

43 | Choosing A or An Read this text and complete it with *a* or *an*. `3.7 A`

Who's Who at <u>a</u> University
₁

Most college professors have ____ doctoral degree[19]. However, sometimes
2

____ university will hire ____ person without one. The university calls this
3   4

person ____ instructor. The instructor works to finish his or her PhD and
5

can become ____ assistant professor after that. Assistant professors don't
6

usually have ____ permanent job or tenure[20]. If they don't receive tenure
7

after 5 to 7 years, they usually have ____ year to find another job.
8

If ____ assistant professor gets tenure, he or she becomes ____ associate
9   10

professor. Later, the associate professor can get ____ position as ____ full
11   12

professor.

____ adjunct professor doesn't have ____ permanent position and
13   14

teaches ____ small number of classes. ____ visiting professor is from one
15   16

university, but teaches at another school for ____ year or two.
17

44 | Using A, An, and Some Complete these questions with *a, an,* or *some*. `3.7 A–B`

1. Do you have ___*some*___ money with you today?
2. Can you drive ___a___ car?
3. Can you give me ___Some___ information about your country?
4. Is there ___a___ bank around here?
5. Do you have ___a___ favorite restaurant?
6. Do you know ___a___ good place for breakfast?
7. Do you live in ___an___ apartment?
8. Can you give me ___Some___ help with my homework?
9. Where's a good place to buy ___Some___ clothes?
10. Would you like ___Some___ coffee right now?
11. Can you name ___Some___ funny movies?

Talk about It Ask a partner the questions above.

A: Do you have some money with you today?
B: Yes, I do. What about you?
A: I do too.

---

[19] **doctoral degree:** the most advanced academic degree; also called a doctorate or PhD

[20] **tenure:** the right to keep a job as long as you want it

Think about It Write each noun phrase in Activity 44 under the correct group in this chart.

A/An + singular count noun	Some + plural noun	Some + noncount noun
		some money

45 | Using *A, An,* and *Some* What would you take on each trip below? Choose two trips and list six things for each trip. Then tell your classmates about the things on your list. **3.7 A–B**

"For trip number 1, I would take some sunscreen, a hat, . . . "

Trip #1: Spend a hot summer day on a sailboat with three friends. Lunch is NOT included.	**Trip #3:** Spend three days in a cabin on a lake. Enjoy the warm weather in a place without electricity.
Trip #2: Take a working vacation. Work on a farm in France for five days. Take care of the farm animals and work in the field. Learn to make cheese. Room and food are included.	**Trip #4:** Spend two nights in one of New York City's best hotels. Free tickets to a Broadway play and the Museum of Modern Art are included.

3.8 Using *The*

A

1 Who is **the new teacher**?

2 Who are **the best students in class**?

3 **The light** in my eyes was too bright.

We can use **the** before:

• singular or plural count nouns, as in **1 – 2**
• noncount nouns, as in **3**

GRAMMAR TERM: *The* is called the **definite article**.

B

4 I met **the new teacher** yesterday.
(I think the listener knows which specific teacher.)

5 **The earth** is in danger of overpopulation.
(There is only one earth.)

6 I need to be at **the airport** by 10:00.
(A city usually has only one airport.)

7 **The computer** in our classroom is old.
("In our classroom" identifies which computer is old.)

8 When's **the last bus**?
(There is only one last bus.)

9 Who is **the youngest person** here?
(There is only one youngest person.)

We can use **the** when:

• we are talking about specific people or things
• and we think our listener knows which one(s) we are talking about, as in **4**

Our listener knows which one we are talking about when:

• there is only one in the world and everyone knows about it, as in **5**
• there is only one in a particular place (such as in a classroom or a city), as in **6 – 7**
• we use the noun with an adjective that describes only one thing, such as *first, last, next, best,* or *oldest,* as in **8 – 9**

C

COMPARE *THE* AND *A/AN*

10a Can you answer **the phone**, please?
(= a specific phone)

10b Do you hear **a phone** ringing?
(= one of many possible phones)

We use **the** when we think the listener can identify the person or thing, as in **10a**.

We use ***a*** or ***an*** when we don't think the listener can identify the person or thing, as in **10b**.

46 | Using *The* with Count Nouns and Noncount Nouns Read this recipe. Write each **bold** noun phrase under the correct group in the chart below. 3.8 A

Singapore Noodles
(Chinese Stir-Fried Rice Noodles)

Ingredients

1 package dried rice noodles
2 tablespoons cooking oil
1 pound shrimp
1 tablespoon garlic, minced
1 tablespoon ginger, minced
1 hot pepper, sliced
1 onion, sliced
1 red bell pepper, sliced

2 tablespoons curry powder
1/2 cup chicken stock
3 tablespoons light soy sauce
2 teaspoons sugar
salt and pepper
2 cups bean sprouts
4 green onions, cut into pieces

Directions

Place **the rice noodles** in a large bowl and cover them with hot water. Soak for 5 to 8 minutes. Drain and rinse with cool water. Drain again and set aside.

Heat **the oil** in a wok over a high flame. Add **the shrimp** and stir-fry for 1 to 2 minutes. Remove the shrimp and set aside.

Add more oil to **the wok** if necessary. Add **the garlic**, **ginger**, and **hot pepper**. Stir-fry for about 30 seconds. Next, add **the onion** and **red pepper** and stir-fry for another 2 to 3 minutes or until **the vegetables** are cooked but still crisp.

Stir in **the curry powder** and stir-fry for about 30 seconds. Then reduce **the heat** to medium and stir in **the chicken stock**, **soy sauce**, **sugar**, **salt**, and **pepper**. Simmer for about a minute.

Stir in **the drained noodles**, **sprouts**, and **green onions**. Toss to coat **the noodles** with **the sauce** and heat them through. Adjust seasoning to taste and serve hot.

> **FYI**
>
> In recipes and instructions, writers sometimes drop *the* before nouns in a series.
>
> Add **the** garlic, ginger, and pepper. =
>
> Add **the** garlic, **the** ginger, and **the** pepper.

The + singular count noun	*The* + plural count noun	*The* + noncount noun
	the rice noodles	

Think about It Was it difficult to group any of the nouns in the recipe above? Why?

47 | Talking about Specific Things Match the sentence beginnings with the sentence endings. **3.8 B**

FACT BOOK

1. **The** first plane flight ___*i*___
2. **The** earth's atmosphere ____
3. **The** first ocean liners ____
4. **The** first trains ____
5. In 2011, **the** tallest building in **the** world ____
6. **The** fastest way to travel ____
7. **The** ground floor of a building ____
8. By **the** 1930s, ocean liners ____
9. **The** capital of Australia ____
10. **The** flag of Singapore ____
11. Countries near **the** equator ____

a. is Canberra.
b. is by plane.
c. crossed **the** Atlantic Ocean in **the** 1840s.
d. is red and white.
e. could cross **the** Atlantic Ocean in about four days.
f. traveled at less than 16 kph (10 mph).
g. are very hot.
h. contains various gases.
i. was in 1903.
j. was in Dubai.
k. is usually **the** first floor.

Think about It Why did the writer use *the* in each sentence above? Choose from these reasons.

a. There is only one in the world and everyone knows about it.
b. The noun is used with an adjective that describes only one thing.

48 | Using *A/An* or *The* Read each conversation and add *a/an* or *the*. Then practice with a partner. **3.8 C**

AT SCHOOL

1. A: Do you know _the_ new science teacher?
   B: Yes, her name is Ms. Hernandez.
2. A: Did you write down ____ homework assignment?
   B: Yes, do you need it?
3. A: Did Mr. Thompson give us _an_ assignment for today?
   B: I hope not.
4. A: Can I borrow _the_ dictionary?
   B: Sorry. This is _the_ only dictionary in the room.
5. A: When is _the_ first day of classes?
   B: _The_ sixth of September, I think.
6. A: Did you find _a_ phone in here?
   B: Does it have _a_ red case?
   A: Yes, that's it.
7. A: Why are you late?
   B: There was _an_ accident on the highway.
8. A: When's _the_ meeting tomorrow?
   B: I think it's at 7.

AT HOME

9. A: Where's _the_ car?
   B: I put it in _the_ garage.
10. A: Could you get me _a_ tomato from _the_ fridge?
    B: Just one?
    A: Yep[21], just one.
11. A: Did you eat _the_ last piece of cake?
    B: Sorry. Were you saving it?
12. A: Do we have _a_ first aid kit?
    B: Yes, it's in _the_ bathroom closet.
13. A: Do you have _the_ remote?
    B: No, it's over there on _the_ chair.
14. A: Please don't play football in _the_ house.
    B: But it's raining outside.
15. A: Did you see _the_ weather forecast for tomorrow?
    B: No, I missed it.
16. A: What's _the_ box for?
    B: I'm sending some things to Ben.

[21] **yep:** yes (informal)

49 | Using *A/An* or *The* Write *a/an* or *the* to complete the sentences in each set. `3.8 C`

1. a. _____ last bus is at 10.

    b. I think there's _____ bus at 10 tomorrow.

    c. Are you going to take _____ 10 o'clock bus?

    d. Is there _____ bus to the zoo?

2. a. We just saw _____ great movie.

    b. I love _____ movie *The Last Emperor*.

    c. We watch _____ movie every weekend.

    d. Is there _____ movie on TV tonight?

3. a. Let's go home _____ different way.

    b. I think this is _____ only way to go.

    c. We went _____ wrong way.

    d. Is there _____ faster way to go?

> **FYI**
>
> When we use *there is* to introduce a new thing or idea, we use *a* or *an* with singular count nouns—NOT *the*.
>
> Hey, **there's a bug** in my soup.
> **There is a great show** on TV tonight.

3.9 Using No Article (Ø)

<table>
<tr>
<td rowspan="1">A</td>
<td>

Ø + PLURAL COUNT NOUN

1 I like Ø **old movies.**
(I enjoy old movies in general.)

2 Are Ø **trains** safe?
(In general, are all trains safe?)

Ø + NONCOUNT NOUN

3 Ø **Life** in the 1800s was difficult.
(a general statement about life in the 1800s)

4 Ø **Education** should be free.
(In general, education should be free.)

</td>
<td>

Sometimes we don't use an article before a noun at all. We use **no article (Ø)** because we are talking about people or things in general, as in **1 – 4**.

We can use no article before:

• plural count nouns, as in **1 – 2**

• noncount nouns, as in **3 – 4**

GRAMMAR TERM: No article (Ø) is also called the **zero article**.

</td>
</tr>
<tr>
<td>B</td>
<td>

COMPARE Ø AND *SOME*

5a I need **some money** for the bus.

5b She always needs Ø **money.**

6a Can we have **some tomatoes** for lunch?

6b He made a pasta dish with Ø **fresh tomatoes.**

7 It's not hard to grow Ø **tomatoes.**
(NOT: It's not hard to grow some tomatoes.)

</td>
<td>

We can use *some* or **no article (Ø)** before a plural count or noncount noun. We use *some* to talk about a small amount, as in **5a – 6a**. When we use no article, we are not giving any information about amount, as in **5b – 6b**.

WARNING! We don't use *some* when we are talking about something in general, as in **7**. Use no article instead.

</td>
</tr>
<tr>
<td>C</td>
<td colspan="2">

CORRECT THE COMMON ERRORS (See page R-16.)

8 ✗ He gave me sandwich for breakfast.   **10 ✗** I learned that the friends are very important.

9 ✗ Tokyo and Kyoto are some cities in Japan.

</td>
</tr>
</table>

GO ONLINE

50 | Writing General Statements Complete these proverbs with the words from the box. (More than one answer may be possible, but only one is correct.) Then say what each proverb means. **3.9 A**

PROVERBS

1. Life is _short_____ .
2. Time is _____ .
3. Knowledge is _____ .
4. Charity[22] begins _____ .
5. Clothes make _____ .
6. Actions speak _____ .
7. Walls have _____ .
8. Money doesn't grow _____ .
9. Misery[23] loves _____ .
10. Laughter is _____ .
11. Bad news travels _____ .

at home
company[24]
ears
fast
louder than words
money
on trees
power
short
the best medicine
the man

> **F Y I**
>
> Proverbs are short, familiar statements. They often give advice or a general truth about life.

Think about It Circle all of the nouns and noun phrases in the proverbs above. Then write them under the correct group in the chart below.

Ø + plural count noun	Ø + noncount noun	*The* + singular count noun	*The* + noncount noun
	life		

Write about It Choose three sentence beginnings above. Think of different ways to complete them.

Money doesn't grow in my wallet.   *Money doesn't grow like weeds.*

51 | Making General Statements Add the missing verb to each sentence. Then check (✓) *Agree* or *Disagree*. **3.9 A**

WHAT'S YOUR OPINION?	AGREE	DISAGREE
1. Life _____ more difficult now than a hundred years ago. (is / are)	☐	☐
2. Women _____ better parents than men. (is / are)	☐	☐
3. Medical care _____ to be free for everyone. (needs / need)	☐	☐
4. People _____ too much free time nowadays. (has / have)	☐	☐
5. Politicians _____ always dishonest. (is / are)	☐	☐
6. Parents _____ to spend time with their children. (needs / need)	☐	☐

---

[22] **charity:** kindness to others
[23] **misery:** great unhappiness

[24] **company:** other people

Talk about It Take turns reading the sentences in Activity 51 aloud with a partner. See if your partner agrees or disagrees and why.

A: *Life is more difficult now than a hundred years ago.*
B: *I agree with that.* OR B: *I'm not sure about that. I think . . .*

52 | **Using *Some* and No Article** Read the texts. Where possible, add *some* before the **bold** words. `3.9 B`

What Do You Like to Do in Your Free Time?

1. When I have *some*
   ^
   free time, I like to sit down and read a good book. I like **novels** best—especially **stories** about **detectives** or **crime**. I often bring **books** to the kitchen so I can read while I am eating. At **night**, I usually read until I fall asleep. Reading lets you enter a different world for a short time. You meet **new people** there and have **exciting adventures**. It is like a vacation from **real life**.

---

2. I enjoy cooking in my free time. I especially like to make **bread** and **fancy desserts**. Usually, **bread** takes a long time to prepare, so I can do other things at the same time. I often put on **good music** and make myself **tea** while I am working in the kitchen.

Write about It What do you like to do in your free time? Write two or three sentences. Then read them to a partner.

53 | **Error Correction** Correct any errors in these sentences. (Some sentences may not have any errors.)

1. I got my high school diploma in 2009, and after that, I went to the college.

   I got my high school diploma in 2009, and after that, I went to college.

2. We took a physical education every year in high school.
3. I hope that I always have a good health.
4. I prefer to travel with friend.
5. When my brother was baby, he was very sick.
6. I like to write an article for my blog.
7. Last night I went to concert of Arabic music.
8. Don't be afraid to ask for a help.
9. My grandmother always had a beautiful clothes.
10. I love this restaurant because it has a delicious food.
11. I want to get better job so that I can get a better health care.
12. I moved here from Colombia after I finished my senior year of the high school.
13. Some money can ruin a good friendship.
14. My goal was to go to the university in my country and get a degree in engineering.

3.10 Using Nouns and Articles in Speaking

A

1 I can't talk now. I'm **in a hurry.** (= "ina hurry")

2 I'll see you **in an hour.** (= "ina nour")

3 Let's sit **in the back.** (= "inthuh back")

4 **In the end**, we got home safely. (= "inthee end")

5 I need **some money.** (= "sm money")

Articles are often difficult to hear. This is because they are short, and we don't usually stress them in conversation. With unstressed articles, we often "reduce" the vowel, as in **1 – 5.**

We pronounce *the* in two ways:

B

We say "thuh" before **consonant sounds**, as in **6 – 9.**

6 | Can I take | the | car?

7 | Please pass me | the | bread.

8 | What's | the | problem?

WARNING! The letter *u* is a vowel, but sometimes it has a consonant sound, as in **9.**

9 | He's a student at | the | university.

We say "thee" before **vowel sounds**, as in **10 – 13.**

10 | I don't understand | the | answer.

11 | The | elevator | isn't working.

12 | Please pass me | the | olives.

WARNING! The letter *h* is a consonant, but sometimes it has a vowel sound, as in **13.**

13 | She belongs to | the | Honor Society.

C

SUGGESTING ANSWERS

14 Who wrote this? **Peter?**

15 What's for dessert? **Ice cream?**

16 Where are you going? To **school?**

We sometimes suggest an answer to our own question. This might be the **name of a person, place, or thing**, as in **14 – 16.**

We usually use rising intonation to suggest an answer.

GO ONLINE

54 | Pronouncing Articles Listen and complete these common expressions. Then practice saying them. Pay special attention to the pronunciation of the articles. **3.10 A**

1. Don't worry about ____a____ thing.
2. Let's try again _____ other time.
3. What's _____ problem?
4. Thank you for _____ lovely evening.
5. I have _____ idea.
6. I'll be with you in _____ minute.
7. Could I leave _____ message?
8. Have _____ good day.
9. Could I have _____ check, please?
10. Give me _____ call later.
11. That's out of _____ question[25].
12. Don't breathe _____ word[26] of this to anyone.
13. Let's call it _____ day[27].
14. I've been under _____ weather[28].

Talk about It Work with a partner. Choose one of the expressions above and use it to create a short conversation. Present your conversation to the class.

A: I don't think I can finish all this work.
B: Don't worry about a thing. I can help you.
A: That would be great. . . .

---

[25] **out of . . . question:** impossible
[26] **don't breathe . . . word:** don't say anything
[27] **call it . . . day:** to stop working for the day
[28] **under . . . weather:** sick

110

55 | Pronouncing _The_ Listen to the questions. Do you hear "thee" or "thuh"? Check (✓) your answers.

3.10 B

	"Thee"	"Thuh"
1.	✓	☐
2.	☐	☐
3.	☐	☐
4.	☐	☐
5.	☐	☐
6.	☐	☐

	"Thee"	"Thuh"
7.	☐	☐
8.	☐	☐
9.	☐	☐
10.	☐	☐
11.	☐	☐
12.	☐	☐

RESEARCH SAYS...

English speakers do not always pronounce _the_ according to the rules in Chart 3.10. You may hear "thee" before consonant sounds and "thuh" before vowel sounds. This does not change the meaning of the nouns.

CORPUS

Talk about It Listen again and write the words you hear after _the_. Then practice saying the questions. Pay attention to the pronunciation of _the_.

DID YOU . . . ?

1. bring the ____umbrella____
2. turn off the _____
3. watch the _____
4. go to the _____

5. read the _____
6. lock the _____
7. eat the _____
8. wash the _____

9. pay the _____
10. stop at the _____
11. go to the _____
12. drink all the _____

56 | Suggesting Answers Choose the correct word(s) from each box on the right to suggest an answer to each question. Then practice with a partner. Be sure to use rising intonation with your suggestion. **3.10 C**

1. A: What do you want for lunch? ____A sandwich____ ?
   B: Sure. Sounds great.

2. A: Where are you going? To _____ ?
   B: No, I have to go to work.

3. A: When are you coming back? _____ ?
   B: Yes, probably.

4. A: What did you buy? _____ ?
   B: No, I didn't buy anything.

5. A: What are you watching? _____ ?
   B: No, it's a movie.

6. A: What are you wearing to the concert? _____ ?
   B: I'm not sure yet.

7. A: How are we going to get there? _____ ?
   B: No, that's too expensive.

8. A: What are you eating? _____ ?
   B: No, it's soup.

1. a restaurant/a sandwich/a glass

2. the gym/a cup of coffee/the teachers

3. the car/tonight/a store

4. the city/a sweater/a new teacher

5. the news/tomorrow/a dictionary

6. the truth/some food/a suit

7. on Monday/some cars/by taxi

8. a cold drink/a new shirt/cereal

Talk about It Ask a partner the questions above again. Use your own ideas to suggest answers.

A: What do you want for lunch? Some soup?
B: Sure. Sounds great.

3.11 Using Nouns and Articles in Writing

A

USING NOUNS IN A LIST

1 My classmates come from **Korea, Turkey, Brazil, and** Spain.

2 **Television, newspapers, and** magazines give too much attention to the lives of famous people.

When we use three or more **nouns in a list**, we separate them with commas, as in **1 – 2**. We use *and* before the last noun only.

WARNING! Some style manuals leave out the comma after the next-to-last noun.

B

FIRST MENTION–SECOND MENTION

3 When I was eight years old, my parents gave me **a gold ring. The ring** wasn't valuable, but I didn't know that. . . .

(The writer starts with *a gold ring* because she is talking about it for the first time. She then says *the ring* because the reader knows what she is talking about.)

We sometimes use *a* or ***an*** to introduce a noun (talk or write about it for the first time). When we mention the noun again, we use *the*, as in **3**.

GRAMMAR TERM: When we introduce a noun with *a/an*, we call it **first mention**. When we later use *the*, we can call it **second mention**.

4 **The first televisions** looked very different from our modern ones. **The screens** were very small, and **the pictures** were only in black and white.

(the screens = the screens on the first televisions)
(the pictures = the pictures on the first televisions)

In writing, we use *the* with nouns that we think the reader already knows. We can also use *the* when a new noun is related to a previous noun, as in **4**.

C

IDENTIFYING NOUNS WITH PREPOSITIONAL PHRASES

5 In Russia, I visited **the homes of some great artists.**

("Of some great artists" identifies which homes.)

6 He stayed there for **the rest of his life.**

("Of his life" identifies what "the rest" is.)

We often use prepositional phrases with *in, on, for, of,* etc., to add information after a noun. Then we can use *the* before the noun phrase because the noun is identifiable, as in **5 – 6**.

57 | Using Nouns in a List **Add the missing commas to these sentences.** `3.11 A`

1. Brazil, Colombia, and Peru are all countries in South America.
2. Hungarian Finnish and Chinese are difficult languages to learn.
3. In biology class, students learn about plants animals and even humans.
4. Playing a sport requires energy concentration and determination.
5. The most important qualities of a good boss are patience fairness and flexibility.
6. The Nigerian writer Chinua Achebe has written novels essays and poems.
7. In a large city, there are many opportunities for work education and entertainment.
8. You can't be a good parent without love caring and commitment.
9. People live longer today because of vaccinations new workplace safety rules and a decrease in smoking.
10. Hemingway Steinbeck and Morrison are well-known writers.

Write about It **Rewrite two of the sentences above with your own ideas.**

Japan, Korea, and Vietnam are all countries in Asia.
Learning a new language requires determination, intelligence, and time.

THE OWL AND THE RABBITS

<u>An</u> owl saw two rabbits on the ground. ____ owl flew down
 1   2
and grabbed one rabbit in each foot. ____ rabbits started
                                       3
running, and they pulled ____ owl behind them. ____ owl's wife
                           4   5
yelled, "Let one of them go."

   "But winter is coming and we'll be hungry," ____ owl replied.
                                                 6
"We'll need both of ____ rabbits."
                      7
   The rabbits ran until they came to ____ big rock. One rabbit ran to ____ left of the rock. ____ other
                                         8   9   10
rabbit ran to ____ right of ____ rock. ____ poor owl hit ____ rock, and ____ two rabbits ran away.
               11   12   13   14   15

THE BOY WHO CRIED WOLF

WOLF!
WOLF!

____ young boy, alone all day, got bored taking care of his
 1
sheep. For fun, ____ boy shouted, "Wolf! Wolf!"
                  2
   People in town heard ____ boy and came running to help him.
                          3
But when they arrived, ____ boy just laughed at them. "I was
                         4
only kidding," ____ boy said to ____ townspeople. "I didn't really
                5   6
see ____ wolf."
     7
   A few days later, ____ boy cried again, "Wolf! Wolf!" Again
                       8
____ people in town came running. And once more, ____ boy
 9   10
laughed at them.

   In time, ____ wolf really did come. ____ boy screamed, "Wolf!
             11   12
Wolf!" But this time no one came.

Think about It Look at the answers for 7 and 11 in the second story above. Why did you choose the article you did?

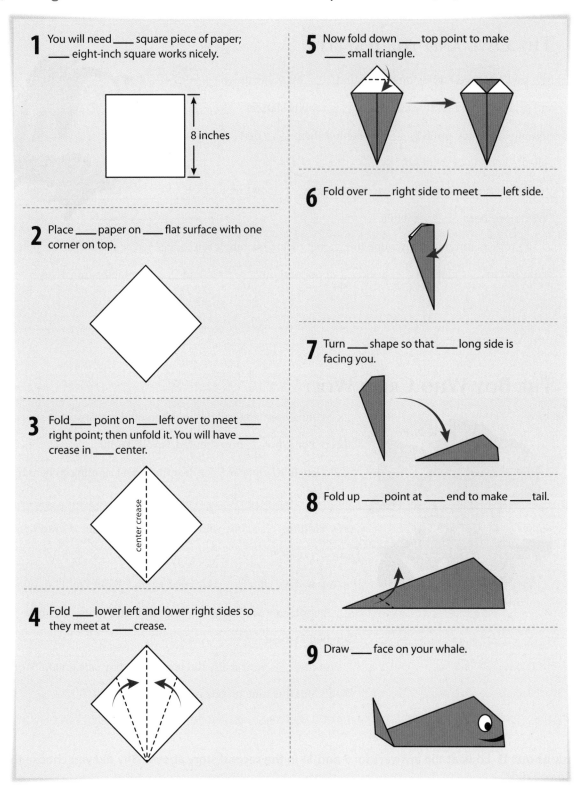

1 You will need ____ square piece of paper; ____ eight-inch square works nicely.

8 inches

2 Place ____ paper on ____ flat surface with one corner on top.

3 Fold ____ point on ____ left over to meet ____ right point; then unfold it. You will have ____ crease in ____ center.

center crease

4 Fold ____ lower left and lower right sides so they meet at ____ crease.

5 Now fold down ____ top point to make ____ small triangle.

6 Fold over ____ right side to meet ____ left side.

7 Turn ____ shape so that ____ long side is facing you.

8 Fold up ____ point at ____ end to make ____ tail.

9 Draw ____ face on your whale.

Write about It Think of something you can do or make. Write the instructions for your classmates to read.

60 | Adding Information to a Noun Look at the **bold** words in these questions. Think of two more prepositional phrases you could use instead. Rewrite the questions with your new ideas. **3.11 C**

1. What is the value **of recreation**?

   What is the value of music?

   _____

2. What are the important qualities **of a good parent**?

   _____

   _____

3. Should the government spend money **on space exploration**?

   _____

   _____

4. Is the traditional role **of fathers** changing?

   _____

   _____

5. What are the main reasons **for poverty**?

   _____

   _____

Write about It Choose two of the questions above. List two or more answers to each question.

What is the value of recreation?
1. Recreation is good for your health.
2. It helps you relax.

WRAP-UP Demonstrate Your Knowledge

A | DISCUSSION Think of at least six things you would find in each place in this chart. Work with a small group to list your ideas.

In an airplane	In a car	In a movie theater	In a kitchen
seats			
seat belts			

Work in your group and look at each list above. Decide which thing on each list is the least important. Why? Report your group's answers to the class.

LEAST IMPORTANT

_____   _____   _____   _____

B | GROUPING NOUNS Study this example. Then choose one of the quotations below and add the **bold** nouns to the correct groups.

Example

Quotation: **Experience** is the **name** everyone gives to their **mistakes**.—Oscar Wilde

Quotation: _____

_____

```
                    NOUNS
        experience, name, mistakes, Oscar Wilde
```

COMMON NOUNS	PROPER NOUNS
experience, name, mistakes	Oscar Wilde

COUNT NOUNS	NONCOUNT NOUNS
name, mistakes	experience

SINGULAR NOUNS	PLURAL NOUNS
name	mistakes

```
                    NOUNS
```

COMMON NOUNS	PROPER NOUNS

COUNT NOUNS	NONCOUNT NOUNS

SINGULAR NOUNS	PLURAL NOUNS

- The **man** who has no **imagination** has no **wings**.—**Muhammad Ali**
- Your **children** need your **presence** more than your **presents**.—**Jesse Jackson**
- **Talent** wins **games**, but **teamwork** and **intelligence** win **championships**.—**Michael Jordan**

C | WRITING Use the pictures below and the words in the box to write a story. Think about how you use *a/an*, *the*, Ø, and *some* in your story.

| ambulance | ice pack | knock herself out | leak | paramedics | plumber | sink | stretcher |

3.12 Summary of Nouns and Articles

NOUNS

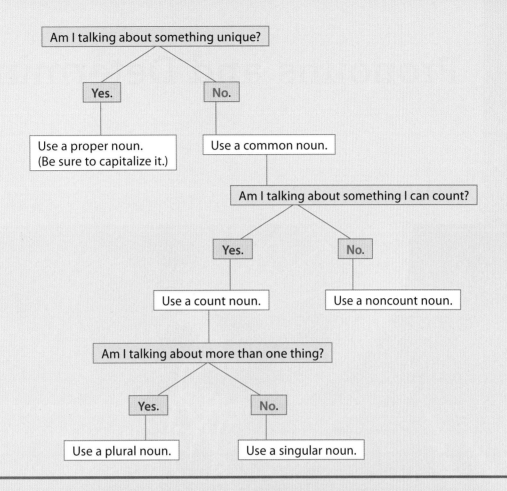

ARTICLES

	COUNT NOUNS		NONCOUNT NOUNS	USE
	SINGULAR	**PLURAL**		
a / an	**a** message (before a consonant sound) **an** answer (before a vowel sound)	–	–	A person or thing that: • the listener can't identify • you talk or write about for the first time
some	–	**some** people	**some** money	Unknown people or things: • a small amount
Ø	–	**Ø** people	**Ø** money	People or things in general
the	**the** message **the** answer	**the** people	**the** money	People or things that: • the listener can identify • were already introduced

4 Pronouns and Determiners

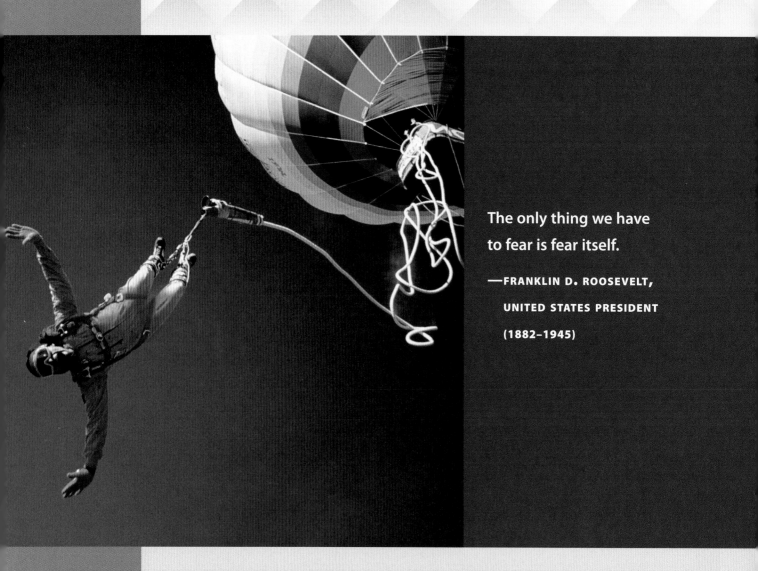

The only thing we have
to fear is fear itself.

—FRANKLIN D. ROOSEVELT,
UNITED STATES PRESIDENT
(1882–1945)

Talk about It What does the quotation above mean? Do you agree or disagree? Why?

WARM-UP

A Match the beginnings of these proverbs with the endings. Then choose one and tell a partner what it means. Do you agree or disagree with it?

Proverbs from Around the World

1. When **the** apple is ripe[1], **it** _d_

2. If **you** want to lose **a** friend, ____

3. To be rich is not **everything**, but ____

4. What belongs to **everybody**, ____

5. **Many** hands ____

6. **You** can't have **your** cake and ____

7. If **you** want **a** thing done well, ____

8. Behind **every** great man, there ____

a. is **a** great woman.

b. do **it yourself**.

c. eat **it** too.

d. will fall.

e. **it** helps.

f. lend **him** money.

g. make light work.

h. belongs to **nobody**.

B Answer these questions about the proverbs above.

1. The words in **blue** are **pronouns**. What are the words?

2. The words in **green** are **determiners**. What are the words?

3. Do we use a verb or a noun after a determiner?

C Look back at the quotation on page 118. Identify any pronouns or determiners.

[1] **ripe:** ready to eat

4.1 Subject Pronouns

A

1 My father came here when **he** was young.
(he = my father)

2 Who are **the people over there**? Are **they** the new teachers? (they = the people over there)

3 My brother and I want to go, but **we** can't.
(we = my brother and I)

We often use a pronoun in place of a noun or noun phrase, as in **1 – 3**. This saves time when we speak or write.

GRAMMAR TERM: We say a pronoun "**refers to**" a noun phrase. For example, in **1**, *he* refers to *my father*.

B

4 A: Is **your brother** here?
B: No, **he's** at home.

5 Ann isn't coming to the meeting. **She's** busy.

6 A: Were **you and Tim** out last night?
B: No, **we** stayed at home.

7 A: Where's **the car**?
B: **It's** in the garage.

8 I love **music**. **It** relaxes me.

9 A: Do you know where **my keys** are?
B: **They're** on the table.

The **subject pronouns** are:

singular	plural
I you he she it	we you they

We use the pronouns *I, you, he, she, we, you,* and *they* to refer to people, as in **4 – 6**.

When we refer to places, things, or ideas, we use:

• *it* in place of a singular count noun, as in **7**
• *it* in place of a noncount noun, as in **8**
• *they* in place of a plural count noun, as in **9**

C

SUBJECT-VERB AGREEMENT

10 I like ice cream, but **it isn't** good for me.

11 My brothers are smart, but **they don't study** very hard.

12 A: Do you know Sam?
B: Sure. **He and I are** good friends.

With subject pronouns, we use:

| a singular pronoun | + a singular verb, as in **10** |

| a plural pronoun | + a plural verb, as in **11** |

| a pronoun + *and* + a pronoun | + a plural verb, as in **12** |

1 | Understanding Subject Pronouns What do the **bold** pronouns refer to in these sentences? Write your answers in the boxes. `4.1 A`

EIGHT FACTS ABOUT NEW ZEALAND

1. The name *New Zealand* comes from the Dutch language. **It** probably means "new sea land."

2. New Zealand and Japan are about the same size, but in other ways, **they** are very different.

3. New Zealand has a population of only 4 million, so **it's** not a very crowded country.

4. People love to watch rugby in New Zealand, but **it** isn't the most popular sport to play. Golf is.

5. The singer Kiri Te Kanawa grew up in New Zealand. **She** has performed around the world and has made many recordings.

6. Sir Edmund Hillary was a famous mountain climber from New Zealand. **He** and Tenzing Norgay were the first people to climb to the top of Mount Everest.

7. Wellington has great weather 12 months a year. **It** is the capital of New Zealand.

8. Kiwi birds live on both the north and the south islands of New Zealand. **They** can't fly, but they can run very fast.

1. it = *New Zealand*

2. they =

3. it =

4. it =

5. she =

6. he =

7. it =

8. they =

Write about It In Activity 1, you read facts about New Zealand. Write three facts about another country. (Use pronouns.)

São Paulo is the largest city in Brazil, but it is not the capital. Brasilia is the capital.

2 | Using Subject Pronouns Replace each **bold** noun phrase with a subject pronoun. `4.1 B`

1. A: Did you like the movie?

   B: Yeah, ~~the movie~~ (it) was great.

2. A: How did your parents get here?

   B: **My parents** took the train.

3. A: Does Maria really like this show?

   B: Yeah, **this show** is her favorite.

4. A: Hi, Mr. Ellis. How are you and Mrs. Ellis?

   B: **Mrs. Ellis and I** are fine, thanks.

5. A: Do you have this shirt in blue?

   B: No, I'm sorry. **This shirt** only comes in red.

6. A: How's your back? Feeling any better?

   B: No, **my back** is worse. Much worse.

7. A: I think Jenna's good at tennis.

   B: Who?

   A: Jenna. **Jenna** plays well.

   B: Oh, I wouldn't know.

   A: Don't you like tennis?

   B: No, **tennis** is boring.

8. A: Look at the two people over there. I think **the two people over there** are teachers at our school.

   B: I think you're right.

9. A: Is your brother still looking for a job?

   B: No, **my brother** just found one.

10. A: Why do you want to study physics?

    B: Because **physics** is interesting.

The movie was great.

My back is worse.

Talk about It Practice the conversations above with a partner. Use contractions where possible.

Think about It Why do we use subject pronouns? What do they help us do?

> **F Y I**
>
> We often contract verbs with subject pronouns. For example:
>
> I am = I'**m**
> you are = you'**re**
> she is = she'**s**

3 | Using the Correct Verb Form Complete these sentences with a pronoun and the simple present form of the verb in parentheses. `4.1 B–C`

GOOD THINGS/BAD THINGS

1. Fried food tastes good, but _____ *it isn't* _____ good for you. (not/be)

2. Coffee may protect you from some kinds of cancer, and _____ good, too. (taste)

3. Games and other kinds of puzzles are fun. _____ your brain active, too. (keep)

4. Exercise is good for you, but _____ kind of boring. (be)

5. Vegetables are good for you, and _____ a lot. (not/cost)

6. The sun feels good, but _____ your skin. (damage)

7. Laughter is good for your health, and _____ free. (be)

8. Cars are useful, but _____ the air. (pollute)

9. It's important to read the news, but sometimes _____ depressing². (be)

10. You can get a lot of information on the Internet, but _____ always accurate. (not/be)

11. Money is useful, but _____ happiness. (not/buy)

12. Volleyball and basketball are good sports for children because _____ dangerous. (not/be)

Write about It Write four sentences about things that are good for you.

_____ *is good for you, but _____.*
_____ *are good for you, but _____.*
_____ *is good for you, and _____.*
_____ *are good for you, and _____.*

4 | Error Correction Correct any errors in these sentences. (Some sentences may not have any errors.)

1. I love my brother. He always make me laugh.

   I love my brother. He always makes me laugh.

2. I and my parents arrived at the same time.
3. When children are young, they a big responsibility.
4. Spanish and electric guitars they have metal strings.
5. I like to eat fresh food because they are good for your health.
6. I and my older sister stayed there for eight days.
7. My brother works hard because he have a big family.
8. Andy and I usually does something together on Saturday night.
9. My friends and I, we always get together on the weekend.
10. My brothers they argue a lot, but we are still good friends.
11. I love music. They really make me happy.
12. Did you hear the news? It's really surprising.
13. She miss her family very much.

> **W A R N I N G !**
>
> We don't use a subject pronoun after a noun subject. We only write the subject one time.
>
> **My friend** lives there.
> (NOT: ~~My friend he lives there.~~)
>
> When we connect two (or more) nouns and pronouns with *and*, the subject pronoun *I* comes last.
>
> **My brother and I live** with my parents.
> (NOT: ~~I and my brother~~ . . .)

² **depressing:** making someone feel very sad

4.2 Subject Pronouns vs. Object Pronouns; *One* and *Ones*

A

SUBJECT PRONOUNS

1 A: Did you call Ann?
B: Yes, but **she** didn't answer.

VERBS + OBJECT PRONOUNS

2 I had Tom's email address, but now I **can't find it.**

3 A: Do you know Tim and Ray?
B: Yes, but I **don't see them** often.

PREPOSITIONS + OBJECT PRONOUNS

4 I have a message **for you.**

5 Tom forgot to bring his cell phone **with him.**

6 A: I'm leaving now.
B: Wait! Don't leave **without** John and **me.**

Like a noun, a pronoun can be:

• a subject, as in **1**
• an object of a verb, as in **2 – 3**
• an object of a preposition, as in **4 – 6**

Notice that **subject pronouns** and **object pronouns** have different forms.

	singular					plural		
SUBJECT	I	you	he	she	it	we	you	they
OBJECT	me	you	him	her	it	us	you	them

B

7 A: May I have a banana, please?
B: I'll have **one**, too. (= I'll have a banana, too.)

8 I hate scary movies. Let's watch **a funny one**.
(= a funny movie)

9 A: Which shoes do you like?
B: I think I like **the red ones.** (= the red shoes)

We can also use **one** or **ones** as pronouns. We use *one* in place of a singular count noun. We use *ones* in place of a plural count noun.

• We can use *one* alone, as in **7**.
• We can use *one* or *ones* after a word like *a* or *the* + an adjective, as in **8 – 9**.

C

CORRECT THE COMMON ERRORS (See page R-17.)

10 ✗ Her father gave she a new computer.

11 ✗ Tom talked to Lisa and I.

12 ✗ He saved some of his money and spent some of them.

13 ✗ We bought a lot of gifts for our friends. I hope they like it.

5 | Using Object Pronouns Complete these conversations with object pronouns. Then practice with a partner. 4.2 A

1. A: What's the problem?

   B: My computer froze and I can't restart ___*it*___.

2. A: Tomorrow is Steve's birthday.

   B: Do you want to make a birthday cake for _____?

   A: Sure. Why not?

3. A: Did you talk to Jen?

   B: Yeah. I told _____ that you were sick yesterday.

4. A: Did you get the tickets for the game?

   B: Yes, I bought _____ yesterday.

5. A: Where's your book?

   B: I left _____ at school.

6. A: Did you call Jill?

   B: No, I asked _____ to call me.

7. A: Goodbye, Joe. I'll call you later.

   B: OK. Talk to _____ then.

8. A: Did you talk to Bob last night?

   B: No. I called _____ but he didn't call _____ back.

9. A: Do you and Chris need some help tomorrow?

   B: No, thanks. Jim is going to help _____.

10. A: Did you get the information?

    B: Yes, I found _____ on the Internet.

11. A: Why are you staring at that man?

    B: I'm not staring at _____. I'm looking at the car behind _____.

12. A: Is Carol late again?

    B: Yes, and I'm getting tired of waiting for _____.

Talk about It Choose one of the conversations in Activity 5. Add three or four more lines. See how many pronouns you can use. Then present it to your classmates.

A: What's the problem?
B: My computer froze, and I can't restart it.
A: Why don't you call Chris? He knows a lot about computers. Maybe he can help.
B: No. I think I'll just unplug it.

6 | Choosing Pronouns Read these paragraphs and complete them with the correct pronouns. `4.2 A`

Favorite Teachers

My favorite teacher in school was my second-grade teacher, Ms. Ellis. ___*She*___ was
                                                                            1
the perfect teacher for young children. Ms. Ellis was strict³, but _____ also treated
                                                                     2
_____ like equals. And when _____ did well, she rewarded⁴ _____. Ms. Ellis
   3   4   5
made it clear that we could talk to _____ about anything. I learned a lot from
                                     6
_____, and I knew that she wanted _____ to be successful.
   7   8

1. she/her
2. she/her
3. we/us
4. we/us
5. we/us
6. she/her
7. she/her
8. I/me

Mr. Ochs was my freshman math teacher. _____ loved math, and by the end of the
                                          9
semester, all of his students loved it, too—and we loved _____. In class, _____
                                                           10   11
usually worked together in groups to solve math problems. For _____, this was
                                                                12
more fun than working alone. Mr. Ochs also encouraged _____ to solve problems in
                                                         13
different ways. He really wanted _____ to be creative thinkers.
                                  14

9. he/him
10. he/him
11. we/us
12. I/me
13. we/us
14. we/us

Write about It Describe one of your favorite teachers. Write three or more sentences.

---

³ **strict:** making people follow rules   ⁴ **reward:** to give something for good work

7 | Using Subject and Object Pronouns Add the missing pronoun to each conversation. Then practice with a partner. `4.2 A`

STATING A FACT

1. A: When's your best friend's birthday?

   B: I think *it* is in March.

2. A: Do you have your book with you today?

   B: No, I left at home.

3. A: Was there a lot of traffic on your way here?

   B: No, was pretty quiet.

4. A: Does your best friend live here?

   B: No, lives in Greece with his family.

5. A: Do you buy your clothes on the Internet?

   B: No, I always buy at a store.

GIVING AN OPINION

6. A: What's your opinion of American food?

   B: I'm not crazy about.

7. A: What did you think of your first teacher?

   B: Was great.

8. A: Do you like classical music?

   B: Yes, I do. I like a lot.

9. A: Do you like French movies?

   B: Yes, I love.

10. A: Do you have a favorite actor?

    B: Well, I'm a great fan of Michael Sheen. I loved in the movie *The Queen*.

Talk about It Ask a partner the questions above. Give your own answers.

A: When's your best friend's birthday?
B: It's on September 22.

8 | Understanding *One* What does the word *one* refer to in each sentence? Write the word(s) in the boxes. `4.2 B`

1. I brought some sandwiches from home today. Do you want **one**?
2. There's an umbrella in the closet if you need **one**.
3. There were fifty questions on the test and I only got **one** wrong.
4. My sister doesn't have a college degree yet, but she plans to get **one**.
5. I have a tissue in my purse if you need **one**.
6. My parents sold their house downtown and bought a new **one** in the country.
7. I didn't like the first book very much, but I liked the second **one** a lot.
8. A new computer is expensive, so I'm waiting until I've saved some more money before I buy **one**.

1. one = *a sandwich*
2. one =
3. one =
4. one =
5. one =
6. one =
7. one =
8. one =

Think about It Read the sentences below. Compare them with sentences 1–3 above. When do we use *it* instead of *one*?

1. I brought a sandwich, but I'm not hungry. Do you want it?
2. If you want my umbrella, it's in the closet.
3. The last question on the test was very hard. I think I got it wrong.

9 | Using *One* or *Ones* Complete these conversations with an adjective from the box + *one* or *ones*. (Use each adjective once.) `4.2 B`

best	important	large	only	right
easy	Italian	new	real	small

1. A: Your car doesn't sound very good.

    B: Yeah, I think I need a _____ new one _____.

2. A: Can you bring home a pizza tonight?

    B: A large one or a _____?

3. A: Which movie do you want to watch first?

    B: Let's put on the _____.

4. A: Oh boy, my suitcase is really heavy.

    B: Why don't you take two small suitcases

    instead of a _____?

5. A: Where do you buy cakes and cookies?

    B: I think Jimmy's Bakery makes the

    _____.

6. A: How many people came to the meeting?

    B: We were the _____ there.

7. A: These are the wrong papers.

    B: Well, where are the _____?

8. A: Did we get any emails?

    B: Yes, but not any _____.

9. A: That's a beautiful diamond!

    B: It's not a _____. It's plastic.

10. A: How was the quiz?

    B: I was worried about it, but it was an

    _____.

Think about It What does the word *one* or *ones* refer to in each conversation above?

Talk about It Work with a partner. Choose one of the adjectives above. Write a new conversation using the adjective + *one* or *ones*. Present your conversation to the class.

A: Your stereo speakers don't sound very good.
B: Yeah, I think I need some new ones.

10 | Error Analysis One sentence in each pair has an incorrect pronoun. Circle the letter of the incorrect sentence and the error.

FAMILY MEMBERS

1. a. My brothers, sisters, and I are very close.

    b. My brothers, sisters, and me are very close.

2. a. I talk to my youngest brother a lot. I tell him everything.

    b. I talk to my youngest brother a lot. I tell her everything.

3. a. My brother helped me a lot. I learned a lot from him.

    b. My brother helped me a lot. I learned a lot from he.

4. a. My parents let my sister and I make our own decisions.

    b   My parents let my sister and me make our own decisions.

WARNING!

We can connect two (or more) nouns and pronouns with *and*. Be careful to use the correct pronoun form after *and*.

Joe and I are going to the movies. (NOT: ~~Joe and me~~)

Do you want to come with **Joe and me**? (NOT: ~~Joe and I~~)

5. a. One of my brothers wants to be an artist, but my parents don't want them to.

 b. One of my brothers wants to be an artist, but my parents don't want him to.

6. a. My oldest sister often helped take care of I because I was the youngest.

 b. My oldest sister often helped take of me because I was the youngest.

7. a. My brothers and sisters and I were good children. My parents hardly ever punished us.

 b. My brothers and sisters and I were good children. My parents hardly ever punished them.

8. a. My sisters and I shared a bedroom. I loved to be with them because we talked and laughed a lot.

 b. My sisters and I shared a bedroom. I loved to be with her because we talked and laughed a lot.

Write about It Write several sentences about your family members like the ones in Activity 10. Pay special attention to the way you use pronouns in your sentences.

I'm the oldest child in my family. I have two younger brothers. I don't see them very often.

4.3 Reflexive Pronouns

A

OBJECT PRONOUNS

1 Sam saw **me** downtown.

2 Jen drove **them** to school.

3 Ian and Linda cooked dinner for **us**.

REFLEXIVE PRONOUNS

4 **Sam** saw **himself** in the mirror. (himself = Sam)

5 **Jen** drove **herself** to school. (herself = Jen)

6 **Ian and Linda** cooked dinner for **themselves**.
(themselves = Ian and Linda)

7 **History** repeats **itself**.

8 **I** told **myself** to hurry.

9 **You** can help **yourselves** to some coffee.

We often use an **object pronoun** after a verb or a preposition, as in **1 – 3**.

However, when the object is the same person or thing as the subject, we use a **reflexive pronoun**, as in **4 – 9**.

	OBJECT PRONOUN	REFLEXIVE PRONOUN
singular	me	myself
	you	yourself
	him	himself
	her	herself
	it	itself
plural	us	ourselves
	you	yourselves
	them	themselves

B

SPECIAL USES OF REFLEXIVE PRONOUNS

10 You have to bag the groceries **yourself**.
(yourself = without help)

11 He wants to tell us **himself**.
(himself = not a different person)

12 I prefer to study **by myself**. (by myself = alone)

We sometimes use a reflexive pronoun to add emphasis, as in **10 – 11**.

We can also use *by* + a reflexive pronoun to mean "alone," as in **12**.

C

CORRECT THE COMMON ERRORS (See page R-17.)

13 ✗ This society must help it self.

14 ✗ We always make tortillas ourself.

15 ✗ I can make a better future for me here.

16 ✗ We made a plan for spending ourself money.

GO ONLINE

11 | Using Reflexive Pronouns Ask a partner these questions. Make notes of your partner's answers.

4.3 A

YOU AND YOUR HABITS

Verb + Reflexive Pronoun

1. Do you like to get up early, or do you have to make yourself get up?

   A: Do you like to get up early, or do you have to make yourself get up?
   B: I usually have to make myself get up.

2. Do you consider yourself to be a good student?
3. Do you ever have to remind yourself to eat?
4. Do you ask yourself questions while you are reading?
5. Did you ever teach yourself to do something?
6. How would you describe yourself in one word?

Preposition + Reflexive Pronoun

7. How often do you look at yourself in a mirror?
8. Do you ever talk to yourself?
9. Do you ever get angry with yourself?
10. Do you usually cook for yourself?
11. Do you ever laugh at yourself?
12. How can you take better care of yourself?

> **PRONUNCIATION**
>
> Be careful not to stress the first syllable in a reflexive pronoun.
>
> NOT: ~~MY~~self

Talk about It Tell your classmates two things you learned about your partner.

"Lin taught herself to play tennis."

12 | Reflexive Pronouns after Verbs Complete these statements with reflexive pronouns. Then draw an arrow from the reflexive pronoun to the subject. 4.3 A

COMMON VERBS

1. If you are feeling anxious, you should remind ____yourself____ to breathe.
2. Linda told _her self_ to get up early this morning, but she didn't.
3. You and Amy need to give _your selves_ more time to relax.
4. I often find _my self_ thinking about work.
5. Sometimes we have to force _our selves_ to smile.
6. If you worry too much, you will make _your self_ sick.
7. What do the Chinese people call _themselves_ ?
8. In the morning, my sister and I found _our selves_ alone in the house.
9. I don't know why my brother lied. He needs to ask _himself_ that question.
10. My parents were in the U.S. for five years, but they didn't consider _themselves_ to be American.

Think about It What verbs do we often use with reflexive pronouns? Make a list of the verbs in the sentences above. Then write a new sentence using each verb with a reflexive pronoun.

told   I told myself to eat a good breakfast this morning.

13 | Reflexive Pronouns after Prepositions Complete these statements with reflexive pronouns. Then check (✓) *Agree* or *Disagree*. 4.3 A

WHAT DO YOU THINK?	AGREE	DISAGREE
1. I **owe it to** _____*myself*_____ to eat well and exercise.	☐	☐
2. If you want to remember someone's name, **repeat it to** _____ a few times.	☐	☐
3. When I tell my friends a secret, I want them to **keep it to** _____.	☐	☐
4. You should always **listen to** _____.	☐	☐
5. Most people like to **hear** good things **about** _____.	☐	☐
6. A newborn⁵ animal can't **take care of** _____.	☐	☐
7. Children need to learn to **think for** _____.	☐	☐
8. You shouldn't **talk about** _____ all the time. It's rude.	☐	☐

Write about It Write a new sentence for each verb + preposition + reflexive pronoun above.

I owe it to myself to do something fun every day.

14 | Pronunciation Note: Reflexive Pronouns Listen to the note. Then do Activity 15.

> When we use a **reflexive pronoun for emphasis**, we often stress the second syllable.
>
> **1** Children shouldn't cook by them**SELVES**.
> **2** It's important to try and do the work your**SELF**.
> **3** Did the boy pay for that him**SELF**?

15 | Giving Emphasis with Reflexive Pronouns Complete these conversations with reflexive pronouns. Then listen and practice with a partner. 4.3 B

1. A: Hey, Bob asked me to invite you to his house for dinner.
   B: Why doesn't he just invite me _____?
   A: I don't know. I guess he's really busy.

2. A: Could you get the phone, Matt?
   B: I can't. You'll have to get it _____.

3. A: Who helped you paint the rooms?
   B: Nobody. We did it _____.

4. A: Sorry I didn't call. I couldn't remember your phone number.
   B: Don't worry about it. I can never remember it _____.

5. A: Why are you upset?
   B: Sarah thinks I lost her phone.
   A: Did you?
   B: No. She lost it _____.

6. A: That's a nice sweater.
   B: Thanks. It's from Anna. She made it _____!

7. A: That was nice of your parents to give you their computer.
   B: Yeah, they didn't need it _____.

8. A: I can't find my cell phone.
   B: It's on the desk. You left it there _____.

⁵**newborn:** just born

Write about It Work with a partner. Write conversations like the ones in Activity 15 for each of these expressions. Then share your ideas with your classmates.

get it yourself   *make it yourself*   *do it yourself*   *just be yourself*

16 | Using Reflexive Pronouns with *By* Write answers to these questions with information about yourself and your opinions. `4.3 B`

DOING THINGS ALONE

1. What are three things you like to do by yourself?
2. What are three things you *don't* like to do by yourself?
3. What are three things young children shouldn't do by themselves?

Talk about It Ask a partner the questions above. Then tell the class about your partner.

"Leila likes to read by herself, but she doesn't like to eat out by herself."

17 | Error Correction Correct any errors in these sentences. (Some sentences may not have any errors.)

1. They expressed themself very well.
2. I ate the whole thing by my self.
3. I finally took my first trip with myself.
4. You should see your person in this picture. You look great.
5. My sister made all of the plans for the trip himself.
6. I often talk or sing to me while I am driving.
7. We had to do everything ourself. No one could help us.
8. Sometimes you need to do things for your family or for your own.

4.4 *Each Other* and *One Another*

A

1 Does Bill know you? Do you know Bill? = Do **you and Bill** know **each other**?

2 **The children** pushed **one another**.
   (= Each child pushed the other children in the group.)

3 **Tom and Joe** are staring at **each other**.
   (= Tom is staring at Joe, and Joe is staring at Tom.)

4 How often do **your friends** talk to **one another**?

We can use **each other** and **one another** to refer back to two or more people. They are an easy way to combine ideas, as in **1**.

We usually use *each other* and *one another* as:

• an object of a verb, as in **1 – 2**
• an object of a preposition, as in **3 – 4**

GRAMMAR TERM: *Each other* and *one another* are called **reciprocal pronouns**.

B

COMPARE RECIPROCAL AND REFLEXIVE PRONOUNS

			reciprocal pronoun
5a	Vera and Tim	were angry with	**each other.**

			reflexive pronoun
5b	Vera and Tim	were angry with	**themselves.**

Reciprocal pronouns and reflexive pronouns have different meanings.

• In **5a**, Vera was angry with Tim, and Tim was angry with Vera.
• In **5b**, Vera was angry with herself, and Tim was angry with himself.

C

CORRECT THE COMMON ERRORS (See page R-18.)

6 ✗ They had a problem each other.

7 ✗ They didn't like one anothers.

8 ✗ My parents have a great relationship. They truly love themselves.

GO ONLINE

18 | Exploring Uses of *Each Other* Read these sentences and check (✓) your opinions. **4.4 A**

HOW IMPORTANT ARE THESE THINGS TO A GOOD MARRIAGE?	VERY IMPORTANT	SOMEWHAT IMPORTANT	NOT AT ALL IMPORTANT
1. A husband and wife should give each other expensive gifts.	☐	☐	☐
2. They shouldn't keep secrets from each other.	☐	☐	☐
3. They should always tell each other the truth.	☐	☐	☐
4. They should talk to each other every day.	☐	☐	☐
5. They should listen to each other carefully.	☐	☐	☐
6. They should spend time away from each other.	☐	☐	☐
7. They should know each other well before they get married.	☐	☐	☐
8. They should agree with each other about everything.	☐	☐	☐
9. They should like (not just love) each other.	☐	☐	☐

Think about It What verbs and expressions above do we use with *each other*? Write each verb and expression under the correct group in the chart below.

Verb + *each other*	Expression with preposition + *each other*
give each other something	*keep (something) from each other*

Write about It What else is important to a good marriage? Write three more sentences and then share them with your classmates.

19 | Using *Each Other* and *One Another* Rewrite each sentence using *each other* or *one another*. **4.4 A**

RELATIONSHIPS

1. I enjoy spending time with my older sister, and she enjoys spending time with me.
   My older sister and I _enjoy spending time with each other_____.

2. My new teacher knows my parents and my parents know my new teacher.
   My new teacher and my parents _____.

3. I email my brothers every day and they email me every day.
   My brothers and I _____.

4. I couldn't look at Sam and Sam couldn't look at me.
   Sam and I _____.

5. Kate respects her boss and her boss respects her.
   Kate and her boss _____.

> **RESEARCH SAYS...**
>
> *Each other* is more common when we are talking about just two people.
>
> My parents love **each other**.
>
> *One another* sounds more formal.
>
> The Internet has changed the way people communicate with **one another**.

CORPUS

6. My brother isn't talking to his best friend, and his best friend isn't talking to him.

My brother and his best friend _____ .

7. I always speak Spanish with my grandfather, and my grandfather always speaks Spanish with me.

_____

8. My father never argues with my mother, and my mother never argues with my father.

_____

20 | *Each Other* or *Themselves*? Complete these sentences with *each other* or *themselves*. Then check (✓) *Agree* or *Disagree*. 4.4 B

WHAT'S YOUR OPINION?	AGREE	DISAGREE
1. People who speak different languages can't understand _____*each other*_____ .	☐	☐
2. Family members shouldn't argue with _____ .	☐	☐
3. It's not unusual for lonely people to talk to _____ .	☐	☐
4. Friends shouldn't lie to _____ .	☐	☐
5. Classmates should give answers to _____ during tests.	☐	☐
6. Most people think they know _____ .	☐	☐
7. It's easier for friends to communicate with _____ these days.	☐	☐
8. It's good for two people to face _____ when they talk.	☐	☐
9. People need to learn to work with _____ .	☐	☐
10. Children should learn to cook for _____ .	☐	☐

Talk about It Take turns reading the sentences above aloud with a partner. See if your partner agrees or disagrees and why.

A: People who speak different languages can't understand each other.
B: I disagree. If you don't speak the same language, you can point or draw pictures.

21 | Error Correction Correct any errors in these sentences. (Some sentences may not have any errors.)

COMMUNICATING AND INTERACTING

1. We talk each other many times during the day.
2. My friends all help each another.
3. In some cultures, people don't look at themselves when they talk.
4. I love my friends. I have a lot of fun with one another.
5. We introduced ourselves to each other.
6. My grandmother and I don't talk on the phone to ourselves very often because she can't hear very well.
7. We use the Internet to communicate with one anothers.
8. My two sisters had a big argument and now they aren't talking to themselves.

4.5 Indefinite Pronouns

A

1 Somebody left a book here.
(A person left a book here. I don't know who.)

2 Please don't touch **anything.**
(Don't touch any of the things here.)

3 He says that to **everyone.**
(He says that to all people.)

4 Luckily, **nobody** got lost.
(Not one person got lost.)

We use **indefinite pronouns** when we can't or don't need to name a specific person or thing, as in **1 – 4.**

INDEFINITE PRONOUNS			
somebody	anybody	nobody	everybody
someone	anyone	no one	everyone
something	anything	nothing	everything

SUBJECT-VERB AGREEMENT

5 Everything is ready. (NOT: ~~Everything are~~ . . .)

6 Somebody has my book. (NOT: ~~Somebody have~~ . . .)

WARNING! Indefinite pronouns are always singular. We use a singular verb with them, as in **5 – 6.**

B

NEGATIVE VERB + *ANYBODY, ANYONE, OR ANYTHING*

7 We **didn't see** anyone there.
(NOT: ~~We didn't see someone~~ . . .)

8 I **can't throw** anything away.

We don't usually use *somebody, someone,* or *something* after *not.* We use *anybody, anyone,* or *anything* instead, as in **7 – 8.**

NOBODY, NO ONE, **AND** *NOTHING* **WITH A POSITIVE VERB**

9 Nobody called. (NOT: ~~Nobody didn't call.~~)

10 There's **nothing** to eat. (NOT: ~~There isn't nothing~~ . . .)

Nobody, no one, and *nothing* have a negative meaning. We don't use them with *not,* as in **9 – 10.**

C

CORRECT THE COMMON ERRORS (See page R-18.)

11 ✗ I didn't see nothing.

12 ✗ I thought everythings were free in the U.S.

13 ✗ Everyone want to come.

14 ✗ I don't want to see somebody.

22 | Understanding Indefinite Pronouns Rewrite these sentences. Replace the **bold** words with *someone, something, everyone, everything, no one, nothing, anyone,* or *anything.* **4.5 A**

1. I thought I heard **a person** outside. I don't know who it was.

   I thought I heard someone outside. I don't know who it was.

2. I like **all of the people** in my class.

3. I moved **all of the things** in my room.

4. **Not one person** called me last night.

5. When there is **a thing** you want to learn, you can look on the Internet.

6. ~~Not one thing~~ *nothing* in the closet belongs to me.

7. We need to find ~~one person~~ *Someone* to help us.

8. ~~Any person~~ *Anybody* can learn this.

9. Do you know ~~all of the people~~ *everybody* here?

10. We didn't see **any person** in the building.

11. Do you want ~~a thing~~ *something* to drink?

12. Did you write down ~~all of the things~~? *everything*

> **F Y I**
>
> We use:
>
> - *some-* for one person or thing
>
> - *every-* for all the people or things in a group
>
> - *any-* for people and things in general
>
> - *no-* to say no people or things

23 | Pronunciation Note: Indefinite Pronouns Listen to the note. Then do Activity 24.

> When an indefinite pronoun is **new or contrasting information**, we can stress the first syllable, as in Example 1. In Example 2, the speaker does not stress the indefinite pronoun. (We don't stress the second syllable in an indefinite pronoun.)
>
> **EXAMPLE 1**
> A: Do you know that man over there?
> B: No, I don't know **ANY**one here.
>
> **EXAMPLE 2**
> A: Why didn't you ask for help?
> B: There was no one there to ask.

24 | Pronouncing Indefinite Pronouns Listen to the song titles and write the missing pronouns. Listen again and repeat the song titles. `4.5 A`

SONG TITLES

1. "_____Everybody_____ Loves Saturday Night"
2. "_____'s Talking"
3. "Say _____"
4. "Money Changes _____"
5. "_____ to Love Me"
6. "_____ Hurts Like Love"
7. "I've Got Plenty of _____"
8. "_____ about You"
9. "_____ Loves _____ Sometime"
10. "I'll Never Need _____ Anymore"
11. "We Must Be Doing _____ Right"
12. "_____ Knows the Trouble I've Seen"
13. "He's Done More for Me Than _____"
14. "Doesn't _____ Want to Be Wanted?"
15. "_____'s Looking for the Same Thing"
16. "_____ Is Different Now"

Write about It Complete these song titles with your own ideas. Then share titles with your classmates.

"Everybody Loves ____"   *"Nobody Knows ____"*
"____ Changes Everything"   *"Somebody Is ____"*
"____ Anything"

25 | Indefinite Pronoun + Verb Complete these conversations with the correct form of the verb in parentheses. Then practice with a partner. `4.5 A`

1. A: Can I help?
   B: No need. Everything _____*is*_____ ready. (be)
2. A: Nothing ever _____ here. (happen)
   B: That's not true.
3. A: Where's Marta?
   B: Nobody __*knows*__. (know)
4. A: ____*is*____ everything OK here? (be)
   B: Yes, I think so.
5. A: __*Does*__ somebody __*have*__ my computer? (have)
   B: Yes, I'm using it.
6. A: Nobody called me last night.
   B: That's because nobody ____*has*____ your new phone number. (have)

RESEARCH SAYS...

More Formal
someone
anyone
no one

Less Formal
somebody
anybody
nobody

CORPUS

134

7. A: _____IS_____ anybody here yet? (be)

   B: Yep[6]. Lisa and Irene are both here.

8. A: Can I start the meeting?

   B: Yes, everyone _____IS_____ here. (be)

9. A: _____Does_____ anyone _____have_____ a question for Mr. Wong? (have)

   B: Yes, I do.

10. A: I forgot to put salt in the soup. I hope nobody _____notices_____. (notice)

    B: Don't worry about it.

Think about It Look at conversations 7–10 above. In each conversation, where do you think the people are? Who are the people? Is the situation more formal or less formal?

26 | Using the Correct Pronoun Choose the correct pronoun to complete these conversations. Then practice with a partner. `4.5 B`

1. A: How was your day?

   B: OK. I didn't do _____anything_____ special.
      (anything / nothing)

2. A: Are you going to play basketball today?

   B: No, there's _____no one_____ to play with.
      (anyone / no one)

3. A: Why didn't Sheila come to the concert?

   B: She said she didn't want to see

   _____anybody_____.
   (anybody / nobody)

4. A: I think there's _____something_____ on the
      (anything / something)
      floor. Be careful!

   B: Don't worry. It's just water.

5. A: Are you going to bring Peter?

   B: No, he doesn't want to do

   _____anything_____ this afternoon.
   (anything / something)

6. A: Was there an accident last night?

   B: Well, I didn't see _____anything_____.
      (nothing / anything)

7. A: What was that noise?

   B: I don't know. I looked outside, but there's

   _____nothing_____ there.
   (nothing / anything)

8. A: Why didn't you come to the meeting?

   B: _____nobody_____ told me about it.
      (nobody / somebody)

9. A: _____Something_____ is wrong with this bill.
      (anything / something)

   B: What do you mean?

   A: The numbers don't add up.

10. A: How come everybody knows my plans?

    B: I don't know. I didn't tell _____anyone_____.
       (anyone / no one)

27 | Usage Note: *Some-* vs. *Any-* Read the note. Then do Activity 28.

> We often use **somebody**, **someone**, and **something** in questions when we expect a particular answer, as in Example 1. We use **anybody**, **anyone**, and **anything** when we don't expect a particular answer, as in Example 2.
>
> **EXAMPLE 1**
> What's that noise? Is **somebody** there?
> (I hear a noise so I expect a "yes" answer.)
>
> **EXAMPLE 2**
> Hello! Is **anybody** home?
> (Someone may or may not be home. I don't know. I have no expectation.)

[6] **yep:** yes (informal)

1. A: Excuse me, waiter?

    B: Yes, can I get you _____?

    A: Could I have some water, please?

    B: Sure.

3. A: What happened?

    B: There was a bad accident.

    A: Has _____ called the police?

    B: I don't know.

2. A: Dinner's almost ready.

    B: Is there _____ I can do to help?

    A: No, I don't think so.

4. A: What's the matter? Did you lose

    _____?

    B: Yeah. I dropped a contact lens.

Think about It Explain each speaker's choice of indefinite pronoun in the conversations above.

29 | Error Correction Correct any errors in these sentences. (Some sentences may not have any errors.)

1. Where were everyone?
2. Everybody in my class have a car except me.
3. We didn't talk to someone while we were in the city.
4. My brother and I are very different. I don't like nothing that he likes.
5. There weren't anythings we could do to help.
6. Everythings went wrong.
7. Is there anything you need?
8. I invited some body to have dinner with us.
9. Can I get you anything?
10. I can't find no one to help me.
11. My brother brought everythings with him. I didn't need to get anything.
12. Everyone in my family have red hair.
13. When my sister got here, she wouldn't talk to no one.
14. When the accident happened, there was no bodies around.
15. I know everybody here and everyone know me.
16. I don't know something about this city.

> **W A R N I N G !**
>
> In informal conversations you may hear some English speakers use a double negative.
>
> "He didn't say nothing."

4.6 Demonstratives

A

DEMONSTRATIVE PRONOUNS

1 | This | **is** | a great movie. | (this = this movie)

2 | These | **are** | my best photos. | (these = these photos)

3 | What | **is** | that | on the roof? | (that = that thing)

4 | Whose books | **are** | those? | (those = those books)

We use the *pronouns this / that / these / those* to point out something, as in **1 – 4**. Notice:

DEMONSTRATIVES		
singular	this	that
plural	these	those

things that are close   things that are farther away

B

DEMONSTRATIVE DETERMINERS

5 | This | information | is very interesting.

6 | These | dishes | are beautiful.

7 | That | window | over there is dirty.

8 | Could you bring down | those | books?

We can also use **this / that / these / those** + a *noun*, as in **5 – 8**. Notice:

| this | that | + singular count noun or noncount noun |

| these | those | + plural count noun |

When we use these words before a noun, they are determiners. Determiners help us "determine" important information about a noun.

GO ONLINE

30 | Distinguishing *This, That, These,* and *Those* Sometimes it's difficult to hear the words *this, that, these,* and *those*. Listen to these sentences and write the missing words. `4.6 A–B`

		PRONOUN	DETERMINER
1. *This cake* _____ is delicious.		☐	☐
2. _____ are mine.		☐	☐
3. Why are _____ here?		☐	☐
4. I can't answer _____.		☐	☐
5. Did you see _____?		☐	☐
6. Do you think _____ is too small?		☐	☐
7. _____ are my friends.		☐	☐
8. _____ works best.		☐	☐
9. _____ isn't possible.		☐	☐
10. Is _____ for sale?		☐	☐
11. _____ were the good days.		☐	☐
12. _____ was difficult.		☐	☐
13. Is _____ your pen?		☐	☐
14. I never saw _____.		☐	☐
15. Do you want _____?		☐	☐

Think about It In each sentence above, is *this, that, these,* or *those* a pronoun or a determiner? Check (✓) your answers.

31 | Using Demonstrative Determiners Choose the correct word to complete these sentences. `4.6 B`

1. I like most movies, but _____*this*_____ movie is terrible.
   (this / these)
2. Do you see _____ students over there? They're teaching assistants.
   (that / those)
3. Do you really know all of _____ people?
   (this / these)
4. Did you hear _____ loud noise?
   (that / those)
5. Are you really going to buy all of _____ things?
   (this / these)
6. _____ information is incorrect.
   (this / these)
7. I have lived in _____ country all my life.
   (this / these)
8. I didn't see _____ holes in the floor.
   (that / those)
9. A very smart person gave me _____ advice. She said, "Listen to yourself."
   (this / these)
10. You are as smart as Tom and Ali. Don't compare yourself to _____ guys.
    (that / those)
11. You know _____ beautiful pictures on our classroom wall? Our teacher painted them.
    (that / those)
12. Turn right here. _____ way is shorter.
    (this / these)

Think about It In which sentences above could you use a different demonstrative?

For number 1, you could say, "I like most movies, but that movie is terrible."
For number 2, you can't use a different demonstrative.

32 | Choosing *This, That, These,* and *Those* Read each situation and answer the question.
Use *this, that, these,* or *those* + a noun in your answer. `4.6 A–B`

1. **Situation:** You are doing homework with a friend. You think the homework is very difficult.
   What do you say to your friend?

   "This homework is really hard."

2. **Situation:** You are wearing some new shoes, and they are hurting your feet. What do you say to yourself?
3. **Situation:** You come home and see some flowers on the table. You want to know where they came from.
   What question do you ask?
4. **Situation:** Your friend made a delicious meal for you. You want to compliment her. What do you say?
5. **Situation:** You are listening to a song, and you don't like it. What do you say?
6. **Situation:** You are at a restaurant. A group of people across the room are very loud.
   What do you say to yourself?
7. **Situation:** There is a man across the room. You think you and your friend have met him.
   What question do you ask your friend?

33 | Error Correction Correct any errors in these sentences. (Some sentences may not have any errors.)

1. I really like these idea.
2. My friend gave me those advices.
3. I don't know all of this things.
4. Here. I want you to have that.
5. Those moneys belong to you.
6. Please take this. I want you to have them.
7. I couldn't do these homeworks.
8. I found this information in a library book.

4.7 Showing Possession

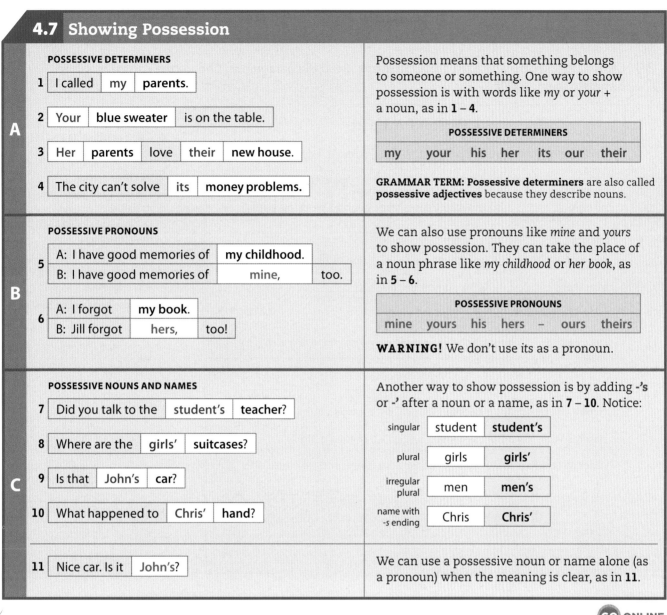

A

POSSESSIVE DETERMINERS

1 | I called | my | parents.

2 | Your | blue sweater | is on the table.

3 | Her | parents | love | their | new house.

4 | The city can't solve | its | money problems.

Possession means that something belongs to someone or something. One way to show possession is with words like *my* or *your* + a noun, as in **1 – 4**.

POSSESSIVE DETERMINERS						
my	your	his	her	its	our	their

GRAMMAR TERM: Possessive determiners are also called **possessive adjectives** because they describe nouns.

B

POSSESSIVE PRONOUNS

5 | A: I have good memories of | my childhood.
  | B: I have good memories of | mine, | too.

6 | A: I forgot | my book.
  | B: Jill forgot | hers, | too!

We can also use pronouns like *mine* and *yours* to show possession. They can take the place of a noun phrase like *my childhood* or *her book*, as in **5 – 6**.

POSSESSIVE PRONOUNS						
mine	yours	his	hers	–	ours	theirs

WARNING! We don't use *its* as a pronoun.

C

POSSESSIVE NOUNS AND NAMES

7 | Did you talk to the | student's | teacher?

8 | Where are the | girls' | suitcases?

9 | Is that | John's | car?

10 | What happened to | Chris' | hand?

Another way to show possession is by adding **-'s** or **-'** after a noun or a name, as in **7 – 10**. Notice:

singular	student	**student's**
plural	girls	**girls'**
irregular plural	men	**men's**
name with -s ending	Chris	**Chris'**

11 | Nice car. Is it | John's?

We can use a possessive noun or name alone (as a pronoun) when the meaning is clear, as in **11**.

GO ONLINE

34 | Using Possessive Determiners Complete the proverbs with *my, your, his, her, its, our,* or *their*. `4.7 A`

PROVERBS

1. A chain is only as strong as ____*its*____ weakest link.

2. Fools[7] and _____ money are soon parted[8].

3. A leopard cannot change _____ spots.

4. A poor workman always blames _____ tools.

5. Cowards[9] may die many times before _____ death.

6. Sticks and stones may break _____ bones, but words will never hurt me.

7. Don't burn _____ bridges behind you.

8. Never judge a book by _____ cover[10].

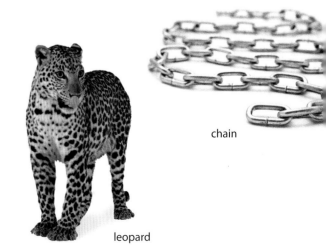

chain

leopard

[7] **fools:** foolish people
[8] **parted:** separated

[9] **cowards:** fearful people
[10] **cover:** the outside part of a book or magazine

Talk about It Choose one of the proverbs in Activity 34. What does it mean to you? Tell your classmates.

35 | Choosing Pronouns and Determiners Read the paragraphs. Choose the correct words to complete them. `4.7 A`

A Person I Admire

I admire my older brother a lot. _____*His*_____ name is Edgar, and
(1. he's / his)

_____ lives in Vancouver with _____ parents. Why do I
(2. he / his)   (3. our / their)

admire _____ so much? Edgar is very good at working with
(4. his / him)

_____ hands. _____ can fix anything. _____ also very
(5. his / him)   (6. he / his)   (7. he's / his)

generous with _____ time. _____ one of his best qualities. If
(8. his / its)   (9. its / it's)

you want _____ to fix something for _____, he'll stop what
(10. his / him)   (11. you / your)

he's doing and fix _____ right away.
(12. it / them)

> **WARNING!**
> Don't confuse *its* and *it's* or *their* and *they're*.
>
> ***its / their* + noun**
> The company lost 25 percent of **its value**.
>
> My three sisters came with **their husbands**.
>
> ***it / they* + be**
> I like this restaurant but **it's** very expensive.
>
> We have two cars but **they're** both old.

I have two older sisters, and I admire _____ both. _____
(13. their / them)   (14. they're / their)

two of the most caring people I know. When I was young, _____
(15. our / us)

parents were very busy because _____ owned a store. _____
(16. their / they)   (17. me / my)

older sisters had to do most of the work at home and take care of

_____. It was probably hard for _____ to take care of
(18. me / my)   (19. their / them)

_____ little sister, but they never complained or got angry
(20. their / them)

about _____.
(21. it / its)

Write about It Write several sentences about someone you admire.

36 | Using Possessive Pronouns Each of these **bold** sentences has a possessive phrase (such as *my new computer*). Change the phrase to a possessive pronoun. Then practice with a partner. `4.7 B`

1. A: I love my new computer.
                        mine
   B: **I like ~~my new computer~~, too.**

2. A: How old is your daughter?

   B: She's five. **Your daughter is seven, right?**

   A: No, she's six.

3. A: Our children love the new teacher.

   B: **Our children do, too.**

4. A: That isn't Tom and Jill's car.

   B: **How do you know it's not their car?**

   A: **Because their car is white.**

5. A: Is this Leila's phone?

   B: **No, her phone is upstairs.**

   A: Then whose is it?

   B: Let me see it. **Maybe it's my phone.**

6. A: Here are your keys. I found them in the car.

   B: **But those aren't my keys.**

   A: Then whose keys are they?

   B: I don't know. Pam was in the car today.

      Maybe they're her keys.

7. A: Can I use your computer?

   B: **What's the matter with your computer?**

   A: It's not working.

8. A: You and George both have nice singing

      voices!

   B: **I think George has a great voice, but my**

      voice is terrible.

   A: Not true. **Your voice is good, too.**

37 | Pronunciation Note: Possessive -'s Listen to the note. Then do Activity 38.

We pronounce the -'s endings on possessive nouns just like the -s endings on plural nouns.					
Usually the -'s ending on a possessive noun is just a consonant sound: / s / or / z /.			When a singular noun ends in a hissing or buzzing sound, the possessive -'s adds another syllable: / əz /. (These words are often spelled with a final -s, -x, -z, -ce, -ge, -se, -ze, -sh, and -ss.)		
1	women	women's clothing	/ z /	**3**	judge	the judge's decision	/ əz / (+ 1 syllable)
2	president	the president's family	/ s /	**4**	Liz	Liz's house

38 | Pronouncing Possessive Nouns Listen to each pair of words and check (✓) the ending you hear on the possessive noun. `4.7 C`

		/ s / OR / z /	/ əz /
1. people	people's problems	☐	☐
2. the horse	the horse's tail	☐	☐
3. a father	a father's role	☐	☐
4. my parents	my parents' friend	☐	☐
5. our children	our children's future	☐	☐
6. someone else	someone else's idea	☐	☐
7. the audience	the audience's response	☐	☐
8. the college	the college's president	☐	☐
9. an employee	an employee's work	☐	☐
10. next month	next month's bill	☐	☐
11. my boss	my boss' boss	☐	☐
12. the earth	the earth's atmosphere	☐	☐
13. a good night	a good night's sleep	☐	☐
14. our nation	our nation's capital	☐	☐

> **F Y I**
>
> We can use a possessive determiner + a possessive noun or name.
>
> **my** friend
> **my parents'** friend
>
> **our** future
> **our children's** future

Write about It Choose five possessive phrases above and write sentences using them.

What's a father's role in a family?

39 | Possessive Names and Nouns Complete each question with the possessive form of the word in parentheses. Then match each question with an answer on the right. `4.7 C`

QUESTIONS ABOUT NAMES AND NOUNS

1. What was ____*Shakespeare's*____ first name? (Shakespeare)
2. What was the name of _____ first movie? (the Beatles)
3. What is the name of a popular _____ toy? (children)
4. What's a popular _____ name? (boy)
5. What is the name of the _____ largest library? (world)
6. What is a scientific name for the _____ moon? (Earth)

____	A Hard Day's Night
____	LEGOs
____	Library of Congress
____	Luna
____	Michael
____	William

7. What is a word for your _____ brother? (father)
8. What do we call our _____ father? (mother)
9. What is the word for an _____ nose? (elephant)
10. What do we call a _____ bed? (baby)
11. What is another word for a _____ bag? (woman)
12. What is one word for a _____ hat? (man)

____	crib
____	fedora
____	grandfather
____	purse
____	trunk
____	uncle

Talk about It Ask a partner the questions above.

40 | Using Possessive Forms Write ten questions using words from each column in the chart. Add -'s or -' after the **bold** noun. `4.7 C`

THE PEOPLE IN YOUR LIFE

What	is are	your best **friend** your **father** your **parents** your **classmates** our **teacher** the **school** your **brother** your **sister** most **children**	name(s)? phone number(s)? address(es)? favorite movie(s)? favorite food(s)? biggest concern(s)? favorite sport(s)?

Talk about It Ask a partner the questions you wrote above.

A: *What is your best friend's favorite food?*
B: *He really likes Japanese food.*

41 | Error Correction Correct any errors in these sentences. (Some sentences may not have any errors.)

1. Do you have mine paper?
2. That's my friend book. Do you want me to give it to her?
3. I want to have a job like my mother job. She is the manager of her parents' clothing store.
4. In my country capital, the street's are crowded, and it takes a long time to get anywhere.

5. My parents are very generous with my. They are helping me start a business.

6. My brother and I argue a lot. I don't always understand he's point of view, and he doesn't understand mine.

7. I live with my aunt. She's home is near the center of town.

8. I can't wear my brother's clothes because he is tall and I am short.

9. Most people know that smoking is not good for you health.

10. While I was there, my friends invited me to them home.

11. I'm lucky because I can watch my TV's roommate.

12. People should take care of theirs health. It's important.

4.8 Overview of Quantifiers

A

QUANTIFIER + SINGULAR NOUN

1 Each **person** is going to help.

2 I called **every** student in the class.

QUANTIFIER + PLURAL NOUN

3 Many **students** today need financial aid.

4 Wow, there are a **lot of** people here!

QUANTIFIER + NONCOUNT NOUN

5 I could use a **little** help.

6 I didn't bring much **money** with me.

We use a special group of determiners to describe *how much* or *how many*, as in **1 – 6**. We call these words **quantifiers**. Notice:

| each each every either neither any | + | singular count noun |
| car book boy |

| a few some any many a lot of | + | plural count noun |
| cars books boys |

| a little some any much a lot of | + | noncount noun |
| time food |

GO ONLINE

42 | Noticing Quantifiers Read the text and circle the quantifiers + nouns. `4.8 A`

What Do You Do to Stay Healthy?

There are (many things) you can do to stay healthy. The right plan is different for every individual, but the most important things are eating right and exercising. I eat a lot of fruit and vegetables during the day, along with some bread and a little meat. I try not to eat many sweets even though I love them. When I can't resist, I try to eat just a few cookies or a little ice cream.

I also try to exercise to stay healthy. Many people go to a gym to exercise, but I prefer to exercise outdoors. Either way will make you feel better. I always feel good after exercising outdoors and have a lot of energy.

Think about It Write each quantifier + noun above under the correct group in the chart below.

Quantifier + singular count noun	Quantifier + plural count noun	Quantifier + noncount noun
	many things	

4.9 Quantifiers with Plural and Noncount Nouns

A

1 I need **some money**.
2 I need **some** new **clothes**.
3 He never has **any money**.
4 I don't have **any clothes** for the baby.

We use **some** and **any** with plural nouns and noncount nouns.

- We can use *some* in a positive statement to talk about a small number or amount, as in **1 – 2**.
- We can use *any* in a negative statement to mean "no," as in **3 – 4**.

B

5 We need **a lot of information**.
6 We didn't receive **many invitations**.
7 I have **a lot of money** with me.
8 I didn't bring **much money** with me.
   (DON'T SAY: I brought much money with me.)

We use **many** or **a lot of** with plural nouns. We use **much** or **a lot of** with noncount nouns.

- We can use *a lot of* and *many* in both positive and negative statements, as in **5 – 7**.
- We usually use *much* in negative, NOT positive, statements, as in **8**.

C

A FEW / FEW + PLURAL NOUN

9 Luckily, **a few people** came. (= a small number)
10 Sadly, **very few people** came. (= almost no people)

A LITTLE / LITTLE + NONCOUNT NOUN

11 It's nice to have **a little** free **time**. (= a small amount)
12 Are you a busy person with **very little** free **time**?
   (= almost no free time)

A *few / few* and **a** *little / little* look similar, but we use them differently. Notice the different meanings in **9 – 12**.

We often use *very* before *few* or *little*, as in **10** and **12**.

D

QUANTIFIERS AS PRONOUNS

13 A: Do you want **some soup**?
   B: Thanks, I'll have **a little**. (a little = a little soup)
   C: And I'll take **a lot**. (a lot = a lot of soup)
14 A: How many of **your friends** did you see today?
   B: **A few**. What about you?
   A: **None**. They were all working.

We can also use a **quantifier as a pronoun** in place of a noun or noun phrase, as in **13 – 14**.

WARNING! When we use *a lot* as a pronoun, we do not use *of*, as in **13**. We use *none* as a pronoun to mean "zero," as in **14**.

GO ONLINE

43 | Some and Any Complete the sentences with *some* or *any*. Then check (✓) *True* or *False*. **4.9 A**

FACTS ABOUT YOU	TRUE	FALSE
1. I like to have _____some_____ fun on the weekend.	☐	☐
2. I ate _____ cereal for breakfast this morning.	☐	☐
3. I didn't have _____ homework last night.	☐	☐
4. I have _____ money in my pocket.	☐	☐
5. I didn't see _____ good movies last year.	☐	☐
6. I have _____ friends in Canada.	☐	☐
7. I have _____ good reasons for studying English.	☐	☐
8. I usually ask _____ questions in class.	☐	☐
9. I never need _____ help with my homework.	☐	☐
10. I have _____ pictures of my family with me today.	☐	☐

	TRUE	FALSE
11. I have _____ concerns about the economy.	☐	☐
12. I don't have _____ trouble making big decisions.	☐	☐
13. I need _____ new clothes.	☐	☐
14. There isn't _____ furniture in my bedroom.	☐	☐

Write about It Rewrite the false statements in Activity 43 to make them true.

There is some furniture in my bedroom.

44 | Much, Many, and A Lot of Complete each sentence with your own ideas. `4.9 B`

1. I don't have many _____ *friends* _____ here.

   _____ at home.

   _____ at school.

   _____ here.

2. I don't have much _____ at home.

   _____ for breakfast.

   _____ here.

3. There are a lot of _____ in a city.

   _____ on TV.

   _____ in the world.

4. There is a lot of _____ in a city.

   _____ on TV.

   _____ in the world.

5. There isn't much _____.

   _____

   _____

6. There are many _____.

   _____

   _____

> **RESEARCH SAYS...**
>
> In general, *a lot of* is less formal than *many* or *much*.
>
> CORPUS

Think about It Share the sentences you wrote above with a partner. How many quantifiers + nouns you can list in the chart below?

Many + plural count noun	*Much* + noncount noun	*A lot of* + plural count noun	*A lot of* + noncount noun
many friends	*much time*	*a lot of people*	*a lot of violence*

45 | A Few/Few and A Little/Little Complete each pair of sentences with the correct words. `4.9 C`

1. a. Everyone needs _____*a little*_____ time to relax.

   b. Hurry up! We have _____ time.

2. a. My brothers live far away, so they are _____ help to my parents.

   b. Could you give me _____ help, please?

3. a. Can you wait ten more minutes? I still have _____ things to do.

   b. My boss is a great person. There are _____ things I dislike about her.

4. a. Let me read this letter while there is still _____ light.

   b. It's difficult to read when there is _____ light.

5. a. Tony Bennett is famous, but _____ people would recognize him.

   b. I thought the movie was funny, but only _____ people laughed.

6. a. My father takes care of himself. He doesn't smoke, and he eats _____ salt.

   b. This soup doesn't have much flavor. I think it needs _____ salt.

7. a. _____ people passed the test, but most didn't.

   b. We were lonely here at first because we knew _____ people.

1. a little/very little
2. a little/little
3. a few/few
4. a little/very little
5. a few/few
6. a little/very little
7. a few/very few

Write about It Look at the sentences above that use (*very*) *few* or (*very*) *little*. Rewrite them with *not . . . many/much*.

Hurry up! We don't have much time.

> **F Y I**
>
> In informal situations, we often use *not . . . many/much* instead of *few* and *little*.
>
> There are**n't many** people here.
> (= There are very few people here.)
>
> He does**n't** have **much** time.
> (= He has very little time.)

46 | Using Quantifiers as Pronouns Choose the correct pronoun to complete each conversation. Then practice with a partner. `4.9 D`

1. A: Can I get you some cake?

   B: Sure. I'd love ____*a little*____.
   (a few / a little)

2. A: Do you have a lot of homework tonight?

   B: No, not ___much___.
   (many / much)

3. A: Where is the coffee?

   B: Oh, we don't have ___any___.
   (any / some)

4. A: Did we get a lot of phone calls?

   B: No, not ___many___.
   (many / much)

5. A: There were only five people there.

   B: That's not very ___many___.
   (many / much)

6. A: Where are all your friends?

   B: Well, ___a few___ are at work.
   (a few / a little)

7. A: Do you want some more coffee?

   B: Sure. Just ___a little___.
   (a few / a little)

8. A: Do you want some potato chips?

   B: OK, but I can't eat very ___many___.
   (many / much)

9. A: Do you have any paper?

   B: Yes, there is ___some___ in the bottom drawer.
   (any / some)

10. A: How many light bulbs should I get?

    B: Just ___a few___.
    (a few / a little)

Think about It What do the underlined words above refer back to? Share ideas with your classmates.

In 1, "a little" refers back to "cake."

47 | How Much and How Many Ask and answer these questions with a partner. Use the pronouns in the box in your answers. `4.9 D`

a lot	not much	a little	a few	none
some	not many	very little	very few	

IN YOUR LIFE

How much / How many . . . ?

1. homework do you have tonight

   A: *How much homework do you have tonight?*
   B: *A little. I'm going to do it after dinner.*

2. meals do you eat at home every week
3. sleep do you get every night
4. text messages do you get a day
5. friends do you have online
6. coffee or tea do you drink in the morning
7. mail do you get every day
8. days off do you have this month
9. rain have we had this month
10. people in your neighborhood do you know

48 | Error Correction Correct any errors in these sentences. (Some sentences may not have any errors.)

1. Each people brought something to eat.
2. Each seasons has different weather.
3. He has had a many exciting adventures.
4. The restaurant serves many kind of fish.
5. You can learn many thing when you travel.
6. We had a lot of funs on our way to the city.
7. He sent me many news about his trip.
8. Lot of people drive too fast.
9. I looked at every channels on TV.
10. My father has a lot of good book in his library at home.
11. If you want to get a good grade in this class, you need to study little.
12. There are a lot of difference between my brother and me.

4.10 Quantifiers with Singular Nouns

A

1 The teacher will speak with **each student** separately.
(= one student at a time)

2 There's a laptop for **every student** in the class.
(= all students in the group)

3 Take **any seat** you want.
(= It doesn't matter which seat you take.)

4 I can visit you **either week**.
(= one week or the other week)

5 **Neither person** had the answer.
(= not one person and not the other)

We can use some quantifiers with singular nouns to describe more than one thing but to talk about them one at a time.

- We use *each*, *every*, and *any* to **talk about a group of things or people**, but we use them differently. Notice the different meanings in **1 – 3**.

- We use *either* and *neither* to **talk about two things or people**, but we use them differently. Notice the different meanings in **4 – 5**.

GO ONLINE

49 | *Each, Every, Any, Either, and Neither* Complete the conversations with the correct word in parentheses. Then practice with a partner. `4.10 A`

1. A: Do you want to leave on Monday or

   Tuesday?

   B: _____*Either*_____ day is fine.
      (either / neither)

2. A: Did you finish the book?

   B: Yep. I read _____ page.
      (either / every)

3. A: What color should we paint the kitchen?

   B: _____ color but yellow.
      (any / neither)

4. A: How many people did you call?

   B: Two, but _____ person
      (either / neither)
      answered.

5. A: Where did you go on vacation?

   B: I spend _____ vacation with
      (every / either)
      my family.

6. A: What kind of ice cream do you want?

   B: _____ kind is fine with me.
      (any / neither)

7. A: How long did it take to correct

   _____ test?
   (each / either)

   B: About 30 minutes.

8. A: Where did you go this summer?

   B: To Mexico. We go there _____ year.
      (every / either)

9. A: Who's going to win the game?

   B: That's hard to say. _____ team is
      (either / neither)
      very good.

10. A: Are you going to study a foreign language?

    B: Yeah, _____ student has to take one.
       (each / every)

4.11 Measure Words

A

COMPARE QUANTIFIERS AND MEASURE WORDS

1a Don't forget to buy **some sugar**.

1b Don't forget to buy **a bag of sugar**.

MEASURE WORD + NONCOUNT NOUN

2 Can I borrow **a piece of paper**?

3 I have **two pieces of advice** for you.

4 I need **two cups of sugar** for this recipe.

MEASURE WORD + PLURAL COUNT NOUN

5 I picked up **a bunch of bananas** at the store.

6 She gave me **two boxes of books**.

7 There are **three pairs of gloves** here.

When we want to describe a specific amount of something, we can use special **measure words + of,** as in **1b**. Notice:

	measure word		
a, an, one	**box cup bunch**	**of**	+ noncount noun / plural count noun

Measure words allow us to "count" noncount nouns, as in **2 – 4**. We can also use them with plural count nouns, as in **5 – 7**.

When we talk about two or more, the measure word is plural, as in **3 – 4** and **6 – 7**. Notice:

	measure word + -s	
two, etc.	**boxes cups bunches**	**of**

For a list of common measure words, see Activity 50, p. 149.

B

CORRECT THE COMMON ERRORS (See page R-19.)

8 ✗ I would like two cup of coffee, please.

9 ✗ He drank two bottle of milks!

10 ✗ Can you get me three boxes of cracker?

11 ✗ My teacher gave us bunch of test.

50 | Learning Measure Words We use certain measure words with certain nouns. Listen to each sentence. What noun do you hear after these measure words? Add it to the chart. `4.11 A`

Measure word	+ of	+ noun
1. bit/bits	of	advice, _____ , money, news, time, trouble
2. bottle/bottles	of	perfume, pills, shampoo, soda, _____
3. box/boxes	of	books, _____ , cereal, clothes, cookies, food, paper
4. bowl/bowls	of	cereal, food, fruit, rice, _____
5. bunch/bunches	of	bananas, carrots, emails, _____ , grapes, people, things
6. cup/cups	of	coffee, soup, sugar, _____
7. glass/glasses	of	ice, juice, milk, _____
8. loaf/loaves	of	_____
9. pair/pairs	of	eyes, glasses, gloves, pants, scissors, shoes, _____
10. piece/pieces	of	advice, cake, equipment, fruit, _____ , information, paper
11. pile/piles	of	books, _____ , dirt, mail, money, papers
12. slice/slices	of	_____ , cake, cheese, pizza

Write about It Choose five measure words above. Write true sentences about yourself using them.

I need a bit of advice.

51 | Listening for Measure Words Listen and write the missing measure words + *of*. `4.11 A`

1. I just put three _____*bottles of*_____ water on the table. Is that enough?
2. Could you please move this _____ papers?
3. Do you want another _____ cake?
4. Can I borrow a few _____ paper?
5. May I offer a _____ advice?
6. There are several _____ books on the floor.
7. I have some useful _____ information for you.
8. What are you going to do with this _____ clothes?
9. Could you get me a _____ cereal?
10. Please help yourself to the _____ fruit on the table.
11. I have a _____ emails to read.
12. How many _____ bread do you need?
13. I need two _____ sugar for this recipe.

> **FYI**
>
> We can use more than one measure word with some nouns. The choice depends on the meaning and the context. Compare:
>
> Could you get me **a loaf of bread** at the store?
>
> Do you want **a slice of bread** with your dinner?

Think about It What other measure word could you use in each sentence above? Compare ideas with your classmates.

"I just put three glasses of water on the table."

52 | Using Measure Words Make these sentences more specific. Replace the **bold** words with *a* + a measure word + *of*. (More than one measure word may be possible.) 4.11 A

a cup of
1. Could I have ~~some~~ coffee?

2. I need **some** information.

3. I gave her **some** perfume.

4. I have **a little** advice for you.

5. Would you like **a little** cake?

6. Can you get me **some** shoes?

7. I'd love **some** pizza.

8. Do you have **some** scissors at home?

9. We need **some** furniture for the bedroom.

10. Why don't you cook **some** rice?

11. My sister gave us **some** flowers.

12. Do you want **some** good news?

Write about It Rewrite each statement above. Use a plural measure word.

Could I have two cups of coffee?

53 | Error Correction Correct any errors in these sentences. (Some sentences may not have any errors.)

1. Could I have cup of tea?
2. I wrote everything on a piece of papers.
3. You should eat at least three piece of fruit every day.
4. You need two slice of bread to make a sandwich.

5. They always sent us box of food for the holiday.
6. These bunch of bananas isn't ripe.
7. I drank some bottle of water.
8. I think we need three loafs of bread.

4.12 Quantifiers for Comparing Amounts

A

1 It's very dry here. We really need **more rain**.
2 There are **more people** in class today.
3 There were **fewer storms** this year than last year.
4 I had **fewer problems** in school this semester.
5 You can lose weight by eating **less food**.
6 I should drink **less coffee**.

We use the quantifiers *more, fewer,* and *less* to compare different amounts or numbers, as in **1 – 6**. We can use:

more	+ a plural noun or a noncount noun
fewer	+ a plural noun
less	+ a noncount noun

B

7 There are **too many people** in New York City.
8 There are **too few days** in the week.
9 I have **too much work**. I'll never finish it.
10 I have **too little time** to finish this.

We can use **too** + some quantifiers, as in **7 – 10**. Notice the different meanings and uses:

	more than you want	less than you want	
too many	too few	+ a plural noun
too much	too little	+ a noncount noun

C

11 A: Are you going to buy this?
   B: Yeah, I think I have **enough money**.
12 A: Did you finish the test?
   B: No, I didn't have **enough time**.

We can use the quantifier **enough** + a plural count noun or a noncount noun, as in **11 – 12**. Notice:

• *enough* = No more is needed.
• *not enough* = More is needed.

 ONLINE

54 | Understanding *More, Fewer,* and *Less* Study the chart and then read the sentences below. Check (✓) *True* or *False*. `4.12 A`

Food	Number of Calories	Amount of Sugar	Amount of Salt
1 banana	105	14.43 grams	1 mg
1 apple	72	14.34 grams	1 mg
1 hamburger (with bun)	270	3.39 grams	369 mg
7 walnuts	185	0.74 gram	1 mg
1 cup of cooked pinto beans	236	0	0
2 slices of white bread	133	2.16 grams	340 mg
1 cup of vanilla ice cream	290	15.28 grams	116 mg

data from www.fatsecret.com

	TRUE	FALSE
1. A banana has more calories than an apple.	☐	☐
2. An apple has fewer grams of sugar than a banana.	☐	☐
3. A banana has less salt than an apple.	☐	☐
4. A hamburger has more calories than a banana and an apple together.	☐	☐
5. Seven walnuts have less sugar than one hamburger.	☐	☐
6. Two slices of white bread have more salt than a hamburger with a bun.	☐	☐
7. A banana has less sugar than an apple.	☐	☐
8. A cup of beans has fewer calories than a cup of ice cream.	☐	☐

Write about It Write four true or false sentences comparing the foods in the chart above. Then read your sentences to your classmates. Ask your classmates if your sentences are true or false.

55 | Using *More, Fewer,* and *Less* Complete each statement with *more, fewer,* or *less*. `4.12 A`

FACT BOOK

1. There are _____*more*_____ sheep in New Zealand than people.

2. There were _____ cars on the road 100 years ago.

3. Warm climates get _____ snow than cold climates.

4. An adult has _____ bones than a baby. An adult has 205 bones, but a baby has over 300.

5. When you wear a seat belt in a car, there is _____ chance you will get injured.

6. Because it's efficient, a refrigerator uses _____ energy than a washing machine or a clothes dryer.

7. There are _____ countries in Africa than in Asia. Asia has 48 countries, while Africa has 54.

8. Researchers say that happy people spend _____ time alone.

9. Most people want to earn _____ money, not less.

10. There are _____ people in New Zealand than in Japan. Japan has the tenth largest population in the world.

Write about It Choose two cities or two countries. Complete these sentences.

____ *has more* ____ *than* ____.   ____ *has fewer* ____ *than* ____.   ____ *has less* ____ *than* ____.

56 | Using *Too* + Quantifier Complete the sentences with *too much, too many, too little,* or *too few*. `4.12 B`

HEALTH PROBLEMS

1. _too much_ sun is bad for your skin.
2. Most people get ___little___ sleep. This can affect your health.
3. Your skin can turn orange from eating _too many_ carrots.
4. Many people eat _too much_ salt.
5. _too little_ exercise can lead to depression.
6. You may not sleep well if you drink _too many_ cups of coffee.
7. If you drink _too little_ water during the day, you may feel tired.
8. In many parts of the world, there are _too few_ doctors.

Write about It Describe four more health problems. Use *too much, too many, too little,* or *too few*.

57 | Understanding *Too Much/Too Many* vs. *Enough* Complete these conversations with *too much, too many,* or *enough*. Then practice with a partner. `4.12 B–C`

1. A: Do you want to go out tonight?
   B: I can't. I have _too much_ homework.
2. A: Why are you studying down here?
   B: There's _too much_ noise upstairs.
3. A: Let's go. There're _too many_ people here.
   B: Yeah, it's really crowded.
4. A: Do you want to watch *2001: A Space Odyssey*?
   B: No, thanks. I've seen it _enough_ times.
5. A: Why are you so hungry?
   B: Because I didn't eat _enough_ for lunch.
6. A: Why did you walk home?
   B: Because I didn't have _enough_ money for the bus.
7. A: Can we stop for a cold drink?
   B: There isn't _too many_ time. The bus leaves in ten minutes.
8. A: Do you want to do something tomorrow?
   B: Sorry, I can't. I have _enough_ things to do this weekend.
9. A: Does the car need gas?
   B: No, I think there's _enough_ for you to get to work.
10. A: You look terrible. Are you OK?
    B: Yeah, I just didn't get _enough_ sleep last night.
11. A: Can you help me bring in the groceries?
    B: Ten bags! I think you bought _too many_ things.

> **F Y I**
>
> We can use words like *more, fewer, less, much, many,* and *enough* as either determiners or pronouns.
>
> We didn't have **enough money**.
> We saved a lot of **money**, but it wasn't **enough** to buy a house.

Talk about It Ask a partner the questions above again. Use your own ideas to answer.

A: Do you want to go out tonight?
B: Sure. I don't have much to do.

4.13 Using Pronouns and Determiners in Speaking

A	***YOU*** **AND** ***THEY*** **FOR PEOPLE IN GENERAL** **1** How do **you** get to the airport? (In general, how does a person do this?) **2** **They** say prices are going up. (In general, people say this.)	We sometimes use **you** and ***they*** to talk about a person or people in general, as in **1 – 2**. • *You* means "any person in general." • *They* means "other people in general."
B	**EXPRESSIONS WITH** ***IT*** **3** Lisa wouldn't stop teasing me, so I finally told her to **cut it out!** (= Stop doing that.) **4** A: I'm still mad at you for being late. B: Can you just **drop it!** (= Stop talking about that.)	We use the pronoun **it** in many informal expressions, as in **3 – 4**. In these cases, it often refers to an action or behavior.
C	**REFERRING BACK WITH** ***THAT*** **5** A: You're always late. B: **That's** not true. **6** A: I don't want to eat anything today. B: **That's** crazy.	In conversation, we often use **that** to refer to something the speaker has just said, as in **5 – 6**.
D	***ME TOO*** **AND** ***ME NEITHER*** **7** A: I'm hungry. B: **Me too.** (= I'm hungry too.) **8** A: I don't want to leave. B: **Me neither.** (= I don't want to leave either.)	In conversation, we sometimes use the expressions **Me too** and **Me neither** to agree with someone, as in **7 – 8**.

58 | Understanding *You* **and** *They* Do the **bold** words refer to specific people or people in general? Circle your answers. Then practice with a partner. `4.13 A`

1. A: Do **you** want to watch a movie tonight?
   B: Sure. That would be fun.

2. A: Should we take a taxi?
   B: No, **you** can't get one at this hour.

3. A: I hope we get a lot of snow this year.
   B: **You** never know.

4. A: Did **you** send the package?
   B: Yes. I sent it yesterday.

5. A: This is a nice neighborhood.
   B: Yeah, **you** need a lot of money to live here.

6. A: **They** say it's going to be cold this winter.
   B: That's OK. I love winter.

7. A: Where did your brothers go?
   B: I don't know. **They** didn't tell me.

8. A: I can't believe my car needs a new engine.
   B: Yeah, **they** don't build very good cars anymore.

1. (a specific person) / any person in general
2. a specific person / any person in general
3. a specific person / any person in general
4. a specific person / any person in general
5. a specific person / any person in general
6. specific people / other people in general
7. specific people / other people in general
8. specific people / other people in general

Talk about It Work with a partner. Create a short conversation using *you* or *they* to talk about people in general. Present your conversation to the class.

🔊 59 | Using Expressions with *It* Listen and write the missing words. Then match each completed expression with a meaning below. Practice the conversations with a partner. **4.13 B**

1. A: I'm leaving.

   B: _____*Hold*_____ **it** for a minute. I need to show you something.

2. A: Dad, this can't be true.

   B: _____ **my word for it**, Ben. It's true.

3. A: I'm sorry I couldn't finish this today.

   B: Don't worry about it. You can _____ **it up** tomorrow.

4. A: Can I go to the movies tonight, Mom?

   B: Absolutely not. You are going to stay here and do your homework. _____ **it**?

5. A: I don't have time to cook dinner tonight.

   B: No problem. _____ **it to me**.

6. A: _____ **it**! There's a car coming.

   B: Thanks. I didn't see it.

7. A: It's five o'clock, and I'm tired.

   B: Me too. **Let's** _____ **it a day**.

   A: Good idea.

8. A: _____ **it off**, kids. You're making too much noise.

   B: OK, Dad.

MEANINGS

____ Stop doing that.   ____ Be careful.   ____ Believe me.   *1* Wait.

____ Stop working.   ____ I'll do it.   ____ Finish it.   ____ Do you understand?

Talk about It Work with a partner. Choose one of the expressions above and use it to create a short conversation. Present your conversation to the class.

60 | Using *That* to Refer Back Give a response for each statement. Use ideas from the box. (Many different responses may be possible.) **4.13 C**

STATEMENTS

1. A: We never have any homework. B: _____
2. A: We have class tomorrow at nine. B: _____
3. A: I saw your brother yesterday. B: _____
4. A: I have some money for you. B: _____
5. A: I'm getting married tomorrow. B: _____
6. A: It's almost three o'clock. B: _____
7. A: It's snowing outside. B: _____
8. A: The sun rises in the west. B: _____
9. A: Men aren't smarter than women. B: _____
10. A: Are you still cooking dinner for the class tomorrow? B: _____

RESPONSES

That's great.
That's fine.
That's interesting.
That's crazy.
That's impossible.
Wait a second. I never said that.
That's nice.
That's true.
That's not true.
That's awful!

Talk about It Work with a partner. One person reads a statement above. The other person gives a response. Then think of your own statements and responses.

A: We never have any homework.
B: That's not true. We had homework yesterday.

61 | Using *Me Too* and *Me Neither* Work with a partner. One person reads a sentence. The other person agrees by saying *Me too* or *Me neither.* `4.13 D`

1. I want to take a vacation.

   A: *I want to take a vacation.*
   B: *Me too.*

2. I had a good time yesterday.
3. I don't like fried food.
4. I have a lot of friends.

5. I didn't do my homework.
6. I'm tired.
7. I don't have any money.
8. I'm not very hungry.
9. I have a headache.

Talk about It Write five statements you think your partner will agree with. Then read your statements aloud and see if your partner agrees.

A: *I really like ice cream.*
B: *Me too. / Oh, I don't.*
A: *I don't like classical music.*
B: *Me neither. / That's interesting.*

4.14 Using Pronouns and Determiners in Writing

A

COMPARE

1a **Dikembe Mutombo** came to the U.S. to study. **Mutombo** wanted to be a doctor, but instead **Mutombo** became a famous basketball player. **Mutombo** wanted to help the people in **Mutombo's** native country, so **Mutombo** helped to build a hospital there.

1b **Dikembe Mutombo** came to the U.S. to study. **He** wanted to be a doctor, but instead **he** became a famous basketball player. **Mutombo** wanted to help the people in **his** native country, so **he** helped to build a hospital there.

Writers often use **pronouns** and **possessive determiners** (such as *his*) in place of nouns and noun phrases, as in **1b**. This makes a piece of writing less repetitious.

It's sometimes necessary to repeat a **noun** or **noun phrase** later in a paragraph, as in **1b**. This helps to make the writing clear for the reader.

GRAMMAR TERM: Clearly connecting sentences to each other in writing is called **cohesion**.

B

FIRST PERSON

2 **My** grandfather was very important to **me**. **My** first memory of him was when I was just three years old. . . .

SECOND PERSON

3 People go on vacation to relax. If **you** don't plan carefully, however, **your** vacation can be a disaster. **You** need to pack carefully. . . .

THIRD PERSON

4 The city of Masdar is in the United Arab Emirates. **It**'s a special city because **it** doesn't use any oil. Instead, the city uses solar power. . . .

When we write a story about our own experiences, we usually use the words *I, me, my, we, us,* and *our*, as in **2**. This is called "first person."

When we write advice or instructions, we often use the words *you* and *your*, as in **3**. It's like speaking directly to the reader. This is called "second person."

For a report or a description, we often use the words *he, him, his, she, her, it, they,* and *them*, as in **4**. It's like being an observer. This is called "third person."

62 | Using Pronouns to Reduce Repetition Read the article. Add the missing pronouns and possessive determiners. **4.14 A**

BLAKE MYCOSKIE

Blake Mycoskie is not an ordinary businessman. _____'s a
1
businessman with a cause[11]. Mycoskie is the owner of TOMS: Shoes for
Tomorrow. _____ cause is making sure that poor children have
2
shoes. Every time _____ company sells a pair of shoes, a child
3
somewhere gets a free pair. People told _____ that _____
4   5
would never succeed, but Mycoskie recently gave away _____
6
millionth pair of shoes.

　　Mycoskie got the idea for _____ company while _____
7   8
was traveling. _____ saw many children without shoes. Because
9
_____ didn't have shoes, _____ weren't allowed to go to
10   11
school. Mycoskie owned a different company at the time. _____
12
sold it to get the money to start _____ shoe company. People like
13
_____ shoes because _____ are comfortable and _____
14   15   16
look cool[12]. In addition to this, when _____ buy a pair of
17
Mycoskie's shoes, _____ are also helping a child live better.
18

Think about It **Answer these questions.**

1. How many times did the writer repeat the name *Mycoskie* in each paragraph above? _____

2. How many times did the writer use *he, him,* or *his* instead? _____

3. What does *they* refer to each time it is used?

　　_____

　　_____

　　_____

　　_____

　　_____

　　_____

[11] **a cause:** something a person cares about and wants to help　　　　[12] **cool:** fashionable; attractive

63 | Using Pronouns in Writing Rewrite these paragraphs. Change some (but not all) of the **bold** nouns to pronouns or possessive determiners. **4.14 A**

CHINUA ACHEBE

The writer Chinua Achebe was born in Nigeria in 1930. **Achebe** wrote novels, essays, poetry, and children's stories. **Achebe** learned English at a young age. **Achebe** enjoyed English literature, but **Achebe** felt that English writers wrote inaccurately[13] about African culture. So **Achebe** wrote about **Achebe's** culture—the Igbo culture into which **Achebe** was born.

Even though **Achebe** spoke Igbo, **Achebe** often wrote **Achebe's** stories in English. **Achebe** believed that storytelling helped people understand themselves and where **people** came from. Unfortunately, **Achebe** was injured in a car accident in 1990. **Achebe** was in a wheelchair after the accident, but **Achebe** continued to write and teach. **Achebe** died in 2013.

Write about It Write a paragraph telling your classmates about a famous person of your choice. Include information that you think will be interesting to your classmates.

64 | Choosing a Point of View Which point of view would you choose for each of these writing topics? Check (✓) your answers. Then compare ideas with your classmates. **4.14 B**

WRITING TOPICS	FIRST PERSON	SECOND PERSON	THIRD PERSON
1. Explain how to buy a plane ticket.	☐	☐	☐
2. Write about an experience that changed your life in some way.	☐	☐	☐
3. Describe a movie you saw last year.	☐	☐	☐
4. Describe the greeting customs in another country.	☐	☐	☐
5. Write instructions for making a cup of coffee.	☐	☐	☐
6. Describe your worst experience in school.	☐	☐	☐
7. Explain how the Internet changed the way people communicate.	☐	☐	☐
8. Your friends plan to visit your favorite city. Suggest what they should do there.	☐	☐	☐

[13]**inaccurately:** incorrectly

A | DISCUSSION Choose one of these questions. In a group, come up with five or more answers. Then share the results of your discussion with the class.

QUESTIONS

1. What's important in a good relationship between friends?
2. What's important in a good employer-employee relationship?
3. What's important in a good father-son relationship?
4. What's important in a good mother-daughter relationship?
5. What's important in a good doctor-patient relationship?

> A: *What's important in a good relationship between friends?*
> B: *I think friends should be honest with each other.*
> C: *And friends should support each other when they are in trouble.*

B | DEMONSTRATION Choose a simple device that you use often. Bring the device to class and explain how to use it.

> *"I think a stapler is a very useful device. You just put some papers together and then slide them between the two parts of the stapler. Then you press down on the stapler, and a staple goes into your papers. Now you can't lose your papers."*

C | SURVEY Choose one of these questions or think of your own. Then ask your classmates the question and record their answers. Report the results of your survey to the class.

QUESTIONS

1. Do you think we get too much homework or too little homework?
2. Do you think university students pay too much, too little, or just enough for their classes?
3. Do you think we take too many tests or too few tests?
4. How important is it for children to study art and music in school?
5. Should girls and boys study together or apart?

A few people said . . .	Some people . . .	Three people think . . .
Everybody thinks . . .	No one . . .	

> *"I asked the question, 'Do you think we get too much homework or too little homework?' No one said we get too little homework, but a few people said we get too much homework. A few people also said we have too many long reading assignments. Everybody else said we get the right amount of homework."*

D | PRESENTATION What should a visitor to your country or city see and do? Think of four or five interesting things. Plan your ideas and make a presentation to the class.

> *"If you visit my hometown, Tokyo, you should definitely go to the fish market at Tsukiji. If you can't sleep after traveling, you can get up early (around 5:30 a.m.) and see the fish buyers there. Then you can go have some fresh sushi for breakfast."*

4.15 Summary of Pronouns and Determiners

						PRONOUN / DETERMINER	
Subject Pronouns	I	you	he	she	it	✓	—
	we	you	they				
Object Pronouns	me	you	him	her	it	✓	—
	us	you	them				
Possessive Pronouns	mine	yours	his	hers	—	✓	—
	ours	yours	theirs				
Reflexive Pronouns	myself	yourself	himself	herself	itself	✓	—
	ourselves	yourselves	themselves				
Reciprocal Pronouns	each other		one another			✓	—

					PRONOUN / DETERMINER	
One/Ones	one ones				✓	—
Indefinite Pronouns	someone somebody something	everyone everybody everything	anyone anybody anything	no one nobody nothing	✓	—

DETERMINERS   PRONOUN / DETERMINER

						PRONOUN / DETERMINER	
Possessive Determiners	my	your	his	her	its	—	✓
	our	your	their				
Measure Words	with plural count nouns a **box** of books a **bunch** of people a **pair** of shoes		with noncount nouns a **bit** of help a **cup** of coffee a **piece** of advice			—	✓

PRONOUN OR DETERMINER   PRONOUN / DETERMINER

				PRONOUN / DETERMINER	
Demonstratives	with singular count nouns this that	with plural count nouns these those	with noncount nouns this that	✓	✓
Quantifiers	with singular count nouns each every* either neither any	with plural count nouns a few some many a lot (of) any	with noncount nouns a little some much a lot (of) any	✓	✓
Quantifiers for Comparing Amounts		with plural count nouns more fewer too many too few enough	with noncount nouns more less too much too little enough	✓	✓

* We don't use *every* as a pronoun.

5 Future Forms

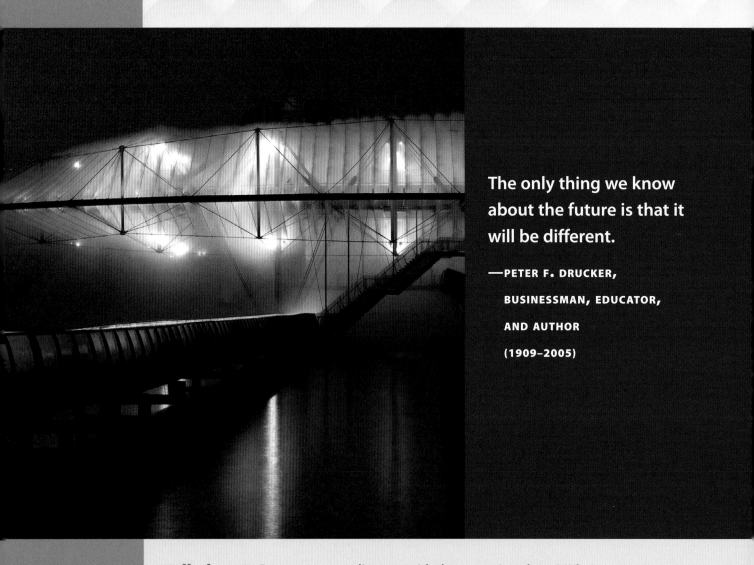

The only thing we know about the future is that it will be different.

—PETER F. DRUCKER, BUSINESSMAN, EDUCATOR, AND AUTHOR (1909–2005)

Talk about It Do you agree or disagree with the quotation above? Why?

WARM-UP

A | Read these sentences and check (✓) *True* or *False*. Then compare answers with your classmates. For each statement, how many people said *true* and how many said *false*?

Your Class

	TRUE	FALSE
1. I'm going to work hard in this class in the future.	☐	☐
2. I'm not going to miss any classes next week.	☐	☐
3. I think I'll learn a lot in this class.	☐	☐
4. We won't have any tests in this class.	☐	☐
5. I'm probably going to pass this class.	☐	☐
6. We aren't going to have class tomorrow.	☐	☐
7. This class is going to be easy.	☐	☐
8. This class finishes in two months.	☐	☐

B | Answer these questions about the sentences above.

1. Which are about a future action or event?
2. Which are predictions?
3. Which are descriptions of plans?
4. What verb forms can we use to talk about the future?

C | Look back at the quotation on page 160. Identify any future verb forms.

5.1 Statements about the Future with *Be Going To*

We use several different verb forms to talk about the future in English. One common form is **be going to**.

To form statements, we use *am / is / are* (+ **not**) + *going to* + the **base form of a main verb**, as in **1 – 6**. In conversation, we often use contractions.

A

POSITIVE STATEMENTS

		be	*going to*	base form
1	I	am 'm	going to	laugh.
2	We You They	are 're	going to	leave.
3	He She It	is 's	going to	work.

NEGATIVE STATEMENTS

		be + not	*going to*	base form
4	I	am not 'm not	going to	cry.
5	We You They	are not 're not aren't	going to	stay.
6	He She It	is not 's not isn't	going to	stop.

Notice: The verb *be* is a helping verb in the *be going to* form.

B

PREDICTIONS

7 The economy **is going to get** better soon.

8 My stomach hurts. I think I**'m going to be** sick.
(evidence = a stomachache)

9 A: The sky is getting dark.
B: Yeah, I think it**'s going to rain**. (evidence = dark sky)

We often use *be going to* when we make a prediction, as in **7 – 9**.

When we have clear evidence or information that something is going to happen, we usually use *be going to*, as in **8 – 9**.

C

PLANS

10 We**'re going to spend** a week in California next summer.

11 My daughter bought a big house with a room for me. I**'m going to move** in with her.

12 Don't be late for dinner. We**'re going to eat** at 7 tonight.

We often use *be going to* when we talk about future plans that we made earlier, as in **10 – 12**.

GO ONLINE

1 | Forming Statements with *Be Going To* Complete these sentences with the correct form of *be going to* and the word(s) in parentheses. Use contractions where possible. **5.1 A**

TALKING ABOUT WHAT TO EXPECT

1. An important package _____*is going to arrive*_____ tomorrow. Let me know when it's here. (arrive)

2. I have some big news to share, but you _____ it. (not/like)

3. Be careful with your money next month. You _____ some extra cash for books. (need)

4. I don't think anything special _____ this week. (happen)

5. Your boss _____ you an interesting offer next week. Think carefully before you make a decision. (make)

6. I don't think you _____ the answer to your question soon. Maybe next week. (get)

7. The quiz _____ difficult this week, but don't worry. You _____. (be) (not/fail)

8. We _____ early tomorrow. Traffic _____ pretty bad. (leave) (be)

9. My brother probably _____ me move. He has to work. (not/help)

10. One of your best friends _____ you a big secret. (tell)

11. Don't lie. He _____ the truth sooner or later. (find out)

12. I _____ my parents soon. I think they miss me. (visit)

2 | Making Predictions with *Be Going To* Match the situations with the predictions. (More than one answer may be possible.) Then compare with a partner. `5.1 B`

SITUATIONS

1. I don't feel well. __j__

2. I studied hard all week. ____

3. The traffic is terrible today. ____

4. I didn't eat breakfast this morning. ____

5. It's only 6 a.m. and it's already 80 degrees. ____

6. The food smells delicious. ____

7. It's a pretty cloudy day. ____

8. My brother failed his final exam. ____

9. This movie has some great actors in it. ____

10. My sister hates her new job. ____

PREDICTIONS

a. This is going to be a great meal.

b. I think it's going to rain.

c. We're going to be late to the meeting.

d. I think I'm going to pass the test tomorrow.

e. I'm going to be really hungry by lunchtime.

f. I think it's going to be really good.

g. It's going to be really hot today.

h. She's probably going to quit soon.

i. Our father is going to be really upset.

j. I think I'm going to faint[1].

Talk about It Work with a partner. Choose three situations above and write a new prediction for each one. Use *be going to.*

"I don't feel well. I think I'm going to be sick."

3 | Describing Future Plans with *Be Going To* Complete these conversations with the correct form of *be going to* and the word(s) in parentheses. Use contractions. Then practice with a partner. `5.1 C`

1. A: Is Ben going to be here for dinner?

   B: No, he __*'s going to work*__ late tonight. (work)

2. A: How are you going to get home?

   B: I _____ a taxi. (call)

3. A: Are you doing anything special tomorrow?

   B: Yeah. We _____ the children to see a movie. (take)

4. A: What do you want for dinner tonight?

   B: I _____ tonight. Something is bothering my stomach. (not/eat)

5. A: Is Pam still angry at Janet?

   B: Yeah, really angry. She says she _____ to Janet ever again. (not/speak)

6. A: Your father sure looks happy these days.

   B: Yeah. He _____ soon. You can tell he's looking forward to it. (retire)

> **RESEARCH SAYS...**
>
> We often use *be going to* in conversation, but we rarely use it in writing. The most common use of *be going to* is to describe personal plans or intentions.
>
> CORPUS

[1] **faint:** to suddenly become unconscious for a short time, for example because you are weak or sick

7. A: When's the meeting tonight?

   B: Eight o'clock, but I _____. I'm too tired. (not/go)

8. A: Why are we getting off the highway?

   B: I _____ some gas. The gas tank is almost empty. (get)

9. A: Are your friends still coming over?

   B: Yes, but they _____ dinner first. (have)

10. A: Are you still working on your paper?

    B: Yeah, and I _____. I need another day. (not/finish)

Talk about It Do you have plans for next weekend? Tell a classmate about them.

4 | Making Predictions with *Be Going To* Use the information in each picture below to write one or more predictions. Use *be going to* and a verb or phrase from the box. (Many different sentences are possible.) **5.1 B**

fall	get burned	have (an accident)	run into
flood (the room)	get hurt	land (on the ground)	tip over

ACCIDENTS WAITING TO HAPPEN

1. _____*He's going to get hurt.*_____   2. _____   3. _____

4. _____   5. _____   6. _____

Talk about It Work with a partner and role-play the situations above. One person gives a warning to the other person.

"Be careful! You're going to get hurt."

5.2 Questions with *Be Going To*

To form *yes/no* questions with **be going to**, we put *am / is / are* before the subject, as in **1 – 2**.
We can give short answers to *yes/no* questions with *am / is / are*, as in **3 – 6**.
In negative short answers, we often use contractions, as in **5 – 6**.

A

YES/NO QUESTIONS

	be	subject	*going to*	base form	
1	Am	I			
	Are	you	going to	stay	here?
	Is	he she it			
2	Are	we you they	going to	help	him?

SHORT ANSWERS

			be
3	Yes,	you	are.
		I	am.
		he she it	is.
4	Yes,	you we they	are.

			be + not
5	No,	you	're not. aren't.
		I	'm not.
		he she it	's not. isn't.
6	No,	you we they	're not. aren't.

B

For *wh-* questions, we use a **wh- word** before *am / is / are* + the subject, as in **7 – 13**.
In **14 – 15**, the *wh-* word is the subject.

WH- QUESTIONS

	wh- word	*be*	subject	*going to*	base form
7	Where	am	I		go?
8	Why		you		leave?
9	Who	are	we	going to	see?
10	What		they		do?

	wh- word	*be*	subject	*going to*	base form
11	How		he		know?
12	Who	is	she	going to	visit?
13	What		it		do?

WH- QUESTIONS ABOUT THE SUBJECT

	subject	*be*	*going to*	base form
14	What	is	going to	happen?
15	Who			help?

GO ONLINE

5 | Asking *Yes/No* Questions with *Be Going To* Unscramble the words and write the questions.

5.2 A

ASKING ABOUT PLANS AND PREDICTIONS

1. you/on your next vacation/anything special/going to/are/do/?

   Are you going to do anything special on your next vacation?

2. go/going to/to school/tomorrow/you/are/?

   _____

3. tomorrow/it/rain/is/going to/?

   _____

4. going to/our next exam/be/is/difficult/?

   _____

5. warmer/it/be/anytime soon/is/going to/?

   _____

RESEARCH SAYS...

Common verbs in yes/no questions with *be going to* include:

be	go	say
do	have	take
get	make	

CORPUS

6. offer/English courses/going to/your school/is/next year/?

____

7. going to/is/soon/anyone in your family/get married/?

____

8. go/after class/you/going to/shopping/are/?

____

9. have/in the next few weeks/you/are/going to/any visitors/?

____

10. we/have/peace in the world/are/ever/going to/?

____

Think about It **Which questions in Activity 5 ask about a future plan? Which ask for a prediction?**

Talk about It **Ask a partner the questions in Activity 5.**

A: Are you going to do anything special on your next vacation?
B: Yes. I'm going to visit my parents.

6 | Usage Note: Future Time Expressions **Read the note. Then do Activity 7.**

We often use a time expression in a sentence about the future. Common time expressions include:

today tonight tomorrow soon someday

next	+	weekend / week / month / semester / summer / year
this		evening / weekend / week / month / semester / summer / year
by		7:00 / lunchtime / tomorrow / this weekend / next year
until		midnight / dinner / tonight / next month / this evening
for		two hours / the next few days / a while / the rest of your life / long
in		a second / the next few minutes / a while / a few weeks / the future

a second / a few minutes / an hour / a week / a month / a year + from now

Time expressions can give more specific times or more general times.

Are you going to be here **tonight / next week / for the rest of your life / a year from now?** (specific times)
I'm going to move out of my parents' home **soon / someday / for a while / in the future.** (general times)

7 | Using Time Expressions **Circle the most logical time expression to make meaningful questions.**

5.2 A–B

ASKING ABOUT FUTURE PLANS

1. Are you going to live here (for the rest of your life / an hour from now / this weekend)?
2. Are you going to be in this room (someday / for a while / soon)?
3. Where are you going to be (tomorrow / for the rest of your life / by 7:00)?

4. Where are you going to be (for long / someday / 50 years from now)?

5. Are you going to buy a house (an hour from now / tomorrow / someday)?

6. Are you going to graduate (by your next birthday / in a while / ten minutes from now)?

7. Is anything surprising going to happen (in the near future / for long / until tomorrow)?

8. Are you going to go anywhere special (this month / for the next few minutes / in a while)?

9. Are you going to have a job (next year / tonight / this weekend)?

10. Is this class going to continue (soon / someday / until next month)?

Talk about It Ask a partner the questions in Activity 7. Then tell your classmates something interesting you learned about your partner.

🔊 **8 | Pronunciation Note: "Gonna"** **Listen to the note. Then do Activity 9.**

In everyday conversation, we often reduce the words *going to*. We say "**gonna**" instead.

WRITTEN FORM	SPOKEN FORM
1 Are they going to leave soon?	"Are they **gonna** leave soon?"
2 Who is going to tell him?	"Who's **gonna** tell him?"
3 What is going to happen?	"What's **gonna** happen?"
4 I am going to stay here.	"I'm **gonna** stay here."
5 Somebody is going to find out.	"Somebody's **gonna** find out."

WARNING! We don't normally use "gonna" in writing.

🔊 **9 | Listening for Reduced Words** **Listen and repeat the spoken form of these questions.** `5.2 A–B`

1. Are you going to do anything special tomorrow?
2. Is it going to rain tomorrow?
3. Are you going to be here in an hour?
4. Are the stores going to be open tomorrow?
5. Are you going to stay up late tonight?
6. What are you going to do tonight?
7. Where are you going to go on your next trip?
8. When are you going to get up tomorrow?
9. How long are you going to stay at school today?
10. How much longer are you going to be here?

Talk about It Choose one of the questions above and interview five classmates. Report the results to the class.

"I asked the question, 'Where are you going to go on your next trip?' Three people are going to visit relatives. One person doesn't know, and one person is going to go someplace warm."

10 | Asking Questions with *Be Going To* Complete these conversations with the correct form of *be going to* and the word(s) in parentheses. Use contractions where possible. `5.2 A–B`

1. A: Do you have plans for the weekend?

   B: Yeah. Josh and I _____*are going to drive*_____ to New York. (drive)

   A: Where _____? (you/stay)

   B: With Josh's friends.

   A: Sounds like fun. _____ a play? (you/see)

   B: Yeah, we have tickets for *Once*.

2. A: Are all these books yours?

   B: Uh-huh.

   A: What _____ with them when you move?

      (you/do)

   B: I _____ them with me. (take)

   A: That _____ expensive. (be)

   B: I know.

3. A: _____ the president's speech tonight?

      (you/watch)

   B: I don't think so. I mean, what _____ that's new?

      (she/say)

   A: Yeah, but it _____ a very long speech. (not/be)

   B: OK, maybe.

4. A: Where is everybody?

   B: They're still at work. It _____ a long night

      for them. (be)

   A: Why do you say that?

   B: Because they have a lot of work to do for the meeting tomorrow.

   A: _____ enough time? (they/have)

   B: I think so.

5. A: _____ a new car? (Anne/really/get)

   B: Yeah, a BMW.

   A: That _____ a lot. (cost)

   B: I know.

   A: Where _____ the money from? (she/get)

   B: I have no idea².

6. A: _____ the project? (they/ever/finish)

   B: I don't know. I think it _____ years. (take)

   A: Years? Really?

   B: Uh-huh. And they _____ a lot of extra help. (need)

> **FYI**
>
> We sometimes use an adverb in a sentence with *be going to*. Notice the placement of the adverb.
>
> Is Tom **really** going to go?
>
> Are we **ever** going to get there?
>
> Are they **still** going to come?
>
> She is **never** going to be happy.

Talk about It Practice the conversations above with a partner. Practice saying *gonna* instead of *going to*.

---

²**have no idea:** don't know

11 | Error Correction Correct any errors in these sentences. (Some sentences may not have any errors.)

1. Is they going to buy a new car?
2. What you going to do tomorrow?
3. How am I gonna do it?
4. What I am going to tell him?
5. What you gonna do?
6. My youngest brother going to college next year.
7. My parents are going to come, but they not going to have dinner with us.
8. Are you going to see your family while you are there?
9. Who are going to be there tomorrow?

5.3 The Future with *Will*

A

POSITIVE AND NEGATIVE STATEMENTS

	will (+ *not*)		base form	
I			**have**	time tomorrow.
We	**will**		**wait**	for you.
You			**find out**	today.
1 They	**'ll**		**know**	the answer.
He	**will not**		**finish**	soon.
She	**won't**		**get**	home before me.
It			**work.**	

YES/NO QUESTIONS AND SHORT ANSWERS

	will	subject	base form	
2	**Will**	I / you / he / she / it / we / they	**be**	late?

			will
3	Yes,	I / you / he / she / it / we / they	**will.**
	No,		**won't.**

WH- QUESTIONS

	wh- word	*will*	subject	base form
4	**How**	**will**	I	**know?**

	subject	*will*	base form	
5	**What**	**will**	**happen**	next?

Another form we use to talk about the future is *will*. (*Will* is a type of helping verb called a **modal**.) We use the same form of *will* with all subjects.

To form statements, we use **will** (+ **not**) + the **base form of a main verb**, as in **1**. In conversation, we often use contractions.

> **won't** = will not

To form *yes/no* questions, we put **will** before the subject, as in **2**. We can give short answers to *yes/no* questions with **will** and **won't**, as in **3**.

For *wh-* questions, we use a *wh-* word before **will**, as in **4 – 5**.

For more information on modals, see Units 6 and 9.

B

PREDICTIONS

6 Many people think the economy **will get** better soon.
(= Many people think the economy is going to get better soon.)

7 In the future, cars **will be** much smaller.

We can use *will* to make a prediction, as in **6 – 7**. It is often similar in meaning to **be going to**.

C

PLANS, PROMISES, OFFERS, AND REQUESTS

8 I'm tired. I think I**'ll go** home.

9 I**'ll see** you tomorrow.

10 Thanks for the money. I**'ll pay** you back tomorrow.

11 I promise I **won't be** late.

12 You rest. I**'ll fix** dinner for everyone.

13 A: Where's my purse?
B: It's on your desk. I**'ll get** it for you.

14 I need to know. **Will** you please **tell** me the truth?

15 **Will** you **do** me a favor?

We can also use *will* for:

- a plan or decision that we make at the moment of speaking, as in **8 – 9**

- a promise, as in **10 – 11**

- an offer of help, as in **12 – 13**

- a request, as in **14 – 15**

12 | Noticing *Will* Read this text. Underline the uses of *will* + a verb. Do you think these are predictions or plans? Why? `5.3 A`

Dreaming for a Better World

We are a second-grade class at Brown Elementary School in Natick. We have been learning about the work of Martin Luther King, Jr. and his dreams. As a class we made a list of our dreams to make the world a better place to live. We have a dream that:

There <u>will be</u> peace.

People will stop smoking.

No one will litter.

There will be no such things as weapons or guns.

Everyone will help each other and get along[3].

There will be no bad guys.

People won't pollute the ocean.

There will be no more violence, swearing[4], stealing, name calling, or mischief[5].

Houses will not burn down.

People will play nicely.

More people will have smiles on their faces.

We hope that our dreams come true.

F Y I

We can use *will be* or *is/are going to be* after *there*.

There will be peace.
There is going to be peace.

---

13 | Making Predictions with *Will* How will things change by 2050? Complete the predictions below with *will* or *won't* and a verb from the box. (You can use a verb more than once.) `5.3 A–B`

be	design	do	have	live	stay	take	use

By the Year 2050

1. Robots _____*will do*_____ most household chores.

2. There _____ only one language in the world.

3. People _____ cars to get around.

4. Students _____ in school until the age of 30.

5. There _____ fewer countries in the world.

6. Most people _____ more than 100 years.

7. People _____ their own clothes.

8. Students _____ all their classes from their homes.

9. Television _____ very different.

---

[3] **get along:** to be friendly
[4] **swearing:** using bad language

[5] **mischief:** activities that cause trouble or harm

10. Self-driving cars _____ commercially available.

11. The world _____ warmer.

12. We _____ enough food for everyone on earth.

Think about It Could you use *be going to* instead of *will* in the sentences in Activity 13?

Talk about It How likely is each prediction in Activity 13? Tell your classmates your ideas.

14 | Pronunciation Note: Contractions with *Will* Listen to the note. Then do Activities 15 and 16.

We often pronounce *will* like *'ll* after pronouns, nouns, question words, and the word *there*.

WRITTEN FORM	SPOKEN FORM
1 I**'ll** call him.	I'll call him.
2 The store **will** open at 10.	The store['ll] open at 10.
3 Where **will** he be?	Where['ll] he be?
4 There **will** be plenty to do.	There['ll] be plenty to do.

WARNING! We can write the contraction *'ll* with subject pronouns (*I, you, he, she, it, we,* or *they*). However, we don't usually write *'ll* with other subjects. We write the full form *will* instead.

The contraction **'ll** is usually easy to hear before a **vowel sound** because the /l/ sound connects with the vowel sound.

5 I**'ll** open the window.
6 My parents['ll] understand.
7 Who['ll] ask him?

The contraction **'ll** is often harder to hear before a **consonant sound** because we don't usually pronounce the /l/ sound clearly.

8 She**'ll** help you.
9 Dinner['ll] be late.
10 Things['ll] get better.

15 | Listening for Contractions Listen and check (✓) the sentence you hear. **5.3 A–C**

1. ☑ a. I drink coffee.
   ☐ b. I'll drink coffee.

2. ☐ a. I do a good job.
   ☐ b. I'll do a good job.

3. ☐ a. We have time.
   ☐ b. We'll have time.

4. ☐ a. They want it.
   ☐ b. They'll want it.

5. ☐ a. You love it.
   ☐ b. You'll love it.

6. ☐ a. I have a salad.
   ☐ b. I'll have a salad.

7. ☐ a. The students get there on time.
   ☐ b. The students['ll] get there on time.

8. ☐ a. People like you better.
   ☐ b. People['ll] like you better.

9. ☐ a. They worry about it.
   ☐ b. They'll worry about it.

10. ☐ a. They show you.
    ☐ b. They'll show you.

11. ☐ a. I put it there.
    ☐ b. I'll put it there.

12. ☐ a. My parents take him to school.
    ☐ b. My parents['ll] take him to school.

13. ☐ a. I come here often.
    ☐ b. I'll come here often.

14. ☐ a. We work hard.
    ☐ b. We'll work hard.

15. ☐ a. Things change.
    ☐ b. Things['ll] change.

16. ☐ a. I try to be nice.
    ☐ b. I'll try to be nice.

Talk about It Work with a partner. Read a sentence in each pair in Activity 15. Ask your partner to say "Sentence A" or "Sentence B."

16 | Listening for Contractions Listen and write the full (uncontracted) form of the missing words.
`5.3 A–C`

1. _____*Everything will*_____ be OK.
2. _____ we get there?
3. _____ be a lot of people there.
4. _____ help you.
5. _____ see.
6. _____ be ready soon.

7. _____ you do there?
8. _____ be a great day.
9. _____ be surprised.
10. _____ do it.
11. _____ you know there?
12. _____ be snow tomorrow.

Talk about It Work with a partner. Choose three of the sentences above and use them to create short conversations. Present one conversation to the class. Say *'ll* where appropriate.

A: Oh, no! I can't find my cell phone.
B: Don't worry. Everything['ll] be OK! I'll help you look for it.

17 | Using *Will* for Promises Complete these promises with *'ll* or *won't*. `5.3 C`

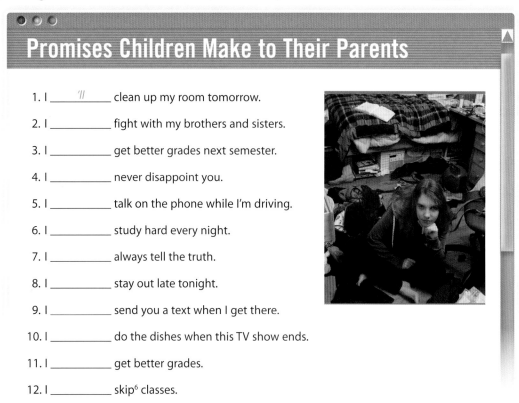

Promises Children Make to Their Parents

1. I _____*'ll*_____ clean up my room tomorrow.
2. I _____ fight with my brothers and sisters.
3. I _____ get better grades next semester.
4. I _____ never disappoint you.
5. I _____ talk on the phone while I'm driving.
6. I _____ study hard every night.
7. I _____ always tell the truth.
8. I _____ stay out late tonight.
9. I _____ send you a text when I get there.
10. I _____ do the dishes when this TV show ends.
11. I _____ get better grades.
12. I _____ skip[6] classes.

Write about It What are some promises that parents make to their children? Write five sentences. Then read your sentences to a classmate.

[6]**skip:** to not attend

18 | Talking about the Future with *Will* Complete the sentences below with *will* or *'ll* and a verb from the box. Then identify how the speaker is using *will*. Write *prediction, plan, promise, offer of help,* or *request*. 5.3 B–C

| bring | forget | get | go | help | join | pay | put | see | take |

PREDICTION, PLAN, PROMISE,
OFFER OF HELP, OR REQUEST?

1. A: Are you coming to lunch with us?

   B: Not today. I don't have time for lunch.

   A: I _____ *'ll bring* _____ you a sandwich. How about that?

   B: Thanks. I _____ you back tomorrow.

> 1A. *offer of help*

> 1B.

2. A: Are you ready to leave?

   B: Not yet. I still have to copy these articles.

   A: I _____ you with that.

   B: Thanks. It _____ faster with two people.

> 2A.

> 2B.

3. A: Is that new pizza place any good?

   B: We like it. We're going to eat there again tonight.

   A: Maybe we _____ you.

> 3.

4. A: It's getting late. I don't think you're going to finish it.

   B: Don't worry. We _____ it done.

> 4.

5. A: Hey, John, can you help me?

   B: Sorry, I'm busy.

   A: But it _____ only _____ ten minutes.

   B: OK, OK.

> 5.

6. A: Time is up. _____ you please _____ your
   pencils down?

> 6.

7. A: Did you have a good trip?

   B: Yeah, I _____ never _____ it.

> 7.

8. A: Are you leaving now?

   B: Yeah, but I _____ you tomorrow.

> 8.

Talk about It Practice the conversations above with a partner.

5.4 Be Going To vs. Will

A

PREDICTIONS

1 The economy **is going to get** better. I'm sure of it.

2 I think the economy **will get** better.

3 Watch out! That tree **is going to fall**.
(NOT: ~~I think it will fall.~~)

4 What's wrong with Sarah? She looks like she**'s going to cry**. (NOT: ~~She looks like she will cry.~~)

5 The first step in finding a job is to write a resume or complete a job application. In most cases, you **will need** a resume to apply for professional job opportunities. For other types of jobs, you **will complete** an application for employment.

We can often use either **be going to** or **will** to make predictions, as in **1 – 2**. However, different things can affect our choice. For example:

- When we have evidence or information that something is going to happen, we usually use *be going to*, as in **3 – 4**.

- When we make predictions in writing, *will* is much more common than *be going to*, as in **5**.

B

PLANS

6 A: Do you have your plane tickets yet?
B: Yeah, we**'re going to leave** on the 5th.

7 Did you hear? Jill**'s not going to take** that job. She**'s going to go** back to school instead.

8 A: What do you want to do tonight?
B: Oh, I**'ll** probably **go** home.

9 A: Can I tell you a secret?
B: Sure. I **won't tell** anyone.

10 A: I'm too tired to cook tonight.
B: That's OK. I**'ll do** it.

11 The library **will be** closed on September 8.

We use both **be going to** and **will** when we talk about future plans, but we use them in different ways.

We often use *be going to* when we talk about a plan made earlier, as in **6 – 7**.

We often use *will* when we make a decision at the moment of speaking, as in **8 – 10**. Using *will* suggests willingness. The speaker is choosing to do something. *Be going to* does not have this meaning.

A decision made at the moment of speaking might be a plan, a promise, or an offer of help.

When we write about future plans, *will* is much more common than *be going to*, as in **11**.

 GO ONLINE

19 | Making Predictions Which future forms can you use in these sentences? Circle one or both forms.

5.4 A

1. Everything **will** / **is going to** be fine.

2. I'm not saying it **'ll** / **'s going to** be easy.

3. It **'ll** / **'s going to** take years to do this.

4. Could you hand me a tissue? I think I **'ll** / **'m going to** sneeze.

5. I **'ll** / **'m going to** be OK. I **'ll** / **'m going to** find a new job soon.

6. Watch out! That bookcase **will** / **is going to** fall over.

7. According to a recent poll, 57 percent of people believe that ordinary individuals **will** / **are going to** travel in space by 2050.

8. An enemy **will** / **is going to** agree with you, but a friend **will** / **is going to** argue. (*Russian proverb*)

Think about It In which sentences above is *be going to* a better choice? Why? In which sentences is *will* a better choice? Why?

20 | Identifying Uses of Future Forms Read these conversations and underline the examples of *be going to* and *will*. Then check (✓) why you think the speaker chose each form. **5.4 A–B**

	PREDICTION	PLAN	PROMISE	OFFER
1. A: Where's Tom? B: He'<u>ll be</u> here any minute.	✓	☐	☐	☐
2. A: Where are you going? B: To Jim's house, but I'll be home early.	☐	☐	☐	☐
3. A: I'm worried about Sarah. B: Really? I think she's going to be OK.	☐	☐	☐	☐
4. A: Tonight's going to be a good night. B: Why do you say that?	☐	☐	☐	☐

5. A: How did you dent the car?
  B: I ran into the side of the garage.
  A: Too bad. Dad's going to be really upset.
	☐	☐	☐	☐

6. A: I think I need a ride to the meeting. B: No problem. I'll drive you.	☐	☐	☐	☐
7. A: Do you need a ride to the meeting? B: No, I'll drive myself.	☐	☐	☐	☐

8. A: Are you busy?
  B: Yeah, I have to finish this paper.
  A: OK. I'll come back at a better time.
	☐	☐	☐	☐

9. A: Where are my glasses? B: I'll get them for you.	☐	☐	☐	☐
10. A: This room is a mess. B: Yeah, it's going to take us all day to clean it.	☐	☐	☐	☐

11. A: Why are you so excited?
  B: I just got a new job! I'm going to move
  to California!
	☐	☐	☐	☐

12. A: Mom's expecting you for dinner tonight. B: Don't worry. I'll be there.	☐	☐	☐	☐

Think about It In which conversations above does the speaker talk about a plan? Is it a plan made earlier or a plan made at the moment of speaking? How do you know?

Talk about It Practice the conversations above with a partner.

21 | Using *Be Going To* and *Will* Read about each situation. Then work with a partner to write answers to the questions. **5.4 A–B**

1. Your doctor's appointment is in 10 minutes, but you are 20 minutes away. You call the doctor's office.

   What do you say to the receptionist?

   "This is Roger Smith calling. My appointment is in 10 minutes, but I'm going to be 10 minutes late."

2. You are on your way to the supermarket. Your aunt tells you that she needs some eggs.

   What do you say?

3. There is a pile of books on your teacher's desk. He needs someone to hand out one book to each student. What do you say to him?

_____

4. Your friend asks about your plans for tonight. You haven't thought about it before now. What do you say?

_____

5. A friend tells you a secret. She doesn't want you to tell it to anyone else. What do you say to her?

_____

6. Your brother sees you wearing fancy evening clothes. He asks why you are wearing these clothes. What do you say?

_____

7. A child is walking out on a frozen lake. You know the ice on the lake is very thin. What do you yell?

_____

8. Your friend is going to go an office supply store this afternoon. You want your friend to get some printer paper for you. What do you say to your friend?

_____

Talk about It Choose one situation in Activity 21 to role-play for your classmates.

A: Hello. Dr. Brown's office. How can I help you?
B: This is Roger Smith calling. My appointment is in 10 minutes, but I'm going to be 10 minutes late.
A: No problem, Mr. Smith. I'll tell the doctor.

5.5 Using Present Forms to Talk about the Future

A

SCHEDULED EVENTS

1 The movie **starts in five minutes**.
2 Jen's flight **arrives at ten tomorrow**.
3 My first exam **is next Monday**.

We sometimes use the **simple present** to talk about a previously scheduled event in the future, as in **1 – 3**. This is especially true when we are talking about timetables and official schedules.

Common verbs used with the simple present to talk about the future include:

arrive	begin	end	leave	start
be	close	finish	open	stop

We usually use a time expression to show that we are talking about the future, as in **1 – 3**.

B

PERSONAL PLANS AND ARRANGEMENTS

4 **I'm leaving at noon tomorrow**.
(= I'm going to leave at noon tomorrow.)

5 A: What **are** you **doing this weekend**?
   B: **I'm taking** my brother to the beach.

We sometimes use the **present progressive** instead of *be going to* when we talk about personal plans and arrangements, as in **4 – 5**.

6 It's going to rain tomorrow.
(NOT: ~~It's raining tomorrow.~~)

We do not use the present progressive to make predictions, as in **6**.

22 | Talking about Scheduled Events Read these sentences and check (✓) *True* or *False* based on the schedules. Then correct the false statements. `5.5 A`

SCHEDULED EVENTS

Flight Departures

Flight Number	Destination	Time	Gate
3988	London	3:52 p.m.	8
3417	Paris	5:15 p.m.	24
315	Cairo	7:35 p.m.	32

	TRUE	FALSE
1. Flight 3988 arrives at ~~3:25~~ *3:52* this afternoon.	☐	✓
2. Flight 3417 leaves from Gate 32.	☐	☐
3. Flight 3417 and Flight 315 depart at the same time.	☐	☐

Fall Term

September 10	Classes begin.
November 13	Classes end.
November 16	Final examination period begins.
November 20	Final examination period ends.

	TRUE	FALSE
4. The fall term ends in September this year.	☐	☐
5. The fall term lasts for about two months.	☐	☐
6. Students finish their final exams on November 16.	☐	☐
7. Classes end two weeks before the final exam period.	☐	☐

Parks and Recreation, Town of Franklin

The Franklin Parks and Recreation Department announces an evening with humorist Tim Widener on Sunday, October 27, at Franklin High School. The event begins at 7 p.m. and doors open at 6 p.m. This is an all-age, family-friendly show.

	TRUE	FALSE
8. The program with Tim Widener takes place on October 27.	☐	☐
9. The doors close at 6 p.m.	☐	☐
10. This program is for adults only.	☐	☐

Talk about It What is on your school schedule for the next few months? Share ideas with your classmates.

23 | Talking about the Future with Present Forms Complete this conversation with the simple present or present progressive form of the verb in parentheses. (In some sentences, either form may be possible.) `5.5 A–B`

A: Do you want to get together sometime next week?

B: I can't next week. I _____ to California.
   (1. go)

A: _____ from Boston?
   (2. you / fly)

B: Yeah, my plane _____ at 7 tomorrow morning.
   (3. leave)

A: How long a trip is it?

B: I _____ planes in Denver, so I don't get to
   (4. change)
   Los Angeles until 4.

A: Long day.

Flight Confirmation

Passenger(s)

Anita Erickson
Jill Erickson

Date	Flight	Departure/Arrival
Nov. 10	1228	7:05 a.m. Depart Boston
		10:05 a.m. Arrive Denver
	2224	2:40 p.m. Depart Denver
		4:00 p.m. Arrive Los Angeles

B: Yeah, but I _____ a good book, and my sister _____ with me.
(5. take)   (6. come)

A: So it's not a work trip?

B: No, we _____ relatives.
(7. visit)

A: Where _____?
(8. you / stay)

B: With our relatives. They live in Pasadena.

A: Well, have fun and call me when you get back.

Think about It In which sentences in Activity 23 is either form possible? Why?

24 | Future or Present Time? Underline the simple present and present progressive verbs in these sentences. Then write *F* over the verbs that refer to the future. `5.5 A–B`

1. Our school football team <u>is traveling</u> all over the country this winter.
   I <u>like</u> to watch them play, so I'<u>m planning</u> to go to a few games.

2. Jon leaves for Peru in three days. His mother is really sad about that.

3. The school is having a job fair in the spring. I'm getting my resume ready now.

4. In two weeks, I have an appointment with my career counselor. He's always very helpful.

5. We usually work from 9 to 5, but tomorrow we are only working until 1.

6. Julia's meeting begins early next Monday, so I'm driving the kids to school.

7. Tomorrow is a holiday, so the stores close at 6 p.m.

8. The concert doesn't end until midnight tonight. Do you still want to go?

9. I'm already at the airport, but my brother's plane doesn't arrive for three more hours.

10. The train is leaving now, but there's another one in 20 minutes.

> **WARNING!**
> We don't use the present progressive to talk about the future when the verb has a non-action meaning.
>
> **Present Time**
> I **have** a doctor's appointment tomorrow. (have = possess)
>
> **Future Time**
> We **are having** a picnic tomorrow. (have = organize)

Think about It Circle the time expressions in the sentences above. Then group them in this chart.

Present time expressions	Future time expressions
	in three days

25 | Error Correction Correct any errors in these conversations. (Some conversations may not have any errors.)

1. A: What are you going to do in Paris?
   B: I'll go to the museums.
2. A: How are you going to get home tonight?
   B: I'm going to take the train.
3. A: Do you think you'll do OK on the test tomorrow?
   B: No, I think I'm failing.
4. A: Do you cook dinner tonight?
   B: No, it's Jill's turn.
5. A: How are you getting to school tomorrow?
   B: My brother takes me.
6. A: Is Sue still here?
   B: Yes, but she leaves soon.
7. A: Do you think Tom will get here on time?
   B: No, I think he's getting here late.
8. A: Is there a movie at 7 tonight?
   B: Yes, I think so.
9. A: Is it snowing tomorrow?
   B: I hope not.

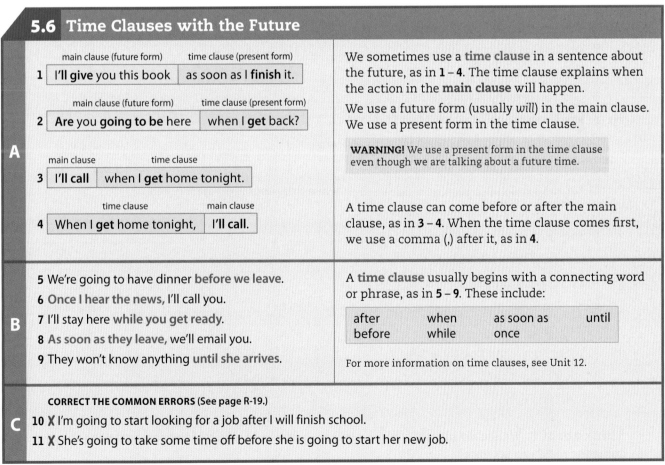

5.6 Time Clauses with the Future

A

	main clause (future form)	time clause (present form)
1	I'll give you this book	as soon as I finish it.

	main clause (future form)	time clause (present form)
2	Are you going to be here	when I get back?

	main clause	time clause
3	I'll call	when I get home tonight.

	time clause	main clause
4	When I get home tonight,	I'll call.

We sometimes use a **time clause** in a sentence about the future, as in **1 – 4**. The time clause explains when the action in the **main clause** will happen.

We use a future form (usually *will*) in the main clause. We use a present form in the time clause.

> **WARNING!** We use a present form in the time clause even though we are talking about a future time.

A time clause can come before or after the main clause, as in **3 – 4**. When the time clause comes first, we use a comma (,) after it, as in **4**.

B

5 We're going to have dinner **before we leave**.
6 **Once I hear the news,** I'll call you.
7 I'll stay here **while you get ready**.
8 **As soon as they leave,** we'll email you.
9 They won't know anything **until she arrives**.

A **time clause** usually begins with a connecting word or phrase, as in **5 – 9**. These include:

after	when	as soon as	until
before	while	once	

For more information on time clauses, see Unit 12.

C

CORRECT THE COMMON ERRORS (See page R-19.)

10 ✗ I'm going to start looking for a job after I will finish school.
11 ✗ She's going to take some time off before she is going to start her new job.

GO ONLINE

26 | Noticing Time Clauses Underline the time clauses in these sentences and circle the connecting word. Then check (✓) *True* or *False* and compare answers with a partner. `5.6 A–B`

	TRUE	FALSE
1. (When) we have our next test, I'll probably do well.	☐	☐
2. I'll probably be tired when this class is over.	☐	☐
3. As soon as the bell rings, I'm going to run out of this room.	☐	☐
4. It won't be dark when I get home tonight.	☐	☐
5. When I get home today, I'll probably study for a while.	☐	☐
6. I will probably have dinner before I do any homework tonight.	☐	☐
7. My parents won't come to visit me until I have a bigger apartment.	☐	☐
8. Once I finish this course, I'm going to look for a job.	☐	☐

27 | Using Time Clauses Complete these conversations with a present or future form of the verb(s) in parentheses. (More than one form may be possible.) Then practice with a partner. `5.6 A–B`

1. A: Are you going to be here late?

   B: Yeah, I'll probably be here until they _____*lock*_____ the doors. (lock)

2. A: Did you buy that book Pat wanted?

   B: Not yet. I _____ it when I go to the bookstore. (get)

3. A: What are your plans for the holiday?

   B: I _____ for Florida as soon as classes end. (leave)

4. A: What are we going to do in the city?

   B: We'll figure it out when we _____ there. (get)

5. A: Can I use your laptop?

   B: Can you wait a few minutes? I _____ you use it as soon as I finish this. (let)

6. A: How long are you going to be in London?

   B: Hard to say. I'll just stay there until my grandmother _____ better. (feel)

7. A: Did you make dinner?

   B: No, not yet. I _____ it when this program is over. (make)

8. A: Can you check this paper for me?

   B: Sure. Just put it over there. I _____ it as soon as I _____ some free time. (do/have)

9. A: Do we have any milk?

   B: No, but Tom _____ some when he _____ to the store. (buy/go)

10. A: When are we meeting tomorrow?

    B: I don't know, but I _____ you as soon as I _____. (call/find out)

Think about It We usually use *will* when we make a promise. In which of the conversations above is someone making a promise?

28 | Completing Clauses Complete these sentences with your own ideas about the future. (Many different answers are possible.) `5.6 A–B`

TIME CLAUSES

1. I'll probably have dinner before *I go to work tonight* _____ .
2. I'm not going to stop studying English until _____ .
3. Things will get better in the world once _____ .
4. I'll probably live here until _____ .
5. I'm going to leave school today as soon as _____ .
6. I'll be happy when _____ .
7. After _____ , I'll have some money.
8. I'm going to be sad when _____ .

MAIN CLAUSES

9. *I'm going to take a nap* _____ as soon as I get home today.
10. When I have some free time, _____ .
11. _____ when we have our next test.
12. _____ until I go on my next vacation.
13. Once this class is over, _____ .
14. _____ when I talk to my parents.
15. Before I do any homework, _____ .
16. _____ when the weather changes.

Talk about It Read five of your sentences above to a partner and ask your partner to respond.

A: I'll probably have dinner before I go to work tonight. What about you?
B: I don't work at night. But I'll have dinner before I do my homework.

B: I'm going to take a nap as soon as I get home today. What about you?
A: Me too. I need a nap after a long day.

29 | Error Correction Correct any errors in these sentences. (Some sentences may not have any errors.)

1. I will study hard until I will graduate from this university.
2. When I get older, I look back on this time and laugh.
3. When my daughter will learn to walk, I will be very excited.
4. When I am in a bad mood, my friends will make me happy.
5. My parents know I will call them when I have a problem.
6. After the exam period will be over, I feel much better.
7. Once my brother is going to get a job, he will get married.

5.7 Using Future Forms in Speaking

A

USING CONTRACTIONS AND FULL FORMS

1 I'll see you later.

2 Please have a seat. The president **will be** here very soon.

3 A: Why won't you help me?
B: But I **will help** you.

In conversation, we usually use the contracted form *'ll* instead of the full form *will*, as in **1**. Using *will* sounds very formal, as in **2**.

However, we sometimes use the full form *will* to emphasize information or to contradict someone, as in **3**.

B

OMITTING WORDS

4 Talk to you later. (= **I'll** talk to you later.)

5 See you tomorrow? (= **Will we** see you tomorrow?)

6 You going to help me next week?
(= **Are** you going to help me next week?)

7 You doing anything tomorrow?
(= **Are** you doing anything tomorrow?)

8 Going home soon? (= **Are you** going home soon?)

In casual conversation, we sometimes omit words in:

• statements with *I'll* or *We'll*, as in **4**

• questions with *Will I* or *Will we*, as in **5**

We sometimes omit words in *yes/no* questions with *be going to* or the present progressive when the subject is *you*, as in **6 – 8**.

C

YES/NO QUESTIONS

9 **Will** you **get** me a dictionary, please?
(= A request: Are you willing?)

10 **Are** you **going to get** me a dictionary?
(= Asking for information: What's your plan?)

11 It's getting late. **Are** you **going to help** me or not?
(The speaker is annoyed.)

We often use *will* in a *yes/no* question to make a request, as in **9**. We use *be going to* when we ask for information about a person's plans or intentions, as in **10 – 11**.

WARNING! Using *be going to* in a question can sometimes suggest that the speaker is annoyed, as in **11**.

 GO ONLINE

30 | 'll or Will? Listen to each conversation. Does the speaker use the contracted form *'ll* or the full form *will*? Circle your answer. Then practice with a partner. **5.7 A**

1. A: Do you want to watch this movie tonight?
   B: No, I don't think so.
   A: But you **'ll** / **will** like it.

2. A: Can you get me a ticket for Saturday?
   B: There aren't any left for this Saturday, but they **'ll** / **will** have some for next Saturday.

3. A: Do you want to meet on Monday?
   B: I'm not coming in on Monday, but I **'ll** / **will** be there on Tuesday.

4. A: Did you call Jessica?
   B: No, I **'ll** / **will** call her tomorrow.

5. A: You need to see a doctor.
   B: I know. I **'ll** / **will** see one—tomorrow.

6. A: Don't forget the meeting tonight.
   B: I won't.
   A: You always say that and then you forget.
   B: But I **'ll** / **will** remember tonight's meeting. I'm the main speaker.

7. A: Are you going to miss me?

   B: Of course.

   A: I'm not sure I believe you.

   B: But I **'ll** / **will** miss you. Honest.

8. A: Why are you so excited?

   B: I **'ll** / **will** tell you later.

   A: No, tell me now.

   B: Nope. I **'ll** / **will** tell you after dinner.

Think about It In which conversations in Activity 30 does the speaker use the full form *will*? Why?

31 | Understanding Sentences with Omitted Words Listen and complete these statements and questions. Then listen again and repeat the sentences. **5.7 B**

1. _Be with you_ in a minute.
2. _____ soon.
3. _____ tonight.
4. _____ you soon?
5. _____ anywhere tomorrow?

6. _____ this afternoon?
7. _____ this weekend?
8. _____ tonight?
9. _____ tomorrow?
10. _____ with us?

Think about It Rewrite the sentences above and add the omitted words.

1. _I'll be with you in a minute._
2. _____
3. _____
4. _____
5. _____

6. _____
7. _____
8. _____
9. _____
10. _____

32 | Making a Request or Asking for Information? Listen to each conversation. Is the speaker making a request or asking for information about the other person's plans? Check (✓) your answer. **5.7 C**

	Making a request	Asking for information
1.	☐	✓
2.	☐	☐
3.	☐	☐
4.	☐	☐
5.	☐	☐
6.	☐	☐
7.	☐	☐
8.	☐	☐

Think about It Listen to the conversations again. Does the speaker sound annoyed in any of the conversations? Which ones?

5.8 Using Future Forms in Writing

A

USING *WILL* IN WRITING

1 Berries are a great source of vitamins. Including berries in your diet **will help prevent** illness and **keep** you healthy. (magazine article)

2 By 18 months, most children **will have** a vocabulary of about 5 to 20 words. By 24 months, their vocabulary **will include** 150 to 300 words. By 36 months, most children **will know** how to use pronouns correctly. (web article)

Will is much more common than *be going to* in writing, as in **1 – 2**. This use of *will* expresses a strong prediction or expectation.

Remember: When we use more than one verb after *will*, it's not necessary to repeat will, as in **1**.

B

INTRODUCING IDEAS

3 This course **will feature** many hands-on activities; students are encouraged to raise questions and issues relevant to the topics covered in class. (from a course syllabus)

4 Each chapter in this book **will first present** the key points of a topic. (from a book introduction)

5 This essay **will discuss** the main causes of pollution in Los Angeles. (from an introduction to an essay)

In formal writing, writers sometimes tell their readers what is coming later in an essay, chapter, or book. They usually use *will* to do this, as in **3 – 5**.

When writers identify the goals of a piece of writing, they often use these verbs:

will describe	will explore
will discuss	will present
will examine	

---

33 | Noticing Future Forms in a Magazine Article Which verbs in this article refer to the future? Underline them. `5.8 A`

ADVICE FOR PARENTS WITH YOUNG CHILDREN

As the school year begins, you can help your child reach her goals in the classroom, stay healthy, and feel good about herself. Model these behaviors now to help your child do her best at school.

Eat breakfast. Get a healthy start to each day by eating breakfast together. It will give your whole family fuel for the day ahead.

Get plenty of sleep. This will help your family start the day alert and refreshed. It also will encourage a positive attitude through the day.

Plan ahead. By getting organized, you and your child can find the right balance of work and play. Your child will learn to manage her time better, and so will you.

Make a schedule. Sit down to plan your activities together. This will help you and your child stay involved in each other's lives.

Think about It Why do you think the writer uses *will* instead of *be going to* above?

Think about It The **bold** sentences above give advice. What do the sentences with the future form do?

34 | Giving Advice and Explanations Choose one of these topics. Write several sentences giving advice. Use a future form to give the reasons for your advice. `5.8 A`

☐ Advice for a New Student at College	☐ Advice for Saving Money
☐ Advice for Someone in a New Country	☐ Advice for Getting Good Grades
☐ How to Take Public Transportation	☐ How to Run a Successful Business

Example: Advice for a New Student at College
Advice: Get a map of the campus and go exploring.   *Reason: This will introduce you to new places at school.*

Advice	Reasons to follow this advice

Write about It Develop your ideas above into a paragraph. Look back at Activity 33 for a model.

35 | Noticing Future Forms in an Essay Circle the future forms in this essay. Underline the time clauses. Then answer the questions below. `5.8 A`

Essay Prompt: What do you hope to accomplish⁵ in the next ten years? Explain.

I want to accomplish a lot of things in the next ten years. I think that this will be a very busy time for me. The first thing I will do is complete my education. I will go to college and study to become a teacher. Getting my degree will be hard work, but it is very important to me. After I get my teaching degree, I will try to find a job in a public school. I think it will be fun to have my own students, and I will work hard to be a very good teacher. Once I have a teaching job, I will think about getting married. Hopefully my partner won't be too hard to find.

> **FYI**
>
> We can also use the simple present form of verbs such as *want, hope,* and *plan* to talk about the future.
>
> I **hope** to go to France next year.
>
> I **want** to run my own business in the future.

QUESTIONS

1. Why do you think the writer uses *will* instead of *be going to* in this essay?
2. Why do you think the writer uses the time clauses? What purpose do they serve?

Write about It What do you hope to accomplish in the next ten years? Write several sentences. Try to use a time clause in your answer.

⁵ **accomplish:** to do; to complete

36 | Identifying the Goals of an Essay Complete these essay outlines with your own ideas. `5.8 B`

Topic: How can students save money while they are going to school?

Overview Statement: This essay will present several ways that students can live cheaply while they are going to school.

The first section will _discuss several ways to save money on food._

_____

The second section will _____

_____

The third section will _____

_____

Topic: What are the problems and concerns of foreign students at universities in this country?

Overview Statement: This essay will _____

_____

The first section will _____

_____

The second section will _____

_____

The third section will _____

_____

WRAP-UP Demonstrate Your Knowledge

A | DISCUSS AND REPORT Work with a partner. Write one or two sentences to answer each question in the chart. Then read your ideas to the class.

How will communication be different in the future?	How will education be different in the future?	How will transportation be different in the future?

"In the future, people will have communication devices inside their heads. We won't need telephones or email."

B | WEB SEARCH Choose a topic from the box and do a web search about how it will be in the future. List five interesting things that you learn.

IN THE FUTURE

| cars | cities | computers | fashion | houses | schools |

C|PLAN AND REPORT Design a holiday weekend for you and your classmates. Choose a place and make a plan for each morning, afternoon, and evening. Take notes in the chart below.

PLACE _____

	Saturday	Sunday
Morning		
Afternoon		
Evening		

Describe your plan above to your classmates. Your class can then choose the best weekend plan.

"For my holiday weekend, we are going to go to Los Angeles, California. On Saturday morning, we're going to drive to Venice Beach. . . ."

5.9 Summary of Future Forms

PREDICTIONS	*will* + base form	You'**ll have** a great time. Everything **will be** fine.	
	be going to + base form	You'**re going to have** a great time. Everything **is going to be** fine.	
	be going to + base form	The weather report says it'**s going to rain** soon.	with clear evidence
		Watch out! You'**re going to fall**.	Person can't control what happens.
PLANS, PROMISES, OFFERS, AND REQUEST	*be going to* + base form	I'**m going to leave** early to pick up my children at school.	plans made in advance
	will + base form	I'**ll be** there in a minute. I just need to finish.	plans made at the moment of speaking
		I **won't be** late. I know you need me.	promises
		I'**ll come** over tonight to help.	offers of help
		Will you **wait** for me?	requests
	present progressive	We'**re leaving** in an hour.	personal plans and arrangements
	simple present	The train **arrives** at 7 tonight.	scheduled events or fixed plans

6 Modals

We must learn to live together as brothers or perish[1] together as fools[2].

—MARTIN LUTHER KING, JR., LEADER IN THE AFRICAN- AMERICAN CIVIL RIGHTS MOVEMENT (1929–1968)

Talk about It What does the quotation above mean? Do you agree or disagree?

[1] **perish:** to die   [2] **fools:** people who do silly things

WARM-UP

A | Read these conversations. Where does each one take place? Tell your classmates.

Overheard Conversations

1. A: **May** I help you with something?
   B: Yeah. Where **can** I find the laundry detergent?
   A: It's in Aisle 5.
   B: **Could** you check for me? I looked, but I **can't** find it anywhere.

2. A: I'm sorry, but you **can't** bring that bag on board.
   B: OK. So what **should** I do?
   A: You **can** give it to me. I'll check it for you.

3. A: That doesn't look right on him.
   B: He **might** want to try a smaller size.
   A: **Would** you grab one for us?
   B: Of course.

B | Answer these questions about the conversations above.

1. The words in **blue** are modals. What verb form comes after a modal?
2. How do you form a negative statement with a modal?
3. How do you form a question with a modal?
4. Is there a different form of the modal for a third-person singular subject?
5. Are these statements about the past, present, or future?

C | Look back at the quotation on page 188. Identify any modal forms.

6.1 Overview of Modals; Statements with Modals

A

WHAT IS A MODAL?

1a

	main verb	
Maria	**swims**	at the Community Center almost every day.

1b

	modal + main verb		
Maria	**can't**	**swim**	on Sundays because the pool is closed.

1c

	modal + main verb		
I think she	**should**	**swim**	on her school swim team. She's really good.

A **modal** is a kind of helping verb. It gives us more information about a **main verb**. Compare:

- Sentence **1a** uses a main verb alone to show a statement of fact.
- Sentences **1b** and **1c** use the modals **can** and **should** to give more information about the main verb *swim*.

The simple (one-word) modals are:

can	may	must	shall	will
could	might		should	would

Most modals have more than one meaning.

GRAMMAR TERM: Helping verbs (such as modals) are also called **auxiliary verbs**.

B

POSITIVE STATEMENTS

2

	modal	base form
I You He She It We You They	can should must	start.

NEGATIVE STATEMENTS

3

	modal + *not*	base form
I You He She It We You They	cannot can't should not shouldn't must not mustn't	start.

To make statements with simple modals, we use a **modal** (+ *not*) + the **base form of a main verb**, as in **2 – 3**. We use the same modal form with all subjects.

We often contract a modal and the word *not*, especially in conversation, as in **3**.

WARNING! We don't use two simple modals together. (NOT: ~~You must can start.~~)

 ONLINE

---

1 | Noticing Modals Circle the modals in these sentences. Underline the main verb that goes with each modal. `6.1 A–B`

PROFESSOR GANTRY'S TIPS FOR IMPROVING YOUR ENGLISH

1. To expand[3] your vocabulary, you (should) <u>read</u> something in English every day.

2. You can keep a vocabulary notebook to help you remember new words.

3. To improve your listening ability, you should watch TV or videos in English every day.

4. You shouldn't stop practicing your English, even during vacations.

5. If you don't know many English speakers, you can meet people online and chat with them.

6. You can keep a journal for everyday writing practice.

7. Remember that you must work hard if you want to improve.

8. Most important, you mustn't get discouraged[4]!

---

[3] **expand:** to increase   [4] **discouraged:** without confidence

Talk about It How many of the suggestions in Activity 1 do you follow? Compare ideas with a partner.

A: I read something in English almost every day.
B: That's good. I don't read something every day, but I watch TV in English.

Write about It Write two or three other ways to improve your English. Share your ideas with your classmates.

2 | Error Correction Correct any errors in these sentences but do not change the modal. (Some sentences may not have any errors.) 6.1 A–B

RULES AND REGULATIONS

1. Students must to come to class on time.

   Students must come to class on time.

2. Customers are can pay with cash or a credit card.
3. Employees don't can wear jeans to work.
4. Guests shouldn't smoking in the rooms.
5. Clerks should be polite and courteous at all times.
6. Employees not can make personal phone calls at work.
7. Students must brought a laptop to class every day.
8. A customer cannot sit in the front seat with the driver.
9. Only a customer can uses the restroom.

Think about It Based on the sentences above, check (✓) the true statements about simple modals. Then share your answers with your classmates.

TRUE

☐ We can use the word *to* directly after a modal.
☐ We can use the verb *be* before a modal.
☐ To make a modal negative, we use *not* after the modal.
☐ We can use a main verb + *-ing* directly after a modal.
☐ We can use a past verb form after a modal.
☐ We use a main verb + *-s* / *-es* after a modal after singular subjects.
☐ We use the same modal form with all subjects.

Talk about It Where might you see each of the rules above? Share your ideas with a partner.

A: The first rule is "Students must come to class on time." You probably see that rule in a class syllabus.
B: Or maybe in a student handbook.

6.2 Questions with Modals

A

YES/NO QUESTIONS

	modal	subject	base form
1	Can / Should	I you he she it we you they	start?

SHORT ANSWERS

			modal (+ *not*)
2	Yes,	you I he she it you we they	can. / should.
	No,		can't. / shouldn't.

To form *yes/no* questions with modals, we put the **modal** before the subject and use the **base form of a main verb**, as in **1**.

We can give short answers to *yes/no* questions with the modal alone, as in **2**. In negative short answers, we often use contractions.

> **WARNING!** We don't begin modal questions with other helping verbs (such as *be* or *do*).
> (NOT: ~~Do I can . . . ?~~ or ~~Are they should . . . ?~~)

B

WH- QUESTIONS

	wh- word	modal	subject	base form	
3	What	should	I	do?	
4	How	can	you	lose	the game?
5	Where	should	Tom	meet	us?
6	When	can	she	come?	
7	Why	should	people	care	about the ocean?

	subject	modal		base form	
8	Who	should		come	to the meeting?
9	What	can		go	wrong?

For *wh-* questions, we use a **wh- word** + a **modal** and the **base form of a main verb**, as in **3 – 9**.

GO ONLINE

---

3 | Identifying Questions and Statements Circle the modals and underline the main verbs in these statements and questions. Then add a period or a question mark to each one. Who says each sentence? Check (✓) your ideas. 6.2 A

AT THE DOCTOR'S OFFICE	DOCTOR	RECEPTIONIST	PATIENT
1. (Can) you please <u>take</u> a deep breath?	✓	☐	☐
2. Patients must sign in here	☐	☐	☐
3. Should I take this medicine every day	☐	☐	☐
4. Visitors can stay until 6 p.m. on weekdays	☐	☐	☐
5. You should make your next appointment now	☐	☐	☐
6. Can I speak to the doctor	☐	☐	☐
7. Should I go back to the waiting room	☐	☐	☐
8. You can go back to work next week	☐	☐	☐

4 | Using *Wh-* Questions with Modals Put the words in the correct order to make *wh-* questions. 6.2 B

ASKING FOR INFORMATION

1. should / I / when / pay / for my classes

   When should I pay for my classes?

2. I / who / should / talk to / about joining

3. I / my account balance / can / find / where

4. can/tickets/buy/we/when
5. what time/we/get in line/should
6. the receipt/we/how long/keep/should
7. my car/can/park/I/where

8. keep/how long/I/can/a book
9. should/what time/we/get together
10. she/where/sign up/can/for that class
11. can/who/a ride/me/give

Talk about It In what situations do people use each question in Activity 4? Share ideas with your classmates.

"The first question is 'When should I pay for my classes?' You probably ask that when you're registering for classes."

6.3 Permission with *Can* and *Could*

A	**GIVING AND DENYING PERMISSION**	
	1 A: Alan **can watch** TV until 5. Then he needs to clean his room before dinner. B: No problem, Mrs. Parker.	In conversation, we often use sentences with **can** to give permission, as in **1 – 2**. This means that something is allowed.
	2 A: Do you want that piece of cake? B: No, I'm full. You **can have** it.	
	3 A: Excuse me. You **can't use** your cell phone in here. B: Oh, sorry! I didn't see the sign.	We use **can't** to refuse permission or say something is not allowed, as in **3 – 4**.
	4 A: Is Tara here? B: She is, but she **can't go out** until she finishes her homework.	Notice: The contracted form *can't* is more common than the full form *cannot*, especially in conversation.

B	**ASKING FOR PERMISSION**	
	5 A: **Can I have** a copy of that article? B: Sure.	To ask for permission, we usually use **can** or **could**, as in **5 – 8**. *Could* usually sounds more polite than *can*.
	6 A: **Can** Tony **stay** for dinner? B: Of course. He's always welcome.	To respond, we usually use expressions like *Sure, Of course,* etc., as in **5 – 7**. To say no politely, we often use *sorry* and give a reason, as in **8**.
	7 A: **Could I look** at that picture again? B: Absolutely. Here you go.	
	8 A: **Could** we **use** your car this afternoon? B: Oh, sorry. I need it today.	**WARNING!** When we respond to a permission question, we don't typically use *can*. (*Yes, you can* is not very common.) Don't use *could* to respond to permission questions. (NOT: ~~Yes, you could~~ or ~~No, you couldn't.~~)

5 | Giving and Refusing Permission with *Can* and *Can't* Complete these statements with *can* or *can't* and a verb from the box. (More than one answer may be possible.) **6.3 A**

THE PERSON IN CHARGE[5]

Bus driver to passenger

1. Please move back behind the line. You _____*can't stand*_____ in this area.

2. Keep your transfer[6]. You _____ it again.

Boss to employee

3. You _____ home a little early today. We're not busy.

4. You _____ personal calls during work hours.

> bring
> buy
> come
> eat
> go
> make
> park
> stand
> start
> use

---

[5] **in charge:** responsible for someone or something

[6] **transfer:** a ticket that a passenger can use to change buses without paying again

Security guard to amusement park guest

5. This area is full right now. You _____ a new line over there along the fence.

6. I'm sorry. You _____ your food on the ride. The trash cans are over there.

Police officer to driver

7. You _____ this way. We're closing the street.

8. You _____ your car over there. See where the other cars are?

Parent to child

9. You _____ whatever you want. It's your money.

10. You _____ candy every day. It'll ruin⁷ your teeth.

bring
buy
come
eat
go
make
park
stand
start
use

Write about It What other things would the people in Activity 5 say to give or deny permission? Write more sentences for three of the people in charge. Use *can* or *can't*.

Boss: I'm sorry. You can't take tomorrow off. We have too much work to do.

6 | Pronunciation Note: *Can/Can't/Could* Listen to the note. Then do Activities 7–9.

In positive statements, we don't usually stress **can**. This means we pronounce it as /kən/ or /kn/. In negative statements, however, we usually stress **can't**. We pronounce it as /kænt°/*.

POSITIVE STATEMENTS (sounds like /kən/ or /kn/)   **NEGATIVE STATEMENTS** (sounds like /kænt°/)

1 You **can** EAT as many vegetables as you want.   3 You **CAN'T** eat dessert yet.

2 You **can** CALL me after 9.   4 You **CAN'T** call before 9.

WARNING! If you stress the word *can* in a statement, listeners may think you said *can't*.

In *yes/no* questions, we don't usually stress **can** or **could**. (We usually pronounce *could* as /kʊd/ or /kd/.) It is often difficult to hear the difference between them in informal speech.

YES/NO QUESTIONS

5 A: **Can** I use this pen? (sounds like /kən/ or /kn/)   6 A: **Could** I take a piece of paper? (sounds like /kʊd/ or /kd/)
   B: Of course.   B: Sure, no problem.

* The symbol ° means a consonant is "unreleased." For example, in the word *can't*, the final t does not make a hard t sound.

7 | Listening for *Can* and *Can't* Listen and circle the modal you hear—*can* or *can't*. 6.3 A

1. You (can) / **can't** have dessert tonight.

2. The children **can** / **can't** stay up late.

3. Students **can** / **can't** bring food to class.

4. You **can** / **can't** use your notes during the test.

5. You **can** / **can't** sell your used books.

6. Customers **can** / **can't** seat themselves.

⁷ **ruin:** to damage something so that it is no longer good

7. Passengers **can / can't** use cell phones during the trip.

8. You **can / can't** enter the building anytime after 6 p.m.

9. You **can / can't** wear T-shirts in the office.

10. Employees **can / can't** park in front of the store.

Talk about It Take turns reading the sentences in Activity 7 to a partner. Use *can* or *can't*. Your partner listens and says yes if you used *can* and no if you used *can't*.

A: You can't stay in this room.
B: No.

8 | Making Statements with *Can* and *Can't* Write *can* or *can't* to make true statements about your school. Take turns reading your sentences to a partner. Discuss any differences between your answers.

`6.3 A`

ON CAMPUS

1. You _____ study in the library after midnight.

2. You _____ make photocopies in the library.

3. Students _____ use the printer in the office.

4. You _____ check out library books for four weeks.

5. You _____ access Wi-Fi everywhere on campus.

6. You _____ buy pizza on campus.

7. Freshmen _____ register for classes before seniors.

8. You _____ pay your tuition with a credit card.

9. You _____ get food late at night.

10. You _____ buy T-shirts in the bookstore.

Write about It Write three more sentences with *can* or *can't* about your school.

🔊 9 | Listening for *Can* and *Could* Listen and circle the modal you hear in each question—*can* or *could*. Then listen again and complete the responses. `6.3 B`

1. A: (Can) / Could I take one of these menus?
   B: _Of course_____. Help yourself.

2. A: **Can / Could** I use your restroom?
   B: _____. It's back there.

3. A: **Can / Could** I call you tomorrow?
   B: _____! I'm looking forward to hearing from you.

4. A: **Can / Could** we sit at a table by the window?
   B: _____. There isn't one available.

5. A: **Can / Could** I borrow your pencil for a minute?
   B: _____. Here you go.

6. A: **Can / Could** I take the car tonight?
   B: _____. You need to study.

> **PRONUNCIATION**
>
> With short answers, we pronounce the full form of *can* and *can't*.
>
> A: Can I leave now?
> B: Yes, you **CAN**. But don't go far.

7. A: **Can** / **Could** I take the test tomorrow instead of today?

    B: _____. But you need to come in early.

8. A: **Can** / **Could** the children go upstairs?

    B: _____. But you need to go with them.

Think about It Which responses in Activity 9 are positive and which are negative? Write them in this chart.

Positive	Negative
Of course.	

Talk about It Practice the conversations in Activity 9 with a partner.

10 | Using *Can* and *Could* for Permission For each situation, write a short conversation using *can* or *could* for permission. Use at least two negative responses. 6.3 A–B

1. Car rental customer: You want to take the car out of the country, and you want your friend to be able to drive the car.

   Car rental clerk: Give or deny permission.

   Customer: Can I take this car out of the country?
   Clerk: Yes, but you'll have to pay for insurance.
   Customer: And can my friend drive the car?
   Clerk: I'm sorry. Only you can drive the car.

2. Tenant: You want to hang pictures on the walls and paint the bedroom.

   Landlord: Give or deny permission.

3. Patient: You want to take medicine in the morning instead of at night, and you want to keep exercising.

   Doctor: Give or deny permission.

4. Customer: You want to return a shirt and receive a refund.

   Store clerk: Give or deny permission.

5. Friend 1: You want to borrow a book and keep it for three days.

   Friend 2: Give or deny permission.

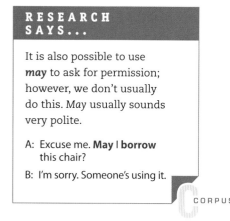

RESEARCH SAYS...

It is also possible to use *may* to ask for permission; however, we don't usually do this. *May* usually sounds very polite.

A: Excuse me. **May I borrow** this chair?

B: I'm sorry. Someone's using it.

CORPUS

Think about It Look at the conversations you wrote above. Write /kn/ over every *can* that you would pronounce without stress. Then practice your conversations and present one to the class.

6.4 Offers with *Can, Could, May,* and *'ll*

A

STATEMENTS

1 A: I **can take** you to the airport.
B: Great! Thanks!

2 A: I **could make** those calls if you want.
B: Thanks so much! I really appreciate that.

3 A: I'm going to be late for work.
B: I**'ll give** you a ride. My car is right outside.

We often use statements with **can** and **could** to make offers, as in **1 – 2**.

We also make offers with **will** using the contraction **'ll**, as in **3**.

B

QUESTIONS

4 A: **Can I open** the door for you?
B: Please!

5 A: **Could** we **help** you with that?
B: That's OK. I've got it.

6 A: **May I take** your jacket?
B: Thank you.

7 Store clerk: **How may I help** you?
Customer: I'm looking for a silver ring.

We also use questions with **can**, **could**, and **may** to make offers, as in **4 – 6**. Notice:

$$\xrightarrow{\text{MORE POLITE}}$$

can	could	may

Store clerks often use **how** with offers of help, as in **7**.

C

POSITIVE RESPONSES	NEGATIVE RESPONSES
Positive responses can be less formal, as in **8 – 9**, or more formal, as in **10 – 11**.	For negative responses, it sounds impolite to just say no. Instead, we usually use an expression like the ones in **12 – 15**.

8 A: I'll lend you my notes. B: **Thanks!**	**12** A: Can I take you home? B: **That's all right.**
9 A: May I help you put things away? B: **Yes, please.**	**13** A: I can pay for the tickets. B: **That's OK, but thanks for offering.**
10 A: I could come in early tomorrow. B: **Great. It's so nice of you to offer.**	**14** A: Could I get you a pillow? B: **That won't be necessary. Thanks.**
11 A: Could I get you a cup of coffee? B: **Thanks. I really appreciate that.**	**15** A: Can I call someone for you? B: **No, but thanks anyway.**

GO ONLINE

11 | Making Offers with *Can, Could,* and *'ll* Complete the offers. Use a subject with *can, could,* or *'ll* and a verb from the box. (More than one answer is possible.) `6.4 A`

A CLASS PRESENTATION

1. A: All right. Who wants to do the research?

   B: *I can look up* _____ the articles and other information.

2. A: Great! And then we need someone to do the writing.

   C: _____ the script.

   A: Perfect!

3. B: _____ the script—to make sure it doesn't have any mistakes.

   A: Good idea.

create	lend	read
find	look up	take
help	proofread[8]	write

[8] **proofread:** to check for mistakes

MODALS   197

4. D: I have a good camera. _____ some pictures.

   A: Oh, wonderful. But we'll need images from the Web, too.

5. E: _____ some images online.

   A: OK. Then someone needs to put it all together.

6. D: Send everything to me. _____ the presentation.

   A: Perfect! Then, once the slides are done, we need to record[9] the narration[10].

7. D: Oh, I don't have a very good microphone on my laptop.

   C: _____ you mine. _____ you with the recording, too.

   D: Thanks.

8. A: Well, I think that's everything. Send it to me when it's all finished and _____ it!

create	lend	read
find	look up	take
help	proofread	write

Talk about It Work in a group of three or four. Choose an activity from this box. Plan the activity. Take turns making offers to help. Continue until everyone has made two offers.

GROUP EVENTS AND PROJECTS

a class picnic	a field trip to a museum	a potluck lunch on campus
a community cleanup project	a grammar presentation	a study group meeting

A: What do you want to bring to the picnic?
B: I'll bring a salad.
C: I can bring a tablecloth.

12 | Noticing Offers with *Can* and *Could* Listen and complete these sentences. Then add a period or a question mark to each sentence. `6.4 A–B`

OFFERS FROM HOTEL EMPLOYEES

1. *I can* _____ carry your luggage.
2. _____ call you a taxi if you want
3. _____ offer you today's newspaper
4. _____ take a message for you
5. _____ take your bags to your room
6. _____ offer you some coffee
7. _____ move you to a different room
8. _____ help you find something
9. _____ charge[11] the bill to your room
10. _____ make a reservation for you

Talk about It Work with a partner. Choose three of the statements or questions above, and use them to create short conversations. Present one of your conversations to the class.

A: I can carry your luggage.
B: Thanks!
A: No problem.

---

[9] **record:** to save words or music using a machine
[10] **narration:** spoken words that explain what is happening

[11] **charge:** to put money you owe on a bill that you pay later

POLITE OFFERS   WHERE?

1. A: Good morning. ___May I help___ you?
   B: Yes. I need to make an appointment.

   | 1. *a doctor's office* |

2. A: _____ your coat?
   B: Thank you.

   | 2. |

3. A: _____ you something to drink?
   B: Yes. Thank you.

   | 3. |

4. A: _____ your order?
   B: Yes, please. I'll have a small salad.

   | 4. |

5. A: _____ you to your table?
   B: Thank you.

   | 5. |

6. A: _____ you a different size?
   B: Sure.

   | 6. |

7. A: _____ you find something?
   B: Yes. I'm looking for some comfortable boots.

   | 7. |

8. A: _____ these to your car for you?
   B: That won't be necessary. Thanks.

   | 8. |

Think about It Why do the speakers use *may* in each of the conversations above?

Write about It Work with a partner. Write another conversation for one of the places above. Use offers
with *may I*.

Doctor's office (on the telephone)
A: Hello. May I speak to Dr. Tam?
B: I'm sorry. He's not available. May I take a message?

🔊 **14 | Usage Note: Using Several Responses** Listen to the note. Then do Activities 15 and 16.

> When responding to an offer, we often use several expressions to give a longer (and more polite) response.
> A: Can I help you with that?   A: Can I help you with that?
> B: **Thanks. I appreciate that. It's so nice of you to offer.**   B: **That's all right, but thanks anyway. I'm OK.**

🔊 **15 | Identifying Responses** Listen to the offers and responses. Check (✓) *Yes* for positive responses
and *No* for negative responses. Then listen again and write each response. Practice the conversations
with a partner. `6.4 C`

		YES	NO
1. A: Can I get the door for you?		✓	☐
B: *Thank you. That would be great.*			
2. A: Could I help you with that?		☐	☐
B: _____			

	YES	NO
3. A: I'll dry the dishes.	☐	☐
B: _____		
4. A: Can I carry that for you?	☐	☐
B: _____		
5. A: I could take those to the office for you.	☐	☐
B: _____		
6. A: Can I call somebody for you?	☐	☐
B: _____		
7. A: We can pay for the supplies.	☐	☐
B: _____		
8. A: Can I bring you something to drink?	☐	☐
B: _____		

Think about It Which speakers in Activity 15 give shorter responses? Why? Discuss your ideas with a partner.

16 | Using Offers and Responses Work with a partner. Write a short conversation for each situation. Use *can*, *could*, *'ll*, and *may*. Then present your conversations to another pair. 6.4 A–C

WHEN PEOPLE NEED HELP

1. A: Your partner doesn't understand the homework. Offer to help.
   B: Accept the offer.

   A: Can I help you with that? I took that class last year.
   B: Thanks! That would be great. I really appreciate it.

2. A: Your friend forgot to bring money for lunch. Offer to pay for today's lunch.
   B: Refuse the offer.

3. A: Your partner looks lost. Offer to help.
   B: Accept the offer. Explain what you are looking for.

4. A: Your teacher is having trouble opening the door because she is holding a large box. Offer to carry the box.
   B: You are the teacher. Accept the offer.

5. A: You have just eaten dinner at your partner's house. Offer to help with the dishes.
   B: Refuse the offer.

6. A: Your partner has just arrived at your home. Offer something to eat or drink.
   B: Accept the offer.

7. A: The class is over and the whiteboard is covered with writing. Offer to help the teacher.
   B: You are the teacher. Accept the offer.

8. A: A friend is having difficulty opening a jar. Offer to help.
   B: Refuse the offer.

Think about It Did any of the conversations you heard above use *may I*? Was the choice appropriate? Why or why not?

6.5 Requests with *Can* / *Could* / *Will* / *Would* and *Would You Mind*

A

MAKING REQUESTS WITH *CAN* / *COULD* / *WILL* / *WOULD*

1 A: **Can** you **please turn off** the light?
B: Sure.

2 A: **Could** you **please repeat** the question?
B: Of course. . . . Where do you live?

3 A: **Will** you **help** me, **please**?
B: No problem. What can I do?

4 A: **Would** you **take** this outside for me?
B: I'm sorry. I hurt my back yesterday and I can't carry anything.

We use **can**, **could**, **will**, and **would** to make requests, as in **1 – 4**. *Could* and *would* usually sound more polite than *can* and *will*.

To make a request more polite, we can put **please** between the subject and the verb, as in **1 – 2**, or at the end, as in **3**.

> **WARNING!** We don't usually use short answers to respond to requests. (NOT: ~~Yes, I can / could / will / would.~~) We usually use expressions like *Sure*, *Of course*, etc., as in **1 – 3**.

B

MAKING REQUESTS WITH *WOULD YOU MIND*

5 A: **Would you mind working** this Saturday?
B: Not at all. What time should I come in?

6 A: **Would you mind moving** that way a little, **please**?
B: No, of course not.

7 A: **Would you mind closing** the shop today?
B: I'm sorry. I can't. I have an appointment.

We also make polite requests with **would you mind** + the **-ing form of a verb**, as in **5 – 7**. We sometimes use **please** at the end of questions with *would you mind*, as in **6**.

Notice: To agree with a request with *would you mind*, we usually use *no* or another negative word, as in **5 – 6**. It's also possible to respond with words such as *Sure* and *OK*.

GO ONLINE

17 | Listening for *Can/Could/Will/Would* in Requests Listen and complete the requests. (Some of the requests include *please*.) Then practice with a partner. `6.5 A`

REQUESTS FOR AN ADMINISTRATIVE ASSISTANT

1. A: _Would you make_____ four copies of this, please?

   B: Of course.

2. A: _____ me the file on the Jones account?

   B: Sure. I'll be right back.

3. A: _____ Martin Garcia for me?

   B: Sure. Right now?

4. A: _____ a meeting with Jill Summers?

   B: Yes, of course.

5. A: _____ the mail, please? I left it on your desk.

   B: OK.

6. A: _____ until 5:30 tonight?

   B: I'm sorry. I can't tonight. I can come in early tomorrow, though.

7. A: _____ a copy of the report? I can't find mine.

   B: No problem.

8. A: _____ tech support to come by? My computer isn't working.

   B: Sure. I'll call them now.

18 | Pronunciation Note: *Would You/Could You* Listen to the note. Then do Activity 19.

> In everyday conversation, we usually pronounce **would you** and **could you** as "wouldja" and "couldja."
>
> **1 Would you** hand me the TV remote?　　*sounds like*　　"Wouldja hand me the TV remote?"
>
> **2 Could you** open the window?　　*sounds like*　　"Couldja open the window?"

19 | Listening for Reduced Questions Listen to and repeat these questions. Then ask and answer the questions with a partner. `6.5 A`

CLASSROOM FAVORS

1. Would you help me with the homework?
2. Could you lend me a pencil?
3. Could you check my paper for mistakes?
4. Would you pronounce this word for me?
5. Would you tell the teacher that I went to the office?
6. Could you hand me a dictionary?
7. Would you trade[12] seats with me?
8. Could you explain the assignment for me?

　　A: *Would you help me with the homework?*
　　B: *We don't have any homework, do we?*

20 | Making Requests with *Would You Mind* Use the verb in parentheses to write a request with *would you mind*. Then listen to the conversations and write the responses. `6.5 B`

GETTING READY FOR A CELEBRATION

1. A: *Would you mind setting* _____ the table? (set)

   B: *Of course not.* _____

2. A: _____ these decorations? (put up)

   B: _____. Where do you want them?

3. A: _____ the napkins? (fold)

   B: _____. Which napkins?

4. A: _____ the glasses? (wash)

   B: _____, but I have to leave for a few minutes.

5. A: _____ some balloons? (blow up)

   B: _____. How many do you want?

6. A: _____ the candles on the cake? (put)

   B: _____

7. A: _____ some ice cream? I forgot to buy it. (pick up)

   B: _____. What kind do you want?

8. A: _____ the chairs? (set up)

   B: _____. I hurt my back.

---

[12] **trade:** to exchange something for something else

202

Think about It Which responses in Activity 20 are positive and which are negative? Write them in this chart.

Positive (agreeing to a request)	Negative (refusing a request)
Of course not.	

21 | Making Requests Read these requests for clarification. Rewrite each one as a question using the words in parentheses. 6.5 A–B

ASKING FOR CLARIFICATION

1. Repeat that. (can/please)

   Can you repeat that, please?

2. Spell that for me. (could/please)
3. Say that again. (would)

4. Say that more slowly. (would you mind)
5. Speak a little louder. (will/please)
6. Say that one more time. (can)
7. Repeat that. (would you mind)
8. Speak more slowly. (would/please)

Talk about It Ask a partner these questions. When your partner answers, ask for clarification using one of the questions you wrote above.

1. What's your family name?

   A: What's your family name?
   B: Reynoso.
   A: I'm sorry. Can you repeat that, please?

2. What street do you live on?
3. What city were you born in?

4. What's your phone number?
5. What was the name of your high school?
6. What is your date of birth?
7. Where are your parents from?
8. What's your favorite kind of music?
9. Who is your favorite actor?

22 | Making Polite Requests Read each informal situation. Then rewrite each conversation to fit the more formal situation. Use a polite form for every request and response. 6.5 A–B

INFORMAL SITUATIONS

1. Mother: Will you close the door when you leave?

   Son: Yeah, sure.

2. Father: Make sure the back door is locked before you go.

   Son: Uh-huh.

3. Friend 1: Could you move your chair? I can't see.

   Friend 2: OK.

4. Friend 1: Can you open the window? It's hot in here.

   Friend 2: That window doesn't open.

FORMAL SITUATIONS

1. Host: _Would you please close the door when you leave?_
   _____

   Houseguest: _Of course._ _____

2. Host: _____
   _____

   Houseguest: _____

3. Stranger 1: _____
   _____

   Stranger 2: _____

4. Stranger 1: _____
   _____

   Stranger 2: _____

INFORMAL SITUATIONS	FORMAL SITUATIONS
5. Friend 1: Could you help me with this? Friend 2: Sure.	5. Worker: _____ _____ Employer: _____
6. Co-worker 1: Could you hand me that paper? Co-worker 2: Here.	6. Worker: _____ _____ Employer: _____
7. Co-worker 1: Can you show me the new printers? Co-worker 2: They're over there.	7. Customer: _____ _____ Clerk: _____
8. Co-worker 1: Wait for me! I'll be done in a minute. Co-worker 2: OK.	8. Worker: _____ _____ Employer: _____

6.6 Desires and Offers with *Would Like*

A

STATING DESIRES

		noun phrase
1	I'd like	some coffee.

		to- infinitive	
2	I'd like	to live	in Paris.

		noun phrase	to- infinitive	
3	I'd like	my friend	to come	for dinner.

We can use **would like** to talk about desires (what someone wants). We can use *would like* with:

- a **noun phrase**, as in **1**
- a **to- infinitive**, as in **2**
- a **noun phrase** + **to- infinitive**, as in **3**

Notice the contractions with *would*:

I'd	you'd	he'd	she'd	*	we'd	they'd

* We don't contract *it would* in writing.

B

ASKING ABOUT DESIRES

4 A: **Would** you **like to live** in Europe someday?
B: Yes, **I would**. / No, **I wouldn't**.

5 A: **What would** Sara **like to study**?
B: I think she**'d like to study** medicine.

We can also use *would like* in questions to ask about desires, as in **4 – 5**.

Notice that when we use *would* in a question, we often use *would* in the answer, too.

C

MAKING OFFERS

6 A: **Would** you **like to come in**?
B: Yes, please. Thank you.

7 A: **Would** you **like some tea**?
B: **I'd love** some, thanks.

8 A: **Would** you **like me to help** you?
B: That **would be** great, thanks.

We use questions with *would you like* to offer something politely, as in **6 – 8**.

To respond to offers with *would you like*, we may use the responses listed in Chart 6.4 C, as in **6**.

We may also respond to these offers with **I'd love** . . . or **that would be** + an adjective, as in **7 – 8**.

MAKING INVITATIONS

9 A: **Would** you **like to have** lunch on Friday?
B: I'm sorry. **I'd love to**, but I have to work.

We often use *would you like to* when we make an invitation, as in **9**.

To say no politely, we often use *I'd love to, but* . . . and give a reason. (A response just with *no* may seem impolite.)

23 | Using _I'd Like_ and _I'd Like To_ Complete each conversation with _I'd like_ or _I'd like to_. Then practice with a partner. **6.6 A**

WHAT DO YOU WANT?

1. A: What do you want to do tonight?

   B: _I'd like to_ _____ go to that new restaurant.

2. A: How can I help you?

   B: _____ two pounds of fish.

3. A: Can I help you?

   B: _____ try on these pants.

4. A: Can I get something for you?

   B: _____ a smaller size, please.

5. A: Good morning. Law Offices.

   B: _____ speak to Mr. Chavez.

6. A: Mr. Chavez is out of the office right now.

   B: _____ leave a message.

7. A: Can I help you find something?

   B: _____ this sweater in red, please.

8. A: Do you need something?

   B: _____ see that paper again.

9. A: Do you want to go to Café Royale?

   B: I think _____ try a new place this week.

10. A: _____ have one of those robot vacuum cleaners.

    B: I wonder how well they work.

> **F Y I**
>
> We can also talk about offers with _want_. However, _would like_ is more polite.
>
> A: What do you want to do tonight?
> B: I **want to go** to that new restaurant.

24 | Using _Would Like_ + Noun Phrase + _To-_ Infinitive Write ten sentences using information from this chart and your own ideas. **6.6 A**

I'd like	movie theaters my friend radio stations textbook writers the administration the cafeteria the management the new student the teacher	to begin . . . to bring . . . to explain . . . to help . . . to make . . . to offer . . . to open . . . to play . . . to prepare . . . to show . . .

I'd like the administration to explain the new schedule.

Talk about It Share some of the sentences you wrote above with a partner. Do you want any of the same things?

A: _I'd like the administration to explain the new schedule._
B: _Me too! I don't understand it._

25 | Talking about Desires with *Would Like* Complete the questions using the verbs in parentheses and *would like*. Write your answer. 6.6 B

1. A: What city _____ *would you like to visit* _____? (visit)

   B: _____

2. A: What famous person from history _____

   to? (talk)

   B: _____

3. A: What famous living person _____? (meet)

   B: _____

4. A: What moment in your life _____? (repeat)

   B: _____

5. A: Where _____ on vacation? (go)

   B: _____

6. A: What _____ for dinner tonight? (eat)

   B: _____

7. A: What superpower[13] _____? (have)

   B: _____

8. A: Where _____ in ten years? (be)

   B: _____

9. A: What other languages _____? (learn)

   B: _____

10. A: What special talent[14] _____? (have)

    B: _____

> **F Y I**
>
> Sometimes *would like* expresses a wish. This may be something possible or impossible.
>
> **Possible**
>
> I'd like to visit Beijing.
>
> **Impossible**
>
> I'd like to talk to Napoleon.

Talk about It Ask a partner the questions above. After your partner answers, ask for more information.

A: What city would you like to visit?
B: I think I'd like to go to Beijing someday.
A: Why?

26 | Making Offers with *Would You Like* Complete these conversations with *would you like to*, *would you like*, or *would you like me to*. Then practice with a partner. 6.6 C

AT A RESTAURANT

1. A: _*Would you like to*_ look at the menu?

   B: Please.

2. A: _____ a salad?

   B: No, just the sandwich.

3. A: _____ bring you some water?

   B: That would be great.

4. A: _____ some dessert?

   B: No, thanks. I'm stuffed[15].

[13] **superpower:** an imaginary ability, such as being very strong, flying, or becoming invisible

[14] **talent:** a natural ability to do something well
[15] **stuffed:** full (informal)

5. A: _____ take these plates?

   B: Yes, please. We're all finished.

6. A: _____ sit near the window?

   B: Yes, perfect.

7. A: _____ anything else?

   B: Just the check, thanks.

8. A: _____ a table or a booth[16]?

   B: A booth, if there's one open.

Talk about It Work with a partner. Take turns asking the questions in Activity 26 again. Give your own responses.

A: Would you like to look at the menu?
B: No, thanks. I'll just have coffee.

27 | Identifying Offers and Desires Listen and complete these conversations. Add a period or a question mark. Then practice with a partner. `6.6 A–C`

AT A CLOTHING STORE

1. Clerk: Can I help you?

   Customer: Yes. *I'd like to* _____ see this in blue.

2. Clerk: _____ keep the hangers

   Customer: Sure.

3. Clerk: _____ a different color

   Customer: No, I think I'll look for something else.

4. Customer: _____ try this on

   Clerk: OK. You can go on into the fitting room.

5. Clerk: Can I help you with anything else?

   Customer: _____ look at some accessories—

   maybe a belt or some jewelry

6. Customer: I don't really like these sleeves.

   Clerk: _____ look for a different style for you

7. Clerk: _____ hold this for you

   Customer: That would be great, thanks.

8. Clerk: _____ help you find something else

   Customer: No, thanks. I'm fine for now.

Think about It Label each sentence you completed above as *D* (desire) or *O* (offer). Then compare with your classmates.

"'I'd like to see this in blue' is a desire."

---

[16] **booth:** a table with benches in a restaurant

28 | Offering Help Write two offers of help for each picture. Remember: Besides *would like*, we can also use *can*, *could*, *may*, and *'ll* to make offers. See Chart 6.4 for more information. `6.6 C`

Talk about It With a partner, choose a role for each picture above. One of you is a person in a picture, and the other is offering help. Role-play a conversation. Don't look at the offers you wrote.

> A: *Can I help you with the door?*
> B: *Yes, please!*
> A: *No problem.*

29 | Making Invitations Work with a partner. One person invites the other to do something from the list on the left. The other person accepts. Then change roles. (Use the information in the boxes to begin and accept.) `6.6 C`

1. have dinner with me

> A: *Are you doing anything tonight?*
> B: *No, not really.*
> A: *Would you like to have dinner with me?*
> B: *That sounds great!*

2. work in my group
3. sit next to me
4. watch a movie with me
5. come to a football game
6. join my group for lunch
7. study together after school
8. go to the park with me

BEGINNING AN INVITATION

Are you busy later today?   Are you doing anything tonight?
Are you free on Saturday?   Do you have plans this weekend?

ACCEPTING AN INVITATION

I'd love to.   That would be great.
Sure. What time?   Yeah. That sounds like fun.

Talk about It Role-play several of the invitations above again. This time, turn down the invitations by saying, "I'm sorry. I'd love to, but . . ." and giving an excuse.

6.7 Preferences with *Would Rather* and *(Would) Prefer*

A

WOULD RATHER* VS. *WOULD PREFER
 	
 1 A: Do you want to go out tonight?
    B: No, **I'd rather stay** home.
 	
 2 A: Would you like some coffee?
    B: **I'd rather not have caffeine** at this hour.
 	
 3 A: Do you know when you want to meet?
    B: Well, **I'd prefer a morning this week** if that works
      for you.
 	
 4 A: Would you like coffee or tea?
    B: **I'd prefer coffee.** Thanks.
	When we prefer one situation to another, we often use *would rather (not)* + the **base form of a main verb**, as in **1 – 2**.
	
	 When we prefer one thing to another, we can use *would prefer* + a **noun phrase**, as in **3 – 4**.
	
	 Notice: It is common to contract *would* as *'d*, especially in everyday conversation.
	
	 For information on using *prefer* + a gerund or *to-* infinitive, see Unit 7, pages 230 and 236.

B

GENERAL PREFERENCES: *WOULD RATHER* AND *PREFER*
 	
 5 Todd **would rather wear jeans than** dress up.
 	
 6 I **would rather watch basketball than** watch baseball any day.
 	
 7 Tina **prefers raspberries to strawberries.**
    (NOT: ~~Tina would prefer raspberries to strawberries.~~)
 	
 8 A: Do you like tea?
    B: Not really. I **prefer coffee to tea.**
    (NOT: ~~I would prefer coffee to tea.~~)
	When we prefer something in general, we can use *would rather*, as in **5 – 6**. We rarely use *would prefer* in this way. Instead, we use *prefer* + a **plural count noun** or **noncount noun**, as in **7 – 8**.
	
	 When we state two choices, we use:
	
	 • *would rather* A **than** B, as in **5 – 6**
	
	 • *prefer* A **to** B, as in **7 – 8**

C

ASKING QUESTIONS ABOUT PREFERENCES
 	
 9 A: **Would you rather live in a cold place or** a
      warm place?
    B: I'd rather live in a warm place.
 	
 10 A: **Would** you **prefer white or wheat bread?**
     B: Wheat, please.
 	
 11 A: Do you **prefer warm weather or cool weather?**
     B: I **prefer warm weather.**
	We can ask about preferences using *would rather*, *would prefer*, and *prefer*. We often use **or** to offer a choice in these questions, as in **9 – 11**.

30 | Using *I'd Rather* and *I'd Prefer* Underline the uses of *I'd rather* and circle the uses of *I'd prefer* in the responses on the right. Then match each sentence on the left with a response. **6.7 A**

1. Would you like to have a picnic? _g_

2. Do you want to have dinner at 9 tonight? ____

3. Let's get pizza for lunch. ____

4. I'd like to go to the beach today. ____

5. What do you think of your phone? ____

6. Do you want to go shopping? ____

7. Do you want to go to a baseball game tonight? ____

8. Do you like this book? ____

a. I don't know. I think I'd rather stay home.

b. Yes, but I'd prefer one with more activities.

c. Can we do something else? I'd rather not spend money.

d. It's OK but I'd prefer a larger screen.

e. I'd rather not*. I have a sunburn.

f. Actually, I'd prefer an earlier time, if that's OK.

g. I'd rather not eat outside. It's kind of cold.

h. I'd prefer Chinese food, if you don't mind.

Talk about It Work with a partner. Take turns reading the sentences on the left above. Give a new response. Try to use *I'd rather* or *I'd prefer*.

---

* I'd rather not can be a polite way to say no to a suggestion.

31 | Stating Preferences Complete this survey with *to* or *than*. Then check (✓) *True* or *False*. `6.7 B`

Survey: What Is Your Work Style?

		TRUE	FALSE
1. I would rather work with others ___*than*___ work alone.		☐	☐
2. I prefer a quiet workplace _____ a noisy one.		☐	☐
3. I'd rather work indoors _____ outdoors.		☐	☐
4. I'd rather wear casual clothes _____ dress up.		☐	☐
5. I prefer a neat desk _____ a messy one.		☐	☐
6. I'd rather work with computers _____ talk to people.		☐	☐
7. I'd rather write _____ work with numbers.		☐	☐
8. I prefer busy days at work _____ slow days.		☐	☐

Write about It Compare your answers to the survey above with a partner. Then write about any differences between you and your partner.

I prefer busy days at work but Maria prefers slow days.

32 | Questions about General Preferences Complete these questions with *would you rather* or *do you prefer*. Add two questions of your own. `6.7 C`

Moving? Take Our Housing Survey

1. ___*Would you rather*___ live in an apartment or a house?
2. _____ downtown or the suburbs¹⁷?
3. _____ live on a busy street or a quiet street?
4. _____ live in a single-story home or a home with two floors?
5. _____ carpeting or wood floors?
6. _____ electric appliances or gas appliances?
7. _____ have a yard or a swimming pool?
8. _____ modern homes or older homes?
9. _____
10. _____

FYI

When two choices repeat the same information, we often omit the repeated words.

Would you rather **live in a cold place** or (live in) **a warm place**?

Do you prefer **busy days at work** or **slow days** (at work)?

Talk about It Ask and answer the questions above with a partner.

A: Would you rather live in an apartment or a house?
B: I think I'd rather live in an apartment.
A: Really? Why?
B: I don't want to take care of a yard.

¹⁷ **suburbs:** parts of a city away from downtown, usually with a lot of houses and not many businesses

6.8 Advice with *Should*, *Ought To*, and *Had Better*

A

1 You **should try** the new café. It's fantastic.

2 It's nice to see you. We **ought to visit** more often.

3 You**'d better hurry**. You're going to miss the meeting.

We make suggestions or give advice with **should**, **ought to**, and **had better**, as in **1 – 3**.

Notice: We usually shorten *had better* to *'d better*, as in **3**, especially in speaking.

B

SHOULD

4 You **should call** your mother. She's lonely.

5 You **shouldn't drink** so much soda. It's bad for you.

6 **Should** I **apply** for this scholarship?

7 What **should** I **take** for a sore throat?

OUGHT TO

8 You **ought to try** these strawberries. They're fantastic.

We use *should (not)* to give advice or to say that something is a good idea, as in **4 – 5**. We also use *should* to ask for advice, as in **6 – 7**.

Ought to is similar to *should*, but we use it much less often, as in **8**. Notice:

| ought to | + | the base form of a verb |

WARNING! We do not usually use *ought to* in negative statements or questions.

C

ADVERBS FOR SOFTENING ADVICE

9 You **should probably call** him tomorrow.

10 You **probably ought to read** the instructions.

11 **Maybe** you **should take** the other class.

12 **Perhaps** you **should call** a lawyer.

We sometimes use the adverbs **probably**, **maybe**, and **perhaps** to soften advice we give. Notice:

• We can use **probably** after *should*, as in **9**.

• We can use **probably** before *ought to*, as in **10**.

• We can use **maybe** and **perhaps** at the beginning of a sentence, as in **11 – 12**.

Perhaps is less common and sounds more formal.

D

HAD BETTER

13 Mother to son: You **had better be** home by 11.

   (= If you aren't home by 11, you're going to get in trouble.)

14 They**'d better finish** the roof soon. It's going to rain next week.

15 I**'d better not stay** any longer. I'm going to be late!

We use *had better (not)* to give strong advice, as in **13 – 15**.

We often use *had better* to emphasize that something needs to happen soon. It often suggests that if the person doesn't follow the advice, something bad will happen.

WARNING! *Had better* does not refer to the past, even though it uses *had* (the past of *have*).

33 | Noticing Advice Underline the advice in this conversation with *should*, *ought to*, and *had better*. `6.8 A`

VISITING A FRIEND

1. A: I'm so glad you're finally coming to see me! Be sure to bring some jeans and good walking shoes.

   B: OK. Are we going hiking or something?

   A: Yes, on Friday. But <u>you should also bring some nice clothes</u>. I made reservations at a really good restaurant for Saturday night.

2. B: Do I need to bring bedding[18]?

   A: No, don't worry about that. My roommate is gone for the weekend. You should probably bring an extra pillow, though. I think she took hers with her.

3. B: So what else are we doing?

   A: Well, it's up to you. Do you want to go shopping? Or would you rather do something like go to a museum? We've got a great science museum.

   B: Both of those sound good to me.

   A: Well, we won't have time for it all . . . you really ought to visit more often!

[18] **bedding:** sheets, blankets, and pillows

4. B: Maybe I should come again in the summer.

   A: That's a great idea! Come in July. I have two weeks off, and it'll be much warmer and drier. Oh, that reminds me: you'd better bring an umbrella. We've been getting a lot of rain lately.

5. B: I'll do that. Listen, I'd better start packing. I'll call you when I land, OK?

   A: Great! Can't wait to see you!

Think about It Is there any other advice in the conversation in Activity 33 that DOESN'T use a modal form?

34 | Using *Should* and *Shouldn't* for Advice Read this advice. Complete the sentences with *should* or *shouldn't* and an appropriate verb. **6.8 B**

Living with Your Roommates: Tips for Getting Along

1. If you have concerns[19], you _____*should talk*_____ to your roommates about them. Communication is important.

2. Talk about what "clean" means. Different people have different ideas about cleanliness. You and your roommates _____ this issue to prevent[20] misunderstandings.

3. Make a cleanup schedule, and put it where everyone will see it every day. You _____ the schedule regularly so that one person isn't always doing the same job.

4. Check with your roommates before you put up pictures or decorations. One roommate _____ these decisions alone. Everyone needs to agree.

5. You _____ dirty dishes in the sink where they can attract[21] insects and other pests. You _____ always _____ your dishes right away.

6. You don't need to tell your roommates about everything you do, but you _____ them if you're going to be gone so they don't worry.

7. Respect each other's property. You _____ your roommates' food or borrow your roommates' clothes without permission.

8. Deal with problems right away. If you aren't happy about something, you _____ your roommates immediately. Otherwise, the problems will probably become worse.

Write about It Write three more tips for roommates like the ones above. Then share them with your classmates.

---

[19]**concerns:** worries or problems
[20]**prevent:** to stop something from happening

[21]**attract:** to make someone or something come somewhere

35 | Asking Questions with *Should* Use *should*, a subject, and a verb from the box to ask for advice about each situation. Then practice with a partner. `6.8 B`

1. A: Can you please go to the supermarket for me?

   B: What _____ *should I get* _____?

2. A: Now, don't stay out too late, OK?

   B: Well, what time _____ home?

3. A: You really need to get another job.

   B: I know, but what kind of job _____?

4. A: I think you need to get some advice.

   B: Who _____?

5. A: You sound terrible. There's some cough syrup in the cabinet.

   B: Good idea. How much _____?

6. A: Could you please call Andrea for me?

   B: _____ her cell?

7. A: Could you bring some chairs in from the other room?

   B: Sure. How many _____?

8. A: The company has really been doing well lately.

   B: Oh yeah? _____ the owner for a raise?

9. A: The new neighbors seem nice.

   B: Yeah, they do. _____ them over for dinner?

10. A: I wonder why the teacher isn't here yet.

    B: No idea. How long _____ for him?

ask
bring
call
come
get
invite
look for
take
talk to
wait

Talk about It Work with a partner. Choose a place from this box. Ask for and give advice for that place.

classroom	doctor's office	mall	school office	train station

Classroom
A: Where should I sit?
B: You should sit in front.

36 | Using Adverbs with *Should* and *Ought To* Rewrite each sentence in the correct order. `6.8 C`

HOW TO MAKE FRIENDS

1. with other people/you/probably/ought to/more time/spend

   You probably ought to spend more time with other people.

2. should/a club/probably/you/join

3. perhaps/join/a study group/should/you

4. you/to/more people/perhaps/introduce yourself/should

5. should/you/be/a little friendlier/maybe

6. volunteer somewhere/you/ought to/perhaps

7. a little more often/should/smile/maybe/you

8. you/ought to/go/maybe/to more social[22] events

Think about It The adverbs in the advice in Activity 36 make it softer. Why and when would we want our advice to be softer?

Write about It Write three more pieces of advice about making friends. Then share them with your classmates.

37 | Using *Had Better* Listen and complete these conversations. Then practice with a partner. **6.8 D**

SHORT ON TIME

1. A: They're waiting for me outside.

   B: _You'd better go._____

2. A: The door says "Private."

   B: OK. _____ here, then. I'm sure she'll

   come out pretty soon.

3. A: _____. I've got a lot to do this afternoon.

   B: OK. It was nice seeing you again!

4. A: _____. I think my boss is coming back.

   B: OK. Call me later.

5. A: They're going to run out of those jeans at that price.

   B: You're right. _____ early tomorrow.

6. A: Why isn't Jack here yet?

   B: I don't know. But _____ a good excuse.

7. A: What's he yelling about?

   B: I don't know. But _____ in there. He'll yell at you, too.

8. A: I'm going to the SuperStore.

   B: _____. They close in a half an hour.

9. A: The car is all fixed now.

   B: _____ about that. It took long enough.

10. A: _____! We're leaving in a couple of minutes.

    B: I'm coming. I'm coming.

> **PRONUNCIATION**
>
> It is often difficult to hear the **'d** in sentences with **had better**.
>
> We say: "You better go."
> We write: You**'d better** go.

Write about It Write four conversations using the sentences in this box. Practice them with a partner.

I'd better get going.	We'd better stay here.	You'd better be careful.	You'd better hurry.

A: Do you know what time it is?
B: It's 3:00.
A: Oh! I'd better get going.
B: OK. See you later.

[22]**social:** connected to doing things with other people

6.9 Suggestions with *May / Might / Could* and Other Expressions

A

COULD, MIGHT, AND MAY **1** You **could wait** until tomorrow. **2** **Maybe** you **could try** again tomorrow. **3** You **might want to think about** that a little more. **4** You **may want to try** that again.	We often use **could** (or **maybe** . . . **could**) to make suggestions, as in **1 – 2**. We also sometimes use the phrase **might / may want to** to make polite suggestions, as in **3 – 4**. In this case, *might* and *may* have a meaning similar to "maybe."

B

WHY DON'T / LET'S / HOW ABOUT / WHAT ABOUT **5** A: **Why don't** you **wear** the blue tie? B: Really? Do you think it looks OK? **6** A: **Why doesn't** Bob **wash** dishes while we make dessert? B: OK. What can I do?	We also use other non-modal expressions to make suggestions. We can use **why don't / doesn't** to make suggestions, as in **5 – 6**.
7 A: So, where should we go for dinner? B: **Let's try** the new Thai place. **8** A: I'm pretty hungry. B: OK. **Let's go out** right now.	We use **let's** to suggest an activity for you and another person, as in **7 – 8**. *Let's* is a short form of *let us*. We rarely use the full form.
9 A: What should I make for lunch? B: **How about a tuna sandwich?** **10** A: Who should I call? B: **What about Martin?** I think he can help you. **11** A: **How about taking a walk with me?** B: That sounds good. **12** A: I don't know where to take my aunt. B: **What about taking her to the History Museum?**	We use **how about** and **what about** to make suggestions—often to respond to a request for a suggestion. They are followed by: • a **noun phrase**, as in **9 – 10** • the **-ing form of a verb**, as in **11 – 12**

38 | Making Suggestions with *Could* and *Might/May Want To* Read these instructions from a teacher to students. Imagine that you have a friend who is not doing well in class. Change the instructions to polite suggestions. Rewrite each sentence with *could*, *might want to*, or *may want to*. **6.9 A**

Having Trouble?
Here's How to Improve Your Grades

1. Form a study group.   *You might want to form a study group.*
2. Do fewer extracurricular activities[23].
3. Take better notes in class.
4. Do the practice problems at the end of the chapter, even if the teacher didn't assign them.
5. Do the reading early, so you have time to reread.
6. Proofread and rewrite your essays before you turn them in.
7. Look for online help.
8. Get a tutor.

F Y I

Sometimes we make suggestions with **might** (without *want to*):

You **might try** the asparagus. I hear it's delicious.

---

[23] **extracurricular activities:** school activities that are not part of the regular class schedule

Write about It Write two suggestions for succeeding in your English class. Share them with your classmates.

39 | Making Suggestions with *Why Don't* Complete these conversations with suggestions, using your own ideas. Then practice with a partner. `6.9 B`

1. A: I need **some new boots**.

   B: Why don't *you try Robert's? They're having a sale.* _____

   A: Sounds good. Let's go!

2. A: I'm so **tired**.

   B: Why don't _____

   A: I probably should.

3. A: Khalid has **a headache**.

   B: Why doesn't _____

   A: That's a good idea. I think I'll suggest that to him.

4. A: I need **a new phone**.

   B: Why don't _____

   A: Good idea.

5. A: I can't hear **the TV very well**.

   B: Why don't _____

   A: Could you do it for me, please?

6. A: Sara doesn't have **anything to do tonight**.

   B: Why doesn't _____

   A: OK, I'll invite her.

7. A: My **computer** isn't working.

   B: Why don't _____

   A: Yeah. I'll probably do that.

8. A: I can't find **my phone**!

   B: Why don't _____

   A: OK. I'll try that.

I need a
new phone.

My computer isn't working.

Talk about It Replace the **bold** words in each conversation above with your own ideas. Make new conversations with a partner.

A: *I need a new computer.*
B: *Why don't we go to OfficeWorld? I need some printer ink.*
A: *Sounds good. Let's go!*

40 | Making Suggestions with *How About/What About* and *Let's* Complete each conversation with a suggestion, using your own ideas. Then practice with a partner. `6.9 B`

1. A: I don't know which classes to take next semester.

   B: How about _____?

2. A: I don't know what to make for dinner.

   B: What about _____?

3. A: My cousin is coming to visit. Where should I take her?

   B: What about _____?

4. A: What should we do tonight?

   B: I don't know. Let's _____.

5. A: Who should we invite to the concert?

   B: How about _____?

6. A: I'm so hungry.

   B: Let's _____.

Talk about It Work with a partner. Choose one of the conversations in Activity 40 (or a similar idea), and continue the conversation. Partner A, reject Partner B's first suggestion. Then present your conversation to another pair.

A: *I don't know which classes to take next semester.*
B: *How about calculus?*
A: *I don't think I need any more math classes.*
B: *Then maybe you could take a business class.*
A: *That's a good idea. I'll do that.*

41 | Giving Advice and Making Suggestions Write three suggestions for each person's problem. Use *should, had better, may/might want to, why don't*, and *what/how about*. `6.9 A–B`

PROBLEMS

1. I can't get to sleep at night. When I lie down in bed, I just can't stop thinking about things. It takes me hours to fall asleep.

   You should try some breathing exercises. Or you might want to play some soft music.

2. I have a co-worker who keeps talking to me while I'm working. It's very annoying. I try not to be very friendly with him, but he doesn't get the hint[24].

3. I'm having trouble getting my homework done because I'm addicted to the Internet. I turn on my computer to study, and pretty soon I'm watching videos and chatting with friends.

4. I'm always losing things. I leave my sweater in the classroom all the time, last week I lost my car keys, and now I can't find my wallet!

5. I have a friend who only calls me when she has a problem. I don't hear from her for weeks and weeks, and then she'll call and ask for help with something.

Write about It Write about a problem that you or someone you know has. Exchange papers with a partner, and write two suggestions or pieces of advice for each other.

[24]**hint:** something that you say, but not in a direct way

6.10 Obligation with *Must, Have To, Had To,* and *Have Got To*

A

MUST (NOT)

1 Schools **must pay** taxes on that income. It is required by law.

2 The government **must cut** spending by 17 percent, or the city will be in trouble.

3 Employees **must not park** in the customer lot.

4 You **mustn't worry** about it.

We use **must**—mostly in writing—to say that something is necessary or is required, as in **1 – 2**.

We use **must not** to say something is not allowed or to strongly advise against something, as in **3 – 4**. We can contract *must not*, as in **4**, but it is not common.

WARNING! Using *must* in this way sounds very formal. We rarely use *must* with this meaning in spoken English.

B

HAVE TO

5 You **have to choose** one of these colors.

6 Everyone **has to help** with the laundry.

7 **Do** you **have to cook** tonight?

8 Why **does** she **have to leave** so early?

9 You **don't have to carry** those books. I'll take them later if you want.

Have to / *has to* also expresses necessity or requirement, as in **5 – 9**. It is much more common than *must* in speaking.

Have to is a **phrasal modal**. Unlike simple modals, *have to* / *has to* must agree with the subject.

We use *do* / *does* to form questions and negatives with **have to**, as in **7 – 9**.

HAD TO

10 A: **Did** he **have to work** late yesterday?
   (NOT: ~~Must he work late yesterday?~~)
   B: No, he didn't. But he **had to work** late on Tuesday.

We use *had to* and *didn't have to* to talk about things that were or were not necessary in the past, as in **10**.

C

DON'T HAVE TO VS. MUST NOT

11a He **doesn't have to park** the car. I'll be right back.
   (This is not necessary. It's a choice.)

11b You **must not park** in a fire lane. (This is not allowed.)

The negative form of **have to**, as in **11a**, means "not necessary." This is not the same meaning as **must not. Must not** means something is not allowed or not advisable, as in **11b**.

D

HAVE GOT TO

12 People are not completing their work on time, and that **has got to change**.

13 I**'ve got to pick up** my brother after school.

14 I **don't have to be** at work until 10.
   (NOT: ~~I don't have got to . . .~~)

We also use *have* / *'ve got to* to say that something is necessary, as in **12 – 13**. It is very common in speaking.

We don't use *have got to* in questions or negative sentences. Instead, we use a form of *have to*.

42 | Using *Must* and *Must Not* Read about the problems in the staff break room. Write a list of rules. Use *must* and *must not*. `6.10 A`

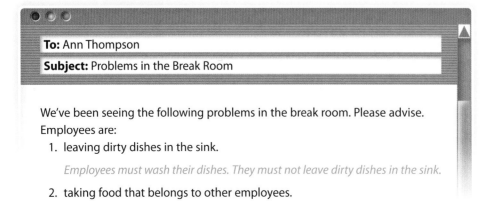

To: Ann Thompson

Subject: Problems in the Break Room

We've been seeing the following problems in the break room. Please advise. Employees are:

1. leaving dirty dishes in the sink.

   Employees must wash their dishes. They must not leave dirty dishes in the sink.

2. taking food that belongs to other employees.

Employees are (*continued*):

   3. leaving old lunches in the refrigerator.

   4. not cleaning up spills in the microwave.

   5. leaving crumbs on the table.

   6. finishing the coffee and not making a new pot.

   7. not returning to work on time.

   8. leaving the lights and the television on when no one is in the room.

43 | Using *Have To/Don't Have To* Use *have to/not have to* to talk to a partner about rules for driving. Use these phrases. Do you and your partner agree on the rules? `6.10 B`

DRIVING

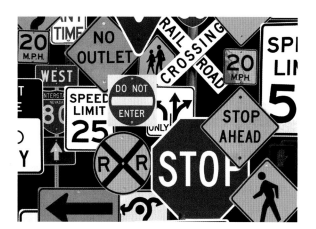

   1. follow the rules of the road

     A: Everyone has to follow the rules of the road.

     B: Well, police officers don't always have to follow them.

   2. wear a seat belt in the back seat

   3. use your headlights in the daytime

   4. go 15 miles per hour near schools

   5. stop at all four-way intersections[25]

   6. stop for ambulances

   7. register[26] your car every year

   8. learn to drive from a professional driving instructor

44 | Using *Have To* and *Had To* Complete these air travel conversations with positive and negative forms of *have to* or *had to* + a subject if necessary. Then practice with a partner. `6.10 B`

AIRPORT AND AIRPLANE CONVERSATIONS

   1. Passenger 1: ___*Do I have to*___ check this bag?

     Passenger 2: I'm not sure. It looks pretty big. It _____ fit under the seat if you want to take it on the plane.

     Passenger 1: Well, I _____ check it last time I flew; they let me put it in an overhead compartment.

   2. Passenger: Where _____ check in?

     Clerk: You already have your boarding pass. You _____ check in. Just go straight to the gate.

   3. Passenger: Why _____ pay for lunch? I _____ pay on this airline last year.

     Flight attendant: Maybe you were on a longer flight? We offer a free meal on flights over six hours long. I can bring you some peanuts. You _____ pay for those.

---

[25] **intersections:** places where two or more roads meet and cross each other   [26] **register:** to put a name on an official list

4. Passenger 1: Hey, what happened?

Passenger 2: My plane was late. I _____ run all the way across the airport to make my connection. I sure hope my bag doesn't get lost.

Passenger 1: Well, the airline _____ pay for your bag if they lose it.

Passenger 2: I'd rather have my bag!

45 | Using *Have To/Don't Have To* and *Must Not* Write sentences about air travel with *have to*, *don't have to*, and *must not*. Use these phrases. `6.10 B–C`

AIRLINE RULES

1. bring knives onto the airplane

   Passengers must not bring knives onto the airplane.

2. turn off your phone during takeoff
3. get out of your seat when the seat belt light is on
4. get a boarding pass
5. carry identification
6. pay for coffee or tea
7. buy a ticket for a baby
8. follow the pilot's instructions

Think about It Look at the sentences you wrote above that use *have to*. In which sentences could you change *have to* to *must*? Why?

Write about It Write four more sentences about air travel like the ones above. Use *must, must not, have to,* and *don't have to.*

46 | Using Modals of Obligation Write four sentences about each profession. Use *have to/don't have to* and *must/must not*. Then compare ideas with your classmates. `6.10 B–C`

JOB REQUIREMENTS

1. doctors
2. teachers
3. accountants
4. professional athletes
5. chefs
6. firefighters
7. computer programmers
8. administrative assistants

Doctors have to go to school for a long time.
Doctors must have a license.

47 | Pronunciation Note: *Got To* Listen to the note. Then do Activity 48.

In speaking, we often pronounce **got to** as "gotta." However, we don't write "gotta."

1 I have got to go.	*can sound like*	"I've **gotta** go."
2 She has got to try harder.	*can sound like*	"She's **gotta** try harder."
3 He has got to understand.	*can sound like*	"He's **gotta** understand."

It is also sometimes difficult to hear the **'ve** in sentences with **have got to**.

4 I have got to go.	*can sound like*	"I **gotta** go."

48 | Using *Have Got To* Look at Mika's calendar. Talk to a partner about what she *has got to/doesn't have to* do. Pay attention to the pronunciation of *got to*. `6.10 C–D`

	Sunday	Monday	Tuesday	Wednesday	Thursday	Friday	Saturday
morning		work 8–12	take Tim to doctor	work 8–12	do homework	clean house	garden
evening	do laundry	go to accounting class		go to accounting class		have dinner with the Wangs	

"On Sunday evening, Mika's got to do laundry."　　　*"She doesn't have to do anything on Tuesday evening."*

Talk about It Complete the calendar for yourself. Tell a partner what you've got to do this week. Pay attention to the pronunciation of *got to*.

	Sunday	Monday	Tuesday	Wednesday	Thursday	Friday	Saturday
morning							
evening							

Write about It Write three sentences about the schedule you made above and three sentences about your partner's schedule. Use *have/has got to* and *don't/doesn't have to*.

49 | Error Correction Correct any errors in these sentences. (Some sentences may not have any errors.)

1. Everyone must to work hard so we can finish on time.

   Everyone must work hard so we can finish on time.

2. I've got get home early today.
3. We must not pay for the concert. It's free.
4. Do the parents must come to the ceremony[27]?
5. He doesn't got to make dinner. I'll do it.
6. She hasn't to come to work early this week. The office is opening late.
7. You don't have to copy a friend's software. It's against the law.
8. Last year, we must pay an entrance fee[28], but it's not required anymore.

---

[27]**ceremony:** a formal event, such as a graduation　　　[28]**fee:** the money you pay to do something

6.11 Using Modals and Related Forms in Speaking

A	**ASKING FOR PERMISSION TO SPEAK OR INTERRUPT** **1** I'm sorry. **Can I say** something? **2 Can I tell** you something? **3** Excuse me. **Could I ask** you a question? **4** I'm sorry. **May I interrupt** for a moment? **5 May I speak** to you for a minute?	We often use the modals **can** and **could** as a polite way of interrupting someone or beginning to speak, as in **1 – 3**. We also use **may** in a similar way, as in **4 – 5**. However, *may* is more formal and less common.
	INTRODUCING RELATED IDEAS **6** A: I don't know how I'm going to finish all the papers we have to write this semester. B: Yes, and **how about** the class project? A: I know! It's a lot of work.	We can use the expressions **how about** and **what about** to introduce a related idea to a conversation, as in **6**.
B	**MAKING A POLITE REQUEST** **7** A: **Can I ask you** to speak a little louder? B: Sure. Can you hear me now? **8** A: **Could I ask you** to close the window? B: Of course. **9** A: **May I ask you** to be a little quieter? B: Oh, sorry!	To make a request more polite, as in **7 – 9**, we sometimes use: | Can Could May	I ask	+	you	+	to- infinitive | We often make requests like these in formal situations and to ask for something difficult or uncomfortable.
C	**USING REDUCED FORMS IN SPEAKING** **10** would you — *sounds like* — "wouldja" **11** could you — "couldja" **12** should you — "shouldja" **13** have got to — "ve gotta" **14** has got to — "sgotta" **15** have to — "hafta" **16** has to — "hasta"	We often use reduced forms with modals in speaking, as in **10 – 16**. **WARNING!** We do not write reduced forms. (NOT: ~~I hafta complete my application by April 1.~~) (NOT: ~~Wouldja please submit your reference by April 1.~~)

GO ONLINE

50 | Asking for Permission to Speak Listen to these conversations and complete the requests. Then practice with a partner. **6.11 A**

1. A: Excuse me, Professor. _Can I ask you_ something?

   B: Yes, of course. What is it?

2. A: Mrs. Taylor?

   B: Yes?

   A: _____ after class?

3. A: . . . and at that point it looked as if the people were going to—

   B: I'm sorry. _____

   A: Sure. What is it?

4. A: Um. _____ something?

   B: Uh-huh.

5. A: So then I told her that I didn't really think that was a good idea, and—

   B: I'm sorry. _____ for a second?

6. A: That was the most boring book I've ever read.

   B: Are you kidding? I loved it! I thought it was really funny.

   A: No way! How about the part when—

   C: Wait. _____

   A: What?

7. A: Excuse me. _____ for a moment?

   B: Of course. Come on in.

8. A: I was telling my friend that he—

   B: Excuse me. I'm sorry. _____

51 | Having a Group Discussion Work in a group. As a group, choose one of these topics to discuss. As you are talking, use the expressions in the box to add new ideas or interrupt. [6.11 A]

1. a local sports team
2. a current news event
3. a famous person
4. a movie or TV show
5. what you're studying right now

> How about/What about . . . ?
> Can I say something?
> Could I ask a question?
> May I speak for a minute?

A: The Panthers played really well last weekend. They got a goal right away.
B: Yeah, and how about when they scored again? Just after halftime.
C: Can I ask you something?
A: Sure.

52 | Asking for a Favor Write a request for a favor for each situation. Use *can*, *could*, or *may* and a *to-* infinitive. Then compare ideas with a partner. [6.11 B]

1. Your professor is speaking very fast.

   I'm sorry. Can I ask you to speak more slowly?

2. You are leaving a restaurant. You drop your keys and they land under someone else's table.
3. You are trying to study in the library and someone is humming.
4. You meet an author and you want him to sign your book.
5. You are trying to hear a lecture, and someone near you is making a lot of noise.
6. You are at a movie and someone sits down in front of you. She is wearing a large hat.
7. Someone calls you when you are very busy.
8. You want to eat lunch at a table in the cafeteria. Someone has spread books and papers all over the table.
9. You want something at the market that is on a high shelf. There's a tall person standing next to you.
10. You forgot your glasses and can't see from the back of the classroom. All of the seats in front are taken.

53 | Listening for Reduced Modals Listen to these conversations and write the missing words, including the subject and the full form of the modal + verb. Then practice with a partner. Use reduced forms. `6.11 C`

1. A: _Could you bring_____ me the flashlight? I can't see what I'm doing.

   B: Sure.

2. A: _____ at 6:00.

   B: OK.

3. A: _____ earlier tomorrow.

   B: OK. I'll tell him.

4. A: _____ these to Sarah? I think she needs them.

   B: No problem.

5. A: When _____ back to the doctor?

   B: In about two months.

6. A: _____ you something.

   B: Yeah? What is it?

7. A: _____ about that already.

   B: How? I didn't tell her.

8. A: Why do _____ this?

   B: The boss wants us to.

6.12 Contrasting Modals in Speaking and Writing

The uses of the modals described in this unit are more common in speaking than in writing.

A

In everyday conversation, we often choose more informal modals or similar expressions, as in **1a – 4a.**

	MORE INFORMAL
1a	I **want to inquire** about the receptionist job.
2a	**Can** you please **send** me the form?
3a	**Can** you **help** me?
4a	Please **call** me at 401-555-0134.

When we do use the modals from this unit in writing, we often choose a more polite form, as in **1b – 4b.**

	MORE POLITE
1b	I **would like to inquire** about the receptionist job.
2b	**Could** you please **send** me the form?
3b	I **would appreciate** your help.
4b	**Could** you please **call** me at 401-555-0134?

B

USING *MAY* FOR PERMISSION IN WRITING

5 Passengers **may use** the bike rack on the back of the bus.

6 Passengers **may not bring** bicycles onto the bus.

We rarely use *may* for permission in speaking. When we do, it usually sounds very formal and unnatural. However, we do use *may* in writing to give and refuse permission, as in **5 – 6.**

 GO ONLINE

---

54 | Making Requests in Writing Rewrite these sentences so that they are appropriate for more formal writing. `6.12 A`

WRITTEN CORRESPONDENCE

1. Please let us use your letter in our advertising.

   Would you please let us use your letter in our advertising?

2. I want to meet with you about a possible salary increase.

3. Can I return this item?

4. I want to ask about any internship possibilities.

5. Please reply as soon as possible.

6. Will you call me at your earliest convenience?

7. Can you look at the enclosed documents?

8. I want to receive the information as soon as possible.

9. Let me know if you have any questions.

10. Will you send me your contact information?

Write about It Choose one of these situations, and write a short email to your professor making a request. Make sure to explain clearly who you are, exactly what you want, and why. Thank him or her.

| a letter of recommendation | extra-credit homework | more time to complete an assignment |

55 | Using *May/May Not* Use these phrases to write about what students *may* and *may not* do at your school or in your class. Share your sentences with a partner. **6.12 B**

School Rules

1. smoke on campus
2. take food into the library
3. bring coffee into the classroom
4. use cell phones during class
5. wear a hat in the classroom
6. speak without raising their hands
7. miss more than five classes
8. contact their instructors at home

1. *Students may not smoke on the central campus.*

Write about It What rules would you add to the ones above? Write two more rules for your school. These can be rules that exist or that you think should exist. Then share your ideas with your classmates.

WRAP-UP Demonstrate Your Knowledge

A | SURVEY Ask five classmates these questions and write down their answers. Ask them for the reasons for their answers. (You can ask follow-up questions.)

1. Do you prefer ice cream or cake?
2. Would you rather have an ordinary home in an exotic place or an extraordinary home in an ordinary place?
3. Would you like to travel to outer space?
4. Would you rather be unusual or completely average?
5. Do you prefer early mornings or late nights?
6. Would you like to know your future?
7. Do you prefer classical music or pop music?
8. Would you like to be really famous?
9. Would you rather win $1 million or get your dream job?
10. Would you like to be able to read minds[29]?

Compare answers with a partner. Are there similarities in the answers you got?

[29] **read minds:** to know what other people are thinking

B | BROCHURE Create a short guide to your city. Think about what you would recommend to a visitor. Tell him or her where to go, what to bring, and how to act. Then create your guide. Include both pictures and text if possible. Then present your guide to your classmates.

"Hong Kong is a great city to visit. It's a very international city—a lot like London or New York. You usually have to get a visa to travel to Hong Kong, but that's pretty easy to do. You shouldn't visit during the summer because there are often cyclones. I think the best time to visit is between October and December. When you arrive, you should get . . . "

Tips for Traveling in Hong Kong

 You shouldn't visit Hong Kong during the summer. There are often cyclones. The best time to visit is between October and December.

 You should get an Octopus Card after you arrive. This is a quick and easy way to pay for the public transport system.

C | PERSONAL REFLECTION Compare your childhood to adulthood. Think about these questions. Then explain your experience (orally or in writing) to your classmates.

1. What chores did/do you do?
2. What was/is your bedtime?
3. Who prepared/prepares your food?

4. Who was/is in charge of your schedule?
5. Who earned/earns money to support you?
6. Who made/makes the decisions for you?

When I was a kid, I was always in a hurry to grow up. Life seemed easier then. I didn't have to worry about a lot. I had to do some chores—like cleaning my room and taking out the garbage. But my parents took care of me. . . .

D | ROLE-PLAY Work with a partner. Write a conversation for each picture. Use the modals from this unit. Include five or six lines in each conversation.

1.
2.
3.

4.
5.
6.

Server: Can I bring you something to eat?
Woman: Yes. I'd like a salad.
Man: Could I get a hamburger with no tomato?
Server: Of course. Would you like anything else?

With your partner, practice your favorite conversation in Activity D. Perform your conversation for the class without reading it. As you listen to other students' role-plays, write down the modals you hear and their uses. For example: *can–permission, should–advice, would you–request.*

6.13 | Summary of Modals I

MODALS	USES	EXAMPLES
can	Permission	**Can** I **bring** my bicycle onto the bus? I'm sorry. You **can't bring** your coffee into class.
	Offers	**Can** I **help** you with that box? It looks heavy.
	Requests	**Can** I **have** a napkin? I spilled something here.
could	Permission	Excuse me. **Could** I **ask** you a question?
	Offers	**Could** I **give** you a ride somewhere? I **could open** that package for you.
	Requests	**Could** you **go** to the store for me? I don't have time today.
	Suggestions	Maybe you **could ask** a friend for help.
had better **('d better)**	Strong Advice Warning	You **had better hurry**! Everyone is leaving soon. You**'d better not try** that again. It's dangerous.
have to (phrasal modal)	Obligation / Lack of Necessity	He **has to take** one more test. Then he's finished for the year. He gave me the tickets. I **didn't have to pay** for anything. I couldn't go out last night because I **had to work**.
may	Permission	**May** I **use** your phone? I left mine in the car.
	Offers	**May** I **help** you with that?
	Suggestions	You **may want to ask** your teacher for help. You **may not want to take** that class—it's very difficult.
might	Suggestions	You **might want to wear** a coat. It's going to get cold tonight. You **might not want to sit** there. The seat is wet.
must	Obligation / Prohibition	Employees **must wash** their hands before returning to work. Employees **must not wear** jeans or sandals.
ought to	Advice	You **ought to try** this game. It's really fun.
will ('ll)	Offers	I**'ll bring** you a sandwich.
	Requests	**Will** you **take** these downstairs for me?
would ('d)	Offers	**Would** you **like** some fruit?
	Desires	I**'d love** some ice cream. Thank you.
	Requests	**Would** you **move** a little to the left? **Would** you **mind** repeating that?
	Preferences	**Would** you **prefer** a sandwich or a salad? I**'d prefer** a salad.
		Would you **rather eat** later? No, I**'d rather eat** now.

7 Gerunds and *To-* Infinitives

By failing to prepare,
you are preparing to fail.

—BENJAMIN FRANKLIN, WRITER,
SCIENTIST, AND STATESMAN
(1706–1790)

Talk about It What does the quotation above mean? Do you agree or disagree?

WARM-UP

A Read these statements and check (✓) *True* or *False* for you. Then compare answers with a partner. How are you the same or different?

WHAT ARE YOUR LIKES AND DISLIKES?

	TRUE	FALSE
1. I enjoy **shopping**.	☐	☐
2. I don't mind **getting up early in the morning**.	☐	☐
3. I love **to watch old movies**.	☐	☐
4. I like **to sing**.	☐	☐
5. I hate **being late**.	☐	☐
6. I'm not interested in **traveling**.	☐	☐
7. I don't like **to exercise**.	☐	☐
8. I can't stand **to eat vegetables**.	☐	☐

B The green phrases in the statements above are gerunds. The blue phrases are *to-* infinitives. Based on the examples, are these statements true or false? Check (✓) your answers.

	TRUE	FALSE
1. A gerund can be one *-ing* word or a group of words with an *-ing* word.	☐	☐
2. A *to-* infinitive includes *to* + the base form of a verb.	☐	☐
3. Both a gerund and a *to-* infinitive can follow the main verb in a sentence.	☐	☐
4. A gerund can follow a preposition (e.g., *by, in, of*).	☐	☐
5. A *to-* infinitive can follow a preposition.	☐	☐

C Look back at the quotation on page 228. Identify any gerunds or *to-* infinitives.

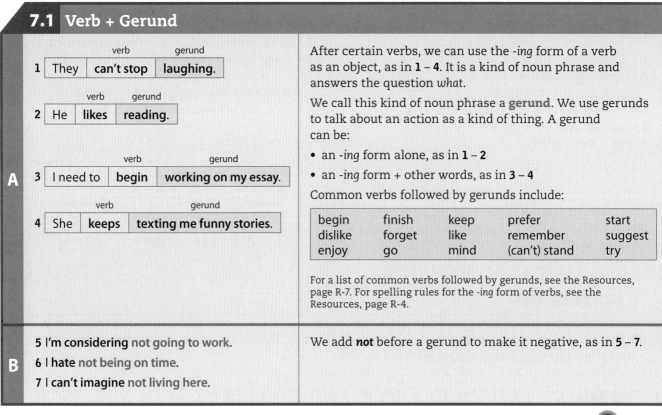

7.1 Verb + Gerund

A

	verb	gerund
1	They **can't stop**	**laughing.**

	verb	gerund
2	He **likes**	**reading.**

	verb	gerund
3	I need to **begin**	**working on my essay.**

	verb	gerund
4	She **keeps**	**texting me funny stories.**

After certain verbs, we can use the *-ing* form of a verb as an object, as in **1 – 4**. It is a kind of noun phrase and answers the question *what*.

We call this kind of noun phrase a **gerund**. We use gerunds to talk about an action as a kind of thing. A gerund can be:

- an *-ing* form alone, as in **1 – 2**
- an *-ing* form + other words, as in **3 – 4**

Common verbs followed by gerunds include:

begin	finish	keep	prefer	start
dislike	forget	like	remember	suggest
enjoy	go	mind	(can't) stand	try

For a list of common verbs followed by gerunds, see the Resources, page R-7. For spelling rules for the *-ing* form of verbs, see the Resources, page R-4.

B

5 I'm **considering** not going to work.

6 I **hate** not being on time.

7 I **can't imagine** not living here.

We add **not** before a gerund to make it negative, as in **5 – 7**.

1 | Using a Verb + Gerund in Conversation
Complete these conversations with the *-ing* form of the verb in parentheses. Then practice with a partner. `7.1 A`

1. A: I really enjoyed _____*meeting*_____ you. (meet)

   B: Me too.

2. A: Are you busy?

   B: No, we just finished _____. (eat)

3. A: Should I get a new computer? My old one is so slow.

   B: You know, I'd suggest _____. I think there might be a sale soon. (wait)

4. A: Do you have that book I lent you?

   B: I don't remember _____ a book from you. (borrow)

5. A: Amanda looks awfully worried these days. What's going on?

   B: I don't know, but I think she's going to quit her job.

   A: But I thought she liked _____ there. (work)

6. A: Why are you in such a hurry?

   B: What do you mean? You know I can't stand _____ late. (be)

7. A: Shhh. Stop _____! (talk)

   B: What's the matter?

   A: I just heard a strange noise.

8. A: Would you like me to drive now?

   B: Not yet. I can keep _____ for a while. (go)

> **PRONUNCIATION**
>
> In everyday conversation, you may hear some English speakers pronounce *-ing* as *-in'*.
>
> Just quit **thinking** about it.
> (may sound like "thinkin'")
>
> She keeps **saying** the same thing.
> (may sound like "sayin'")

9. A: I'm going to buy a magazine.

   B: Well, don't be long. They're going to begin _____ the airplane

   in a few minutes. (board[1])

10. A: When are you going to start _____ an apartment? (look for)

    B: Next week.

11. A: Does anyone know the answer to the question? Khalid? What do you think?

    B: Would you mind _____ the question? (repeat)

12. A: Would you ever want an office job?

    B: Never! I really dislike _____ all day. (sit)

Think about It Circle the gerunds in Activity 1. Then write each gerund under the correct group in this chart.

A gerund can be an *-ing* form alone.	A gerund can be an *-ing* form + other words.
	meeting you

Think about It Look at the examples in the chart above. What kinds of other words can follow an *-ing* form?

2 | Asking Questions with a Verb + Gerund Complete these questions with the *-ing* form of the verb in parentheses. **7.1 A**

Personal Questions

1. Do you enjoy _____*cooking*_____? (cook)

2. Did you like _____ to school as a child? (go)

3. When did you begin _____ English? (study)

4. Did you start _____ any sports as a child? (play)

5. What is one thing you can remember _____ angry about? (get)

6. What do you usually do after you finish _____ dinner? (eat)

7. What do you suggest _____ for a headache? (take)

8. Is there anything you can't stand _____? (do)

Talk about It Ask a partner the questions above. Then tell the class one thing you learned about your partner.

"Ben doesn't enjoy cooking."

[1] **board:** to get on a bus, train, ship, plane, etc.

3 | Usage Note: *Go* + Gerund Read the note. Then do Activity 4.

> We often use ***go*** + a **gerund** for types of fun activities and recreation.
>
> | | | |
> |---|---|---|
> | **go** camping | **go** jogging | **go** shopping |
> | **go** exploring | **go** riding | **go** swimming |
> | **go** hiking | **go** running | **go** walking |

4 | Using *Go* + Gerund Complete the questions below with a word or phrase from the box. Use the *-ing* form of the **bold** verb. (Many different questions are possible.) **7.1 A**

camp (in the woods)	**hike** (in the mountains)	**shop** (for clothes)	**swim** (in the ocean)
explore (in your city)	**jog** (in the morning)	**shop** (for food)	**walk** (with friends)

YOUR HABITS AND YOUR TOWN

1. How often do you go _____?
2. Where do you usually go _____?
3. When did you last go _____?
4. Where did you last go _____?
5. Where can you go _____?
6. Do you enjoy going _____?
7. Do you ever go _____?
8. Would you like to go _____ someday?

Talk about It Ask a partner the questions you wrote above. Then tell the class one thing you learned about your partner.

"Maria never goes jogging."

5 | Using *Not* + Gerund Complete these sentences with the *-ing* form of the verb in parentheses. Use *not* where appropriate to make the sentences true. **7.1 B**

PEOPLE'S PREFERENCES

1. Most children love _____ candy. (eat)
2. Most children dislike _____ to bed early. (go)
3. Most children start _____ around age 1. (walk)
4. Most students like _____ a midterm test. (have)
5. Most students prefer _____ lots of homework every night. (do)
6. Many people prefer _____ alone. (travel)
7. Most people dislike _____ on holidays. (work)
8. Most doctors recommend _____. (exercise)
9. Some doctors recommend _____ after 8 p.m. (eat)

Write about It Write six sentences about what you *love, dislike, prefer,* or *recommend.*

I dislike going to bed early.

6 | Error Correction Correct any errors in these sentences. (Some sentences may not have any errors.)

1. She didn't remember she meets me.
2. I finished study at 8 and went out.
3. I like learned languages a lot.
4. We continued walk for a while.
5. I do not like be alone.
6. My grandfather continued worked until he was 80.
7. Many children start learn a second language when they are very young.
8. He speaks English well because he began studied at a young age.
9. I hope you don't mind to answer this question.
10. You can't avoid to make mistakes when you speak a second language.

7.2 Preposition + Gerund

	PREPOSITION + GERUND	
A	1 He left **without** saying anything. 2 You can improve your grades **by** studying more. 3 You can learn a lot **from** traveling.	We sometimes use the **prepositions** *without*, *by*, and *from* + a **gerund** to answer the question *how*, as in **1 – 3**.
B	ADJECTIVE + PREPOSITION + GERUND 4 I'm **tired of** watching this. 5 Aren't you **sick of** working on this? 6 I'm **shy about** giving orders.	Certain adjectives go together with specific prepositions. We often use a gerund after these **adjectives** + **prepositions**, as in **4 – 6**. For a list of common adjectives + prepositions followed by gerunds, see the Resources, page R-8.
C	VERB + PREPOSITION + GERUND 7 I don't **feel like** cooking tonight. 8 She's **thinking about** quitting her job. 9 We **look forward to** seeing them.	Certain verbs go together with specific prepositions. We often use a gerund after these **verbs** + **prepositions**, as in **7 – 9**. For a list of common verbs + prepositions followed by gerunds, see the Resources, page R-8.

 GO ONLINE

7 | Using a Preposition + Gerund Match the first part of each sentence on the left with a preposition + gerund on the right. (More than one answer may be possible.) **7.2 A**

EDUCATION

1. You won't do well on tests __d__
2. You can't learn a foreign language ____
3. You will learn a lot ____
4. You won't make your teacher happy ____
5. You can make your teacher happy ____

a. by coming to class on time.
b. by skipping class.
c. without practicing.
d. without studying.
e. from taking notes in class.

HEALTH

6. You probably won't lose weight ____
7. Your skin can turn orange ____
8. You can get lung cancer[2] ____
9. You can damage your skin ____
10. You can lose weight easily ____

f. by eating less.
g. from eating too many carrots.
h. from smoking cigarettes.
i. without exercising.
j. by sitting in the sun.

[2] **cancer:** a serious disease

Write about It Think of a different way to complete the first part of each sentence in Activity 7. Use *without, by,* or *from* + a gerund.

You won't do well on tests by not studying.

8 | Using an Adjective + Preposition + Gerund Write ten meaningful questions using ideas from this chart. Use each gerund in the right column only once. (Many different questions are possible.) `7.2 B`

	Adjective + preposition		Gerund		
Are you	afraid of capable of good at	interested in nervous about tired of	becoming a doctor? being a student? doing puzzles? giving speeches?	getting hurt? listening? teaching?	being a chef in a restaurant? running a business? saying something stupid?

Talk about It Ask a partner the questions you wrote above.

A: Are you interested in becoming a doctor?
B: Do you mean a medical doctor? No, not really.

9 | Using a Verb + Preposition + Gerund Complete each set of sentences with a verb + preposition from the box. `7.2 C`

1. It's getting late. We should _____*think about*_____ going to bed.
2. Elderly people often _____ falling down.
3. We should probably _____ going swimming. It's too cold.
4. Students often _____ having too much homework.

complain about
forget about
think about
worry about

5. Lots of young people _____ becoming an actor or musician.
6. Did you ever _____ doing something that you didn't do?
7. Most people don't _____ working when they are sick.

admit to
dream of
feel like

8. What do you _____ doing next year?
9. Are you going to _____ getting better grades?
10. Some parents don't _____ using physical punishment[3].
11. You should _____ being late to class.

apologize for
believe in
plan on
work on

12. My friends and I _____ doing scary things, but we never actually do them.
13. What can you _____ starting a fire?
14. It's dark outside, but I'm going to _____ looking for my lost watch.

keep on
talk about
use for

Write about It Write sentences about yourself using four of the verbs + prepositions above with gerunds.

I sometimes think about changing schools.

---

[3] **physical punishment:** hitting someone because he or she did something bad

10 | Using a Preposition + Gerund in Conversation Underline the gerunds. What comes before each gerund? Circle the form and check (✓) your answers. Then practice with a partner. `7.2 A-C`

	PREPOSITION ALONE	ADJECTIVE + PREPOSITION	VERB + PREPOSITION
1. A: What's the matter? B: Nothing really. I'm just (tired of) <u>watching this</u>.	☐	✓	☐
2. A: Are you doing anything special for the holiday? B: Yeah. I'm thinking of having some friends over.	☐	☐	☐
3. A: What are you planning on doing tomorrow? B: I'm probably just going to stay home.	☐	☐	☐
4. A: I need to leave early tomorrow. B: OK, but don't go without saying goodbye.	☐	☐	☐
5. A: Did you call David back? B: No. I don't feel like talking to him right now.	☐	☐	☐
6. A: You're really good at making presentations. B: You think so? A: Yeah.	☐	☐	☐
7. A: Are you still looking for an apartment? B: Yes, but I don't have much hope of finding one.	☐	☐	☐
8. A: I'm excited about working together. B: Me too.	☐	☐	☐
9. A: Are you going home soon? B: No, I'm going to keep on studying for a while.	☐	☐	☐

11 | Stating Ideas with Gerunds Complete these sentences with your own ideas. Use gerunds. `7.2 B-C`

ALL ABOUT ME

1. I'm good at _____.
2. I'm afraid of _____.
3. I sometimes worry about _____.
4. I'm not capable of _____.
5. I dream of _____.
6. As a child, I sometimes complained about _____ _____.
7. I often feel like _____.
8. I think people should apologize for _____ _____.

> **W A R N I N G !**
>
> Be careful not to confuse a verb + the preposition *to* (which is followed by a gerund) with a *to*- infinitive (*to* + the base form of a verb).
>
> I **look forward to** seeing you.
> (NOT: ~~I look forward to see you.~~)
> I **want to see you later.**

Talk about It Compare your ideas above with your classmates. Make a list of all your different ideas.

I'm good at . . . organizing things
playing soccer
spending money

7.3 Verb + To- Infinitive

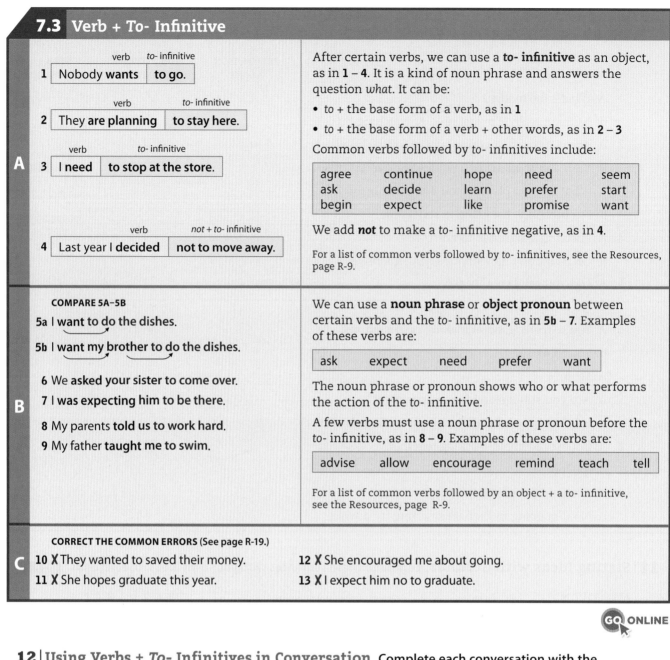

A

	verb	to- infinitive
1	Nobody **wants**	**to go.**

	verb	to- infinitive
2	They **are planning**	**to stay here.**

	verb	to- infinitive
3	I **need**	**to stop at the store.**

	verb	not + to- infinitive
4	Last year I **decided**	**not to move away.**

After certain verbs, we can use a **to- infinitive** as an object, as in **1 – 4**. It is a kind of noun phrase and answers the question *what*. It can be:

• *to* + the base form of a verb, as in **1**

• *to* + the base form of a verb + other words, as in **2 – 3**

Common verbs followed by *to*- infinitives include:

agree	continue	hope	need	seem
ask	decide	learn	prefer	start
begin	expect	like	promise	want

We add **not** to make a *to*- infinitive negative, as in **4**.

For a list of common verbs followed by *to*- infinitives, see the Resources, page R-9.

B

COMPARE 5A–5B

5a I **want to do** the dishes.

5b I **want my brother to do** the dishes.

6 We **asked your sister to come over.**

7 I **was expecting him to be there.**

8 My parents **told us to work hard.**

9 My father **taught me to swim.**

We can use a **noun phrase** or **object pronoun** between certain verbs and the *to*- infinitive, as in **5b – 7**. Examples of these verbs are:

ask	expect	need	prefer	want

The noun phrase or pronoun shows who or what performs the action of the *to*- infinitive.

A few verbs must use a noun phrase or pronoun before the *to*- infinitive, as in **8 – 9**. Examples of these verbs are:

advise	allow	encourage	remind	teach	tell

For a list of common verbs followed by an object + a *to*- infinitive, see the Resources, page R-9.

C

CORRECT THE COMMON ERRORS (See page R-19.)

10 ✗ They wanted to saved their money.

11 ✗ She hopes graduate this year.

12 ✗ She encouraged me about going.

13 ✗ I expect him no to graduate.

12 | Using Verbs + *To*- **Infinitives in Conversation** Complete each conversation with the *to*- infinitive form of a verb from the box. Then practice with a partner. **7.3 A**

1. A: Do you want _____*to do*_____ something tonight?

   B: Sure. Let's eat out somewhere.

2. A: Is Hassan still sick?

   B: Yes, but I think he's starting _____ a little better.

3. A: Can I start the meeting?

   B: Go ahead. Everyone seems _____ here.

4. A: What's the matter?

   B: I can't continue _____ with Mika. She's driving me crazy.

5. A: I'll see you later.

   B: Yes, I hope _____ you soon.

be
do
feel
see
work

6. A: How did you learn _____ a car?

   B: My father taught me.

7. A: Are you ready?

   B: For what?

   A: Come on. You agreed _____ me with my homework.

   B: OK. OK.

8. A: I thought you were going to a movie.

   B: I decided _____.

9. A: What did you get Anna for her birthday?

   B: Do you promise _____ her?

   A: Of course.

10. A: Are you leaving soon?

    B: No, I expect _____ here for another hour.

be
drive
(not) go
help
(not) tell

🔊 **13 | Pronunciation Note: *To*** **Listen to the note. Then do Activities 14 and 15.**

> With a *to-* infinitive, we usually pronounce **to** like /tə/ or sometimes just /t/. It can be difficult to hear.
>
> **1** She wants **to learn to speak** Chinese.   *sounds like*   "She wants /tə/ learn /t/ speak Chinese."
>
> When **to** is the last word in a sentence, speakers pronounce its full sound. It sounds like /tu/.
>
> **2** A: Did you pay the rent?
>   B: Oh, no. I forgot **to**.

🔊 **14 | Pronouncing *To-* Infinitives** **Listen to each question and write the verb + *to-* infinitive you hear. Then practice saying the questions.** `7.3 A`

YOUR SCHEDULE

1. Where do you _____*expect to be*_____ at this time tomorrow?

2. Where do you _____ tomorrow?

3. What do you _____ tonight?

4. Who do you _____ tomorrow?

5. What do you _____ in the morning?

6. Where do you _____ the afternoon tomorrow?

7. When do you _____ tomorrow?

8. When do you _____ a vacation?

9. What do you _____?

10. How many times a day do you _____?

Write about It **Write answers to the questions above. Use complete sentences.**

1. I expect to be at home at this time tomorrow.

15 | Listening for a Verb (+ Noun Phrase) + *To*- Infinitive Listen and check (✓) the sentence you hear. `7.3 B`

1. ☐ a. I don't want to do the dishes.
   ☑ b. I don't want him to do the dishes.

2. ☐ a. She doesn't want to go.
   ☐ b. She doesn't want them to go.

3. ☐ a. They didn't ask to help.
   ☐ b. They didn't ask us to help.

4. ☐ a. My brother doesn't need to be there.
   ☐ b. My brother doesn't need me to be there.

5. ☐ a. I expect to call her at noon.
   ☐ b. I expect her to call at noon.

6. ☐ a. Do you want to go with them?
   ☐ b. Do you want me to go with them?

7. ☐ a. Did she ask to come over?
   ☐ b. Did she ask him to come over?

8. ☐ a. Do you want to go somewhere?
   ☐ b. Do you want her to go somewhere?

9. ☐ a. Do you want to stay?
   ☐ b. Do you want me to stay?

10. ☐ a. When do they expect to get there?
    ☐ b. When do they expect you to get there?

Talk about It Work with a partner. Read a sentence in each pair above. Ask your partner to say "sentence A" or "sentence B."

16 | Using a Verb (+ Noun Phrase) + *To*- Infinitive Use each quotation to write a new sentence. Some sentences will need a noun phrase before the *to*- infinitive, and some will not. `7.3 B`

REPORTING STATEMENTS

1. Toshi: "I don't expect my brother to help."

   Toshi doesn't expect _his brother to help_____.

2. Emma: "I expect to be there by 7."

   Emma expects _____.

3. Kate: "I want John to read something."

   Kate wants _____.

4. Carlos: "I really want to see that movie."

   Carlos _____.

5. Sam: "I need someone to give me a ride to school."

   Sam _____.

6. Mary: "I advised David to get there early."

   _____

7. Isabel: "I told my brother to do his homework."

   _____

8. Rob: "I encouraged Amanda to take the job."

   _____

9. Sarah: "I taught my sister to ride a bike."

   _____

10. Matt: "I really don't want to leave."

    _____

17 | Using a Verb + Noun Phrase + *To-* Infinitive Write six meaningful questions using ideas from the chart. (Many different questions are possible.) [7.3 B]

EXPECTATIONS

		advise allow ask encourage expect need tell want		
What do What should	parents children teachers students	advise allow ask encourage expect need tell want	their children their parents their students their teachers	to do?

What do children need their parents to do?

Talk about It Ask a partner the questions you wrote above.

A: What do children need their parents to do?
B: They need their parents to keep them safe.

18 | Error Correction Correct any errors in these sentences. (Some sentences may not have any errors.)

1. We hoped getting there early.
2. I helped they to move to a new apartment.
3. He doesn't want lose his job.
4. They invited her about going.
5. They expected he to do well in school.
6. I never offered him to help.
7. My parents gave us lots of advice. For example, they told to work very hard.
8. We must encourage to be good students and listen carefully.

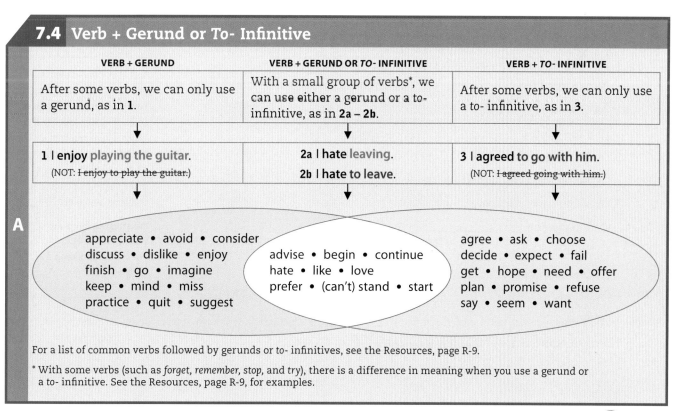

7.4 Verb + Gerund or *To-* Infinitive

VERB + GERUND	VERB + GERUND OR *TO-* INFINITIVE	VERB + *TO-* INFINITIVE
After some verbs, we can only use a gerund, as in **1**.	With a small group of verbs*, we can use either a gerund or a to-infinitive, as in **2a – 2b**.	After some verbs, we can only use a to- infinitive, as in **3**.
1 | enjoy playing the guitar. (NOT: ~~I enjoy to play the guitar.~~)	**2a | hate leaving.** **2b | hate to leave.**	**3 | agreed to go with him.** (NOT: ~~I agreed going with him.~~)

A

appreciate • avoid • consider
discuss • dislike • enjoy
finish • go • imagine
keep • mind • miss
practice • quit • suggest

advise • begin • continue
hate • like • love
prefer • (can't) stand • start

agree • ask • choose
decide • expect • fail
get • hope • need • offer
plan • promise • refuse
say • seem • want

For a list of common verbs followed by gerunds or to- infinitives, see the Resources, page R-9.

* With some verbs (such as *forget, remember, stop,* and *try*), there is a difference in meaning when you use a gerund or a *to-* infinitive. See the Resources, page R-9, for examples.

19 | Listening for a Verb + Gerund or *To*- Infinitive Listen and complete these conversations. Then practice with a partner. `7.4 A`

1. A: Why didn't you ask me for help?

   B: You know I _____*hate to ask*_____ for help.

2. A: What do you _____ tomorrow?

   B: Nothing special.

3. A: How do you like that book?

   B: I don't know. I just _____ it.

4. A: Why do you _____ your brother?

   B: Because I'm worried about him.

5. A: Why can't I go out tonight?

   B: Because you _____ your homework.

6. A: Let's have dinner here tonight.

   B: Are you sure? I don't mind going out.

   A: No, really. It's no problem. I _____.

7. A: Are you ready to leave?

   B: Give me 20 more minutes.

   A: I _____ this but we are going to be late.

8. A: Why did you turn the TV off?

   B: Because I _____ reality TV shows. They're terrible.

Why didn't you ask me for help?

Think about It In which of the conversations above could you use either a gerund or a *to*- infinitive?

20 | Gerund or *To*- Infinitive? Complete these conversations with the gerund or *to*- infinitive form of the verb in parentheses. (More than one answer may be possible.) Then practice with a partner. `7.4 A`

1. A: I hope you feel better tomorrow.

   B: Me too. I hate _____*being*_____ sick. (be)

2. A: How was your trip?

   B: I can't begin _____ it. (describe)

3. A: How's John doing?

   B: Better. He even started _____ a bit. (eat)

4. A: Where are you going?

   B: I just want _____ some fresh air. (get)

5. A: Where's Anna?

   B: She didn't plan _____ with me. (come)

6. A: Would you mind _____ me a soda from the fridge? (get)

   B: Sure.

7. A: I'm worried about that test tomorrow.

   B: I know. I don't even like _____ it. (think about)

8. A: I hate my job.

   B: Well, maybe you should consider _____ a new one. (look for)

> **F Y I**
>
> We usually avoid using two *-ing* forms right next to each other (one as a progressive main verb and one as a gerund). This is especially true after verbs like *begin, continue,* and *start.*
>
> **I'm starting keeping** a journal. (awkward)
>
> **I'm starting to keep** a journal. (better)

9. A: Are we having lunch with James?

   B: Yeah. He suggested _____ at his office. (meet)

10. A: Can I help you?

    B: Sure. I'd love _____ some help. (have)

11. A: How's your car?

    B: It seems _____ OK. (be)

12. A: I don't think we should continue _____ on this. (work)

    B: I don't either.

Think about It In which of the conversations in Activity 20 could you use either a gerund or a *to-* infinitive?

21 | Changing Forms Circle the gerunds and underline the *to-* infinitives in these sentences. Then rewrite the sentence using the other form when possible. `7.4 A`

About Me

1. I decided <u>to start</u> (running) and (being more active outdoors.)

   I decided to start to run and be more active outdoors.

2. I like to ride my bike and play football.

3. I don't enjoy watching horror films because I don't like to feel scared.

4. I can't imagine having the same job my whole life.

5. I started to study English when I was a child.

6. In the next ten years, I hope to become a doctor.

7. I'm a very competitive[4] person and I hate to lose to someone else.

8. I miss seeing my family and eating my mother's cooking.

9. I can't stand to make bad decisions.

10. I don't mind working hard when I want to accomplish something.

11. I am a morning person. I love to exercise early in the morning and eat a big breakfast.

12. I started playing tennis when I was very young, and I hope to keep playing throughout my life.

F Y I

When we use a series of *to-* infinitives, it is not necessary to repeat the word *to*.

I like **to ride my bike** and (to) **play football**.

Think about It Sentences 1 and 12 above contain both *to-* infinitives and gerunds. What do you notice about how they are used together?

Talk about It Take turns reading the sentences above aloud with a partner. Say if any of the sentences are true for you.

Write about It Think of a different way to complete each sentence above with a gerund or *to-* infinitive. Write about yourself and say what you decided, like, don't enjoy, etc.

I decided to stop eating fast food.   I like to read and go for long walks.

---

[4] **competitive:** wanting to win or be better than other people

7.5 Infinitives of Purpose

A

1 I exercise **to stay healthy.**
2 I just called **to ask a question.**
3 A: Why did you bring your computer?
  B: **To show you some pictures.**

4 We left at 5 **in order to get there on time.**
5 We need to wait another month **in order to be** absolutely certain.

We sometimes use a **to- infinitive** as a kind of adverb. It answers the question *for what purpose* or *why*, as in **1 – 5.**

We sometimes use the words **in order** before the **to- infinitive**, as in **4 – 5.**

22 | Identifying Infinitives of Purpose Underline the infinitive of purpose in each question. Then answer the questions. 7.5 A

Survey Questions

1. What do you like to do <u>to relax</u>?

   I like to read a good book to relax.

2. What do you like to do to challenge yourself?
3. What do you need to do to get good grades in school?
4. What can you do to improve your English?
5. What should you keep doing in order to stay healthy?
6. What do you have to do to be successful in life?
7. What do you need to do to find a good job?
8. What skills do you need to run your own business?
9. What do children need in order to have a happy childhood?
10. What changes would you need to make to spend more time with your family?

Talk about It Choose one of the questions above and interview your classmates. Then report their answers to the class.

"I asked the question, 'What do you like to do to relax?' Most people said they like to watch TV to relax, and a few people like to listen to music."

23 | Choosing Infinitives of Purpose Complete each sentence below with an idea from the box. 7.5 A

| to borrow some books | to cut the meat | to get some bread | to ride a bicycle |
| to buy a book | to earn money | to get to work | to wash the dishes |

WHAT IS THE PURPOSE?

1. He put on an apron *to wash the dishes* .
2. He went to the library _____.
3. She went to a bookstore _____.
4. She used a sharp knife _____.

apron

5. She put on a helmet _____.

6. He takes a bus _____.

7. She goes to work _____.

8. He went to the grocery store _____.

helmet

Write about It Think of different ways to complete the sentences in Activity 23 with infinitives of purpose.

He put on an apron to cook dinner.   *She put on a helmet to go skiing.*

24 | Using Infinitives of Purpose Write as many answers as you can for each question. Try to use infinitives of purpose. `7.5 A`

1. Why do you use the Internet?

   To email my friends. To shop . . .

2. Why do you study English?

3. Why do people exercise?

4. Why do people travel?

5. Why do people work?

6. Why do people eat?

Why do you use the Internet?

Talk about It Compare your ideas above with your classmates. Make a list of all your different ideas.

7.6 Gerunds and *To-* Infinitives as Subjects

A

GERUND AS SUBJECT

	gerund	verb	
1	**Staying healthy**	**is**	important.

	gerund	verb	
2	**Being good parents**	**isn't**	easy.

	gerund	verb	
3	**Cooking a good meal**	**takes**	time.

	gerund	verb	
4	**Not getting enough sleep**	**can make**	you sick.

We can use a **gerund** as the subject of a sentence, as in **1 – 4**. Notice that we use a singular verb when the subject is a gerund.

Remember: We use *not* to make a gerund negative, as in **4**.

B

TO- INFINITIVE AS SUBJECT

	to- infinitive	verb	
5	**To learn a new language**	**isn't**	easy.

IT + BE + ADJECTIVE + TO- INFINITIVE

6	**It** isn't	easy	**to learn a new language.**

(= To learn a new language isn't easy.)

7	**It's**	nice	**to be here.**

(= To be here is nice.)

It is uncommon and very formal to use a **to-infinitive** as the subject of a sentence, as in **5**.

Instead, we sometimes begin a sentence with *it* and use an adjective + a *to-* infinitive, as in **6 – 7**. *It* is a placeholder for the subject.

Common adjectives followed by a *to-* infinitive are:

bad	easy	hard	impossible
difficult	good	important	possible

25 | Identifying Gerund Subjects Underline the gerund subject in each sentence. Circle the verb. Then check (✓) *Agree* or *Disagree*. `7.6 A`

HEALTH	AGREE	DISAGREE
1. <u>Learning a new language</u> (is) good for your brain.	☐	☐
2. Riding a bike is good exercise.	☐	☐
3. Exercising makes you strong.	☐	☐
4. Eating fish makes you smart.	☐	☐
5. Smoking is bad for your health.	☐	☐
6. Drinking a glass of warm milk helps you fall asleep.	☐	☐
7. Sitting too close to your computer screen will ruin[5] your eyes.	☐	☐
8. Swimming is good for your body.	☐	☐
9. Feeling a lot of stress isn't good for you.	☐	☐
10. Eating a lot of carrots improves your eyesight.	☐	☐

Talk about It Take turns reading the sentences above aloud with a partner. See if your partner agrees or disagrees and why.

A: Learning a new language is good for your brain.
B: I agree with that. **OR** *B: I'm not sure. Sometimes it gives me a headache.*

Write about It Think of a different subject for each sentence above, and write new sentences.

Doing puzzles is good for your brain.

26 | Using Adjectives + *To-* Infinitives Choose adjectives from the boxes to complete the questions. Use each adjective only once. (More than one adjective may be possible.) `7.6 B`

WHAT'S YOUR OPINION?

1. Why is it _____ to be a good parent?
2. Is it ever _____ to cry at work or school?
3. Is it _____ to vote?
4. Is it _____ to travel alone?
5. Is it _____ to spend a lot of money when you travel?

| dangerous |
| difficult |
| important |
| necessary |
| OK |

6. Why is it _____ to get a good education?
7. Is it _____ to skip classes?
8. When is it _____ to dress up?
9. Why is it _____ to divide by zero?
10. Is it _____ to learn English?

| bad |
| easy |
| important |
| impossible |
| necessary |

Talk about It Ask a partner the questions above.

A: Why is it difficult to be a good parent?
B: I don't know. I guess because a child needs a parent for everything....

[5] **ruin:** to damage something so that it no longer is good

27 | Using *It* with *To-* Infinitives Rewrite each sentence using *it* + *be* + an adjective + a *to-* infinitive. `7.6 B`

1. Skiing can be dangerous.

   It can be dangerous to ski.

2. Having a day off is nice.
3. Eating sweet things is OK sometimes.
4. Learning a new language isn't easy.
5. Getting some exercise every day is important.
6. Traveling is exciting.
7. Sitting all day is bad for your health.
8. Finding a good job isn't hard.
9. Getting up early can be difficult.
10. Knowing another language is helpful.

Write about It Think of a different *to-* infinitive for each sentence above, and write new sentences.

It can be dangerous to drive on the highway.

7.7 Using Gerunds and To- Infinitives in Speaking

A	**PRONOUNCING *WANT* + *TO-* INFINITIVE** **1** What do you **want to do?** (sounds like "wanna do") **2** I **want to go.** (sounds like "wanna go") **3** He didn't **want to talk about it.** (sounds like "wanna talk")	The verb **want** + **to-** infinitive is very common in conversation, as in **1 – 3**. We often pronounce *want to* as "wanna." **WARNING!** We do not use "wanna" in writing.
B	**MAKING A REQUEST WITH *WOULD YOU MIND*** **4** A: Would you mind **taking this for me?** B: No problem. (= No, I wouldn't mind.) **5** A: Would you mind **giving me a ride?** B: No, not at all. (= No, I wouldn't mind.) **6** A: Would you mind **coming over here?** B: OK.	In speaking, we often use *would you mind* + a **gerund** to make a polite request, as in **4 – 6**. Notice: We often use a negative response to agree to a request with *would you mind*. Some examples are: No problem. No, of course not. No, not at all. No, that's fine.

GO ONLINE

28 | Pronouncing *Want* + *To-* Infinitive Listen and write the missing words. Then practice with a partner. Practice the pronunciation of *want to* as "wanna." `7.7 A`

1. A: What do you _____ after class?

   B: Nothing special.

2. A: Do you _____ for a cup of coffee?

   B: Sure.

3. A: Tell me about yourself.

   B: What do you _____?

   A: Well, where did you grow up?

   B: In Turkey.

4. A: I don't _____ anything tonight.

   B: I don't either.

5. A: Where do you _____ today?

   B: Doesn't matter to me.

6. A: Let's see a movie tonight.

   B: Not tonight. I really just _____ home.

7. A: Where's Amanda?

   B: She didn't _____.

8. A: Is your brother coming with us?

   B: No, he doesn't _____ right now.

9. A: Do you _____ with us?

   B: Sure. I'd love to.

10. A: Do you _____ me later?

    B: Sure. What time?

Talk about It Work with a partner. Choose three of the sentences you completed in Activity 28. Write new conversations with them. Then present one conversation to the class.

A: What do you want to do after class?
B: I don't know. Maybe we should see a movie.

29 | Using *Would You Mind* + Gerund Rewrite each conversation. Use *would you mind* + a gerund in the request. Remember that a negative response means you agree. `7.7 B`

MAKING REQUESTS

1. A: Could you open the door for me, please?

   B: Sure.

2. A: Would you please turn the TV down?

   B: OK.

3. A: Can you give me a ride to work tomorrow?

   B: Of course. What time?

4. A: Could you go to the store for me?

   B: Sure. What do you need?

5. A: Could you bring me another glass of water, please?

   B: Yes, I'll be right back with it.

6. A: Could you pass me the salt, please?

   B: Sure.

7. A: Could you wait for just a minute?

   B: OK, but I don't want to be late.

8. A: Could you take our picture?

   B: Sure. I'd be happy to.

REQUEST WITH WOULD YOU MIND

1. A: *Would you mind opening the door for me, please?*

   B: *No, of course not.*

2. A: _____
      _____

   B: _____

3. A: _____
      _____

   B: _____

4. A: _____
      _____

   B: _____

5. A: _____
      _____

   B: _____

6. A: _____
      _____

   B: _____

7. A: _____
      _____

   B: _____

8. A: _____
      _____

   B: _____

Talk about It Where would you hear each request above? Discuss your ideas with your classmates.

7.8 Using Gerunds and To- Infinitives in Writing

A

USING THE SAME FORM IN LISTS

1 Group decision making involves three steps:

- writing the discussion questions
- brainstorming alternatives
- evaluating alternatives

2 A good introduction has several functions:

- **to get the attention of the audience**
- **to state the purpose of the presentation**
- **to describe the presenter's qualifications**

We sometimes use **gerunds** and **to- infinitives** when we write lists of items, as in **1 – 2**.

Notice that the items in each list have the same grammatical form. We don't mix grammatical forms in a list.

GRAMMAR TERM: When we use the same grammatical form in this way, we call it **parallelism**.

B

USING THE SAME FORM IN A SERIES OF IDEAS

3 **Eating well**, **exercising**, and **not worrying** are good for your health.

4 In the next few years, I hope **to finish my education, get a job**, and **maybe start a family.**
(= to finish my education, to get a job, and maybe to start a family)

When we write a series of ideas, we make them parallel—they use the same grammatical form.

- Sentence **3** has three subjects: *eating well, exercising,* and *not worrying.* The writer uses the same grammatical form for each one.
- Sentence **4** has three objects of the verb *hope.* Remember: When we use a series of *to-* infinitives, it is not necessary to repeat the word *to.*

 GO ONLINE

30 | Listing Ideas Add another idea to each list. Use the same form as the other ideas in the list. (Make them parallel.) `7.8 A`

THREE THINGS

1. Parents have many important responsibilities:

   - keeping their children safe
   - modeling[6] good behavior
   - _____

2. You can use the Internet to do many useful things:

   - to look for a job
   - to read the news
   - _____

3. Three simple things can help you stay healthy:

   - eating good food
   - getting enough sleep
   - _____

[6] **model:** to show or demonstrate

4. Children can learn several important things from playing sports:
   - to value[7] physical activity
   - to work together as a team
   - _____

5. The United Nations has several important functions:
   - to keep peace in the world
   - to help solve economic problems
   - _____

31 | Using a Series of Ideas Complete these sentences with your own ideas. Use the same form as other ideas in the series. (Make them parallel.) `7.8 B`

1. Lots of people go to local parks to have a picnic and _____*get some exercise*_____.
2. Skiing and _____ are popular cold-weather sports.
3. On a sunny day, most people enjoy being outside, _____, and _____.
4. Parents should encourage their children to be polite, _____, and _____.
5. Parents can teach their children good behavior without yelling at them or _____.
6. Before you get on an airplane, it's necessary to go through security and _____.
7. People join clubs to have fun and _____.
8. On a vacation, many people enjoy visiting new places, _____, and _____.
9. Lots of people dream of making a lot of money and _____.
10. You can learn a lot from reading, _____, and _____.

WRAP-UP Demonstrate Your Knowledge

A | DISCUSSION Work with a partner. Find something both of you can't stand doing, dislike doing, enjoy doing, etc. Then report your answers to the class.

are good at	are interested in	can't stand	dislike	enjoy	hate	like	want

"Both of us can't stand getting up early in the morning."
"Both of us enjoy . . ."
"Both of us hate . . ."

[7] **value:** to think that something is important

B | SURVEY Ask your classmates questions to find the information below. Use the verb and the correct form of the phrase in parentheses. When someone answers yes, write the person's name in the box.

A: Do you like to play football?
B: No, I don't.

A: Do you like to play football?
C: Yes, I do.

FIND SOMEONE WHO . . .

1. like (play football) Name: _____	4. worry about (find a job) Name: _____	7. plan (study tomorrow) Name: _____
2. plan on (go to school next year) Name: _____	5. enjoy (cook) Name: _____	8. expect (take a trip soon) Name: _____
3. like (play board games) Name: _____	6. is good at (play the piano) Name: _____	9. want (work in the medical field) Name: _____

C | WRITING What is one of your future goals? How do you plan to reach that goal? Answer these questions in a short piece of writing.

Becoming a teacher of young children is one of my future goals. I plan to reach this goal by studying hard and getting good grades. I hope to go to graduate school to get a master's degree in education. I am also interested in . . .

7.9 Summary of Gerunds and *To-* Infinitives

GERUNDS

VERB + GERUND	I just **started** writing. I can't **imagine** writing a computer program. I **finished** writing my paper last night.
PREPOSITION + GERUND	I got a blister **from** writing. I'm **tired of** writing these letters. I **feel like** writing her a message.
GERUND AS SUBJECT	Writing was never a great subject for me. Writing in a journal is a creative outlet. Writing is like a muscle. You need to exercise it.

TO- **INFINITIVES**

VERB + *TO-* **INFINITIVE**	Do you **promise to write**? I **need to write** a business plan.
VERB + OBJECT + *TO-* **INFINITIVE**	Do you **want me to write** this? I **told my brother** to write to you.
INFINITIVE OF PURPOSE	She wrote **to ask for money**. I need a computer **in order to write this report**.
TO- **INFINITIVE AS SUBJECT**	**To write badly** is easy. (not typical) **To write in your own words** is important. (not typical)
IT + BE + **ADJECTIVE +** *TO-* **INFINITIVE**	**It**'s easy to write badly. **It** is important **to write in your own words**.

8 Present Perfect and Past Perfect

Two roads diverged in a wood, and I—
I took the one less traveled by,
And that has made all the difference.

—ROBERT FROST, POET

(1874–1963)

Talk about It What does the quotation above mean to you?

WARM-UP

A | Check (✓) the sentences that describe you. Then compare with a partner. Who is the most adventurous person in the class?

How Adventurous Are You?

☐ 1. I **have given** one or more speeches in my life.
☐ 2. I **have traveled** to a place where I couldn't speak the language.
☐ 3. I **have tried** a somewhat[1] dangerous sport such as surfing.
☐ 4. I **have done** something even though I was afraid.
☐ 5. I **have eaten** unusual foods from other countries.
☐ 6. I **have** always **enjoyed** trying new things.
☐ 7. I **have tried** to do something difficult and failed.
☐ 8. I **have taken** a trip alone.

• If you checked 7 to 8 boxes, you are extremely adventurous.
• If you checked 5 to 6 boxes, you are very adventurous.
• If you checked 2 to 4 boxes, you are somewhat adventurous.
• If you checked 0 to 1 box, you might need a little more adventure in your life.

B | The verbs in blue above are present perfect verbs. Based on these examples, what can you say about the present perfect? Check (✓) *True* or *False*.

	TRUE	FALSE
1. We usually form the present perfect with the helping verb *have* + the *-ed/-en* form of the main verb (the past participle).	☐	☐
2. The past participle is always the same as the simple past form.	☐	☐
3. We use the present perfect to talk about a specific time in the past (such as *last year* or *yesterday*).	☐	☐

C | Look back at the quotation on page 250. Identify any present perfect verb forms.

[1] **somewhat:** a little bit

A

1 I**'ve lived** here **all my life**.
(= I've lived here from the time I was born up until now.)

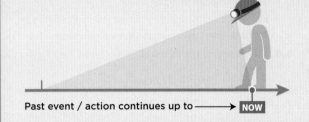

Past event / action continues up to ⟶ **NOW**

2 A: Nice car! Is it new?
B: No, I**'ve had** it **since 2010**.
(= I've had the car from 2010 up until now.)

3 Carl **has always been** a good friend. (= Carl was a good friend in the past, and he is a good friend now.)

When we want to show that something started in the past and continues up to the present (the moment of speaking), we often use the **present perfect** form of a verb, as in **1 – 3**.

Some common verbs for this use of the present perfect are:

be	have	live
feel	know	work

Notice: We sometimes use a **time expression** in a sentence with a present perfect verb, as in **1 – 3**.

B

POSITIVE AND NEGATIVE STATEMENTS

4

	have (+ *not*)	past participle		
I You We They	**have** **'ve** **have not** **haven't**	**lived**	there	for years.

5

	has (+ *not*)		past participle	
He She It	**has** **'s** **has not** **hasn't**	always	**lived**	there.

We form the present perfect with *have / has* (+ ***not***) + the **past participle of a main verb**, as in **4 – 5**. In conversation, we often use contractions.

Notice: We use the verb *have* as a helping verb in the present perfect form.

C

The past participle of regular verbs looks the same as the simple past form, as in **6**. We add -(e)d to the base form. The past participle of many (but not all) irregular verbs is different from the simple past, as in **7**.

6

REGULAR VERBS		
base form	simple past	past participle
like	lik**ed**	lik**ed**
live	liv**ed**	liv**ed**
want	want**ed**	want**ed**
work	work**ed**	work**ed**

7

IRREGULAR VERBS		
base form	simple past	past participle
be	was/were	**been**
feel	felt	**felt**
have	had	**had**
know	knew	**known**

For spelling rules of -*ed* endings, see the Resources, page R-5.

For a list of past participles of irregular verbs, see the Resources, page R-3.

1 | Noticing the Present Perfect Underline the present perfect verb forms in these conversations. Then practice with a partner. 8.1 A

1. A: Are you OK?
   B: I'm not sure. I<u>'ve had</u> a headache all day.
2. A: You look tired.
   B: I am. I've worked hard all week.
3. A: Is Amanda a good cook?
   B: She should be. She's worked in restaurants all her life.
4. A: Do you know David?
   B: Sure. I've known him all my life.
5. A: I'm sleepy.
   B: Me too. I've been up since 3 this morning.
6. A: Nice coat. Is it new?
   B: No, I've had it since November.
7. A: Where should I stay in San Francisco?
   B: Email James Bailey and ask him. He's lived there for years.
8. A: What's the matter?
   B: I don't know. I haven't felt good all day.
9. A: We're going to Chicago next weekend. Do you want to come?
   B: Sure. I've always wanted to go there.
10. A: You're a good student.
    B: Thanks. I like to study. I've always liked to study.

Are you OK?

Is Amanda a good cook?

Think about It Make a list of the time expressions in sentences with the present perfect above.

all day, all week,

Think about It Circle the other verb forms in the conversations above. What other verb forms often appear together with the present perfect?

2 | Usage Note: *For and Since* Read the note. Then do Activity 3.

> We can use the time expressions *for* and *since* in sentences with the present perfect.
>
> **1** To show "for how long," we use *for* + **a length of time**.
>
> We haven't lived there **for 5 years.** (= for the past 5 years / from 5 years ago until now)
> I've known him **for 23 years.** (= for the past 23 years / from 23 years ago until now)
>
> **2** To show "from when," we use *since* + **a specific time in the past**.
>
> We've lived here **since 1995.** (= from 1995 to now)
> She hasn't felt good **since the picnic.** (= from the day of the picnic until now)
>
> **3** We can also use *since* in a **time clause** (with a subject and a verb).
> We usually use the simple past in the time clause.
>
> I've known him **since we were children.** (= from the time we were children to now)

3 | Using *For* and *Since* Underline the present perfect verbs in these sentences. Then complete the sentences with *for* or *since*. 8.1 A–B

DESCRIBING RELATIVES

My sister Anna

1. She <u>has lived</u> in Vancouver ___*since*___ she graduated from college in 2001.

2. She has been married _____ a few years.

3. She has been an art teacher _____ 12 years.

4. She has taught at an elementary school _____ the past 4 years. Before that she taught at a private school.

5. She and her husband have lived in their present apartment _____ 2010.

My grandfather John

6. He has lived in California _____ he was a child.

7. He has lived in the same house _____ most of his life.

8. He has lived alone _____ his wife died.

9. He hasn't worked full-time _____ he was 70 years old.

10. He has been a chess player _____ most of his adulthood.

Write about It What do you know about these two people now (in the present)? Use present verb forms to write as many sentences as you can about the two people above.

Anna lives in Canada.
She has a college degree.

4 | Forming Present Perfect Statements Choose verbs from these charts to complete the sentences on page 255. (More than one verb may be possible.) Use the present perfect and contractions where possible. Then check (✓) *True* or *False*. 8.1 B–C

REGULAR VERBS		
Base form	**Simple past**	**Past participle**
enjoy	enjoyed	**enjoyed**
like	liked	**liked**
live	lived	**lived**
own	owned	**owned**
want	wanted	**wanted**
work	worked	**worked**

IRREGULAR VERBS		
Base form	**Simple past**	**Past participle**
be	was / were	**been**
feel	felt	**felt**
have	had	**had**
know	knew	**known**
make	made	**made**
say	said	**said**
teach	taught	**taught**

MY FAMILY	TRUE	FALSE

1. My parents _____ *have* _____ always _____ *lived* _____ in the same city. ☐ ☐

2. My parents _____ married for a long time. ☐ ☐

3. They _____ a car since they got married. ☐ ☐

4. They _____ each other since they were children. ☐ ☐

5. My father _____ always _____ at the same place. ☐ ☐

6. My father _____ at a high school for many years. ☐ ☐

7. My mother _____ many different jobs. ☐ ☐

8. My mother _____ always _____ me laugh. ☐ ☐

9. My aunts and uncles _____ never _____ to this country. ☐ ☐

10. No one in my family _____ in a movie. ☐ ☐

11. My relatives _____ always _____ important in my life. ☐ ☐

12. People in my family _____ always _____ that I have a
    talent for sports. ☐ ☐

13. My parents _____ always _____ me to become a doctor. ☐ ☐

14. My mother and her mother-in-law _____ always _____
    each other. ☐ ☐

15. The people in my family _____ always _____
    getting together. ☐ ☐

Write about It Write six sentences about your family. Use *always, since,* or *for* and the present perfect form of a verb from the charts in Activity 4.

My parents have always lived in Barcelona.

5 | Error Correction Correct any errors in these sentences. (Some sentences may not have any errors.)

1. He hasn't in this country eight years.
2. I has been here only since last week.
3. My sister been in the United States from the last seven months.
4. She hasn't lived here for very long.
5. My father has worked for the same company since ten years.
6. I loved scary movies since I was a child.
7. We have only knew him since we moved here.
8. Football haven't always been my favorite sport.
9. This city has changed a lot since I came here.
10. A: Is that a new computer?
    B: No, I had it for almost a year.
11. A: Do you know Sam Davidson?
    B: Of course. I've known him since a year.
12. A: Did you talk to Anne?
    B: Not yet. She been on the phone.

> **FYI**
>
> Sometimes we use an expression for a finished time (*yesterday, last week,* etc.) after *since.* The main clause still uses the present perfect.
>
> I haven't seen him **since I talked to him** yesterday.
>
> We haven't gone anywhere **since last week**.

8.2 Using the Present Perfect (II); *Yes/No* Questions

A

1 I've **finished** the book. Do you **want** to read it?

Past event / action connected to ⟶ NOW

2 She **has talked** to her boss about the problem, but he **refuses** to do anything about it.

3 My brother **knows** a lot about Canada. He's **been** there several times.

Happened more than one time and connected to ⟶ NOW

Sometimes we want to talk about something that started and ended in the past but has **a connection to the present**. In these situations, we use the **present perfect**, as in **1 – 2**.

We can also use the present perfect to talk about something that happened more than one time in the past and has **a connection to the present**, as in **3**.

Remember: We form the present perfect with *have / has* (+ *not*) + the past participle form of a main verb.

B

For *yes/no* questions, we use *have / has* and the **past participle of a main verb**, as in **4 – 5**.
We can give a short answer with *have* or *has*, as in **6 – 9**.
In negative short answers, we often use contractions, as in **8 – 9**.

YES/NO QUESTIONS

	have/has		*past participle*
4	**Have**	I you we they	**eaten?**
5	**Has**	he she it	**eaten?**

SHORT ANSWERS

		have/has	
6	Yes,	you I you they	**have.**
7	Yes,	he she it	**has.**

		have/has + not	
8	No,	you I you they	**haven't.**
9	No,	he she it	**hasn't.**

GO ONLINE

6 | Connecting to the Present Match each past event with a connection to the present. `8.2 A`

PAST ACTIONS OR EVENTS

1. I've lost Ahmad's phone number. __d__
2. We have never eaten Japanese food. ____
3. My brother has had a few accidents with his car. ____
4. Matt has missed a lot of classes. ____
5. I've stopped caring about football. ____
6. I haven't found my keys. ____
7. Mr. Jones has already gone. ____
8. I've studied this subject before. ____

CONNECTIONS TO THE PRESENT (NOW)

a. I don't think he's a very good driver.
b. I can't open the door.
c. I don't want to watch the game.
d. I can't call him.
e. He's not here now.
f. I know a lot about it.
g. He's in trouble with his teacher.
h. I don't know what it tastes like.

Think about It Underline the present perfect verb in the sentences in Activity 6. Does the verb describe something that happened one time or more than one time in the past? Share ideas with your classmates.

Write about It Choose three past actions or events in Activity 6. Write another sentence showing a connection to the present.

7 | **Usage Note: Irregular Past Participles** Study the chart. Then answer the questions below.

GROUP 1		
base form	simple past	past participle
cut	cut	cut
put	put	put

GROUP 2		
base form	simple past	past participle
become	became	become

GROUP 3		
base form	simple past	past participle
eat	ate	eaten
fall	fell	fallen
see	saw	seen
show	showed	shown
write	wrote	written

GROUP 4		
base form	simple past	past participle
find	found	found
leave	left	left
lose	lost	lost
say	said	said

GROUP 5		
base form	simple past	past participle
break	broke	broken
forget	forgot	forgotten

GROUP 6 (OTHER)		
base form	simple past	past participle
begin	began	begun
fly	flew	flown

QUESTIONS

1. What is similar about the form of the verbs in each group? Use the colors to help you identify a pattern. Then share ideas with your classmates.

   "In group 1, the base form, the simple past, and the past participle are the same."

2. Add these verbs to the correct groups in the chart above. Then think of six other verbs to add to the chart.

buy/bought/bought	go/went/gone	speak/spoke/spoken
do/did/done	hurt/hurt/hurt	take/took/taken
get/got/gotten	make/made/made	think/thought/thought
give/gave/given	run/ran/run	throw/threw/thrown

8 | Using the Present Perfect Complete these conversations with the present perfect form of a verb from Activity 7. Use contractions where possible. Then practice with a partner. 8.2 A

1. A: Do you still have Emma's phone number?

   B: No, I ___'ve lost___ it.

2. A: I _____ some coffee. Do you want some?

   B: Sure. Thanks.

3. A: Are the children doing their homework?

   B: No, they _____ already _____ it.

4. A: Are you hungry?

   B: No, I _____ already _____.

5. A: Why don't we go to Art Café anymore?

   B: It _____ too popular. It's always crowded.

6. A: Do you want to go to the science museum with me today?

   B: I don't think so. I _____ several times this year. That's enough for me.

7. A: Where is Carlos?

   B: They _____ him to the hospital. He fainted!

8. A: Who's the new student in your class?

   B: I _____ her name. Ask Mary. She'll know it.

9. A: Nice jacket. Is it new?

   B: You _____ it before. I wore it last week.

10. A: Don't forget to take your lunch. I _____ your name on the bag.

    B: OK. Thanks, Mom.

> **RESEARCH SAYS...**
>
> Common verbs used with the present perfect in speaking and writing include:
>
> | | | |
> |---|---|---|
> | be | give | say |
> | become | go | see |
> | call | have | show |
> | come | lose | take |
> | do | make | think |
> | get | put | win |
>
> CORPU

Think about It Why do you think the speakers chose to use the present perfect in each conversation above?

Talk about It Choose one of the conversations in Activity 8. Add three or four more lines. Try to use other present forms. Then present it to your classmates.

9 | Usage Note: *Just, Recently, and Finally* Read the note. Then do Activity 10.

> We sometimes use *just*, *recently*, and *finally* with the present perfect. We often do this when we are talking about something that started and ended in the past but has a connection to the present.
>
> **1 *Just*** means "a very short time ago." We use *have/has* + *just* + the past participle.
>
> I think somebody's **just** knocked on the door. Can you get it?
>
> **2 *Recently*** means "not long ago." We can use *recently* in different places in a sentence.
>
> She **has recently completed** a degree in architecture, and now she is looking for a job in New York.
>
> **Recently**, she **has completed** a degree in architecture, and now she is looking for a job in New York.
>
> She **has completed** a degree in architecture **recently**, and now she is looking for a job in New York.
>
> **3 *Finally*** means "after a long time." We can use *finally* in different places in a sentence.
>
> My brother **has finally found** a new job. He's really excited about it.
>
> **Finally**, my brother **has found** a new job. He's really excited about it.
>
> My brother **has found** a new job **finally**. He's really excited about it.

10 | Using the Present Perfect with *Just, Recently,* **and** *Finally* **Complete these sentences with the words in parentheses. Use the present perfect form of the bold verb and contractions where possible.** `8.2 A`

1. We ___'ve recently gotten___ a new cell phone, and I'm having trouble using it. (**get**/recently)
2. The snow _____. Let's go outside. (**stop**/finally)
3. I don't want to go jogging now. I _have just eaten_. (**eat**/just)
4. My father has a lot more free time now because he _has finally retired_ (**retire**[2]/finally)
5. Our school _has recently begun_ a new program for foreign students. (**begin**/recently)
6. I'm tired of winter. I'm glad that warmer weather _has finally arrived_. (**arrive**/finally)
7. Sarah is pretty angry because Rob _has just lost_ her new laptop. (**lose**/just)
8. Everyone is celebrating because peace _has finally come_ to the country. (**come**/finally)
9. The college _has recently published_ a handbook with study tips. (**publish**/recently)
10. Hurry up. The movie _has just started_. I don't want to miss the beginning. (**start**/just)

Write about It Which sentences above can you rewrite and put the time word in a different place?

1. Recently, we've gotten a new cell phone. OR *We've gotten a new cell phone recently.*

11 | Asking *Yes/No* **Questions** Ask a *yes/no* question with the present perfect and write an answer with *yes* or *no* and more information. Then compare and practice with a partner. `8.2 B`

1. A: I can't find my laptop. _Have you seen it?_ (you/**see**/it)
   B: _Yes, I have. It's on the kitchen table._ (yes)
2. A: _____ (anyone/**call**/today)
   B: _____ (yes)
3. A: _____ (Sam/**leave**)
   B: _____ (no)
4. A: _____ (the movie/**begin**)
   B: _____ (no)
5. A: _____ (you/**take** your medicine)
   B: _____ (yes)
6. A: _____ (the plane/**land**)
   B: _____ (no)
7. A: _____ (you/**talk** to your parents/recently)
   B: _____ (yes)
8. A: _____ (the rain/**stop**)
   B: _____ (no)
9. A: I'm going to Costa Rica next year. _____ there before? (you/**be**)
   B: _____ (no)
10. A: _____ (you/**have** lunch)
    B: _____ (yes)

[2] **retire:** stop working because you are a certain age

12 | Usage Note: *Ever* and *Never* Read the note. Then do Activity 13.

We sometimes use *ever* and *never* with the present perfect.

1 We can use *ever* in questions to ask: Has something happened "at some time before now"?

A: **Have** you **ever been** to Spain?　　　A: I need a good book to read.

B: No, I haven't. Why do you ask?　　　B: **Have** you **ever** **read** *The Road*? It's great.

2 We use *ever* in negative statements. It means something has not happened "before now."

I **haven't ever visited** Hawaii. I want to go.　　Nobody **has** ever **called** me lazy.

3 We can use *never* in positive statements. It also means something has not happened "before now."

I**'ve never visited** Hawaii. I want to go.　　　A: Do you like Vietnamese food?

B: I don't know. I**'ve never tried** it.

WARNING! We don't usually use *ever* in a statement without a negative word (*not, nobody*, etc.).
NOT: ~~I have ever been to Hawaii.~~

---

13 | Using *Ever* and *Never* Complete these conversations with the words in parentheses. Use the present perfect form of the **bold** verb and contractions where possible. Then practice with a partner. `8.2 A–B`

1. A: What does a cheetah look like?

   B: I don't know. I _____*haven't ever seen*_____ one. (**see**/not/ever)

2. A: You're a really good football player.

   B: Really? You _have never said_ that before. (**say**/never)

3. A: _have you ever been_ the band Snow Patrol?

   (you/**hear**/ever)

   B: Sure. Why do you ask?

   A: Because they're playing at the university tonight. Do you want to go?

4. A: Do you like Indian food?

   B: I don't know. I _have never tried_ it. (**have**/never)

5. A: Look at the water. _have you ever seen_ a blue like that? (you/**see**/ever)

   B: No, it's beautiful.

6. A: You're a really good cook. _have you ever thought of_ opening a restaurant?

   (you/**think of**/ever)

   B: I have, but it's a lot of work.

7. A: Tom and I are going skateboarding this afternoon. Want to join us?

   B: I don't know. I _haven't ever tried_ it. (**try**/not/ever)

   A: Oh, come on. I think you'll like it.

8. A: What do you do when you get a parking ticket?

   B: I don't know. I _have never gotten_ one. (**get**/never)

Think about It Look at the sentences you completed above. Which ones could you rewrite using *ever* instead of *never* or *never* instead of *ever*?

1. I've never seen one.

260

14 | Usage Note: _Yet_ and _Already_ Read the note. Then do Activity 15.

We sometimes use _yet_ and _already_ with the present perfect to talk about our expectations.

1 We use **yet** and **already** in questions when we expected something to happen.
   We ask: Has it happened?

   A: **Have you finished** your essay **yet**?
   B: No, I'm still working on it.

   A: **Have you eaten** already?
   B: Actually, I haven't.
   A: Good. Then let's eat out.

2 We use **yet** in negative statements. It means something we expected has not happened.

   Sit down. I **haven't excused** you **yet**.

   A: Where's Nick?
   B: I don't know. I **haven't seen** him **yet**.

3 We use **already** in positive statements. It means something has happened earlier than we expected.

   A: Do you want to pay for that now?
   B: I've **already paid** for it.

   A: Don't forget to do your homework.
   B: I've **already done** it.

15 | Using _Yet_ and _Already_ Complete these conversations with the words in parentheses. Use the present perfect form of the bold verb and contractions where possible. `8.2 A–B`

1. A: We're going to the National Museum this weekend. Do you want to come?
   B: Thanks, but I ___'ve already been___ there. (**be**/already)

2. A: Where's Isabel?
   B: She _hasn't arrived yet_. (**arrive**/not/yet)

3. A: _Have you already eaten_? (you/**eat**/already)
   B: Sorry. I was really hungry.

4. A: What's the score?
   B: There is no score. The game _hasn't started yet_. (**start**/not/yet)

5. A: Where do you want to go for dinner?
   B: I _haven't decided yet_. (**decide**/not/yet)

6. A: Do you like that new software?
   B: Yeah. It _has already been_ very useful. (**be**/already)

7. A: Toshi isn't going to be here tomorrow.
   B: Yeah, he _has already told_ me. (**tell**/already)

8. A: _Has anything happened yet_? (anything/**happen**/yet)
   B: No, we are still waiting.

9. A: Do you need any help with the picnic?
   B: No, Amanda _has already taken care of_ everything. (**take care of**/already)

10. A: Come on. Let's go.
    B: Wait. We _haven't finished yet_. (**finish**/not/yet)

11. A: Why don't you want to watch this movie with us?
    B: Because I _have already seen_ it. (**see**/already)

8.3 Wh- Questions with the Present Perfect

When we ask *wh-* questions with the present perfect, we use a **wh- word** + *have / has* and the **past participle of a main verb**, as in **1 – 10**.

A

WH- QUESTIONS

	wh- word	have	subject	past participle
1	What		I	done?
2	Why		you	called?
3	Where	have	we	been?
4	Who		the people	elected?
5	How		they	changed?

	wh- word	has	subject	past participle
6	What		he	done?
7	Where		she	gone?
8	How	has	it	changed?
9	Who		your sister	invited?
10	Why		the store	closed?

WH- QUESTIONS ABOUT THE SUBJECT

	subject	has	past participle	
11	Who		been	there?
12	What	has	happened?	

Sometimes the *wh-* word is the subject of the sentence, as in **11 – 12**.

B

13	How long	have you been here?
14	How far	have the children gone?
15	How many times	has he called you today?
16	How many cups	of coffee have you had today?
17	How much coffee	have you had today?

We sometimes ask questions with:
- *how* + an adjective, as in **13 – 14**
- *how* + *many* + a plural noun, as in **15 – 16**
- *how* + *much* + a noncount noun, as in **17**

16 | Forming Wh- Questions with the Present Perfect Complete these questions with the words in parentheses. Use the present perfect form of the **bold** verb. **8.3 A**

QUESTIONS FROM INTERVIEWS WITH FAMOUS PEOPLE

1. How ____*has the president done*____ so far?
   (the president / **do**)
2. What _____ from this experience?
   (you / **learn**)
3. What _____ your biggest frustration[3]?
   (**be**)
4. Who _____ the most fun with on a movie set?
   (you / **have**)
5. Why _____ to make this change and why now?
   (you / **decide**)
6. How _____ to keep your positive attitude?
   (you / **manage**)
7. How _____ your family life?
   (your success / **affect**)
8. What _____ since you lost weight?
   (**change**)
9. What _____ to prepare for this movie?
   (you / **do**)
10. Where _____ ?
    (the money / **go**)

FYI

We often use the present perfect to describe experiences that we bring to present situations, such as interviews.

[3]**frustration:** a feeling of anger because you cannot do what you want to do

11. Why _____?
   (unemployment / **go down**)
12. Why _____ a comedy?
   (you / **make**)

Talk about It For each question in Activity 16, do you think the interviewer is talking to a politician, an entertainer (actor, comedian, etc.), and/or an athlete? Why? Share ideas with your classmates.

17 | Asking Questions with *How* and the Present Perfect Complete the conversations below with words from the box. Then practice with a partner. 8.3 B

how far	how long	how many	how much

1. A: Do we have enough money to go out tonight?

   B: I don't know. ___*How much*___ have we spent this week?

   A: Not much. About $50.

2. A: Mika wants another aspirin. Can I give her one?

   B: _____ has she had so far today?

   A: Only one.

   B: OK then. Let her have another one.

3. A: Are we there yet?

   B: No, not yet.

   A: _____ have we gone?

   B: About 300 miles.

4. A: I hear you're going back home this summer.

   B: Yeah, I'm really excited.

   A: _____ has it been since you were there?

   B: Just three years.

5. A: I can't work on this paper anymore.

   B: _____ hours have you spent on it?

   A: Seems like a million.

6. A: Hey, Carlos, are you still asleep? It's ten o'clock.

   B: No, I'm reading.

   A: _____ have you been awake?

   B: About an hour. I've already had two cups of tea.

7. A: Do you want to go out?

   B: I can't. I'm still doing today's reading assignment.

   A: _____ have you gotten?

   B: I'm only up to page 32.

8. A: Have you finished your homework yet?

   B: No, not yet.

   A: Well, _____ have you done?

   B: About half of it.

> **RESEARCH SAYS...**
>
> When we ask a present perfect question with *when*, we are often making a complaint. (These questions are not common.)
>
> **When have** you ever **done** the dishes?
>
> **When have** you **been** on time to class?
>
> CORPUS

8.4 The Simple Past vs. the Present Perfect

<table>
<tr>
<td rowspan="2">A</td>
<td>

THE SIMPLE PAST

We often use the **simple past** to describe something that began and ended in the past. It is *no longer connected to now* (the moment of speaking), as in **1a – 3a**.

1a Nobody lived here in 1990. It was very quiet then.

2a I saw Linda at the theater last night.

3a We read that book several times in high school. It was one of my favorite books.

</td>
<td>

THE PRESENT PERFECT

We usually use the **present perfect** to describe something that started or happened in the past but is *still connected to now*, as in **1b – 3b**.

1b Nobody has lived here since 1990. I wonder why.

2b I've seen Linda today, but I don't know where she is now.

3b We've read that book several times. It's great.

</td>
</tr>
</table>

<table>
<tr>
<td rowspan="2">B</td>
<td>

TIME EXPRESSIONS WITH THE SIMPLE PAST

We use the simple past with time expressions that identify a *finished time*, including:

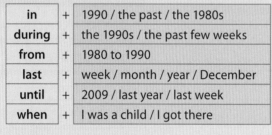

in	+	1990 / the past / the 1980s
during	+	the 1990s / the past few weeks
from	+	1980 to 1990
last	+	week / month / year / December
until	+	2009 / last year / last week
when	+	I was a child / I got there

a day / a month / a year / soon	+	after that
two days / a week / a few years	+	ago
several days / a month / a year	+	later

</td>
<td>

TIME EXPRESSIONS WITH THE PRESENT PERFECT

We use the present perfect with time expressions that identify a time period *up until now*, including:

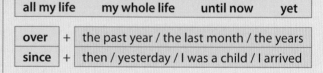

all my life	my whole life	until now	yet

over	+	the past year / the last month / the years
since	+	then / yesterday / I was a child / I arrived

</td>
</tr>
</table>

<table>
<tr>
<td rowspan="2">C</td>
<td>

THE SIMPLE PAST

4a I **always** did well in school. My parents were very proud of me.

5a I was in Spain **for a week**. I didn't want to leave.

THE PRESENT PERFECT

4b I have **always** done well in school. My parents are very proud of me.

5b I have been in Spain **for a week**. I don't want to leave.

</td>
<td>

We can use some time expressions with either the simple past or the present perfect, including:

already	before	never	today
always	ever	recently	

this	+	week / month / year
for	+	an hour / a day / five years / a long time

The choice of verb form depends on how we interpret the event and when it happened, as in **4 – 5**.

</td>
</tr>
</table>

GO ONLINE

---

18 | Choosing the Correct Time Expressions Underline the verbs in these sentences. Then circle the correct time expression in **bold**. **8.4 A–B**

Sports

1. Gymnastics <u>is</u> a very popular sport. It <u>has been</u> in every Olympic Games **in 1896 /** (**since 1896.**)

2. Brazil has won five World Cups **several years ago / over the past 60 years**.

3. Professional tennis players started using yellow balls **in 1986 / since 1986** so that TV viewers could see the ball.

gymnastics

4. **Over the years / In 2012**, the Korean archery team has won many Olympic medals.

5. In 1954, Roger Bannister became the first person to run a mile in less than four minutes. **During the 1990s / Since then**, many runners have broken his record.

6. Tennis became an Olympic sport **more than 20 years ago / over the past 20 years**.

7. **A long time ago / Over the years**, there have been many football-like games.

8. The astronaut Alan Shepard hit a golf ball **when he was on the moon / since he was on the moon**.

9. Golf has become a popular sport in Denmark **a year ago / recently**. It is especially popular among people over age 24.

10. **In the early 1900s / Since the early 1900s**, baseball players wore leather helmets[4]. Head injuries were common.

11. Queenie Newall was 53 years old **when she won an Olympic gold medal / since she won an Olympic gold medal** in 1908.

12. Tug of war was an Olympic event **from 1900 to 1920 / since 1920**.

13. Runners didn't use a crouching[5] position at the start of a race **since 1908 / until 1908**. This change helped them to finish a race much faster.

14. Since the first World Cup in 1930, European teams have reached the final **every year / last year** except 1930 and 1950.

archery

tug of war

Think about It Choose five sentences in Activity 18. Change the verb form in each sentence so that you can use the other time expression in **bold**. You may also need to make other changes.

Gymnastics was in the Olympic Games in 1896.

19 | Simple Past or Present Perfect? Complete these sentences with the simple past or present perfect form of the verb in the box. `8.4 A–C`

ACCOMPLISHMENTS

win

1. I think Taylor Swift is an accomplished[6] musician. She _____ *has won* _____ many awards this year, and she continues to make hit songs.

2. The actress Meryl Streep _____ an Academy Award in 2012. She got the award for playing British Prime Minister Margaret Thatcher in *The Iron Lady*.

3. Lawrence Bragg was just 25 years old when he _____ the Nobel Prize in Physics.

---

[4] **helmet:** a hard hat that keeps your head safe
[5] **crouching:** bending low or close to the ground

[6] **accomplished:** skillful; very good

travel

4. On her flight around the world, Amelia Earhart _travelled_ about 23,000 miles before her plane disappeared.

5. Dr. Helen Caldicott is a famous anti-nuclear activist[7]. She _has travelled_ around the world many times on lecture tours.

6. Karen Bass _has travelled_ to every continent to make films. She has recently finished a TV series on the natural history of North, South, and Central America.

be

7. Will Smith _has been_ an actor for a long time. His most recent film is *After Earth*.

8. William Shakespeare _was_ an actor before he started writing plays.

9. The inventor Thomas Edison _was_ a very creative person. During his lifetime, he invented 1,093 different things.

10. Brenda Brathwaite _has been_ an important figure in the field of game design for the past decade.

write

11. Naguib Mahfouz _wrote_ many good books during his lifetime. His best book was probably *Midaq Alley*.

12. Toni Morrison _has written_ many good books. Her most famous book is probably *Beloved*.

13. Cameron Crowe _has written_ his first movie script in the early 1980s. Since then, he _wrote_ _has written_ the stories for many famous movies.

14. Rodney Mullen is one of the most famous skateboarders in the world. In 2003, he _wrote_ an autobiography titled *The Mutt: How to Skateboard and Not Kill Yourself.*

Toni Morrison

Talk about It Choose three of the people from the sentences in Activity 19. Look online to find more information about them, and share information about their other accomplishments with your classmates.

[7] **activist:** a person who works to make changes in the world

20 | Error Correction Correct any errors in these sentences. (Some sentences may not have any errors.)

1. On that day we celebrated my father's birthday. We've invited more than 40 people to our house for dinner.

2. I have ever been to England. I learned that it is a very interesting place.

3. When I came here, I have studied the language and gotten a job.

4. Did you ever feel that life is very difficult?

5. I really miss my friend Erica. I haven't seen her since one year ago.

6. Recently this profession became more popular among young people.

7. When we arrived here, we have known we were lucky.

8. Lee is my new best friend. I met him last year when I started this class.

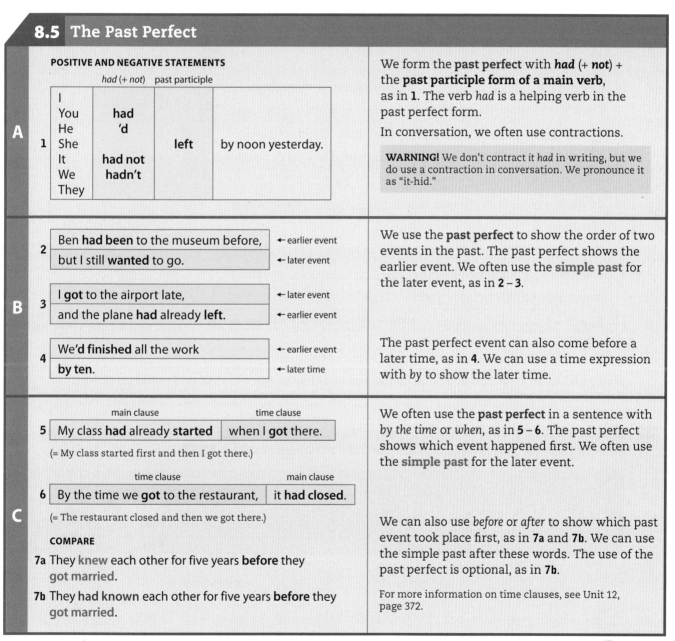

8.5 The Past Perfect

A

POSITIVE AND NEGATIVE STATEMENTS

	had (+ *not*)	past participle	
I You He She It We They	**had** **'d** **had not** **hadn't**	**left**	by noon yesterday.

(1)

We form the **past perfect** with ***had*** (+ ***not***) + the **past participle form of a main verb**, as in **1**. The verb *had* is a helping verb in the past perfect form.

In conversation, we often use contractions.

WARNING! We don't contract *it had* in writing, but we do use a contraction in conversation. We pronounce it as "it-hid."

B

2. Ben **had been** to the museum before, ← earlier event
   but I still **wanted** to go. ← later event

3. I **got** to the airport late, ← later event
   and the plane **had** already **left**. ← earlier event

4. We**'d finished** all the work ← earlier event
   by ten. ← later time

We use the **past perfect** to show the order of two events in the past. The past perfect shows the earlier event. We often use the **simple past** for the later event, as in **2–3**.

The past perfect event can also come before a later time, as in **4**. We can use a time expression with *by* to show the later time.

C

main clause	time clause
5. My class **had** already **started**	when I **got** there.

(= My class started first and then I got there.)

time clause	main clause
6. By the time we **got** to the restaurant,	it **had closed.**

(= The restaurant closed and then we got there.)

COMPARE

7a. They **knew** each other for five years **before** they **got married.**

7b. They **had known** each other for five years **before** they **got married.**

We often use the **past perfect** in a sentence with *by the time* or *when*, as in **5–6**. The past perfect shows which event happened first. We often use the **simple past** for the later event.

We can also use *before* or *after* to show which past event took place first, as in **7a** and **7b**. We can use the simple past after these words. The use of the past perfect is optional, as in **7b**.

For more information on time clauses, see Unit 12, page 372.

21 | Forming the Past Perfect Complete these sentences with the past perfect. Then read each sentence again and check (✓) *That's surprising!* or *That's not surprising.* 8.5 A

GREAT ACCOMPLISHMENTS?	THAT'S SURPRISING!	THAT'S NOT SURPRISING.
1. By age 8, the Bangladeshi artist Sunny Sanwar _____*had learned*_____ six languages. (learn)	☐	☐
2. By age 8, I _____ a few words in another language. (memorize)	☐	☐
3. By age 23, Facebook CEO Mark Zuckerberg _____ a billionaire. (become)	☐	☐
4. By age 23, I _____ a lot of money to pay for my education. (borrow)	☐	☐
5. By age 9, March Tian Boedihardjo _____ his studies at a Hong Kong university. (start)	☐	☐
6. By age 17, I _____ my university studies. (begin)	☐	☐
7. The actress Shirley Temple began her career in movies at the age of 3. By age 20, she _____ more than 25 films. (make)	☐	☐
8. By age 3, I _____ a few movies, but I don't remember them. (watch)	☐	☐
9. By the age of 12, Lope de Vega _____ his first play. (write)	☐	☐
10. By the age of 12, I _____ in several school plays. (be)	☐	☐
11. The Australian artist Aelita Andre _____ paintings worth over $30,000 by age 4. (sell)	☐	☐
12. By age 4, I _____ some pictures that my mother liked. (make)	☐	☐

Write about It What had you done by the age of 5? By the age of 15? Write several sentences.

22 | Simple Past or Past Perfect? Complete these sentences with the verbs in parentheses. Use the simple past or the past perfect form and contractions where possible. 8.5 B

I Can't Believe I Did It!

1. I _____*mailed*_____ the letter but I _____*hadn't put*_____ any stamps on it.
   (mail)   (not put)
2. I ____*turn*____ _*on*_ the washing machine but I __*hadn't put*__ in the clothes.
   (turn on)   (not put)
3. Dinner ____*was*____ in the oven for an hour, but I __*had forgotten*__ to turn the oven on.
   (be)   (forget)

4. I ___got___ to the airport in time but I ___hadn't brought___ my passport.
   (get)   (not bring)

5. My phone ___didn't work___ yesterday because I ___hadn't charged___ it.
   (not work)   (not recharge)

6. My computer ___crash___ and I ___hadn't backed___ anything.
   (crash)   (not back up)

7. I ___went___ to the store to buy some things, but I ___had left___ my wallet at home.
   (go)   (leave)

8. I ___sent___ a message to my brother, but I ___had used___ an old email address, so
   (send)   (use)

   he ___didn't receive___ it.
   (not receive)

Think about It Which action or event happened first in each sentence in Activity 22? Write the number *1* over it.

23 | Combining Sentences with the Past Perfect Underline the time expressions in the sentences. Then connect each pair of sentences using the words in parentheses. Change one of the verbs to the past perfect, and leave out the underlined time expressions. | 8.5 C |

WHAT HAPPENED FIRST?

1. I got to school at 9:10. My class started at 9. (already/by the time)

   By the time I got to school, my class had already started.

2. She finished the report at 9:30 on Monday. The meeting started at 10. (just/when)

   She had just finished when the meeting started

3. It started to rain at 6:45. The football game began at 7. (just/when)

   It had just started to rain when the game began.

4. The big sale took place in August. I spent all my savings in July. (already/by the time)

   By the time the sale took place, I had already spent

5. My friends ate breakfast at 7. I woke up at 8. (already/by the time)

   My friends had already breakfast by the time I woke up

6. The movie started at 7. I got to the movie theater at 7:15. (already/when)

   The movie had already started when I got to the

7. Hassan didn't finish his work on Friday. He went on vacation on Saturday. (still/when)

   Hassan still hadn't finished his work when

8. On Wednesday afternoon, I decided to go to the concert. On Wednesday morning, they sold out of tickets. (by the time)

   by the time I decided to go to the concert, they had

9. David's mother ate dinner at 8. She made dinner for her kids at 7. (before)

   David's mother had made dinner for her kids before

10. I ate dinner at 7. I was still hungry at 8. (after)

    I had eaten, but I am still hungry

24 | Analyzing the Past Perfect in a Text Read this article and underline the verb forms. Then answer the questions below. **8.5 A–C**

A BATTLE FOR NO REASON

Fast and clear communication has always been very important. Without the correct information, people can lose money, time, or even their lives. One clear example of this happened during the War of 1812 when Britain and the U.S. were fighting. During the Battle of New Orleans, hundreds of people died.

Soon after the battle, the British and the Americans discovered some shocking news—they had not needed to fight at all. Two weeks before the battle, the U.S. and Britain had signed a peace treaty[8] in Ghent, Belgium. However, this information had not reached the U.S. when the Battle of New Orleans began. Because information about the peace treaty had not arrived quickly enough, many people had died unnecessarily.

General Andrew Jackson at the Battle of New Orleans

QUESTIONS

1. What verb forms did this writer use? List them.
2. List any time words (time expressions, frequency expressions, or time clauses).

VERB FORMS	TIME WORDS
has been (present perfect)	always

3. Why do you think the writer used the past perfect instead of some other verb form?
4. Why do you think the news of the treaty didn't reach the U.S. in time?

25 | Error Correction Correct any errors in these sentences. (Some sentences may not have any errors.)

1. She had had a difficult life, but she never gives up.
2. After the accident, we thought my brother died.
3. When I was in high school, I had been a poor student.
4. It started to rain and then the game had begun.
5. This past weekend, my brothers had opened their new business.
6. By the time I had made that decision, I had already started high school.
7. When I got to work, I realized I didn't bring my keys with me.
8. Because of the bad weather, our class had started at 10 yesterday.

[8] **treaty:** a written agreement between countries

8.6 Using the Present Perfect in Speaking

A

EXPANDING AN ANSWER TO A *YES/NO* QUESTION

1 A: Do you know Jack Browne?
B: Of course. We**'ve been** friends for years.

2 A: Do you speak Arabic?
B: Well, I**'ve studied** it for a few years, but I **don't speak** it very well.

3 A: Have you seen Jack today?
B: No, he **didn't come** in today.

When we answer a *yes/no* question, we often say *yes* or *no* (or use a similar expression). Then we expand our answer to give more information. We can use:

- the **present perfect**—for past events connected to the present, as in **1 – 2**
- the **simple present**—for generally true statements, as in **2**
- the **simple past**—for finished events in the past, as in **3**

B

USING CONTRACTIONS IN SPEAKING

4 A: Do you like the new volunteers?
B: Yeah. They**'ve already been** really helpful.

5 A: Hi, Mom. I'm home.
B: It's late. Where[**'ve**] you **been**?

6 A: What's the matter?
B: I have bad news. There**'s been** an accident.

7 A: How is your sister in Canada doing?
B: Great. My parents[**'ve**] **visited** her twice already.

8 A: You did a great job today.
B: Really? No one**'s said** that to me before.

When we use the present perfect in speaking, we often contract *have / has*, as in **4 – 8**.

WARNING! We can write the contractions *'s* and *'ve* with pronouns. With nouns and question words, however, we usually write the full forms.

WRITTEN FORM	SPOKEN FORM
no one's	no one's
they've	they've
my sister has	my sister['s]
where have	where['ve]

Contractions are harder to hear when the main verb begins with the same or a similar sound, as in **7 – 8**.

 GO ONLINE

---

26 | Expanding Your Answer Work with a partner. Take turns asking these questions. Answer *yes* or *no* and then add more information. (Many different answers are possible.) **8.6 A**

1. Do you live here?

   A: Do you live here?
   B: Yes, I do. I've lived here for about two years.

2. Do you play a musical instrument?

3. Have you ever tried Thai food?

4. Do you know how to cook any dishes from your country?

5. Have you seen any good movies recently?

6. Do you like to travel?

7. Do you watch much television?

8. Have you lived in any other cities?

9. Have you already graduated from college?

10. Do you like to surf?

> **RESEARCH SAYS...**
>
> The most common verbs used with the present perfect in conversation are *be, do, get, go,* and *have.*
>
> CORPUS

Talk about It How many different ways can you answer each question above? Share ideas with your classmates.

27 | Listening for Contractions Listen and repeat the sentences. Then write the full, written form of each sentence. `8.6 B`

CONTRACTED, SPOKEN FORM

FULL, WRITTEN FORM

1. Where['s] she gone?   *Where has she gone?*
2. What['s] happened here?
3. Somebody's taken my book.
4. How long['s] she been there?
5. Nobody's heard from him.
6. The snow['s] stopped.
7. The weather['s] been nice lately.
8. Everyone's heard of Einstein.
9. Where['ve] the kids been?
10. Why['ve] you come?
11. Why['s] he left?
12. My family['s] been through a lot.
13. The president['s] made a decision on that.
14. This country['s] been good to me.
15. Things['ve] changed.

28 | Listening for Contractions Listen to the conversations and check (✓) the sentence you hear in each pair. `8.6 B`

1. ☑ a. I've voted in every election.
   ☐ b. I voted in every election.

2. ☐ a. He's lost a lot of weight.
   ☐ b. He lost a lot of weight.

3. ☐ a. She's set herself a difficult goal.
   ☐ b. She set herself a difficult goal.

4. ☐ a. They've decided to go on a trip.
   ☐ b. They decided to go on a trip.

5. ☐ a. I've paid for it already.
   ☐ b. I paid for it already.

6. ☐ a. She's studied Chinese for several years.
   ☐ b. She studied Chinese for several years.

7. ☐ a. We've visited them several times.
   ☐ b. We visited them several times.

8. ☐ a. What['s] he done?
   ☐ b. What['d] he do?

9. ☐ a. Where['s] everyone gone?
   ☐ b. Where['d] everyone go?

10. ☐ a. How long['s] she studied there?
    ☐ b. How long['d] she study there?

11. ☐ a. Mika['s] told me already.
    ☐ b. Mika told me already.

12. ☐ a. Well, John['s] heard all about it.
    ☐ b. Well, John heard all about it.

13. ☐ a. Sure. It's stopped snowing.
    ☐ b. Sure. It stopped snowing.

14. ☐ a. Yes, but he's always hated it.
    ☐ b. Yes, but he always hated it.

Think about It Which contractions above were especially difficult to hear? Why?

Talk about It Work with a partner. Read a sentence in each pair above. Ask your partner to say "Sentence A" or "Sentence B."

8.7 Using the Present Perfect and Past Perfect in Writing

A

MAKING GENERAL STATEMENTS

1 The basic design of a bicycle **hasn't changed** very much since the 1880s. Every bike still **uses** a foot-powered cog-and-chain system. . . .

2 A dance-fitness program called Zumba **has become** popular in recent years. Zumba **combines** salsa, merengue, and other forms of Latin American music. Alberto "Beto" Perez of Colombia **created** Zumba in the 1990s. Since then, it **has spread** around the world. . . .

We sometimes use the **present perfect** to make a general statement about something that has changed from a past time up until now. We then give more information using the **simple present** or the **simple past**, as in **1 – 2**.

Common verbs for this use of the present perfect include:

become	get better	increase	improve
change	get worse	decrease	grow

Remember: We use the simple present to describe things that are generally true. We usually use the simple past to describe specific past events.

B

SUPPORTING GENERAL STATEMENTS

3 Béatrice Coron **is** an artist with an interesting background. She **has been** a truck driver, factory worker, cleaning lady, and New York City tour guide. She **has lived** in France, Egypt, Mexico, and China.

When we describe someone or something in the present, we sometimes begin with a general statement, as in **3**. We then use the present perfect to show how actions and events in the past support our general statement.

C

GIVING BACKGROUND INFORMATION

4 In 1932, Robert Fulton **was** 24 years old. He **had** already **graduated** from Harvard University. He **had** recently **completed** advanced studies in Austria. He **was planning** to return to the U.S. . . .

When we write about someone or something in the past, we sometimes use the **past perfect** to give background information, as in **4**.

 ONLINE

---

29 | Writing about Change Complete these sentences with the simple present, simple past, or present perfect form of the verb in parentheses. **8.7 A**

HOW HAS IT CHANGED?

1. Tennis _____*has changed*_____ a lot over the past 50 years. For many
   (change)
   years, players _____ heavy wooden tennis rackets.
   (use)
   Then, in the 1980s, very light metal rackets _____
   (become)
   available.

2. Computers _____ a lot smaller in the past 50 years.
   (become)
   The first computer _____ bigger than a small
   (be)
   house and _____ 33 metric tons. Computers today
   (weigh)
   _____ tiny and easy to carry around.
   (be)

3. Families _____ much smaller in the past 50 years.
   (get)
   Large families _____ common years ago, but today
   (be)
   many people only _____ one or two children.
   (have)

The Wimbledon Championships, 1924

4. Bicycles _____ over the years. The first bicycles _____ pedals.
   (improve)   (not have)

   Instead, riders _____ the ground with their feet.
                        (push)

5. The number of cars on the road _____ dramatically over the past 30 years. In 1986,
                                         (increase)

   there _____ 500 million cars in the world. By 2010, there _____ more
            (be)   (be)

   than a billion.

Write about It Think of something else that has changed, gotten better, or gotten worse over the years. Write several sentences about it like the ones in Activity 29.

30 | Connecting the Past to the Present Complete each description with the words in parentheses. Use the simple present or the present perfect. `8.7 B`

Describing People

1. Amy Tan is a very talented writer. She _____*has written*_____
                                                      (write)
   a number of well-known novels, and one of her books, *The Joy*

   Luck Club, _____ a successful movie.
                        (become)

2. My oldest brother is the most hard-working person I know.

   He _____ a demanding job, and he
          (always / have)

   _____ a day of work. Sometimes I worry
        (never / miss)
   that he works too hard.

Amy Tan

3. My youngest brother is only 14 years old, but he is already

   very spoiled. My parents _____ him everything he wants. He
                                    (always / give)

   _____ work for anything.
        (never / have to)

4. My cousin Matt is a very good athlete. He _____ a star basketball player,
                                                        (be)

   and he _____ in several 10-kilometer races. He still runs several times a
              (also / compete)
   week, and now he is learning to ski.

5. My sister is an excellent student. She _____ good grades and she
                                                  (always / get)

   _____ many academic awards. I'm sure she will do well in college.
        (win)

Write about It Choose three people you know well. Write a general statement about each person. Then give more information to support your statement.

31 | Using the Past Perfect to Give Background Information Complete these paragraphs with the words in parentheses. Use the simple past or the past perfect. **8.7 C**

PAST EVENTS

1. One of the most important events in my life was when I

   moved to Costa Rica. Even though I was 26 years old, I

   ___*had never lived*___ outside of my small town,
         (never / live)

   and I _____ communicate in a second
         (never / have to)

   language. That year my life _____ forever.
                  (change)

2. One of the most exciting days in my life was when I graduated from university. No one else in my

   family _____ to college. Both of my parents _____ to work
         (ever / go)   (start)

   at a young age, and my older sister _____ married right after high school. All
                     (get)

   of my relatives _____ to my graduation ceremony, and I know my parents were
         (come)

   very proud of me.

3. One of my best memories was when my father took me to a baseball game. I

   _____ only ten years old at the time, and I _____
         (be)   (never / see)

   a real baseball game. My father and I _____ early that day and
                (get up)

   _____ a bus into the city. I was so excited just to spend a whole day with
         (take)

   my father.

4. One of my worst memories took place when I was in elementary school. My family

   _____ to a new city, and I _____ at a new school. This
         (just / move)   (just / start)

   new school _____ ahead of my old school in math. The students at my new
            (be)

   school _____ to multiply numbers, but this was new to me. On my first day,
         (already / learn)

   the teacher _____ me to go to the board to multiply some numbers in front of
            (ask)

   the whole class. I just _____ at the board because I didn't know what to do.
                 (stand)

   I _____ so embarrassed!
     (be)

Think about It Which sentences in each paragraph above give background information?

Write about It Choose one of these topics and write several sentences about it. Give some background information in your writing.

- One of the most important events in my life was when . . .
- One of the most exciting days in my life was when . . .
- One of my best memories was when . . .

WRAP-UP Demonstrate Your Knowledge

A | INTERVIEW Work with a partner. Ask your partner each question. Ask follow-up questions to get more information, and take notes on your partner's answers. Then tell the class about your partner.

QUESTIONS

1. Do you play a musical instrument?
2. What sports do you play?
3. What languages do you speak?

A: Do you play a musical instrument?
B: No, I don't.
A: Does anyone in your family?
B: My father plays the piano.
A: How long has he played the piano?

A: Do you play a musical instrument?
B: Yes, I do. I play the guitar.
A: How long have you played the guitar?
B: Since high school.

B | WEB SEARCH Do an online search for the phrase "has gotten better" or "has gotten worse." Copy the five most interesting sentences you find, and then share them with your classmates.

C | TIC-TAC-TOE Follow these instructions:

1. Work with a partner. Student A is X. Student B is O.
2. Student A: Choose a square. On another piece of paper, answer the question in a complete sentence.
3. Students A and B: Check the sentence together. If the sentence has no errors, write an X in the square. If the sentence is not correct, do not write an X in the square.
4. Student B: Take your turn. Write an O for each correct answer.
5. The first person to get 3 Xs or 3 Os in a line is the winner.

What is the nicest city you have ever visited?	What is something that you have had since you were a child?	Who has been your good friend over the years?
What sports have you tried?	What's the scariest thing you have ever done?	What is something that you have always wanted to buy?
How many schools have you attended?	What are three things you had done by 9 this morning?	Where had you studied English before you started this course?

8.8 Summary of the Present Perfect and Past Perfect

PRESENT PERFECT

STATEMENTS

I You We They My friends	have 've have not haven't		
He She It My sister	has 's has not 's not hasn't	been	there before.

YES/NO QUESTIONS WITH THE PRESENT PERFECT

Have	I / you / we / they	left?
Has	he / she / it	

WH- QUESTIONS WITH THE PRESENT PERFECT

Where	have	I / you / we / they	gone?
	has	he / she / it	

What	has happened?

USES

We use the **present perfect** to describe something in the past that is connected to now. This could be something that:

- started in the past and continues to now
- started and ended in the past but has a connection to now
- happened more than one time in the past but has a connection to now

PAST PERFECT

STATEMENTS

I You We They My friends He She It My brother	had 'd had not hadn't	arrived	by noon.

YES/NO QUESTIONS WITH THE PAST PERFECT

Had	I / you / we / they	left?
	he / she / it	

WH- QUESTIONS WITH THE PAST PERFECT

Where	had	I / you / we / they	gone?
		he / she / it	

What	had happened?

USES

We use the **past perfect** to show that one event in the past took place before another event or time in the past.

9 Modals II

Knowledge can be communicated, but wisdom cannot.

—HERMAN HESSE, GERMAN-BORN
SWISS NOVELIST AND POET
(1877–1962)

Talk about It What does the quotation above mean? Do you agree or disagree?

WARM-UP

A | Match the beginnings and endings of these quotations. What does each quotation mean? Share your ideas with the class.

Famous Quotations

1. Failure is not fatal[1], but _____

2. If you **can** find a path with no obstacles[2], _____

3. **Perhaps** too much of everything _____

4. By the time a man realizes that **maybe** his father was right, he usually has a son _____

5. Whenever people agree with me, I always feel _____

6. When I was a boy I was told that anybody **could** become President. _____

a. I'm beginning to believe it. _(Clarence Darrow, lawyer)_

b. is as bad as too little. _(Edna Ferber, writer)_

c. who thinks he's wrong. _(Charles Wadsworth, classical pianist)_

d. I **must** be wrong. _(Oscar Wilde, writer and poet)_

e. failure to change **might** be. _(John Wooden, basketball player and coach)_

f. it **probably** doesn't lead anywhere. _(Frank A. Clark, cartoonist)_

B | Answer these questions about the sentences above.

1. Circle the words in **blue** that are modals. How do you know they are modals?

2. What kinds of words come before the modals? What kind of words come after them?

3. The other **blue** words are adverbs. Are these words followed directly by a verb?

C | Look back at the quotation on page 278. Identify any modal forms.

---

[1] **fatal:** causing death

[2] **obstacles:** things that make it difficult for you to do something

9.1 Present and Future Ability with *Can*

A

CAN FOR PRESENT ABILITY

1 Emma **can speak** three languages.

2 I **can't cook.** No one ever taught me.

3 A: **Can** Rob **run** a mile in eight minutes?
B: I don't think so.

4 Excuse me, Professor. I **can't see** the board.

5 A newborn baby **cannot see** very far.

We often use **can** to talk about abilities in the present. It may have a meaning similar to:

- "know how to," as in **1 – 2**
- "have the ability," as in **3 – 5**

Notice: The contracted form *can't* is more common in conversation, as in **4**. The full form *cannot* usually appears in writing, as in **5**.

CAN WITH THINKING AND FEELING VERBS

6 You're not happy. I **can see** it in your face.

7 I **can't hear** the announcer. It's too noisy.

8 I **can understand** what you mean. I feel the same way.

We often use *can* with thinking and feeling verbs, as in **6 – 8**. Some common thinking/feeling verbs we use with *can* include:

believe	hear	see
guess	imagine	understand

B

CAN FOR FUTURE ABILITY

9 Mika works in the evenings, so she **can't study** with us tonight.

10 I'm going to the library tomorrow, so I **can pick up** that book for you.

In some situations, we also use *can* to talk about abilities in the future, as in **9** and **10**.

It is possible to use *can* in this way when a specific situation or decision leads to the future ability. These situations are often related to planned events.

🔊 **1 | Pronunciation Note: *Can* and *Can't*** Listen to the note. Then do Activity 2.

Remember: In positive statements, **can** is not usually stressed. In negative statements, however, we usually stress **can't**.

POSITIVE STATEMENTS

1 Emma **can** SPEAK three languages.

2 I **can** UNDERSTAND what you mean.

NEGATIVE STATEMENTS

3 She **CAN'T** speak Spanish.

4 We **CAN'T** understand the homework.

🔊 **2 | Listening for *Can* and *Can't*** Listen and circle the modal you hear—*can* or *can't*. Then listen again and repeat the sentences. **9.1 A**

1. I **can** / **can't** understand that.

2. I **can** / **can't** see why.

3. She **can** / **can't** believe it.

4. They **can** / **can't** hear you.

5. We **can** / **can't** talk about it later.

6. He **can** / **can't** leave at 3:00.

7. They **can** / **can't** hear the TV.

8. She **can** / **can't** come tomorrow.

9. You **can** / **can't** believe him.

10. I **can** / **can't** tell you now.

Talk about It Take turns reading the sentences in Activity 2 to a partner. Use *can* or *can't*. Your partner listens and says yes if you used *can* and no if you used *can't*.

A: *I can't understand that.*
B: *No.*

3 | Statements with *Can* and *Can't* Complete each fact below with *can* or *can't* and a verb from the box. 9.1 A

breathe	eat	live	see	swim
climb	fly	run	sting[3]	walk

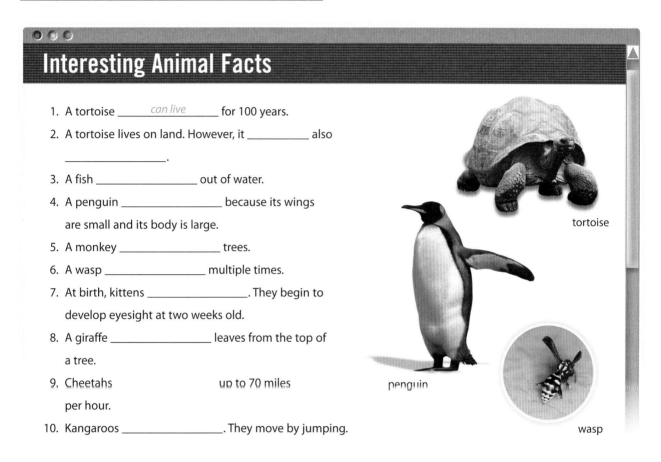

Interesting Animal Facts

1. A tortoise _____*can live*_____ for 100 years.
2. A tortoise lives on land. However, it _____ also _____.
3. A fish _____ out of water.
4. A penguin _____ because its wings are small and its body is large.
5. A monkey _____ trees.
6. A wasp _____ multiple times.
7. At birth, kittens _____. They begin to develop eyesight at two weeks old.
8. A giraffe _____ leaves from the top of a tree.
9. Cheetahs _____ up to 70 miles per hour.
10. Kangaroos _____. They move by jumping.

tortoise

penguin

wasp

Write about It Write four more sentences about the animals in this box with *can* or *can't*. Look for the information online if necessary.

bee	horse	shark
cow	monkey	snake
elephant	ostrich	wolf

[3] **sting:** to hurt (someone) by pushing a sharp, pointed part into the skin

4 | Questions with *Can* Complete the survey questions below. Use *can*, the subject *you*, and a verb from the box. (More than one answer may be possible.) Then guess your own answer for each question. **9.1 A**

add	keep	reach	run	stand
jump	name	read	spell	write

MAKE A GUESS   **YOUR ANSWER**

1. How high _____*can you reach*_____ with your arms outstretched? _____
2. How high _____? _____
3. How long _____ without stopping? _____
4. How many countries _____ in 30 seconds? _____
5. How long _____ on one leg? _____
6. How many English verbs _____ in 15 seconds? _____
7. How fast _____ 1,364, 267, and 4,897? _____
8. From how far away _____ the title of this book? _____
9. How long _____ your eyes open without blinking? _____
10. How many names of vegetables _____ correctly in 30 seconds? _____

Talk about It Ask a partner the survey questions above. Then "test" one or two of your answers to see if you guessed correctly.

5 | *Can* and *Can't* with Thinking/Feeling Verbs Complete the sentences below with *can* or *can't* and a verb from the box. Add a subject if necessary. Then practice with a partner. **9.1 A**

believe	guess	hear	imagine	see	understand

1. A: Where's the dictionary?
   B: I'm sorry. I _____*can't hear*_____ you. Could you say that a little louder?
   A: I said, "Where's the dictionary?"
2. A: Is that an *A* or an *E*? I _____ it. It's too small!
   B: I think that's an *E*.
3. A: Do you think it's going to rain?
   B: Yeah, I do. I _____ storm clouds in the distance.
4. A: What is he saying? _____ him?
   B: Not a word. I don't think he's speaking English.
5. A: That guy is really rich. What do you think that's like?
   B: I have no idea. I can't even pay my rent. I _____ having that much money.
6. A: I've read this three times, but I _____ it. Can you explain it to me?
   B: Sure.

7. A: Hello? Hello? _____ me?

   B: Not very well. We have a bad connection.

8. A: I think that's the house. _____ the address?

   B: No, I _____ anything.

9. A: What do you think I have in this bag?

   B: I don't know.

   A: No idea?

   B: No! I _____. Just tell me!

10. A: Did you hear that Ramon quit yesterday?

    B: Wow, I _____ that. I thought he loved this job.

Write about It Work with a partner. Write a short conversation using *can* or *can't* with a thinking or feeling verb. Present your conversation to another pair.

6 | Can or Can't for Future Ability Look at Paula's to-do list. Complete the sentences below about the things she can and can't do tomorrow. `9.1 B`

To Do:
make dentist appointment
buy gift for Tony
call cable company
pick up coffee
do laundry
finish chemistry homework
get books

1. She _____ the laundry because she has class all day.

2. She has a long break, so she _____ her chemistry homework in the library between classes.

3. She has about an hour free in the afternoon, so she _____ the dentist appointment then.

4. She _____ the cable company because that might take a long time.

5. The store is open until 11 p.m., so she _____ some coffee on the way home.

6. She _____ Tony's gift until she gets paid.

7. She _____ her books until her check comes, either.

Talk about It Make a list of things you need to do soon. Show it to a partner, and explain which things you can and can't do tomorrow. Explain why.

9.2 Present and Future Ability with *Be Able To*

A

CAN VS. *BE ABLE TO*

1a Robert **can speak** several languages.
(simple modal)

1b Robert **is able to speak** several languages.
(phrasal modal)

***BE ABLE TO* FOR PRESENT ABILITY**

	subject	*be able to*	main verb	
2	I	'm (not) able to 'm unable to		
3	He	's (not) able to 's unable to	run	very fast.
4	They	're (not) able to 're unable to		

Like **can**, we use the phrasal modal **be able to** to talk about abilities in the present, as in **1a – 1b**. However, **can** is more common.

Unlike simple modals, phrasal modals include a verb like *be*. The verb must agree with the subject, as in **2 – 4**.

Notice: *Unable is another way to say not . . . able.*

Remember these contractions:

am = 'm   **are** = 're   **is** = 's

B

***BE ABLE TO* FOR FUTURE ABILITY**

5 My parents are going to be able to come to the wedding.

6 I won't be able to leave early.

7 Students will be unable to use the computer without a password.

8 I'm not going to be able to give you an answer.

9 **Prediction:** In the future, we will be able to power whole cities with solar energy.
(NOT: ~~In the future, we can power~~ . . .)

We can also use **be able to** after a future form, as in **5 – 9**. In this case, the verb *be* does not change forms. Notice:

will (not) am/is/are (not) going to	be (un)able to	main verb

WARNING! We use *not* or *unable*, not both.

When we make a prediction about a future ability, we usually use *be able to*, as in **9**. We do not use **can** for predictions.

C

QUESTIONS ABOUT THE PRESENT

10 Is Lisa able to take time off work in the mornings?

11 How often are you able to see your family?

We can ask questions about the present with **be able to**, as in **10 – 11**. Notice:

am/is/are	subject	able to	main verb

QUESTIONS ABOUT THE FUTURE

12 Will you be able to come tomorrow?

13 Are you going to be able to make the deadline?

14 When will you be able to retire?

We can also ask questions about the future with **be able to**, as in **12 – 14**. Notice:

will am/is/are	subject	— going to	be able to	main verb

7 | *Be Able To* for Present Ability Rewrite these sentences with *be (not) able to* or *be unable to* and frequency adverbs. `9.2 A`

ABILITIES AT DIFFERENT AGES

1. A 16-year-old can drive safely.

   A 16-year-old is often able to drive safely.

2. Eighty-year-olds can be good employees.

3. An 80-year-old can't learn a new language.

4. A 1-year-old can't walk.

5. Four-year-olds can read.

> **F Y I**
>
> You can use *never, rarely, sometimes, often, usually,* and *always* with *be able to*. We usually put them after *am/is/are* or after *not*.
>
> Young children **are sometimes able to follow** directions quite well.
>
> A 40-year-old **is not usually able to run** as fast as a teenager.

6. A 60-year-old can understand the problems of a 16-year-old.

7. A 16-year-old can understand the problems of a 60-year-old.

8. A young person without a college degree can find a good job.

9. A full-time college student can work a full-time job.

10. Teenagers can't control their emotions.

Talk about It Read the sentences you wrote in Activity 7 to a partner. See if your partner agrees or disagrees and why.

A: A 16-year-old is often able to drive safely. I was a good driver when I was 16.
B: I don't know. I think 16-year-olds get in a lot of accidents. They aren't able to make good decisions.

8 | *Be Able To* for Future Ability Complete these statements. Use a future form with *be able to* and the verb in parentheses. 9.2 B

1. I'm sorry, but we _____ *aren't going to be able to attend* _____ your wedding.
(attend)

2. I _____ early tomorrow.
(come in)

3. I'm afraid I _____ you next weekend.
(help)

4. I hope that you _____ us.
(assist)

5. I _____ working on Monday.
(start)

6. We're sorry that we _____ you the job.
(offer)

7. You _____ that after you open it.
(return)

8. I'm sorry. You _____ that item.
(exchange)

9. I _____ that information for you.
(provide)

10. I _____ the job on time.
(finish)

> Michelle
> &
> Steven
>
> PLEASE REPLY
> BEFORE MAY 8
>
> *Linda Lee*
> NAME
>
> ☐ will be attending
> ☑ not able to attend

Talk about It Where might you hear the sentences above? Who would say them? Share your ideas with a partner.

9 | *Can* vs. *Be Able To* Can these sentences be rewritten with *can* instead of *be able to*? Check (✓) *Yes* or *No*. Then rewrite the sentences you checked *Yes*. 9.2 B

IN THE FUTURE	YES	NO
1. Next year we'll be able to take English 3.	☐	☐
2. We're going to be able to go home early on Friday.	☐	☐
3. Someday we'll be able to travel to other solar systems.	☐	☐
4. We won't be able to study tonight.	☐	☐
5. Our grandchildren won't be able to see many of the animals that are alive today.	☐	☐
6. In the future, more people are going to be able to work at home.	☐	☐
7. It's going to be sunny on Saturday. We're going to be able to go swimming.	☐	☐
8. The ocean levels are rising. Someday people won't be able to live along the coast.	☐	☐

Write about It Write three of your own predictions with *be able to*. Read your predictions to a partner. See if your partner agrees or disagrees and why.

10 | Asking Questions with *Be Able To* Complete these conversations with questions. Use a present or future form with *be able to*, a subject, and a verb from the box. Then practice with a partner. 9.2 C

1. A: The Crows are playing hard today!

   B: _Will they be able to win?_ _____

   A: I don't know. We'll see.

2. A: Thanks for the invitation!

   B: _____

   A: I'm not sure. I'll tell you tomorrow.

3. A: My cousins are coming to visit me.

   B: That's nice. How long _____?

   A: I'm not sure. I think about a week.

4. A: _____ home every weekend?

   B: No, I live too far away for that. I only go home on vacations.

5. A: I'm saving up for a new car.

   B: When _____ one?

   A: This summer, I think.

6. A: So, you have three roommates? How _____

   on your studying?

   B: I don't study at home. I go to the library.

7. A: I'm so tired of working.

   B: When _____ a vacation?

   A: Not until March.

8. A: I'm going back to my hometown for a few days.

   B: Nice! _____ your brother?

   A: No, unfortunately. He's away at school.

9. A: They're painting our building. It smells terrible.

   B: Oh, no! How _____ tonight?

   A: They're moving us out for a couple of days.

10. A: How often _____ dinner at home?

    B: Not often. I'm just too busy.

buy
come
concentrate
cook
go
see
sleep
stay
take
win

9.3 Past Ability with *Could* and *Was / Were Able To*

A	**GENERAL ABILITY IN THE PAST** **1** When I was young, **I could stay up** all night and still have energy the next day. **2** My brother **couldn't speak** until he was five. **3** Mike **was able to run** a mile in ten minutes. **4** **Could** you **hear** the speaker? It was really loud in that room. **5** **Were** you **able to speak** to the professor?	We use **could (not)** or ***was / were (not) able to*** to talk about a past ability in general, as in **1 – 5**.
B	**SPECIFIC ACTION WE HAD THE ABILITY TO DO** **6** Yesterday, Tom **was able to attend** the meeting. (NOT: ~~Yesterday, Tom could attend~~ . . .) **7** We **were able to improve** our sales last year. (NOT: ~~We could improve~~ . . .) **8** I pushed and pushed, but I **couldn't open** the door. **9** Mike **was unable to** participate in sports last year.	To talk about a specific past action that we had the ability to do, we don't usually use *could*. We use *was / were able to*, as in **6 – 7**. In negative sentences, we may use *couldn't* or *was / were not able to*, as in **8 – 9**.
C	**USING ADVERBS WITH *COULD*** **10a** I **could only get** three tickets to the game, so one of us will have to stay home. **10b** I **was only able to get** three tickets. **11a** He was so tired that he **could barely walk**. **11b** He **was barely able to walk**.	We also use *could* with adverbs like **only** and **barely**, as in **10a – 11b**. Notice that we put *only* and *barely* after the first helping verb (*could* or *was / were*). • *Only* means "and nothing else." • *Barely* means "almost not." **WARNING!** We don't usually use *only* and *barely* in this way in negative sentences. (NOT: ~~I couldn't barely walk.~~)

11 | General Ability in the Past and Present Use phrases from this box to write sentences about your past abilities and present abilities. 9.3 A

IN THE PAST

climb a tree	play a sport well
cook my own dinner	see without glasses
do complicated math problems	speak English
drive a car	stand on my hands
focus on my studies	stay up all night

When I was a kid, I could stand on my hands. I still can!
When I was a teenager, I wasn't able to focus on my studies.
Now I'm a much better student.

Talk about It Compare the sentences you wrote above with a partner. Discuss which things have changed and why.

stand on my hands

12 | General Ability vs. Specific Action in the Past Does each sentence describe a past ability in general or a specific action that someone did in the past? Check (✓) your answers. 9.3 A–B

School opportunities	General ability	Specific action
1. a. At my high school, students were able to take college courses in the summer before senior year.	☐	☐
b. I was able to take a college biology course before my senior year. I got four units of credit.	☐	☐
2. a. We were also able to get college credit by passing Advanced Placement tests[4].	☐	☐
b. I was able to get 15 credits this way.	☐	☐
3. a. Because of my extra credits, I was able to enter college as a sophomore.	☐	☐
b. This was great for me because sophomores were able to take more interesting classes.	☐	☐
4. a. Students were able to use the job placement service to search for internships[5].	☐	☐
b. I was able to find a paying internship in my senior year. I was very lucky.	☐	☐
5. a. Interns[6] were able to apply for full-time jobs after graduation.	☐	☐
b. I didn't get hired at first, but I was able to get a job three months later.	☐	☐

Think about It Which sentences above can you rewrite using *could*? Rewrite them. What happens to the meaning in the other sentences if you try to rewrite them?

13 | Understanding When to Use *Could* and *Couldn't* Read this text. Underline all the examples of (*not*) *be able to*. Rewrite the sentences using *could* or *couldn't* if possible. 9.3 A–B

The Amazing Ancients

1. The ancient Egyptians did not have the wheel, but they had thousands of workers who were able to move large stones. They also had advanced mathematical knowledge. Because of this, they were able to build the Pyramids of Giza.

Pyramids of Giza

2. The ancient Polynesians didn't have compasses[7], but they were able to navigate[8] using the stars. Many scientists believe that they were able to travel from Taiwan to Micronesia over 3,000 years ago.
3. Using the abacus, the ancient Chinese were able to add, subtract, multiply, and divide with amazing speed.

ancient Chinese abacus

4. There were no cows or horses in ancient America, so the Aztecs were not able to use these animals for farming. However, the Aztecs had advanced farming technology, and they were able to grow enough food for their large population.
5. The ancient Mayans had excellent astronomers and were able to develop an accurate[9] calendar.

Mayan calendar

[4] **Advanced Placement tests:** tests that secondary students can take to earn college credit
[5] **internships:** on-the-job training
[6] **interns:** people working at internships
[7] **compasses:** devices for finding directions
[8] **navigate:** to plan a route
[9] **accurate:** correct

6. The ancient Greeks had indoor plumbing. They were able to bathe inside the house.
7. The ancient Romans built thousands of miles of roads across Europe, so their army was able to travel long distances quickly. The longest and most famous road was the Appian Way. The Romans were able to build it in less than a year.
8. The Babylonians had very advanced astronomy and mathematics. They were able to predict lunar eclipses[10] with great accuracy.

Write about It Work with a partner. Write four more sentences about things ancient people could or couldn't do. Look for information online if necessary.

14 | Questions for Present, Future, and Past Ability Complete these conversations. Use *can*, *could*, or a form of *be able to* and a verb from the box. (More than one answer may be possible.) If necessary, look back at Charts 9.1–9.2 for information on the present and future uses. `9.3 A–B`

1. A: _Can you feel_____ that?

   B: Yes! That hurts! That's my sore tooth.

2. A: _____ last night?

   B: No, I was awake all night. Now I'm exhausted.

3. A: I'm confused. _____ that lecture?

   B: No, the teacher speaks too fast.

4. A: _____ the sales report?

   B: No, I'm sorry. But I'll finish it this afternoon.

5. A: _____ this dish without onions?

   B: Yes, of course. We can prepare it any way you'd like.

6. A: _____ it by tomorrow?

   B: No, there's too much damage. But I think I can fix it by Saturday.

7. A: _____ this if I don't like it?

   B: Certainly. Just keep the receipt.

| feel |
| finish |
| make |
| repair |
| return |
| sleep |
| understand |

Think about It Which questions above are about the past, the present, or the future?

Talk about It Practice the conversations above with a partner.

15 | Using *Only/Barely* with *Could* Complete each sentence with *could* and *only* or *barely*. Make sure that the sentences are logical and meaningful. `9.3 C`

HEALTH COMPLAINTS

1. My head hurt so much that I _____*could barely*_____ think.

2. My eyes were so sore. I _____ open them.

3. My tooth hurt so badly that I _____ eat very soft food.

4. My back hurt so much that I _____ walk.

My tooth hurt so badly!

[10] **lunar eclipses:** occasions when the moon passes into the earth's shadow

5. I wanted to sleep on my stomach, but I _____ lie on my side.

6. I was really weak. When I got out of bed, I _____ stand up.

7. After the operation[11], I _____ lift things weighing less than 2 pounds.

8. I had trouble swallowing[12], so I _____ drink water and broth.

Write about It Rewrite the sentences in Activity 15 with *be able to*.

My head hurt so much that I was barely able to think.

Talk about It Have you ever had any of the health complaints in Activity 15? Tell your classmates.

"Last week, my head hurt so much that I could barely move. I think I hadn't eaten enough."

16 | Error Correction Correct any errors in these sentences. (Some sentences may not have any errors.)

1. Last night I went to bed and could fall asleep right away.

Last night I went to bed and was able to fall asleep right away.

2. I'm so happy I could go to the picnic next weekend.
3. Sorry I can't come to the dinner last night.
4. She wasn't able to finish the project on time.
5. I studied every day and finally I can pass the test. I got a 90.
6. That runner was really tired. He couldn't barely finish the race.
7. Why can't you come to school yesterday?
8. Someday we can run a whole city on solar power.
9. I worked a lot of hours last week, but I could only make $300.
10. I'm sorry. I can't be able to see you next week.

9.4 | Strong Certainty about the Present

We often use modals to show how certain we are that something is true. Charts 9.4 – 9.6 show how different modals express different degrees of certainty.

A

POSITIVE STATEMENTS

1 He answered all the questions correctly. He **must be** pretty smart.

2 She worked all night. She **has to be** exhausted.

3 You **have got to be** kidding. I don't believe you.

NEGATIVE STATEMENTS

4 That **can't be** true.

5 You **couldn't possibly** understand this.

6 You don't know about that place? You **must not live** around here. (NOT: ~~You mustn't live around here.~~)

We use some modals to express strong certainty about things in the present. Usually our belief is based on other information (or evidence) we have.

- We can use **must**, **have / has to**, and **have / has got to** when we are almost sure that something is true, as in **1 – 3**.

- We often use **can't**, **couldn't**, and **must not** to express disbelief or surprise, as in **4 – 6**. We do not usually contract *must not* in this case.

WARNING! We do not use these modals in this way to talk about the future. (NOT: ~~He couldn't come to work tomorrow.~~)

---

[11] **operation:** the act of cutting into the body to fix or remove something   [12] **swallowing:** making food or drink move down your throat

17 | Expressing Strong Certainty with *Must* Match each statement with the correct picture. 9.4 A

PEOPLE WATCHING

a. He looks nervous. He must have a test.

b. He's in good shape. He must run a lot.

c. She must be a mom.

d. She must be pretty hungry.

e. He must have a headache or something.

f. They sure must like that toy.

1. ____

2. ____

3. ____

4. ____

5. ____

6. ____

Write about It What else do you believe about the people above? Write another statement for each person. Use *must*. Then read your sentences to a partner. Are all of them logical?

1. She must have a small child.

18 | Using Modals for a Strong Degree of Certainty Complete these conversations with *have to*, *have got to*, *must (not)*, *can't*, or *couldn't*. (More than one answer may be possible.) Then practice with a partner. 9.4 A

SERVICE PROBLEMS

1. A: I'm really sorry. Your order isn't ready yet.

   B: Are you sure? It ____*has got to*____ be ready. I brought it in two days ago.

   A: Unfortunately, we couldn't finish it because the computer crashed.

   B: But you _____ have more than one computer, right?

   A: We do. But the whole system crashed.

2. A: I'm sorry, but no one can see you today. Can you come back tomorrow?

   B: Are you sure? You _____ be that busy. I mean, there's nobody here.

   A: Oh, it'll get crowded in just a few minutes. Our schedule is full this afternoon.

   B: Maybe I can wait. People _____ cancel sometimes, right?

3. A: Where's the server? I'm starving.

   B: Oh, they're always slow here. You _____ come here very often.

   A: No, I don't. But the food _____ be fantastic.

   B: Why do you say that?

   A: Because the service is so slow, but it's still really popular.

> **RESEARCH SAYS...**
>
> We don't often use *must* in informal speaking. However, when we do, we usually use it to express strong certainty.
>
> CORPUS

4. A: This _____ be someone else's order.

   B: I'm pretty sure it's yours, actually.

   A: No. It _____ be mine. This lists four cups of coffee and I only ordered one.

5. A: This place is always empty.

   B: I know. Everyone buys books online nowadays. The owners _____ be worried.

   A: Maybe. They _____ pay very much rent, though. This neighborhood is pretty cheap, and they've had the store for years.

Talk about It Where are the people in each conversation in Activity 18? Share your ideas with classmates.

19 | Strong Certainty vs. Obligation Underline the uses of *must* (*not*), *have to*, and *have got to*. Do they express strong certainty or an obligation? Check (✓) your answers. Then practice with a partner. 9.4 A

A MEETING	STRONG CERTAINTY	OBLIGATION
1. A: You've got to wear a suit and tie to the meeting. B: I know.	☐	✓
2. A: You must be very important! They've seated you at the main table. B: That's because I'm speaking today.	☐	☐
3. A: You must remember Dr. Alton. You met her last year. B: Of course. Nice to see you again.	☐	☐
4. A: We have to present our report at 3. B: That's fine. We'll be ready.	☐	☐
5. A: Mr. Rand is still running the company. But he's got to be 80 years old. B: Hmm. I wonder if he's going to retire.	☐	☐
6. A: We have to wait until 11 before we can take a break. B: OK.	☐	☐
7. A: That must be the new manager. B: It is. I met him yesterday.	☐	☐
8. A: Can you read that sign? B: Yeah. It says, "Every attendee must wear identification."	☐	☐
9. A: The CEO[13] and the CFO[14] must not like each other very much. They haven't spoken all day. B: Yeah, I noticed that.	☐	☐
10. A: I'm so tired. This has to be the last presentation, right? B: Nope. There's one more after this.	☐	☐

FYI

We can use the modals **must**, **have to**, and **have got to** to talk about **certainty** or to talk about **obligation**.

You **must be** pretty smart. (I'm certain.)

You **must be** on time. (This is required.)

Think about It Compare your answers above with your classmates. For each conversation, what helped you decide between the two meanings?

[13] **CEO:** chief executive officer   [14] **CFO:** chief financial officer

20 | Strong Certainty vs. Ability Underline the uses of *can't* and *couldn't* in these conversations. Do they mean "impossible" or "not able"? Write *I* (impossible) or *NA* (not able) above each use. If necessary, look back at Chart 9.1 for information on *can* for ability. **9.4 A**

1. A: Is that Tom in the water?

   B: No way! That can't be Tom!

   A: Why not?

   B: Because he can't swim.

2. A: It can't be 8 already!

   B: I'm afraid it is. Why?

   A: I didn't realize how late it was. Now I can't go shopping.

3. A: This answer can't be right. But I'm not sure what I did wrong.

   B: Sorry, I can't help you with that. I'm terrible at math.

4. A: I think Amin is awake.

   B: No, he couldn't be awake already.

   A: Why not?

   B: He was up until 3 last night. He couldn't fall asleep.

5. A: Where's Bill? He's usually here by now.

   B: He couldn't come to class. He had to pick up his dad from the airport.

   A: Well, he's with someone in the cafeteria right now, but it couldn't be his dad. He looks so young!

Talk about It Practice the conversations above with a partner.

9.5 Weaker Certainty about the Present and Future

We can use the modals *might (not)*, *may (not)*, and *could* to express weaker certainty about a situation. It means we believe something is possible, but we aren't sure.

We can use *might (not)*, *may (not)*, and *could* to talk about present situations, as in 1 – 5.

WARNING! We do not contract *might not* or *may not*. (NOT: ~~mightn't / mayn't~~)

A

	POSITIVE STATEMENTS ABOUT THE PRESENT		NEGATIVE STATEMENTS ABOUT THE PRESENT
1	She's not in her office. She **might be** at lunch.	4	These documents **might not be** important, but I'm keeping them just in case.
2	All the lights are off. They **may be closed** today.	5	I always serve a vegetarian dish because some guests **may not eat** meat.
3	You have a fever. You **could have** the flu.		

Remember: *Couldn't* expresses stronger certainty (see Chart 9.4).

We can also use *might (not)*, *may (not)*, and *could* to talk about future situations, as in 6 – 10.

B

	POSITIVE STATEMENTS ABOUT THE FUTURE		NEGATIVE STATEMENTS ABOUT THE FUTURE
6	If they go up too high, gas prices **might affect** the local economy.	9	He's sick. He **might not come** to work tomorrow.
7	The team has been training hard. They **may win** the game tomorrow.	10	There's a lot to do. They **may not finish** by tomorrow.
8	We're hoping for a donation. Additional money **could help** our cause.		

21 | Expressing Weaker Certainty about the Present Complete each answer below with *might (not)*, *may (not)*, or *could* and a verb from the box. (More than one answer may be possible.) 9.5 A

be	feel	have	know	like

1. Why is Donna smiling?

   It _____*may be*_____ her birthday.

   She _____ in a good mood.

   She _____ about the bad news.

2. Why is that man wearing a blue uniform?

   He _____ a mail carrier.

   It _____ comfortable to wear.

   He _____ a job at an airport.

3. Why isn't Marco in class today?

   He _____ sick.

   He _____ a doctor's appointment.

   He _____ we have class today.

4. Why is the clerk so unfriendly?

   She _____ good.

   She _____ sick.

   She _____ her job.

5. Why is Sam's face so red?

   He _____ embarrassed.

   He _____ out of breath[15].

   He _____ sick.

Talk about It Talk to a partner. Make statements about these pictures like the statements above using *might (not)*, *may (not)*, or *could*.

22 | Making Guesses Read these facts. Write guesses about why they are true. Use *might (not)*, *may (not)*, or *could*. Then compare with a partner. Which are the best guesses? 9.5 A

Fascinating Facts

1. You burn more calories[16] sleeping than watching TV.

   We might move around a lot when we are sleeping.
   We may not move very much when we watch TV.

2. Women live longer than men.
3. People eat more when they are in groups than they do when they're alone.
4. If one person sees someone in trouble, he or she will usually help. But if a crowd of people sees someone in trouble, sometimes nobody helps.
5. People are about one centimeter taller in the morning than in the evening.
6. It is easier to remember facts if you read them in an unusual, difficult-to-read font[17].
7. Smiling can make you feel happier.
8. People usually do not notice small mistakes in books or movies.

[15]**out of breath:** having trouble breathing, for example, after exercise

[16]**calories:** units for measuring the energy value of food
[17]**font:** a style of printed letters

23 | Weaker Certainty vs. Permission Underline the uses of modals in these conversations. Do they express weaker certainty or permission? (Remember: The modal *may* can express weaker certainty or permission.) Check (✓) your answers. `9.5 A`

EMPLOYEES AND EMPLOYERS	WEAKER CERTAINTY	PERMISSION
1. Employees <u>may not make</u> personal phone calls at work.	☐	☑
2. If employees have flexible work hours, they might be less likely to quit.	☐	☐
3. Family problems could distract[18] employees from their work.	☐	☐
4. Employees can retire at the age of 65 and collect full benefits[19].	☐	☐
5. An older employee may have more experience than a younger one.	☐	☐
6. An older employee might not work for a small salary.	☐	☐
7. New employees may not take vacation in their first three months of employment.	☐	☐
8. New employees may not feel comfortable asking for help.	☐	☐
9. A young employee may not be interested in staying at the same company for a long time.	☐	☐
10. A younger employee could have more energy than an older one.	☐	☐
11. Employees cannot leave before 5:00.	☐	☐
12. Employers may hire anyone, as long as they don't practice discrimination[20].	☐	☐

Talk about It Talk with a partner about the sentences above. Do you agree with them? Why or why not?

A: *Employees may not make personal phone calls at work.*
B: *I don't think that's right. People should be able to make a short phone call.*

24 | Expressing Weaker Certainty about the Future Tell a partner which things you *may*, *might*, or *could* do on this list. Explain your answer. (You can use a form like *be going to* to talk about things you are definitely going to do.) `9.5 B`

1. take a trip on an airplane	6. buy someone a present
2. buy a car or a bike	7. get a new phone
3. read more than two books	8. get a new computer
4. go to the beach	9. go to a museum
5. visit a different country	10. change your hairstyle

I might take a trip on an airplane next summer. I'm thinking about going to China.
I'm definitely going to buy a bike. I want to start riding to work.

Write about It Write three sentences about three other things you are thinking of doing. Share them with your classmates.

---

[18] **distract:** to stop you from thinking about what you are doing
[19] **benefits:** money that is paid by a company when someone stops working
[20] **discrimination:** treating someone in an unfair way

25 | Making Guesses Look at the headlines. Do you think these might be real news stories someday? Write a sentence about each headline with *might (not)*, *may (not)*, or *could*. You can use *by* + a year to say when. ▮9.5 B▮

1. Humans Put Building on Moon

   Humans may put a building on the moon by 2020.

2. Scientists Find Cure for Common Cold
3. World Uses More Solar Power than Oil
4. 90% of Homes Have 3-D Televisions
5. Most Cars Run on Autopilot[21]
6. Technology Ends World Hunger
7. Private Spaceship Flies to Mars
8. Governments Stop Printing Paper Money

> **F Y I**
>
> We sometimes use the frequency adverbs *never* and *(not) ever* with *may* and *might* to make a negative statement.
>
> Humans **might never put** a building on the moon.
>
> Humans **may not ever put** a building on the moon.

Talk about It Read the sentences you wrote above to a partner. Explain your predictions.

"Humans may put a building on the moon by 2020. Many countries are already able to go to the moon."

9.6 Expectations about the Present and Future with *Should*

A

POSITIVE STATEMENTS

1 The store **should be** open now. It usually opens at 7 a.m.

2 Don't worry. He **should be** here soon. He's almost never late.

NEGATIVE STATEMENTS

3 She lost her keys. I **shouldn't be** surprised—she loses things all the time.

4 The test **shouldn't be** difficult for you. You're very well prepared.

We can use **should (*not*)** to express our expectations about present or future situations, as in **1 – 4**. *Should* expresses moderate certainty—not as strong as *have to* or *must*.

We often contract *should not* as **shouldn't** in negative statements, as in **3 – 4**.

 ONLINE

---

26 | Expectations with *Should* and *Shouldn't* Match the questions with the answers. Then practice with a partner. ▮9.6 A▮

EXPECTATIONS

1. Will your teacher be late to your next class? ____
2. What will the weather be like tomorrow? ____
3. Where is your best friend right now? ____
4. Who will you see next weekend? ____
5. Will you have a good day tomorrow? ____
6. When will the store open? ____
7. When are you getting home? ____
8. Will you be at work Friday? ____

a. It should be warmer than today.
b. He should be at work.
c. I should. It's my day off.
d. It should open at 7.
e. I shouldn't be. But my boss may call me in.
f. She shouldn't be. She's usually on time.
g. I should be there around 5.
h. I should see my brother. He usually comes over on Sunday.

---

[21] **autopilot:** a device that controls a plane, car, etc., for the pilot or driver

Write about It Write your own responses to these questions. Use *should* or *shouldn't*.

1. How will the weather be tomorrow?
2. What will the teacher cover in your next class?
3. When will you finish your studies?
4. Where will you be three hours from now?

27 | Advice vs. Expectations Do these sentences express advice or an expectation? Check (✓) your answers. 9.6 A

	Advice	Expectation
1. You really should eat more vegetables. Your diet isn't very healthy.	☐	☐
2. She should have some money left. I gave her quite a bit yesterday.	☐	☐
3. They should be pretty happy. They got everything they wanted.	☐	☐
4. He should be careful. That road is dangerous this time of year.	☐	☐
5. You shouldn't worry about her. She'll be fine.	☐	☐
6. You shouldn't be so tired. You just woke up!	☐	☐
7. They say the storm is over. It should be beautiful tomorrow.	☐	☐
8. You shouldn't have any trouble finding my house. It's right on the corner.	☐	☐

28 | Using Modals for Certainty and Expectation Use the modals in this box to complete the conversations below. Some modals can work in more than one place. Look back at Charts 9.4–9.6 for all the uses. 9.6 A

STRONG CERTAINTY		EXPECTATIONS	WEAKER CERTAINTY	
must (not)	can't	should(n't)	might (not)	could
have (got) to	couldn't		may (not)	

1. A: Look! I see a whale!

   B: I don't know what that is, but it _____ be a whale.

   We never see whales around here.

2. A: What is that awful noise?

   B: I don't know. The neighbors are out of town, so it

   _____ be them.

3. A: Why are all the lights off?

   B: It _____ be closed. There's no one here.

   A: Hmm. I wanted to buy some batteries.

   B: We _____ need any. I bought some just a few days ago.

4. A: Did you finish Chapter 5?

   B: I did. I stayed up all night.

   A: You _____ be exhausted!

   B: Yeah, I am. But that chapter _____ be on the test, so I wanted to finish it.

5. A: Peter ate all the cherries and left all the chocolates.

   B: He _____ like chocolate very much.

whale

STRONG CERTAINTY		EXPECTATIONS	WEAKER CERTAINTY	
must (not)	can't	should(n't)	might (not)	could
have (got) to	couldn't		may (not)	

6. A: I _____ be here tomorrow. I have to pick up my uncle from the airport,

   but I'm not sure what time.

   B: That's OK. We _____ be fine without you for one day.

7. A: So what do you think? Are they going to win?

   B: I'm afraid they _____. They're not playing very well.

Think about It Compare your answers in Activity 28 with a partner. Explain your modal choices. Then practice the conversations with your partner.

9.7 Expressing Certainty with Linking Verbs

A

SEEM, LOOK, AND *SOUND*

1a He **must be** tired. He keeps making mistakes.
1b He **seems** tired. He keeps making mistakes.

2 A: Did you like the cake? It **looked** delicious.
   B: It was!

3 A: I'm afraid to take that class. It **sounds** really difficult.
   B: Really? I think it **sounds** interesting.

Sometimes we use the linking verbs *seem*, *look*, and *sound* to express fairly strong certainty, as in **1a – 1b**. This is similar to a **modal** meaning.

We usually use:
- *look* for things we can see, as in **2**
- *sound* for things we have heard or read about, as in **3**

Notice: We usually use adjectives after linking verbs.

B

LOOK LIKE AND *SOUND LIKE*

4 This **looks like** a good idea. I think we should try it.
5 The new plan **sounds like** an answer to our problems.

6 They're ahead by two goals. It **looks like** they are going to win.

7 It **sounds like** you'll really enjoy it.

We can also use *look like* and *sound like* to express certainty. These expressions are often followed by:
- a **noun phrase**, as in **4 – 5**
- a **clause**, as in **6 – 7**

 GO ONLINE

29 | Using *Seem, Look,* and *Sound* Complete these conversations. Use the correct form of *seem*, *look*, or *sound* and an adjective from the box. (More than one answer may be possible.) Then practice with a partner. **9.7 A**

IMPRESSIONS

1. A: I cut my finger last night.

   B: Ooh. That _____ *looks painful* _____.

   A: It is. I had to get four stitches[22].

2. A: That guy never does any of his work. He _____ really _____.

   B: Actually, he has two jobs. I think he's just too tired to do his schoolwork.

3. A: Why is Ben eating lunch by himself?

   B: I don't know, but he _____. Let's invite him to eat with us.

angry
annoying
disappointed
lazy
lonely
lost
painful
scary

[22] **stitches:** short pieces of thread that doctors use to sew the edges of a cut together

4. A: There's no way I'm going on that roller coaster. It _____!

   B: Oh, come on.

5. A: Did you hear Lee this morning? He _____ really _____.

   B: I know! I wonder who he was yelling at.

6. A: I felt bad for Tony when he lost the race. He _____ so _____.

   B: Yeah. Poor guy.

7. A: My neighbor is practicing the piano again. She practices every night at 11.

   B: That _____.

   A: It is. Especially since she's not very good at it.

8. A: You _____. Can I help you?

   B: Yes, thanks. I can't find Market Street.

Think about It Work with a partner. Look at each sentence you completed in Activity 29. How could you rewrite it using a modal?

Write about It Write six sentences with *seem*, *look*, and *sound* about people and things you know. Use adjectives from this box or your own ideas. Then share your sentences with your classmates.

delicious	exciting	fun	happy	intelligent	nice
easy	friendly	great	helpful	interesting	wonderful

Myung Ja looks happy today.   *The new James Bond movie sounds exciting.*

30 | Using *Look Like* and *Sound Like* Use the correct form of *look like* and *sound like* to complete the responses. Then practice with a partner. 9.7 B

1. A: Did you hear those guys cheering?

   B: Yep. It _____*sounds like*_____ the Tigers are winning.

2. A: Where is Christine?

   B: I don't know. It _____ she's absent today.

3. A: I read four chapters last night! I'm really tired.

   B: It _____ you were up late.

4. A: Carla was packing her suitcase this morning.

   B: Hmm. It _____ she's going away.

5. A: Who is that?

   B: I don't know. She _____ she might be a professor.

6. A: Do you know when the meeting is going to be over?

   B: Everyone is standing up. It _____ they're finishing now.

7. A: He's always complaining about his job lately.

   B: I know. It _____ he's going to quit.

8. A: Let's go out for dinner tonight.

   B: That _____ a good idea.

9.8 Expressing Certainty with Adverbs

Another way to express certainty is with **adverbs**. Different adverbs express different degrees of certainty.

definitely / clearly = I am certain.

apparently = I'm almost certain. The evidence suggests this is true.

probably = This is very possible.

maybe / perhaps = This is possible.

A

Notice the placement of adverbs, as in **1 – 8**.

SENTENCES WITH A SIMPLE VERB

	subject	adverb	main verb	
1	My sister	**probably**	**knows**	the answer.
2	She	**apparently**	**works**	for that company.

SENTENCES WITH *BE* AS A MAIN OR HELPING VERB

	subject	*be*	adverb	
3	We	**are**	**definitely**	going to change our plans.
4	This	**is**	**clearly**	very important.

NEGATIVE SENTENCES

	subject	adverb	negative verb	
5	Sam	**probably**	**won't be**	home tonight.
6	The discussion	**clearly**	**isn't going**	well.

SENTENCES WITH *MAYBE / PERHAPS*

	adverb	subject	verb	
7	**Maybe**	they	**took**	the bus.
8	**Perhaps**	Lela	**isn't**	interested.

31 | Adding Adverbs Read the first sentence of each pair. Add *clearly, apparently, probably, definitely,* or *maybe* to the second sentence. (More than one answer may be possible.) **9.8 A**

probably

1. The student is failing his classes. He doesn't understand the material.

2. They took a popular dish off the menu. There are going to be a lot of complaints.

3. Pablo has a lot of soccer trophies[23]. He's a good player.

4. The students finished the test in ten minutes. It was too easy.

5. The children left most of their food on the plates. They didn't like it.

6. I'm not sure where she is. She went to the store.

7. The audience is laughing and cheering. They love the show.

8. That coffee shop has opened five new stores in this area. It is doing very well.

9. Everyone is reading that book lately. It is a big seller.

Think about It Take turns reading your sentences above aloud with a partner. If your adverb choices are different, discuss whether they both make sense.

---

[23] **trophies:** silver cups, etc., that you get for winning a sports event

32 | Using Adverbs to Write Formal Statements Rewrite these sentences using *clearly, apparently, probably, definitely,* or *perhaps* instead of *must* or *may*. (More than one answer may be possible.) `9.8 A`

IN COURT

1. The defendant must be worried.

   The defendant is definitely worried.

2. The jury must not believe him.
3. The defendant's lawyer must be nervous.
4. The judge must be tired.
5. The defendant's lawyer may ask for a break soon.
6. This trial[24] may last for many days.
7. The witness must know the defendant.
8. The police officer may speak tomorrow.

33 | Using Modals, Verbs, and Adverbs Use the words in this box to complete the text below. You will use one word twice. If necessary, look back at Charts 9.4, 9.5, and 9.7. `9.8 A`

might	seems	clearly	maybe
must	looks	definitely	probably

The Grand Canyon

The Grand Canyon ____*must*____ be one of the most
                            1
beautiful places in the world. Millions of people visit every year.

It _____ like most visitors stay up near the rim of
        2
the canyon rather than hiking down the trails. The steep trails

are _____ too difficult for many people. But if
        3
you're an experienced hiker, you _____ want to try
                                        4
hiking down. If you don't like to hike, _____ you'd
                                              5
enjoy a helicopter tour. It is _____ expensive,
                                    6
but thrilling!

   Most people visit the South Rim of the canyon. It is easy to get there, and there are many places to stay

nearby. However, if you don't like crowds, the North Rim is _____ a better choice for you.
                                                                    7
It takes a long time to drive to the North Rim, so there are fewer visitors. If it _____ like you
                                                                                        8
will have enough time, the North Rim is _____ worth the trip.
                                              9

Think about It Which words in the box above could fit in more than one place in the text?

Write about It Write four sentences about a beautiful place. Use words from the box above. Then read your sentences to a partner.

[24]**trial:** the process in a court of law

9.9 *Used To* for Past Habits and States

A

POSITIVE STATEMENTS

1 My mother **used to make** our lunches every morning.

2 My friends and I **used to take** the bus to school on Mondays and Wednesdays.

3 I **used to live** in Paris. I moved to New York three years ago.

4 He **used to have** a moustache. He shaved it off last week.

5 In high school, I **worked** hard to get good grades.
(NOT: ~~I used to work hard to get good grades.~~)

NEGATIVE STATEMENTS AND QUESTIONS

6 That **didn't use to bother** us.

7 A: **Did** you **use to have** long hair?
B: Yeah, it was pretty long.

We use *used to* + the **base form of a main verb** to talk about past habits, as in **1** and **2**. It means that something happened regularly in the past, but it doesn't happen now—something has changed.

Used to can also describe states or situations that are different now from the past, as in **3** and **4**.

> **WARNING!** We can't use *used to* with every past verb. We don't use it to simply talk about events that began and ended in the past, or if the state or action only happened once, as in **5**.

Notice that we use the base form **use** in negative statements, as in **6**, and questions, as in **7**.

B

USING *NOW*, *THEN*, **AND** *ANYMORE*

8 He **used to be** rich, but **then** he lost all his money. **Now** he has to work two jobs. He's **not** very happy **anymore**.

We can use *used to* with expressions like *now*, *then*, and *not . . . anymore* to emphasize the change between past and present, as in **8**.

• *Now* and *then* usually come before the subject.

• We use *anymore* at the end of a clause.

C

ADVERBS OF FREQUENCY WITH *USED TO*

9 We **always used to visit** my grandparents during summer vacation. We **sometimes used to stay** until September.

10 I **never used to exercise.**

We can use **adverbs of frequency** before *used to*, as in **9**.

Never makes a sentence negative, as in **10**. It is more common than *didn't use to*.

 GO ONLINE

🔊 **34 | Pronunciation Note:** *Used To/Use To* **Listen to the note. Then do Activity 35.**

In everyday speech, we reduce *used to* to "usta." As a result, *use to* and *used to* sound the same.

COMPARE

1a She **used to live** on another street.

1b She **didn't use to live** near here.

1c **Did** she **use to live** near you?

🔊 **35 | Identifying** *Used To* **and** *Use To* **Listen to the sentences and circle the correct form. Notice that the forms sound the same.** `9.9 A`

COMPLAINTS ABOUT HOW THINGS HAVE CHANGED

1. used to   use to   3. used to   use to   5. used to   use to   7. used to   use to
2. used to   use to   4. used to   use to   6. used to   use to   8. used to   use to

🔊 **Talk about It** Listen again. Take notes about the complaints you hear. Do you agree with any of the complaints? Tell your classmates.

"One complaint was, 'People used to be more polite.' I agree with that."

36 | Using *Used To* for Past Habits and States Work with a partner. Ask questions with *did . . . use to* for each of these things. `9.9 A`

CHILDHOOD

1. walk to school
2. play outside all day
3. eat breakfast with your parents
4. have to go to bed early

5. hide when you were in trouble
6. suck your thumb
7. like dinosaurs
8. have a lot of toys

A: *Did you use to walk to school?*
B: *Sometimes. But I usually took the bus.*

Write about It Write five sentences with *used to* about your habits, routines, likes, and dislikes from the past.

I didn't use to enjoy reading.

37 | *Used To* vs. the Simple Past Read these sentences about great soccer stars. Rewrite the **bold** verb with *used to* if possible. `9.9 A`

SOCCER GREATS

Pelé

1. Pelé **grew up** in poverty in Brazil.
2. He **earned** extra money by working in tea shops.
3. He **practiced** soccer using a sock stuffed with newspapers.
4. He **tried out** for Santos Football Club when he was 15 years old.

Zinedine Zidane

5. Zidane's parents **immigrated** to France from Algeria.
6. He **practiced** his soccer skills in the streets of Marseille.
7. When he was 14 years old, he **joined** the Association Sportive de Cannes Football youth division.

Diego Maradona

8. Maradona **received** his first soccer ball as a gift when he was 3 years old.
9. He **became** a ball boy for a professional team when he was 12.
10. During halftime, he **amazed** audiences with his tricks with the ball.

Think about It Which sentences above could you NOT rewrite using *used to*? Why?

38 | Using Expressions to Compare Time Complete the comparisons with *then*, *now*, or *anymore*.
`9.9 B`

CHANGING PLACES

1. This area used to be farmland. _____*Now*_____ it is covered with homes and shopping malls.
   You don't see farms around here _____.
2. This store used to be very busy. _____ they built the big shopping mall, and _____
   people don't come here _____.
3. This school used to be much smaller. _____ there are a lot more students. It's not easy
   to get into classes _____.

4. That house used to be in good shape. Nobody lives there _____, and the paint is peeling and the grass is brown.

5. This restaurant didn't use to be very popular. _____ they changed the menu. _____ it's crowded every night.

6. It used to be easy to get into this university. _____ thousands of students apply every year. It's hard to get admitted _____.

Write about It Write two or three sentences about changes in these places: your hometown, your neighborhood, your favorite restaurant, and your school. Use *used to*, *now*, *then*, and *anymore*.

39 | Adverbs of Frequency with *Used To* Think of a teacher you had. Use these ideas to write about things that teacher *sometimes*, *always*, and *never* used to do. Add two ideas of your own. **9.9 C**

A TEACHER FROM THE PAST

1. assign a lot of homework
2. sing in class
3. show videos
4. give us free time in class
5. allow students to eat in class
6. allow students to sleep in class

He always used to assign a lot of homework.

9.10 Using Modals in Speaking

A

COMMON EXPRESSIONS WITH *CAN* AND *CAN'T*

The expressions in **1 – 13** are very common in spoken English.

The negative expressions with *can't* are more common than the positive ones.

1 I **can't help it.** (= I can't control myself.)

2 I **can't wait.** (= I'm excited about it.)

3 I **can wait.** (= I don't mind waiting.)

4 I **can't stand it.** (= I hate it.)

5 I **can stand it.** (= It doesn't bother me.)

6 I **can't imagine.** (= I have no idea.)

7 I **can imagine.** (= I can picture the situation.)

8 I **can't afford it.** (= I don't have enough money to buy it.)

9 I **can afford it.** (= I have enough money to buy it.)

10 I **can't believe it.** (= I don't think it's true. OR "Wow!")

11 I **can believe it.** (= It's easy for me to think it's true.)

12 I **can't deal with it.** (= I can't manage the situation.)

13 I **can deal with it.** (= I can manage the situation.)

B

USING MODALS IN SHORT ANSWERS

14 A: Will he **come** to the meeting?
B: He **can't.** He doesn't have time.

15 A: Is the plumber going to **come** today?
B: She **may.** But she hasn't called.

16 A: Does Mark **have** the keys?
B: He **must.** He had them this morning.

17 A: **Is** he at work?
B: He **might be.** He left about 20 minutes ago.

18 A: **Is** she **talking** on the phone?
B: She **must be.** There's no one else in the room.

We can use most **modals** as short answers to questions, as in **14 – 16**.

Notice: When we use a modal as a short answer, we understand that the modal refers back to the main **verb** in the question.

When the main verb is *be* or when we use a present progressive form, we use modal + **be** in the short answer, as in **17 – 18**.

40 | Using Expressions with *Can* and *Can't* Complete each response with *can* or *can't*. `9.10 A`

1. A: Do you like working nights?

   B: No! I ___*can't*___ stand it.

2. A: Is he going to buy that car?

   B: Maybe. He _____ afford it, but he's

   not sure he wants it.

3. A: Should you be eating all that chocolate?

   B: I shouldn't. But I _____ help it!

4. A: Would you rather come back tomorrow?

   B: No, it's OK. I _____ wait.

5. A: Where is Mark?

   B: I _____ imagine. I'm surprised he's

   not here.

6. A: The Rangers lost the game.

   B: I _____ believe it! They always win.

7. A: There's so much work to do around here.

   B: Don't worry. I _____ deal with it.

8. A: Are you going to Hawaii?

   B: Yes, next week. I _____ wait!

41 | Using Expressions with *Can* and *Can't* Complete these conversations with expressions from Chart 9.10. Two answers are positive and the rest are negative. `9.10 A`

1. A: Shh. Don't talk so loud.

   B: Sorry. I _____*can't help*_____ it. My voice gets loud when

   I'm excited.

   A: Why are you so excited?

   B: My husband just bought a new car. I _____

   to see it!

2. A: What's the matter?

   B: I have so much housework and yard work to do. I just _____ it.

   A: Why don't you pay someone to help you?

   B: I'd love to, but I _____ it.

3. A: Please turn off that noise. I _____ it!

   B: It's great music. It's not noise.

   A: Yes, it is. I _____ why you listen to that stuff.

4. A: I _____ that the rent is so high now! It used to be much cheaper to live here.

   B: I know. But don't worry. We _____ it. I just got a raise.

5. A: Just think, Sara is traveling around the world right now.

   B: I _____ that. She always was adventurous.

Write about It Choose four of the expressions from Chart 9.10 A. Work with a partner to write a conversation that includes the four expressions. Then read your conversation to another pair.

42 | Using Modals for Short Answers Write a short answer for each question. Use *can't*, *couldn't*, *may*, *might*, and *must* (+ *be*). (More than one answer may be possible.) `9.10 B`

1. A: Will you lend me a thousand dollars?

   B: I _____. I don't have that much money!

2. A: Is your friend working today?

   B: He _____. He usually works on

   Tuesday, and that's today.

3. A: Are you going out for dinner on Friday?

   B: I _____. It depends on whether

   I get paid.

4. A: Are you going to vote next month?

   B: I _____. I'm not a citizen yet.

5. A: Does your teacher have a computer at home?

   B: She _____. She works a lot at home.

6. A: Are you going to bed early tonight?

   B: I _____. I need the sleep.

7. A: Is your friend coming to the movie with us?

   B: She _____. I'm not sure yet.

8. A: Did you read this chapter last night?

   B: I _____. I had other homework.

Talk about It Ask and answer these questions with a partner. Use a short answer with a modal, and give more information about your answer.

1. Are you going out for dinner this weekend?

   "I might. I'm going to see how I feel Saturday night."

2. Are you doing something fun next summer?

3. Are you going to study tonight?

43 | Using Modals for Short Answers Write a question for each answer so that the answer is true for you. Don't use the modal in the question. Then add more information to the answer. **9.10 B**

1. _____

   I might. _____

2. _____

   I couldn't. _____

3. _____

   I used to. _____

4. _____

   I can't. _____

5. _____

   I should. _____

6. _____

   I have to. _____

Talk about It Take turns asking and answering the questions you wrote above with a partner.

9.11 Using Modals in Writing

A	**CAN AND MAY FOR POSSIBILITY** **1** February **can be** very cold in this area. Temperatures often **drop** below zero. (= Perhaps not every day in February is cold.) **2** Active worker bees only **live** for a few weeks, but the queen bee **may live** for a year or more. (= Not every queen bee lives more than one year.) **3** Many visitors **come** through the museum's doors, but they **may not see** all of the exhibits.	We usually use the **simple present** to talk about facts and make general statements. However, we sometimes use the modals **may** and **can** to make our writing more exact, as in **1 – 2**. With the modal, the statement describes what happens some of the time (not always). We also use the negative form of *may* this way, as in **3**.
B	**WOULD FOR PAST HABITS** **4 When I was young**, I **would fall** asleep on the sofa and wake up in my bed. **5 In my old neighborhood**, the kids **would play** in the street until sunset. **6** My father **used to work** until 7 or 8 in the evening. We **would** always **wait** until he got home to eat dinner. I **used to get** so hungry! But Mom **wouldn't let** us eat dinner until he got there.	We sometimes use **would** in writing to describe past habits and things we often did. However, we usually introduce the past time before using *would*. For example: • In **4 – 5**, **When I was young** and **In my old neighborhood** introduce the past context. • In **6**, the first sentence with **used to** tells us that we are talking about the past. It is very common to use *used to*, *would*, and the simple past together. **WARNING!** We cannot use *would* to describe a past state. *He used to live in Miami.* (NOT: ~~He would live in Miami.~~)

44 | Using *Can* and *May* Read this text. Rewrite the underlined part of the sentences using *can* or *may*. (Sometimes the modal is given in parentheses.) `9.11 A`

Barcelona

<u>It's very hot</u> and humid in Barcelona in the summer. If you go in August,
₁
<u>you see</u> a lot of empty streets because so many of the local people are on
₂
vacation. And if you try to go shopping in the middle of the day,
<u>you discover</u> that the grocery store is closed. Fortunately, <u>you always find</u>
₃   ₄
lots of fresh fruit and vegetables at the farmers' market downtown. On the
wide street called The Ramblas, <u>you find</u> flowers and birds for sale. Even at
₅
night, <u>the street is</u> full of people. The beaches south of the city are lovely, but
₆
<u>you want to bring</u> sunscreen. It's almost always sunny!
₇

1. (can)   *It can be very hot and humid in Barcelona in the summer.* _____
2. (may)   _____
3. (may)   _____
4. (can)   _____
5.   _____
6.   _____
7.   _____

Write about It Write a paragraph about where you live. Use *may* and *can* in two or three sentences.

45 | Noticing *Would* and *Used To* Read this text. Circle the examples of *would* and *used to*. Underline the verbs in the simple past. `9.11 B`

LAURA INGALLS WILDER

Laura Ingalls Wilder grew up in the late 1800s. She wrote many books about her childhood that children still read today. When Laura was a little girl, she lived in a cabin in the woods. Her father used to hunt and fish for most of their meat. He would bring the meat home, and then the family would work together to prepare the meat for winter. One day he brought home a bear. Laura's mother used to grow onions, potatoes, and carrots. She would store the vegetables in the cool cellar below the house. The family would live through the winter on the food they had prepared and stored in the spring. One winter was very long and cold, and the family almost didn't survive.

Think about It Why did the writer choose *used to* and *would* for some of the verbs in the text above? Which verbs have to be in the simple past? Were there any other verb forms used? Why?

46 | Using *Would* Read these sentences. Rewrite six of the sentences with *would* instead of *used to*. Two of the sentences would not be correct with *would*. 9.11 B

Ancient Rome

1. Much of western and central Europe used to be part of the Roman Empire.
2. The Romans used to build roads to the areas they conquered.
3. They used to bring their advanced plumbing technology with them.
4. They used to fight huge battles with thousands of soldiers.
5. Rich Romans used to eat food imported from Asia and other parts of Europe.
6. They used to lie on couches while they ate.
7. They used to decorate their houses with colorful mosaics[25].
8. Rome used to be the center of power in the Western world.

mosaic

WRAP-UP Demonstrate Your Knowledge

A | DISCUSSION Work with a group. Write as many sentences as you can to make guesses about each picture below. Use words from the box.

must (not)	might (not)	definitely	seems
have (got) to	may (not)	clearly	looks (like)
can't	could	apparently	
couldn't		probably	

1   2   3

1. It might be New York. It's clearly cold.

B | WRITING Use these sentence starters to write about the past. Use *could, couldn't, (not) be able to, used to,* and *would.*

1. When I was three years old,
2. Five years ago,
3. Before I came to this school,
4. When I first started learning English,
5. Before my parents met,

6. Before there were televisions,
7. Before there were airplanes,
8. In the 1800s,
9. During ancient times,
10. Before there were computers,

Choose one of the sentence starters above and develop it into a topic sentence. Write a paragraph.

[25] **mosaics:** pictures made from small pieces of glass

9.12 Summary of Modals II

ABILITY

Present / Future		
• simple modal	can / can't	She **can play** the piano very well.
• phrasal modal	am / is / are able to	They **are able to attend** all of the meetings.
	will be able to	We'll **be able to fix** this mistake very soon.
Past		
• simple modal	could / couldn't	When I was young, I **could speak** a little Chinese.
• phrasal modal	was / were able to	They **were able to attract** new customers.

CERTAINTY

STRONGER CERTAINTY

Present		
• simple modals	must (not)	It's 10 degrees. You **must be** cold!
	can't	You **can't be done** yet. The test is 30 pages.
	couldn't	This **couldn't be** mine. I lost mine.
• phrasal modals	has / have to	It's 6:00. They **have to be** home by now.
	has / have got to	He's not here, so he**'s got to be** at the office.
Present / Future		
• verbs	seem	She **seems** very tired lately. She falls asleep in class.
	look (like)	They **look** happy. They're all laughing.
	sound (like)	He **sounded** upset. I don't know what was wrong.
• adverbs	clearly	She's **clearly** the top student in the class.
	definitely	They're **definitely** not going to come.
	probably	They are **probably** out of town.
	apparently	He **apparently** doesn't have any money.
Present / Future		
• simple modals	should / shouldn't	Can you wait? She **should be** here any minute.
• simple modals	could	He **could be** in the library, but I doubt it.
	might (not)	She **might know** the answer. Why don't you ask her?
	may (not)	I **may have** time to help you tomorrow. I'll let you know.
• adverbs	maybe	**Maybe** he's coming later.
	perhaps	**Perhaps** we should stop now.

(EXPECTATION) →

WEAKER CERTAINTY

PAST HABITS

PAST STATES

Past		
• phrasal modal	used to	My brother **used to tease** me a lot.
• simple modal	would	When I was a kid, my parents **would take** us to the park every weekend.
• phrasal modal	used to	The neighborhood **used to be** very quiet.

Adjectives and Other Forms That Describe Nouns

The beautiful thing about learning is nobody can take it away from you.

—B. B. KING, AMERICAN MUSICIAN
(1925–)

Talk about It What does the quotation above mean? Do you agree or disagree?

WARM-UP

A | Match each picture with a dictionary definition below.

Weather Conditions

 a.

 b.

 c.

 d.

 e.

 f.

_____ 1. A breeze is a **light** wind.

_____ 2. A blizzard is a very **bad** storm <u>with snow and strong winds</u>.

_____ 3. A tornado is a **violent** storm <u>with a very strong wind</u> *that blows* <u>*in a circle*</u>.

_____ 4. Smog is **dirty, poisonous** air *that can cover a whole city*.

_____ 5. An avalanche is a **large** amount <u>of snow</u> *that slides quickly* <u>*down a mountain*</u>. It can be **dangerous**.

_*a*_ 6. A hurricane is a storm <u>with very strong winds and heavy rain</u>, <u>over or near the ocean</u>.

B | The words in **blue** above are adjectives. The <u>underlined</u> words are prepositional phrases. The *italicized* words are adjective clauses. Based on the examples, answer these questions.

1. Can we use two **adjectives** together?
2. Does an **adjective** always come before a noun?
3. Does a <u>prepositional phrase</u> always begin with the word *of*?
4. Does an *adjective clause* come after a noun?
5. Do **adjectives**, <u>prepositional phrases</u>, and *adjective clauses* give information about nouns?

C | Look back at the quotation on page 310. Identify any forms used to describe nouns.

10.1 Overview of Adjectives and Other Forms That Describe Nouns

A

We have many different ways to describe or give more information about nouns (people, places, things, and ideas). This unit looks at how we use adjectives, prepositional phrases, and adjective clauses to describe nouns, as in **2 – 4**.

noun	adjective + noun	noun + prepositional phrase	noun + adjective clause

1 a **car**

2 an **old car**

3 a **car** with a racing stripe

4 a **car** that can carry six surfboards

B

5 Cape Town is a **great place** for a holiday.
    adjective   prepositional phrase

6 I live in a **small town** that doesn't have many stores.
    adjective   adjective clause

7 Jan has **a good idea for our discussion**.
    noun phrase

8 She's **an excellent judge of character**.
    noun phrase

In a sentence, we often use more than one way to give information about a noun, as in **5 – 6**.

A noun + its descriptive words = a **noun phrase**, as in **7 – 8**.

Remember: A determiner (*a, the, my, this,* etc.) also gives important information about a noun. A determiner is part of a noun phrase, as in **7 – 8**.

---

1 | Noticing Descriptive Words Underline the descriptive words in each phrase. Then match each phrase with a picture below. Write the descriptive phrase under the picture.

1. a <u>blue</u> car
2. an old car without a roof
3. a car that was in an accident
4. a red car that goes on water

5. a new car with stripes
6. a car with grass on it
7. a red car with big wheels
8. a red car with four people

a. *a car with grass on it*

b. _____

c. _____

d. _____

e. _____

f. _____

g. _____

h. _____

Talk about It What do you like or dislike about each car in Activity 1? Tell your classmates.

312

Think about It In the descriptions in Activity 1, find an example of these ways to describe nouns:

- determiner + adjective + noun *a blue car*
- determiner + noun + prepositional phrase
- determiner + noun + adjective clause

2 | Understanding Descriptive Words in Conversation Check (✓) the correct picture for each conversation. Then practice with a partner. `10.1 A–B`

IN A RESTAURANT

1. A: Can I help you?
   B: Yes, **a small coffee with cream**, please.

2. A: What's the special tonight?
   B: We're serving **a baked fish with tomatoes and onions**.

3. A: What can I get for you?
   B: **A hamburger with lettuce and tomato**, please.

4. A: Could we have **a table for two near the window**, please?
   B: Sure. Follow me.

IN AN OFFICE SUPPLY STORE

5. A: What kind of chair are you looking for?
   B: **A chair with wheels**.

6. A: Can I help you?
   B: Yes, I need **some white paper for my printer**.

7. A: Are you looking for something special?
   B: Yeah, I need **a printer that prints on both sides of the page**.

8. A: What kind of pens do you want?
   B: I need **some pens that don't have caps**.

Think about It Look again at each **bold** noun phrase in Activity 2. Write the words in the correct column.

NOUN PHRASES				
Determiner	Adjective	Noun	Prepositional phrase	Adjective clause
1. *a*	*small*	*coffee*	*with cream*	
2.				
3.				
4.				
5.				
6.				
7.				
8.				

10.2 Using Adjectives and Noun + Noun Combinations

A

ADJECTIVE + NOUN

1 My favorite **sport** is football.

2 That was a terrible **meal**.

LINKING VERB + ADJECTIVE

3 My **room** is getting cold.

4 You look familiar.

INDEFINITE PRONOUN + ADJECTIVE

5 Did you buy **anything** new?

6 He cooked **something** delicious.

We use **adjectives** to give important information about a noun. We generally use adjectives in three main places:

- before a noun (after a determiner), as in **1 – 2**
- after a linking verb in a statement, as in **3 – 4**. The adjective describes the subject of the sentence. Common linking verbs are:

be	feel	grow	seem
become	get	look	

- after (not before) an indefinite pronoun, as in **5 – 6**

For a list of common adjectives, see the Resources, page R-11.

B

NOUN + NOUN

7 I just had a **phone** conversation with her.

8 I haven't had my **morning** coffee yet.

9 Do you have a **credit** card?

10 My brother is a **university** student.

ADJECTIVE + NOUN + NOUN

11 He's a professional **football** player.

12 It's a beautiful **beach** area.

13 Did you get a new **cell** phone?

We can also use a **noun** to describe another noun. The first noun functions like an adjective: it gives information about the second noun, or main noun, as in **7 – 10**.

Notice that we often use an adjective before a noun + noun combination, as in **11 – 13**.

For a list of common noun + noun combinations, see the Resources, page R-11.

314

3 | Noticing Adjectives Read these comments and underline the adjectives. `10.2 A`

COURSE NAME	STUDENT COMMENTS ON PROFESSORS
Biology 124	1. <u>Excellent</u> professor! Dr. Franklin is very <u>nice</u> and always helpful. His class can be difficult but I definitely recommend it.
Biology 124	2. Dr. Franklin's lectures are very clear and his *PowerPoint* presentations are awesome. His tests aren't easy, but go to class and do the homework, and you'll be fine.
Biology 124	3. Great professor! His lectures are interesting because he tells a lot of personal stories. Tests are very long but that's not really a bad thing.
Management 103	4. Awesome teacher! She's very helpful and enthusiastic about the subject. I can't think of anything negative about her class.
Management 103	5. One of my favorite professors! The class is easy and enjoyable.
Public Speaking 101	6. I just want to say that I'm a very shy person but this class was terrific. There was nothing scary about it at all. Professor Lane really helped me overcome[1] my fear of public speaking.

Think about It Group the adjectives from the sentences above in this chart.

Adjective + noun	Linking verb + adjective	Indefinite pronoun + adjective
excellent professor	*is nice*	

Write about It Write three sentences about a teacher you liked. Use adjectives in your sentences.

4 | Using Adjectives in Different Places Put the words in the correct order to make statements. Check (✓) *Compliment* or *Criticism*. Then compare answers with your classmates. Do you agree? `10.2 A`

	COMPLIMENT	CRITICISM
1. a / is / nice / person / he *He is a nice person.*	✓	☐
2. food / good / tastes / this _____	☐	☐
3. wasn't / answer / clear / your _____	☐	☐
4. apartment / I / love / new / your _____	☐	☐
5. looks / nice / your / hair _____	☐	☐

[1] **overcome:** to control something

	COMPLIMENT	CRITICISM

6. good/you/coffee/make   ☐ ☐

_____

7. she/person/is/a/lazy   ☐ ☐

_____

8. did/you/great/a/job   ☐ ☐

_____

9. wasn't/good/there/anything/on TV   ☐ ☐

_____

10. never/do/anything/for me/nice/you   ☐ ☐

_____

11. looks/perfect/it   ☐ ☐

_____

Talk about It Work with a partner. Choose one compliment and one criticism in Activity 4, and use each of them to create a short conversation.

5 | Usage Note: Placement of Adjectives Read the note. Then do Activity 6.

Most **adjectives** can go either before a noun or after a linking verb. However:

ADJECTIVE + NOUN

A few adjectives normally go **before a noun only**. Examples of these adjectives include:

entire	introductory	maximum
former	main	previous

The **entire class** is here. (NOT: ~~The class is entire.~~)

LINKING VERB + ADJECTIVE

A few adjectives normally go **after a linking verb only**. Examples of these adjectives include:

afraid	alone	glad	ready	sure
alive	asleep	ill	sorry	well

The boy **was afraid**. (NOT: ~~He was an afraid boy.~~)

6 | Using Adjectives in the Correct Place Choose an adjective from the box to complete each conversation below. Then practice with a partner. `10.2 A`

afraid	entire	glad	previous	tired	well
asleep	full	northern	sorry	unusual	

1. A: Why aren't you going outside?

   B: Because it's dark and I'm _____*afraid*_____.

2. A: Where do you live in the city?

   B: In the _____ part.

3. A: Where do you live now?

   B: 223 Ridgewood Road.

   A: And what was your _____ address?

   B: 182 Center Street.

4. A: Jack didn't look right today.

   B: Yeah, I don't think he's _____.

5. A: Is Barbara at home?

   B: Yes, but she's _____.

6. A: Do you want to do something tomorrow?

   B: I'm _____ but I have a meeting all day.

7. A: Thank you for the beautiful sweater.

   B: I'm _____ you like it.

8. A: How was the movie?

   B: I don't know. I didn't get to see it.

   A: What happened?

   B: The theater was already _____ when I got there.

9. A: Do you know this city very well?

   B: I should. I've lived here my _____ life.

10. A: You look _____.

    B: I am. I'm taking seven classes this semester.

    A: Is that _____?

    B: Yeah, four or five is more common.

Think about It Which adjectives in Activity 6 can you use both before a noun and after a linking verb?

---

7 | Using Noun + Noun Combinations Choose a noun from the box to complete each question. **(More than one noun may be possible.)** `10.2 B`

1. Do you have a _____*road*_____ map of this area?

2. Did you take a long _____ trip last year?

3. Does anyone help you with your _____ work?

4. Are you a _____ fan[2]?

5. Do you have _____ insurance?

6. What is your favorite _____ memory?

7. How long was your _____ vacation from school?

8. Do you usually carry _____ identification?

9. Do you make your own _____ arrangements?

10. Do you hope to be a _____ owner someday?

11. Do you enjoy going to _____ museums?

12. Do you have a _____ degree?

art
baseball
business
childhood
health
photo
road
school
summer
train
travel
university

Talk about It Ask a partner the questions above. (Just say "I'd rather not answer that" if you don't want to answer a question.)

Think about It Answer these questions.

1. Which questions above use an adjective before a noun + noun combination?
2. What other adjectives could you use in each question?

Do you have a(n) [electronic/good/clear/new] road map of this area?

---

8 | Forming Noun + Noun Combinations Use the words in this box to make as many different noun + noun combinations as you can. Then compare your list with a partner. `10.2 B`

business	environment	hospital	manager	office	record	school	teacher
emergency	guide	library	notebook	paper	room	supplies	worker

Write about It Choose three of the noun + noun combinations you made above and use each in a sentence.

[2] **fan:** a person who likes, for example, a singer or a sport very much

10.3 Using a Series of Adjectives

A

We use **adjectives** to give many different types of information. For example:

TYPE OF INFORMATION	EXAMPLES
OPINION	beautiful, delicious, familiar, favorite, interesting, safe, terrible, tired
SIZE	big, enormous, huge, large, little, short, small, tall, tiny
SHAPE	flat, oval, round, square
AGE	ancient, elderly, new, old, young
COLOR	black, brown, green, red, white, yellow
NATIONALITY	Canadian, Chinese, Spanish
MATERIAL	cotton*, paper*, plastic*, sandy, wool*
PURPOSE / TYPE	international, national, private, public, social

*Words like *cotton*, *paper*, *plastic*, and *wool* function as both nouns and adjectives.

B

ADJECTIVES + NOUN

1 This restaurant serves **fresh, simple meals**.
2 My phone has a lot of **interesting new features**.

We sometimes (but not often) use two or three adjectives before a noun, as in **1 – 2**. When two adjectives come before a noun, people sometimes put a comma between them.

> It's not easy to know when to add a comma between two adjectives that come before a noun. For now, just be aware that you will see this done.

LINKING VERB + ADJECTIVES

3 We were **tired and hungry**.
4 Bicycles are **safe, fun, and economical**.

After a linking verb, we add *and* between two adjectives, as in **3**. We use commas between three adjectives; we use *and* before the last adjective, as in **4**.

C

ORDER OF ADJECTIVES

5 He gave me a **beautiful ceramic bowl**.
6 She teaches **traditional Chinese cooking**.
7 I just found an **interesting new website**.
8 I want to go somewhere with **white sandy beaches**.
9 This restaurant serves **simple, delicious food**.
10 Everyone should have **good, clean water**.

When we use two or more adjectives together, they often (but not always) follow the order in Section A above. For example:

- We usually use an adjective of opinion before other types of adjectives, as in **5 – 7**.
- We usually use an adjective of color before an adjective of material, as in **8**.

We often use two adjectives of opinion together, as in **9 – 10**. The more general adjective usually comes first. In this case, we usually use a comma between the adjectives.

GO ONLINE

9 | Categorizing Adjectives Underline the adjectives in these statements and check (✓) *True* or *False*. Then group the adjectives in the chart on page 319. (More than one answer may be possible.) `10.3 A`

	TRUE	FALSE
1. I've been really <u>busy</u> lately.	☐	☐
2. I'm taking an interesting course this semester.	☐	☐
3. I think it's really noisy in here.	☐	☐
4. I just learned something new.	☐	☐
5. I never do anything wrong.	☐	☐
6. My previous school was in a different city.	☐	☐

	TRUE	FALSE
7. I had a big breakfast this morning.	☐	☐
8. I love Japanese food.	☐	☐
9. I don't like using plastic shopping bags.	☐	☐
10. I don't eat enough green vegetables.	☐	☐
11. I've had a lot of hard jobs.	☐	☐
12. I'm tired now.	☐	☐
13. The earth is flat.	☐	☐
14. The United Nations is an international organization.	☐	☐

Opinion	Size	Shape	Age	Color	Nationality	Material	Purpose/ Type
busy							

Think about It Which type of adjective seems to be the most common? Which adjectives were hard to put in a category?

Write about It Rewrite each false statement in Activity 9. Use a different adjective to make the statement true.

10 | Using a Series of Adjectives Choose a series of adjectives from the box to complete the sentences below. Add commas and use *and* where necessary. (More than one answer may be possible.) 10.3 B

big/beautiful	clean/safe	good/hot	pleasant/residential
busy/industrial	friendly/cozy	helpful/nice/caring	spacious[3]/clean/comfortable
busy/main	friendly/helpful	nice/quiet	

○ ○ ○

Hotel Kashmir

1. Great place to stay in Agra. The staff was _____*friendly and helpful*_____, and my room was _____.

2. This was my favorite hotel in India. It's on a _____ street yet close to a _____ road.

3. Agra is a _____ city, but the hotel is in a _____ _____ area. It's a _____ place to stay.

[3] **spacious:** with a lot of space inside

4. The hotel itself is a _____ house with a nice garden, and there was very _____ water.

5. This hotel has a _____ atmosphere, and its staff is _____ as well.

Think about It Which series of adjectives in Activity 10 need commas? Why?

Think about It Writers use a series of adjectives when they need to get a lot of descriptive information into a few words. Can you think when this might be necessary?

Talk about It Talk to a partner. Describe the last hotel where you stayed.

11 | Which Adjective Comes First? What type of information do you think each **bold** adjective gives? Choose your answers from the box. (Some adjectives are difficult to categorize.) `10.3 C`

opinion	size	shape	age	color	nationality	material	purpose/type

1. I own a **beautiful Persian** carpet.   _opinion_   _nationality_
2. Kimchi is a **traditional Korean** dish.   _____   _____
3. Can you hand me that **big plastic** spoon?   _____   _____
4. I went to a **large private** school.   _____   _____
5. You can't live without **good, clean** water.   _____   _____
6. **Small, solar-powered** cars will be available in the future.   _____   _____
7. There's a **new green** space around my house.   _____   _____
8. Fast food is **tasty, convenient**, and **cheap**.   _____   _____   _____
9. A banana is a **long, curved, yellow** fruit.   _____   _____   _____
10. The National Council of La Raza (NCLR) is a **large national Hispanic** organization.   _____   _____   _____

Think about It Which adjectives above were hard to put in a category? What does this suggest about why the order of adjectives isn't always the same?

12 | Error Correction Correct any errors in these sentences. (Some sentences may not have any errors.)

1. Friends are always honest supportive and loyal.
2. The leader of a country needs to be intelligence and truthful.
3. My parents' house is modern, and comfortable.
4. Good neighbors are caring, collaborative[4], and sociable.
5. Chinese food is healthy delicious.
6. I try to write good and interesting paragraphs.

[4]**collaborative:** able to work with others on a project

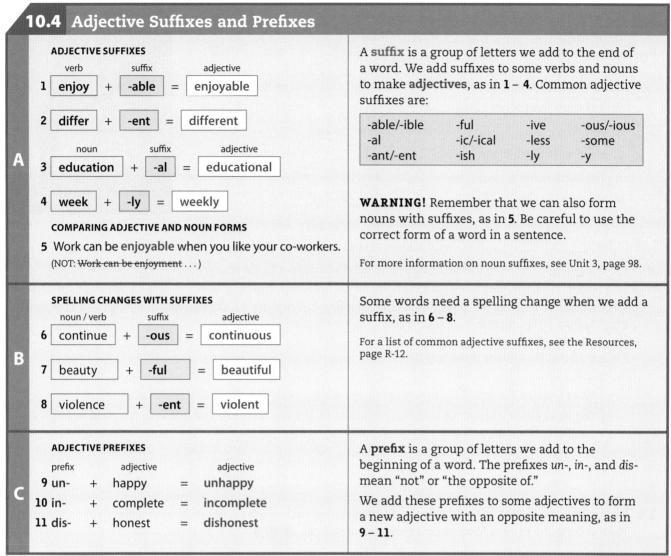

10.4 Adjective Suffixes and Prefixes

A

ADJECTIVE SUFFIXES

1. enjoy (verb) + -able (suffix) = enjoyable (adjective)

2. differ (verb) + -ent (suffix) = different (adjective)

3. education (noun) + -al (suffix) = educational (adjective)

4. week (noun) + -ly (suffix) = weekly (adjective)

COMPARING ADJECTIVE AND NOUN FORMS

5. Work can be **enjoyable** when you like your co-workers.
   (NOT: Work can be ~~enjoyment~~ ...)

A **suffix** is a group of letters we add to the end of a word. We add suffixes to some verbs and nouns to make **adjectives**, as in **1 – 4**. Common adjective suffixes are:

-able/-ible	-ful	-ive	-ous/-ious
-al	-ic/-ical	-less	-some
-ant/-ent	-ish	-ly	-y

WARNING! Remember that we can also form nouns with suffixes, as in **5**. Be careful to use the correct form of a word in a sentence.

For more information on noun suffixes, see Unit 3, page 98.

B

SPELLING CHANGES WITH SUFFIXES

6. continue (noun / verb) + -ous (suffix) = continuous (adjective)

7. beauty + -ful = beautiful

8. violence + -ent = violent

Some words need a spelling change when we add a suffix, as in **6 – 8**.

For a list of common adjective suffixes, see the Resources, page R-12.

C

ADJECTIVE PREFIXES

9. un- (prefix) + happy (adjective) = unhappy (adjective)

10. in- + complete = incomplete

11. dis- + honest = dishonest

A **prefix** is a group of letters we add to the beginning of a word. The prefixes *un-*, *in-*, and *dis-* mean "not" or "the opposite of."

We add these prefixes to some adjectives to form a new adjective with an opposite meaning, as in **9 – 11**.

13 | Noticing Suffixes   How is each adjective formed? Complete this chart. Then complete each sentence on page 322 with an adjective from the chart. (More than one answer may be possible.)   `10.4 A`

Adjective	= Verb/Noun + suffix		Adjective	= Verb/Noun + suffix
1. attractive	= ___*attract*___ + ___*ive*___		10. healthy	= _____ + _____
2. available	= _____ + _____		11. important	= _____ + _____
3. awesome	= _____ + _____		12. monthly	= _____ + _____
4. careless	= _____ + _____		13. national	= _____ + _____
5. comfortable	= _____ + _____		14. poisonous	= _____ + _____
6. emotional	= _____ + _____		15. powerful	= _____ + _____
7. fashionable	= _____ + _____		16. professional	= _____ + _____
8. foolish	= _____ + _____		17. reasonable	= _____ + _____
9. harmful	= _____ + _____		18. successful	= _____ + _____

1. Looking at the stars through a telescope is an _____ sight.
2. Smoking is _____ to your health.
3. _____ clothes usually aren't fashionable.
4. Chocolate will kill some animals. It is _____ to them.
5. Most fast food is not _____.
6. Not all _____ people earn a lot of money.
7. Heat and electricity are usually _____, not weekly, expenses.
8. There are some _____ programs on TV.
9. You should never become _____ at work.
10. When you are _____, you often make poor decisions.
11. A _____ artist should never give away his or her work.
12. It's _____ to walk a mile in about 15 minutes (1.6 kilometers).

Talk about It Look at the statements you completed in Activity 13. Do you disagree with any of them? Why? Tell your classmates.

Think about It Answer these questions.

1. Are the adjectives in the chart in Activity 13 formed from nouns or verbs? Write *N* (noun) or *V* (verb) next to each. (If the word can be either, write both *N* and *V*.) Use a dictionary if necessary.

2. What nouns do we often use with the adjectives in Activity 13? Do an online search to find examples.

attractive: woman, people, images, face, personality

14 | Recognizing Adjective vs. Noun Forms Label each word on the right as *A* (adjective) or *N* (noun). Then choose the correct form to complete the sentences. 10.4 A

DESCRIBING WEBSITES

1. This website produces _____ podcasts[5] of stories translated into Spanish.
   ___ freedom   ___ free

2. This is a _____, educational website just for children.
   ___ safe   ___ safety

3. This poetry website provides examples of _____ styles of poetry.
   ___ different   ___ difference

4. This website offers university courses with both _____ and practical value.
   ___ academy   ___ academic

5. This website is a _____ resource for teachers.
   ___ wonder   ___ wonderful

6. People of all ages will find a _____ of weekend activities on this website.
   ___ variety   ___ various

7. This website provides _____ activities on math and geography.
   ___ interactive   ___ interaction

8. These free lectures and podcasts are a _____ resource for students.
   ___ value   ___ valuable

---

[5] **podcasts:** recordings that you can take from the Internet and watch or listen to on your computer or MP3 player

9. Learn how to run a _____ business through these free online courses.   ___ successful   ___ success

10. This website has a science _____ for everyone.   ___ active   ___ activity

15 | Making Spelling Changes Complete these questions with the adjective form of the word in parentheses. If necessary, use a dictionary to make the spelling changes. [10.4 B]

1. Do you feel _____ on an airplane? (nerve)
2. What's the name of a _____ movie? (fun)
3. Have you ever met anyone _____? (fame)
4. How can you learn about _____ differences? (culture)
5. Do you like to read _____ materials? (science)
6. What are three _____ things that everyone needs? (base)
7. Are you in _____ health? (excellence)
8. Can you study in a _____ room? (noise)
9. What is an example of a _____ disaster? (nature)
10. Are you a _____ person? (create)
11. Were you _____ when you were a child? (cooperate)

> **STUDY STRATEGY**
> There is no easy way to know which suffix to add to a word. You learn suffixes by seeing the words and using them. Reading a lot helps. You can also look in a dictionary.

Talk about It Ask a partner the questions above.

16 | Spelling Note: The Prefix *In-* Read the note. Then do Activity 17.

When we add the prefix *in-* to some adjectives, we make a spelling change.

- When the adjective begins with *p* or *m*, the prefix *in-* changes to **im-**:
  possible   **im**possible   mature   **im**mature

- When the adjective begins with *r*, the prefix *in-* changes to **ir-**:
  regular   **ir**regular   relevant   **ir**relevant

- When the adjective begins with *l*, the prefix *in-* changes to **il-**:
  logical   **il**logical   legal   **il**legal

17 | Using Adjective Prefixes Add a prefix to make a new adjective with the opposite meaning. Make any necessary spelling changes. (Use a dictionary to check the meaning of any words you don't know.) [10.4 C]

un-					
afraid	_____	comfortable	_____	fashionable	*unfashionable*
attractive	_____	connected	_____	interested	_____
breakable	_____	conscious	_____	kind	_____
certain	_____	equal	_____	professional	_____
clear	_____	fair	_____	safe	_____

in- / im- / ir- / il-					
patient	_____	replaceable	_irreplaceable_	separable	_____
practical	_____	resistible	_____	significant	_____
rational	_____	reversible	_____	sincere	_____
regular	_____	secure	_____	valid	_____
relevant	_____	sensitive	_____		

dis-					
agreeable	_____	interested	_____	orderly	_____
connected	_____	loyal	_____	respectful	_____
graceful	_____	obedient	_____	similar	_____

Think about It Which adjectives in Activity 17 can use more than one negative prefix? Can you explain the differences in the meaning of each pair of adjectives?

Write about It Read these questions. Use five of the adjectives in Activity 17 to write five more questions. Then ask a partner the questions.

1. What do you think is fashionable these days? What's unfashionable?
2. What is irreplaceable to you?
3. Do you own something unbreakable?
4. Have you ever been disloyal to a good friend?
5. What food is irresistible to you?

6. _____

7. _____

8. _____

9. _____

10. _____

18 | Error Correction Correct any errors in these sentences. (Some sentences may not have any errors.)

1. My wife is a kindness woman.
2. Traveling by plane is very convenience.
3. A success person is willing to work long, hard hours.
4. When I am loneliness, I try to do something fun with my friends.
5. My sister is an optimist person.
6. You need many different skills to be succeed in the world.
7. We are not safety here.
8. There are many things you can do to stay health.
9. I think confident makes us cheerful and grateful.
10. Life needs to be colorful and adventure.

Introduction to -*ing* and -*ed* Adjectives

We sometimes use the -**ing** and -**ed** forms of verbs as adjectives. With adjectives for feelings, we can often use both forms, but we use them in different ways, as in **1a – 2b**.

X CAUSES A FEELING

1a A bear is a **frightening** animal.
A bear is **frightening**.
(A bear causes fright.)

2a That man is an **amazing** skier.
That man is **amazing**.
(The man causes amazement.)

X FEELS SOMETHING

1b Tom was a **frightened** little boy.
Tom felt **frightened**.
(Something makes Tom feel fright.)

2b She performed to an **amazed** audience.
The audience felt **amazed**.
(Something makes the audience feel amazement.)

With many other -*ing* and -*ed* forms, only one form commonly functions as an adjective, as in **3a – 4b**.

3a We moved the meeting to the **following** week.

3b Not used as an adjective: ~~followed~~

4a This problem is **complicated**.

4b **Less common:** The problem has a number of **complicating** factors.

GRAMMAR TERMS: We call the -*ing* form of a verb the **present participle**. The -*ed* form of a verb is the **past participle**.

19 | Noticing -*ing* and -*ed* Adjectives Underline the -*ing* and -*ed* adjectives and complete the sentences with your own ideas. Then compare with your classmates. `10.5 A`

1. _____ is an interesting book.

2. _____ is a tiring activity.

3. _____ is a confusing topic for an essay.

4. _____ is an exciting sport.

5. I am interested in _____.

6. I feel tired when _____.

7. I feel confused when _____.

8. I feel excited when _____.

20 | Using -ing and -ed Adjectives Complete the sentences below with adjectives from the box. (More than one answer may be possible.) `10.5 A`

encouraging	exciting	increasing	outstanding	relaxing

1. Climbing a mountain is not a _____relaxing_____ way to spend your vacation.

2. Traveling around the world would be an _____ adventure.

3. Do we need to worry about the _____ number of people who try to climb Mount Everest every year?

4. I could use a few _____ words before I take my driver's test.

5. This is an _____ book. You really should read it.

RESEARCH SAYS...

Common -ing adjectives include *amazing, boring, encouraging, exciting, following, increasing, interesting, outstanding,* and *working.*

CORPU

complicated	determined	disappointed	exhausted	organized

6. An _____ person can find things quickly.

7. A _____ person doesn't give up easily.

8. A _____ math problem is difficult to solve.

9. It's not unusual to feel _____ when you don't reach a goal.

10. He was _____ after taking a long hike in the mountains.

RESEARCH SAYS...

Common -ed adjectives include *advanced, ashamed, bored, complicated, confused, determined, disappointed, educated, excited, exhausted, frightened, interested, pleased, surprised,* and *tired.*

CORPU

21 | -ing or -ed Adjective? Complete each conversation with an adjective from the box. Then practice with a partner. `10.5 A`

1. A: That was really scary.
   B: I don't know. I thought it was sort of _____.

2. A: I have a surprise for you but don't get too _____.
   B: What is it?
   A: We're going to San Francisco!

exciting/excited

3. A: Let's do something different because this is really _____.
   B: I agree.

4. A: What did you think of the movie?
   B: I didn't really like it but I wasn't _____ at all.

boring/bored

5. A: How was the show?
   B: It was pretty _____.

6. A: Did you see the car hit the fence?
   B: Yeah, I'm _____ the driver didn't get hurt.

amazing/amazed

7. A: Are you nervous about the exam?

   B: No, I feel pretty _____ .

8. A: Do you want to do something special?

   B: No, let's just stay here and have a _____ day.

relaxing/relaxed

10.6 Multi-Word Adjectives

We sometimes put two or more words together to make a **multi-word adjective**, as in **1 – 7**. Some common combinations include:

A

1	ADJECTIVE + NOUN	a last-minute **plan**, a full-length **movie**, a high-risk **investment**, a fast-food **restaurant**
2	NOUN + ADJECTIVE	a smoke-free **office**, an ice-cold **drink**, a world-famous **singer**
3	ADJECTIVE + ADJECTIVE	a bluish-gray **car**, a dark-gray **suit**, a light-blue **sweater**
4	ADJECTIVE + -ING FORM	a high-ranking **person**, a long-lasting **friendship**, an English-speaking **country**
5	NOUN + -ING FORM	a confidence-building **activity**, a hair-raising **experience**, a mouth-watering **smell**
6	ADJECTIVE + -ED FORM	an open-ended **question**, a ready-made **meal**, an old-fashioned **kitchen**
7	NOUN + -ED FORM	a world-renowned **doctor**, a health-related **issue**, sun-dried **fruit**

B

8 I'm looking for a **full-time** job.

9 He's a **good-looking** man.

10 The test had a lot of **open-ended** questions.

11 I have more health problems now that I'**m middle aged**.

12 This phone **isn't** very **user friendly**.

When a multi-word adjective comes before a noun, we usually write it with a hyphen (-), as in **8 – 10**.

We don't usually use a hyphen when a multi-word adjective follows a linking verb, as in **11 – 12**.

GO ONLINE

22 | Noticing Multi-Word Adjectives
Underline the multi-word adjective in each sentence. Then group the multi-word adjectives in the chart on page 328. **10.6 A**

1. A sloth is a <u>strange-looking</u> animal.
2. Spinach is an iron-rich food.
3. Most people have long-distance service on their phones.
4. This isn't a very user-friendly website.
5. Jogging in waist-high water is good for you.
6. Driving through the mountains can be a nerve-racking experience.
7. It's easy to move a free-standing mirror.
8. Physically inactive people have more health-related problems.
9. Not all trees have dark-green leaves.
10. The average life expectancy of a family-owned business is 24 years.
11. Businesses spend a lot of money on eye-catching advertisements.
12. My advice for the new employees is to stay open minded.

sloth

Adjective + noun	
Noun + adjective	
Adjective + adjective	
Adjective + -*ing* form	*strange-looking*
Noun + -*ing* form	
Adjective + -*ed* form	
Noun + -*ed* form	

Talk about It What other multi-word adjectives can you think of for each group above?

Write about It Choose three of the multi-word adjectives in the chart above. Use them in your own sentences.

23 | Using Multi-Word Adjectives Choose a multi-word adjective from the box to complete each sentence below. Add a hyphen if necessary. `10.6 B`

big name	funny looking	side view	time consuming
bright yellow	home cooked	Spanish speaking	year round
family owned	life prolonging	sugar free	world famous

F Y I

We sometimes use another adjective with a multi-word adjective.

I'm looking for a **permanent** full-time job.

The test had a lot of **difficult** open-ended questions.

1. IZZE is a _____ *sugar-free* _____ soda. They make it with fruit juice.

2. People in Brazil speak Portuguese. Brazil is not a

   _____ country.

3. My grandfather started this company 100 years ago. It is a

   _____ business.

4. Britain, New Zealand, and Australia have _____ schools.

   This means there are shorter summer vacations and more frequent breaks.

5. People everywhere have heard of Barack Obama. He's _____.

6. Writing good tests is a difficult, _____ task.

7. The red-shanked douc is a _____ monkey that looks a lot like a clown.

8. Cars have _____ mirrors so you can see passing cars.

9. Most people have heard of Apple. It's a _____ company.

10. I usually eat a lot of meals out, so I always enjoy a _____ meal.

11. In some countries, taxis are _____. That makes them easy to see.

12. Exercising regularly is a _____ activity.

Think about It In which sentences above did you use a multi-word adjective without a hyphen? Why?

10.7 Prepositional Phrases That Describe Nouns

A

	noun	prepositional phrase
1 They have	a **house**	**with** a pool.

preposition + noun phrase

2 You'll love the white sandy **beaches of Cape Town**.
(Which beaches?)

3 The school has made several **changes in the schedule**. (What kind of changes?)

4 Berries are a great **source of vitamins**.
(What kind of source?)

5 He didn't give a **reason for the gift**.
(What kind of reason?)

6 It's a small **city with narrow streets**.

7 What are the **causes of climate change**?

Like an adjective, we can use a **prepositional phrase** to give more information about a **noun**, as in **1**. The prepositional phrase comes after the noun.

A prepositional phrase often answers the question *what kind* or *which one*, as in **2 – 5**.

Common prepositions include:

as	by	from	like	on	with
at	for	in	of	to	

Notice that we sometimes add an **adjective** or **noun** before the noun in a prepositional phrase, as in **6 – 7**.

B

Remember: Not every prepositional phrase functions like an adjective. Many give information about an action or a whole sentence.

COMPARE

8a | My **brother** in Canada | is a doctor. | (Which brother? In Canada. = acts like an adjective)

8b | I visited my father | **in Canada**. | (Visited where? In Canada. = acts like an adverb)

We sometimes use several prepositional phrases after a noun, as in **9 – 10**. Each prepositional phrase adds information to the noun before it.

9 | What is the salary | of the top football player | in the world? |

10 | There has been a noticeable increase | in the number | of cars | on the road. |

GO ONLINE

24 | Noticing Prepositional Phrases Underline the prepositional phrases in these sentences. Circle the noun that each prepositional phrase describes. Then check (✓) *True* or *False* for you. **10.7 A**

	TRUE	FALSE
1. I have had more than 15 (years) of education.	☐	☐
2. I have an apartment with big windows.	☐	☐
3. I'm a member of an organized group or club.	☐	☐
4. I've met a few people from Germany.	☐	☐
5. I have great respect for my parents.	☐	☐
6. I have a strong interest in science.	☐	☐
7. I have a large collection of jazz music.	☐	☐
8. I have studied the history of China.	☐	☐
9. I have some experience as a teacher.	☐	☐
10. I enjoy unusual food like squid[6] and okra[7].	☐	☐

[6] **squid:** an animal that lives in the ocean. It has a soft body and ten long legs

[7] **okra:** a vegetable with long green pods that are used in soups and stews

	TRUE	FALSE
11. I have recently made some important changes in my life.	☐	☐
12. I think freedom of expression is important.	☐	☐
13. I have a good sense of humor.	☐	☐
14. I know a lot about life in Saudi Arabia.	☐	☐

Talk about It Which sentences in Activity 24 are true for you? Compare with a partner.

Think about It How many adjectives can you find in the sentences in Activity 24? Make a list and compare with a classmate. Which adjectives come before the noun in the prepositional phrase?

25 | Usage Note: Learning Noun + Preposition Combinations Read the note. Then do Activity 26.

We often use nouns with specific prepositions. It's helpful to learn the two words together.

NOUN + *OF*		NOUN + *IN*	NOUN + *FOR*	NOUN + *ON*
cause of	quality of	change in	explanation for	data on
cost of	result of	confidence in	reason for	effect on
development of	role of	difference in	respect for	emphasis on
effect of	sense of	experience in	responsibility for	focus on
form of	series of	increase in	room for	impact on
history of	source of	interest in	time for	influence on
importance of	understanding of	role in	way for	research on
knowledge of	way of	success in		
process of				

Notice that some nouns combine with more than one preposition.

What is the **role of** the United Nations Security Council?
My aunt played an important **role in** my childhood.
For many people, moving to a new country also gives them a new **way of** life.
The company offers new **ways for** people to connect.

26 | Learning Nouns + Prepositional Phrases Choose a noun from the Usage Note above to complete each question. You may need to use a plural form of the noun. (More than one noun may be possible.) **10.7 A**

of

1. Do you have a good _____*sense*_____ of direction?

2. Do you have a good _____ of English grammar?

3. What is the _____ of a college education?

4. What are the _____ of wind on water?

5. What is one common _____ of war?

6. What is one common _____ of stress?

wind on water

in

7. Have you noticed any _____ in your memory recently?

8. Has there been an _____ in the price of food over the past ten years?

9. Do you have any _____ in computer programming?

for

10. Is there _____ for a cell phone in your pocket?

11. What is a good _____ for celebration?

12. Why is it important to have _____ for differences?

on

13. Would you enjoy doing _____ on animal behavior?

14. Did your parents put an _____ on grades when you were young?

15. Where can you get _____ on the changing population?

animal behavior

Talk about It Ask a partner the questions in Activity 26.

A: Do you have a good sense of direction?
B: I guess so. I don't usually get lost.

27 | Noticing Prepositional Phrases in a Row Read the building descriptions and follow these steps.

`10.7 B`
- Underline the prepositional phrases that describe nouns. (Remember: Not every prepositional phrase describes a noun.)
- Circle the noun that each prepositional phrase describes.
- Look at the pictures on page 332. Match each picture with the correct building name.

Famous Buildings

Citigroup Center	1. The (Citigroup Center) in New York is a tall, modern (building) with a (triangle) at the top.
Flatiron Building	2. New York's Flatiron Building is a tall, triangular building at the intersection of two streets.
Casa Milà	3. The Casa Milà in Barcelona is a fascinating example of the work of the architect Antoni Gaudí. There is usually a long line to get in, but there is a great view of the city from the rooftop.
Bank of Asia	4. This famous building is in Bangkok. Some people say that its robotic appearance is a symbol of the modernization of banking.
Sydney Opera House	5. The design of the Sydney Opera House in Sydney, Australia, copies the appearance of the sailboats in Sydney Harbor. The view of the harbor from the inside of the building is breathtaking.
Oriente Station	6. The design of this beautiful train station in Lisbon, Portugal, is light and airy. The designer, Santiago Calatrava, wanted people to feel close to nature while they were in his building.
Hundertwasserhaus	7. Artist/architect Friedensreich Hundertwasser designed this multi-colored apartment building in Vienna, Austria. It has windows of various shapes in many sizes. There are a total of 19 terraces for residents in the building.
National Aquatics Center (Water Cube)	8. The National Aquatics Center's cube shape is a representation of the Chinese symbol for Earth. The outer wall is designed like a pattern of bubbles from soap.

a. _Hundertwasserhaus_

b. _____

c. _____

d. _____

e. _____

f. _____

g. _____

h. _____

Talk about It Work with a partner. Describe other famous buildings you know of. Try to use prepositional phrases.

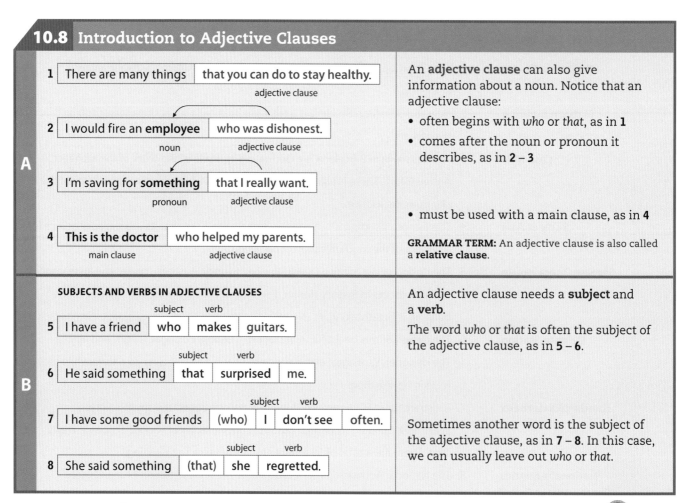

10.8 Introduction to Adjective Clauses

A

1 There are many things | that you can do to stay healthy.
adjective clause

2 I would fire an **employee** | who was dishonest.
noun · adjective clause

3 I'm saving for **something** | that I really want.
pronoun · adjective clause

4 **This is the doctor** | who helped my parents.
main clause · adjective clause

An **adjective clause** can also give information about a noun. Notice that an adjective clause:

- often begins with *who* or *that*, as in **1**
- comes after the noun or pronoun it describes, as in **2 – 3**

- must be used with a main clause, as in **4**

GRAMMAR TERM: An adjective clause is also called a **relative clause**.

B

SUBJECTS AND VERBS IN ADJECTIVE CLAUSES

5 I have a friend | *subject* who | *verb* makes | guitars.

6 He said something | *subject* that | *verb* surprised | me.

7 I have some good friends | (who) | *subject* I | *verb* don't see | often.

8 She said something | (that) | *subject* she | *verb* regretted.

An adjective clause needs a **subject** and a **verb**.

The word *who* or *that* is often the subject of the adjective clause, as in **5 – 6**.

Sometimes another word is the subject of the adjective clause, as in **7 – 8**. In this case, we can usually leave out *who* or *that*.

28 | Noticing Adjective Clauses Circle the adjective clauses and underline the main clauses. Then match each definition with a picture. `10.8 A`

DEFINITIONS OF ANIMALS

1. <u>A frog is a small green animal</u> (that lives in and near water). _c_

2. A grasshopper is an insect that can jump high in the air. ____

3. A hippopotamus is a large African animal that has thick skin and lives near the water. ____

4. A jellyfish is an animal with a soft, pale body that lives in the ocean. ____

5. A lizard is a small animal that has four legs and a long tail. ____

6. A moth is an insect with big wings that flies at night. ____

a.

b.

c.

d.

e.

f.

DEFINITIONS OF TOOLS/EQUIPMENT

7. A printer is a machine that prints words and pictures from a computer. ____

8. A helmet is a hard hat that keeps your head safe. ____

9. A javelin is a long, pointed stick that people throw as a sport. ____

10. A padlock is a lock that you use on things like gates and bicycles. ____

11. A compass is an instrument for finding direction, with a needle that always points north. ____

12. A hammer is a tool that you use to hit nails into things. ____

g.

h.

i.

j.

k.

l.

All dictionary entries are from the *Oxford Basic American Dictionary for learners of English*
© Oxford University Press 2011.

Think about It In the sentences above, draw an arrow from each adjective clause to the noun it describes.

A frog is a small green animal (that lives in and near water).

Think about It What adjectives and prepositional phrases does the writer use to describe each thing in the sentences above?

frog = small/green

29 | Usage Note: Choosing *Who* or *That* Read the note. Then do Activities 30 and 31.

To give more information about a person, we can begin an adjective clause with **who** or **that**.

He's the person **who helped me.**
She's not the one **that got the job.**

There are some people here **that you should meet.**
I have some friends **who you know.**

To give more information about a thing, we often begin an adjective clause with *that*.

That's the dog **that bit me.**
Could you hand me the book **that's on the table?**

I heard something **that you should know.**
I found the key **that you lost.**

---

30 | Adding Information Complete each sentence with an adjective clause on the right. `10.8 A–B`

1. Friendship is a relationship _*h*_
2. Anger is a feeling ____
3. A good friend is someone ____
4. A freshman is a student ____
5. Freshman composition is a course ____
6. A hero is a person ____
7. A dolphin is an intelligent animal ____
8. The Coast Guard is an organization ____
9. An explorer is someone ____
10. A school counselor is a person ____

   a. who is in the first year of college.
   b. who has done something brave or good.
   c. that everyone experiences in life.
   d. that lives in the ocean.
   e. who students can go to for help.
   f. that helps people who are in danger at sea.
   g. who travels around a new place to learn about it.
   h. that takes time to build.
   i. who is loyal.
   j. that students take in their first year of college.

Talk about It Do you disagree with any of the statements above? Why? Tell your classmates.

Think about It In which sentences above can you leave out *who* or *that*? Why?

---

31 | Using *Who* or *That* Circle the correct pronoun(s). Then practice with a partner. `10.8 A–B`

1. A: Do you know Mr. Lucas?
   B: Yeah, he's the teacher (who / that) gave me an F in Biology.

2. A: *Ci vediamo domani.*
   B: Uh, I don't understand a word (who / that) you are saying.
   A: Oh, sorry. You don't speak Italian, do you?
   B: No, unfortunately.

3. A: Who's Anna?
   B: She's someone (who / that) I met at school.

4. A: Do we have to go out tonight?
   B: But you're the one (who / that) didn't want to stay at home.

5. A: What's all this stuff?
   B: It's everything (who / that) I want to sell.

6. A: Is there something special (who / that) you are looking for?
   B: No, I'm just looking.

7. A: Do you know anyone (who / that) wants an old TV?
   B: Sure. I'll take it.

8. A: Don't leave yet. There's something (who / that) I think you should see.
   B: But I'm in a hurry.
   A: OK then. I'll show you later.

Think about It In which sentences above can you only have one answer? Why? In which sentences can you leave out *who* or *that*? Why?

10.9 Using Adjectives and Other Forms That Describe Nouns in Speaking

A	1 A: Which book do you want?
	   B: **The one about the economy.**
	
	2 A: Here are your books.
	   B: Oh. Those aren't **the ones** I wanted.
	
	3 A: Which keys are yours?
	   B: **The ones on the table.**
	
	4 A: This is a really silly movie.
	   B: Yeah, sorry. I'm **the one** who wanted to see it.
		We use **the one(s)** + a **prepositional phrase** or an **adjective clause** to identify a particular noun from a group of similar nouns, as in **1 – 4**. We can use it to answer the question *which*.
		
		For more information on *one(s)*, see Unit 4, page 123.

B	5 A: Hey, you're standing on my foot!
	   B: Whoops! **Sorry!** (Sorry! = I'm sorry.)
	
	6 A: My cell is 555-0199.
	   B: **Sorry?** (Sorry? = Excuse me, I didn't understand.)
	   A: You wanted my cell number. It's 555-0199.
	
	7 A: **Nice shirt!**
	   B: Thanks.
	
	8 A: **Great meal!**
	   B: I'm glad you liked it.
		We often respond to another person or introduce a topic with a single **adjective** or an adjective + noun, as in **5 – 8**.

C	9 A: Did you get the **stuff** that I sent?
	   B: Yeah, it just arrived.
	
	10 A: Is there **anything** I can get you?
	    B: I'd love a glass of water.
	
	11 A: Here. I brought you something special.
	    B: Oh, this is **something** I've always wanted.
		We sometimes use an **adjective clause** to add more information to:
		• a noun with a general meaning, such as *thing* or *stuff*, as in **9**
		• an indefinite pronoun, such as *anything* or *something*, as in **10 – 11**

GO ONLINE

32 | Identifying *Which One(s)* Listen and write the missing words. Circle the person or thing in the picture that Speaker B identifies. Then practice with a partner. `10.9 A`

1. A: Are those your shoes?

   B: No, mine are the ones _____.

2. A: Which key opens the garage door?

   B: The one _____.

3. A: Is your brother the one _____?

   B: No, he's on the left.

4. A: Who's that man?

   B: You mean the one _____?

   A: Yeah.

   B: I don't know.

5. A: Which questions do I need to answer?

   B: Just the ones _____.

6. A: Which sandwich is the one _____?

   B: The one _____.

33 | Using Adjectives in Conversation Use the adjectives in the box to complete the conversations below. (More than one answer may be possible.) 10.9 B

Big	Delicious	Nice.	Sorry?	Super!	Terrible.
Boring	Fine.	Poor	Sorry.	Sure.	

1. A: Could you open the door for me?

   B: _Sorry?_

   A: The door. Could you open it, please?

   B: _____

2. A: _____ James.

   B: Why? What happened?

   A: He wrecked his car yesterday.

3. A: Ouch! That hurt.

   B: _____

4. A: _____ day today.

   B: I know. I hope I get the job.

5. A: I don't want to go out today.

   B: _____ Stay here.

6. A: _____ meal.

   B: I'm glad you enjoyed it.

7. A: What's for dinner?

   B: Pizza.

   A: _____

8. A: Did you draw this?

   B: Yeah.

   A: _____

   B: You really think so?

   A: Yeah. I like it a lot.

9. A: How was your day?

   B: _____

   A: What happened?

   B: I lost my wallet.

10. A: _____ movie.

    B: Yeah, it almost put me to sleep.

🔊 **Talk about It** Listen and check your answers. Were your choices the same? Then practice the conversations with a partner.

Think about It Which adjectives above are used alone and which are used with a noun?

◄)) 34 | Adding Information to General Nouns and Indefinite Pronouns Listen and write the missing adjective clauses. Then practice with a partner. `10.9 C`

1. A: Is there anything special _____?
   B: No, let's just stay home.

2. A: Do we have any plans for today?
   B: Nope. You can do anything _____.

3. A: There's something _____.
   B: Sorry. I'm in a hurry. Can you tell me later?
   A: I guess so.

4. A: Are you going to finish painting the door today?
   B: I don't have time.
   A: Come on. You never finish anything

   _____.

5. A: Do you know anyone _____?
   B: No. Why do you ask?
   A: Because I'm going there next month.

6. A: Is there any stuff here _____?
   B: Yeah, you can take the magazines.

7. A: Are you going to the meeting tonight?
   B: I can't. There's some stuff

   _____ at home.

8. A: There are two things _____
   about Anita.
   B: What?
   A: She's quiet but she can be demanding.

9. A: We're having a guest for dinner.
   B: Is it someone _____?
   A: I can't tell you. It's a surprise.

10. A: What's that big black thing you

   _____?
   B: It's just an old radio. I don't want
   it anymore.
   A: I can see why.

Think about It How many adjective clauses above use *who* or *that*? Can those words be left out? Why or why not?

10.10 Using Adjectives and Other Forms That Describe Nouns in Writing

A	PREPOSITIONAL PHRASES	Prepositional phrases are common in written English, especially after a noun with a general meaning, such as *way, idea, method, tool, quality,* etc., as in **1–2**.
	1 The Internet is a useful **tool** for education.	
	2 Decisiveness is an important **quality** of a good boss.	
	3	A child's **education**	during the first years	of life	is very important.	Writers often use two or three prepositional phrases together, as in **3–4**.
	4	She has a master's **degree**	in business	from the University	of North Carolina.	

B	COMPARING SPOKEN AND WRITTEN LANGUAGE	In conversation, we often describe a noun with just one adjective or other form, as in **5**.
	5 A: Are you a writer? B: No, I'm an actor. A: Oh, yeah? What kind **of stuff**? B: A lot **of TV**. A: Anything <u>I'd know</u>? B: Maybe. (from the movie *Sideways*)	In writing, we tend to combine a lot of information into longer, complete sentences, as in **6**. **Adjectives, noun + noun combinations, prepositional phrases**, and <u>adjective clauses</u> are four ways we can put more information into a sentence.
	6 I have a **well-known actor friend** <u>who has been in a number of TV shows</u> <u>that you probably have seen.</u>	

35 | Using Prepositional Phrases Choose a prepositional phrase to complete each sentence. `10.10 A`

1. One of the most dangerous ways _____ is by car.

2. Foreign travel makes you question your way _____.

3. People have many different ways _____.

4. Many people _____ change careers.

5. Relaxing before you go to bed will help to improve the quality

   _____.

6. The cell phone is a convenient tool _____.

7. The goal _____ is to make money.

8. Wearing white coats became a tradition _____.

9. The students _____ stayed awake for 24 hours.

10. This study shows the differences _____ among residents

    of Paris, Madrid, and London.

11. Doctors say you should eat a variety of types _____.

12. The Internet gives people instant access to large amounts _____.

13. A number of studies have shown that walking _____ gives you energy.

14. It sometimes takes a disaster for people to see the need _____.

for change
for doctors
for work
in cell phone behavior
in the research study
in the woods
in their fifties
of any business
of dealing with stress
of doing things
of food
of information
of traveling
of your sleep

Think about It In which sentences above are two or more prepositional phrases used together? What noun or pronoun does each prepositional phrase describe?

Write about It Choose a sentence above. Write two to three more sentences to support or explain it.

36 | Using Prepositional Phrases in a Text Complete the article below with the prepositional phrases from the box. `10.10 A`

about kindness and taking care of the planet	of animated films	of the world's greatest directors
at drawing	of art	of young people
at the Japanese Academy Awards	of audiences and critics[8]	with magical abilities
of airplanes	of his own	

HAYAO MIYAZAKI: DIRECTOR OF ANIMATED FILMS

Many people regard Hayao Miyazaki as one _of the world's greatest directors_
                                           1

_____. Viewers love his imaginative animation,
          2

adventurous characters, and thrilling plots[9]. He is famous not just in Japan but

throughout the world.

   Miyazaki began his career as an animator in 1963. His skill _____ earned him the
                                                                              3

admiration[10] _____. He directed his first feature anime[11] film 16 years later. Then he
               4

---

[8]**critics:** people who say that someone or something is good or bad
[9]**plots:** the things that happen in stories, plays, or movies

[10]**admiration:** the feeling that someone or something is very good
[11]**anime:** Japanese style of cartoons or animation

started a movie company _____ 5 _____ in 1985. In 2001, his movie *Spirited Away* won

Best Film _____ 6 _____. It was also the first anime film to win an American

Academy Award.

Miyazaki's movies are often about the adventures _____ 7 _____

_____ 8 _____. As a boy, Miyazaki loved to draw pictures _____ 9 _____.

In his movies, people can sometimes fly. One character even turns into a bird. His movies also teach

lessons _____ 10 _____. Miyazaki's movies aren't cartoons;

they are works _____ 11 _____.

Think about It Circle the adjectives the writer used in Activity 36. Put a box around any nouns used to describe other nouns. In which sentences did the writer use two prepositional phrases together? Underline the noun that each prepositional phrase describes.

37 | Noticing Different Forms of Adjectives Read these job descriptions. Then group the **bold** descriptive words in the chart below. `10.10 B`

CAFÉ HELP

We are hiring **full-time counter staff** for our **busy café**. We ask for a **high level** of **friendly customer service** from our staff. Patience, punctuality[12], and an **outgoing personality**—all these **positive qualities** will help. Both **morning shifts**[13] and **evening shifts** are available. All applicants must be at least 18 years old. Please send your resume, including **phone number**, and also tell us something about your idea of **excellent customer service**!

CONSTRUCTION COMPANY SEEKS CARPENTERS

Previous experience is essential. The **successful applicant must be good** with **hand tools** and **reliable**. Must be able to lift **heavy objects**. We are a **well-run**, **progressive company** with opportunities for growth and advancement.

Multi-word adjective + noun + noun	Adjective + noun + noun	Multi-word adjective + adjective + noun	Adjective + noun	Linking verb + adjective	Noun + noun
full-time counter staff					

Talk about It Which job above sounds more interesting to you? Why? Tell your classmates.

[12] **punctuality:** the quality of arriving or doing something at the right time, not late

[13] **shifts:** periods of time in the working day

ADJECTIVES AND OTHER FORMS THAT DESCRIBE NOUNS 339

38 | Comparing Texts Look at the two versions of this article. Version 2 has more details and descriptive information than Version 1. Underline the information in Version 2 that does not appear in Version 1. **10.10 B**

The Importance of Early Learning

VERSION 1

An American study shows the importance of early education. The study involved 111 young children.

Researchers put the children in two groups. One group of children attended an all-day program at a childcare center. It offered some programs. The other group did not attend the childcare center. However, both groups went to public school.

The two groups were similar when they were babies, but different after the age of about 18 months. As babies, both groups had similar results in tests. However, the children in the childcare program scored much higher in tests after the age of 18 months.

The children took tests again at the ages of 12 and 15 years. Again, the children had better test scores.

The study suggests that education is important for all later development. Children may be more successful if they have early education. They may do better in school, go to college, and get better jobs. The researchers believe their study shows a need to spend money on public education. They believe these kinds of programs could create better success in schools.

VERSION 2

A major American study from the University of North Carolina shows the importance of early education for poor children. The long-term study involved 111 young children from poor families.

Researchers put the children in two groups. One group of children attended an all-day program at a high-quality childcare center. It offered some social, health, and educational programs. The other group did not attend the childcare center. However, both groups went to public school after the age of 5.

The two groups were similar when they were babies, but different after the age of about 18 months. As babies, both groups had similar results in tests for mental and physical skills. However, the children in the educational childcare program scored much higher in tests after the age of 18 months.

The children took tests again at the ages of 12 and 15 years. Again, the children who had been in the childcare center had better test scores.

The study suggests that education during the first months and years of life is important for all later development. Poor children may be more successful if they have early education. They may do better in school, go to college, and get better jobs. The researchers believe their study shows a need for the government to spend money on public education at an early age. They believe these kinds of programs could create better success in American schools.

Think about It What kinds of words, phrases, and clauses did the writer add to Version 2 above?

ADJECTIVES	PREPOSITIONAL PHRASES	ADJECTIVE CLAUSES
major	from the University of North Carolina	
	for poor children	

WRAP-UP Demonstrate Your Knowledge

A | DISCUSSION What are the characteristics of a good teacher? In a group, consider the qualities in this box or other qualities. Decide on the top three qualities. Then say why and give examples from your own experience. Share the results of your discussion with the class.

expects a lot from students	has a sense of humor	is very strict
explains things clearly	has knowledge of his or her subjects	makes the class interesting
gives a lot of homework	is considerate of students' feelings	spends time to help students

B | WRITING Describe your best friend. What is special about this person, and why is he or she your best friend?

My best friend is Thomas, and he is someone who can always make me laugh. We met when we were working together a few years ago. He's a little quiet, so we didn't become friends right away. But after a while, I realized he had a really clever sense of humor. That's when we started spending more time together. . . .

Exchange descriptions with a partner and answer these questions.

1. Does your partner's description give a clear mental picture of the subject? What other information do you want to know?
2. How did your partner use adjectives and other forms to describe nouns? Identify the uses.

C | RESEARCH Look at the back cover of several books to find excerpts of praise for the book from different sources. Find examples of the types of adjectives, noun + noun combinations, prepositional phrases, and adjective clauses from this unit, and share them with your classmates.

"A funny, profound, emotionally generous, and wonderfully human story." —Joe Lansdale
"A truly interesting, engaging, and fascinating memoir."—Lou Schuler

D | WEB SEARCH Look online for an interesting apartment for rent. Print out the advertisement, and underline the words, phrases, and clauses that describe nouns. Then write an advertisement for your ideal apartment.

Apartment for Rent

This <u>amazing</u> unit is in a <u>prime</u> <u>14th Street</u> location <u>with elevator and laundry</u> <u>in the building</u>. This <u>bright</u> unit has <u>big</u> windows and a <u>private</u> patio!!!! The windows are a <u>unique</u> feature <u>that you will not find anywhere else</u>. There is a lot of <u>closet</u> space and an <u>additional</u> <u>storage</u> loft. The kitchen has <u>new</u> <u>full-sized</u> appliances. Don't miss out on this <u>great</u> deal! Call or txt today for more information on your <u>new</u> home!! Contact Franklin at 555-1212.

10.11 Summary of Adjectives and Other Forms That Describe Nouns

We use adjectives, prepositional phrases, nouns, and adjective clauses to give more information about a **noun** (a person, place, thing, or idea).

		noun			
I went to	a	restaurant.			

		noun	noun		
I went to	a	family	restaurant.		

		adjective	noun		
I went to	an	American	restaurant.		

		adjective	multi-word adjective	noun	
I went to	an	American	fast-food	restaurant.	

		adjective	multi-word adjective	noun	adjective clause
I went to	an	American	fast-food	restaurant	that has a playground.

		adjective	multi-word adjective	noun	adjective clause	prepositional phrase
I went to	an	American	fast-food	restaurant	that has a playground	for children.

11

Adverbs and Prepositional Phrases

Live simply, that others may simply live.

—MAHATMA GANDHI,

INDIAN LEADER

(1869–1948)

Talk about It What does the quotation above mean? Do you agree or disagree?

WARM-UP

A | Check (✓) the sentences that describe your study habits. Then compare answers with your classmates and share other study habits.

Study Habits

☐ 1. I usually take notes in class.
☐ 2. I often look up new words in a dictionary.
☐ 3. I review my textbook before class.
☐ 4. Unfortunately, I don't always do my homework.
☐ 5. I study regularly outside of class.
☐ 6. I pay attention during class.
☐ 7. I like to study with a group of friends.
☐ 8. Surprisingly, I prefer to study in noisy places.

B | The words in blue above are adverbs. The words in green are prepositional phrases. Based on these examples, what can you say about adverbs and prepositional phrases? Check (✓) *True* or *False*.

	TRUE	FALSE
1. Adverbs always end in *-ly*.	☐	☐
2. We can use adverbs in different places in a sentence.	☐	☐
3. We use some adverbs and prepositional phrases to give information such as *when, where, how,* and *how often*.	☐	☐
4. We use some adverbs to give an opinion about the information in a statement.	☐	☐

C | Look back at the quotation on page 342. Identify any adverbs or prepositional phrases.

11.1 What Is an Adverb?

A

1 The movie started **late**. (when)

2 The train is **always** late. (how often)

3 No one is going to be **there**. (where)

4 Some people learn languages **easily**. (how)

5 We were **very** tired. (to what degree)

We often need to explain *when, how often, where, how,* or *to what degree* something happens. We can use **adverbs** to do this, as in **1 – 5**.

B

```
        adverb   adjective
6  | I feel | pretty | good. |
```

```
          adverb    adverb
7  | They left | very | quickly. |
```

```
         verb    adverb
8  | Did you | look | outside? |
```

```
           verb phrase          adverb
9  | You | need to do your homework | now. |
```

```
    adverb          whole sentence
10 | Unfortunately, | I'm busy tomorrow. |
```

An adverb can add information to:

• an adjective, as in **6**

• another adverb, as in **7**

• a verb or verb phrase, as in **8 – 9**

• a whole sentence or clause, as in **10**. Notice that these adverbs sometimes give the speaker's opinion about the information in the sentence.

Notice: We use adverbs in several different places in a sentence.

C

WHEN

11 She arrived **in the evening**.

12 He'll probably get here **before lunch**.

WHERE

13 He lives **at home**.

14 There's a good restaurant **near here**.

HOW

15 She didn't want to go **with me**.

16 I'm going to go **by myself**.

WHY

17 They canceled the meeting **because of the weather**.

18 **Thanks to the Internet**, I can do all my research from home.

We often use a **prepositional phrase** to explain *when, where, how,* or *why,* as in **11 – 18**. In these sentences, the prepositional phrase functions like an adverb.

GO ONLINE

1 | Noticing Adverbs Decide if the **bold** adverb in each conversation explains *when, how often, where, how,* or *to what degree*. Check (✓) your answers. Then practice with a partner. `11.1 A`

	WHEN?	HOW OFTEN?	WHERE?	HOW?	TO WHAT DEGREE?
1. A: David, I need you here **immediately**. B: I'll be right there.	✓	☐	☐	☐	☐
2. A: Have you been checking your messages? B: Yes, **obsessively**[1].	☐	☐	☐	☐	☐

[1] **obsessively:** without being able to stop

	WHEN?	HOW OFTEN?	WHERE?	HOW?	TO WHAT DEGREE?
3. A: I'll see you **later**. B: OK. Sounds good.	☐	☐	☐	☐	☐
4. A: That's a nice sweater. B: Thanks. I made it years **ago**.	☐	☐	☐	☐	☐
5. A: You look **really** familiar. Have we met before? B: I don't think so.	☐	☐	☐	☐	☐
6. A: Could you please give this package to Mr. Jones? B: Certainly. I'll deliver it **personally**.	☐	☐	☐	☐	☐
7. A: Is anyone here yet? B: Yeah, a few people. They're waiting for you **upstairs**.	☐	☐	☐	☐	☐
8. A: Could you wait **outside**, please? B: Of course. Is there a problem? A: I'm not really sure.	☐	☐	☐	☐	☐
9. A: What are you doing now? B: Setting up my new computer. A: Well, be sure you follow the instructions **carefully**.	☐	☐	☐	☐	☐
10. A: Have you ever been to Canada? B: **Once**, but it was a long time ago.	☐	☐	☐	☐	☐
11. A: Do you talk to Amanda very often? B: No, but she sends text messages **hourly**.	☐	☐	☐	☐	☐
12. A: How do you find anything here? B: It's a mess, isn't it? I just can't throw anything **away**.	☐	☐	☐	☐	☐

Think about It Circle any other adverbs in the sentences in Activity 1. What kind of information do they give?

2 | What Does the Adverb Describe? What part of the sentence does each **bold** adverb describe? Draw an arrow to it. Then check (✓) *Agree* or *Disagree* for each statement. `11.1 B`

Sentences from Student Essays

	AGREE	DISAGREE
1. A good teacher must be able to explain things **clearly**.	☐	☐
2. You can play tennis **indoors**.	☐	☐
3. All public buildings should be **easily** accessible[2].	☐	☐
4. Employers should treat all of their employees **equally**.	☐	☐

[2] **accessible:** possible to enter

	AGREE	DISAGREE
5. **Hopefully**, scientists will find life on other planets.	☐	☐
6. Card games are a good form of entertainment because you can play them **anywhere**.	☐	☐
7. Feeling a lot of stress is a **very** good thing.	☐	☐
8. The average life expectancy[3] has increased **greatly** since 1900.	☐	☐
9. Learning languages is not an **especially** difficult thing to do.	☐	☐
10. Today people can communicate **instantly** by using email.	☐	☐
11. In stressful situations, you should try to breathe **slowly**.	☐	☐
12. Running your own business can be **extremely** rewarding.	☐	☐

Think about It Replace each **bold** adverb in Activity 2 with a different one. Do your classmates agree or disagree with your new statement?

"A good teacher must be able to explain things simply."

3 | Noticing Prepositional Phrases What does each **bold** prepositional phrase explain? Write *when*, *where*, *how*, or *why* above the phrase. `11.1 C`

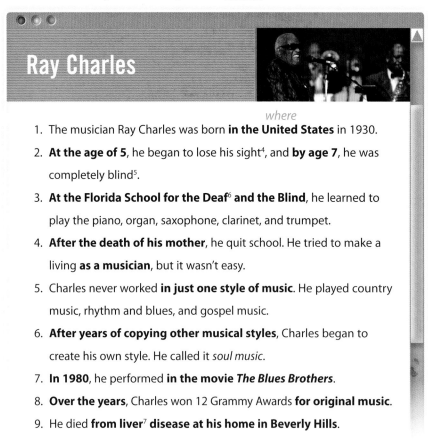

Ray Charles

where

1. The musician Ray Charles was born **in the United States** in 1930.
2. **At the age of 5**, he began to lose his sight[4], and **by age 7**, he was completely blind[5].
3. **At the Florida School for the Deaf[6] and the Blind**, he learned to play the piano, organ, saxophone, clarinet, and trumpet.
4. **After the death of his mother**, he quit school. He tried to make a living **as a musician**, but it wasn't easy.
5. Charles never worked **in just one style of music**. He played country music, rhythm and blues, and gospel music.
6. **After years of copying other musical styles**, Charles began to create his own style. He called it *soul music*.
7. **In 1980**, he performed **in the movie *The Blues Brothers***.
8. **Over the years**, Charles won 12 Grammy Awards **for original music**.
9. He died **from liver[7] disease at his home in Beverly Hills**.

---

[3] **life expectancy:** how long we believe someone or something will live
[4] **sight:** the ability to see

[5] **blind:** not able to see
[6] **deaf:** not able to hear
[7] **liver:** the part of the body that cleans the blood

Think about It How many prepositional phrases do you see in each sentence in Activity 3? Is it possible to put two or more prepositional phrases together in a row?

Talk about It Was any of the information in the article in Activity 3 surprising to you? Discuss with a partner.

4 | Usage Note: Adjective or Adverb? Read the note. Then do Activity 5.

An adverb adds information to a verb, an adjective, an adverb, or an entire sentence or clause. An adjective adds information to a noun. Sometimes a word or prepositional phrase can function like an adverb in one context and like an adjective in another context.

FUNCTIONS LIKE AN ADVERB	FUNCTIONS LIKE AN ADJECTIVE
1a I don't have any classes **on Tuesday**.	**1b** My class **on Tuesday** is bigger than my class **on Friday**.
2a My brother works **hard**.	**2b** My brother is a **hard** worker.
	2c The test was **hard**.

5 | Adjective or Adverb? Does each **bold** word or prepositional phrase function like an adjective or an adverb? Check (✓) your answers. **11.1 A–C**

	ADJECTIVE	ADVERB
1. The window **in my bedroom** is broken.	✓	☐
2. I'm going to study **in my bedroom**.	☐	☐
3. Why do you drive so **fast**?	☐	☐
4. You're a **fast** learner.	☐	☐
5. You shouldn't work so **hard**.	☐	☐
6. That test was **hard**.	☐	☐
7. Try to get here **early**, please.	☐	☐
8. Let's have an **early** lunch today.	☐	☐
9. Most of my friends **at school** are from this area.	☐	☐
10. I've made a lot of good friends **at school**.	☐	☐
11. I think there's someone **at the door**.	☐	☐
12. Who's the man **at the door**?	☐	☐
13. Who put the picture **on the wall**?	☐	☐
14. The picture **on the wall** is of my grandparents.	☐	☐

Write about It Choose a prepositional phrase, and write your own pair of sentences like the ones above. Ask your classmates to identify how the prepositional phrase functions in each sentence (like an adverb or like an adjective).

11.2 Explaining *When* and *How Often*

A

EXPLAINING *WHEN*

1 They're having dinner **now**.

2 No one has arrived **yet**.

3 That happened **in the past**.

4 I'll see you **in a while**.

COMPARE

5a They **arrived after lunch**. (simple past)

5b I**'ll be** there **after lunch**. (future with *will*)

5c He usually **takes** a nap **after lunch**. (simple present)

6a She **met** him **a long time ago**. (simple past)

6b **Have** you **met** him **lately**? (present perfect)

We can use certain **adverbs** and **prepositional phrases** in time expressions to explain *when* something happens, as in **1 – 4**.

We use many time expressions with more than one verb form, as in **5a – 5c**.

However, we use some time expressions together with particular verb forms (simple past, present perfect, etc.), as in **6a – 6b**.

B

EXPLAINING *HOW OFTEN*

7 **Sometimes** we stayed late but not **always**.

8 He's **always** leaving his clothes on the floor.

9 They're **usually** a few minutes late.

10 It's important to exercise **regularly**.

11 **Year after year**, she won the competition.

We can use adverbs of frequency and certain prepositional phrases to explain *how often* something happens, as in **7 – 11**. Examples include:

- always, constantly, continuously, over and over
- usually, regularly, normally
- often, frequently, again and again
- sometimes, occasionally, from time to time
- rarely, seldom, infrequently
- never, no longer
- hourly, daily, monthly, year after year

C

PLACEMENT OF TIME AND FREQUENCY EXPRESSIONS

12 A: Do you have any meetings this week?

B: **On Tuesday** I'm meeting with the design team, and **on Wednesday** I have a budget meeting.

13 She **never goes** there.

14 They **are constantly** bothering me.

15 Some people **are always** happy.

16 I don't cook **in the evening** when I'm tired.

We use different time and frequency expressions in different places in a sentence. For example, we use some of them:

- at the beginning of a clause or sentence, as in **12**
- before a single main verb, as in **13**
- after the first helping verb, as in **14**
- after the verb *be*, as in **15**
- at the end of a clause or sentence, as in **16**

6 | Noticing Time Expressions Underline the time expressions in these conversations. Then practice with a partner. **11.2 A**

1. A: Do you want some coffee?

   B: No, thanks. Not <u>now</u>.

2. A: Hey, James. Where are you?

   B: Relax. I'll be there in a second.

3. A: Bye. I'll call you later.

   B: OK. Bye.

4. A: Have you eaten yet?

   B: No, I just got home five minutes ago.

5. A: What do you want to do?

   B: I don't know, but we need to decide soon.

6. A: Is Anna there?

   B: No, but she'll be back in a few minutes.

7. A: What's the matter?

   B: I'm in trouble again.

   A: So what else is new?

8. A: John is coming over in a while.
      Do you want to join us?

   B: Sure. I haven't seen him in years.

9. A: Ready for your job interview on Friday?

   B: I think so.

10. A: Can I talk to you?

    B: Yes, but just for a second. I'm late for class.

11. A: Is Emma here?

    B: No, but she should get here before long.

12. A: Have you looked outside lately?

    B: No. Why?

    A: It's snowing.

Think about It What verb form did the speaker use with each time expression in Activity 6?

1. I don't want any coffee now. (simple present)

7 | Explaining *How Often* Circle the correct frequency expression to complete each sentence. `11.2B`

MAKING TRUE STATEMENTS

1. The average person laughs **constantly** / **occasionally**.

2. Too many people talk on the phone while they are driving.
   This is **frequently** / **infrequently** the cause of accidents.

3. It's important to brush your teeth **from time to time** / **regularly**.

4. You can learn the words to a song by repeating them
   monthly / **over and over**.

5. It's not unusual for a husband and wife to argue
   from time to time / **hourly**.

6. Many people pay their bills **hourly** / **monthly**.

7. Children **usually** / **continuously** start walking around age 1.

8. If you store honey in a tight jar, it will **never** / **usually** go bad.

9. An annual flower blooms[8] and then dies, but a perennial blooms **again and again** / **once**.

10. Languages are **constantly** / **never** in contact with each other and affect each other in many ways.

11. Many languages have 50,000 words or more, but people **infrequently** / **normally** use the same few
    hundred words in everyday conversation.

12. The earth moves around the sun **continuously** / **infrequently**.

Talk about It What other frequency expressions could you use in each sentence above? Share ideas with
your classmates.

8 | Usage Note: Using Noun Phrases like Adverbs Read the note. Then do Activity 9.

> We sometimes use just a **noun phrase** to explain *when, how long,* or *how often.* We almost always use
> these noun phrases at the very beginning or very end of a sentence or clause.
>
> **1** You should eat breakfast **every morning.**   **4** I've been here **all day.**
>
> **2 Next week** I can't travel.   **5** We shop there **all the time.**
>
> **3** Are you going anywhere **today?**   **6** Maybe I should come back **another time.**

[8] **bloom:** to produce a flower

9 | Using Noun Phrases and Prepositional Phrases like Adverbs Look at the answers to these questions. Label each one as *NP* (noun phrase), *A* (adverb), or *PP* (prepositional phrase). Then circle the answers that are true for you. Add your own answer if necessary. **11.2 B**

Personal Survey

1. When did you last eat something?

   a. a few minutes ago *NP*   c. yesterday
   b. an hour ago   d. other: _____

2. How often do you work out?

   a. six times a week   c. once a week
   b. twice a week   d. other: _____

3. When are you going to take your next vacation?

   a. this time next year   c. in a couple of years
   b. this spring   d. other: _____

4. How often do you change your passwords?

   a. never   c. every day
   b. every few months   d. other: _____

5. How often do you use your phone to make actual phone calls?

   a. rarely   c. 30 minutes a month
   b. quite a bit   d. other: _____

6. When did you last go to a movie theater?

   a. last month   c. years ago
   b. last year   d. other: _____

7. How long have you lived here?

   a. my whole life   c. since 2011
   b. for a couple of years   d. other: _____

8. How long have you been in this room?

   a. all morning   c. for about an hour
   b. all afternoon   d. other: _____

Talk about It Compare your answers above with your classmates. Who has the most unusual answer?

Think about It What other time expressions could you use to answer each question above?

Write about It Work with a partner. Write a short quiz like the one above using the question words *when* and *how often*. Then give your quiz to your classmates.

1. How often do you miss class?
   a. never   c. from time to time
   b. almost never   d. frequently

10 | Noticing the Position of Expressions Underline the time and frequency expressions in these paragraphs. Then answer the questions below. **11.2 C**

When Do You Function⁹ Best?

I am a morning person. I get up <u>at 5:00</u> <u>every morning</u>. My mind is fresh and clear then. I feel energetic. I like to exercise early in the morning and do things around my apartment. Then I feel ready to go to work. I can get a lot of things done at this time of day.

   After lunch, things slow down for me. I don't work very well between 2:00 and 3:00. By the end of the workday, I am very tired. I don't usually go out in the evening because I just don't have any energy. Instead, I relax at home. By 9:30, I can't keep my eyes open anymore. I know that some people feel wide awake at night, but I'm not like that at all.

> **W A R N I N G !**
>
> A few time adverbs have the same form as adjectives: *early, late, daily, weekly, monthly,* and *yearly.*
>
> We left **early**. (adverb)
> I had an **early** breakfast. (adjective)

QUESTIONS

1. Which sentences have two time or frequency expressions in a row? Which expression comes first— the more specific one or the more general one?
2. How many sentences begin with a time expression?
3. Which time or frequency expression does the writer use after a helping verb?
4. Which time or frequency expressions does the writer use at the end of a clause or sentence?

Write about It When do you function best? Write several sentences to read to your classmates.

11.3 Explaining *Where*

A

1 Your friends are **upstairs.**
2 Go **away.**
3 What's happening **outside?**
4 A: A large coffee, please.
   B: For **here?**
   A: No, make it to go.

We often use **adverbs** of place to explain *where* someone or something is, as in **1 – 4**. This information usually comes at the end of a sentence. Common adverbs of place include:

ahead	backward	down	here	outside
away	behind	far	inside	somewhere
back	close	forward	nearby	there

B

5 I left my things **at home.**
6 The World Court is **in the Netherlands.**
7 He yelled at me **in front of the whole office.**

We can also use certain **prepositional phrases** to explain *where,* as in **5 – 8**. Some common prepositions used this way are:

at	home, school, work, war, sea, college
in	the kitchen, the city, China, the world, my backyard
on	Fifth Avenue, the floor, the ground, the table
to	school, work, the hospital, the store

8 She worked **in Singapore** **in 2012.**
(*in Singapore* = where; *in 2012* = when)

Notice that we often use several prepositional phrases together, as in **8**. These expressions may give different kinds of information.

9 Please **put the milk** **in the refrigerator.**
(NOT: ~~Please put in the refrigerator the milk.~~)

WARNING! We don't normally use an expression of place between a verb and its object, as in **9**.

⁹**function:** to work or do other tasks

11 | Noticing Place Expressions Underline the expressions that explain *where* in these conversations. Then practice with a partner. `11.3 A-B`

1. A: Do you work <u>here</u>?
   B: Yeah. Let me show you around.

2. A: Are you in the attic? What are you doing up there?
   B: I'm looking for something.

3. A: Where are you going now?
   B: Relax. I'm not going far. I'll be back in a second.

4. A: What's the matter?
   B: I can't find my glasses. I know I put them somewhere.
   A: Did you look in the kitchen?
   B: I've looked everywhere.

5. A: The door is open. Do you think it's OK to go inside?
   B: I don't know. It's kind of dark in there. You go ahead. I'll follow right behind in a few seconds.

6. A: What's that on the ground?
   B: I don't know. Don't get close to it. It might be dangerous.

7. A: Where have you been?
   B: Nowhere.
   A: You mean you've been at home all day?
   B: That's right.

8. A: Could everyone please step forward?
   B: Why? What's going on?
   A: Nothing. But you're blocking the sidewalk.

9. A: What are you cooking?
   B: Don't look! Go away! It's a surprise.

10. A: Is there anything interesting in the news?
    B: Not really.

11. A: Is this your laptop?
    B: Oh, thanks. I've been looking all over for it.

12. A: Can I borrow your phone?
    B: Sure, but don't forget to bring it back.

13. A: How's the fish? Is it OK?
    B: Actually, it's a little raw inside.

14. A: How many people were at your old school?
    B: About a hundred.
    A: Really! That's small.
    B: How many go here?
    A: About two thousand.

> **F Y I**
>
> Many words function in more than one way. For example, the word *inside* can function as an adverb, a preposition, an adjective, or a noun.
>
> He went **inside**. (adverb)
> We saw smoke **inside the house**. (preposition)
> He put the letter in his **inside** pocket. (adjective)
> He locked the door from the **inside**. (noun)

Think about It How many time expressions can you find in the conversations above? Circle them.

12 | Explaining *Where* Complete the article below with the correct expressions of place from the box.

`11.3 A–B`

above the ground	on the wheel
away	to a mechanic
in its place	to the side of the road
in the hubcap	under the car
in your car	

○ ○ ○

How to Fix a Flat Tire

Nobody wants to get a flat tire, but you always need

to be prepared.

Make sure you have the following things

_____*in your car*_____ : a jack,
　　　　　　　1

a wrench, and a spare tire.

If you get a flat tire, pull over

_____. Take off the hubcap and use the wrench to loosen the nuts.
　　　　2

Don't take them off yet. Place the jack _____ near the flat tire. Then
　　　　　　　　　　　　　　　　　　　3

raise the car a few inches _____. Remove the nuts and put them
　　　　　　　　　　　　　4

_____ so you don't lose them. Next, remove the flat tire and put the spare tire
　　　5

_____. Put the nuts back _____ and tighten them
　　　6　　　　　　　　　　　　　　　7

well. Replace the hubcap, lower the car with the jack, and put your tools _____. Take
　　　　　　　　　　　　　　　　　　　　　　　　　　　　　　　　8

your car _____ to repair the flat tire.
　　　　　9

nuts　　　jack

hubcap

spare tire　　　wrench

13 | Usage Note: Using Place, Time, and Frequency Together Read the note. Then do Activities 14 and 15.

We often use **place expressions** with **time expressions** or **frequency expressions**. The expression of place usually comes first.

		where	when
1	We left	**for school**	at 8:00.

		where	when
2	Have you looked	**outside**	lately?

		where	how often
3	I read the newspaper	**online**	every morning.

14 | Explaining *Where* and *When* Complete these sentences with information about yourself, and share them with your classmates. `11.3 A–B`

PERSONAL BACKGROUND

1. I was born _____
   (where / when)

   _____ .

2. I went to high school _____
   (where / when)

   _____ .

3. I worked _____
   (where / when)

   _____ .

4. I met my best friend _____
   (where / when)

   _____ .

5. My parents met _____
   (where / when)

   _____ .

6. Yesterday I went _____
   (where / when)

   _____ .

FYI

For most places, we use *to* + determiner + noun: *to the store, to my friend's house.*

For a small group of places, we use *to* + noun: *to work, to school.* This means *to my regular place of work, to my school.*

For a few others, we can use the noun alone: *home, downtown, uptown.*

15 | *Where* or *When*? Do these underlined words and phrases answer the question *where* or *when*? Write your answers above the words and phrases. `11.3 A–B`

Starting a New Job

It's important to make a good impression <u>on your first day</u> *(when)* <u>at a new job</u>.

<u>Here</u> are some tips to help you:

- Be sure to arrive <u>at work</u> <u>on time</u>.

- <u>Before your first day</u> <u>at work</u>, find out about the company's dress code[10].

- What are the lunch-hour rules <u>at your new job</u>? Find out.
  For example, do people eat <u>at their desks</u>, or does everyone take a full hour <u>outside the workplace</u>?

- You should never make personal phone calls <u>from your office</u> <u>during work hours</u>.

- Don't send personal emails <u>from your office computer</u>.

- <u>At the end of your first day</u> <u>at work</u>, make sure your desk is neat.

FYI

A prepositional phrase can function like an adverb in one context and like an adjective in another context.

I was **at work** by 7:00.
(= adverb; I was *where* at 7:00?)

I met a lot of people on my first day **at work**.
(= adjective; *which* first day?)

Think about It In which sentences above does the time information come before the place information? Why is that?

[10]**dress code:** a set of rules about what you are allowed to wear

11.4 Explaining *How*

A

1 She **has done** well so far.

2 Please **come** quickly.

PLACEMENT OF ADVERBS OF MANNER

3 **Don't forget to speak** slowly.

4 My parents **dropped by** unexpectedly.

5 We **need to finish this work** quickly.

6 **Can** we **do this** together?

7 They **ate dinner** quickly.
(NOT: ~~They ate quickly dinner.~~)

We can use **adverbs** of manner to describe how something is done, as in **1 – 2**.

We often use these adverbs of manner:

- after the **complete verb**, as in **3 – 4**
- after the **complete verb** and its **object**, as in **5 – 6**

WARNING! We don't usually use an adverb between a verb and its object, as in **7**.

B

FORMING ADVERBS OF MANNER

adjective		-ly		adverb
8	sad	+	-ly	=	sadly
9	strange	+	-ly	=	strangely
10	careful	+	-ly	=	carefully

We form many adverbs of manner by adding -ly to an adjective, as in **8 – 10**.

WARNING! Not all words ending in -ly are adverbs. Some are adjectives, such as *friendly*, *costly*, and *lovely*.

For a list of spelling rules, see Activity 17.

C

11 I don't want to go by myself.

12 With difficulty, he climbed out of the tiny car.

13 A: Can I take your order?
B: Just a cup of coffee, please. With extra cream.

14 She left the house without a word to anyone.

15 They left in a hurry.

16 He works as a waiter.

We can also use certain **prepositional phrases** to explain *how*, as in **11 – 16**. Some common prepositions used this way are:

as		a waiter, a child, a team, a student
by		car, bus, mistake, myself
in	+	a hurry, a low voice, a new way
with		people, friends, water, difficulty, a smile
without		a doubt, a word, question, hesitation

 ONLINE

---

16 | Using Adverbs of Manner Circle the adverbs that best describe you. Then compare with a partner.

`11.4 A`

YOUR BEHAVIOR

1. I usually eat **quickly / slowly**.

2. I do my homework **carefully / carelessly**.

3. I tend to walk **fast / slowly**.

4. My friends and I usually study **alone / together**.

5. I usually treat other people **nicely / rudely**.

6. I drive **cautiously / recklessly**[11].

7. Normally I speak **loudly / softly** in class.

8. When I was a child, I played sports **awkwardly / gracefully**.

9. I usually dress **elegantly / simply**.

10. I speak my first language **poorly / well**.

> **WARNING!**
>
> The word *good* is an **adjective**. The related adverb is *well*.
>
> He's a **good** singer. (adjective)
> He sings **well**. (adverb)
>
> Some adverbs of manner and adjectives have the same form:
>
> **fast**–fast
> **hard**–hard
> **wrong**–wrong

[11] **recklessly:** dangerously and without thinking

Think about It Can you change the placement of the adverb of manner in any of the sentences in Activity 16? Why or why not?

Write about It Write three more sentences about your behavior. Use an adverb of manner from Activity 16 in each sentence.

I tend to read slowly.

---

17 | Spelling Note: Spelling -*ly* Adverbs Read the note. Then do Activities 18–20.

We can form **adverbs** from many adjectives.

	ADJECTIVE	ADVERB
1 For many adverbs, simply add -*ly* to the adjective.	natural	natural**ly**
2 When the adjective ends in -*le*, change the -*e* to -*y*.	simp**le**	simp**ly**
3 When the adjective has two syllables and ends in -*y*, change the -*y* to -*i* and then add -*ly*.	craz**y**	craz**ily**
4 When the adjective ends in -*ic*, add -*ally*.	bas**ic**	bas**ically**

WARNING! Some adjectives end in -ly. We can't change these adjectives into adverbs. We use a **prepositional phrase** instead; for example, *friendly* becomes *in a friendly way*.

---

18 | Spelling -*ly* Adverbs Write the adverb form of each adjective. Then use ten of the adverbs to complete the sentences below. (More than one answer may be possible.) `11.4 B`

ADJECTIVE	ADVERB	ADJECTIVE	ADVERB
1. greedy	*greedily*	10. enthusiastic	_____
2. angry	_____	11. irritable	_____
3. brave	_____	12. accidental	_____
4. thoughtful	_____	13. hungry	_____
5. weary	_____	14. happy	_____
6. rude	_____	15. loud	_____
7. anxious	_____	16. frantic	_____
8. easy	_____	17. repeated	_____
9. hasty	_____	18. comfortable	_____

HOW DID THEY SAY IT?

1. "Can I have three more cookies?" Kate asked _____*greedily*_____.

2. "No, no, no," the man said _____.

3. "I'm really nervous about the exam," Matt said _____.

4. "I can't walk any farther," the child said _____.

5. "Why did you throw my computer out the window?" the woman asked _____.

6. "My vacation starts tomorrow," Rob said _____.

7. "Stop, thief!" the woman yelled _____.

8. "Come on, everyone. This is going to be fun!" Sam said _____.

9. "Is there anything to eat?" the child asked _____.

10. "Someone has been hurt! We need a doctor now!" Mary yelled _____.

19 | Using -ly Adverbs Choose an adverb from Activity 18 to complete these sentences. (More than one answer may be possible.) `11.4 B`

Good Advice

1. Don't answer test questions _____*hastily*_____. Slow down and you'll make fewer mistakes.

2. Don't let children play with matches¹². They might _____ start a fire.

3. Use new words _____. That will help you learn them.

4. Don't speak _____ to anyone. You may regret what you say.

5. In a dangerous situation, act _____ but don't do anything foolish.

6. In a store, don't speak _____ on your cell phone. No one else wants to hear your conversation.

7. It's important to dress _____ when you take a long plane trip.

8. Don't speak _____ to your elders. Speak politely.

> **F Y I**
>
> Sometimes we can use an adverb before a main verb to give emphasis to other words in the sentence. Compare:
>
> Don't answer the test questions **hastily**.
>
> Don't **hastily answer** the test questions.

Think about It Can you change the placement of the adverb of manner in each sentence above? Why or why not?

Write about It Write three sentences with good advice. Use an adverb of manner in each sentence.

20 | Using -ly Adverbs Rewrite the questions. Use the adverb form of the **bold** adjective. `11.4 B`

1. Are you a **careful** writer?   Do you write _____*carefully*_____?
2. Are you a **positive** thinker?   Do you think _____?
3. Do you want to be a **good** writer?   Do you want to write _____?
4. Are you an **attentive**¹³ listener?   Do you listen _____?
5. Are you a **confident** speaker?   Do you speak _____?
6. Have you ever done something **courageous**¹⁴? Have you ever acted _____?
7. Are you an **independent** person?   Do you like to make decisions _____?
8. Are you a **careless** driver?   Do you drive _____?
9. Are you an **enthusiastic** sports fan?   Do you cheer _____?
10. Are you **irritable** in the morning?   Do you behave _____ in the morning?
11. Is learning a new language **easy** for you? Do you learn new languages _____?
12. Are you a **selfish** person?   Do you ever act _____?

Talk about It Ask a partner the questions in the second column above.

¹²**matches:** short pieces of wood that you use to light a fire
¹³**attentive:** watching, listening to, or thinking about someone or something carefully

¹⁴**courageous:** brave; not afraid

21 | Usage Note: *By/Without* + Gerund Read the note. Then do Activity 22.

> We sometimes use a prepositional phrase formed with *by* + a **gerund** or *without* + a **gerund** to express *how*.
>
> **1** I learn new words **by repeating them.**   **4** She left **without saying goodbye.**
>
> **2** You can log in **by using your password.**   **5** Don't cross the street **without looking both ways.**
>
> **3** You can help **by making lunch.**   **6** You can't play the game **without knowing the rules.**

22 | Using Prepositional Phrases to Explain *How* Match each question with an answer. `11.4 C`

HOW SHOULD YOU DO IT?

1. How should you answer the phone in English? __b__
2. How should you talk on the phone in public? ____
3. How should you choose a husband or wife? ____
4. How should you come into class late? ____
5. How should you climb a mountain? ____
6. How do people often greet each other in business situations? ____
7. How can you see the surface of the moon? ____
8. How can you get good grades? ____
9. How should you eat potato chips? ____
10. How should you speak to an angry child? ____

a. With great care.
b. By saying hello.
c. Without making any noise.
d. In a soft voice.
e. By shaking hands and saying hello.
f. Without looking down.
g. Without eating the whole bag.
h. Without yelling.
i. With a telescope.
j. By studying hard.

Write about It Write three of your own questions that begin with *how should you*. Ask your classmates your questions.

23 | Explaining *How* Complete each definition below with a word or phrase from the box. `11.4 A–C`

| by radio or television | in an angry way | loudly | quietly | with great force |
| by using your hands | lightly | quickly | strongly | with your arms and head first |

DICTIONARY DEFINITIONS

1. **demand**   to say _____ *strongly* _____ that you must have
   something: *The workers are demanding more money.*

2. **dive**   to jump into water _____:
   Sam dove into the pool.

3. **argue**   to talk with someone _____ because
   you do not agree: *My co-workers argue a lot about schedules.*

4. **whisper**   to speak _____ to someone so that
   others cannot hear you: *He whispered so that he wouldn't wake up the baby.*

5. **broadcast**   to send out sound or pictures _____:
   The Olympics are broadcast live around the world.

6. **exclaim**   to say something suddenly and _____ because you are surprised or angry: *"I don't believe it!" she exclaimed.*

7. **dab**   to touch something _____ and quickly: *She dabbed the cut with a cotton ball.*

8. **dart**   to move _____ and suddenly: *He darted across the road.*

9. **fling**   to throw something carelessly or _____: *She flung her coat on the chair.*

10. **grope**   to try to find something _____ when you cannot see: *He groped for the light switch.*

24 | Explaining *When, Where,* and *How* Underline the words and phrases that explain *when, how long, where,* and *how.* Write *when, how long, where,* or *how* over the words. (Look back at Charts 11.2, 11.3, and 11.4 for more information if necessary.)

How to Calculate Your Life Expectancy

Note: This quiz is just for fun!

1. Start with the number 79.   *79*

2. Are you male? *Subtract 3.* Are you female? *Add 4.*   ____

   where
3. Do you live <u>in a large city</u>? *Subtract 2.* Do you live in a small town? *Add 2.*   ____

4. Do you live with a relative or friend? *Add 5.* Do you live alone? *Subtract 1.*   ____

5. Do you eat fresh fruit and vegetables every day? *Add 3.*   ____

6. Do you sleep more than ten hours a night or fewer than five? *Subtract 2.*   ____

7. Do you exercise hard for at least 30 minutes three or four times a week? *Add 2.*   ____

8. Do you plan to work behind a desk for most of your life? *Subtract 3.* Are you physically active at work? *Add 2.*   ____

9. Do you expect to work after age 65? *Add 3.*   ____

10. Do you get angry easily? *Subtract 3.* Are you easygoing and relaxed most of the time? *Add 3.*   ____

11. Are you usually happy? *Add 1.*   **TOTAL** ____

Talk about It   Answer the questions above to find your life expectancy. Share your results with your classmates.

11.5 Explaining *Why*

A	**1** We didn't leave the house **because of the weather.** **2** There were 50,000 deaths last year **due to car crashes.** **3** **Thanks to the Internet,** we can now get information quickly.	We can use certain **prepositional phrases** to explain *why* (or give a reason), as in **1 – 3.** These are more common in writing. For more information on giving reasons, see Unit 12, Chart 12.3, page 383.

25 | Explaining *Why* Complete each sentence with a reason from the box. `11.5 A`

GIVING REASONS

1. People live longer today in part _____*because of advances in medicine*_____.

2. _____, many people spend one or two hours a day just driving to their jobs.

3. Many areas aren't getting enough rain _____.

4. She's a great singer, and _____, she's had many opportunities to travel.

5. They couldn't fit the box into the car _____.

| because of advances in medicine |
| because of climate[15] change |
| because of crowded roads |
| because of its size |
| because of that |

6. The city is becoming crowded _____.

7. _____, Europe has become largely multilingual.

8. Men are more likely to miss a day of work _____.

| due to a cold or flu |
| due to the arrival of foreigners |
| due to the growing population |

9. The beaches are crowded _____.

10. _____, I'm in good shape now.

11. _____, I can wake up to music.

| thanks to the arrival of tourists |
| thanks to my clock radio |
| thanks to yoga |

Write about It Think of another way to complete each sentence above.

People live longer today in part because of better food.

11.6 Explaining *To What Degree*

A

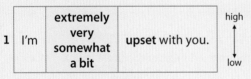

ADVERBS OF DEGREE

| 1 | I'm | extremely
very
somewhat
a bit | upset with you. |

high ↑↓ low

WITH ADJECTIVES OR ADVERBS

2 He's **perfectly capable** of doing it.

3 I think I did **pretty well** on the test.

4 I'm **fairly certain** about this.

5 Where can I hang my jacket? It's **slightly wet**.

WITH VERBS

6 We **completely forgot**.

7 I don't **quite understand** this.

8 The car **nearly hit** the wall.

We can use **adverbs** of degree to explain *to what degree*. We use different adverbs to express different degrees of strength, as in **1**.

We can use adverbs of degree with adjectives and other adverbs, as in **2 – 5**. Some common examples include:

high ← → low

| completely
exactly
extremely
perfectly | awfully
pretty
quite
really
so
very | fairly
rather
somewhat | a (little) bit
kind of
slightly |

We can use some adverbs of degree with verbs, as in **6 – 8**. Some common examples include:

high ← → low

| absolutely
completely
definitely
totally | quite
really | almost
nearly |

GRAMMAR TERM: Adverbs of degree are also called **intensifiers**.

ONLINE

[15] **climate:** the normal weather conditions of a place

26 | Noticing Adverbs of Degree Underline the adverbs of degree in these conversations. Then practice with a partner. `11.6 A`

1. A: How do you feel today?
   B: <u>Pretty</u> good. And you?
   A: I don't know. I'm kind of tired.
2. A: Is something wrong?
   B: No, I'm just a bit hungry.
3. A: This is so pretty!
   B: I'm glad you like it.
4. A: It's sort of hot in here.
   B: Yeah, it is a bit.
5. A: This is a serious problem.
   B: You're absolutely right.
6. A: What are you doing?
   B: Packing my suitcase.
   A: So you're definitely going?
   B: Yep. I've already called a taxi.
7. A: What's the value of the euro now?
   B: I'm not exactly sure.

8. A: How was the weather in London?
   B: Terrible. It almost ruined my trip.
9. A: When are you leaving?
   B: Right now. Are you coming with me?
   A: Hold on. I'm almost ready.
10. A: Can I use your computer tonight?
    B: It works somewhat differently from yours, but help yourself.
11. A: When will you have the answer?
    B: I should be able to find out pretty quickly.
12. A: How was your trip?
    B: It was OK, but I couldn't completely enjoy myself because of work.
13. A: I don't understand the homework assignment.
    B: I don't quite understand it myself.
14. A: How did you do on the test?
    B: Really well. I don't think I made any mistakes.
    A: Good for you.

Think about It Does each adverb of degree above describe an adjective, another adverb, or a verb?

27 | Usage Note: Placement of Adverbs of Degree Read the note. Then do Activity 28.

When an **adverb** of degree describes an adjective or another adverb, it usually comes before the adjective or adverb.

I'm not **quite certain.**   They left **rather quickly.**   She told the story **somewhat differently.**

When *almost*, *nearly*, *quite*, and *really* describe a single verb, they usually come before the main verb. When there is one (or more) helping verb, they usually come after the first helping verb.

He **almost fell down.**   They had **nearly forgotten.**   I don't **quite believe** her.

A few adverbs of degree can come before the main verb, after the main verb, or after an object.

I **completely agree.**   I **agree completely.**   I **don't understand you completely.**

28 | Placing Adverbs of Degree Write the adverb of degree in parentheses in the correct place in the sentence. (More than one answer may be possible.) Then check (✓) *True* or *False* for you. `11.6 A`

Personal Statements

	TRUE	FALSE
pretty 1. I'm a good student. (pretty)	☐	☐
2. I'm hard-working. (incredibly)	☐	☐

	TRUE	FALSE
3. I like ice cream. (really)	☐	☐
4. I usually do my homework carefully. (fairly)	☐	☐
5. I missed the bus today. (nearly)	☐	☐
6. I don't understand the news in English. (quite)	☐	☐
7. I have lived here for a long time. (very)	☐	☐
8. I have changed over the past year. (completely)	☐	☐
9. I am certain about my future. (absolutely)	☐	☐
10. I prefer food that is spicy. (slightly)	☐	☐

Think about It Which adverb of degree in Activity 28 can you use in more than one place in the sentence?

Write about It Rewrite the false statements in Activity 28 to make them true for you.

29 | Usage Note: *Too* and *Enough* Read the note. Then do Activity 30.

We often use **too** <u>before</u> an adjective or adverb to mean "more than is good or possible."

    These shoes are **too small**.   He speaks **too quickly**.   The test was not **too hard**.

We can use the adverb *enough* <u>after</u> an adjective, adverb, or verb. *Enough* means "to the necessary amount or degree."

    These shoes aren't **big enough**.   She doesn't speak **clearly enough**.   She doesn't **read enough**.

We can use an **infinitive** in a sentence with *too* and *enough*. The infinitive shows a result.

    I'm **too tired to study**.   She speaks **too softly to hear**.
    The kids are **old enough to stay home alone**.   I didn't get up **early enough to go to the gym**.

30 | Using *Too* and *Enough* Complete these conversations with the word in parentheses and *too* or *enough*. Then practice with a partner. `11.6 A`

1. A: Who did you vote for?

   B: I didn't vote. I'm not _____. (old)

2. A: What do you think of my cake?

   B: It's _____ to eat. (pretty)

   A: Oh, come on. Have a piece.

3. A: What's that music?

   B: I can't tell. It's not _____. (loud)

4. A: How was your vacation?

   B: Absolutely wonderful, but it ended

     _____. We didn't have time

   to see everything. (soon)

5. A: Can you translate this Spanish song for me?

   B: Oh, sorry. My Spanish isn't

     _____. (good)

6. A: What's for dinner?

   B: I don't know. I'm _____ to cook.

   (tired)

7. A: OK. I'm finally ready to go.

   B: It's _____ to go to the store.

   (late) It's closed.

8. A: Who's that over there? Can you see?

   B: No. He's not _____. (close)

9. A: Are you _____ to help
   me move this sofa? (strong)

   B: I think so. Let's try.

10. A: Wait for me. You're getting
    _____ ahead. (far)

    B: Sorry. I'll slow down.

31 | Using *Too/Enough* with Infinitives Write ten logical questions using ideas from this chart. Use each infinitive in the right column only once. (Different questions are possible.) `11.6 A`

Are you	fit[16] enough humble[17] enough old enough strong enough tall enough too busy too nervous too old too shy too smart too tired	to apologize when you make a mistake? to ask for help? to be fooled? to give answers in class? to lift a friend? to reach the top shelf? to remember when no one had a cell phone? to run a marathon? to see your friends? to start a new career? to stay up late?

Talk about It Ask a partner the questions you wrote above.

A: Are you fit enough to run a marathon?
B: Well, I'm in good shape, but I don't think so.

11.7 Other Uses of Adverbs

A

1 There is **certainly** no secret formula for being a good boss.

2 I'll be at the meeting, **of course**.

3 **Without a doubt**, Yosemite is one of the most beautiful spots in the U.S.

4 We'll **probably** take the train.

5 Yosemite is **maybe** one of the most beautiful spots in the U.S.

6 I planned to leave by 7:00, but I **actually** didn't leave until 9:00.

7 I know Sarah's coming. **In fact**, she's bringing all the food.

8 **Luckily**, no one got hurt in the accident.

9 **Unfortunately**, it rained all day.

10a This story is true, **really**.

10b This story is **really** long.

11a **Clearly** we're going to be late.

11b You need to explain your ideas **clearly**.

We sometimes use an **adverb** or **prepositional phrase** to show our attitude or feelings about the information in a clause or sentence. For example, we may:

• show certainty, as in **1 – 3**
• show doubt, as in **4 – 5**

• emphasize that something is true or factual, as in **6 – 7**

• make an evaluation or judgment, as in **8 – 9**

Notice that many of these adverbs can also function as **adverbs of degree** or **manner**, as in **10a – 11b**.

---

[16] **fit:** healthy and strong

[17] **humble:** not thinking that you are better than other people

32 | Noticing Adverbs In these sentences, which adverbs show the writer's attitude or feelings about the information in the sentence? Circle them. Then write them under the correct group in the chart below. `11.7 A`

Sentences from Student Essays

1. Many people fear or dislike anger, but anger is (actually) a very important emotion.
2. Sadly, we had to leave the area when I was only three.
3. It was really the best advice that I had ever received.
4. We need to address the causes of climate change. Fortunately, advances in technology will help us do this.
5. I have read a lot of books about Mahatma Gandhi. He has definitely inspired me in my life.
6. I try to put some money in the bank every month. Perhaps I will use this money to start a business or go back to school.
7. Recreation[18] can make families and friends closer. Taking a trip or playing a sport gives them something to remember for the rest of their lives. Of course, not all these memories will be good.
8. There are certainly many important problems in the world today.
9. Obviously, you have more space in the suburbs than in the city.
10. The Internet will bring people around the world closer together. In fact, it already does every day.
11. Without a doubt, Yosemite is one of the most beautiful spots in the U.S.
12. Coal[19] is a major source of air pollution. Unfortunately, we can't live without it.
13. When I think about my future, I plan big things. Maybe I will be a fashion designer or perhaps an art buyer.
14. At the age of 25, he had no money and no job. Clearly he needed to change his situation.

Certainty	Doubt	Actuality/Truth	Evaluation
		actually	

Think about It Are there any words or phrases in the sentences above that say *when, where, how, why,* or *to what degree*? Underline them and say what kind of information they give.

very—to what degree

---

[18] **recreation:** relaxing and enjoying yourself, when you are not working

[19] **coal:** a black mineral used as fuel

33 | Using Adverbs in Conversation Circle the best adverb to complete each conversation. Then practice with a partner. `11.7 A`

1. A: Do you still have five dollars?

   B: **Actually / Of course**, I have eight dollars, not five.

2. A: Do you really enjoy swimming?

   B: I love it. I would do it every day, but I can't, **luckily / sadly**.

3. A: I had a good time tonight, **really / unfortunately**.

   B: Good. So did I.

4. A: Do you want to come over on Tuesday?

   B: Um, **actually / maybe**, I have football practice on Tuesday.

   A: Well, **certainly / maybe** Wednesday then.

   B: I'm kind of busy Wednesday.

5. A: You did the dishes!

   B: **Maybe / Of course** I did the dishes. I always do the dishes.

6. A: Why am I always the last person to get here?

   B: **Actually / Luckily**, Carlos and David aren't here yet.

7. A: Is there anything left to eat?

   B: **Fortunately / Probably**, I saved something for you.

8. A: Are you really going to sell your car?

   B: Sure. **In fact / Really**, two people have already looked at it.

9. A: Do you need to sit down?

   B: No, I'm OK, **obviously / really**.

10. A: What are you going to do next year?

    B: I don't know. I might take some time off.

    A: What for?

    B: **Clearly / Maybe** to do some traveling.

Do you still have five dollars?

Are you really going to sell your car?

34 | Using Adverbs Rewrite each sentence or pair of sentences using one of the adverbs in the box. `11.7 A`

1. I don't think he will come back.

   He probably won't come back.

2. I am sure she will be here soon.
3. You aren't happy here. That's obvious.
4. I'm telling you the truth. I didn't do it.

5. The traffic was terrible this morning, but I still got to my job interview on time. That was lucky.
6. I really mean it. You should stay in bed today.
7. I don't know the answer to your question. That's the truth.
8. We might go to Spain next summer.

| certainly |
| clearly |
| honestly |
| probably |

| actually |
| luckily |
| maybe |
| seriously |

Talk about It Work with a partner. Choose one of the sentences you rewrote in Activity 34, and use it to create a short conversation. Present your conversation to the class.

A: When is Jake coming back?
B: You know, he probably won't come back. He wasn't feeling well.
A: Oh, too bad!

11.8 Using Adverbs in Speaking

A

1 A: When are you leaving?
  B: **In a minute.**

2 A: Let's stay home tomorrow.
  B: **Seriously?**
  A: Yeah, I'm kind of tired.

3 A: I think it's going to rain again.
  B: Yeah, **probably.**

In conversation, speakers sometimes use **adverbs** or **prepositional phrases** alone, as in **1 – 3**.

B

SOFTENING A SUGGESTION

4 A: I think I'll leave now.
  B: It's raining pretty hard. **Maybe** you should wait until later.

5 A: What time is it?
  B: It's late. You should **probably** get going.

6 A: Could I **just** interrupt you for a minute?
  B: Sure. What do you need?

Speakers sometimes use an adverb to soften a suggestion, as in **4 – 5**. These are usually adverbs showing doubt, but we also use *just* in this way, as in **6**.

GO ONLINE

35 | Using Adverbs Alone Listen and complete these conversations with the missing words. Then practice with a partner. `11.8 A`

1. A: I like your new haircut.

   B: _____

   A: Yeah, it looks very good on you.

2. A: Do you really think I can do it?

   B: _____

3. A: Are you sure you want to go?

   B: _____

4. A: Will you be ready to leave in ten minutes?

   B: Yeah, _____.

5. A: Do you still want to look at my pictures?

   B: Oh, yeah. _____. Of course.

6. A: I'm proud of you.

   B: _____

   A: Yes. You did a great job.

7. A: Do you want dinner now?

   B: No, _____.

8. A: Did you like the movie?

   B: _____

9. A: How did the meeting go?

   B: _____

10. A: Are you hungry?

   B: Yes, _____.

Talk about It Practice the conversations above again. This time, respond with a different adverb or prepositional phrase.

A: I like your new haircut.
B: Really?

36 | Softening a Suggestion Add *probably, perhaps, maybe,* and *just* to soften the suggestions in the box, and use each suggestion in a conversation below. Then practice with a partner. **11.8 B**

> Well, you should tell him about it.   You should apologize.   You should lie down for a while.
> You need to leave home earlier.   You should call him.

1. A: Toshi hasn't called in days. I hope he's OK.

   B: *Perhaps you should call him.*

2. A: Why is Isabel so angry?

   B: I forgot to go to her picnic and now she won't talk to me.

   A: _____

3. A: My head's killing me.

   B: _____

4. A: I just can't get to class on time.

   B: _____

5. A: Does your father know about your accident?

   B: No, I don't think so.

   A: _____

11.9 Using Adverbs and Prepositional Phrases in Writing

Writers use certain **adverbs** and **prepositional phrases** to connect sentences in a piece of writing, as in **1**. We call them **linking expressions**.

1 | I spend a lot of time planning for the future. | **However,** | this is usually more stressful than helpful. |

sentence 1   sentence 2

A

2 It's fun to look for cultural differences when you travel. | For example, | people in a different place may eat very different food.

3 I would need a good reason to fire an employee. | For instance, | I would fire someone who stole from the company.

4 As a child, I wanted to become a great athlete or movie star. | However, | now my goals are more realistic.

5 At first I couldn't communicate in Spanish very well. | However, | after several months, my Spanish got better.

Like traffic lights and road signs, linking expressions signal (or tell the reader) the kind of information that is coming. The most common linking expressions in academic writing are *for example* and *however*.

• We use *for example* or *for instance* to signal an example of something mentioned earlier, as in **2 – 3**.

• We use *however* to signal that contrasting information is coming next, as in **4 – 5**.

B

6 Most children take their first steps between 10 and 16 months. | At this age, | the child is still somewhat unstable.

7 A fad is something that is very popular for a short time. One summer everyone wears the same kind of shirt. | The next summer, | people wear something totally different.

Writers sometimes use time, place, and manner expressions at the beginning of a sentence to connect the sentence back to a previous sentence and to add details, as in **6 – 7**.

GO ONLINE

37 | Adding Examples in Writing Match the sentences on the left with examples on the right. `11.9 A`

THE ENGLISH LANGUAGE

1. Many words in English come from other languages. ____

2. We are constantly adding new words to the language or new meanings to old words. ____

3. The main part of a word is called the root. Many words in English come from the same root. ____

4. Some prefixes, such as *in-* and *un-*, can reverse the meaning of a word. ____

5. Many words in English have more than one meaning. ____

6. Synonyms are words that are similar in meaning. ____

7. We form an acronym by using the first letters of a group of words. ____

a. For example, the word *incomplete* is the opposite of *complete*.

b. For example, the words *biography*, *biology*, and *biochemistry* come from the root *bio*, which means "life."

c. The word *so*, for example, can mean "consequently," "thus," "to a great extent," "also," "apparently," or "true."

d. The word *scuba*, for example, means "self-contained underwater breathing apparatus."

e. For instance, computers introduced a new meaning for the word *mouse*.

f. The word *chocolate*, for example, comes from the Aztec word *xocolatl*, which means "bitter water."

g. For instance, you can use the word *large* in place of *big* with little change in meaning.

38 | Using Linking Expressions Complete each sentence with *however* or *for example*. `11.9 A`

1. It's not always possible to exercise every day. _____, most people should be able to go for a walk or play a sport several times a week.

2. Sometimes a little stress is good for me. _____, feeling a little stress before an exam makes me study harder.

3. A few years ago, experts thought that computers would replace books. Now, _____, they are saying that books won't disappear.

4. I'm usually quite tired in the afternoon. By evening, _____, I usually feel pretty alert and energetic.

5. In my culture in the past, a girl's parents chose a husband for her. Today, _____, this happens less often.

6. I moved here with my family ten years ago. At first I was very unhappy because I didn't know anyone. _____, after I started school, I made lots of new friends and I didn't feel lonely anymore.

7. In many parts of the world, the average life expectancy has increased greatly. _____, in the U.S., life expectancy was 47 years in 1900. Today it is 77 years.

8. A few bilingual people speak two languages equally well. Normally, _____, bilingual people speak one language more fluently.

9. I would need a good reason to fire an employee. _____, I would fire someone who kept missing work without a good excuse.

10. When you sleep, you dream about 20 percent of the time. _____, a person who sleeps for eight hours dreams for about 96 minutes.

11. I am very hard-working and I get along well with other people. _____, I am not very organized.

39 | Connecting Ideas in Writing Complete each sentence with your own ideas. Then compare with your classmates. (Many different answers are possible.) `11.9 A`

1. There are many different ways to greet someone. For example, _____.

2. There is always something interesting to do here. For example, _____.

3. There are many things that can make a person angry. For instance, _____.

4. Some great cities are not very well known. For instance, _____.

5. The way people live has changed tremendously[20] in the past 50 years. For example, _____
   _____.

6. Traveling alone can be fun. However, _____.

7. Air travel is relatively safe. However, _____.

8. It's not easy to learn a foreign language. However, _____.

9. Many people would like to work fewer hours. However, _____.

40 | Using Time and Place Expressions to Connect Ideas Read two versions of each essay. Underline the new information in Version 2. Then answer the questions below. `11.9 B`

Version 1	Version 2
THE AIRCAR	**THE AIRCAR**
Would you like to drive and fly? You may be able to. Ken Wernicke is building a car that you can both drive and fly. He calls it an Aircar. Wernicke's Aircar is wide enough to fly but narrow enough to fit on the road. This unusual car will have a maximum speed of 310 miles per hour (499 kilometers per hour). It will go 65 miles per hour (105 kilometers per hour). This two-person vehicle will be able to travel 1,300 miles (2,092 kilometers) or 2,000 miles (3,219 kilometers).	Would you like to drive to the airport and then fly to another city—without ever leaving your car? Someday you may be able to. Ken Wernicke is building a car that you can both drive and fly. He calls it an Aircar. Wernicke's Aircar is wide enough to fly but narrow enough to fit on the road. In the air, this unusual car will have a maximum speed of 310 miles per hour (499 kilometers per hour). On the highway, it will go 65 miles per hour (105 kilometers per hour). With two 50-gallon (189-liter) fuel tanks, this two-person vehicle will be able to travel 1,300 miles (2,092 kilometers) in the air or 2,000 miles (3,219 kilometers) on the road.
THE FIRST AIRPLANE	**THE FIRST AIRPLANE**
Orville Wright flew the first successful airplane. He and his brother Wilbur took turns as pilot and flew. They went a little bit farther. Wilbur was able to travel 852 feet. The two brothers from Ohio had invented powered flight.	On December 17, 1903, Orville Wright flew the first successful airplane for 120 feet on a beach in Kitty Hawk, North Carolina. He and his brother Wilbur took turns as pilot and flew three more times that day. On each flight, they went a little bit farther. On their final flight, Wilbur was able to travel 852 feet in 59 seconds. The two brothers from Ohio had invented powered flight.

1. How is Version 1 of each story different from Version 2?

2. In Version 2 of each story, which time, place, and manner expressions does the writer use at the beginning of a sentence? What purpose do they serve? Write *when*, *where*, or *how* next to each expression.

[20] **tremendously:** a lot

WRAP-UP Demonstrate Your Knowledge

A | GIVING ADVICE Choose an adverb of manner. List five things you should do using the adverb of manner. Then read your list to the class, and ask your classmates to add more ideas.

carefully
- *You should drive carefully.*
- *You should answer questions on a test carefully.*
- *You should choose a spouse carefully.*

B | WRITING Study the pictures and complete the accident reports with your own ideas. (Many different answers are possible.) Try to use all of the adverbs and prepositional phrases in the box.

Accident Report #1

Employee's name: Sandra Woods

Describe accident: ___On Saturday,___

___Sandra Woods had almost finished with___

___the lunch service.___

_____

_____

_____

_____

_____

_____

_____

_____

_____

_____

actually
almost
however
luckily
maybe
on the floor
pretty
suddenly
usually

Accident Report #2

Employee's name: Jeff Sawyer

Describe accident: _____

_____

_____

_____

_____

_____

_____

_____

_____

_____

_____

_____

backward
carelessly
however
probably
really
unexpectedly
unfortunately
without looking

C | RESEARCH Choose a well-known person—someone you admire—and research biographical information about him or her. Then write a short biography about this person for your classmates to read. Be sure to include details about *when*, *why*, and *how*.

D | PRESENTATION Explain to your classmates how to do something simple. Try to use adverbs and prepositional phrases in your presentation.

How to Wash Your Hands
1. *Put water on your hands.*
2. *Add soap to your hands.*
3. *Rub your hands together vigorously for about 20 seconds.*
4. *Rinse your hands well.*
5. *Dry your hands with a paper towel.*

E | WEB SEARCH Look online for the script of a movie you enjoyed seeing. Search in the script for three examples of degree adverbs from Chart 11.6. Copy the sentences with the examples from the script, and ask your classmates to use the sentences to make a new conversation.

from the movie <u>Moonstruck</u>:
What exactly does your husband do?   *That's very sad.*   *It's really cold.*

11.10 Summary of Adverbs and Prepositional Phrases

TYPE	PURPOSE	EXAMPLES IN BOOK TITLES
TIME	to explain *when*	***Now**, Discover Your Strengths* by Marcus Buckingham and Donald O. Clifton
FREQUENCY	to explain *how often*	***Seldom** Right But Never in Doubt: Essays, Journalism, and Social Commentary* by Joseph Dobrian and Dorothy Parker
PLACE	to explain *where*	*Difficult People: Dealing With Difficult People **at Work*** by Colin G. Smith
MANNER	to explain *how* or *in what way*	*How to Take Great Notes **Quickly** And **Easily**: A Very Easy Guide* by John Connelly
REASON	to explain *why*	***Because of You*** by B. G. Hennessy and Hiroe Nakata
DEGREE	to explain *to what degree* to strengthen or weaken a verb, adjective, or adverb	*The **Perfectly** Roasted Chicken: 20 New Ways to Roast* by Mindy Fox
ATTITUDE / FEELINGS	to show certainty	*The Underground Baseball Encyclopedia: Baseball Stuff You Never Needed to Know and Can **Certainly** Live Without* by Robert Schnakenberg
	to show doubt	*Baking Soda: Over 500 Fabulous, Fun, and Frugal Uses You've **Probably** Never Thought Of* by Vicki Lansky
	to emphasize the truth	*Your First $1000—How to Start an Online Business that **Actually** Makes Money* by Steve Scott
	to make an evaluation or judgment	***Unfortunately**, It Was Paradise: Selected Poems* by Mahmoud Darwish, Munir Akash, Carolyn Forché, and Sinan Antoon
LINKING	to connect clauses in a piece of writing	*You're Not Old Until You're Ninety: Best to Be Prepared, **However*** by Rebecca Lattimer

12 Adverb Clauses

If you wait for perfect conditions, you'll never get anything done.

—ANONYMOUS

Talk about It What does the quotation above mean? Do you agree or disagree? Why?

WARM-UP

A | Complete this questionnaire. Check (✓) *True* or *False*. Then compare answers with your classmates. Would you be better at starting a new business if you checked more *Trues* or *Falses*?

SHOULD YOU START YOUR OWN BUSINESS?

	TRUE	FALSE
1. I like to try new things because I enjoy taking risks.	☐	☐
2. I'll do something by myself if no one can help me.	☐	☐
3. When I make a mistake, I try to learn from it.	☐	☐
4. I don't get stressed when I don't have a lot of money.	☐	☐
5. In the past, when something went wrong, I stayed calm and focused.	☐	☐
6. I am willing to listen when someone disagrees with me.	☐	☐
7. I'll keep working until a job is finished.	☐	☐
8. I have been able to do unpleasant tasks if they were necessary.	☐	☐

B | The words in blue in each sentence above form an adverb clause. Based on these examples, what can you say about adverb clauses? Check (✓) *True* or *False*.

	TRUE	FALSE
1. An adverb clause has a subject and a verb.	☐	☐
2. An adverb clause always comes at the end of a sentence.	☐	☐
3. An adverb clause always begins with the word *when*.	☐	☐
4. An adverb clause always uses a present verb form.	☐	☐
5. We always use a comma in a sentence with an adverb clause.	☐	☐

C | Look back at the quotation on page 372. Identify any adverb clauses.

12.1 What Is an Adverb Clause?

A

	main clause	adverb clause
1	You should leave	while you still have time.

2 He was fine **when I last saw him.** (when)

3 She didn't do anything **because it was so hot.** (why)

4 **If you want to call,** our number is 555-0199.
(under what conditions)

			subject	verb	
5	He called	**because**	**he**	**needed**	something.

		subordinator	
6	Call me on my cell phone	**if**	**you go out.**

COMPARE

7a We had dinner together **before she left.**

7b **Before she left,** we had dinner together.

We use an **adverb clause** to add information to a **main clause**, as in **1**. This unit looks at how we use adverb clauses to explain *when*, *why*, or *under what conditions*, as in **2 – 4**.

Notice that an adverb clause:
- has a subject and a verb, as in **5**
- begins with a connecting word called a **subordinator**, as in **6**
- can come before or after the main clause, as in **7a – 7b**

Notice: When the adverb clause comes first, we use a comma (,) to separate it from the main clause, as in **7b**.

B

PRESENT TIME FRAME

8 I **like** football **because** it's fast-paced.
(simple present / simple present)

9 **Come** back **when** you **can stay** longer.
(imperative / *can* + base form)

10 I'm good at tennis **because** I've played it for a long time. (simple present / present perfect)

PAST TIME FRAME

11 He **got** excited **when** he **heard** the news.
(simple past / simple past)

12 I **couldn't believe** it **when** he **told** me the news.
(*couldn't* + base form / simple past)

13 She **was** upset **because** I **had forgotten** to call.
(simple past / past perfect)

MIXED TIME FRAME

14 Here **is** a picture of me **when** I **was** 12 years old.

15 He **isn't going to go because** he's still sick.

It's important to pay attention to the form of the verbs in the **main clause** and the **adverb clause**.

When both verbs refer to a present time frame, we use present verb forms, as in **8 – 10**.

When both verbs refer to a past time frame, we use past verb forms, as in **11 – 13**.

When both verbs refer to future time, we use verb forms in a special way. See Chart 12.2.

When the verbs in the two clauses refer to different time frames, we use different verb forms, as in **14 – 15**.

1 | Understanding Adverb Clauses Underline the subject and verb in each **bold** adverb clause. `12.1 A`

Learning to Play the Piano

1. I started playing the piano **when I was 10 years old**.
2. At first I didn't like playing the piano **because I wasn't very good at it**.
3. I didn't like my teacher either **because she made me practice every day**.
4. **Even when I was on vacation**, I had to practice.
5. My first piano teacher was also very impatient. **If I made a mistake**, she always yelled at me.
6. Of course, **when she yelled at me**, I got nervous and made more mistakes.

---

7. Luckily, **when I was 13 years old**, my family moved to another city and I got a new piano teacher.
8. My new piano teacher was very different from my first teacher. **Whenever I made a mistake**, she raised her eyebrows but she never yelled at me.
9. She also made me practice a lot, but not **while I was on vacation**.
10. **Because I practiced a lot**, I'm now a pretty good piano player.
11. **Whenever I have some free time**, I sit down at the piano.
12. I play a lot of jazz **because it's my favorite type of music**.

Think about It How many different subordinators can you find in the sentences in Activity 1? What are they? Which adverb clauses are followed by a comma? Why?

Talk about It What did you learn about the writer? Without looking back, tell a partner three things.

2 | Identifying the Time Frame Look again at the sentences in Activity 1. Complete this chart. Write the verb in the main clause, the verb in the adverb clause, and the time frame. `12.1 B`

Verb in main clause	Verb in adverb clause	=	Time frame: present, past, mixed?
1. *started*	*was*	=	*past*
2.		=	
3.		=	
4.		=	
5.		=	
6.		=	
7.		=	
8.		=	
9.		=	
10.		=	
11.		=	
12.		=	

3 | Using the Correct Verb Form Complete each sentence with the correct form of the verb in parentheses. (Hint: In these sentences, the verbs in the main clause and the adverb clause refer to the same time frame.) Then check (✓) *True* or *False* for you. `12.1 B`

	TRUE	FALSE
1. I _____*like*_____ to read in bed before I go to sleep. (like)	☐	☐
2. I studied English when I _____ a child. (be)	☐	☐
3. Because I _____ English fairly well, I feel comfortable speaking in public. (speak)	☐	☐
4. I couldn't go to school last year because I _____ a job. (have)	☐	☐

5. When this course _____, I didn't know anyone in my class. (start) ☐ ☐

6. I know a lot about Canada because I _____ there several times. (be) ☐ ☐

7. I like to listen to music while I _____. (study) ☐ ☐

8. I don't like to exercise when it _____ very hot. (be) ☐ ☐

9. I can't study while other people _____. (talk) ☐ ☐

10. I'm not usually hungry in the morning because I _____ dinner late. (eat) ☐ ☐

11. I was tired this morning because I _____ really late last night. (stay up) ☐ ☐

12. I _____ satisfied after I've had a good meal. (feel) ☐ ☐

Write about It Rewrite the false statements in Activity 3 to make them true for you.

I usually watch TV before I go to sleep.

12.2 Adverb Clauses of Time

A

EVENTS THAT HAPPEN AT THE SAME TIME

1 You shouldn't use your phone **while you're driving**.

2 We were eating **when the phone rang**.

3 The phone went dead **as she was dialing his number**.

4 **Whenever I call**, he's busy.

We can use an **adverb clause of time** to explain when something happened or happens.

We use some subordinators to show that two events happen at the same time, as in **1 – 4**.

- *while* = during the time that, as in **1**
- *when* = at the time that, as in **2**
- *as* = while; when; during the time that, as in **3**
- *whenever* = every time that, as in **4**

EVENTS THAT HAPPEN IN A SEQUENCE

5 You can't stop the process **after it begins**.

6 I had just fallen asleep **when the phone rang**.

7 I usually get up **as soon as I hear the alarm**.

8 **Once it started to rain**, they stopped the game.

9 I didn't know her **before I moved here**.

10 **By the time I called**, everyone was asleep.

We use some subordinators to show that one event happens before or after another event.

- *after* = at a later time, as in **5**
- *when* = and then, as in **6**
- *as soon as* = immediately after, as in **7**
- *once* = as soon as; anytime after, as in **8**
- *before* = at an earlier time, as in **9**
- *by the time* = before that time or event, as in **10**

OTHER TIME RELATIONSHIPS

11 I decided to stay **until my parents arrived**.

12 It has been a month **since we talked**.

13 I'm going to stay **as long as I can**.

Other time subordinators include:

- *until* = up to that time, as in **11**
- *since** = from that time until now, as in **12**
- *as long as* = for the length of time that, as in **13**

* When we use *since* in a time clause, the verb must refer to an earlier time (simple past, present perfect, past perfect, etc.).

B

FUTURE TIME CLAUSES

14 I'll wait **until you get here**.

(NOT: ~~I'll wait until you will get here.~~)

15 I'm going to call **as soon as I get there**.

(NOT: ~~I'm going to call as soon as I will get there.~~)

We can also use an adverb clause to tell when something will happen in the future. We use the simple present form in a time clause to express future time, as in **14 – 15**.

4 | Noticing Adverb Clauses of Time Check (✓) the sentences that describe you. Then underline the adverb clauses of time. `12.2 A`

Unusual Habits

□ 1. I always count the stairs <u>as I go up</u>.
□ 2. I like to drink several glasses of water while I eat.
□ 3. When I'm alone, I talk to myself.
□ 4. Whenever I'm scared, I laugh.
□ 5. I like to sing when I'm driving alone.
□ 6. When I get out of the shower, I put on a pair of plastic slippers.
□ 7. I have to open the windows as soon as I get in a car, or I'll get carsick.
□ 8. I always turn on a fan before I go to bed, even when it's cold.
□ 9. I bite my tongue whenever I'm concentrating.
□ 10. When I'm out in public, I almost always wear sunglasses.
□ 11. I never answer the phone until it rings three times.
□ 12. As soon as I wake up in the morning, I drink a full glass of warm water.
□ 13. I have to wear socks when I sleep—even if it's hot.
□ 14. Before I go to bed, I eat a couple of crackers so I don't feel hungry.
□ 15. Ever since I was a child, I've been able to fall asleep almost anywhere.

Think about It Which sentences describe two events that happen at the same time? That happen in a sequence?

Talk about It What are some other unusual habits that people have? Share ideas with your classmates.

Write about It Use these adverb clauses to write sentences about your habits.

- Whenever I'm nervous, . . .
- Before I go to sleep, . . .
- Whenever I'm scared, . . .
- . . . while I eat.

5 | Punctuating Time Clauses Underline each time clause and add a comma (,) where necessary. `12.2 A`

Eating Customs

1. Brazil
- <u>When you go into a restaurant</u>, you should greet the people who work there.
- It's rude to make noise while you are eating.
- Before they start to eat Brazilians usually say "bom apetite" to their friends.

2. Turkey
- You shouldn't talk when you have food in your mouth.
- You should keep your mouth closed while you are eating.
- In a restaurant, you should order your food before you order your drinks. While the kitchen is preparing your food the server can bring your drinks.

3. Japan

- You shouldn't start eating until everyone is at the table.
- When you eat a bowl of rice or soup you may lift the bowl to your mouth.
- People often say "gochiso-sama deshita" when they finish eating.

4. Korea

- When you are eating with an older person you should wait until he or she starts eating.
- Try not to make any noise while you are chewing[1] your food.
- You shouldn't leave the table before the oldest person finishes eating.

Write about It Write two true sentences and one false sentence about eating customs in your culture. Read your sentences to the class, and ask your classmates to identify the false sentence.

6 | Understanding Subordinators Decide if each pair of sentences is similar in meaning or different. Write *S* (similar) or *D* (different). `12.2 A`

_S_ 1. Make a wish while you blow out the candles.
Make a wish when you blow out the candles.

____ 2. You shouldn't use your phone while you are driving.
You shouldn't use your phone when you are driving.

____ 3. I had just fallen asleep when the phone rang.
I fell asleep just before the phone rang.

____ 4. I decided to stay until my parents left.
I decided to stay before my parents left.

____ 5. He had just arrived when the fire broke out.
He arrived when the fire broke out.

____ 6. You can't stop the process once it begins.
You can't stop the process after it begins.

____ 7. Whenever I talk to her, she always makes me laugh.
She always makes me laugh when I talk to her.

____ 8. I'll tell you all about it when I get back.
I'll tell you all about it after I get back.

____ 9. I've played the piano since I was a child.
I played the piano when I was a child.

____ 10. I don't want to do anything until he gets here.
I don't want to do anything before he gets here.

[1] **chew:** to use your teeth to break up food in your mouth while you are eating

7 | Using Time Subordinators Choose the subordinator in parentheses that best completes each sentence. Then check (✓) the good study habits. **12.2 A**

Good Study Habit or Bad Study Habit?

☐ 1. _____ I have homework, I do it right away.
      (while / until / whenever)

☐ 2. I often study at night _____ I go to bed.
      (since / as soon as / before)

☐ 3. I like to listen to loud music _____ I am studying.
      (since / before / while)

☐ 4. I am ready to start learning _____ I get to class.
      (as soon as / until / since)

☐ 5. I often skip² class _____ I'm tired.
      (by the time / after / when)

☐ 6. I often daydream³ _____ the teacher talks.
      (as / before / after)

☐ 7. I take notes in class _____ my teacher talks.
      (before / whenever / until)

☐ 8. _____ I've read a chapter in my textbook, I never look at it again.
      (before / as / once)

☐ 9. _____ I read a new word, I write it in my notebook.
      (whenever / since / before)

☐ 10. I haven't opened a book _____ the semester started.
       (before / since / when)

Talk about It What are some other good and bad study habits? Share ideas with your classmates.

8 | Usage Note: Reduced Clauses with *When* and *While* Read the note. Then do Activities 9 and 10.

We can sometimes shorten or reduce an adverb clause of time. We can do this when:
- the adverb clause begins with *when* or *while*, and
- the subject of the main clause and the subject of the adverb clause are the same, and
- the adverb clause has a form of the verb *be* (as a helping verb or main verb).

We reduce the clause by removing the subject and the verb *be*.

FULL ADVERB CLAUSES	REDUCED ADVERB CLAUSES
1a She had a job **when she was studying there**.	1b She had a job **when studying there**.
2a We didn't meet anyone **while we were in Rome**.	2b We didn't meet anyone **while in Rome**.

When the main clause and the adverb clause have different subjects, we can't reduce the adverb clause.

  3 She had a job **while her husband** was studying there. (NOT: She had a job while studying there.)

---

² **skip:** to not do something that you should do

³ **daydream:** to think happy thoughts that make you forget what you should be doing

9 | Using Reduced Clauses Read these sentences and check (✓) *True* or *False*. Where possible, rewrite the sentence with a reduced clause. 12.2 A

TRUE OR FALSE?

	TRUE	FALSE
1. Scientists often wear a special coat or jacket when they are doing experiments.	☐	☐
Scientists often wear a special coat or jacket when doing experiments.		
2. When you quit smoking, your heart rate⁴ goes up right away.	☐	☐
The adverb clause can't be reduced.		
3. While you're resting, you burn a lot of body fat.	☐	☐
4. Most professional tennis players started playing while they were very young.	☐	☐
5. Many people like to read while they're traveling on public transportation.	☐	☐
6. When you are feeling relaxed, you can usually think more clearly.	☐	☐
7. When you are breathing deeply, your chest expands, or gets bigger.	☐	☐
8. Many university students have jobs while they are in school.	☐	☐
9. Most athletes don't do extra training before they have competitions.	☐	☐
10. Your body will let you know when you are working too hard.	☐	☐
11. Very few people listen to music while they are driving.	☐	☐
12. Most people do things outdoors when the weather is nice.	☐	☐
13. Only very intelligent people dream while they are sleeping.	☐	☐
14. When a parent sings to a baby, the baby's breathing speeds up.	☐	☐
15. Most athletes don't drink enough water when they are exercising.	☐	☐

Think about It Tell a partner which sentences above can't be reduced. Explain why not.

Talk about It Tell your partner why you said true or false for each sentence above.

⁴ **heart rate:** the speed at which the heart pumps blood through the body

10 | Using Reduced Clauses Complete these sentences with information about yourself. Then rewrite each sentence with a reduced adverb clause. `12.2 A`

YOUR HABITS

1. I usually _____*listen to music*_____ when I am _____*resting*_____.
   _____*I usually listen to music when resting.*_____

2. I never _____ while I am _____.
   _____

3. I like to _____ while I am _____.
   _____

4. I didn't _____ while I was _____.
   _____

5. I always _____ while I am _____.
   _____

6. I never _____ when I am _____.
   _____

7. I dislike _____ when I am _____.
   _____

8. I enjoy _____ while I am _____.
   _____

Talk about It Ask a partner questions based on the sentences you wrote above. Does your partner have similar habits?

A: *Do you usually listen to music when resting?*
B: *No, I usually like it to be quiet.*

11 | Talking about the Future Complete these conversations with the simple present or a future form of the verb in parentheses. Then practice with a partner. `12.2 B`

1. A: Why hasn't Annie called?

   B: Relax. I'm sure she'll call as soon as she _____ back. (get)

2. A: Could you give this to Andy?

   B: Sure. I'll give it to him when I _____ him tomorrow. (see)

3. A: Aren't you going to be late?

   B: Yes, but I'm not going to leave until Bob _____. (call)

4. A: How was the meeting?

   B: I _____ you about it as soon as I'm back home. (tell)

5. A: Can I borrow a little money from you?

   B: Sure. Is this enough?

   A: Yeah, thanks. I _____ you back as soon as I can. (pay)

6. A: Where are you now?

   B: I'm still pretty far away. I'm probably not going to see you before you

   _____. (leave)

7. A: What time do you get out of work today?

   B: I'm not sure.

   A: Well, I'll come get you when you _____ ready to leave. Just call me. (be)

8. A: What are you going to do while your friends _____ here? (be)

   B: I'll just show them around, take them a few places, you know.

9. A: What did they say? Did you get the job?

   B: I won't know until they _____ me. (call)

10. A: What do you want to do now?

    B: I'm going to take a shower before I _____ anything else. (do)

Think about It Underline the future forms in the conversations in Activity 11. Then look at the uses of future forms in this box. Why is the future form used in each conversation?

USES OF FUTURE FORMS

| to talk about a future plan | to make a prediction | to make a promise | to offer some help |

12 | Using Future Time Clauses Read these clauses and think about the sequence of events. Combine the clauses using the adverb in parentheses. Use a simple present and a future verb form. (More than one answer may be possible.) 12.2 B

PLANNING A WEDDING

1. have an engagement party/start planning the wedding (before)

   We're going to have an engagement party before we start planning the wedding.
   We're going to start planning the wedding before we have an engagement party.

2. announce the engagement/tell our families (after)
3. decide on a date/make a budget[5] for the wedding (once)
4. look for a wedding location/make a guest list (while)
5. choose a location/send the invitations (when)
6. hire a band/decide on the kind of music we want (once)
7. taste the food/not choose the menu (until)
8. ask some friends for advice/hire a photographer (after)
9. not think about wedding clothes/do everything else (until)
10. go shopping for clothes/take my best friend (when)

Think about It Which sentences above are logical when written in either sequence?

13 | Error Correction Correct any errors in these sentences. (Some sentences may not have any errors.)

1. Until I came to this country, then I went to school.
2. I will take care of my parents when they will be older.
3. When the movie finish, I went home.
4. I want to go back home as long as I can.
5. Before leave, you have to sign out.
6. After they got married. They moved to Spain.

[5] **budget:** a plan for how much money you will have and how you will spend it

7. When I woke up I realized the house was freezing.

8. When I feel sad my sister told me a funny story.

9. I met him six months ago when he start this class.

10. My mother left Hungary in 1998. When she arrived here, she doesn't like it.

11. My sister went to school in Los Angeles. While she studying there, she made a lot of friends.

12. Our needs change as we get older. When we are children, we spend a lot of time with our parents. Since we are teenagers, we do more things with our friends.

13. At home we always did the same thing in the evening. Around 7:00, we had something for dinner, and then as soon as we finish, we played chess.

12.3 Adverb Clauses of Reason

<table>
<tr>
<td rowspan="1">A</td>
<td>main clause   reason clause

1   I like Thai food | **because it's spicy.**

2 **Since my phone wasn't working,** I couldn't call.

3 Don't bother to call me **because I won't answer.**

4 I can't invite you in **because I have to leave now.**</td>
<td>We use an **adverb clause of reason** to explain why something in the main clause happens or happened, as in **1**.

Adverb clauses of reason usually begin with the subordinators **because** or **since**, as in **1 – 4**.</td>
</tr>
<tr>
<td rowspan="1">B</td>
<td>5 A: Why didn't you call me back?
   B: **Because I fell asleep.**

6 The traditional role of fathers is changing. **Since many mothers now work outside the home,** fathers must help out more at home.</td>
<td>In conversation, speakers sometimes leave out the main clause when they answer a question, as in **5**.

In writing, however, we need to use a main clause with the adverb clause, as in **6**. Otherwise, the sentence is incomplete.</td>
</tr>
<tr>
<td rowspan="1">C</td>
<td>**OTHER WAYS TO EXPLAIN** *WHY*

main clause + *so* + main clause
7a **They were doing construction on the street outside, so I couldn't sleep.**

main clause with *because of* + noun phrase
7b I couldn't sleep **because of the construction.**</td>
<td>Notice the other ways we explain why something happens in **7a – 7b**.

  • *so* = a conjunction
  • *because of* = a phrasal preposition

Because of is followed by a noun phrase, not a clause, as in **7b**. The information that follows *because of* is usually shorter or more concise.</td>
</tr>
<tr>
<td rowspan="1">D</td>
<td colspan="2">**CORRECT THE COMMON ERRORS** (See page R-20.)

8 ✗ I was happy because learned something important.

9 ✗ I'm proud of myself because now I could communicate with people in English.

10 ✗ I was sad because I have to leave soon.

11 ✗ We stayed at home. Because it was so hot.</td>
</tr>
</table>

14 | Noticing Adverb Clauses of Reason Underline each adverb clause of reason. Then circle the verbs in each main clause and adverb clause. `12.3 A`

Sentences from Student Essays

1. I try to eat well and exercise every day. I (think) I (feel) better <u>because I (do) these things</u>.

2. My grandfather didn't spend much time with his children because he worked very long hours.

3. Because we live in a multilingual world, I think everyone should study a foreign language.

4. My favorite game is sudoku because I can play it by myself.

5. In a big city, you can stay out late because there is always something open.

6. I have always wanted to be a teacher. I think this is because I have always had great teachers.

7. People like to use the Internet because it gives them instant access to a lot of information.

8. I avoid coffee and tea late in the day because they will interfere[6] with my sleep.

9. My watch is special to me because it was a gift from my parents.

10. Since my family is Polish, I want to learn about the history of Poland.

11. Since many people have moved here from other countries, you hear many different languages on the street.

12. Since many mothers are now working outside the home, fathers are helping more with the children.

Think about It Look again at the sentences in Activity 14. Complete the chart. Then answer the questions below.

Verb in main clause	Verb in adverb clause	Verb in main clause	Verb in adverb clause
1. *think, feel*	*do*	7.	
2.		8.	
3.		9.	
4.		10.	
5.		11.	
6.		12.	

QUESTIONS

1. For each sentence, how are the verb forms similar or different in the two clauses?
2. In which sentences do both clauses refer to the same time frame?

15 | Usage Note: Using *Since* in Time Clauses and Reason Clauses Read the note. Then do Activity 16.

We can use *since* to introduce a **time clause** or a **reason clause**, but the meaning of the word is different.

Time clause: I haven't done anything since I got home. (*since* = from the time that)
Reason clause: Since no one is here, you should probably lock the door. (*since* = because)

In conversation, we use *since* more often to introduce a time clause. In writing, we use *since* more often to introduce a reason clause.

[6]**interfere:** to stop something from being done well

16 | Adverb Clause of Time or Reason? Underline the adverb clauses in these sentences. Then check (✓) *Time Clause* or *Reason Clause*. `12.3 A`

		TIME CLAUSE	REASON CLAUSE
1.	I have wanted to be a doctor <u>since I was a small child</u>.	✓	☐
2.	Since the front door wasn't locked, I let myself in.	☐	☐
3.	Since it began in the 1980s, the organization has attracted many new members.	☐	☐
4.	Since we had to leave right away, we didn't have time to pack a suitcase.	☐	☐
5.	We've known her since we were four or five.	☐	☐
6.	Since I had already studied English for several years, I got into an advanced class.	☐	☐
7.	I haven't been to that museum since it reopened in 2012.	☐	☐
8.	Since you need more money, maybe you should get a better-paying job.	☐	☐
9.	I've been a fan of Alan Rickman since I saw him in a play several years ago.	☐	☐
10.	The new technology led to smaller devices[7] since designers could use smaller batteries.	☐	☐
11.	It has been a long time since we went to that restaurant.	☐	☐
12.	Since we didn't speak the same language, we spent a lot of time smiling at each other.	☐	☐

17 | Pronunciation Note: *Because* Listen to the note. Then do Activity 18.

> In conversation, we often pronounce **because** as /cɔs/ or /cəz/.
>
> **1** A: Why aren't you coming with us?   **2** A: How come you're still here?
>   B: **Because** /cəz/ I'm tired.   B: **Because** /cɔs/ I still have work to do.
>
> **WARNING!** We do not use /cəz/ or /cɔs/ in writing.

18 | Listening for Reasons Listen and complete these conversations. Then listen again and check (✓) the pronunciation: *because* or /cɔs/ /cəz/. `12.3 B`

		BECAUSE	/cɔs/ /cəz/
1.	Friend A: Why didn't you call?	☐	✓
	Friend B: Because *I left my phone at school* _____.		
2.	Friend A: Why are you watching this movie again?	☐	☐
	Friend B: Because _____.		
3.	Wife: I think we should take flowers or something.	☐	☐
	Husband: What for?		
	Wife: Because _____.		

---

[7] **devices:** specialized tools or pieces of equipment

		BECAUSE	/cɔs/ /cəz/

4. Wife: Why are you telling me about this?

   Husband: Because _____. ☐ ☐

5. Sister: I'm so sorry. Really. ☐ ☐

   Brother: Sorry? Why are you sorry?

   Sister: Because _____.

6. Teacher: Why didn't you finish the test? ☐ ☐

   Student: Because _____.

7. Teacher: You have very good ideas. Why don't you say more in class? ☐ ☐

   Student: Because _____.

8. Teacher: Why are you late? ☐ ☐

   Student: Because _____.

9. Teacher: Do you have your homework? ☐ ☐

   Student: I'm sorry, I don't.

   Teacher: Well, why not?

   Student: Because _____.

10. Teacher: Why weren't you here yesterday? ☐ ☐

    Student: Because _____.

Talk about It Practice the conversations in Activity 18 with a partner. Try using /cɔs/ or /cəz/ instead of *because*.

Talk about It What other reasons could each person give for the questions in Activity 18? Share ideas with your classmates.

Write about It Rewrite each person's answer in Activity 18 as a complete sentence.

I didn't call because I left my phone at school.

19 | Explaining *Why* Rewrite each sentence using a different way to explain *why*. In some cases, you may need to add more information so that the meaning is complete. **12.3 C**

1. The airport shut down because of bad weather.

   The weather was bad, so the airport shut down. **OR**
   The airport shut down because the weather was bad.

2. I couldn't go because of an illness.
3. My sister didn't want to go, so I didn't go.
4. I lost my job because of an injury.
5. I joined the chess club because he did.
6. The roads were really bad, so we stayed at home.
7. He had to stop working because he got sick.
8. My sister quit her job because she didn't like her boss.

Think about It How does the information we give change if we use *because of* versus *so*? Which expression lets us give more information?

20 | Error Correction Correct any errors in these sentences. (Some sentences may not have any errors.)

1. My brother wants to graduate this year, because he needs to get a job.
2. My birthday is the happiest day of my life because my family was there.
3. I couldn't sleep last night. Because it was hot.
4. I was an only child, I was often lonely.
5. Because the war, my parents had to leave their home.
6. We traveled a lot because of my father worked for the United Nations.
7. Since I didn't know English very well I can't understand anyone.
8. It has become easy to travel around the world, knowing a foreign language is more important than before.

12.4 Present and Past Real Conditionals

A

main clause | conditional clause

1 | He always feels better | if he goes swimming.

condition | result

2 | If I go to bed late, | (then) I can't get up early.

A conditional statement has a **main clause** and a **conditional clause**, as in **1**.

The adverb clause states a condition, and the main clause gives the result, as in **2**.

> Notice: Conditional clauses usually begin with the word *if*. When the main clause comes second, it sometimes begins with the word *then*.

B

PRESENT REAL CONDITIONALS

3 If you live in a city, you **have** many job opportunities.

4 If you go to a shopping mall on the weekend, it's usually very crowded.

5 If I'm running late, I usually **take** the bus.

6 If I've done a lot of work, I **feel** good.

PAST REAL CONDITIONALS

7 If it rained, she always **took** the bus.

8 I always **did** the dishes if he cooked.

COMPARE *IF* AND *WHEN*

9a The alarm rings if **someone opens the window**.

9b The alarm rings when **someone opens the window**.

A present real conditional describes:

• a fact or general truth, as in **3 – 4**

• something that happens regularly and its result, as in **5 – 6**

A past real conditional describes something that happened regularly in the past and its result, as in **7 – 8**.

With present and past real conditionals, we can use *when* or *whenever* instead of *if* with very little difference in meaning, as in **9a – 9b**.

Notice that we use many different verb forms in present and past real conditional statements. Some common verb forms are:

	conditional clause	main clause
PRESENT REAL CONDITIONALS	simple present present progressive present perfect	simple present *should* + base form *can* + base form
PAST REAL CONDITIONALS	simple past past progressive	simple past *used to* + base form

> **GRAMMAR TERMS:** Conditional clauses are also called *if-* **clauses**. Present and past real conditionals are also called **zero conditionals**.

ONLINE

21 | Noticing Conditional Clauses Put a slash (/) between the two clauses in these sentences. Write *C* above the conditional clause and *R* above the result clause. Then check (✓) *True* or *False* according to your experience. **12.4 A**

Getting Around

	TRUE	FALSE
1. You save a lot of money^R /if you use public transportation^C instead of a car.	☐	☐
2. If you travel by train during rush hour⁸, your ticket usually costs less.	☐	☐
3. You can't buy a car if you are younger than 21.	☐	☐
4. It's fun to drive long distances if you have a comfortable car.	☐	☐
5. You don't need a map if you have GPS⁹ in your car.	☐	☐
6. If you drive and text at the same time, you are asking for an accident.	☐	☐
7. You need to be careful if you ride a bike in a city.	☐	☐
8. You couldn't go very far in the 1800s if you didn't have a horse.	☐	☐
9. If you ride a motorcycle, you have to wear a helmet¹⁰.	☐	☐
10. You need a special driver's license if you want to drive a motorcycle.	☐	☐
11. If you traveled overseas in the 1800s, you probably went by plane.	☐	☐
12. If you travel by boat today, it's very expensive.	☐	☐

Write about It Choose four of the conditional clauses above. Add a different result clause to them.

You can read or do work if you use public transportation instead of a car.

> **F Y I**
> We sometimes use the word *you* in a real conditional sentence to refer to people in general.

22 | Understanding Conditional Clauses Read the sentences below and underline the conditional clauses. Then decide what each sentence describes. Choose the correct answer from the box. **12.4 B**

> a. a fact or general truth
> b. something that happens regularly
> c. something that happened regularly in the past

___b___ 1. Cell phones are very useful. <u>If you are waiting somewhere,</u> you can call a friend and have a nice chat.

_____ 2. Busy people eat out a lot. If they have children, they may go to fast-food restaurants.

_____ 3. New York is a nice place to live if you don't have a car.

_____ 4. I don't feel good if I don't do a good job on something.

_____ 5. If I'm feeling stressed, I like to go for a long walk.

---

⁸**rush hour:** a time when there is a lot of traffic because people are traveling to or from work

⁹**GPS:** Global Positioning System; a piece of equipment that shows your location and helps you get somewhere

¹⁰**helmet:** a hard hat that keeps your head safe

_____ 6. It's not fair if some students cheat[11] on a test.

_____ 7. My mother punished me if I misbehaved—not my father.

_____ 8. When I was a child, if there was a lot of snow, we didn't have class.

_____ 9. No country is really developed if it has money but no technology.

_____ 10. My brother always helped me if I was having trouble with something.

_____ 11. If my mother gets home from work and she's really tired, she usually takes a nap[12].

_____ 12. We always had a big meal if we had company for dinner.

Think about It What verb form does each speaker use in the main clause and the conditional clause in Activity 22? Complete this chart and then answer the question below.

Verb in main clause	Verb in conditional clause	Verb in main clause	Verb in conditional clause
1. can call, have	are waiting	7.	
2.		8.	
3.		9.	
4.		10.	
5.		11.	
6.		12.	

QUESTION

Which sentences in Activity 22 use the same time frame in both the main clause and the conditional clause?

23 | Using Conditional Clauses Complete these sentences with information about your habits now and in the past. 12.4 B

PRESENT HABITS

1. If I don't get enough sleep, _____ I feel tired _____.

2. If I need to relax, _____.

3. If I don't eat breakfast, _____.

4. I _____ if I'm hungry between meals.

5. I _____

   if I'm tired.

> **F Y I**
>
> We sometimes use *will* in a main clause to predict something that commonly happens.
>
> If you don't get enough sleep, you **will feel** tired.

PAST HABITS

6. If I helped my mother when I was a child, _____.

7. If I didn't like the food we were eating, _____.

8. If I wanted something, _____.

9. If I couldn't go to sleep, _____.

10. _____ if I felt sick.

[11] **cheat:** to do something that is not honest   [12] **nap:** a short sleep during the day

12.5 Future Real Conditionals

A

1 **If she doesn't want me there,** I'll leave.

2 **If you like movies with a good story,** you'll probably like *Sense and Sensibility.*

3 I'll buy it for you **if you really like it.**

4 **If you get an email from him,** can you send it to us?

5 You might feel better **if you take a nap.**

6 **If you're not doing anything tomorrow,** come over.

In a future real conditional statement, the **adverb clause** states a condition, and the main clause gives the likely results in the future.

We sometimes use a future real conditional when we make:

- a plan, as in **1**
- a prediction, as in **2**
- a promise, as in **3**
- a request, as in **4**
- a suggestion, as in **5 – 6**

B

PRESENT CONDITION / FUTURE RESULT

7 How **is** she **going to pay** the bills **if she's not working** now? (*be going to* + base form / present progressive)

8 You**'ll figure** it **out if** you **haven't done** so already. (*will* + base form / present perfect)

PAST CONDITION / FUTURE RESULT

9 **If you did** all the homework last week, you**'ll do** well on the test. (simple past / *will* + base form)

10 You **won't be** hungry later **if** you **ate** a good breakfast. (*will* + base form / simple past)

FUTURE CONDITION / FUTURE RESULT

11 **If I have** time tomorrow, I **might go** downtown. (simple present / *might* + base form)

12 **If you don't go** to work tomorrow, **call** me. (simple present / imperative)

In a future real conditional, we can use many different verb forms in the conditional clause and the main clause, as in **7 – 12**. Some common verb forms are:

conditional clause	main clause
simple present	*will*
present progressive	*might*
present perfect	*should* + base form
can/can't + base form	*be going to*
simple past	imperative

WARNING! We don't normally use *will* in the conditional clause even when it refers to the future, as in **11 – 12**.

GRAMMAR TERM: The future real conditional is also called the **first conditional**.

 GO ONLINE

24 | Listening for Conditional Clauses Choose the correct conditional clause from the box to complete each conversation below. Listen and check your answers. Then practice with a partner. `12.5 A`

if we don't have any money	if you tell me
if you decide to visit again	if you want to read something
if you get lost	if you're late for dinner
if you keep bugging[13] me	if you've heard this before
if you need me	if you've really learned it

1. A: Don't be nervous about the exam. You've studied really hard.

   B: But I'm afraid I'm going to forget everything.

   A: Relax. *If you've really learned it* _____, you won't forget it.

2. A: Where were you?

   B: Nowhere special.

   A: Come on. _____, I won't get mad. I promise.

[13] **bug:** to bother or worry someone

390

3. A: Are you really going to drive there alone?

   B: Sure. Why not?

   A: Well, what will you do _____?

   B: But I won't get lost.

4. A: Nice meeting you, Jean.

   B: Nice meeting you, too. _____, call me.

   A: Thanks. I will.

5. A: I'm leaving now. _____, just call me at home.

   B: OK. Get some rest.

6. A: Sorry to bother you again.

   B: Look, I'm not going to get any work done _____.

7. A: Where are you?

   B: I'm still at school.

   A: Well, you'd better hurry home. Your father will be mad _____.

8. A: It's still raining and I'm bored.

   B: Well, _____, here's a good book.

9. A: Have I told you about the time I lost my phone at the beach?

   B: I don't think so.

   A: Well, stop me _____.

10. A: How much money do we have?

   B: Zero. None.

   A: But _____, we won't be able to go anywhere next week.

   B: That's true.

Think about It Look again at the sentences in Activity 24 with future real conditionals. How is the sentence used? Write a use from this box next to each sentence. (More than one answer may be possible.)

| a plan | a prediction | a promise | a request | a suggestion |

25 | Identifying Verb Forms Look again at the future real conditionals in Activity 24. What verb form does the speaker use in the main clause and the conditional clause? Complete this chart. `12.5 B`

Verb in main clause	Verb in conditional clause	Verb in main clause	Verb in conditional clause
1. *won't forget*	*'ve learned*	6.	
2.		7.	
3.		8.	
4.		9.	
5.		10.	

Think about It For each sentence, how are the verb forms similar or different in the two clauses? In which sentences do both clauses refer to the same time frame? Discuss ideas with your classmates.

26 | Matching Conditions and Results Use the information in this chart to match each condition below with a possible result. `12.5 B`

How the Vitamins in Food Can Help You

Vitamin	Food sources	What it does
Vitamin A	Liver[14], eggs, milk, carrots, tomatoes, apricots, cantaloupe, fish	Promotes[15] good eyesight; helps form and maintain healthy skin; may reduce the risk of some cancers
Vitamin C	Citrus fruits, strawberries, tomatoes	Promotes healthy teeth; helps heal[16] cuts more quickly
Vitamin D	Milk, fish; also produced by the body in response to sunlight	Builds strong bones and teeth
Vitamin E	Nuts, vegetable oils, whole grains, olives, asparagus, spinach	Helps in the formation of red blood cells[17]
Vitamin B2	Nuts, dairy products, liver	Helps change food into energy

CONDITIONS

1. If you eat a lot of fruit, ____
2. If you want to have healthy skin, ____
3. If you eat a lot of nuts, ____
4. If you want to have good teeth, ____
5. If you work outdoors in the sun, ____
6. If you don't eat fruit, ____
7. If you eat liver once a week, ____
8. If you don't have a lot of energy, ____
9. If you want your cuts to heal faster, ____
10. If you eat a lot of whole grains, ____

POSSIBLE RESULTS

a. you'll get a lot of vitamins E and B2.
b. drink plenty of milk and eat lots of fish.
c. you'll get plenty of vitamin D.
d. you'll get a lot of vitamins C and A.
e. you won't get a lot of vitamin C.
f. you'll get vitamins A and B2.
g. your body can form red blood cells more easily.
h. eat more citrus fruits and strawberries.
i. eat plenty of fish, carrots, and tomatoes.
j. you should eat more nuts, dairy products, and liver.

27 | Using Conditional Clauses Complete these sentences with your own ideas. Use a modal (*should*, *will*, etc.) or an imperative in the result clause. `12.5 B`

THINGS PARENTS SAY TO THEIR CHILDREN

1. If you want to go out, *put on your shoes* _____.
2. If you want to earn some money, _____.
3. If your grades don't improve, _____.
4. If you don't clean your room, _____.
5. If you say that word again, _____.

---

[14] **liver:** the part of the body that cleans the blood
[15] **promote:** to help be better

[16] **heal:** to make well again
[17] **cells:** the smallest parts of any living thing

6. If you are late to class one more time, _____.

7. If you don't work harder, _____.

8. If you need some extra help, _____.

9. If you have any questions, _____.

10. If you have finished the test, _____.

Think about It Read one of the sentences you wrote in Activity 27 to the class. Ask your classmates if your sentence identifies a plan, prediction, promise, request, or suggestion.

A: *If you want to go out, please be back by dinnertime.*
B: *I think that's a request.*

28 | Noticing Conditional Clauses in a Text Read this student essay and underline all the conditional clauses. Then answer the questions below.

Three Good Reasons Not to Be a Workaholic

A workaholic is a person who works all the time. My uncle Mario is an example of a workaholic. He starts working early in the morning, and he doesn't stop until late at night. He almost never takes a day off from work, and in 20 years, he has taken only a few weeks of vacation. Most workaholics say they like to work, but I don't think it's good to be a workaholic.

What is bad about being a workaholic? If you are a married workaholic, you probably aren't going to have a very good relationship with your spouse[18]. How could you? You are never around to do things together or to help out at home.

If you are a workaholic with children, the consequences are even worse. If you don't spend time with your children, they might do poorly in school or have emotional problems.

Being a workaholic isn't good for your health either. Most workaholics don't have time to eat properly, exercise regularly, or relax and have fun. And if you don't do these things, you probably won't live a very long life.

QUESTIONS

1. How many present real conditionals did you find? How many future real conditionals?

2. If you take out the conditional clauses, what happens to the piece of writing? How is it different?

[18] **spouse:** husband or wife

12.6 Using Adverb Clauses in Speaking

<table>
<tr>
<td rowspan="1">A</td>
<td>
1 A: How long have you known each other?
B: Since we were 12.
2 A: Are you going to leave soon?
B: If I can.
3 A: Why are you leaving?
B: Because I'm tired.
</td>
<td>
In conversation, we sometimes answer a question with an adverb clause alone, as in 1 – 3.
</td>
</tr>
<tr>
<td>B</td>
<td>
4 Tell me the truth if you can.
5 Watch it again if you want.
6 I need some help if you don't mind.
</td>
<td>
We sometimes use a conditional clause to soften a suggestion, request, or command, as in 4 – 6.
</td>
</tr>
<tr>
<td>C</td>
<td>
7 A: How are you going to fix your computer?
B: I'm just going to reinstall the software.
A: What if it doesn't work?
   (= What are you going to do if it doesn't work?)
B: Then I'll think of something else.

8 A: Where's my laptop?
B: Bill has it.
A: What if he forgets to bring it?
   (= What are we going to do if he forgets to bring it?)

9 A: When do you want to go?
B: What if we leave in an hour?
   (= Is it OK if we leave in an hour?)
A: That's fine with me.
</td>
<td>
In conversation, speakers sometimes ask a question with <i>what if</i>, as in 7 – 9. <i>What if</i> can mean a number of different things. For example:

What if =	What are you going to do if . . . ? Is it OK if . . . ? Do you mind if . . . ? What will happen if . . . ? How would it be if . . . ?
</td>
</tr>
</table>

GO ONLINE

29 | Using Adverb Clauses in Conversation Complete these conversations with the correct form of the verb in parentheses. Use contractions where possible. Then listen and check your answers. `12.6 A`

1. A: Why didn't you follow my instructions?

   B: Because they _____*weren't*_____ clear to me. (not be)

2. A: When do you want to go?

   B: Whenever you _____ ready. (be)

3. A: Do you want to go out tonight?

   B: Sure, if it _____ you happy. (make)

4. A: Why are you being so quiet?

   B: Because I _____ tired. (be)

5. A: Can I speak to Bob?

   B: If he _____ still here. (be)

6. A: If Bill calls, tell him I'll be late.

   B: Sure, if he _____. (call)

7. A: How long will you be there?

   B: Until I _____ everything. (finish)

8. A: Are you coming with us?

   B: If you _____. (not mind)

9. A: When are we going to have dinner?

   B: As soon as your father _____ home. (get)

10. A: When do you want to look at my homework?

    B: After we _____ dinner. (eat)

11. A: Hurry up. You're going to be late.

    B: Not if I _____ right now. (leave)

12. A: Why didn't you stop at the store?

    B: Because I _____ time. (not have)

13. A: How long has your sister played soccer?

    B: Since she _____ in high school. (be)

14. A: When did Sarah clean up the kitchen?

    B: Before she _____ to work. (go)

Talk about It Practice the conversations in Activity 29 with a partner.

Write about It What is Speaker B really saying in each conversation in Activity 29? Write the complete sentence.

I didn't follow your instructions because they weren't clear to me.

30 | Softening a Suggestion, Request, or Command Add a conditional clause from the box to soften each statement below. (You will use some conditional clauses more than once. More than one answer is possible.) **12.6 B**

if you want to	if you can	if that makes sense to you
if you don't want to	if you don't mind	if you want my advice
if it's OK with you	if you have time	

1. You don't have to go _if you don't want to_____.

2. I think we should leave early tomorrow _____.

3. Could you help me with my homework tonight _____?

4. Please try to come home early _____.

5. _____, I'd like to eat out tonight.

6. Call me later _____.

7. _____, I think you should put the money in the bank.

8. I'd like to talk to you for a few minutes _____.

9. I'd like to stay home tonight _____.

10. I don't want to go away for the weekend _____.

Talk about It Work with a partner. Choose one of the sentences you wrote above, and use it to write a conversation. Present your conversation to the class.

A: Are you going out this evening?
B: Yeah, I have a meeting but I really don't want to go.
A: You don't have to go if you don't want to.
B: But it's important and I really should go.

31 | Listening for Questions with *What If* Listen to these conversations and write the questions. Then practice with a partner. `12.6 C`

1. A: Let's eat out tonight.

   B: With the baby? _What if she starts crying?_____

   A: Then we'll leave.

2. A: I really don't want to go skiing.

   B: Oh, come on. You'll have fun.

   A: But _____

   B: Why do you worry about everything?

3. A: I've been thinking about our trip to L.A.

   B: And?

   A: Well, _____? We'll save a lot of time.

   B: That's fine with me.

4. A: Did you call the store?

   B: Yeah, but no one answered.

   A: Well, _____

   B: Then we'll go somewhere else.

5. A: What do you want to do tonight?

   B: I don't know. _____

   A: Fine with me.

6. A: Are you really going to invite Bill for dinner?

   B: Sure. Why not?

   A: Well, _____

   B: Well, so what?

7. A: What time do you want to get together?

   B: _____

   A: That works for me.

8. A: Where's Jim? He's awfully late.

   B: I know. _____

   A: Then you'll have to run the meeting.

9. A: Are you going to answer the phone?

   B: Do I have to?

   A: _____

   B: OK, OK.

10. A: What did you get Ann for her birthday?

    B: A pair of shoes.

    A: Shoes? Really? _____

    B: Well, she can exchange them.

Write about It What does each *what if* question in Activity 31 mean? Write your ideas.

What are we going to do if she starts crying?

12.7 Using Adverb Clauses in Writing

A

GIVING BACKGROUND INFORMATION

1 When I was eight years old, my father took a new job in Canada. My whole family . . .

2 Before I learned to drive, I went everywhere on my bicycle. Some days I rode for hours. . . .

3 Because I love to travel, I'm always packing my bags to go somewhere. Last year, . . .

We sometimes use an **adverb clause** at the beginning of a sentence or paragraph to set the scene or give background information, as in **1 – 3**.

B

VARYING SENTENCES WITH ADVERB CLAUSES

4a In 2002, I was an architecture student. I had to present my final project to a committee. I prepared my presentation carefully. I practiced it many times. I was very nervous. I couldn't sleep the night before the presentation. . . . (no adverb clauses)

4b When I was an architecture student in 2002, I had to present my final project to a committee. I prepared my presentation carefully, and I practiced it many times. Because I was very nervous, I couldn't sleep the night before the presentation. . . .

Writers sometimes use adverb clauses to vary the length and structure of the sentences in a paragraph, as in **4b**. This helps to make a piece of writing more interesting.

C

SUPPORTING OPINIONS

5 Stress can be a good thing. For example, if students are feeling stressed, they may study more.

6 It's not good to be a workaholic. If you work long days, you don't have time to do things with your friends and family.

7 Good bosses need to be good at their job. If they aren't, their employees won't respect them.

Writers often give their opinion in a piece of writing. They might then use a sentence with a **conditional clause** to give an example to support their opinion, as in **5 – 7**.

GO ONLINE

32 | Giving Background Information Complete these sentences with information about yourself. Then add a second sentence with more information. **12.7 A**

1. When I was a child, _____.
   _____

2. Before I started school, _____.
   _____

3. Because I like _____, I _____.
   _____

4. When I started studying English, _____.
   _____

5. I _____ because I enjoy _____.
   _____

6. When I was 16, _____.
   _____

7. Ten years ago, while I was living in _____, I _____.
   _____

8. Because I've studied _____, I _____.
   _____

Write about It Choose one of the sentences you wrote in Activity 32 as a topic sentence, and develop it into a paragraph.

33 | Adding Sentence Variety Rewrite these paragraphs. Make them more interesting by adding several adverb clauses. You can also make other changes. (Many different answers are possible.) `12.7 B`

A	B
The most important qualities of a good parent are patience, creativity, and a sense of humor. Having children can be very stressful. There are things that a good parent can do to make life less stressful. Children ask a lot of questions. Parents have to answer those questions. Children also need entertainment. Young children can get bored easily and have a shorter attention span[19] than adults.	There are two important skills you need to run your own business: organization and the ability to make decisions. You must be very organized. You need to keep track of many things. For people who work from home, it's especially important to be well organized. It's easy to mix up your personal papers and your business papers. Business owners must be intelligent, too. You have to make many decisions, often very quickly. You need to make those decisions intelligently.

Think about It Compare the paragraphs you wrote above with a partner. How did you rewrite them differently?

34 | Analyzing Conditional Clauses in Writing Read this text and underline the conditional clauses. Then answer the questions on page 399. `12.7 C`

What Is the Most Useful Invention of the Past 50 Years?

The most useful invention of the past 50 years is the cell phone because it has made long-distance communication much easier. The cell phone is an especially convenient tool at work. If you go out for a business appointment, your clients and co-workers can easily contact you by phone. And if you need to travel out of town, the cell phone makes it easy to stay in touch with the office.

The cell phone has also made it easier to stay in touch with friends and family. If you are out shopping, you can call someone and ask for advice. Or if you are just waiting somewhere, you can call a friend for a chat. It's also easier to make last-minute plans when you have a cell phone. In general, cell phones have made our daily lives much easier.

[19] **attention span:** the amount of time someone can look or listen carefully

1. Why do you think the writer uses the conditional clauses? What purpose do they serve?

2. What other adverb clauses does the writer use? Circle them.

Write about It Rewrite the text in Activity 34. For example, you might want to combine the information in different ways or use different examples with conditional clauses.

The most useful invention of the past 50 years is the cell phone. It is an especially convenient tool if you need to communicate over long distances quickly. . . .

35 | Using Conditional Clauses to Support an Opinion Write a sentence with a conditional clause to support each opinion. `12.7 C`

1. The most useful invention of the past 50 years is the cell phone. _____
   _____

2. Computers have completely changed the way people work. _____
   _____

3. Electric cars are a great idea. _____
   _____

4. People should recycle. _____
   _____

5. Quitting smoking is very important. _____
   _____

6. Learning a new language is useful. _____
   _____

7. Everyone should exercise every day. _____
   _____

8. Eating vegetables is good for your health. _____
   _____

Think about It Compare your answers above with your classmates. How many different ways did you find to support each opinion?

Write about It Choose one of the statements above, and develop your ideas into a cohesive paragraph.

The most useful invention of the past 50 years is the cell phone. If you have a cell phone, you can communicate with someone immediately. You can also get information online, send emails, or take pictures. . . .

A | WRITING Study this picture. Work with a partner and identify the parts of the machine using the words in the box. Then write sentences to explain how the machine works. Use time, reason, and conditional clauses. (Many different answers are possible.)

THE *TURN ON A LIGHT BULB* MACHINE

PARTS OF THE MACHINE
ax
birdcage
bowling ball
bowling pin
boxing glove
hammer
iron
jug
light bulb
pool ball
pulley
rope
scale
track

When the glove hits the bowling ball, the ball rolls down and hits the bowling pin.
When the bowling pin falls, it pulls on the rope.

B | PERSONAL REFLECTION Choose one of these statements to agree or disagree with. Make some notes to support your opinion, and give examples from your experience. Then explain to your classmates why you agree or disagree with the statement.

STATEMENTS

1. Everyone should do some charity work.
2. Studying a language is essential.
3. Nothing is impossible.
4. Actions are better than words.
5. Confidence is all you need to be successful.
6. Traveling is the best kind of education.

"I agree with the second statement. If you don't learn English, you can't get a job so easily. When I was 12, I decided to learn both English and Spanish. I chose those languages because so many people speak them. Before you choose a language, you should think about the kind of life you want. For example, if you want to travel a lot, English is very useful. If you want to earn a lot of money, maybe it's better to choose a different language, like Chinese. One day, I want to learn Chinese because I want to be a translator."

C | MAKING SUGGESTIONS Choose a city you know well. What should someone do there? Think about the topics in the box, and write as many suggestions as possible. Use conditional clauses in your suggestions.

art	great view	music	shopping
famous sites	interesting buildings	parks	sports
food	museums	places to walk	

If you are interested in art, go to the Museum of Modern Art.
If you like good music, try the Poisson Rouge.
If you like good food, you'll probably enjoy my favorite restaurant. It's called . . .

12.8 Summary of Adverb Clauses

We use **adverb clauses** to add information to a **main clause**. For example:

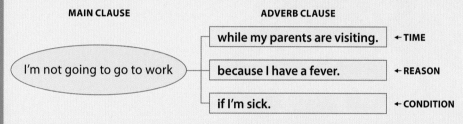

MAIN CLAUSE	ADVERB CLAUSE	
I'm not going to go to work	while my parents are visiting.	← TIME
	because I have a fever.	← REASON
	if I'm sick.	← CONDITION

An adverb clause:

- can come before a main clause.

adverb clause	main clause
If we don't leave soon,	we'll be late.
Whenever you're ready,	we can go.

- can come after a main clause.

main clause	adverb clause
We'll be late	if we don't leave soon.
We can go	whenever you're ready.

- has a subject and verb.

Call me on my cell	if	**you**	**go out**.
			adverb clause

- begins with a connecting word, or subordinator.

I couldn't read the sign	**because**	the print	was so small.
	subordinator	adverb clause	

We use different subordinators to introduce different types of adverb clauses. Some common subordinators are:

TIME CLAUSES			REASON CLAUSES	CONDITIONAL CLAUSES
after	by the time	when	because	if
as	once	whenever	since	
as long as	since	while		
before	until			

13 Comparisons

It's better to know some of the questions than all of the answers.

—JAMES THURBER,
CARTOONIST AND AUTHOR
(1894–1961)

Talk about It What does the quotation above mean? Do you agree or disagree?

WARM-UP

A Read these sentences and check (✓) *True* or *False*. Then compare with your classmates. How many do you agree on?

Geography Trivia

	TRUE	FALSE
1. Africa is **larger than** Asia.	☐	☐
2. The Gobi Desert isn't **as hot as** the Sahara Desert.	☐	☐
3. The Nile is **the longest** river in the world.	☐	☐
4. Russia has **more trees than** Mexico.	☐	☐
5. Texas is almost **as big as** Chile.	☐	☐
6. A sea is **the same as** an ocean.	☐	☐
7. The Arctic has land all around it. Antarctica, **in contrast,** is surrounded by water.	☐	☐
8. The Amazon flows **faster than** most other rivers.	☐	☐

B The phrases in blue in each sentence above are different ways we compare and contrast things. Based on the examples, answer these questions.

1. Which sentences describe things that are the same or similar?
2. Which sentences describe things that are different?
3. Which blue phrases include an adjective? Which ones include a noun? Which one includes an adverb?
4. Which sentence compares information with the sentence before it?

C Look back at the quotation on page 402. Identify any comparisons.

13.1 Showing Similarities and Differences

We use many different forms and expressions to compare things. For example, comparisons can describe **similarities**, as in **1 – 9**, and **differences**, as in **10 – 18**.

A

SIMILARITIES	DIFFERENCES
DESCRIBING HOW THINGS ARE THE SAME	**DESCRIBING HOW THINGS ARE DIFFERENT**
1 I can throw **as far as** my coach can.	**10** The problem is **not as simple as** you think it is.
2 He doesn't run any **faster than** his brother.	**11** The streets are **narrower** in the old part of town.
3 My sister looks **like** my aunt.	**12** The knitting class is **less popular than** the cooking class.
4 The new program is very **similar to** the old one— they only changed a few things.	**13** Could you please speak **more slowly**?
5 **Both** children **and** adults will enjoy this story.	**14** My opinion is a bit **different from** yours.
DESCRIBING NO CHANGE OVER TIME	**DESCRIBING A CHANGE OVER TIME**
6 His hair is **as black as** it ever was.	**15** My niece has gotten a lot **taller**.
7 She's wearing **the same clothes** again.	**16** My job seems **more difficult** lately.
8 They **aren't playing** any **better** this year.	**17** He's **working more than** he used to.
9 We don't have **homework** this year.	**18** Grandma seems to have **less energy** these days.

1 | Identifying Similarities and Differences Do these sentences describe similarities or differences? Check (✓) your answer. `13.1 A`

COMPARING THINGS ON THE JOB	SIMILARITY	DIFFERENCE
1. I worked just as hard as he did.	☑	☐
2. Her ideas are very similar to mine.	☐	☐
3. This job isn't as difficult as my previous job.	☐	☐
4. I would like a bigger desk.	☐	☐
5. Both the manager and the assistant manager are on vacation today.	☐	☐
6. The two offices are almost the same.	☐	☐
7. Amanda comes to work on time and does everything that is required of her. However, some of her co-workers don't share that work ethic[1].	☐	☐
8. The new computer system is more powerful than the old one.	☐	☐
9. He does his work a little more enthusiastically[2] these days.	☐	☐
10. She sounds just like my old boss.	☐	☐
11. We've been getting a lot more customers lately.	☐	☐
12. That job certainly pays more than it used to.	☐	☐

Think about It Which sentences above compare the qualities of two things? Which sentences describe a change over time? What kinds of words tell us that a change is happening over time?

---

[1] **share that work ethic:** to have the same belief that hard work is important   [2] **enthusiastically:** with excitement and interest in something

13.2 Using (Not) As . . . As with Adjectives, Adverbs, and Nouns

A

adjective

1	Your bedroom is	as	**big**	as	my living room.
2	This restaurant isn't	as	**good**	as	it used to be.

adverb

3	She works	as	**hard**	as	the men do.
4	He doesn't play	as	**often**	as	his friend does.

much / many + noun

5	That fruit juice has	as	**much sugar**	as	a candy bar.
6	They don't have	as	**many bills**	as	we do.

We often use (*not*) *as . . . as* to say that things are the same or different. We can use (*not*) *as . . . as* with:

• an **adjective**, as in **1 – 2**

• an **adverb**, as in **3 – 4**

• *much* / *many* + a **noun**, as in **5 – 6**

B

COMPLETING (*NOT*) *AS . . . AS*

first clause with *as . . . as* — noun phrase

	first clause with *as . . . as*	noun phrase
7	I'm **as tall as**	**my father.**
8	This stove is **as old as**	**the house.**
9	Anna's hair is **as long as**	Sarah's hair.
10	Your guess is **as good as**	mine.

first clause with *as . . . as* — noun phrase — verb

	first clause with *as . . . as*	noun phrase	verb
11	He **isn't as tired as**	I	am.
12	I**'ve been** there as many times as	she	has.
13	I **can't run as fast as**	my brother	can.
14	He **didn't sleep as long as**	the other boys	did.
15	He **visits as often as**	his sister	does.
16	She **talks** just as fast as	her mother	did.

We sometimes complete (*not*) *as . . . as* with a **noun phrase** alone, as in **7 – 10**.

We can also use a **noun phrase** and a **verb** to complete (*not*) *as . . . as*:

• For sentences with a helping verb or the main verb *be*, use a form of the helping verb or *be*, as in **11 – 14**.

• For sentences with no helping verb, use *do*, *does*, or *did*, as in **15 – 16**.

GO ONLINE

2 | Noticing (*Not*) As . . . As Underline the comparison in each sentence. Is (*not*) *as . . . as* used with an adjective, an adverb, or *much*/*many* + noun? Check (✓) your answers. **13.2 A**

TWO RESTAURANTS	ADJECTIVE	ADVERB	MUCH/MANY + NOUN
1. The Lunch Place <u>isn't as expensive as</u> Café Bravo.	✓	☐	☐
2. I think the food at The Lunch Place isn't quite as good as at Café Bravo.	☐	☐	☐
3. It seems that Café Bravo isn't as busy as The Lunch Place.	☐	☐	☐
4. Café Bravo has as many customers as The Lunch Place does.	☐	☐	☐
5. I like The Lunch Place, but not as much as I like Café Bravo.	☐	☐	☐
6. Café Bravo isn't as big as The Lunch Place, so it seems crowded.	☐	☐	☐
7. Café Bravo fills up at lunchtime, so get there as early as you can.	☐	☐	☐

	ADJECTIVE	ADVERB	MUCH/MANY + NOUN
8. The servers at Café Bravo aren't as friendly as the ones at The Lunch Place.	☐	☐	☐
9. Café Bravo doesn't have as many items on the menu.	☐	☐	☐
10. I don't go to The Lunch Place nearly as often as I go to Café Bravo.	☐	☐	☐

3 | Using *As* + Adjective + *As* Expressions that compare one thing to a very different thing are called similes. Many similes in English use *as . . . as*. Work with a partner. Match the beginnings of these similes with the endings. `13.2 A`

COMMON SIMILES WITH AS . . . AS

1. The twins are as alike as ___*i*___
2. I've been as busy as ____
3. The sound was as clear as ____
4. This room is as cold as ____
5. The desert felt as dry as ____
6. Don't worry—this recipe is as easy as ____
7. I took the books out of my bag, and now it's

   as light as ____
8. That song is as old as ____
9. Even though my grandmother is 80, she's still

   as sharp as ____
10. His face turned as white as ____
11. There are no mountains here. The whole area is

    as flat as ____
12. Classes ended today and I feel as free as ____

a. A, B, C.
b. a bee.
c. a pancake.
d. a bone.
e. the hills.
f. two peas in a pod.
g. snow.
h. a bell.
i. a tack.
j. a bird.
k. ice.
l. a feather.

peas in a pod

tack

feather

Talk about It What does each simile above mean? Share ideas with your classmates.

Talk about It There are many common expressions with *as . . . as* in English. What similar expressions do you have in your language? Tell them to a partner.

4 | Usage Note: Making (*Not*) *As* . . . *As* Stronger or Softer Read the note. Then do Activity 5.

> We can use the adverbs **almost** and **just** in statements with **as . . . as**. We use *just* to make the statement stronger. We use *almost* to make the statement softer.
>
> **1** Her car was **just as expensive as** mine. (emphasizes that things are the same)
>
> **2** This table is **almost as old as** the house is. (Things are close to the same.)
>
> We can use the adverbs **nearly** and **quite** in statements with **not as . . . as**. We use *nearly* to make the negative statement stronger. We use *quite* to make the statement softer.
>
> **3** This class isn't **nearly as difficult as** the last one.
>
> **4** He doesn't have **quite as much experience as** you do.

5 | Using _As_ + Adjective/Adverb/Noun + _As_ Complete these sentences using _as . . . as._
Use the words in parentheses and _much_ or _many_ if necessary. `13.2 A`

MY NEW NEIGHBORHOOD

1. My new neighborhood isn't _____ as expensive as _____ my
   old one. (expensive)
2. It's just _____ the old one. (safe)
3. It doesn't have _____ the old one did. (trees)
4. It's almost _____ the old one was. (pretty)
5. I like living here _____ I liked living in my
   old neighborhood. (much)
6. My old neighbors weren't _____ the ones
   I have now. (friendly)
7. In the old neighborhood, people didn't spend _____
   _____ they do here. (time outside)
8. That neighborhood wasn't nearly _____ this
   one is. (convenient)
9. I don't drive _____ I used to. (much)
10. This neighborhood isn't quite _____ the old one. (quiet)

my old neighborhood

my new neighborhood

Think about It Circle _almost_, _just_, _nearly_, and _quite_ in the sentences above. Add one of those words to
the sentences that don't include them. How does the meaning of the sentence change?

My new neighborhood isn't quite as expensive as my old one.

Write about It Write three sentences to compare two neighborhoods you know.

6 | Usage Note: _As Possible_ and _As . . . Can_ Read the note. Then do Activity 7.

> We often complete **as . . . as** with **possible** or a **noun phrase** + **can**.
>
> Please come **as soon as possible**. (= as quickly as you are able to)
> I got here **as early as possible**. (= as early as I was able to)
> I'm running **as fast as I can**. (= as fast as I am able to)
> She needs to earn **as much money as she can** before summer. (= as much money as she is able to)
> We tried to make our guests **as comfortable as possible**. (= as comfortable as we were able to)

7 | Listening for _As . . . As_ Listen and complete these conversations. Then practice with a partner. `13.2 A`

1. A: Hurry up!
   B: I'll be there in a minute. I'm going _____ as fast as _____ I can.
2. A: What do you think of the new clerk?
   B: He's pretty good. But he doesn't know _____ the last one.

3. A: Can you finish it tomorrow?

   B: I'm not sure. I'll finish it _____ possible.

4. A: What time do you need me here?

   B: _____ possible, please.

5. A: Toshi didn't do very well on the test.

   B: I don't think he studied _____ we did.

6. A: I'm sorry. I'm not quite ready yet.

   B: No worries. Take _____ you need.

7. A: Are you going to the gym again?

   B: Yeah. I go _____ I can.

8. A: Emma has a lot of energy.

   B: That's because she didn't work _____ we did.

9. A: Please fill this out _____ possible.

   B: Of course.

10. A: I'm a little nervous about learning the routine.

    B: Don't worry. We're going to make it _____ possible for you.

11. A: They didn't finish _____ the last group.

    B: They did a good job, though.

12. A: I'm trying _____ I can, but I just don't understand this.

    B: I know what you mean.

Think about It Which conversations in Activity 7 include *as possible* and *as . . . can*? Can you think of a different way to express the same idea?

I'm going as fast as I can. = I'm going as quickly as possible.

8 | Completing (*Not*) As . . . As Complete each sentence with a form of *be* or a helping verb. 13.2 B

My Best Friend and I

1. My best friend is almost as tall as I _____ *am* _____.

2. Her hair is as black as mine _____.

3. She likes to swim and run as much as I _____.

4. I don't have as many books as she _____.

5. I haven't traveled as much as she _____.

6. My house isn't as big as hers _____.

7. I'm almost as tall as she _____.

8. She hasn't lived here as long as I _____.

9. I like music as much as she _____.

10. I'm not quite as friendly as she _____.

Talk about It Tell a partner some things you have in common or don't have in common with a friend or family member. Use (*not*) *as . . . as.*

Write about It Write three of the facts you told your partner.

9 | Usage Note: (*Not*) As . . . As to Compare Times Read the note. Then do Activity 10.

> Sometimes we describe a change over time using (*not*) *as . . . as*. To help complete the comparison, we may use a **clause with *used to***, a **time clause**, or a **time expression**. Notice: We sometimes use a time expression by itself to complete the comparison.
>
> | **AS . . . AS WITH *USED TO*** | **AS . . . AS WITH A TIME CLAUSE OR TIME EXPRESSION** |
> |---|---|
> | I don't work as hard as **I used to**. | I don't work as hard as **I did when I was younger.** |
> | I don't have as much time as **I used to**. | I don't have as much free time **lately.** |
> | This place isn't as cheap as **it used to be**. | This place isn't as cheap **anymore.** |
> | I'm just as busy as **I used to be**. | I'm just as busy as **I was last year.** |

10 | Comparing Times with (*Not*) As . . . As Complete the descriptions below with the words from the box. (More than one answer is possible.) Then answer the questions that follow. `13.2 A–B`

difficult	fun	homework	shy	video games
friends	good	often	time	worried

THEN AND NOW

1. When I was younger, I didn't like to meet new people. Nowadays, I have just as many _____*friends*_____ as I used to, but I'm a lot more comfortable with strangers. I'm not as _____ anymore.

2. I don't like _____ as much as I did when I was younger. I used to play all day long. I still spend as much _____ on the Internet these days, though.

3. I think this school year is going to be just as _____ as last year. I don't have as much _____ this year, but I'm working more hours at my job.

4. I don't go to the movies as _____ as I used to. Theaters are so expensive, and watching movies at home on my big TV is just as much _____.

5. I used to get so nervous whenever I took a test, but I'm not as _____ anymore. Of course, I still do my work and I study, but now I try to relax and get a good night's sleep before exams. And my grades are just as _____ as they used to be.

QUESTIONS

1. Was each missing word an adjective, adverb, or noun?
2. Which comparisons include *used to*? A time expression? A time clause?
3. Which comparison does not have a second part? Why?

Write about It Write three sentences about ways that you have changed and one about how you have not changed since you were younger. Use (*not*) *as . . . as*. Share your sentences with a partner.

13.3 Using -er / More / Less with Adjectives and Adverbs

<table>
<tr><td rowspan="2" style="vertical-align:middle">**A**</td><td>

DESCRIBING DIFFERENCES WITH ADJECTIVES

1 The train is **faster** than the bus is.

2 I'm a lot **happier** than I used to be.

3 This new doctor seems a lot **friendlier** than my last one.

4 My life was **simpler** before I got promoted.

5 I decided to drop accounting and take biology. I think biology is **more interesting**.

6 The new rules are **less confusing**.

7 The chocolate ice cream is **better** than the vanilla.

</td><td>

We often use **adjectives** to describe differences. We can do this by adding:

- **-er** to most one-syllable and some two-syllable adjectives, as in **1 – 4**
- **more / less** before other adjectives with two or more syllables, as in **5 – 6** (*Less* is the opposite of *more*.)

Some adjectives have irregular comparative forms, as in **7**. These include:

bad – worse	far – farther / further	good – better

</td></tr>
<tr><td>

DESCRIBING DIFFERENCES WITH ADVERBS

8 Kate has always worked **harder** than I do.

9 Bob usually eats **more quickly** than his sister.

10 I see David a lot **less often** these days.

11 She sang the song **better** than her teacher did.

12 Thanks to online shopping, we can buy things **more easily** now. (NOT: ~~buy more easily things~~)

</td><td>

We describe differences with **adverbs** in a similar way as adjectives, as in **8 – 12**. Some adverbs have irregular comparative forms, as in **11**. These include:

badly – worse	far – farther / further	well – better

WARNING! We do not usually put an adverb between a verb and its object, as in **12**.

For information on the spelling of *-er* forms, see Activity 12, page 411.

</td></tr>
<tr><td>**B**</td><td>

COMPLETING *-ER, MORE,* AND *LESS* SENTENCES

13 The chocolate ice cream is **better than** the vanilla.

14 Bob usually eats **more quickly than** his sister.

15 Kate has always worked **harder than** I do.

16 The train is **faster than the bus is**.

17 I'm a lot **happier than I used to be**.

18 I see David a lot **less often** these days.

19 My life was **simpler** before I got promoted.

</td><td>

Often, we don't mention the second thing that we are comparing because it's obvious. If we do, we may use **than** with:

- a noun phrase, as in **13 – 14**
- a noun phrase + a main verb or helping verb, as in **15 – 16**

When we describe a change over time, we may use a clause with *used to*, a time expression, or a time clause to help complete the comparison, as in **17 – 19**.

</td></tr>
</table>

11 | Noticing *-er/More/Less* Forms Find the comparisons in this text. Circle the adjective forms and underline the adverb forms. Then answer the questions on page 411. 〔13.3 A〕

My Dream Home

There are some major differences between my dream home and my real home. First of all, my dream home is much (larger). My real home has two bedrooms, so I have to share one with my brother. In my dream home, we each have our own huge bedroom. Of course, I'm older, so my room should be a little bigger than his. And size isn't the only difference. My dream home is also newer and more modern than my real one. The air conditioner works better, and it has smarter temperature controls. Also, my dream home is less noisy at night. Now we live on a big street, so I can always hear the traffic. My dream home is right next to the beach, and the only thing I hear at night is the waves.

QUESTIONS

1. How many comparisons use adjective forms? How many comparisons use adverb forms?
2. How many of the comparisons use *than* to say which two things are being compared? Why do you think most of the comparisons do not include *than*?

Talk about It How is your dream home different from your real home? Tell a partner. Use comparative adjectives and adverbs.

12 | Spelling Note: *-er* Adjectives and Adverbs Read the note. Then do Activity 13.

SPELLING RULES FOR ONE- AND TWO-SYLLABLE ADJECTIVES AND ADVERBS	EXAMPLES	
	adjective or adverb	*-er* form
1 For most one-syllable adjectives and adverbs, **add *-er*.** When a one-syllable adjective or adverb ends in *-e*, **add *-r*.**	fast high wide	**faster** **higher** **wider**
2 When a one-syllable adjective ends in a **c**onsonant + **v**owel + **c**onsonant (CVC), **double the final consonant and add *-er*.**	**big** **hot**	**bigger** **hotter**
3 When a two-syllable adjective ends in *-ow*, **add *-er*.** When a two-syllable adjective ends in *-le*, **add *-r*.**	nar·**row** sim·**ple**	**narrower** **simpler**
4 When a two-syllable adjective or adverb ends in *-y*, **change the *-y* to *-i* and add *-er*.**	ea·**sy** friend·**ly** an·**gry**	**easier** **friendlier** **angrier**

13 | Using *-er/More/Less* Forms Complete these sentences with the correct form of the adjectives and adverbs in parentheses. **13.3 A**

Things Are Improving

1. My life is getting _____ *better* _____ than it used to be. (good)
2. My job is a little _____, but it's also _____. (difficult/interesting)
3. My new co-workers are _____ than the ones I worked with before. (friendly)
4. I get home _____ now, which is really nice. (early)
5. My noisy roommate moved out, so my apartment is _____. (quiet)

FYI

We can use some two-syllable adjectives with either *-er* or *more*.

narrow**er**	**more** narrow
ang**rier**	**more** angry
simpl**er**	**more** simple

6. My new roommate works _____ than I do,
   so I have time alone in the apartment. (late)

7. I've been eating _____ so I'm feeling
   _____. (good/healthy)

8. I think I'm a little _____, too. (thin)

9. I also started exercising and I'm getting _____.
   (strong)

10. I'm feeling _____ and I fall asleep
    _____ at night. (relaxed/fast)

Talk about It Tell a partner about three things that have improved in your life.

14 | Completing Comparisons Match the beginnings of these sentences with the endings.
Underline the two different things that are compared. (More than one answer is possible.) `13.3 B`

LIFE STAGES

1. Underline{Teenagers} are more independent __*a*__   a. than underline{younger children}.

2. Parents are sometimes stricter[3] ____   b. than a 1-year-old.

3. A 20-year-old can usually run faster ____   c. than grandparents.

4. A teenager is often more emotional ____   d. than middle-aged people.

5. Small children usually cry louder ____   e. than an adult.

6. A college student often stays up later ____   f. than a 20-year-old.

7. Most elderly people walk
   more slowly ____   g. than older children.

                                                h. than a younger child.

8. Sometimes an older child will be
   more helpful ____   i. than a 50-year-old.

                                                j. than a high
9. A 60-year-old has had more   school student.
   experiences ____

10. A 3-year-old can speak more clearly ____

Think about It Look at the second part of each sentence above. Add a verb after the noun phrase that
matches the verb in the first part of the sentence.

Teenagers are more independent than younger children are.

Talk about It What are some things we expect of young people? What are some things we expect
of older people? Why do we expect these things? Is it different in different cultures? Share ideas with
your classmates.

Write about It Write one or two paragraphs about life stages. Try to use comparisons with adjectives
and adverbs.

[3] **stricter:** more likely not to let people behave badly

15 | Usage Note: Making *-er/More/Less* Forms Stronger or Softer Read the note. Then do Activity 16.

We can use many expressions to make *-er*, **more**, and **less** forms stronger or weaker. They express "how much." We often use *a lot*, *even*, **much**, and *far* to express a greater difference. We often use *a bit* and *a little* to express a smaller difference.

EXAMPLES WITH ADJECTIVES	EXAMPLES WITH ADVERBS
My new computer is **a lot** faster.	They visit **much** more frequently than they used to.
The strawberries are great, but the raspberries are **even** more delicious.	His co-worker works **far** less often than he does.
The tests were almost the same, but the second one was **a bit** more difficult.	Things are changing **a little** faster than I expected.

WARNING! We do not use *very* to make *-er*, *more*, and *less* forms stronger or weaker.
(NOT: ~~My computer is very faster.~~)

16 | Using *-er/More/Less* Forms Complete the sentences below. Use the words from the box with *-er*, *more*, or *less*. (More than one answer is possible.) `13.3 A-B`

complicated	dangerous	efficient	often	powerful
convincing	easy	expensive	popular	smart

Technology—Now vs. Ten Years Ago

1. Computers are much _____*more powerful*_____ now.
2. Cell phones are a lot _____ now. They used to just make calls and take pictures.
3. TV remotes are much _____ now. They used to just control the TV and the DVD player—now they control everything.
4. Free Wi-Fi is _____ to find now.
5. Ten years ago, cars didn't have as many airbags[4] and they were _____.
6. There weren't as many hybrids[5], and cars in general were _____ than they are now.
7. Large headphones are _____ now. It seems as if everyone is using them.
8. People were using the Internet a lot ten years ago, but we use it even _____ nowadays. Many of us use it all day long.
9. Good cameras are a little _____ than they used to be. And even the low-priced cameras take good pictures.
10. Special effects[6] are far _____ than they used to be. Sometimes it's hard to tell what's real and what's not.

Think about It Circle *a lot*, *a little*, *even*, *much*, and *far* in the sentences above. Would you add any of these words to the sentences that don't have them? Which words would you use?

---

[4] **airbags:** bags in the car that fill with air during an accident to protect the people inside
[5] **hybrids:** cars that run on two sources of power, usually electricity and gasoline

[6] **special effects:** parts of movies that are made on a computer

Write about It Write four sentences comparing technology today with the same technology ten years ago. Use at least one adverb to compare them. Share sentences with your classmates.

17 | Error Correction Correct any errors in these sentences. (Some sentences may not have any errors.)

1. My new sofa is much more comfortable that the one I used to have.
2. This car isn't as bigger as the other one.
3. I think this class is more hard this semester.
4. Matt isn't as experienced than his co-workers.
5. I'm much more happier now than I was last year.
6. Hassan works longer hours than John is.
7. The oranges are more good today.
8. This show is more bad than the last one we watched.
9. Mika comes here more often than her children does.
10. It seems as if this year's strawberries are more sweeter.

> **FYI**
>
> *Not as . . . as* has a similar meaning as *less* + an adjective/adverb.
>
> The movie is **not as interesting as** the book. (= The movie is **less interesting than** the book.)

13.4 Using *More / Less / Fewer* with Nouns and Verbs

A

DESCRIBING DIFFERENT AMOUNTS WITH NOUN PHRASES

		more + noun	*than*	
1	Matt takes	**more breaks**	than	I do.
2	The Lees have	**more money**	than	we do.

		less + noncount noun	*than*	
3	Jenni has	**less difficulty**	than	she used to.

		fewer + count noun	*than*	
4	This store has	**fewer workers**	than	the other one does.

5 I should eat **less sugar**.
6 It's nice to spend **more time** with my family.

We can use **more**, **less**, and *fewer* in **noun phrases** to describe different amounts. We can use:

- *more* with plural count nouns and noncount nouns, as in **1 – 2**
- *less* with noncount nouns, as in **3**
- *fewer* with plural count nouns, as in **4**

For more information on *more*, *fewer*, and *less*, see Unit 4, page 150.

When the meaning is clear, we sometimes use the noun phrase without *than* and the second part, as in **5 – 6**.

B

DESCRIBING DIFFERENCES WITH VERBS

		subject + verb (+ object)	*more / less*	*than*	
7	He **talks**		more	than	I do.
8	She **weighs** ten pounds		less	than	she weighed before.

9 I should really try to **eat less**. (= less than I do now)
10 I hope he **tells** us **more**. (= more than he told us before)

We can also use **more** and **less** by themselves after **verbs** to describe differences, as in **7 – 8**.

When the meaning is clear, we can omit *than* and the second part, as in **9 – 10**.

414

18 | Comparing Amounts Read this nutritional information. Write comparisons with *more/less/fewer* in the noun phrase. Use the words below in the order provided. `13.4 A`

Nutritional Information Per Serving					
Small donut		**Salmon (3 oz)**		**Medium fresh peach**	
Protein	2.34 g	Protein	16.86 g	Protein	1.36 g
Fat	10.30 g	Fat	5.39 g	Fat	0.38 g
Fiber	0.7 g	Fiber	0	Fiber	2.2 g
Salt	181 mg	Salt	86 mg	Salt	0
Sugar	11 g	Sugar	0	Sugar	12.58 g
Calories	192	Calories	121	Calories	58
Slice of wheat bread		**Steak (3 oz)**		**Canned peach in syrup**	
Protein	3.01 g	Protein	16.67 g	Protein	0.76 g
Fat	1 g	Fat	15.44 g	Fat	0.26 g
Fiber	1.2 g	Fiber	0	Fiber	1.8 g
Salt	151 mg	Salt	42 mg	Salt	9 mg
Sugar	1.76 g	Sugar	0	Sugar	21.40 g
Calories	78	Calories	210	Calories	105

1. a donut/calories/a slice of wheat bread   *A donut has more calories than a slice of wheat bread.*
2. a slice of wheat bread/fat/a donut   _____
3. a donut/fiber/a slice of wheat bread   _____
4. salmon/calories/steak   _____
5. salmon/protein/steak   _____
6. a canned peach/salt/a fresh peach   _____
7. a fresh peach/calories/a canned peach   _____
8. a canned peach/sugar/a donut   _____
9. a donut/protein/a fresh peach   _____
10. a slice of wheat bread/fiber/a fresh peach   _____

Talk about It Tell your classmates the foods you should or would like to eat more, less, or fewer of.

"I should eat more fish."   *"I'd like to eat more dessert!"*

19 | *More/Less* with Nouns and Verbs Find the comparisons in these conversations. Circle noun phrases with *more/less/fewer*. Underline *more/less* by itself after a verb. Then practice with a partner. `13.4 A–B`

1. A: Could you get me more cough syrup?
   B: Yes, of course. I'll be right back.

2. A: This car has more power than my old one.
   B: It probably uses more gas, too.

3. A: These light bulbs use less energy than those.

 B: I know, but they cost a lot more.

4. A: Did you injure your back?

 B: Yeah. I'm afraid the exercises did more harm than good[7].

5. A: He got in another car accident?

 B: Yep. Fortunately there was less damage[8] this time.

6. A: How's the new job?

 B: It's great, but I have a lot less free time than I used to.

7. A: You're giving her more credit than she deserves.

 B: I don't think so. She worked hard on this project.

8. A: Do you think Rob will help us?

 B: Probably. He has more time than money right now.

9. A: Your piano playing has really improved.

 B: Well, I'm practicing more.

10. A: Was the meeting helpful?

 B: Not really. I still have more questions than answers.

Think about It Look at each comparison you circled in Activity 19. Is *more/less* used in a noun phrase or by itself after a verb? Write *NP* (noun phrase) or *AV* (after a verb) next to each one.

20 | Using *More/Less/Fewer* with Nouns and Verbs Complete these questions. Use the words in parentheses and *more*, *less*, or *fewer*. (More than one answer is possible.) `13.4 A-B`

LIFESTYLE

1. Do you _____exercise more_____ than you did last year? (exercise)

2. Do you _____ on Monday than on Friday? (study)

3. Do you _____ than you did when you were younger? (take naps)

4. Do you _____ now than you did last year? (go out to eat often)

5. Do you _____ now than you did two years ago? (do homework)

6. Do you _____ than you used to? (eat healthy food)

7. Do you _____ than you used to? (work hours)

8. Do you _____ than you had three years ago? (have friends)

9. Do you _____ on the weekends than on the weekdays? (sleep)

10. Do you _____ than you used to? (own books)

> **F Y I**
>
> Sometimes you will hear people use *less . . . than* (instead of *fewer . . . than*) with plural count nouns.
>
> There are a lot **less cars** on the road today.

Talk about It Ask and answer the questions you completed above with a partner. Use complete sentences. For negative answers, use *less* or *fewer*.

A: Do you exercise more than you did last year?
B: No. I exercise less.

Think about It Which of the questions you completed above use *more*, *less*, or *fewer* in a noun phrase? Which use *more*, *less*, or *fewer* after a verb?

---

[7] **do more harm than good:** to have a bad result instead of being helpful

[8] **damage:** physical harm that is done to something

13.5 Repeated Comparisons and Double Comparisons

A	**REPEATED COMPARISONS** **1** She's getting **thinner and thinner**. **2** The salespeople here are getting **more and more aggressive**. **3** I think these pills are **less and less effective**. **4** These problems are occurring **more and more frequently**. **5** The bus has been coming **less and less often**. **6** **More and more applications** are coming in every week. **7** I see **fewer and fewer people** smoking.	We sometimes repeat an **-er, more**, or **less form** to show that something is continuing to change over time, as in **1 – 5**. We can repeat comparisons with: • adjectives, as in **1 – 3** • adverbs, as in **4 – 5** • nouns, as in **6 – 7**
B	**DOUBLE COMPARISONS** **8** **The more** you practice, **the better** you get. (If you practice more, you get better than you used to be.) **9** **The older** I get, **the less** I understand about people. (As I get older, I understand less about people than I did before.)	We can use **double comparisons** to show that one change causes another change, as in **8 – 9**. To do this, we use *the* + *more*, *less*, or an *-er form* in both clauses.

21 | Using Repeated Comparisons Describe each situation with a repeated comparison. (More than one answer may be possible.) Then share your sentences with a partner. `13.5 A`

ONGOING CHANGES

1. There was a tiny crack in the window. A few days ago it was two inches long. Now it's four inches long.

   It's getting longer and longer.

2. The first test in your class was easy. The second was harder. The last one was very difficult.

3. Your uncle used to weigh 170 pounds. Two years ago, he weighed 185. Now he weighs 200 pounds.

4. First, one new student came to class. Then three more came. Last week, five new students came to class.

5. He traveled abroad twice a couple of years ago. Last year, he traveled abroad four times. This year, he is traveling abroad eight times.

6. The first show was OK. The second show was pretty good. The most recent show was fantastic.

7. Grandfather used to walk at a normal pace. Then he started walking more slowly. Now he walks very slowly.

8. A few people used to eat dinner at that restaurant. Last year, more people started eating there. Now there are a lot of people there every night.

9. In her 20s, she was very interested in politics. In her 30s, she wasn't as interested in politics. Now she's not very interested in politics at all.

10. Two years ago, his aunt and uncle gave him some money. Last year, they gave him more money. This year, they gave him even more money.

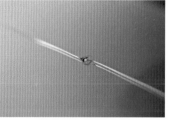

crack

Think about It Do the sentences you wrote above use repeated comparisons with adjectives, adverbs, or nouns?

Write about It Write three sentences about continuing changes in your life. Use repeated comparisons.

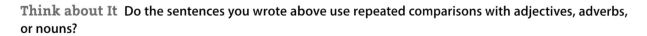

22 | Using Double Comparisons Complete each double comparison with your own ideas. Then share your sentences with a partner. `13.5 B`

LIFE LESSONS

1. The older you get, _the less sleep you need_ _____.
2. The harder you work, _____.
3. The more you practice your English, _____.
4. The more money you save now, _____.
5. The more you exercise, _____.
6. The later you stay up at night, _____.
7. The closer you get to graduation, _____.
8. The more often you go out to eat, _____.
9. The more new friends you make, _____.
10. The more time you spend on computer games, _____.

13.6 Other Ways of Comparing

THE SAME, SIMILAR, AND DIFFERENT

A

	subject	verb (+ adverb)	noun phrase with *the same / similar / different*
1	My father and my brother	have	the same name.
2	My two co-workers	have	similar ideas.
3	These	are	different problems.
4	My friends and I	like totally	different kinds of music.

	subject	linking verb (+ adverb)	*the same / similar / different*
5	Our names	aren't	the same.
6	Their ideas	are	similar.
7	These problems	seem completely	different.

	subject	linking verb (+ adverb)	*the same as / similar to / different from*	noun phrase
8	Your shoes	are	the same as	mine. (my shoes)
9	This laptop	looks	similar to	the one at school.
10	This painting	isn't really	different from	the others.

We sometimes use *the same*, *similar*, and *different* to compare. We can use them:

• in a noun phrase, as in **1 – 4**

• after *be* or other linking verbs, as in **5 – 7**

We also use *the same as*, *similar to*, and *different from* to compare, as in **8 – 10**.

LIKE AND ALIKE

B

	subject	verb	*like*	noun phrase	
11	She	is		a sister	to me.
12	Your phone	sounds	like	a bird.	
13	That house	looks		a castle.	
14	That boy	speaks		an adult.	

	subject	verb (+ adverb)	*alike*
15	My brother and I	look	
16	We	aren't at all	alike.
17	You and I	think a lot	

We can use *like* to say that two things are similar (or act in a similar way), as in **11 – 14**. In these sentences, we are comparing qualities of one thing with another.

We also use *alike* after a verb to compare the qualities of two things, as in **15 – 17**.

418

23 | Using *The Same/Similar/Different* Look at the picture and complete these sentences. (More than one answer may be possible.) `13.6 A`

SIMILARITIES AND DIFFERENCES

1. Carlos and Toshi are wearing _____*the same*_____ hat.
2. Their shirts are _____.
3. They have _____ watches.
4. Their bags are _____.
5. They are waiting at _____ bus stop.
6. They aren't _____ age.
7. Their pants are _____.
8. Their shoes look _____.
9. They have _____ phones.
10. They are doing _____ thing—using their phones.

Write about It Rewrite five of the sentences above in a different way.

Their hats are the same.

Talk about It Work with a partner. Compare two classmates in the room. Talk about how they are the same, similar, or different.

24 | Usage Note: Making *The Same*, *Similar*, and *Different* Stronger or Softer Read the note. Then do Activity 25.

We can use many expressions to make **the same** (*as*), **similar** (*to*), and **different** (*from*) stronger or softer.

EXAMPLES WITH *THE SAME* (*AS*)

Sam and I are **about** the same age.

That blouse is **almost** the same color as your eyes.

They walked in at **more or less** the same time.

Venus and Earth are **nearly** the same size.

Those pictures look **exactly** the same.

The chairs look similar, but they aren't **quite** the same.

EXAMPLES WITH *SIMILAR* (*TO*)

A peach and a nectarine are **very** similar.

You don't look **very** similar to your mother.

Those girls aren't related, but they look **quite** similar.

EXAMPLES WITH *DIFFERENT* (*FROM*)

My opinion is **a bit** different from yours.

Something looks **a little** different, but I'm not sure what.

The new model isn't **very** different from last year's.

College is **completely** different from what I expected.

25 | Using *The Same As/Similar To/Different From* Complete these conversations. Choose the correct words and phrases in parentheses. Listen and check your answers. Then practice with a partner. `13.6 A`

SHOPPING

1. A: This shampoo is _____*exactly the same as*_____ that one, but it's much cheaper.

   B: Well, it's not _____*quite the same*_____. It doesn't smell as good.

   (exactly / quite / the same as / the same)

2. A: Do you think these shoes look _____ those?

   B: Not at all! The color is _____, but the style is _____.

   (completely/the same as/similar/different)

3. A: This belt is _____ the one I already have.

   B: How about this one instead? It's _____.

   (totally/almost/the same as/different)

4. A: These sandals are _____ those.

   B: Yeah, they are. But they're _____.

   (very/a bit/similar to/different)

5. A: These jeans are _____ the ones they used to have.

   B: Actually, I'd say they're _____!

   (a little/totally/different/different from)

6. A: Which shirt would look better on me?

   B: I don't know. They're _____.

   A: I know, but they're _____.

   (about/a little/different/the same)

7. A: We came here at _____ time yesterday, and it wasn't this busy!

   B: That's because yesterday was Sunday. It's _____ on the weekends.

   (completely/more or less/the same/different)

8. A: Do these colors match?

   B: I don't think so. They're _____, but they're not _____.

   (exactly/quite/similar/the same)

26 | Using *Like* Expressions that compare one thing to a very different thing are called similes. Many similes in English use *like*. Match the beginnings of these similes with the endings. **13.6 B**

COMMON SIMILES USING *LIKE*

1. She swims like _b_   a. a horse.
2. This suit fits like ____   b. a fish.
3. He's sleeping like ____   c. a glove.
4. This school runs like ____   d. the back of my hand.
5. He eats like ____   e. a baby.
6. Your words cut like ____   f. a chicken with its head cut off.
7. I want to fly like ____   g. a well-oiled⁹ machine.
8. Please hurry. Run like ____ h. a knife.
9. I know this city like ____   i. an eagle.
10. She's running around like ____ j. the wind.

glove

eagle

Talk about It What does each simile above mean? Share ideas with your classmates.

Talk about It There are many common expressions with *like* in English. What similar expressions do you have in your language? Tell them to a partner.

⁹ **a well-oiled machine:** a machine that runs smoothly because its parts have been oiled

27 | Usage Note: Making *Like* and *Alike* Stronger or Softer Read the note. Then do Activity 28.

We can use many expressions to make **like** and ***alike*** stronger or softer.

EXAMPLES WITH *LIKE*	**EXAMPLES WITH *ALIKE***
It smells **a little** like gas in here.	I think Mary and her sister look **a bit** alike.
He's not **a bit** like my old boss.	We're **a lot** alike in some ways.
The new store is **somewhat** like the old.	David and James talk **just** alike. It's amazing.
The leaves tasted **a lot** like spinach.	I don't think John and Matt look alike **at all**!
Her voice sounds **exactly** like my mother's.	
Your car looks **just** like mine. I can't even tell them apart.	
She doesn't look **very much** like her aunt.	

28 | Using *Like* and *Alike* Unscramble the words to make sentences about family similarities. `13.6 B`

FAMILY SIMILARITIES

1. My son and my father are both very athletic and they both love sports.
   They are very much alike. _____ (are/much/they/alike/very)

2. My son and my husband are both tall with curly back hair.
   _____ (like/looks/my son/a lot/my husband)

3. One of my sisters is tall and the other is short.
   _____ (don't/they/alike/at all/look)

4. When he answers the phone, I always think he is his father.
   _____ (sound/they/alike/exactly)

5. My daughter is outgoing and friendly, but my son is shy and quiet.
   _____ (a bit/they/are/not/alike)

6. My uncle likes to sing and tell jokes and so does my father sometimes.
   _____ (like/acts/my uncle/my father)

7. Both my mother and my grandmother like to read, but they are very different otherwise.
   _____ (a little/is/my mother/my grandmother/like)

8. My cousins Rob and Sam are twins.
   _____ (like/looks/Rob/just/Sam)

9. My sister and I like similar things, but our personalities are very different.
   _____ (I/my sister/are/and/alike/somewhat)

10. If you look at her mouth and chin, you can see they are similar to her mother's.
   _____ (her mother/she/a little/looks/like)

Write about It Choose five of the sentences above and write different sentences with a similar meaning.

My son is a lot like my father.

Talk about It Tell a partner about the family resemblances in your family or in another family you know. Use *like* and *alike*.

29 | Error Correction Correct any errors in these sentences. (Some sentences may not have any errors.)

1. My niece looks alike my grandmother.
2. Those two books are exactly like.
3. My uncle and my brother have same name.
4. Your bag is very similar as mine.
5. This class is very different to my old one.
6. My car is the same almost as yours.
7. I think my problem is different a little from yours.
8. Those two movies have very similar story.
9. This room isn't look like the one we had last year.
10. Mittens and gloves are similar to.

13.7 Using *the* + *-est* / *Most* / *Least* Forms of Adjectives and Adverbs

We use *the* + *-est* / *most* / *least* forms of **adjectives** and **adverbs** to compare one thing to **the other members of a group it belongs to**, as in **1 – 3**.

1 I'm **the shortest person in my family.** (group = my family)

2 Hassan always finishes his work **the fastest of everyone in class.** (group = the class)

3 This is **the most interesting trip we've ever taken.** (group = all of the trips we've taken)

GRAMMAR TERM: We call expressions using *-est* / *most* / *least* the **superlative forms**.

A

4 I'm not sure which color I want. Just give me **the lightest one.**

5 Everyone did a good job, but Sara worked **the hardest.**

6 The simplest explanation is usually right.

7 Matt gets up **the earliest,** so he can make coffee in the morning.

8 What's **the most delicious thing** on the menu?

9 That shipment arrived **the most recently.**

10 I bought the white shirt because it was **the least expensive.**

11 He speaks **the least fluently** of everyone in the class.

12 That place serves **the best breakfast** in town.

13 I sang **the worst** of all.

- With most one-syllable and some two-syllable adjectives and adverbs, we add *-est*, as in **4 – 7**.

- With most other adjectives and adverbs with two or more syllables, we use *most / least*, as in **8 – 11**.

- Some adjectives and short adverbs have irregular *-est* forms, as in **12 – 13**. These include:

bad – worst	far – farthest / furthest	good – best
badly – worst	far – farthest / furthest	well – best

For information on the spelling of *-est* forms, see Activity 31, page 423.

B

COMPLETING *-EST, MOST,* AND *LEAST* SENTENCES

14 Julie is **the most reliable of my employees.**

15 Amanda works **the fastest of all the students.**

16 Mika is **the shortest student in the school.**

17 She works **the hardest in her family.**

18 He is **the nicest person (that) I know.**

19 This is **the best fish (that) I've ever tasted.**

Often, we don't mention the group of people or things that we are comparing because it's obvious. If we do, we often use a **prepositional phrase** with

- *of* to describe a group that something or someone belongs to, as in **14 – 15**

- *in / on / at*, etc., to describe a group or a place, as in **16 – 17**

We also use **adjective clauses** in sentences with *-est* / *most* / *least* forms, as in **18**. These adjective clauses often have present perfect verbs, as in **19**.

30 | Noticing *the* + *-est/Most/Least* Forms Read these sentences and underline the uses of *-est/most/least* forms. `13.7 A`

Hotel Reviews

RATING	COMMENT
★★★★	1. The room wasn't very big, but it had <u>the most comfortable</u> bed I've ever slept in.
★★★★★	2. They served the tastiest[10] appetizers[11] before dinner, and the dinner was delicious, too.
★	3. I ended up paying a lot less than the lowest online price, but it still wasn't worth it.
★★	4. I heard that the West Tower was the newest, so I booked my room there. But when I got there I discovered that it is also the farthest from the beach.
★★★★★	5. The hotel staff has some of the kindest, most generous people you'll ever meet.
★★★★	6. The hotel is one of the largest in the world, so don't be surprised if you get lost!
★★★	7. Bring your GPS[12]—this is not the easiest place to find.
★★★★★	8. We chose this hotel because it was the least expensive one on the beach, so we were surprised at how nice it was.
★★★	9. My biggest complaint is that the free Wi-Fi was really weak.
★★★★	10. Our group was staying in three different rooms. I liked my room because it had the best view of the ocean.

Think about It Are the forms you underlined above adjectives or adverbs?

Think about It Which *-est/most/least* forms are part of noun phrases? Which come after a form of *be*?

> **FYI**
>
> Sometimes we use a possessive determiner before an *-est/most/least* form instead of *the*.
>
> She spent **her** happiest years in that house.

31 | Spelling Note: *-est* Adjectives and Adverbs Read the note. Then do Activities 32–33.

SPELLING RULES FOR ONE- AND TWO-SYLLABLE ADJECTIVES AND ADVERBS	EXAMPLES	
	adjective or adverb	*-est* form
1 For most one-syllable adjectives and adverbs, **add -*est*.** When a one-syllable adjective or adverb ends in -*e*, **add -*st*.**	fast high wide	**fastest highest widest**
2 When a one-syllable adjective ends in a **consonant + vowel + consonant (CVC), double the final consonant and add -*est*.**	**big hot**	**biggest hottest**
3 When a two-syllable adjective ends in -*ow*, **add -*est*.** When a two-syllable adjective ends in -*le*, **add -*st*.**	nar•**row** sim•**ple**	**narrowest simplest**
4 When a two-syllable adjective or adverb ends in -*y*, **change the -*y* to -*i* and add -*est*.**	ea•**sy** friend•**ly**	**easiest friendliest**

[10] **tastiest:** most delicious; best to eat
[11] **appetizers:** small amounts of food that you eat as the first part of a meal

[12] **GPS:** Global Positioning System, a piece of equipment that tells your location and helps you get somewhere

32 | Using *the* + *-est/Most* Forms with Prepositional Phrases Complete the beginning of each sentence with *the* + the *-est/most* form of the adjective in parentheses. Then match it with the correct prepositional phrase. `13.7 A–B`

Geography Facts

1. The Step Pyramid of Djoser is ____*the oldest*____   _*j*_   a. in recorded history.
   (old)
2. Mount McKinley is _____ mountain   ___   b. in the United States.
   (tall)
3. São Paulo is _____ city   ___   c. of the world's oceans.
   (large)
4. The Great Wall is _____ landmark[13]   ___
   (famous)
5. Oymyakon, Siberia is one of _____   ___
   (remote)
   places
6. The eruption of Krakatoa was _____   ___
   (big)
   explosion
7. The Eiffel Tower is one of _____   ___
   (popular)
   tourist destinations
8. The Atlantic is _____   ___
   (salty)
9. With an average elevation of 330 meters, Australia is

   _____   ___
   (low)
10. Mount Fuji is one of _____ places   ___
    (recognizable)

a. in recorded history.
b. in the United States.
c. of the world's oceans.
d. in South America.
e. on earth.
f. in China.
g. of all the continents.
h. in Japan.
i. in France.
j. of the pyramids in Egypt.

Step Pyramid of Djoser

Write about It Look online to find more information about the places and things above. Can you write any other sentences using *the* + the *-est/most* forms of adjectives?

> **F Y I**
>
> We often use *one of the* before an *-est/most/least* adjective + plural noun.
>
> That is **one of the oldest buildings** in the city.

33 | Using *the* + *-est/Most/Least* Forms of Adverbs Add *the* + the *-est/most/least* form of the adverb in parentheses to these questions. (More than one answer may be possible.) `13.7 A`

IN YOUR CLASS

                         the earliest
1. Who usually gets to class? (early)
2. Who travels to get to school? (far)
3. Who is late to class? (frequently)
4. Who do you remember being absent from class? (recently)
5. Who gives the right answer? (often)
6. Who speaks English? (fluently)

---

[13]**landmark:** a big building or another thing that you can see easily from far away

7. Who finishes their homework? (fast)

8. Who does their homework? (carefully)

9. Who do you think works? (hard)

10. Who writes? (neatly)

11. Who can draw? (good)

12. Who talks? (loud)

13. Who talks? (quietly)

14. Who laughs? (easily)

15. Who dresses? (fashionably)

Talk about It Take turns asking and answering the questions in Activity 33 with a partner. Make notes of your answers. Then compare with your classmates. How many answers do you agree on?

A: Who usually gets to class the earliest?
B: Uh . . . probably Sarah.

34 | Using *the* + *-est/Most* Forms with Adjective Clauses Match the first part of each sentence with the correct adjective clause. Then complete each sentence with information about yourself, and share with a partner. 13.7 B

MY EXPERIENCES

1. _____ was the most expensive thing ___*b*___   a. I know.
   (thing)
2. _____ is the most delicious thing ___   b. I bought this year.
   (food)
3. _____ miles is the farthest ___   c. I've ever walked.
   (number)
4. _____ is the most generous employer ___   d. I've ever eaten.
   (person or company)
5. _____ hours is about the longest ___   e. I've ever stayed awake.
   (number)
6. _____ is the most beautiful place ___   f. I've ever visited.
   (place)
7. _____ is the funniest person ___   g. I've ever been.
   (person)
8. _____ was the scariest experience ___   h. I've studied.
   (something that happened)
9. _____ is the most difficult subject ___   i. I've ever had.
   (school subject)
10. _____ is the most interesting city ___   j. I've ever worked for.
    (city name)

Think about It Which sentences above can you rewrite using *one of the* + a plural noun? Which ones can you not restate? Why not?

My new computer was one of the most expensive things I bought this year.

Write about It Choose four of the adjective clauses above, and write new sentences with *the* + *-est/most*. Use *one of the* if necessary.

35 | Usage Note: -est/Most/Least vs. -er/More/Less Read the note. Then do Activity 36.

We use *the* + *-est / most / least* forms of adjectives and adverbs when we compare something to the rest of a group it belongs to. We usually describe the group with a prepositional phrase or an adjective clause.	We use *-er / more / less* forms of adjectives and adverbs when we compare one thing to another. We often introduce the second thing with *than*.
COMPARE	
1a He's **the tallest student in the classroom.**	**1b** He's **taller than the other students in the class.**
2a He's **the nicest person that I've ever met.**	**2b** He's **nicer than most other people.**
3a She talks **the loudest of all of us.**	**3b** She talks **louder than the rest of us do.**

36 | Using -est/Most/Least and -er/More/Less Use the correct form to complete each sentence. (More than one answer may be possible.) `13.7 A–B`

Vacations

1. I think the beach is _____*the best*_____ place to take a vacation. (good)

2. Lying on the beach is _____ than sightseeing. (relaxing)

3. _____ vacation that I ever had was a trip with my family. (stressful)

4. Exploring a place on my own is _____ than taking a tour. (exciting)

5. I'd love to visit all _____ places in the world. (beautiful)

6. My parents think going to museums is _____ than lying on the beach. (interesting)

7. For me, visiting museums and looking at buildings is _____ way to spend a vacation. (bad)

8. _____ I've ever traveled is about 2,000 miles. (far)

9. Someday when I have more money, I'll travel _____. (often)

10. Small towns are much _____ than big cities, and they can be very interesting, too. (cheap)

Talk about It Do you agree or disagree with each statement above? Tell a partner.

Think about It How did you know whether to use *-est/most* or *-er/more* in the sentences above?

37 | Error Correction Correct any errors in these sentences. (Some sentences may not have any errors.)

1. His computer is fastest than mine.
2. Old Town is the more interesting part of this city.
3. My mom makes best cookies.
4. Traffic today is the most slowest that it has been in a long time.

5. It was the most large turtle that I had ever seen.

6. All three books are pretty good, but I liked that one the less.

7. For the interview, she wore her nicer dress.

8. City Hall is the tallest building of my city.

9. This is the bigger meal that I've ever eaten.

10. I'm having the most difficulty with this job than the last one.

13.8 Using *the + Most / Least / Fewest* with Nouns and Verbs

		the most / least / fewest with nouns	
A	**1**	Matt takes	the most breaks	at work.
	2	Whoever has	the most money	should pay!
	3	He puts	the least effort	into his job.
	4	This group has	the fewest problems.	

		subject + verb (+ object) *the most / least*	
5	She **talks** to me	the most	of all.
6	I probably **work**	the least	in my family.

We can use **the most**, **the least**, and **the fewest** in **noun phrases**. We can use:

- **the most** with plural count nouns and noncount nouns, as in **1 – 2**
- **the least** with noncount nouns, as in **3**
- **the fewest** with plural count nouns, as in **4**

We can also use **the most / the least** by themselves after **verbs**, as in **5 – 6**.

 ONLINE

38 | Using *the + Most/Least/Fewest* with Nouns and Verbs Complete these sentences with *the most*, *the least*, or *the fewest*. Compare your answers with a partner.   `13.8 A`

A RESTAURANT HOST

1. I spend _____*the most*_____ time figuring out where to seat people.

2. The part of the job I like _____ is talking to rude customers.

3. We usually get _____ customers on weekday mornings.

4. The servers with _____ experience sometimes get promoted to host.

5. Customers like the window seats _____.

6. They like the seats next to the kitchen _____.

7. It seems as if large parties always come in when we have _____ tables available.

8. Teenagers usually make _____ noise and older people make _____.

9. The servers share their tips with me, so I make _____ money when we're busy.

Think about It In each sentence above, is *the most/the least/the fewest* used in a noun phrase or by itself after a verb? Write *NP* (noun phrase) or *AV* (after a verb) next to each one.

Talk about It Tell a partner four things about your job or about school. Use *the least*, *the most*, and *the fewest* with a noun or verb.

13.9 Using Comparisons in Speaking

A

COMPARE

1a She's as old as **I am.**

1b She's as old as **me.**

2a He has the same job as **I do.**

2b He has the same job as **me.**

3a I'm older than **she is.**

3b I'm older than **her.**

4a I have more experience than **he does.**

4b I have more experience than **him.**

5a He has lived longer than **we have.**

5b He has lived longer than **us.**

When speakers make comparisons in informal conversation, they sometimes use an **object pronoun** instead of a **subject** + **verb**, as in **1 – 5**.

People do this because it is a shorter way to compare two things. Many people consider this incorrect in written English.

B

6 A: I don't like the new model.
B: Why not? It's just **as good.** (= as good as the old model)

7 A: Do you want to go to the park?
B: Let's go tomorrow. It's not quite **as crowded** on Mondays. (= not as crowded as it is on other days)

8 A: This looks a lot like the other apartment, doesn't it?
B: It's **bigger.** (= bigger than the other apartment)

9 A: How are you feeling?
B: **Better.** (= better than I was feeling before)

When we can understand the context from a conversation, we often use **unfinished comparisons**.

With *as . . . as* comparisons, we may not include the second part of the *as* form, as in **6 – 7**.

With *-er/more/less*, we often omit *than* and the information that follows, as in **8**.

We can even use a single comparative adjective as a response if the context is clear, as in **9**.

39 | Noticing Object Pronouns in Comparisons Listen and complete each conversation with a comparison using an object pronoun. Then practice with a partner. `13.9 A`

1. A: I can't reach the top shelf.
   B: Sure you can. You're just
   _____*as tall as me*_____ .

2. A: How can they afford that car?
   B: Well, they have a lot
   _____ .

3. A: I heard Kate got a raise.
   B: I don't know why. We work
   _____ .

4. A: John's playing is getting a lot better.
   B: I know. I should practice
   _____ .

5. A: Why are they leaving already?
   B: They got here _____ .

6. A: How long have you worked here?
   B: Two years. Not _____ !

7. A: My sister is a lot _____ .
   B: Don't be silly. You're just as pretty as she is.

8. A: How many years has she lived here?
   B: Five or so. About _____ .

9. A: Are you _____ ?
   B: No, we're about the same height.

10. A: David can go out, but you need to stay home.
    B: Why? I'm almost _____ .

Think about It Rewrite each comparison above using subject + verb. Then practice the conversations again using your new comparisons.

A: I can't reach the top shelf.
B: Sure you can. You're just as tall as I am.

428

40 | Noticing Unfinished Comparisons Use the comparisons in the box to complete the conversations below. Listen and check your answers. Then practice with a partner. `13.9 B`

as big	better	harder	more interesting	more talented	shorter
as funny	better	more difficult	more often	older	taller
as weak					

1. A: He grew three inches this year.

   B: I thought he looked _____*taller*_____!

2. A: Remember how you used to stay up all night?

   B: Well, I'm _____ now and I know _____.

3. A: How's the new class?

   B: It's _____, but also _____.

4. A: How's your mom feeling?

   B: A lot _____. Not _____.

5. A: How's the new apartment?

   B: It's not _____, but it's nice.

6. A: What does she look like now?

   B: Pretty much the same. Her hair is _____.

7. A: So, are you still working as hard as you used to?

   B: _____

8. A: Do you think she's as talented as her sister?

   B: Possibly _____.

9. A: How was the new show?

   B: It was OK. It wasn't _____.

10. A: Boy, Anna really knows her way around this place.

    B: Well, she comes here _____.

Think about It How could you complete each comparison above? Why do you think we don't usually use the complete forms in speaking?

41 | Using Unfinished Comparisons Ask and answer these questions with different classmates. Use short, unfinished comparisons with *-er/more* and *not as . . . as*. Try not to use the same adjective twice. `13.9 B`

CHANGES

1. How is this school different from your last school?

   A: How is this school different from your last school?
   B: It's bigger. And there are more students.

2. How is your current home different from a place where you used to live?
3. How is the weather today different from the weather three months ago?
4. How is our teacher different from your last teacher?

5. How is this grammar book different from your last grammar book?

6. How is this classroom different from your living room?

7. How is fast food different from home-cooked food?

8. How is your life different this year compared to last year?

13.10 Using Comparisons in Writing

A

USING LINKING EXPRESSIONS

1 If you go to Mayfield Park in the morning, you'll see lots of moms with babies, small children in the playground, and maybe a few adults jogging or exercising. **On the other hand**, if you visit at night, you'll probably only see teenagers in the park.

2 Many companies charge hundreds of dollars for this service. **In contrast**, our services are far less expensive.

3 The old system caused a lot of problems for our staff. The new system, **however**, has been working well ever since we installed it.

4 The employees complained about the night manager. **Similarly**, they criticized the general manager for not acting sooner.

5 You know that we must invest money in our future. **In the same way**, we must invest our time.

When we compare ideas in a paragraph, we often use linking expressions to show differences and similarities. For example:

• *On the other hand*, *in contrast*, and *however* introduce differences, as in **1 – 3**.

• *Similarly* and *in the same way* express similarities, as in **4 – 5**.

We usually use linking expressions like these at the beginning of a clause or sentence, as in **1 – 2** and **4 – 5**. However, we can also sometimes use them between the subject and the verb, as in **3**.

B

BOTH (OF) AND NEITHER (OF)

My two grandfathers have a lot in common:

6 **Both men** grew up on farms.

7 **Both of them** moved to a big city.

My two grandmothers are very different, but they have a few things in common:

8 **Neither woman** was born in this country.

9 **Neither of them** learned English as a child.

plural noun
10 **Both chairs** are broken.

singular noun
11 **Neither child** is at school today.

plural noun phrase
or plural pronoun

12	Both of	the chairs/them	are fine.
13	Neither of	the children/us	likes tomatoes.

We often use *both* or *both of* for a positive similarity between two things, as in **6 – 7**, and *neither* or *neither of* for a negative similarity, as in **8 – 9**. Although we can use these words in conversation, they are more common in written English.

We use:

• *both* + a plural noun phrase, as in **10**

• *neither* + a singular noun phrase, as in **11**

• *both of / neither of* + a plural noun phrase or plural pronoun, as in **12 – 13**

We usually use *both* or *both of* + a noun phrase with a **plural verb**, as in **10** and **12**, and *neither* or *neither of* with a **singular verb**, as in **11** and **13**.

C

BOTH . . . AND / NEITHER . . . NOR

14 **Both the government and the corporations** are responsible for the current situation.

15 **Neither the customer inside nor the people** waiting outside were able to hear the announcement.

In more formal writing, we *sometimes* use *both . . . and . . .* and *neither . . . nor . . .* to say that two things are similar or perform (or do not perform) the same action.

• *Both . . . and* uses a plural verb, as in **14**.

• *Neither . . . nor* uses a verb that agrees with the subject closest to it, as in **15**.

 GO ONLINE

42 | Noticing Comparisons Circle the words and expressions in this passage that show contrast and similarity. `13.10 A`

The Internet

The Internet has changed the way people communicate. Communication across cities, states, and countries has never been easier, and an average person can now instantly connect with friends, family, and strangers. (On the other hand), people now spend less time on face-to-face communication. So the question is this: does the Internet bring us closer together or push us further apart?

It is unfortunate that we don't communicate in person as much as we used to, but new technology provides many social benefits. First, we can communicate with a far greater number of people because of the Internet. When it was necessary to see people in person, write letters, or talk on the telephone, most of us couldn't communicate with very many people every day. Most people would see or speak to a few friends and family members. Similarly, we saw only a few co-workers and couldn't work with large numbers of people.

Second, the Internet becomes a more powerful social tool every year. Both friends and family can stay in closer contact because of online video telephoning and chatting. In the same way, people who meet each other briefly in person can get to know each other better online. Some people have become more isolated because they interact online instead of going out. However, in general, the Internet has brought us closer together.

FYI
We don't usually use linking expressions more than once in the same paragraph; we usually use them in longer pieces of writing.

Think about It Underline the other types of comparisons used in the passage above.

43 | Using Linking Expressions for Similarity and Contrast Add the linking expressions in parentheses to these paragraphs. `13.10 A`

Student Paragraphs

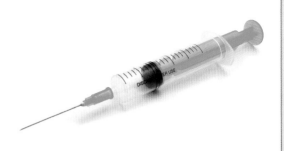

1. (in contrast) Years ago, diseases like measles[14] and polio[15] were common. Children often got them, and if you grew up in that time, you probably knew someone who got one of them. People nowadays are often not even aware of these diseases. They get vaccinated as children, and they may go their whole lives without meeting someone who has had measles or polio.

2. (on the other hand) I like to eat in restaurants. It's nice to sit down while someone serves me a meal. I like eating dishes that I never make at home. I am a pretty good cook. Sometimes I enjoy spending hours in the kitchen preparing a great meal.

3. (similarly) It's easier to eat healthy food if you cook at home. You can choose the ingredients that you want to cook with. You can control how much salt and sugar are added to your food.

4. (in contrast) Bicycles are a safe, fun, and economical form of transportation. When you ride a bicycle, you don't have to spend money on gas. You can also get a good workout from riding a bicycle. Cars use a lot of expensive fuel, and driving everywhere doesn't give you any of the benefits of exercise.

5. (however) Online classes are very convenient. You can study when you want to for as long as you want to. I sometimes prefer a traditional class.

6. (in the same way) Sometimes when I'm doing homework, I get distracted by the Internet. Instead of studying, I go online to see what my friends are doing or to watch a movie. I can get distracted during an online class.

7. (on the other hand) Small schools are nice because you get to know all of the students. When you start a new class, you see a lot of the same people, so you feel comfortable and relaxed. Big schools have more programs and more opportunities for study.

8. (similarly) If you have lived in a small town, you know that it can get boring. Sometimes you want to see new things and meet new people. A small school can seem boring after a while.

Write about It Choose one of the comparisons above. Write your own short paragraph comparing the two things. Use a linking expression to show contrast or similarity.

---

[14] **measles:** an illness that makes small red spots appear on your skin

[15] **polio:** a serious disease that makes a person unable to move certain muscles

44 | Using *Both* (*of*) and *Neither* (*of*) Complete these sentences with *both*, *neither*, *both of*, or *neither of*.

`13.10 B`

Barcelona and Los Angeles

1. _Both of_ the cities are near the coast.
2. _____ one gets very cold in the winter.
3. _____ them have a lot of traffic.
4. _____ are quite crowded.
5. _____ city is the capital of its country.
6. _____ Barcelona and Los Angeles have large, diverse[16] populations.
7. _____ them have a lot of good restaurants.
8. _____ Barcelona nor Los Angeles has a lot of green space.
9. _____ the cities have hosted the Summer Olympics.
10. _____ the cities has hosted the Winter Olympics.

Barcelona

Los Angeles

Write about It Write four sentences about two places that you know. Use *both*, *neither*, *both of*, and *neither of* to describe what they have in common.

45 | Using *Both* . . . *And* and *Neither* . . . *Nor* Write a single sentence about each situation. Use *both . . . and . . .* or *neither . . . nor . . . .* Pay careful attention to whether the verb you use is singular or plural. `13.10 C`

Playing Games

1. Chess is difficult to play well.
   Go is difficult to play well.

   Both chess and go are difficult to play well.

2. Board games can be a great way for people to socialize.
   Sports can be a great way for people to socialize.
3. Tennis provides a good workout.
   Swimming provides a good workout.
4. Computer games are not good for physical fitness.
   Board games are not good for physical fitness.
5. Soccer is a fast-moving sport.
   Basketball is a fast-moving sport.
6. Soccer doesn't require a lot of equipment.
   Basketball doesn't require a lot of equipment.
7. Adults like to play games.
   Children like to play games.
8. Card games can be fun for the family.
   Board games can be fun for the family.
9. Chess isn't a game for small children.
   Bridge isn't a game for small children.

chess

go

bridge

[16] **diverse:** very different from each other

46 | Error Correction Correct any errors in these sentences. (Some sentences may not have any errors.)

1. Both my school and my job is on Cuesta Avenue.
2. Neither of brothers is married.
3. Nor my high school teacher nor my college teacher told me about this rule.
4. Both parent told me to study tonight.
5. Neither the movies we saw was very good.
6. Both my sister love that song.
7. Neither the strawberries nor the lemons is ripe yet.
8. Both of computers have been having problems lately.
9. Neither the classes is very difficult.
10. Neither the printer nor the scanner are working.

WRAP-UP Demonstrate Your Knowledge

A | GROUP DISCUSSION Work in a group. Take turns discussing these topics. Talk about each topic one at a time. Use expressions from the box below to make comparisons about the topic. When everyone has spoken about the topic, go on to the next topic.

"An SUV is not as much fun as a sports car."
"A sports car goes faster than an SUV."

TOPICS

1. a sports car vs. an SUV
2. a school cafeteria vs. a restaurant
3. taking a bus vs. driving a car
4. a supermarket vs. a small grocery store
5. running vs. swimming
6. reading a book vs. watching a movie
7. a university vs. a high school
8. one famous person vs. another (your choice)

EXPRESSIONS		
(not) as . . . as	different (from)	neither
-er than	like	neither of
more than	alike	both . . . and . . .
the same (as)	both	neither . . . nor . . .
similar (to)	both of	

B | SURVEY Work with a small group. Follow these instructions to complete a group survey.

1. Work together to complete these survey questions. As a group, write three more questions to add to the survey.

2. Use the survey questions to interview several classmates who are not in your group. Write short answers.

3. Return to your group and report back on your classmates' answers.

"The most interesting place Isabel has ever visited is Malaysia."

Questions	Answers
1. What's the most interesting _____ you have ever _____?	
2. What's the best _____ you have ever _____?	
3. Who is the _____ person you know?	
4. What is the _____ place you have ever _____?	
5. What is the most difficult _____ you have ever _____?	
6. What is the worst _____ you have ever _____?	
7. What is one of your least favorite _____?	
8.	
9.	
10.	

C | **WEB SEARCH** Look online for descriptions of two similar products or places; for example, two tourist destinations, hotels, restaurants, cars, or phones. Write sentences to compare the two things.

Museums of Mexico

MEXICO CITY

MONTERREY

The National Museum of Anthropology was established in 1964. It gets about two million visitors a year. The museum has 23 rooms and many outdoor gardens. The exhibits include thousands of items that show the history of Mexico.

Open Tues.–Sun. from 9 a.m. to 7 p.m.

General admission: $57 MN[17]

The Museum of Contemporary Art was established in 1991. It has 11 rooms and covers 5,000 square meters, with a large central garden. It gets thousands of visitors a year. The exhibits include paintings from contemporary Latin American artists.

Open Tues. and Thurs.–Sun. from 10 a.m. to 6 p.m., Wed. from 10 a.m. to 8 p.m.

General admission: $70 MN

The two museums are not in the same city.
The Museum of Contemporary Art is newer.
The National Museum of Anthropology is bigger and gets more visitors.
The Museum of Contemporary Art isn't open as many hours.

D | **WRITING** Choose one of the topics from this box or another topic, and write a paragraph about it. Use some of the language for expressing comparisons that you learned in this unit.

TOPICS
two ways of losing weight
a good boss and a bad boss
this decade and another decade
two famous stories or movies
driving a car vs. taking public transportation
a warm-weather vacation vs. a cold-weather vacation
working as a server in a restaurant vs. working as a flight attendant

Some people try to lose weight by eating <u>fewer</u> calories, and some people try to lose weight by exercising. Exercise is important because it helps you build muscle, and muscles burn calories <u>faster</u> than fat does. Exercise also makes you feel good, so you are <u>less likely</u> to go off your diet. <u>However</u>, most overweight people need to change their diets, too. You don't need to count every calorie. If you choose <u>healthier</u> food and eat <u>smaller</u> servings, you will lose weight. <u>Both</u> exercise <u>and</u> diet are important for losing weight.

[17] **MN:** national money of Mexico

DESCRIBING SIMILARITIES	as + adjective / adverb + as as + much / many + noun + as	His hair is just **as black as** it used to be. I can run **as fast as** you can. I have **as much time as** you need.
	the same (as)	This picture is **the same as** that one. These pictures are **the same**.
	similar (to)	Your idea is **similar to** mine. Our ideas are **similar**.
	like	The clouds look **like** a herd of white elephants.
	alike	Their stories are very much **alike**.
	similarly	They finished the highway very quickly last year. **Similarly,** the bridge is going to be finished early this year.
	in the same way	Your teachers give you exams to learn your progress. **In the same way,** your employers will do evaluations of your work.
	both / both of	**Both** cars are very old. But **both of them** run quite well.
	neither / neither of	**Neither** book is very interesting. Fortunately, **neither of them** is required for this class.
	both . . . and	**Both** Spain **and** Portugal are located on the Iberian Peninsula.
	neither . . . nor	**Neither** this school **nor** my old one has a cafeteria.
DESCRIBING DIFFERENCES	not as + adjective / adverb + as not as much + noncount noun / many + count noun + as	I'm **not as energetic as** my sister. I can't run **as fast as** you can. I don't have **as much time as** I used to.
	-er / more / less forms of adjectives and adverbs	This view is even **lovelier** than the last one. She talks **louder** than I do. He's running **less often** these days.
	more / less / fewer + noun	Coffee has **more caffeine** than soda. They're making soy sauce with **less salt** in it now.
	verb + more / less	He **calls more** than he should. They **are eating less** than they used to.
	different (from)	Her left shoe is **different from** her right shoe. They like **different** kinds of food.
	in contrast	Our public transportation is fast, efficient, and cheap. **In contrast,** private cars get stuck in traffic and use expensive gasoline.
	on the other hand	He is very smart and does excellent work. **On the other hand,** he doesn't get along with his co-workers very well.
	however	It sounds like a good idea. **However,** I don't know all of the details yet, so I might be wrong.
-EST / MOST / LEAST ADJECTIVES AND ADVERBS	the + -est / most / least forms of adjectives and adverbs	That's **the yellowest rose** I've ever seen. Khalid runs **the fastest** of all of us. That is **the least attractive** option.
	the most / least / fewest + noun	Could you give me the one with **the least sugar**? John has **the most experience** with these things.

14 Sentence Patterns

We don't laugh because we're happy—we're happy because we laugh.

—WILLIAM JAMES,
AMERICAN PHILOSOPHER
(1842–1910)

Talk about It What does the quotation above mean? Do you agree or disagree?

WARM-UP

A | Match the beginnings of these proverbs with the endings. What does each proverb mean? Is there a similar one from your culture? Share your ideas with the class.

PROVERBS FROM AROUND THE WORLD

1. Make money, ____
2. It is the grass that suffers[1] ____
3. Men learn little from success, ____
4. Hope is a great breakfast, ____
5. Don't count your chickens ____
6. Wait until night ____

a. when elephants fight. (*African*)
b. but it is a poor dinner. (*Czech*)
c. before you say it has been a fine day. (*French*)
d. but they can learn much from failure. (*Arabian*)
e. but don't let money make you. (*Danish*)
f. before they hatch[2]. (*Greek*)

B | Answer these questions about the sentences above.
1. Circle the verbs in each sentence. Do all the sentences have verbs in both halves?
2. Underline the subjects in each sentence. Do all the sentences have subjects in both halves?
3. What words connect the two parts of each sentence?
4. Could the part on the left be a complete sentence? Could the part on the right be a complete sentence? If not, why not?
5. Which verbs (besides *be*) are followed by a noun or noun phrase?

C | Look back at the quotation on page 438. Identify all the verbs and any connecting words.

---

[1] **suffer:** to experience something bad

[2] **hatch:** to come out of an egg

14.1 Sentences, Clauses, and Phrases

A

SIMPLE SENTENCES WITH ONE CLAUSE

subject (noun phrase)	predicate (the verb and everything after it)
1 My uncle	is going to go to the store.
2 My friend	had never ridden a bicycle before today.

SENTENCES WITH TWO CLAUSES

subject	predicate	subject	predicate
3 The flight	arrived early	but there	wasn't a gate for the plane.

subject	predicate	subject	predicate
4 He	couldn't sleep last night	because the rain	was so loud.

Most sentences contain one or more **clauses**. Every clause has two main parts, as in **1 – 2**:

• a **subject**—a noun phrase near the beginning of the clause

• a **predicate**—one (or more than one) verb and everything that comes after it

Many sentences contain more than one clause, as in **3 – 4**. See Chart 14.8 for more information about these kinds of sentences.

B

PHRASES

noun phrase	verb	noun phrase and other phrase types
5 A child		a big responsibility. (noun phrase)
6 She	is	really happy. (adjective phrase)
7 Your mother		on the phone. (prepositional phrase)
8 My grandmother	walks	very slowly. (adverb phrase)

Within clauses, we use words together in natural groups called **phrases**. Examples of some phrase types are shown in **5 – 8**.

WARNING! A phrase is not a complete sentence.

GRAMMAR TERMS: A complete clause is also called a **main** or **independent clause**.

 GO ONLINE

1 | Identifying Subjects and Predicates Underline the subject of each clause. Circle the predicate.

14.1 A

HIGHLAND UNIVERSITY

Office of Admissions

Dear Amanda:

Congratulations! You have been accepted to Highland University!

Highland University has a lot to offer you. Our faculty can provide you with an excellent education, and we have many exciting student organizations. We offer small classes, active learning, and many opportunities for international study.

The registration form is enclosed[3]. If you would like a place in our fall class, you must mail this form to us no later than May 1.

Our Spring Orientation programs begin in April. I hope to see you on campus then.

Sincerely,

Michaela Turner

Michaela Turner
Director of Admissions

Think about It Which sentences above have one clause? Which have two clauses?

[3] **enclosed:** in the envelope

2 | Identifying Phrases and Clauses Label the phrases *P* and the clauses *C*. Add a capital letter and final punctuation to each complete sentence. `14.1 A`

SUMMER FUN

_P_ 1. my favorite time of year

____ 2. to the beach for the day

____ 3. I love to swim in the ocean

____ 4. the community swimming pool

____ 5. the water is a nice escape[4] from the heat

____ 6. my family sometimes eats dinner in the backyard

____ 7. on warm July evenings

____ 8. the long days pass quickly

____ 9. delicious summer fruit

____ 10. six weeks of vacation

> **F Y I**
>
> In writing, we add a capital letter and final punctuation (usually a period or a question mark) to a clause to make **a simple sentence**.

Write about It Write complete sentences using the phrases above.

1. Summer is my favorite time of year.

Think about It What did you add to each phrase above to make it a complete sentence? Did you add a subject? A predicate? Something else?

3 | Identifying Kinds of Phrases Study the information in the box. Then label the highlighted phrases below as noun phrases (*NP*), prepositional phrases (*PP*), adjective phrases (*AdjP*), and adverb phrases (*AdvP*). `14.1 B`

> **Noun phrase** = (determiner) + (adjective) + noun + (prepositional phrase/adjective clause): *the young men in my class*
> **Prepositional phrase** = preposition + noun phrase: *at the bank*
> **Adjective phrase** = (adverb) + adjective: *extremely difficult*
> **Adverb phrase** = (adverb) + adverb: *very slowly*

Albert Einstein

                                           PP

1. Albert Einstein was born in Germany   in 1879.

2. When he was a child, his head was unusually large.

3. His parents were quite worried about him.

4. In addition, he began speaking fairly late.

5. But his parents didn't worry for very long.

6. When he was a young boy, he was very interested in his father's compass[5].

7. He learned advanced mathematics very quickly.

8. He always got excellent scores on physics and math tests.

9. Before World War II, Einstein moved to the United States.

10. Most people consider him   one of the world's most brilliant scientists.

---

[4] **escape:** a way of getting away from a place or situation

[5] **compass:** a thing for finding directions, with a needle that always points north

A

	subject	verb	direct object
1	Sarah	found	**a key.** (Found what?)
2	He	is holding	**the baby.** (Holding what?)

	subject	verb	indirect object	direct object
3	Tom	got	**his son** (For whom?)	**a computer.**
4	She	is making	**them** (For whom?)	**lunch.**

	subject	verb	direct object	indirect object
5	Ron	brought	**presents**	**for the children.**
6	They	gave	**the check**	**to us.**

To give a complete meaning, some verbs need a **direct object** (usually a kind of noun phrase), as in **1 – 2**. We call these **transitive** verbs.

We can use some transitive verbs with two objects—direct and indirect. An **indirect object** answers the question *to or for whom or what.*

- We usually place indirect objects before direct objects in a sentence, as in **3 – 4**.
- Sometimes we put an indirect object after a direct object using **to** or **for**, as in **5 – 6**.

EXAMPLES OF VERBS THAT ARE USED TRANSITIVELY

VERBS THAT CAN USE A DIRECT OBJECT				
carry	find	know	put	see
catch	forgive	like	raise	take
create	get	lose	receive	use
enjoy	hold	need	remember	want
expect	keep	push	say	watch

VERBS THAT CAN USE BOTH A DIRECT AND AN INDIRECT OBJECT		
buy	give	promise
bring	hand	sell
cook	make	teach
get	offer	throw

4 | Identifying Direct and Indirect Objects Underline the direct objects and circle the indirect objects in this article. `14.2 A`

Salt

Salt has been very important in human history. We need <u>salt</u> to live, and we also preserve[6] food with salt. Long ago, people followed animals to find salt, and when they ate a lot of meat, they got all the salt they needed. However, when people began farming, they needed more salt and it became very valuable.

People traded[7] salt around the world. In some places, traders exchanged gold for an equal amount of salt. Egyptian ships brought salt to the Greeks. In Abyssinia, people used rock salt as money. The Romans gave salt to their soldiers as part of their pay. The English word *salary* comes from this ancient use of salt.

Nowadays, of course, many people eat too much salt. We put it on almost everything we eat.

[6] **preserve:** to keep something in good condition   [7] **trade:** to buy and sell

Think about It What kinds of verbs use indirect objects? Do you notice any similar meaning or pattern among them?

5 | Using Indirect Objects Complete these sentences with direct and indirect objects and your own ideas. `14.2 A`

THINGS I'VE NEVER DONE

1. I've never taught _____*my classmates*_____ _____*a Chinese song*_____.
2. I've never made _____ _____.
3. I've never cooked _____ for _____.
4. I've never thrown _____ _____.
5. I've never brought _____ for _____.
6. I've never bought _____ for _____.
7. I've never offered _____ _____.
8. I've never given _____ to _____.

Talk about It Share your sentences above with a partner. Tell your partner if you would like to do any of the things you wrote about.

"I'd like to teach my classmates a Chinese song."

Write about It Rewrite each sentence above, changing the order of the direct and indirect object. Add a preposition if necessary.

1. I've never taught a Chinese song to my classmates.

6 | Using Direct and Indirect Objects Complete the chart below. Write sentences about things that have happened recently. Use the verbs in the box. (Some sentences will not have an indirect object.) `14.2 A`

ask	enjoy	give	hand	leave	offer	remember	send	tell

IN THE LAST WEEK				
Subject	**Verb**	**Indirect object**	**Object**	**Rest of sentence**
1. *My teacher*	*handed*	*me*	*my last test*	*yesterday.*
2.				
3.				
4.				
5.				
6.				
7.				
8.				
9.				

7 | Error Correction Correct any errors in these sentences. (Some sentences may not have any errors.)

1. It remembered me my last day of school.
2. My uncle is teaching to me the family business.
3. We bought that software because we really needed.
4. He says me, "Good morning" every day.
5. He brought to her a chocolate cake.
6. No, thanks. I don't want.
7. Thank you so much for giving it us.
8. We enjoyed very much the dinner.

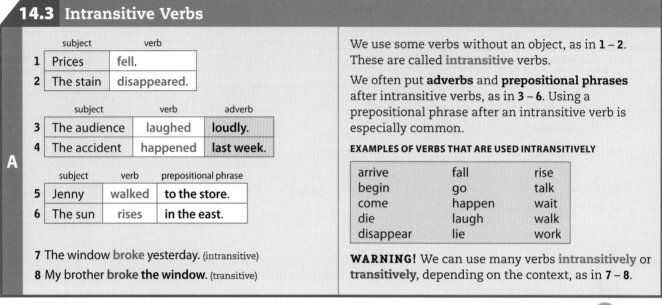

14.3 Intransitive Verbs

A

	subject	verb
1	Prices	fell.
2	The stain	disappeared.

	subject	verb	adverb
3	The audience	laughed	**loudly.**
4	The accident	happened	**last week.**

	subject	verb	prepositional phrase
5	Jenny	walked	**to the store.**
6	The sun	rises	**in the east.**

7 The window **broke** yesterday. (intransitive)
8 My brother **broke the window.** (transitive)

We use some verbs without an object, as in **1 – 2**. These are called **intransitive** verbs.

We often put **adverbs** and **prepositional phrases** after intransitive verbs, as in **3 – 6**. Using a prepositional phrase after an intransitive verb is especially common.

EXAMPLES OF VERBS THAT ARE USED INTRANSITIVELY

arrive	fall	rise
begin	go	talk
come	happen	wait
die	laugh	walk
disappear	lie	work

WARNING! We can use many verbs **intransitively** or **transitively**, depending on the context, as in **7 – 8**.

8 | Identifying Transitive and Intransitive Verbs Read this article. Write *I* above the **bold** intransitive verbs and *T* above the **bold** transitive verbs as they are used in the article. `14.3 A`

The Invisible Gorilla

It is a simple test: **watch** a video of people playing basketball. Some players **are wearing** white shirts and some are wearing black shirts. **Count** the passes of the players in white shirts.

Christopher Chabris and Daniel Simons first **gave** people this test in 1999. Participants counted the passes without any problem. But something unusual **happened** during the game: a man in a gorilla suit **walked** by. About half of the test participants didn't see him.

Since that time, Chabris and Simons have the given "the invisible gorilla" test hundreds of times. The same thing always **happens**. When the gorilla **arrives**, almost half of the people don't **notice** him because they are concentrating on something else. In one version of the experiment, participants **talked** on a cell phone while they counted the passes. About 90 percent of these people **did not see** the gorilla.

Because "the invisible gorilla" became world-famous, Simons decided to try again in 2010 with a different test. This time, people knew about the gorilla test, so they **expected** something unusual to happen. In the new video, a gorilla **appears** in the middle of a basketball game and **stands** in front, so everyone **sees** him. However, two other unexpected things also happen: one of the players **disappears** and the curtain behind them changes color. When Simons gave this test, only 17 percent of the people **noticed** these two things. This shows that even when we are **prepared** for them, we are not good at noticing unusual events.

Think about It Find the intransitive verbs in Activity 8 that are followed by prepositional phrases. Circle the prepositional phrases.

9 | Using Intransitive Verbs Write complete answers to these questions. Then ask and answer the questions with a partner. `14.3 A`

GETTING TO KNOW YOU

1. When was the last time you laughed a lot? What were you laughing at?

   I laughed a lot on Saturday night. I was laughing at a TV show.

2. Who was the last person you talked to? What did you talk about?
3. Where would you like to work someday?
4. How often do you cook? Who do you cook for?
5. Besides the people you live with, who do you talk to the most? How do you communicate? (For example, in person, online, or on the phone?)
6. Have you ever fallen and hurt yourself? What happened?
7. Where do you go during your free time?
8. What do you really hate to wait for?
9. How often do you sing? Where do you sing?

Think about It Underline the verbs in the answers you wrote above. How many did you follow with a prepositional phrase? What is after the other verbs?

Think about It Which of the verbs above can you use transitively? Write a sentence using the verb transitively if possible.

10 | Error Correction Correct any errors in these sentences. (Some sentences may not have any errors.)

1. The teacher handed my test.
2. The accident happened us yesterday.
3. She was very angry at her parents, but she finally forgave.
4. Someone disappeared the car!
5. He arrived school early this morning.
6. I saw to her in the bus station last night.
7. My boss promised to me a raise.
8. He waited me for a long time yesterday.
9. I used to have a bicycle, but someone stole.
10. The teacher talked us about the schedule.

14.4 Linking Verbs

A

LINKING VERB + ADJECTIVE COMPLEMENT

1 She **seems** tired.

2 Your job **sounds** really exciting.

3 Marty **looks** upset. I wonder what**'s** wrong.

4 After two years, he **became** very ill.

5 When I told her what happened, she **got** really mad.

LINKING VERB + OTHER COMPLEMENTS

6 My sister **became** a doctor after many years of study*.

7 He **is** a very nice man.

8 The dishes **are** in the cabinet.

9 I **am** certain about this. (NOT: ~~I am certainly about this.~~)

Linking verbs are a special type of intransitive verb. However, like transitive verbs, they need something else to make them complete—called a **complement**.

For all linking verbs, we can use an adjective complement, as in **1 – 5**.

EXAMPLES OF COMMON LINKING VERBS

be	feel	look	smell
become	get	seem	sound

We can also use *become* and *be* with other forms:

• *become* + noun phrase*, as in **6**

• *be* + noun phrase*, as in **7**

• *be* + prepositional phrase, as in **8**

*Notice that a noun phrase after *be* or *become* is not a direct object—it tells more about the subject. It does not receive the action of the verb.

WARNING! We do not use an adverb as a complement for a linking verb, as in **9**.

 ONLINE

11 | Identifying Linking Verbs Underline the linking verbs in these conversations. Then practice with a partner. `14.4 A`

CONVERSATIONS ON CAMPUS

1. A: Your friend <u>seems</u> really nice.

   B: She is. We should all have lunch sometime.

   A: Sounds good!

2. A: I was looking for you yesterday.

   B: I wasn't on campus. I was at work, actually.

   A: Oh, you got a job? Congratulations!

3. A: Your lunch smells delicious! What is it?

   B: Noodle soup. My mom made it.

4. A: Do you know that guy?

   B: Yeah, I do. He's in my business class.

   A: He looks very excited about something.

   B: He is. He just won the student council[8] election.

5. A: I haven't seen Joseph lately.

   B: I know. He got sick last week and hasn't come back yet.

6. A: I can't find my phone. I've looked everywhere!

   B: Did you try Lost and Found? It's in the main office.

7. A: Did you hear they're going to put in a new engineering building?

   B: No, where?

   A: Right behind the old one. It's going to be very nice.

   B: Well, I hope they finish it before I graduate!

8. A: Have you heard about the new economics professor?

   B: Yeah. Everyone is talking about him. His classes sound very interesting.

[8] **student council:** student government

WARNING!

We can use some verbs as both **linking** verbs and **transitive** verbs.

That pot roast really **smells delicious**! (linking verb)

I can really **smell the flowers** at this time of year. (transitive verb)

9. A: Marco is in really good shape.

   B: He spends a lot of time at the gym. I think he wants to become a personal trainer.

Think about It Circle the complement of each linking verb in Activity 11. Is it an adjective phrase, a prepositional phrase, or a noun phrase? Which linking verbs do not include the complement? Why?

Talk about It Talk with a partner about your impressions of people and things at school. Use *be*, *seem*, *become*, *feel*, *look*, *sound*, and *smell*.

12 | Error Correction Correct any errors in these sentences. Use the same verb. You may need to write a new complement. (Some sentences may not have any errors.)

1. This class seems a lot of difficulty.
2. Your father sounds a nice man.
3. Sora had no one to talk to at the picnic. She felt out of place.
4. That chair looks really comfortably.
5. Did I cook this too long? It smells burning.
6. Why does Matilda look so seriously? Did something happen?
7. Sang isn't here. He got too much anger and walked out.
8. She became very famously, but she was still unhappy.

14.5 Questions

YES/NO QUESTIONS

—	first helping verb or *be*	subject	rest of the sentence
1	Are	they	going?
2	Has	he	ever **been** there?
3	Do	you	have a dollar?

MOST WH- QUESTIONS

	wh- word	first helping verb	subject	rest of the sentence
4	What time	does	he	leave tonight?
5	Where	did	you	go on vacation?
6	What	are	they	doing?
7	Why	have	they	left so early?

In *yes/no* questions and most *wh-* questions, the first helping verb (or *be*) comes before the subject, as in **1 – 7**.

WH- QUESTIONS ABOUT THE SUBJECT

	wh- word (subject)	helping and main verbs	—	rest of the sentence
8	Who	has been		here before?
9	What	is going on		downtown?
10	What	happened		yesterday?
11	Who	comes		to these meetings?

In some *wh-* questions, the *wh-* word is the subject. We put the *wh-* question word first, followed by the rest of the sentence, as in **8 – 11**.

WARNING! Simple present and simple past questions about the subject do not need a helping verb, as in **10 – 11**.

NEGATIVE YES/NO QUESTIONS

12 A: **Isn't** Anna **coming** home for dinner? I expected her at 5.
   B: Yeah, she is. She'll be here in a few minutes.

13 A: **Doesn't** Alan **like** the food?
   B: No, he doesn't.
   A: I'm surprised. I thought he loved this dish.

We sometimes use **negative yes/no questions** to confirm an expectation, as in **12 – 13**. We ask the question with a negative because something didn't happen (or isn't happening) in the way we expected.

13 | Forming Questions Write questions about activities. Use your own ideas. Then, for each question, circle the first helping verb (or the main verb *be*), and underline the subject. `14.5 A`

Activity Survey

1. What _____ (are) you doing _____ tomorrow?
2. What _____ yesterday?
3. Have you ever _____?
4. Are you going to _____ next week?
5. Did you _____ last week?
6. Where does _____?
7. Where is _____?
8. How often _____?
9. Are you _____?
10. Where do you _____?
11. Were you _____?
12. Does _____?

Talk about It Compare your questions above with a partner. How did you complete them differently? Then ask and answer the questions.

A: *What are you doing tomorrow?*
B: *Well, I have class and then I have to work.*

14 | Identifying *Wh-* Questions about the Subject Circle the *wh-* questions about the subject in this conversation. (Not every numbered item has a *wh-* question about the subject.) `14.5 A`

THE NEXT DAY

1. A: So who came to the dinner?

   B: Carlos, Amy, Kevin, Rita . . . the usual people.

2. A: Did you see Lisa?

   B: Yeah, she was there. She got into an argument with Rita.

   A: Really? What happened?

   B: Someone told Lisa that Rita was talking about her.

3. A: Who told her that?

   B: I have no idea. But Lisa was mad! Rita denied⁹ it, though.

4. A: Did Lisa believe her?

   B: I think so. Rita is a nice person. . . . So where did you go last night?

5. A: I went to work. Someone called in sick, so I worked some extra hours.

   B: Who called in sick?

   A: Matt.

   B: Oh, really? That's funny. Matt was at dinner with us!

⁹**deny:** to say something isn't true or didn't happen

15 | Writing *Wh-* Questions Read this article about the explorers. Then complete the questions below about each explorer. `14.5 A`

EXPLORERS

1. The Vikings were early explorers from Northern Europe. They built long wooden boats and explored great distances. From the eighth to the twelfth centuries, they explored as far east as Constantinople and as far west as Newfoundland.
2. Later, there was a lot of exploration from Southern Europe. Ferdinand Magellan sailed from the Atlantic to the Pacific Ocean and then across the Pacific. His expedition[10] was the first one to travel around the globe. Magellan didn't make the whole voyage[11], though, because he died in battle in the Philippines.
3. Hernán Cortéz traveled from Spain to the Americas about the same time as Magellan. He led the expedition that caused the Aztec empire to fall.
4. Francisco Pizarro was also from Spain. He was a distant cousin of Hernán Cortéz. He conquered the Inca empire in Peru.
5. Europeans were not the only explorers. Ahmad ibn Fadlan was an Arab explorer in the tenth century who traveled to what is now Central Russia. He described the people he saw there. Today many scholars believe these are the earliest descriptions of the Vikings.
6. Zheng He was a Chinese explorer who led voyages to Southeast Asia, the Middle East, and East Africa. He lived from 1371 to 1433.

QUESTIONS

1. Question: ___Who built_____ long wooden boats for exploration?
   Answer: The Vikings.
   Question: Where _____?
   Answer: Northern Europe.

2. Question: _____ an expedition that traveled around the globe?
   Answer: Magellan.
   Question: _____ the whole voyage?
   Answer: Because he died in the Philippines.

3. Question: _____ travel?
   Answer: About the same time as Magellan.
   Question: _____ his expedition do?
   Answer: It caused the fall of the Aztec empire.

4. Question: _____ a distant cousin of Cortéz?
   Answer: Pizarro.
   Question: _____ conquer?
   Answer: The Inca empire in Peru.

> **STUDY STRATEGY**
> Writing questions about the material you're studying can help you prepare for tests.

[10] **expedition:** a long trip for a special purpose   [11] **voyage:** a long trip by ship or in space

5. Question: _____ to Central Russia

in the tenth century?

Answer: Ahmad ibn Fadlan.

Question: _____

Answer: The people he saw there. (Possibly the Vikings.)

6. Question: _____ to Southeast Asia,

the Middle East, and East Africa?

Answer: Zheng He.

Question: _____

Answer: From 1371 to 1433.

Talk about It Ask and answer the questions in Activity 15 with a partner. Try to answer from memory.

16 | Usage Note: Answering Negative Questions Read the note. Then do Activity 17.

Answer **negative questions** the same way you would answer **positive questions**. In other words, answer them according to the truth of the situation.

TRUTH: MARIA GOT HERE AT 9:00.

A: **Did** Maria get here at 9?
B: **Yes, she did.** ⟶ A: **Didn't** Maria get here at 9?
B: **Yes, she did.**

A: **Did** Maria get here at 8?
B: **No. She got here at 9.** ⟶ A: **Didn't** Maria get here at 8?
B: **No. She got here at 9.**

17 | Asking Negative Questions Complete these conversations. Write negative questions using the verbs in parentheses. (Many different questions are possible.) Then practice with a partner. `14.5 B`

1. A: All I see are sandals and tennis shoes. _Don't you sell boots?_ _____ (sell)

   B: I'm sorry. We only sell boots in the fall and winter.

2. A: Why do we need to have a conference? _____ (be)

   B: Oh, yes. Kate's a wonderful student. I'm making appointments with all of the parents.

3. A: It's so crowded here already! _____ (open)

   B: Yes, we just opened last weekend. Our food has been getting great reviews.

4. A: Those are all so big! _____ (have)

   B: No, I'm sorry. This is the smallest soda we have.

5. A: I can't believe she doesn't want any! _____ (like)

   B: Yeah, she likes ice cream, but she just ate. She's full.

6. A: It's cold out here! _____ (need)

   B: I left my sweatshirt in the car. But I'll be OK once we start running.

7. A: He doesn't seem to understand me. _____ (speak)

   B: Yes, he can speak English. You just talk really fast.

8. A: You're going out tonight. _____ (study)

   B: Yeah, I should. But I don't feel like it.

Talk about It For each conversation in Activity 17, where do you think the people are? Who do you think is speaking?

Talk about It Choose one of the situations in Activity 17 and add three or four more lines. Try to use one more negative question.

14.6 Tag Questions

A

main clause with helping verb or *be*	helping verb or *be*	subject pronoun	
1 She **didn't go**,	did	she?	
2 You **aren't** worried,	are	you?	negative statement + positive tag
3 He **shouldn't go** alone,	should	he?	
4 They're **leaving** soon,	aren't	they?	
5 We've **been** here before,	haven't	we?	

main clause with no helping verb	*do* helping verb	subject pronoun	
6 They **live** here,	don't	they?	positive statement + negative tag
7 She **likes** garlic,	doesn't	she?	
8 You **met** the lawyer,	didn't	you?	

Tag questions are a kind of *yes/no* question. We often use them to confirm information in a statement.

- For main clauses with helping verbs or *be*: Repeat the helping verb or *be* + the subject pronoun, as in **1 – 5**.
- For main clauses with no helping verb: Use *don't*, *doesn't*, or *didn't* + the subject pronoun, as in **6 – 8**.

If the statement is negative, the tag is positive, as in **1 – 3**. If the statement is positive, the tag is negative, as in **4 – 8**.

18 | Pronunciation Note: Tag Questions Listen to the note. Then do Activity 19.

When we don't know if a statement we've made is true, we use a tag with rising intonation.

LESS CERTAIN STATEMENTS + TAG WITH RISING INTONATION

1 A: You live near here, **don't you?**
B: Yes. Just a few blocks away.

2 A: He isn't sick, **is he?**
B: No, I don't think so.

When we are fairly sure a statement we've made is true, we use a tag with falling intonation.

MORE CERTAIN STATEMENTS + TAG WITH FALLING INTONATION

3 A: You told her the answer, **didn't you?**
B: Yes, I did. Sorry.

4 A: You've been here before, **haven't you?**
B: Yes. A couple of times.

19 | Identifying Tag Question Intonation Listen to the questions. Draw a rising ⤴ or falling ⤵ intonation line over each tag. Then practice with a partner. **14.6 A**

1. A: You're staying for dinner, aren't you?
   B: I can't. I've got too much work to do.

2. A: You wanted coffee, didn't you?
   B: That's OK. Tea is fine.

3. A: He's visiting his sister, isn't he?
   B: I think he's on a business trip.

4. A: She isn't sick, is she?
   B: Nope. I just saw her at the mall.

5. A: You don't like cherries, do you?

   B: I like them. I just can't eat them—I'm allergic.

6. A: He's already taken this class, hasn't he?

   B: Yep. He took it last year.

7. A: The neighbors weren't home last night, were they?

   B: I didn't see them.

8. A: You'll call tomorrow, won't you?

   B: I promise.

> **F Y I**
>
> We answer tag questions in the same way we answer positive or negative questions. In other words, answer them according to the truth of the situation.
>
> A: You've finished, haven't you?
> B: Yes, I have. Thanks. / No, not yet.

20 | Using Tag Questions Complete these trivia questions. Add positive or negative tag questions to the main clauses for 1–10. In 11–18, use the verbs in parentheses to complete the main clauses with positive or negative forms. `14.6 A`

Trivia

1. Mount Everest is in the Himalayas, _____isn't it_____?

2. The Chinese invented paper, _____?

3. Jonas Salk developed the first polio vaccine[12], _____?

4. India doesn't border Russia, _____?

5. The Nile is the longest river, _____?

6. Humans can't see ultraviolet light, _____?

7. Delhi has a large population, _____?

8. Thomas Edison didn't invent the telephone, _____?

9. Switzerland doesn't have a coastline, _____?

10. Humans have walked on the moon, _____?

11. The Aztecs _____lived_____ in Mexico, didn't they? (live)

12. Sweden _____ an Olympics, hasn't it? (hold)

13. Cleopatra _____ Egypt, didn't she? (rule)

14. Shakespeare _____ English novels, did he? (write)

15. Benjamin Franklin never _____ as U.S. president, did he? (serve)

16. The world population _____ a lot, hasn't it? (increase)

17. Nelson Mandela _____ the president of South Africa, wasn't he? (be)

18. In the 1400s, many people _____ from the Black Plague[13], didn't they? (die)

Thomas Edison

Nelson Mandela

Talk about It Ask and answer the questions above with a partner. How many statements are true?

A: Mount Everest is in the Himalayas, isn't it?
B: Yes, it is.

Write about It Work with a partner. Write four trivia tag questions. Write two correct questions and two incorrect questions. Find a new partner and ask each other your questions.

---

[12] **polio vaccine:** a substance that protects against the disease polio

[13] **Black Plague:** a disease that spread quickly and killed many people

452

21 | Using Questions Complete these conversations. Write positive tag questions, negative questions, or questions about the subject for the responses. (Many different questions are possible.) If necessary, look back at Charts 14.5–14.6 for information on a question form.

1. A: Have you seen Tony today?

   B: *No. Isn't he at work?*

   A: Oh, you're right. I guess I'll see him later.

2. A: Here are the groceries.

   B: _____

   A: Oh, I forgot! I'll have to go back.

3. A: I think we're out of rice.

   B: _____

   A: No, we don't. I used it yesterday.

4. A: I don't think Sarah has finished the project.

   B: _____

   A: I don't know. I'll ask her.

5. A: We can't afford a new car.

   B: _____

   A: Yes, but we need to save that money for tuition.

6. A: It seems as if Ted is not talking to Alan.

   B: _____

   A: I don't know. I didn't hear about that.

7. A: I'm starving[14]!

   B: _____

   A: Maybe. I'll look.

8. A: I didn't get all the reading done.

   B: _____

   A: I don't know. I hope that's true!

9. A: Someone stole my bike last night.

   B: _____

   A: I thought I did. Maybe I forgot.

10. A: Paul still isn't here.

    B: _____

    A: Yes, but he isn't answering his phone.

Talk about It Compare the questions you wrote above with a partner. How did you complete the conversations differently? Then practice with your partner.

Think about It How can you rewrite each of your questions above using a different form? Does the meaning of the question change in any way? How?

1. He's at work, isn't he? **OR** *Is he at work?*

---

[14] **starving:** very hungry

14.7 Multi-word Verbs

A

1 Do you want to **try on** this shirt?

2 Did you **fill out** all the forms?

3 You need to **calm down**.

4 Watch out! The floor is slippery.
(watch out = be careful)

5 I **came across** an interesting article online.
(came across = found)

6 You really can't **do without** a car here.
(do without = manage not having)

We use some verbs together with a small word like *on*, *out*, *across*, and *down*, as in **1 – 3**. We call these verbs **multi-word verbs**.

Multi-word verbs function as a single word. They often have a meaning that is different from the meanings of the individual words, as in **4 – 6**.

GRAMMAR TERMS: Phrasal verbs and **prepositional verbs** are two kinds of **multi-word verbs**.

B

TRANSITIVE MULTI-WORD VERBS

7 Please **put away** your books.

8 Don't forget to **hand in** your homework.

9a She **turned down** a good job.

9b She **turned** a good job **down**.

9c She **turned down** a really good job at an entertainment company.

9d She **turned** it **down**.

We can use many multi-word verbs transitively (with an **object**), as in **7 – 8**.

One group of multi-word verbs are separable; the object can come in two places:

- directly after the multi-word verb, as in **9a**
- between the verb and the small word, as in **9b**

When the object is a long noun phrase, it usually comes directly after the multi-word verb, as in **9c**.

When the object is a pronoun, it usually comes between the verb and the small word, as in **9d**.

For a list of common transitive multi-word verbs, see the Resources, page R-6.

C

INTRANSITIVE MULTI-WORD VERBS

10 She isn't **coming back**.

11 My parents **dropped by** yesterday.

12 Wake up! It's already 10 o'clock.

We can use some multi-word verbs intransitively (without an object), as in **10 – 11**.

Notice that we often use intransitive multi-word verbs as imperatives, as in **12**.

For a list of common intransitive multi-word verbs, see the Resources, page R-7.

 ONLINE

22 | Understanding Multi-Word Verbs Complete each set of questions with the correct form of a multi-word verb from the box. `14.7 A`

1. How do you feel when you _____*get back*_____ from a long trip?

2. When do you usually _____ on the weekend?

3. Do you and your best friend always _____?

4. What is one good way to _____ in your career?

> **get ahead** = become more successful in something
> **get along** = have a friendly relationship
> **get back** = return
> **get up** = get out of bed

5. Do you _____ your mother or your father?

6. Is there a sport you would like to _____ someday?

7. Why do some people _____ more work than they can possibly do?

8. Do you usually _____ notes during class?

take after = be or look like an older member of your family

take down = write down something that is said

take on = accept or decide to do something

take up = start doing something regularly (for example, as a hobby)

9. How carefully do you _____ your homework before you hand it in?

10. When did you last _____ a word in a dictionary?

11. Why do people _____ holidays?

12. Who _____ you when you were a child?

look after = be responsible for or take care of someone or something

look forward to = wait for something with pleasure (because you expect to enjoy it)

look over = read something to see how good, interesting, etc., it is

look up = search for information—usually in a book

Talk about It Ask and answer the questions in Activity 22 with a partner.

A: How do you feel when you get back from a long trip?
B: I'm usually pretty happy to be home.

Talk about It Join another pair. Tell them three things you learned about your partner.

23 | Using Transitive Multi-Word Verbs Underline each multi-word verb in these conversations and circle the object. Then match each multi-word verb with a definition on the right. `14.7 B`

1. A: I can't figure out this remote.
   B: Yeah, it's really confusing. Did you try turning off the TV?
   A: Yes, but it didn't work.
   B: I have the manual if you want to look up the instructions.
   A: OK.

a. _____ = move the switch on a machine, etc., to stop it from working

b. _____ = search for information

c. _*figure out*_ = understand; find the answer to

2. A: I hear Tomas Garcia is taking over the accounting department.
   B: That's good news. He'll do a good job.

3. A: My brother turned down the job at the movie theater.
   B: How come?
   A: He got a better job at a restaurant.

4. A: Where is everyone?
   B: Maria called off the meeting. Didn't you hear?
   A: No, no one told me.

d. _____ = cancel

e. _____ = say no to something

f. _____ = take control or responsibility for something

5. A: Are you going to try on that shirt?

   B: Nah. I can't afford it anyway.

   A: I can lend you the money if you want.

   B: Really? Thanks. I'll pay back every cent.

6. A: You need to fill out this application today.

   B: Can't I do it tomorrow?

   A: You know, you really shouldn't put off

      something so important.

g. _____ = complete a printed form

h. _____ = delay doing something

i. _____ = give money back to the
   person you borrowed it from

j. _____ = put on clothing to see if it fits
   you and how it looks

Talk about It Practice the conversations in Activity 23 with a partner. Then practice them again and move the object between the verb and the small word.

*A: I can't <u>figure</u> **this remote** <u>out</u>.*
*B: Yeah, it's really confusing. Did you try <u>turning</u> **the TV** <u>off</u>?*

24 | Using Separable Multi-Word Verbs Work with a partner. Take turns reading a sentence aloud. The other person responds with a multi-word verb and *I've already . . . (pronoun) . . .* [14.7 B]

1. Don't forget to take out the trash.

   A: Don't forget to take out the trash.
   B: I've already taken it out.
   A: Thanks.

2. Don't forget to check over your homework.
3. Don't forget to fill out the form.
4. Don't forget to clean out the refrigerator.
5. Remember to turn down the heat before you go.

6. Don't turn the job down yet.
7. Remember. You promised to clean off the table.
8. Could you open up the windows for me?
9. Don't forget to put away the dishes.
10. Remember to shut off the lights upstairs.
11. Please don't throw out your drawings.
12. Remember to write down the directions.
13. Don't forget to pay back your sister.

Think about It Why does person B above answer with a pronoun instead of a noun phrase?

STUDY STRATEGY

To learn separable multi-word verbs, practice saying them in three different ways:

hand in my paper / **hand** my paper **in** /
hand it **in**

25 | Transitive or Intransitive? Is the writer using the **bold** multi-word verb transitively or intransitively? Write *T* (transitively) or *INT* (intransitively) above the verb. [14.7 C]

                 T
1. The best way to **work out** your problems is to talk about them.

2. When I spend a lot of time exercising, I sleep better at night.

   Then I feel more energetic when I **wake up** in the morning.

3. In 2011, Reza Pakravan **set out** on a 1,200-mile trip across the

   Sahara desert.

4. When I was ten years old, my parents gave me a special gold ring

   for my birthday. I wore it every day and never **took** it **off**.

FYI

Some multi-word verbs have a transitive meaning in one context and an intransitive meaning in another.

pay off (something) = pay all the money that you owe for something

pay off = be successful

5. After I **pay off** my school loans, my credit will get even better.

6. I **grew up** as a middle child. I have an older sister and younger brother.

7. When I feel stressed, I try to **slow down** my breathing, quiet my thoughts, and relax my muscles.

8. With my pale skin, green eyes, and red hair I definitely **stood out**.

9. On my first job I had to **show up** at 7:00 in the morning. The owner needed me to be there at that time and no later.

10. A good businessperson has to be able to make a plan for a successful business and then be able to work hard to **carry out** the plan. If your plan is a good one, then your hard work will **pay off** in the end. If you are not dedicated enough, then you may **give up** before your business has a chance to be successful.

Think about It What do you think each **bold** verb in Activity 25 means? Compare ideas with your classmates. Then check your answers by looking the verbs up in a dictionary.

Write about It Use each of the multi-word verbs in Activity 25 in a sentence of your own.

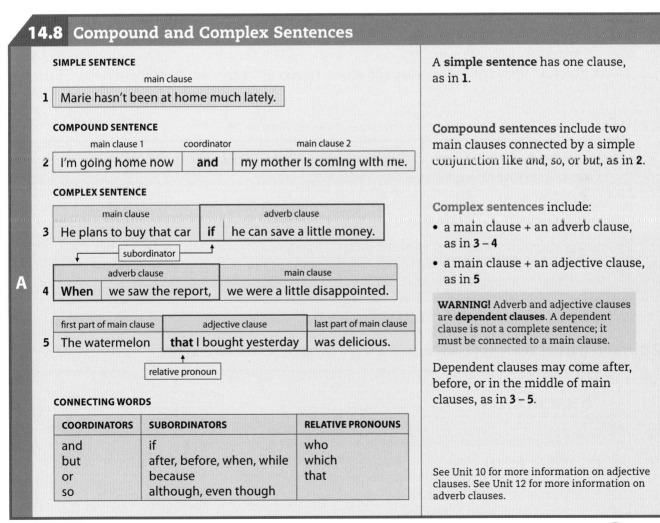

14.8 Compound and Complex Sentences

A

SIMPLE SENTENCE

main clause

1 | Marie hasn't been at home much lately. |

COMPOUND SENTENCE

main clause 1 | coordinator | main clause 2

2 | I'm going home now | **and** | my mother is coming with me. |

COMPLEX SENTENCE

main clause | adverb clause

3 | He plans to buy that car | **if** | he can save a little money. |

subordinator

adverb clause | main clause

4 | **When** | we saw the report, | we were a little disappointed. |

first part of main clause | adjective clause | last part of main clause

5 | The watermelon | **that** I bought yesterday | was delicious. |

relative pronoun

CONNECTING WORDS

COORDINATORS	SUBORDINATORS	RELATIVE PRONOUNS
and	if	who
but	after, before, when, while	which
or	because	that
so	although, even though	

A **simple sentence** has one clause, as in **1**.

Compound sentences include two main clauses connected by a simple conjunction like *and*, *so*, or *but*, as in **2**.

Complex sentences include:
• a main clause + an adverb clause, as in **3 – 4**
• a main clause + an adjective clause, as in **5**

WARNING! Adverb and adjective clauses are **dependent clauses**. A dependent clause is not a complete sentence; it must be connected to a main clause.

Dependent clauses may come after, before, or in the middle of main clauses, as in **3 – 5**.

See Unit 10 for more information on adjective clauses. See Unit 12 for more information on adverb clauses.

GO ONLINE

26 | Identifying Simple, Compound, and Complex Sentences Label each sentence as simple (*S*), compound (*CD*), or complex (*CX*). `14.8 A`

Travel Advice: Rio de Janeiro

1. We took two tours, and they were both great. _CD_

   The guides[15] who showed us around were very helpful. ____

2. If you haven't been to Sugar Loaf mountain, you really should go. ____

   The views from the top are amazing. ____

3. I recommend the hang-gliding tour. ____

   It's an incredible experience and it's not too expensive. ____

4. You can see some local art in the Centro Cultural Banco do Brasil. ____

   There are also a library and a cinema inside, so it's easy to spend a

   day there. ____

5. At Tijuca National Park, you can explore a tropical[16] forest right in the

   middle of the city. ____

   I recommend taking a tour because you can really see the less-visited

   places. ____ It's just beautiful. ____

Think about It Underline the adjective and adverb clauses in the complex sentences above.

---

27 | Usage Note: Using Commas Read the note. Then do Activity 28.

> We use a comma after an adverb clause when it comes before the main clause.
>> **If she wants to have dinner,** she should be here by 6:00.
>
> We usually do not use a comma before coordinators when they join two short main clauses.
>> He lives here **and** he works in Milton.
>
> However, if the clauses are long, we sometimes add a comma. The comma shows where one main clause ends and the next one begins.
>> We were going to come by after work, **but John's meeting didn't end until almost 8:00.**

---

28 | Punctuating Sentences Add a comma to the sentences if necessary. `14.8 A`

SHACKLETON

1. Ernest Henry Shackleton first went to Antarctica in 1901 but he became
   ill and had to go home.
2. He wanted to explore Antarctica so he returned there in 1907.
3. Because he went farther south than anyone else had the king of England
   honored him when he returned.

---

[15] **guides:** people who show places to tourists   [16] **tropical:** coming from the hottest, wettest parts of the world

4. Although he got close Shackleton was not the first person to reach the South Pole.
5. Roald Amundsen got to the South Pole first but Shackleton went back to Antarctica later for more exploration.
6. While his ship was approaching Antarctica it became trapped in the ice.
7. Shackleton hoped the ship would be able to escape when the warmer weather came in the spring.
8. The ship was destroyed and Shackleton and his men had to stay on the ice for almost 500 days. They all survived.

Think about It Look at the sentences above where you added a comma. How does having a comma help you understand the sentence better?

29 | Using Complex Sentences Rewrite these compound sentences as complex sentences with adverb clauses. Use the word in parentheses. Add a comma if necessary. `14.8 A`

City News

1. A new store opened in the mall yesterday, and traffic was terrible on Third Street. (because)

   Because a new store opened in the mall yesterday, traffic was terrible on Third Street.

2. The electricity went out, and a lot of people went to the park to keep cool. (when)
3. The city tore down some historical buildings and people are angry. (because)
4. The town opened a new library, but the old one is still crowded. (although)
5. They were putting in the new highway, and they discovered some ancient artifacts[17]. (while)
6. Some people are finding work, but unemployment is still high. (even though)
7. There was a third robbery at the gas station, and the police installed new security cameras. (after)
8. They cut a lot of trees down and they repaired the sidewalks[18]. (before)

Think about It Which of the sentences above sound better with a subordinator? Why?

30 | Using Complex Sentences Rewrite each compound sentence as a complex sentence with an adjective clause. `14.8 A`

SCHOOL DAYS

1. The students took the train today and they were late to class.

   The students who took the train today were late to class.

2. The teacher assigned a new book and it was really hard.
3. The counselor visited class last week and she spoke really fast.
4. We watched a video and I had seen it before.
5. The group presented first and they talked about Chile.

---

[17] **artifacts:** objects of historical interest

[18] **sidewalks:** raised surfaces on the side of a street for people to walk on

6. I spoke to a new student and she's from Morocco.

7. I bought a notebook for class and it was not the right size.

8. The teacher gave a lecture, and it really helped me understand the chapter.

31 | Combining Sentences Rewrite the sentences. Use the correct connecting word in parentheses. `14.8 A`

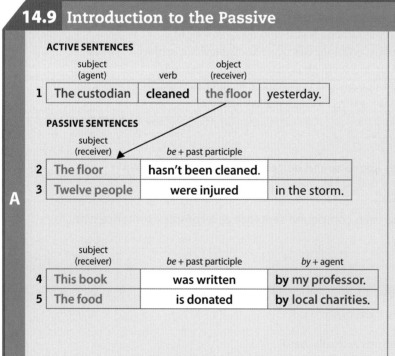

Restaurant Reviews

1. Try the delicious lobster. Stay away from the meat dishes. (although/but)

   Try the delicious lobster but stay away from the meat dishes.

2. Order any of their popular dishes. You'll be happy with your meal. (if/or)

3. I had a bowl of soup. It was the best I've ever tasted. (but/that)

4. The service at the Bamboo Restaurant was bad. They were very busy. (because/who)

5. The server was unfriendly. He brought our lunch. (and/who)

6. I've been to lots of steakhouses. I've never found a better one than Nico's. (because/but)

7. We were waiting for a table. They gave us a free cup of coffee. (if/while)

8. I heard that this was the best sushi place in town. I really wanted to try it. (after/so)

14.9 | Introduction to the Passive

ACTIVE SENTENCES

subject (agent)	verb	object (receiver)	
1 The custodian	**cleaned**	**the floor**	yesterday.

PASSIVE SENTENCES

subject (receiver)	*be* + past participle	
2 The floor	**hasn't been cleaned.**	
3 Twelve people	**were injured**	in the storm.

A

subject (receiver)	*be* + past participle	*by* + agent
4 This book	**was written**	**by** my professor.
5 The food	**is donated**	**by** local charities.

Most English sentences are **active**. In active sentences, we focus on the person or thing that causes or does the action—the **agent**, as in **1**.

Sometimes we want to focus on the **receiver** of the action instead of the agent—the person or thing that the action happens to. In this case, we use a **passive** verb form, as in **2 – 3**.

We use **be** + the **past participle of a main verb** (*-ed* / *-en* form) to form the passive. See Chart 14.12 for more examples.

We mention the agent only when it is important information. Then we often do it in a prepositional phrase with **by** + a noun phrase, as in **4 – 5**.

WARNING! We can only use transitive verbs in passive sentences (verbs with an object).

32 | Identifying Passive Verbs Circle the passive verb forms in these sentences. `14.9 A`

EARTHQUAKES

1. Earthquakes are caused by movements in the earth's crust[19].
2. Small earthquakes happen every day around the world.
3. They are measured using instruments called seismometers.
4. Most people don't notice earthquakes of magnitude[20] 2 and lower.
5. On the other hand, magnitude 7 earthquakes can cause a lot of damage.
6. Some earthquakes are deep and some are shallow.
7. The worst damage is usually caused by shallow earthquakes.
8. Other geological events[21], like tsunamis and volcanic eruptions, are sometimes caused by earthquakes.

Think about It How many of the sentences above have *by* phrases? In each case, can you explain why the *by* phrase was included?

33 | Using the Passive Circle the verbs in these sentences. Then rewrite each sentence in the passive. Do not include the agent. `14.9 A`

CRIME AND PREVENTION

1. Someone took a girl's bicycle.

   A girl's bicycle was taken.

2. Someone robbed the jewelry store three times.
3. Robbers stole money and jewelry from the safe.
4. Men guard both entrances to the bank.
5. An employee takes the money to the bank every day.
6. Cameras videotape the customers in the store.
7. The store owners always prosecute[22] shoplifters[23].
8. Police caught the thief in the park.
9. The police arrested the thief.
10. People steal things from supermarkets every day.

Think about It Why was the *by* phrase not necessary in the sentences above?

---

[19] **crust:** a hard layer on the surface of something
[20] **magnitude:** the power of an earthquake
[21] **geological events:** things that affect the land in a particular area

[22] **prosecute:** to officially charge someone with a crime in court
[23] **shoplifters:** people who steal from a store while pretending to be customers

34 | Using the Passive with *By* Phrases Complete the sentences below with the things and people in the boxes. You can look online for help if necessary. 14.9 A

CREATIONS, INVENTIONS, AND DISCOVERIES

the Eiffel Tower

Marie Curie

THINGS	
Don Quixote	the *Mona Lisa*
radium	the Olympics
the Eiffel Tower	the printing press
the Great Pyramid	*Titanic*

PEOPLE	
Gustave Eiffel	Marie Curie
James Cameron	Miguel de Cervantes
Johannes Gutenberg	the ancient Egyptians
Leonardo da Vinci	the ancient Greeks

1. *Radium* _____ was discovered by _____ *Marie Curie* _____ .
2. _____ was written by _____ .
3. _____ was invented by _____ .
4. _____ was directed by _____ .
5. _____ was built by _____ .
6. _____ was painted by _____ .
7. _____ were started by _____ .
8. _____ was designed by _____ .

Write about It Choose three of the passive verbs + *by* phrases above. Complete the sentences using other discoveries, inventions, or creations. Share your sentences with a partner.

35 | Using the Present Passive Rewrite the sentences that you think would sound better in the passive. Include the *by* phrase only if it seems important. Then compare your choices with classmates. 14.9 A

JOB ORIENTATION

1. The receptionists answer the phones.
2. You won't need to worry about the phone calls.
3. Someone opens the doors at 7 a.m.
4. Saul and Remy do most of the filing.
5. People store the office supplies in that cabinet.
6. You can call me if you need any help.
7. Someone picks up the mail in the afternoon.
8. Someone sets the alarm every evening.

14.10 Using Clauses and Phrases in Speaking

A

STRINGING TOGETHER SEVERAL CLAUSES

1 A: I went to the bank yesterday **and** I ran into Jeff, **and** he is doing great these days, **but** we didn't have too much time to talk **'cuz** I had to go to school, **but** I'm definitely going to call him soon and catch up more.
   B: Well, say hi for me.

In speaking, we often string together several clauses or phrases using **connecting words**, as in **1**.

The most common connecting words in speaking are *and*, *but*, *or*, *so*, and *because* (often pronounced /cos/ or /cuz/).

B

2 A: Why didn't you come with us last night?
   B: Because I just didn't have enough time.

3 A: I sold my guitar yesterday. . . .
   B: Which is a good thing. You needed the money.
   A: I know. Gonna miss it, though.

We often use just a **phrase** or a **dependent clause** alone as a response to a question or statement, as in **2 – 3**.

WARNING! We do not use dependent clauses alone in writing.

C

4 You can't wear that because of the dress code.

5 We have coffee, tea, and orange juice.

6 I stayed up late last night watching TV, / so I'm really tired today.

7 He's at home. / At least, / I think he is.

We use intonation and pauses to make our speech easier to understand.

- We often use falling intonation at the end of a clause or a series of words, as in **4 – 5**.
- We also sometimes put short pauses (/) after phrases and clauses. When you read aloud, punctuation can help you know when to pause, as in **6 – 7**.

D

USING *DO / DOES / DID* TO EMPHASIZE INFORMATION

8 A: Too bad you didn't go to the concert. It was great.
   B: I **DID** go! I was in the back, so you didn't see me.

9 A: Tom doesn't want to stay here, does he?
   B: He **DOES** want to stay. He's just not feeling well.

10 A: Did you live in Paris?
   B: Well, I didn't live in Paris, but I **DID** live in France for a while.

11 A: Didn't she take out the trash?
   B: She **did NOT** take out the trash. I took it out.

When we want to emphasize a contrast or unexpected information, we sometimes use the helping verbs **do / does** and **did** in positive statements, as in **8 – 10**. We **stress** the helping verb in these sentences.

We often do this to show emphasis or to disagree with another speaker's statement.

For negative statements, we sometimes use the full, uncontracted form for emphasis, as in **11**. In these sentences, we stress **not**.

GO ONLINE

36 | Identifying Connecting Words in Speaking Listen to the story about James Holman. Check (✓) the correct box each time you hear a connecting word. **14.10 A**

And	But	Or	So	Because ('cuz)

Think about It Which connecting word above is not used? Why do you think this is?

Talk about It Listen to the story again. Then retell the story to a partner. When you listen to your partner tell the story, note how many times he or she uses *and*, *but*, *or*, *so*, and *because*.

37 | Identifying Dependent Clauses and Phrases in Speaking Listen and write the responses to complete these conversations. Then practice with a partner. `14.10 B`

MAKING PLANS

1. A: Let's go for a walk. I need to wake up.

   B: *After I finish my essay.*

   A: OK. But how long will that take?

   B: _____

2. A: Let's invite Rosa.

   B: _____

   A: Yeah, her.

3. A: Why are you taking next week off?

   B: _____

   A: Nice! Post some pictures.

   B: _____

4. A: When are you going on vacation?

   B: _____

   A: I know what you mean.

5. A: Are you going to the show on Friday?

   B: _____

   A: Wow! You're really a fan.

6. A: Are you going to fold the laundry?

   B: Yeah. _____

   A: OK.

7. A: I hear you're leaving town for a few days.

   B: Yep. _____. Why not?

   A: Have fun.

8. A: When should we have dinner?

   B: _____. I'm starving.

38 | Using Phrases and Clauses in Speaking Complete each conversation with a clause. Use the connecting word provided and your own ideas. `14.10 B`

1. A: I love that game. It's so much fun.

   B: And _____.

   A: Yeah, that's true, too.

2. A: I fell asleep at 7 yesterday.

   B: Because _____?

   A: Well, maybe.

3. A: When should I make the rice?

   B: While _____?

   A: That's a good idea.

4. A: I kind of want to stay home tonight.

   B: But _____?

   A: Exactly.

5. A: Will you finish the reading on time?

   B: If _____.

6. A: When did you go to the restaurant?

   B: After _____.

7. A: When should we buy the cake?

   B: Before _____.

8. A: Why did you turn your phone off?

   B: Because _____.

Talk about It Compare the answers you wrote in Activity 38 with a partner. How did you complete the conversations differently? Then practice the conversations.

39 | Identifying Pauses Listen to the article. Mark every pause with a /. `14.10 C`

Shark Attack

A teenager was attacked by a shark on Saturday. / Matt Adama and a few friends were surfing when he fell off his board and felt a pain in his foot. At first he thought the pain was from stepping on a rock, but then he realized it was something much worse. He swam back to the shore, where a man helped him. The man, who had military training, tied something around Adama's leg to stop the bleeding. When paramedics[24] carried him off the beach, the teen was surprisingly cheerful, even smiling for the cameras. The wound[25] required 40 stitches[26], and doctors say it will take six weeks to recover. Adama says that he'll be back on his surfboard as soon as possible.

Talk about It Compare your answers above with a partner. Then take turns reading the story aloud. Remember to use falling intonation at the end of each sentence.

40 | Using Emphatic *Do* Ask and answer these questions with a partner. Give answers that describe your own life. Use emphatic responses, and provide an additional explanation or contrasting statement. `14.10 D`

EMPHASIZING CONTRASTING INFORMATION

1. You didn't wake up on time this morning, did you?

   "I DID wake up on time. I woke up as soon as my alarm rang."
   OR   *"You're right. I didn't wake up on time. I woke up an hour late."*

2. Didn't you work today?

---

[24] **paramedics:** people who have special training in helping sick or injured people but are not doctors
[25] **wound:** an injury, especially a cut

[26] **stitches:** short pieces of thread that doctors use to sew the edges of a cut together

3. You didn't use your computer last night, did you?
4. You don't really like school, do you?
5. Doesn't your best friend live in this city?
6. Didn't you eat breakfast this morning?
7. You don't study very much, do you?
8. You didn't watch TV last night, did you?

FYI

In sentences that use *be* as a main verb or have a helping verb (such as *be, have,* or *can*), we often show emphasis by using the uncontracted form.

A: You're not a student here.

B: I AM a student! Look—here's my ID.

14.11 Using Linking Expressions and Sentence Variety in Writing

A

USING LINKING EXPRESSIONS

1 We are selling very few of that model lately, and the prices have gone up. **As a result,** we're not going to order any more for next year.

2 She couldn't find the type of sugar she normally used in the cake recipe. **Instead,** she used regular brown sugar, and the cake was not as good as usual.

3 You need to watch the plants carefully and take care of any problems immediately. **For instance,** if the leaves begin to turn brown, you may need to water more often.

4 Technologies in food growing may end hunger in this century. **In addition,** as we learn how to cure more diseases, more people will live longer.

In addition to coordinators and subordinators, writers sometimes use **linking expressions** to connect ideas. Linking expressions include single adverbs, prepositional phrases, and other forms.

The most common way we use linking expressions is at the beginning of the second clause or sentence, followed by a comma, as in **1 – 4**. Linking expressions signal what comes next. For example:

- *as a result*: a result or consequence
- *instead*: The next sentence contrasts with an earlier statement.
- *for instance*: An example is coming next.
- *in addition*: We are adding new information.

See the Resources, page XXX, and Unit 11, Chart 11.9, for more linking expressions.

B

USING SENTENCE VARIETY

5 Many forms of exercise are good for you, **and** it's important to choose an enjoyable one. **For instance,** I love to play volleyball with friends. Volleyball gets you running and jumping. It also exercises your arms **as** you reach up to hit the ball. Stress is one of the worst things for your health, **but** enjoying yourself in a game helps to relieve stress. **While** you are playing, you forget about any problems or responsibilities you face.

In good writing, it is important to use a variety of sentence patterns. This makes our writing more interesting. The paragraph in **5** contains simple, compound, and complex sentences and a variety of connecting words.

GO ONLINE

41 | Identifying Linking Expressions Underline the linking expressions in this text. Then write *result*, *contrast*, *example*, or *new information*. **14.11 A**

Health

1. Your mental health is just as important as your physical health. Take time to do things that relieve stress and make you feel good. <u>For instance</u>, make sure that you spend some time with friends and family every day. _____*example*_____

2. Some people believe that it's not necessary to spend a lot of time exercising. Instead, they say, you should exercise hard for half an hour every day. _____

3. In many countries, fast food is becoming more and more popular, and people are exercising less. As a result, more people are overweight. _____

4. Heavily processed foods like packaged food, frozen food, or white bread often don't have enough nutrients and fiber. In addition, many processed foods have a lot of salt. _____

5. Many people feel that they don't have enough time to exercise, but you don't need to spend an hour at the gym every day. Instead, take a fast walk around your neighborhood in the evenings. _____

6. Processed carbohydrates like white bread quickly turn into sugar when you eat them. As a result, blood sugar rises quickly and then falls. This makes you feel hungry again sooner. _____

7. Different kinds of fruits and vegetables provide different vitamins, so you should eat a variety every day. For instance, you could eat berries with breakfast, an orange for a snack, and both a green and a yellow vegetable with dinner. _____

8. Eating a wide variety of fruits and vegetables helps you get all of the vitamins you need. In addition, if you eat a variety of foods, you are less likely to become bored with your diet. _____

processed foods   foods with many nutrients and fiber

42 | Using a Variety of Connecting Words Use the connecting words in the box to complete this essay. 14.11 A–B

Food Preparation: Then and Now

People are better off now than in the past _____because_____ they don't have to spend so

much time preparing food. In the old days, people had more free time, _____

life is very busy now. People don't want to spend all day in the kitchen.

    Now, anyone can make a delicious meal in 30 minutes. _____, people

have more time to do other things, like work or spend time with family. Even kids don't

have to wait for their mom or dad to prepare food anymore. _____, they can

heat up a frozen pizza or make a quick sandwich _____ they get hungry.

Kids are busy, too!

    People can still spend hours in the kitchen making a big meal _____ they

want to, but they don't have to anymore, _____ that's why easier preparation

is an improvement. Now there is a choice.

| and |
| as a result |
| because |
| but |
| if |
| instead |
| when |

43 | Using Linking Expressions Connect the ideas in the paragraphs below using the words and phrases in the box. 14.11 A

| as a result | instead | for instance | in addition |

SPORTS

1. American football players wear a lot of protection so that they don't get injured during the game. All players wear helmets and padding[27] to protect their bodies. _____, some players wear special collars to protect their necks.

American football

2. English rugby is a very physical game, but the players rarely wear any kind of padding or protection. _____, they play in jerseys[28] and shorts, with only a mouth guard to protect their teeth.

3. Ping-Pong is a very popular sport in China, and many people begin playing at a young age. _____, it's not surprising that many of the world's best players are Chinese.

rugby

4. Soccer is the most popular sport in the world. It is played in over 200 countries by more than 250 million people. Many people say that soccer became so popular because it doesn't require any expensive equipment except a ball. _____, it doesn't require a special field and can be played in any open space.

5. In soccer, players pass the ball with their feet, but in American football, players don't kick the ball that often. _____, for most of the game, they hand or throw the ball to each other.

Ping-Pong

6. In the past, very few women participated in the Olympics. _____, in the 1952 Summer Olympics, fewer than 12 percent of the athletes were women. At the 2012 Summer Olympics, over 40 percent of the athletes were women.

7. When most people think of golf, they imagine players walking slowly on a grassy field. It seems as if golf players wouldn't get injured very often. But golf players use the same arm movements many times during every game. _____, injuries to the elbow, back, and shoulders are quite common.

golf

[27] **padding:** soft material used for protection

[28] **jerseys:** shirts that are part of a sports uniform

44 | Identifying Sentence Variety Read this paragraph. Write *simple, compound,* or *complex* above each sentence. `14.11 B`

THE TURTLE AND THE RABBIT

complex
There once was a rabbit who passed by a turtle walking slowly down the road. The rabbit stopped and laughed because the turtle was so very slow. The rabbit said, "I'll race you to the top of the hill." The turtle agreed. The rabbit laughed again, and he ran quickly to the bottom of the hill. When he looked back, the turtle was very far behind. The rabbit didn't think he needed to hurry. Instead, he decided to sleep for a while. "I'll wait until he gets here. Then I'll run up the hill," he thought. When the turtle got to the bottom of the hill, he saw the rabbit sleeping.  He kept walking. He walked all the way to the top of the hill. Finally the rabbit woke up. When he ran to the top of the hill, he discovered that the turtle was already there.

45 | Using Sentence Variety Study this chart. Then rewrite the paragraph below. Change some of the simple sentences to compound and complex sentences. Add connecting words if necessary. `14.11 B`

Connecting words		
Coordinators connect two equal main clauses.	**Subordinators** connect a main clause and a dependent clause.	**Linking expressions** usually come at the beginning of a sentence or clause and connect it to the ideas that came before.
and, but, or, so	if after, before, when, while because although, even though	as a result instead for instance in addition

Listening

Listening is an important skill. It can help you become a success in the world. I listen to my parents. I find out important information. I find out what time we'll have dinner! I listen to my teachers. I learn when my homework is due. I listen to my friends. I discover what is going on with their lives. Sometimes they are having a hard time. Just listening to them will make them feel better. Business owners need to listen to their customers. They want to know what products customers want. Politicians need to listen to the people. They can take care of the people's needs. Teachers should listen to their students. They'll know what students need to learn. By listening we make life better for ourselves and for others.

Listening is an important skill, and it can help you become a success in the world. . . .

Talk about It Share the paragraph you rewrote above with a partner. What different choices did you make to rewrite the paragraph?

WRAP-UP Demonstrate Your Knowledge

A | GAME Work with a group. Share information about your past.

a. Use ten index cards or pieces of paper. On each card or piece of paper, write one of the following: *but, or, so, that, which, because*, and three linking expressions.

b. Stack the cards upside down. Take turns picking up a card and answering the first question below. Use the word on the card and two clauses in your answer. Once everyone has answered, move on to the next question. When all the cards have been used, shuffle them and put them back in a pile. Continue until everyone has answered all eight questions.

c. Choose one group member to write down each sentence. Work as a group to check that each one is correct.

QUESTIONS

1. What did you do in the summers when you were younger?

   It's very hot in my town, so I went swimming a lot.

   | so |

2. What was your favorite free-time activity when you were a child?
3. What was your favorite school subject when you were young?
4. What was your hometown like?
5. What did you want to be when you grew up?
6. What was difficult for you when you were a child?
7. What was easy for you?
8. Who was one of your favorite people?

B | CONFIRMING INFORMATION What do you know about your classmates? Write negative and tag questions about ten different classmates to confirm things that you think you know.

1. *You work at a restaurant, don't you?*
2. *Doesn't your brother go to this school?*

Ask each person his or her question. Tell the class how many you got right.

C | RECORDING A STORY Follow these instructions to record a story on an audio recording device.

1. Record yourself telling a short story about someone you know. It can be a friend, a family member, or a famous person. Spend a minute or two preparing, but don't write down what you are going to say.
2. Play the recording for a group. Listen to each person's story twice. Write down every use of *and, but, or, so,* and *because*. Talk about the story. Was it easy to follow? Were the relationships between ideas clear?

D | TELLING A STORY Work with a partner. Write a short story that you are both familiar with. It can be a fairy tale (like "Cinderella"), a traditional story, or a story from a movie. Use at least one simple, one complex, and one compound sentence and one linking expression. Meet with another pair and share your stories.

470

14.12 Summary of Sentence Patterns

CLAUSES AND SIMPLE SENTENCES

SUBJECT	PREDICATE	
subject	intransitive verb	adverb or prepositional phrase
My grandfather	walks	slowly.
		to the store.

subject	linking verb	complement	
That recipe	sounds/looks	delicious.	← adjective
Bill	seems	a little worried.	← adjective phrase
Sasha	is becoming	a lawyer.	← noun phrase — only with *be* or *become*
My sister	is	in Chicago.	← prepositional phrase — only with *be*

subject	transitive verb	direct object
Hiro	sold	the house.

subject	transitive verb	indirect object	direct object
The lecture	gave	me	an interesting idea.

subject	transitive verb	direct object	*to/for* phrase (indirect object)
Rolando	brought	presents	for the children.

PASSIVE SENTENCES

subject	passive verb		
The trash	is picked up	at 6:00.	← simple present
His house	was damaged	in the storm.	← simple past
The street	hasn't been cleaned	yet.	← present perfect
You	will be taken care of	as soon as possible.	← future with *will*
Broccoli	can be eaten	cooked or raw.	← modal
Plans	are being made	to improve the city.	← present progressive

LINKING EXPRESSIONS

SENTENCE	LINKING EXPRESSION + CLAUSE
He lost his job and had no savings.	**As a result**, he couldn't pay his rent.
Many of her hobbies seem very dangerous to me.	**For instance**, she likes to go mountain climbing alone.

COMPOUND SENTENCES

MAIN/INDEPENDENT CLAUSE	COORDINATOR	MAIN/INDEPENDENT CLAUSE
They came early,	**so**	they got the best seats.
He lost his wallet,	**but**	someone returned it.

COMPLEX SENTENCES

ADVERB/DEPENDENT CLAUSE	MAIN/INDEPENDENT CLAUSE
Before you decide,	look at all the facts.
If you want more dessert,	just help yourself.

MAIN/INDEPENDENT CLAUSE	DEPENDENT CLAUSE
You can watch TV	**if** you get home early.

BEGINNING OF MAIN CLAUSE	ADJECTIVE/DEPENDENT CLAUSE	END OF MAIN CLAUSE
The woman	**that** Maria introduced us to	was really smart.

Resources

I. Non-Action Verbs

agree	consist of	fear	include	mind	recognize	think
appear	contain	feel	involve	need	remember	understand
appreciate	cost	fit	know	owe	see	want
be	dislike	hate	like	own	seem	weigh
believe	doubt	have	look	possess	smell	wish
belong	envy	hear	love	prefer	suppose	
conclude	equal	imagine	mean	realize	taste	

Remember:

- A non-action verb describes a state (an unchanging condition).
- Non-action verbs are also called **stative verbs**.
- Some verbs have more than one meaning. They can function as a non-action verb in one context and an action verb in another.

II. Linking Verbs

appear	become	get*	look	seem	sound	turn*
be	feel	grow*	remain	smell	taste	

* with a meaning of *become*

Remember: A linking verb can have an adjective as a complement.

III. Irregular Verbs

BASE FORM	SIMPLE PAST	PAST PARTICIPLE
beat	beat	beaten
become	became	become
begin	began	begun
bend	bent	bent
bet	bet	bet
bite	bit	bitten
bleed	bled	bled
break	broke	broken
bring	brought	brought
build	built	built
burn	burned	burned
buy	bought	bought
catch	caught	caught
choose	chose	chosen
come	came	come
cost	cost	cost
cut	cut	cut
dig	dug	dug
draw	drew	drawn
dream	dreamed	dreamed
drink	drank	drunk
drive	drove	driven
eat	ate	eaten
fall	fell	fallen
feed	fed	fed
feel	felt	felt
fight	fought	fought
find	found	found
fly	flew	flown
forbid	forbade	forbidden
forget	forgot	forgotten
forgive	forgave	forgiven
freeze	froze	frozen
get	got	gotten
give	gave	given
go	went	gone
grow	grew	grown
hear	heard	heard
hide	hid	hidden
hit	hit	hit
hold	held	held
hurt	hurt	hurt
keep	kept	kept
know	knew	known
lay	laid	laid
lead	led	led
leave	left	left
lend	lent	lent

BASE FORM	SIMPLE PAST	PAST PARTICIPLE
let	let	let
lose	lost	lost
make	made	made
mean	meant	meant
meet	met	met
pay	paid	paid
put	put	put
quit	quit	quit
read	read	read
ride	rode	ridden
ring	rang	rung
rise	rose	risen
run	ran	run
say	said	said
see	saw	seen
sell	sold	sold
send	sent	sent
set	set	set
sew	sewed	sewn
shake	shook	shaken
shoot	shot	shot
show	showed	shown
shut	shut	shut
sing	sang	sung
sink	sank	sunk
sit	sat	sat
sleep	slept	slept
speak	spoke	spoken
speed	sped	sped
spend	spent	spent
spill	spilt/spilled	spilt/spilled
spread	spread	spread
stand	stood	stood
steal	stole	stolen
swear	swore	sworn
sweep	swept	swept
swim	swam	swum
take	took	taken
teach	taught	taught
tear	tore	torn
tell	told	told
think	thought	thought
throw	threw	thrown
understand	understood	understood
wake	woke	woken
wear	wore	worn
win	won	won
write	wrote	written

IV. Spelling Rules for the -s/-es Form of Verbs

To form the third-person singular *(he/she/it)* for the simple present:

1 Add *-es* to verbs that end in *-sh, -ch, -ss, -s, -x,* or *-z.*

| finish | finishes | touch | touches | pass | passes | relax | relaxes |

2 For verbs ending in a consonant + *-y,* change the *-y* to *-i* and add *-es.*

| study | studies | worry | worries | deny | denies | fly | flies |

3 Three verbs have a special spelling:

| go | goes | do | does | have | has |

4 For all other verbs, add *-s.*

| like | likes | buy | buys | see | sees | speak | speaks |

V. Spelling Rules for the -ing Form of Verbs

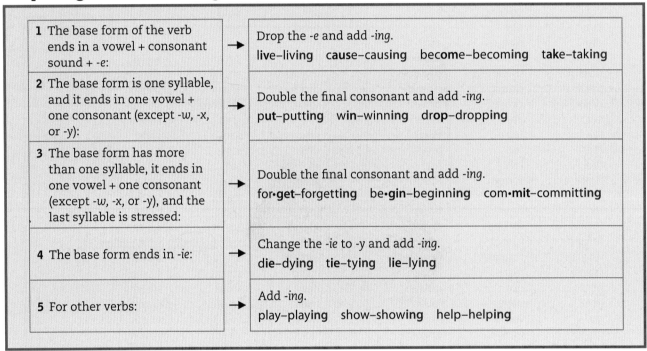

1 The base form of the verb ends in a vowel + consonant sound + *-e*:	Drop the *-e* and add *-ing*. **live**–living **cause**–causing **become**–becoming **take**–taking
2 The base form is one syllable, and it ends in one vowel + one consonant (except *-w, -x,* or *-y*):	Double the final consonant and add *-ing*. **put**–putting **win**–winning **drop**–dropping
3 The base form has more than one syllable, it ends in one vowel + one consonant (except *-w, -x,* or *-y*), and the last syllable is stressed:	Double the final consonant and add *-ing*. for·**get**–forgetting be·**gin**–beginning com·**mit**–committing
4 The base form ends in *-ie*:	Change the *-ie* to *-y* and add *-ing*. **die**–dying **tie**–tying **lie**–lying
5 For other verbs:	Add *-ing*. **play**–playing **show**–showing **help**–helping

VI. Spelling Rules for the -ed Form of Verbs

SPELLING RULES	base form	simple past
When the base form of a regular verb ends in -e, **add -d**.	close refuse	closed refused
When the base form ends in a consonant + **-y, change the -y to -i and add -ed**.	study worry identify	studied worried identified
When the base form has one syllable and ends in a **c**onsonant + **v**owel + **c**onsonant (CVC), **double the final consonant and add -ed**. (Warning! Do not double a final w, x, or y: play / played, wax / waxed, row / rowed.)	plan jog drop	planned jogged dropped
When the base form of a two-syllable verb ends in a **c**onsonant + **v**owel + **c**onsonant (CVC) and the last syllable is stressed, **double the final consonant and add -ed**.	re•**fer** re•**gret**	referred regretted
For all other regular verbs, **add -ed**.	open destroy	opened destroyed

VII. Common Transitive Verbs

VERB + DIRECT OBJECT

Examples: *begin the day; believe everything; bring a sweater*

allow	close*	end*	include	love	raise	show	visit*
ask*	complete	enjoy	intend	make	read*	speak*	want
attempt	consider	expect	introduce	mean	receive	start*	wash*
begin*	create	feel*	invent	meet*	recognize	study*	watch*
believe*	cut*	find	involve	move*	refuse	surround	win*
bring	describe	follow*	keep*	need	remember*	take	write*
build	design	forgive	know*	pass*	save	teach	
buy	destroy	hear*	leave*	pay*	say	tell	
call*	develop	help*	lend	produce	see*	think*	
carry	discover	hold*	like	provide	send	throw	
cause	do	identify	lose*	put	serve	use	

* verbs that we can also use intransitively (without a direct object)

Remember: Transitive verbs need an object (a noun phrase or pronoun) to complete their meaning.

VERB + INDIRECT OBJECT + DIRECT OBJECT

Examples: *ask the teacher a question; bring your sister a sweater*

ask	forgive	lend*	pay	save	teach*
bring	give*	make	promise*	send*	tell*
buy	hand*	offer*	read*	serve*	throw*
find	leave*	owe*	refuse	show*	wish*

* The indirect object can come before or after the direct object.

VIII. Common Intransitive Verbs

Examples: *The movie begins at 8:00. She doesn't hear very well.*

agree	cough	freeze*	lie	remember*	stop*
appear	cut*	go	live	ring*	study*
arrive	decrease*	happen	look	rise	swim
begin*	die	hear*	lose*	see*	visit*
belong	disappear	help*	matter	shake*	wait
bleed	dream*	hide*	meet*	sit	walk*
break*	drown	hurt*	move*	sleep	wash*
burn*	end*	increase*	pass*	sneeze	watch*
call*	fall	laugh	rain	snow	win*
close*	follow*	leave*	read*	start*	work
come					

* verbs that we can also use transitively (with a direct object)

Remember: Intransitive verbs make sense without an object.

IX. Common Transitive Multi-Word Verbs

act out	clear out	finish off	keep out	pay off	set aside	think of
blow away	close down	finish up	laugh off	pick out	set down	think over
blow up	come across	flag down	lay aside	pick up	shake up	think up
break down	cover up	get across	lay down	pin down	shave off	throw away
break off	cut off	get along with	leave out	play back	shut down	throw down
bring out	cut out	get into	let down	point out	shut off	throw out
bring up	dig out	get off	let out	pour out	sign up	try on
call off	dig up	get on	lock up	put aside	slow down	turn back
call on	do away with	get over	look after	put away	sort out	turn down
call up	do over	give away	look down on	put down	stretch out	turn off
carry on	do without	give out	look forward to	put off	sweep away	use up
carry out	drop off	give up	look over	put on	take after	wake up
check into	dry off	hand in	look up	put up with	take back	wash off
check off	dry out	hand out	look up to	read back	take down	wash out
check out	eat up	heat up	make up	read over	take off	wear down
check over	empty out	help out	mix up	ring up	take on	wear out
cheer up	figure out	hold off	move out	round off	take out	work out
chop down	fill out	hold up	open up	run over	take over	write down
clean off	fill up	hunt down	pass over	save up	take up	write off
clean up	find out	jot down	pay back	see through	tell off	

Remember: Transitive multi-word verbs need an object (a noun phrase or pronoun) to complete their meaning.

Some multi-word verbs have more than one meaning. We can use them transitively in one context and intransitively in another.

Examples: They **broke down** the door to get inside. (transitive)

My car **broke down** on the bridge. (intransitive)

You can't **turn back** the clock. (transitive)

Let's **turn back** now. (intransitive)

X. Common Intransitive Multi-Word Verbs

back up	cry out	get up	keep out	pull up	sign off	start off
blow out	dig in	go off	melt away	quiet down	sit up	take off
break down	drive off	grow back	move in	rest up	slow down	turn over
calm down	eat out	grow up	move out	roll over	slow up	turn up
carry on	end up	hang on	pass by	run away	speak up	wake up
catch on	fade away	heat up	pass on	set off	speed up	wear down
catch up	fall over	hurry up	pass out	show off	split up	wear off
cool off	get back	join in	pull through	shut up	stand up	

Remember: An intransitive multi-word verb = a multi-word verb that can be used without an object.

Some multi-word verbs have more than one meaning. We can use them transitively in one context and intransitively in another.

Examples: You need to **cheer up.** (intransitive)

I tried everything, but I couldn't **cheer her up.** (transitive)

Don't **give up**! You can do it. (intransitive)

I **gave up soda** and lost five pounds. (transitive)

XI. Common Verbs Followed by Gerunds

VERB + GERUND

Examples: *appreciate having; avoid getting; denied knowing*

admit	continue*	enjoy	love*	prefer*	risk
advise	defend	finish	mean**	quit	start*
appreciate	delay	forget**	mention	recall	stop**
avoid	deny	hate*	mind	recommend	suggest
begin*	detest	imagine	miss	regret**	tolerate
can't help	discuss	involve	need**	remember**	try**
can't stand*	dislike	keep	postpone	resist	
consider	dread*	like*	practice	resume	

* can also be followed by a to- infinitive   ** can be followed by a to- infinitive but with a change in meaning

VERB + OBJECT + GERUND

Examples: *hear him talking; saw my friends leaving; found them sitting*

discover	feel	find	hear	notice	see	watch

XII. Common Verbs + Prepositions Followed by Gerunds

Examples: *argue about going; apologize for being; cope with losing; dream of becoming*

VERB + *ABOUT*	VERB + *AT*	VERB + *FOR*	VERB + *IN*	VERB + *INTO*
argue about care about complain about forget about talk about think about worry about	aim at work at	apologize for blame for care for forgive for thank for use for	believe in result in specialize in succeed in	look into

VERB + *LIKE*	VERB + *OF*	VERB + *ON*	VERB + *TO*	VERB + *WITH*
feel like	accuse of approve of dream of hear of think of	concentrate on depend on go on insist on keep on plan on work on	admit to confess to object to	cope with deal with

XIII. Common Adjectives + Prepositions Followed by Gerunds

Examples: *afraid of being; bad at making; excited about going*

ADJECTIVE + *OF* + GERUND	ADJECTIVE + *AT* + GERUND	ADJECTIVE + *ABOUT* + GERUND
afraid of aware of capable of fond of incapable of proud of tired of	bad at better at effective at good at great at successful at upset at	bad about concerned about enthusiastic about excited about happy about nervous about serious about sorry about worried about

ADJECTIVE + *FROM* + GERUND	ADJECTIVE + *IN* + GERUND	ADJECTIVE + *FOR* + GERUND
different from evident from exempt from free from obvious from safe from tired from	crucial in effective in important in interested in involved in useful in	available for crucial for famous for important for necessary for responsible for sorry for suitable for useful for

XIV. Common Verbs Followed by To- Infinitives

VERB + *TO*- INFINITIVE

Examples: *agree to go; asked to leave; decide to stay*

afford	can't stand*	desire	hope	plan	remember**	threaten
agree	claim	dread*	intend	prefer*	request	try**
aim	consent	fall	learn	prepare	say	volunteer
appear	continue*	forbid	like*	pretend	seek	vow
ask	dare	forget**	love*	proceed	seem	wait
attempt	decide	get	manage	promise	start*	want
beg	decline	hate*	mean**	prove	stop**	wish
begin*	demand	help	need**	refuse	struggle	
bother	deserve	hesitate	offer	regret**	tend	

* can also be followed by a gerund   ** can be followed by a gerund but with a change in meaning

VERB + OBJECT + *TO*- INFINITIVE

Examples: *advised me to go; reminded me to call; helped them to move*

advise**	beg*	encourage**	hate*	know**	permit**	teach**
allow**	believe**	expect*	help*	like*	persuade**	tell**
appoint**	challenge**	forbid**	imagine**	love*	prefer*	urge**
ask*	choose*	force**	instruct**	need*	promise*	want*
assume**	consider**	get*	judge**	order**	remind**	warn**

* object is optional   ** object is required

XV. Common Verbs Followed by Gerunds or To- Infinitives

Examples: *begin working / begin to understand; continue talking / continue to work*

begin	forget*	love	prefer	start
can't stand	hate	mean*	regret*	stop*
continue	like	need*	remember*	try*

* with a change in meaning

XVI. Examples of Differences in Meaning Between Gerunds and To- Infinitives

VERB	GERUND	TO- INFINITIVE
forget	I'll never **forget watching** her win the race. (= I'll never forget the time I watched her win the race.)	I **forgot to watch** the race on TV. (= The race was on TV but I didn't watch it.)
mean	Being an adult **means having** responsibilities. (= involves/necessitates responsibilities)	I **meant to call** but I didn't have time. (= intended/planned to call)
remember	I **remembered seeing** his picture in the newspaper. (= First I saw his picture; later I remembered it.)	I **remembered to call** him. (= First I remembered and then I called him.)
stop	She finally **stopped talking.** (= She was talking and then she stopped.)	She **stopped to talk** to me. (= She stopped first so she could talk to me.)
try	I **tried calling** but no one was at home. (= I made the phone call but no one answered.)	I **tried to call** but my phone wasn't working. (= I made the effort but I couldn't call.)

XVII. Common Noncount Nouns

advice	coffee*	flour	homework	medicine*	peace	snow
air	confidence	fruit*	information	milk	physics	soap
baggage	courage	fun	glass*	money	progress	spaghetti
beauty	economics	furniture	heat	music	rain	sugar
behavior*	electricity	gasoline	jewelry	news	research	traffic
blood	entertainment	grammar	knowledge	noise*	rice	truth*
bread	equipment	hair*	literature	organization*	safety	violence
cash	evidence	happiness	luck	oxygen	salt	water
chemistry	excitement	health	luggage	paint*	sand	weather
clothing	experience*	help	mathematics	patience	smoke	work*

* often has a count meaning or a noncount meaning

XVIII. Common Noun Suffixes

SUFFIX	EXAMPLES
-age	shortage storage
-ance -ence -ancy -ency	appearance existence vacancy frequency
-ant -ent	assistant consultant president student
-ation	examination organization
-cracy	autocracy democracy
-ee	employee trainee

SUFFIX	EXAMPLES
-er	painter singer
-hood	brotherhood childhood neighborhood sisterhood
-ian	comedian historian librarian
-ics	athletics physics
-ion	action connection
-ist	artist capitalist scientist

SUFFIX	EXAMPLES
-ity	inequality purity
-ment	announcement development excitement resentment
-ness	gentleness kindness loneliness sadness
-ology	biology ecology psychology
-or	actor conductor inventor
-ship	citizenship friendship

XIX. Common Noun + Noun Combinations

family	+	business / friend / history / life / member / room / support / values
government	+	agency / employee / official / policy / program / regulation / spending
police	+	car / chief / department / force / interview / officer / station
world	+	bank / championship / cup / economy / leader / record / trade / view / war
business	+	administration / community / leader / owner / people / plan / school / world
car	+	accident / company / crash / door / keys / radio / seat / wash / window
city	+	center / council / government / hall / limits / manager / official / police / street
health	+	benefits / care / insurance / officials / problems / professionals / services
labor	+	costs / day / force / market / movement / party / relations / statistics / union
TV	+	ad / camera / commercial / guide / movie / news / series / set / show / station

XX. Common Adjectives

These are the 100 most common adjectives in English in order of frequency.

other	little	human	full	current	serious	religious
new*	important	local	special	wrong*	ready	cold
good*	political	late	easy	private	simple	final
high	bad	hard*	clear	past	left	main
old*	white*	major	recent	foreign	physical	green
great	real	better	certain	fine	general	nice*
big*	best	economic	personal	common	environmental	huge
American	right*	strong	open	poor	financial	popular
small	social	possible	red	natural	blue	traditional
large	only	whole*	difficult*	significant	democratic	cultural
national	public	free	available	similar	dark	
young	sure*	military	likely	hot	various	
different*	low	true*	short	dead*	entire	
black*	early	federal	single	central	close	
long*	able*	international	medical	happy*	legal	

* common in conversation

XXI. Common Adjective Suffixes

SUFFIX	MEANING	EXAMPLE
-able -ible -ble	possible to	acceptable noticeable divisible
-al	connected with	environmental experimental
-ant -ent	having a particular quality	different
-centric	concerned with or interested in	egocentric
-ed	having a particular state or quality	bored patterned
-ese	from a place	Chinese Japanese
-free	without the thing mentioned	fat-free tax-free
-ful	having a particular quality	helpful useful
-ial	typical of	dictatorial
-ical	connected with	economical physical

SUFFIX	MEANING	EXAMPLE
-ing	producing a particular state or effect	exciting interesting
-ish	describing nationality or language	English Spanish
-ive	having a particular quality	attractive effective
-less	not having something	fearless hopeless
-like	similar to	childlike
-looking	having the appearance	good-looking odd-looking
-most	the furthest	southernmost topmost
-ous	having a particular quality	dangerous religious
-proof	to protect against the thing mentioned	soundproof waterproof
-y	having the quality of the thing mentioned	fatty rainy thirsty

Taken from *Oxford American Dictionary for learners of English*

XXII. Common Adverbs of Degree

absolutely	entirely	highly	quite	slightly	too*
almost	exactly*	more	rather	so	totally
awfully	extremely	nearly	real*	somewhat	utterly
completely	fairly	perfectly	really*	terribly	very*
definitely	fully	pretty*	relatively	thoroughly	

* common in conversation

COMMON ERRORS CORRECTIONS

1.2 Simple Present Statements (page 7)

CORRECTION

14 ✗ She don't have time for this.

✓ She **doesn't** have time for this.

15 ✗ He email his family a lot.

✓ He **emails** his family a lot.

16 ✗ She is a housewife and **have** three children.

✓ She is a housewife and **has** three children.

17 ✗ It make me happy.

✓ It **makes** me happy.

EXPLANATION

I / You / We / They	don't have . . . email . . . have . . . make . . .

He / She / It	doesn't have . . . emails . . . has . . . makes . . .

1.5 Using Time Expressions with the Simple Present (page 20)

CORRECTION

16 ✗ He walks to school **usually** every morning.

✓ He **usually** walks to school every morning.

17 ✗ They **always are** busy.

✓ They **are always** busy.

EXPLANATION

Notice the correct order of words:

subject	adverb of frequency	verb

subject	verb *be*	adverb of frequency

18 ✗ They always don't leave a tip.

✓ They **don't always** leave a tip.

✓ They **never** leave a tip.

Notice the correct order of words:

subject	helping verb	adverb of frequency	verb

There are two ways to correct this sentence:

They don't always leave a tip means "Sometimes they *do* leave a tip, but sometimes (about 10 to 50 percent of the time) they *don't* leave a tip."

They never leave a tip means "They leave a tip 0 percent of the time."

19 ✗ John **don't never** visit us.

✓ John **never visits** us.

We don't use *not* with a negative adverb (*hardly ever, rarely, seldom, almost never, never*).

1.8 Comparing the Simple Present and Present Progressive (page 29)

C

CORRECTION	EXPLANATION
7 ✗ I'm usually **going** to school on Monday. ✓ I usually **go** to school on Monday.	We usually describe present habits with simple present verbs (**go**), not present progressive verbs ('*m going*).
8 ✗ He **cooks** dinner right now. ✓ He **is cooking** dinner right now.	We describe things in progress now with present progressive verbs (**is cooking**), not simple present verbs (*cooks*).
9 ✗ You're always **make** fun of me. ✓ You always **make** fun of me.	For the simple present, we don't use a form of *be* ('*re*) with the main verb. We just use the main verb (**make**).
10 ✗ They **watching** TV every evening. ✓ They **watch** TV every evening.	For the simple present of most verbs, we use *they* + base form (**watch**), not the -*ing* form (*watching*).

2.2 Simple Past Statements with Regular and Irregular Verbs (page 47)

C

CORRECTION	EXPLANATION
12 ✗ He **attend**, but he **fail**. ✓ He **attended**, but he **failed**.	For the simple past of regular verbs, we add -**d** or -**ed** to the base form.
13 ✗ He **teached** me everything. ✓ He **taught** me everything.	*Teach* is an irregular verb. The simple past form is **taught**.
14 ✗ I sat and **think** for a while. ✓ I sat and **thought** for a while.	The simple past form of the verb *think* is **thought**.
15 ✗ My grandfather **dead** five years ago. ✓ My grandfather **died** five years ago.	The word *dead* is an adjective. The verb form is *die*. The simple past form is **died**.

2.3 Simple Past Negative Statements and Questions (page 52)

D

CORRECTION	EXPLANATION
12 ✗ They **don't go** shopping last weekend. ✓ They **didn't go** shopping last weekend.	We use **didn't** (not *don't*) + base form for simple past negative statements. (We use *don't* for simple present negative statements.)
13 ✗ I **no hear** the news last night. ✓ I **didn't hear** the news last night.	For simple past negative statements, we use *did* + *not* (**didn't**) + base form.
14 ✗ Who **go** with you? ✓ Who **went** with you?	When the *wh-* word is the subject, we use: 	*wh-* word	+	past form of main verb	
15 ✗ When you **get** there? ✓ When **did** you get there?	For *wh-* questions, we use: | *wh-* word	+	*did*	+	subject	+	base form	

2.4 Simple Past of the Verb *Be* (page 56)

D

CORRECTION	EXPLANATION
17 ✗ I absent yesterday. ✓ I **was** absent yesterday.	*Absent* is an adjective. We use: subject + verb *be* + adjective
18 ✗ It was rain yesterday. ✓ It was **rainy** yesterday. ✓ It **rained** yesterday.	*Rain* is a regular verb; *rainy* is an adjective. We use: it + verb *be* + adjective (**rainy**) or it + verb (**rained**)
19 ✗ Was you late again? ✓ **Were** you late again?	Was I / he / she / it . . . ? Were you / we / they . . . ?
20 ✗ Where you were last night? ✓ Where **were** **you** last night?	Notice the correct order of words: *wh-* word + verb *be* + subject . . . ?

2.6 Time Clauses with the Simple Past (page 62)

C

CORRECTION	EXPLANATION
8 ✗ After left the class, something happened. ✓ After (**I, we, everyone, the teacher,** etc.) left the class, something happened.	A clause needs a **subject** and a verb.
9 ✗ I **meet** her last week when I **start** the class. ✓ I **met** her last week when I **started** the class.	We don't use present verb forms (*meet, start*) with the time expression *last week*. The simple past forms are **met** and **started**.
10 ✗ I left, before she got there. ✓ I left before she got there. ✓ **Before she got there,** I left.	We use a comma (,) at the end of a time clause when it comes before (not after) the main clause. no comma main clause | time clause comma time clause | , | main clause
11 ✗ He **gave** me advice when I **need** it. ✓ He **gave** me advice when I **needed** it. ✓ He **gives** me advice when I **need** it.	When the main clause and the time clause refer to the same time frame, we use similar verb forms (*gave / needed; gives / need*).

3.5 Subject-Verb Agreement (page 95)

D

CORRECTION	EXPLANATION
11 ✗ My family **help** me a lot. ✓ My family **helps** me a lot. 12 ✗ My husband **miss** us when he is away. ✓ My husband **misses** us when he is away. 13 ✗ That person **don't** know my name. ✓ That person **doesn't** know my name.	The words *family*, *husband*, and *person* are singular count nouns. We use them with singular (not plural) verbs.
14 ✗ Some people in my class **is** never on time. ✓ Some people in my class **are** never on time.	The word *people* (a plural count noun) is the subject of the sentence. We use a plural verb (**are**) with a plural count noun.

3.6 Noun Suffixes (page 98)

C

CORRECTION	EXPLANATION
6 ✗ My **happy** did not continue very long. ✓ My **happiness** did not continue very long. 7 ✗ I think his **lazy** hurt him. ✓ I think his **laziness** hurt him. 8 ✗ The most important thing is **appreciate** for my parents. ✓ The most important thing is **appreciation** for my parents. 9 ✗ My parents taught me that **educate** is important. ✓ My parents taught me that **education** is important.	When a word functions as a noun, it's important to use the noun form of the word. adjective + suffix = noun happy + -ness = happiness lazy + -ness = laziness verb + suffix = noun appreciate + -ion = appreciation educate + -ion = education

3.9 Using No Article (Ø) (page 107)

C

CORRECTION	EXPLANATION
8 ✗ He gave me **sandwich** for breakfast. ✓ He gave me **sandwiches** for breakfast. ✓ He gave me **a sandwich** for breakfast.	We can use no article (Ø) before a plural count noun (*sandwiches*). We can use *a*, *an*, or *the* before a singular count noun (*sandwich*).
9 ✗ Tokyo and Kyoto are **some** cities in Japan. ✓ Tokyo and Kyoto are cities in Japan. 10 ✗ I learned that **the** friends are very important. ✓ I learned that friends are very important.	We don't use *some* or *the* when we are talking about something in general. We use no article (Ø) instead.

4.2 Subject Pronouns vs. Object Pronouns; *One* and *Ones* (page 123)

C

CORRECTION	EXPLANATION
10 ✗ Her father gave **she** a new computer. ✓ Her father gave **her** a new computer. 11 ✗ Tom talked to Lisa and **I**. ✓ Tom talked to Lisa and **me**.	<table><tr><td>Subject Pronouns</td><td>I / you / he / she / it / we / you / they</td></tr><tr><td>Object Pronouns</td><td>me / you / him / her / it / us / you / them</td></tr></table>
12 ✗ He saved some of his money and spent some of **them**. ✓ He saved some of his money and spent some of **it**. 13 ✗ We bought a lot of gifts for our friends. I hope they like **it**. ✓ We bought a lot of gifts for our friends. I hope they like **them**.	*Money* = a noncount noun; we use **it** to refer back to a noncount noun. *Gifts* = a plural count noun; we use **them** to refer back to a plural count noun.

4.3 Reflexive Pronouns (page 127)

C

CORRECTION	EXPLANATION
13 ✗ This society must help **it self**. ✓ This society must help **itself**. 14 ✗ We always make tortillas **ourself**. ✓ We always make tortillas **ourselves**.	The reflexive pronouns are: <table><tr><td>myself</td><td>yourself</td><td>himself</td><td>herself</td><td>itself</td></tr><tr><td>ourselves</td><td>yourselves</td><td>themselves</td><td></td><td></td></tr></table>
15 ✗ I can make a better future for **me** here. ✓ I can make a better future for **myself** here.	When the subject and the object are the same person, we use a reflexive pronoun (**myself**), not an object pronoun (*me*).
16 ✗ We made a plan for spending **ourself** money. ✓ We made a plan for spending **our** money. ✓ We made a plan for spending **the** money **ourselves**.	Before a noun (*money*), we can use a possessive determiner (**our**, *my*, *your*, etc.), not a reflexive pronoun (*ourself*). We sometimes use a reflexive pronoun at the end of a clause to give emphasis (*spending the money* **ourselves**).

4.4 Each Other and One Another (page 130)

C

CORRECTION	EXPLANATION
6 ✗ They **had a problem** each other. ✓ They **had a problem with** each other.	We use: had a problem **with** + noun / pronoun
7 ✗ They didn't like **one anothers**. ✓ They didn't like **one another**. ✓ They didn't like **each other**. ✓ They didn't like **one another's** spouses.	*One another* does not have a plural form.
8 ✗ My parents have a great relationship. They truly love **themselves**. ✓ They truly love **each other**.	**They truly love themselves** = "My mother loves herself and my father loves himself." **They truly love each other** = "My mother loves my father and my father loves my mother."

4.5 Indefinite Pronouns (page 133)

C

CORRECTION	EXPLANATION
11 ✗ I didn't see **nothing**. ✓ I didn't see **anything**. ✓ I saw **nothing**.	We don't normally use *nobody*, *no one*, or *nothing* in a sentence with *not*.
12 ✗ I thought **everythings were** free in the U.S. ✓ I thought **everything was** free in the U.S. ✓ I thought **all things were** free in the U.S. **13** ✗ Everyone **want** to come. ✓ Everyone **wants** to come. ✓ Everyone **wanted** to come.	Indefinite pronouns are always singular. We use a singular verb (**was**, **wants**) with them.
14 ✗ I don't want to see **somebody**. ✓ I don't want to see **anybody**. ✓ I **want** to see somebody.	We don't usually use *somebody*, *someone*, or *something* after *not*.

4.11 Measure Words (page 148)

B

CORRECTION	EXPLANATION
8 ✗ I would like two **cup** of coffee, please. ✓ I would like two **cups** of coffee, please. 9 ✗ He drank two **bottle** of milks! ✓ He drank two **bottles** of milk! 10 ✗ Can you get me three boxes of **cracker**? ✓ Can you get me three boxes of **crackers**?	We use *two* + a **plural** measure word (*cups*) + *of* + a noncount noun (*coffee / milk*) or plural count noun (*crackers*).
11 ✗ My teacher gave us bunch of **test**. ✓ My teacher gave us **a** bunch of **tests**.	We use *a / an / one* + a singular measure word (*bunch*) + *of* + a plural count noun (*tests*) or noncount noun.

5.6 Time Clauses with the Future (page 179)

C

CORRECTION	EXPLANATION
10 ✗ I'm going to start looking for a job after I **will finish** school. ✓ I'm going to start looking for a job after I **finish** school. 11 ✗ She's going to take some time off before she **is going to start** her new job. ✓ She's going to take some time off before she **starts** her new job.	We sometimes use a time clause in a sentence about the future. We use a **present form** in the time clause even though we are talking about the future.

7.3 Verb + To- Infinitive (page 236)

C

CORRECTION	EXPLANATION
10 ✗ They wanted to **saved** their money. ✓ They wanted to **save** their money. 11 ✗ She hopes graduate this year. ✓ She hopes **to** graduate this year.	A *to-* infinitive = *to* + the **base form** of a verb (**save**), not *to* + the simple past form (*saved*).
12 ✗ She encouraged me **about going**. ✓ She encouraged me **to go**.	We use: *encourage* + object pronoun (*me*) or noun phrase + to- infinitive
13 ✗ I expect him **no** to graduate. ✓ I expect him **not** to graduate.	To make a *to-* infinitive negative, we use **not** + *to-* infinitive.

12.3 Adverb Clauses of Reason (page 383)

D

CORRECTION	EXPLANATION
8 ✗ I was happy because learned something important. ✓ I was happy because I learned something important.	A clause needs both a **subject** and a verb.
9 ✗ I'm proud of myself because now I **could** communicate with people in English. ✓ I'm proud of myself because now I **can** communicate with people in English. **10** ✗ I was sad because I **have to** leave soon. ✓ I'm sad because I have to leave soon. ✓ I was sad because I **had to** leave soon.	When the verb in the main clause and the verb in the adverb clause refer to a present time frame, we use present verb forms. When both verbs refer to a past time frame, we use past verb forms.
11 ✗ We stayed at home. **Because** it was so hot. ✓ We stayed at home **because** it was so hot.	In writing, it's necessary to use an adverb clause in a sentence with a main clause. An adverb clause alone (*Because it was so hot.*) is an incomplete sentence.

Index

Multi-word adjectives, 327, 328, 341
Multi-word verbs, 39, 454–456
   intransitive, 454, R-7
   transitive, 454, R-6
Must and ***must not***
   for certainty, 290, 292, 309
   for obligations, 218, 292
      vs. *have to/don't have to*, 218

N

Names, possessive, 139
Negative, double, 136
Negative statements
   ever in, 20, 260
   future forms
      be going to, 162
      will, 169
   modals, 190, 194, 211, 280, 290, 293, 296
   with past perfect, 252, 277
   with past progressive, 65, 75
   with present progressive, 23, 41
   with simple past, 52, 75
      of *be*, 56, 75
   with simple present, 7, 41
      of *be*, 16, 41
   yet in, 261
Negative *yes/no* questions, 447
Neither, 143, 147, 159
Neither . . . nor, 430
Neither (of), 430
Never with present perfect, 260
No article, 107, 117
Non-action verbs, 30, 178, R-2
   defined, 4
Noncount nouns
   defined, 90
   common, R-10
   how questions with, 19
   quantifiers +, 143, 144, 159
   subject-verb agreement with, 95
No one, nothing. *See* Indefinite pronouns
(Not) as . . . as, 405, 409. *See also* Comparisons
Noun phrases, 78, 80
   defined, 312
   parts of, 78
   with prepositional phrases, 80, 329
   that function like adverbs (e.g., *today*), 349
   uses of, 312
   in writing, 155
Nouns, 78–99, 110–112
   defined, 78
   adjectives before, 314, 316
   common, 81, 117
   as complements, 78
   connecting with *and*, 126
   count, 90, 117
   first and second mention of, in writing, 112

in lists, 112
   more/less/fewer with, 414
   the + most/least/fewest with, 427
   noncount, 19, 90, 117, 143, 144, R-10
   (not) as . . . as with, 405
   in noun + noun combinations, 314, R-11
   as objects of prepositions, 78
   as objects of verbs, 78
   possessive, 139
   with prepositional phrases, 78, 112, 329, 330
   proper, 81, 82, 117
   quantifiers
      with plural and noncount nouns (e.g., *a few people, a little sugar*), 150
      with singular nouns (e.g., *each student*), 147
   singular and plural, 85, 117
   in speaking, 110
   as subjects, 78
   summary of, 117
   uses of, 78
   in writing, 112
Noun suffixes, 98, 99, R-10

O

Object pronouns (e.g., *me, him*), 123, 127, 159
   in comparisons (e.g., *older than me*), 428
   vs. reflexive pronouns, 127
   vs. subject pronouns, 123
Objects
   direct, 442, 471
   indirect, 442, 471
Obligations with *must, have to, had to,* and *have got to*, 218, 227
Offers
   with *can* and *could*, 197, 199, 227
   with *may*, 197
   responding to, 199
   with *will*, 169, 227
   with *would*, 227
   would like in making, 204
One another, 131
One/ones, 159
Or, 69, 457, 463
Ought to for advice, 211, 227

P

Parallelism, 247
Passive sentences, 460
Past participle. See also *-ed* form of verbs
   of irregular verbs, 47, 252, 257, R-3
   of regular verbs, 47, 48, 50, 252
Past perfect
   negative statements in, 267, 277
   positive statements in, 267, 277
   questions in, 277
   vs. simple past, 267
   time expressions with, 269

Class Audio Track List

GO ONLINE For these audio tracks and the audio scripts, go to the Online Practice.

Unit	Activity	Track File Name
Unit 1	Activity 8, p. 9	ELM2_U01_Track01_Activity08.mp3
	Activity 9, p. 9	ELM2_U01_Track02_Activity09.mp3
	Activity 17, p. 14	ELM2_U01_Track03_Activity17.mp3
	Activity 18, p. 15	ELM2_U01_Track04_Activity18.mp3
	Activity 19, p. 15	ELM2_U01_Track05_Activity19.mp3
	Activity 20, p. 15	ELM2_U01_Track06_Activity20.mp3
	Activity 21, p. 15	ELM2_U01_Track07_Activity21.mp3
	Activity 40, p. 27	ELM2_U01_Track08_Activity40.mp3
	Activity 41, p. 27	ELM2_U01_Track09_Activity41.mp3
	Chart 1.10, p. 35	ELM2_U01_Track10_Chart1.10.mp3
	Activity 54, p. 36	ELM2_U01_Track11_Activity54.mp3
	Activity 56, p. 37	ELM2_U01_Track12_Activity56.mp3
Unit 2	Activity 5, p. 48	ELM2_U02_Track01_Activity05.mp3
	Activity 6, p. 48	ELM2_U02_Track02_Activity06.mp3
	Activity 6, p. 48	ELM2_U02_Track03_Activity06.mp3
	Activity 7, p. 49	ELM2_U02_Track04_Activity07.mp3
	Activity 8, p. 49	ELM2_U02_Track05_Activity08.mp3
	Chart 2.8, p. 69	ELM2_U02_Track06_Chart2.8.mp3
	Activity 38, p. 69	ELM2_U02_Track07_Activity38.mp3
	Activity 39, p. 70	ELM2_U02_Track08_Activity39.mp3
	Activity 40, p. 70	ELM2_U02_Track09_Activity40.mp3
Unit 3	Activity 4, p. 80	ELM2_U03_Track01_Activity04.mp3
	Activity 5, p. 81	ELM2_U03_Track02_Activity05.mp3
	Activity 13, p. 86	ELM2_U03_Track03_Activity13.mp3
	Activity 14, p. 86	ELM2_U03_Track04_Activity14.mp3
	Activity 15, p. 86	ELM2_U03_Track05_Activity15.mp3
	Activity 25, p. 92	ELM2_U03_Track06_Activity25.mp3
	Chart 3.10, p. 110	ELM2_U03_Track07_Chart3.10.mp3
	Activity 54, p. 110	ELM2_U03_Track08_Activity54.mp3
	Activity 55, p. 111	ELM2_U03_Track09_Activity55.mp3
Unit 4	Activity 14, p. 129	ELM2_U04_Track01_Activity14.mp3
	Activity 15, p. 129	ELM2_U04_Track02_Activity15.mp3
	Activity 23, p. 134	ELM2_U04_Track03_Activity23.mp3
	Activity 24, p. 134	ELM2_U04_Track04_Activity24.mp3
	Activity 28, p. 136	ELM2_U04_Track05_Activity28.mp3
	Activity 30, p. 137	ELM2_U04_Track06_Activity30.mp3
	Activity 37, p. 141	ELM2_U04_Track07_Activity37.mp3
	Activity 38, p. 141	ELM2_U04_Track08_Activity38.mp3
	Activity 50, p. 149	ELM2_U04_Track09_Activity50.mp3
	Activity 51, p. 149	ELM2_U04_Track10_Activity51.mp3
	Chart 4.13, p. 153	ELM2_U04_Track11_Chart4.13.mp3
	Activity 59, p. 154	ELM2_U04_Track12_Activity59.mp3
Unit 5	Activity 8, p. 167	ELM2_U05_Track01_Activity08.mp3
	Activity 9, p. 167	ELM2_U05_Track02_Activity09.mp3
	Activity 14, p. 171	ELM2_U05_Track03_Activity14.mp3
	Activity 15, p. 171	ELM2_U05_Track04_Activity15.mp3
	Activity 16, p. 172	ELM2_U05_Track05_Activity16.mp3
	Chart 5.7, p. 182	ELM2_U05_Track06_Chart5.7.mp3
	Activity 30, p. 182	ELM2_U05_Track07_Activity30.mp3
	Activity 31, p. 183	ELM2_U05_Track08_Activity31.mp3
	Activity 32, p. 183	ELM2_U05_Track09_Activity32.mp3
Unit 6	Activity 6, p. 194	ELM2_U06_Track01_Activity06.mp3
	Activity 7, p. 194	ELM2_U06_Track02_Activity07.mp3
	Activity 9, p. 195	ELM2_U06_Track03_Activity09.mp3

Unit	Activity	Track File Name
Unit 6 (cont.)	Activity 12, p. 198	ELM2_U06_Track04_Activity12.mp3
	Activity 13, p. 199	ELM2_U06_Track05_Activity13.mp3
	Activity 14, p. 199	ELM2_U06_Track06_Activity14.mp3
	Activity 15, p. 199	ELM2_U06_Track07_Activity15.mp3
	Activity 17, p. 201	ELM2_U06_Track08_Activity17.mp3
	Activity 18, p. 202	ELM2_U06_Track09_Activity18.mp3
	Activity 19, p. 202	ELM2_U06_Track10_Activity19.mp3
	Activity 20, p. 202	ELM2_U06_Track11_Activity20.mp3
	Activity 27, p. 207	ELM2_U06_Track12_Activity27.mp3
	Activity 37, p. 214	ELM2_U06_Track13_Activity37.mp3
	Activity 47, p. 220	ELM2_U06_Track14_Activity47.mp3
	Chart 6.11, p. 222	ELM2_U06_Track15_Chart6.11.mp3
	Activity 50, p. 222	ELM2_U06_Track16_Activity50.mp3
	Activity 53, p. 224	ELM2_U06_Track17_Activity53.mp3
Unit 7	Activity 13, p. 237	ELM2_U07_Track01_Activity13.mp3
	Activity 14, p. 237	ELM2_U07_Track02_Activity14.mp3
	Activity 15, p. 238	ELM2_U07_Track03_Activity15.mp3
	Activity 19, p. 240	ELM2_U07_Track04_Activity19.mp3
	Chart 7.7, p. 245	ELM2_U07_Track05_Chart7.7.mp3
	Activity 28, p. 245	ELM2_U07_Track06_Activity28.mp3
Unit 8	Chart 8.6, p. 271	ELM2_U08_Track01_Chart8.6.mp3
	Activity 27, p. 272	ELM2_U08_Track02_Activity27.mp3
	Activity 28, p. 272	ELM2_U08_Track03_Activity28.mp3
Unit 9	Activity 1, p. 280	ELM2_U09_Track01_Activity01.mp3
	Activity 2, p. 280	ELM2_U09_Track02_Activity02.mp3
	Activity 34, p. 302	ELM2_U09_Track03_Activity34.mp3
	Activity 35, p. 302	ELM2_U09_Track04_Activity35.mp3
	Chart 9.10, p. 304	ELM2_U09_Track05_Chart9.10.mp3
Unit 10	Chart 10.9, p. 335	ELM2_U10_Track01_Chart10.9.mp3
	Activity 32, p. 335	ELM2_U10_Track02_Activity32.mp3
	Activity 33, p. 336	ELM2_U10_Track03_Activity33.mp3
	Activity 34, p. 337	ELM2_U10_Track04_Activity34.mp3
Unit 11	Chart 11.8, p. 366	ELM2_U11_Track01_Chart11.8.mp3
	Activity 35, p. 366	ELM2_U11_Track02_Activity35.mp3
Unit 12	Activity 17, p. 385	ELM2_U12_Track01_Activity17.mp3
	Activity 18, p. 385	ELM2_U12_Track02_Activity18.mp3
	Activity 24, p. 390	ELM2_U12_Track03_Activity24.mp3
	Chart 12.6, p. 394	ELM2_U12_Track04_Chart12.6.mp3
	Activity 29, p. 394	ELM2_U12_Track05_Activity29.mp3
	Activity 31, p. 396	ELM2_U12_Track06_Activity31.mp3
Unit 13	Activity 7, p. 407	ELM2_U13_Track01_Activity07.mp3
	Activity 25, p. 419	ELM2_U13_Track02_Activity25.mp3
	Chart 13.9, p. 428	ELM2_U13_Track03_Chart13.9.mp3
	Activity 39, p. 428	ELM2_U13_Track04_Activity39.mp3
	Activity 40, p. 429	ELM2_U13_Track05_Activity40.mp3
Unit 14	Activity 18, p. 451	ELM2_U14_Track01_Activity18.mp3
	Activity 19, p. 451	ELM2_U14_Track02_Activity19.mp3
	Chart 14.10, p. 463	ELM2_U14_Track03_Chart14.10.mp3
	Activity 36, p. 463	ELM2_U14_Track04_Activity36.mp3
	Activity 37, p. 464	ELM2_U14_Track05_Activity37.mp3
	Activity 39, p. 465	ELM2_U14_Track06_Activity39.mp3

OXFORD
UNIVERSITY PRESS

198 Madison Avenue
New York, NY 10016 USA

Great Clarendon Street, Oxford, OX2 6DP, United Kingdom

Oxford University Press is a department of the University of Oxford.
It furthers the University's objective of excellence in research, scholarship,
and education by publishing worldwide. Oxford is a registered trade
mark of Oxford University Press in the UK and in certain other countries.

© Oxford University Press 2014

The moral rights of the author have been asserted.

First published in 2014
2018 2017 2016 2015 2014
10 9 8 7 6 5 4 3 2 1

Director, ELT New York: Laura Pearson
Head of Adult, ELT New York: Stephanie Karras
Publisher: Sharon Sargent
Senior Development Editor: Andrew Gitzy
Senior Development Editor: Rebecca Mostov
Development Editor: Eric Zuarino
Executive Art and Design Manager: Maj-Britt Hagsted
Content Production Manager: Julie Armstrong
Image Manager: Trisha Masterson
Image Editor: Liaht Pashayan
Production Artists: Elissa Santos, Julie Sussman-Perez
Production Coordinator: Brad Tucker

ISBN: 978 0 19 402823 3 Student Book 2 with Online Practice Pack
ISBN: 978 0 19 402842 4 Student Book 2 as pack component
ISBN: 978 0 19 402879 0 Online Practice website

Printed in China

This book is printed on paper from certified and well-managed sources.

ACKNOWLEDGEMENTS

*Although every effort has been made to trace and contact copyright holders before publication,
this has not been possible in some cases. We apologize for any apparent infringement of
copyright and if notified, the publisher will be pleased to rectify any errors or omissions at the
earliest opportunity.*

*The authors and publisher are grateful to those who have given permission to reproduce the
following extracts and adaptations of copyright material:* p. 31 definitions reproduced
by permission of Oxford University Press from *Oxford Basic American Dictionary*
© Oxford University Press 2011; p. 35 "Advice on Writing from the Poet Gwendolyn
Brooks" from "Gwendolyn Brooks," as appeared in *The Place My Words Are Looking For:
What Poets Say About and Through Their Work* by Paul B. Janeczko. Reprinted by Consent
of Brooks Permissions; p. 38 reprinted with the permission of Simon & Schuster
Publishing Group from *The Book of Answers* by Barbara Berliner with Melinda Corey
and George Ochoa. Copyright © 1990 by The New York Public Library and The
Stonesong Press, Inc. All rights reserved; p. 59 "How to Make an Origami Whale,"
The World Almanac for Kids, 2000, Elaine Israel, editor. Copyright © 1999 by PRIMEDIA
Reference Inc. Reprinted by permission of Infobase Publishing; p. 64 reproduced
by permission of Oxford University Press from *IE Transitions Student Book Level 2* by
Linda Lee © Oxford University Press 1999; p. 311 and p. 333 definitions reproduced
by permission of Oxford University Press from *Oxford Basic American Dictionary*
© Oxford University Press 2011.

Illustrations by: 5W Infographics: p. 55, 66, 74, 177, 221, 252, 256, 285. Mark Duffin:
p. 312 (top, 4 cars), 313. Dermot Flynn/Dutch Uncle: p. 73, 113, 335, 336, 469.
Jerome Mireault: p. 208. Kevin Rechin/Mendola: p. 116. Tablet Infographics: p. 22,
90, 114, 158. Joe Taylor/Mendola: p. 136, 226, 301, 353, 370, 415, 419, 467.

We would also like to thank the following for permission to reproduce the following photographs:
Cover: blinkblink/shutterstock; back cover: lvcandy/Getty Images; global: Rodin
Anton/shutterstock; p. 2 Giorgio Fochesato/istockphoto; p. 5 OUP/pdesign, OUP/
Graphi-Ogre; p. 6 Newton Daly/Getty Images, Simon Jarratt/Corbis, Gene Chutka/
istockphoto, Blend Images/SuperStock, Andres Rodriguez/Alamy, Image Source/
Alamy, Clerkenwell/Getty Images; p. 8 Paul Simcock/Blend Images/Corbis; p. 19
Brasil2/istockphoto, Bettmann/Corbis; p. 22 Blend Images/Alamy; p. 32 AP Photo/
Phil Klein, Dave M. Benett/Getty Images, Walter McBride/Corbis; p. 35 AP Photo;
p. 39 Archer Street/Delux/Lion's Gate/Pathe/The Kobal Collection/BUITENDIJK, JAAP,

Tiger Moth/Miramax/The Kobal Collection; p. 42 Blend_Images/istockphoto;
p. 44 Visions of America/SuperStock; p. 46 Reuters/Corbis; p. 51 Gabriel Bouys/
AFP/Getty Images; p. 57 The Francis Frith Collection/Corbis, Caro/Alamy; p. 61
Prisma Archivo/Alamy; p. 62 Lordprice Collection/Alamy; p. 63 Grant Dixon/
Hedgehog House/Minden Pictures/Corbis; p. 64 Hulton Archive/Getty Images;
p. 66 kreego/shutterstock; p. 72 RW Photographic/Masterfile, Lei Wang; p. 76
Angela Waye/shutterstock; p. 78 Jiri Hera/Alamy, Hans Laubel/istockphoto,
Bombaert Patrick/shutterstock, Karl Weatherly/Corbis, Hanka Steidle/shutterstock,
Worldgraphics/shutterstock; p. 79 Clint Hughes/Getty Images; p. 84 Atlaspix/
shutterstock, Pedro Ladeira/AFP/Getty Images; p. 96 ClassicStock/Masterfile; SuperStock;
Lauri Patterson/istockphoto; p. 118 Actionplus/AGE fotostock; p. 121 PhotoAlto/Corbis; p. 160
Alamy, jump fotoagentur Susanne Treubel/Alamy; p. 127 OUP/Fuse; p. 139 Cannon Fagan/
Photodisc, valzan/shutterstock; p. 143 Rich Wheater/All Canada Photos/Sy ages, Masterfile,
p. 156 Donato Sardella/WireImage/Getty Images; p. 157 Jurgen Frank/Co ettmann/Corbis,
Paul Raftery/VIEW/Corbis; p. 164 Troy Wayrrynen/NewSport/Corbis, Sha Aspen Photo/
Getty Images, David H. Lewis/istockphoto, Henrik Sorensen/Getty Im 8 KidStock/Blend
MM Productions/Corbis; p. 168 Jerry Dohnal/Getty Images; p. 170 M/Masterfile; p. 195
Javier Pierini/Getty Images; p. 172 john lund/Getty Images; p. 17 es; p. 200 Lucenet
Shutterstock.com; p. 184 Christopher Futcher/istockphoto; p. 18 svetikd/Getty Images;
Images/Corbis; p. 191 BlueLela/shutterstock; p. 192 Cultura R y/WireImage/Getty Images;
Phil Schermeister/Corbis; p. 198 Massimo Merlini/Getty Imag /Corbis, ThinkDeep,
Patrice/Oredia Eurl/SuperStock; p. 201 Mika/Corbis; p. 202 , Russell Shively/shutterstock;
p. 206 Steve Debenport/Getty Images; p. 207 Kevin P. Case , Radharc Images/Alamy; p. 228
p. 212 Monalyn Gracia/Corbis; p. 216 ClarkandCompany stockphoto; p. 232 Gelpi JM/
istockphoto; p. 217 Kelvin Murray/Getty Images; p. 219 9 Jose Luis Pelaez, Inc./Blend
p. 223 Westend61/Getty Images; p. 226 AP Photo/NASA 242 frytka/istockphoto; p. 243 Blaz
Ann Cutting/Getty Images; p. 231 Neustockimages/ E fotostock; p. 245 Aurora Photos/
Shutterstock; p. 237 luciaserra/Shutterstock; p. 2 dge/Getty Images, PhotosIndia/AGE
Images/Corbis; p. 240 Jerzyworks/Masterfile; p. k, Stan Honda/AFP/Getty Images; p. 250
Kure/Shutterstock, Jochen Tack/imagebrok/AG OCK4B-RF/Getty Images, Sollina Images/
Masterfile; p. 247 JGI/Getty Images, Klaus Tie Blend Images/Alamy; p. 260 Eric Isselée/
fotostock; p. 248 imagebroker.net/SuperSto s; p. 264 PCN Photography/Alamy; p. 265
Panoramic Images/Getty Images; p. 253 ST ympic Museum/Allsport/Getty Images; p. 266
Blend Images/Corbis; p. 254 MBI/Alamy, otostock/SuperStock; p. 270 Niday Picture
istockphoto; p. 262 Gabe Palmer/Corbis /Getty Images; p. 274 Marc Brasz/Corbis; p. 278
Jewel Samad/AFP/Getty Images, IOC O stockphoto, Leksele/shutterstock, hnijjar007/
Colin McPherson/Corbis; p. 268 AGE utterstock; p. 287 Jose Luis Pelaez, Inc./Blend
Library/Alamy; p. 273 Hulton Archive old Images, Ekkapon/shutterstock, Dimedrol68/
khoa vu/Getty Images; p. 281 rusm/i istockphoto; p. 291 Paul Prescott/shutterstock,
istockphoto; p. 283 arek_malang/sh, Randy Faris/Corbis, Aping Vision/STS/Getty Images,
Images/Corbis; p. 288 OUP/Jon Arn orbis, Andrew Rich/Getty Images; p. 294 Annie Engel/
shutterstock; p. 289 GlobalStock IP/SuperStock; p. 297 AlaskaStock/Masterfile; p. 301
Andreas Rodriguez/istockphot rstock; p. 305 JGI/Jamie Grill/AGE fotostock; p. 307
Andersen Ross/Blend Images/C catwalker/Shutterstock.com; p. 308 Vanni Archive/
Corbis, LAURENT/GAELLE/BS ert Harding World Imagery/Corbis, Frank Fennema/
prochasson frederic/shutte uel Robbins/Corbis; p. 310 epicurean/istockphoto; p. 311
fotoVoyager/Getty Images y, Eye Ubiquitous/Alamy, Beverly Armstrong/Getty Images,
Corbis, Ellen Rooney/Ro 11, Ocean/Corbis, Eric Nguyen/Science Photo Library; p. 312
shutterstock, David San ly, Ralph Lauer/ZUMA Press/Corbis, CB2/ZOB WENN Photos/
ZUMA Press, Inc./Alam Towers Picture Library/Alamy, Lisa S./shutterstock, XiXinXing/
OUP/Ellen McKnight Culture/Getty Images, Road & Track Magazine/Guy Spange/
MS Bretherton/Alam ; p. 319 OUP/Photodisc; p. 322 Craig Joiner Photography/Alamy;
Newscom, Alvey & ead/shutterstock, KidStock/Blend Images/Corbis, stockstudioX/
Getty Images, Car Anne-Marie Palmer/Masterfile; p. 327 Minden Pictures/Masterfile; p. 330
Transtock/Corbis ience Faction/SuperStock; p. 331 OUP/Digital Vision; p. 332 Doug
p. 325 Scott E R fotostock, Sylvain Sonnet/Getty Images, Alan Schein Photography/
Getty Images, Lewis/Alamy, SeanPavonePhoto/Shutterstock.com, View Stock Stock
Norbert Wu/Sc USA/Newscom, PjrTravel/Alamy, Iain Masterton/AGE fotostock; p. 333
Pearson/AGE nan/shutterstock, Mikhail Melnikov/shutterstock, OUP/David Cook/
Corbis, Barry dios, Sirikorn Techatraibhop/shutterstock, Anan Kaewkhammul/
Connection k, Lingbeek/istockphoto, ConstantinosZ/shutterstock, OUP/D. Hurst,
Robert Eastn hutterstock, wikanda/shutterstock, Gunnar Pippel/shutterstock, JM-Design/
blueshiftstu ck; p. 338 Armando Gallo/Retna Ltd./Corbis; p. 342 Charles Gullung/
shutterstoc p. 346 SGranitz/WireImage/Getty Images; p. 349 OUP/BLOOMimage; p. 351
f9photos/s cks/Corbis; p. 358 Mark Poprocki/shutterstock; p. 365 Tetra Images/Corbis,
shutterstoc Diebel/Getty Images; p. 368 Radius Images/Corbis; p. 371 OUP/BlueMoon
Images; p. 372 Andrea Pattaro/AFP/Getty Images; p. 377 olaser/Getty Images, pdesign/
Jon Hick rstock, Artgraphixel.com/shutterstock; p. 378 OUP/Graphi-Ogre, Globe
Martin r/shutterstock, Jessica Peterson/Tetra Images/Corbis; p. 379 wavebreakmedia/
Stock; erstock; p. 382 Lindsay & Gavin Fries, silentwings/shutterstock; p. 386
shutter layton/AGE fotostock; p. 388 Abel Mitja Varela/Getty Images; p. 393 Alija/
Turne kphoto; p. 398 pictafolio/istockphoto; p. 400 Jeffrey Coolidge/Getty Images;
shutt 02 OJO Images Ltd/Alamy; p. 406 OUP/David Cook/www.blueshiftstudios.co.uk,
Lex R /Dennis Kitchen Studio, Inc, anafcsousa/istockphoto; p. 407 VI_K/Alamy,
istoc mysh/shutterstock; p. 410 Jo Ann Snover/shutterstock; p. 412 Blend Images/
p. 4 ny; p. 417 B Calkins/shutterstock; p. 420 mathom/shutterstock, Mary Nguyen
OUP shutterstock; p. 424 James Morris/Axiom Photographic/Design Pics/SuperStock,
kara 26 BlueOrange Studio/shutterstock; p. 7 John Lund/Marc Romanelli/Getty
Alam ges; p. 431 Zoonar GmbH/Alamy; p. 432 arasov/shutterstock; p. 433 Junko
NG/ ba/Getty Images, Proehl Studios/Corbis, UP/BananaStock, Wouter van Caspel/
p. 4 ty Images, Seokyong Lee/Bloomberg via Getty Images; p. 436 Album/Raga/Prisma/
Imag wscom, REUTERS/Tomas Bravo; p. 438 Chris Crisman/Corbis; p. 441 Keystone
Chi tures USA/Alamy; p. 442 Tsuji/istockphoto; p. 444 Rich Legg/istockphoto; p. 446
Ge Ooms/Masterfile; p. 448 Sherrie Nickol/Citizen Stock/Corbis; p. 449 Sigurgeir
Ne asson/Getty Images; p. 452 Bettmann/Corbis, Peter Yates/Corbis; p. 458 Richmatts/
Pic ockphoto; p. 459 Corbis; p. 460 picturepartners/shutterstock, Denys Kurbatov/
Roy 461 Naypong/shutterstock; p. 462 Ruy Barbosa Pinto/Getty Images,
Jon oto Researchers/Alamy; p. 464 Johner Images/Johnér Images/Corbis; p. 465
isto athan Blair/Corbis; p. 468 Aspen Photo/Shutterstock.com, PhotoStock10/
shu utterstock.com, esting/Shutterstock.com, Justin Horrocks/istockphoto.

ELEMENTS *of* SUCCESS
Online Practice

How to Register for Elements of Success Online Practice

Fol...

...low these steps to register for *Elements of Success Online Practice*:

1. Go ...
2. Read a ...to www.elementsofsuccessonline.com and click **Register**
3. Enter the ...nd agree to the terms of use. **I Agree.**

   the inside ba... Access Code that came with your Student Book. Your code is written on
   ...ck cover of your book.

4. Enter your persona... information (first and last name, email address, and password). **Enter**

5. Click the Student Bo... ...ok that you are using for your class.

   It is ...
   You a...
   Please **very important to select your book.**
   ...are using Elements of Success 2.
   ...click the **GREEN** Elements of Success 2 cover.

   If you don't know which book ...

   ...to select, **STOP**. Continue when you know your book.

6. Enter your class ID to join your cl... ...ass, and click NEXT. Your class ID is on the
   line below, or your teacher will g... ...ive it to you on a different piece of paper.
   _____
   You don't need a class ID code. If y... **Next**
   To enter this code later, choose Join... ...ou do not have a class ID code, click Skip.
   ...a Class from your Home page.

7. Once you're done, click Enter Online ...
   Online Practice.
   ...Practice to begin using *Elements of Success*

   Enter Or... ...**line Practice**

   Next time you want to use *Elements of S...*
   www.elementsofsuccessonline.com and l... ...*uccess Online Practice*, just go to
   ...g in with your email address and password.